lonely

ITALY

Turin & Piedmont, p158

Milan & the Lakes, p224

Dolomites & the Northeast, p314

Venice, p268

Italian Riviera, p190

Bologna & Emilia-Romagna, p362

Florence, p402

Tuscany, p448

Umbria & Le Marche, p504

Lazio & Abruzzo, p130

ROME, P58

Naples & Campania, p544

Puglia, p594

Sardinia, p708

Calabria & Basilicata, p622

Sicily, p656

Duncan Garwood,
Federica Bocco, Julia Buckley, Virginia DiGaetano,
Stefania D'Ignoti, Benedetta Geddo, Paula Hardy,
Phoebe Hunt, Sara Mostaccio, Stephanie Ong,
Kevin Raub, Eva Sandoval, Nicola Williams, Angelo Zinna

CONTENTS

SERGIO DELLE VEDOVE/SHUTTERSTOCK ©

Basilica di Santa Croce, Florence (p429)

TOP: VALERIOMEI/SHUTTERSTOCK ©

Parco Nazionale d'Abruzzo, Lazio e Molise (p153)

ITALY
THE JOURNEY BEGINS HERE

Walking Rome's subdued streets in the immediate aftermath of Italy's strict lockdown was a strange and unsettling experience. It was as if the volume had been turned to zero; it wasn't right. The city needed the noise and energy of its usually crowded pavements and piazzas. Almost two years on and the volume is back. Life has returned to normal, only now even the most simple of pleasures seems precious. And Italy is a country that excels at the simple pleasures: a pasta carbonara at a favourite trattoria, a glass of red wine with a bowl of baked *taralli* (pretzel-like biscuits), an uplifting walk in the autumnal hills. It's pretty good at those big, bucket-list experiences too, those 'see the Sistine Chapel' moments or day trips to Pompeii. Really, if any one country can revive your appetite for travel, Italy can.

My favourite experience is hiking through the beech forests and mountains of the Parco Nazionale d'Abruzzo, Lazio e Molise. I haven't seen a bear yet but there's always next time.

Duncan Garwood

🗩 *@DuncanGarwood*

Based in Rome, Duncan is a travel writer and guidebook author specialising in Italy and the Mediterranean.

WHO GOES WHERE

Our writers and experts choose the places which, for them, define Italy

The **Basilica di San Marco** (p278) sums up Venice – not just for its sublime beauty, but because it tells the often-overlooked history of La Serenissima. Much of what's in there was looted from other countries; there's even a mosaic outside boasting of the theft of St Mark's relics. It's also suffered heavily from flooding – that it's still standing is testament to Venetians' extraordinary resilience.

Julia Buckley
🐦 @juliathelast

Julia swapped life as an editor for UK newspapers for freelance life from the floating city and weekends exploring Italy's rail network.

Like most European castles, the **Reggia di Venaria Reale** (p171) just outside Turin feels like something out of a fantasy book. Nothing beats finding the Galleria Grande almost or completely empty – the resulting pictures are out of this world. Then there's the old town of **Parasio** (p222), overlooking Imperia – every corner a composition of twisting alleys, cascades of greenery and the blue sea.

Benedetta Geddo
🐦 @beegeddo 📷 @beegeddo

Benedetta writes guides, news and features for Lonely Planet; the rest of her writing relies on the vast expanse of her nerd culture.

The **Supramonte mountain range** (p723) in northern Sardinia is so colossal that you cannot help but feel utterly dwarfed by it. But it is not just the size that is striking. Something in it is both forbidding and inviting, beckoning you with one breath as it warns you off with another. It offers you a choice: freedom or restraint. It is exhilarating and brave by its very existence alone, just like the island it calls home.

Virginia DiGaetano
Virginia is a writer and translator who never meant to live in Italy and now finds it hard to imagine living anywhere else, mostly due to the coffee.

Puglia (p595) is a sunny region located in the heart of the Mediterranean. But it's beyond just a land of warm hospitality – it's a magical combination of cultural history, wild nightlife and unspoilt nature. Here, small villages shine through a unique light, and the flavours of a simple cuisine are reminiscent of a past where each civilisation that has come and gone left its indelible traces.

Stefania D'Ignoti
🐦 @stef_dgn

Stefania is a journalist and writer specialising in Italian culture and society, which she has written about for National Geographic, BBC Travel and more.

The Calabrian village of **Badolato** (p649) is fascinating because it encapsulates both the struggles and potential of this unsung part of Italy. Emptied by emigration in the 1970s, its kindness in welcoming a ship of refugees in 1997 initiated a dramatic revival. Staying here not only gives you an insight into the intense close-knit relationships of a mountain town, but makes you think deeply about the issue of migration and how that shapes places.

Paula Hardy

@paulahardy

A travel journalist for over 20 years, Paula contributes regularly to Lonely Planet and newspapers like the Financial Times, The Telegraph and The Guardian.

Milan Design Week (p230) is my favourite time of year. It's an intense week, crowded with locals and foreigners rushing to back-to-back events. But it's all worth it to see something clever, unexpected or beautiful in a hidden corner of Milan, from a former factory to an ancient cloister. I love the energy and creativity that pours into the city during this time, which gets bigger every year and shows just how quickly Milan and this region are growing.

Stephanie Ong

Stephanie is a Melbourne-born writer who made her home in Milan 10 years ago and hasn't looked back.

I live in Bologna, where locals are conditioned to scoff at **Modena** (p375), but my crush runs deep (many *bolognesi* have never even been!). It's home to some of my favourite restaurants in Italy, my favourite coffeehouse, my favourite gelateria and my favourite food market. I love the colours – Modena's rusty oranges and fiery reds moodily tilt according to the sunlight's will. It's a small town but managed to gift the world Ferrari, balsamic vinegar and Pavarotti. Don't listen to the *bolognesi*.

Kevin Raub

@RaubontheRoad @RaubontheRoad

Kevin is a Bologna-based travel journalist and craft-beer connoisseur – and the co-author of over 110 Lonely Planet guidebooks on four continents.

Naples (p544) may have a rough exterior, but scratch beneath its graffiti-streaked surface to unearth treasures beyond your imagination. You'll find Roman ruins layered upon 3000-year-old Greek streets, magical saints' blood, frilly baroque palaces, and the best pizza you've ever had in your life. Take it slow; Naples is a Russian doll to be pried open one layer at a time, lest its contents overwhelm.

Eva Sandoval

@ieatmypigeon @ieatmypigeon

Eva writes about food and travel for publications like Condé Nast Traveler, BBC Future and Fodor's Travel. She divides her time between Italy and the US, eating as much as she can in both countries.

When the island vibe beckons, I head to **Favignana** (p706) in Sicily's Egadi Islands. I can't get enough of its unpretentious cuisine and the nonchalance with which quarried tufa blocks are scattered around like Lego bricks. Islanders here make no attempt to manicure their island. Favignana is, first and foremost, their home where the day's catch ends up in brown-paper cones of deep-fried *frittura mista* (mixed seafood) and wild botanicals with salty water from an artisan well end up in Isola di Favignana craft gin.

Nicola Williams

🐦 *@tripalong* 📷 *@tripalong*

Nicola is a travel writer, trail runner and mountain addict.

Walking on the mountain ridges above **Carrara** (p479) produces an odd mixture of awe and bitterness. Embraced by raw wilderness, the seemingly pixelated quarries of white marble are evidence of the environment's finitude. As the mountains recede, the sites Michelangelo visited to select his sculptures' material now appear like photographs of the Anthropocene – places worth seeing to carefully think about what is worth building and what is worth preserving.

Angelo Zinna

📷 *@angelo_zinna*

Angelo is a Florence-based writer, editor and photographer, passionate about odd architecture, the environment and the former Soviet region.

CONTRIBUTING WRITERS

Federica Bocco

📷 *@fedaenerys*

Federica contributed to the Naples & Campania chapter. Federica is a traveller by passion and a writer by natural necessity, although she sometimes wishes it was the other way around.

Phoebe Hunt

📷 *@phoebetravelpig*

Phoebe contributed to the Tuscany chapter. Phoebe is travel writer who lives in Florence – she has worked on four guidebooks and countless articles about Italy and beyond.

Sara Mostaccio

📷 *@fritha*

Sara contributed to the Sicily chapter. She is a journalist and a podcaster.

8

Turin
Admire royal palaces in the city's hinterland (p164)

Milan
Shop for the latest designer fashions (p230)

The Dolomites
Hike amid soaring rock cathedrals (p314)

Venice
Marvel at the canal city's architectural bombast (p268)

Urbino
Revel in Renaissance art without the crowds (p521)

Tuscany
Cycle your way through Chianti wine country (p448)

200 km
100 miles

BUDAPEST

HUNGARY

SERBIA

BOSNIA &
HERZEGOVINA

MONTENEGRO

PODGORICA

Dubrovnik

SLOVENIA

LJUBLJANA

Klagenfurt

Salzburg

Munich

GERMANY

AUSTRIA

Innsbruck

Tarvisio

Cortina
d'Ampezzo

Dolomites

Udine

FRIULI
VENEZIA
GIULIA

Trieste

CROATIA

Rijeka

Pula

Cres

Krk

Brač

Hvar

Vis

Korčula

Split

Zadar

Adriatic
Sea

Ancona

Ascoli
Piceno

Pescara

ABRUZZO

L'Aquila Monte Amaro

Corno
Grande

LAZIO

Viterbo

Orvieto

Terni

Tevere

UMBRIA

Assisi

Perugia

LE MARCHE

Urbino

SAN MARINO

Rimini

Ravenna

Ferrara

EMILIA-ROMAGNA

Bologna

Modena

Padua

Venice

Treviso

Belluno

TRENTINO

Trento

Cima
Brenta

Bolzano

Merano

Vicenza

Verona

VENETO

Lago di
Garda

Mantua

Parma

Piacenza

Po

Cremona

Brescia

Bergamo

LOMBARDY

Lago di
Como

Como

Lugano

Lago
Maggiore

Monte
Rosa

Zürich

SWITZERLAND

Rhein

Geneva

Mont Blanc
(Monte Bianco)

Gran
Paradiso

Aosta

PIEDMONT

Turin

Briançon

FRANCE

Cuneo

Asti

Alba

Alessandria

Savona

San Remo

Nice

MONACO

CORSICA

Bastia

Elba

Giglio

Orbetello

Grosseto

TUSCANY

Livorno

Pisa

Lucca

The Apuane
Alps

Monte
Pisanino

Pistoia

San
Gimignano

Siena

Arno

Florence

Arezzo

Milan

Genoa

LIGURIA

Gulf of
Genoa

La Spezia

Po

Mantua

Milan

Pula

Rhein

Munich

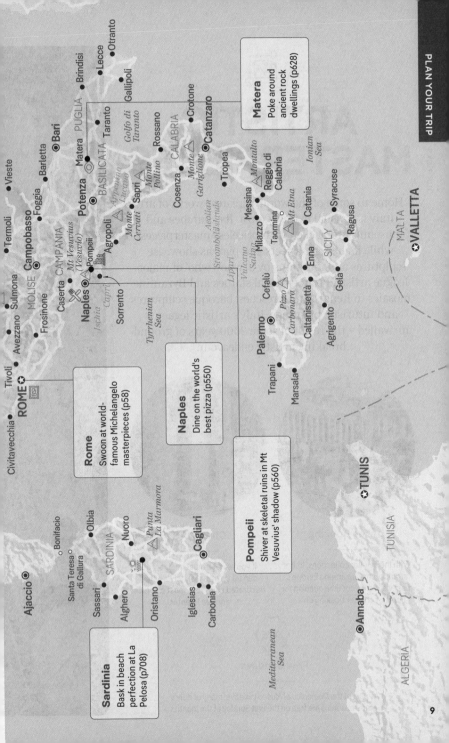

Rome
Swoon at world-famous Michelangelo masterpieces (p58)

Naples
Dine on the world's best pizza (p550)

Pompeii
Shiver at skeletal ruins in Mt Vesuvius' shadow (p560)

Sardinia
Bask in beach perfection at La Pelosa (p708)

Matera
Poke around ancient rock dwellings (p628)

9

ARTISTIC MASTERPIECES

Home to some of the world's greatest works of art, Italy is a visual extravaganza. Its churches and museums are packed with priceless masterpieces, while its historic streets and piazzas showcase sculptures and fountains by a 'who's who' of major-league artists. From classical statues and Byzantine mosaics to Renaissance frescoes, baroque sculptures and futuristic paintings, Italy's artistic legacy is unrivalled – the result of some 3000 years of ground-breaking artistic endeavour.

Online Booking

With their stellar collections, Italy's art museums are among Europe's most visited. To cut time queuing for tickets, consider booking online.

Church Art

If you're not a museum fan, you can fill up on art at Italy's richly decorated churches, most of which are free to enter.

FREE

Free Sundays

As part of the *Domenica al Museo* initiative, many of Italy's state museums are free on the first Sunday of the month.

BEST ART EXPERIENCES

Gaze heavenwards at Michelangelo's celebrated frescoes in the **Sistine Chapel ❶**, the papal church and the grand finale in the Vatican Museums. (p95)

Pay homage to Leonardo da Vinci's version of *The Last Supper*, on show at the **Basilica di Santa Maria delle Grazie ❷** in Milan. (p231)

Go face to face with world-famous Renaissance paintings at Florence's premier art museum, the **Galleria degli Uffizi ❸**. (p411)

Witness dazzling displays of Early Christian mosaics at the **Basilica di San Vitale** (p396) and **Basilica di Sant'Apollinare Nuovo** (p398) ❹ in Ravenna.

Marvel at the seemingly soft marble used to wrap Jesus in the *Cristo velato*, the highlight of the **Cappella Sansevero ❺** in Naples. (p550)

ANCIENT RELICS

From temples and cemeteries to amphitheatres, arenas and aqueducts, Italy's ancient past is writ large on the country's landscape. The Greeks and Etruscans paved the way, but it was the Romans who left the biggest mark, producing monumental buildings, major highways and sophisticated urban infrastructures. More than 2000 years on and their legacy is woven into the fabric of the nation: roads run past ancient aqueducts, metro stations incorporate underground ruins, opera rings out in gladiatorial arenas.

Best Times

Visit big sites in the early morning or late afternoon to avoid the worst heat and crowds. Spring and autumn are the best periods for sightseeing.

Read Up

Signposting and information panels are often in short supply at Italy's archaeological parks, so it pays to have a map or written guide.

Cultural Events

Many ancient monuments host concerts and cultural events, particularly in summer. It's always worth checking.

❸

❹ ❶

❷

❺

BEST ANCIENT EXPERIENCES

Summon the roar of the crowds as you scale the stands of the **Colosseum** ❶, the greatest gladiatorial amphitheatre in the Roman world. (p66)

Retrace the daily steps of the ancients who lived, worked and died at **Pompeii** ❷, the infamous town destroyed by Mt Vesuvius' devastating eruption. (p560)

Soar to the sound of music in Verona's **Roman Arena** ❸, the magnificent setting for the city's annual opera festival. (p352)

Discover erotic frescoes and kilometres of haunting Hobbit-like tombs in the Etruscan cemeteries of **Cerveteri** and **Tarquinia** ❹ in northern Lazio. (p140)

Delight in the symmetrical beauty and engineering genius of the Greek temples in Agrigento's **Valley of the Temples** ❺. (p696)

WONDERS OF THE TABLE

Few countries have mastered the joys of the table as well as Italy. Dishes are prepared with fresh seasonal produce and a culinary know-how honed over the generations, while historic piazzas and seafront promenades provide a ready supply of memorable settings. Regional specialities abound, but wherever you go in this food-mad country you'll eat well – whether in a family-run trattoria, a boisterous backstreet pizzeria or a chic harbourside restaurant.

Where to Eat

In addition to trattorias and *ristoranti* (restaurants), you can also chow down in pizzerias, *osterie* (taverns/ wine bars) and *agriturismi* (farm-stays).

What Time?

As a rough guide: *pranzo* (lunch) 1pm to 2.30pm, *aperitivo* (pre-dinner drinks) 5pm to 8pm, *cena* (dinner) 7.30pm to 9.30pm. Southern Italians generally eat later than northerners.

The Full Meal

A full meal consists of an *antipasto* (starter), *primo* (pasta or rice dish), *secondo* (meat or fish), *contorno* (salad or vegetable side dish) and *dolce* (dessert).

BEST FOOD EXPERIENCES

Taste the best wood-fired pizza of your life in **Naples ❶**, the city that created the margherita in honour of Queen Margherita di Savoia. (p550)

See how it's really done – dig into *tagliatelle al ragù* (the original spag bol) in a **Bologna ❷** trattoria. (p368)

Snack on sublime street food in **Palermo ❸**. Star of the show is the *arancino*, a fried rice ball encasing a drop of *ragù* and molten cheese. (p662)

Do as the Romans do and head to the **Castelli Romani ❹** hills to feast on *porchetta* (boneless herbed roast pork) and other specialities at a *fraschetta*. (p148)

Learn how to prepare Puglia's trademark *orecchiette*, or 'little ears' pasta, in a *trullo* (circular stone-built house) in **Alberobello ❺**. (p600)

ARCHITECTURAL TOURS DE FORCE

Architects have long looked to Italy for inspiration. Throughout history, the country's scene-stealing classical monuments have provided a benchmark for architectural ambition and engineering innovation. The Church has also played a starring role, sponsoring the great architects of the day to push boundaries and build ever greater churches. The result is a country awash with extraordinary buildings, from Gothic cathedrals and Renaissance palaces to baroque basilicas and contemporary eco-skyscrapers.

FROM LEFT: ANDREA IZZOTTI/SHUTTERSTOCK ©; ARJMA/SHUTTERSTOCK ©; DAVE G KELLY/GETTY IMAGES ©

Free for All

Admiring Italy's architectural icons often involves little more than keeping your eyes open as you roam around its historic towns and cities.

Golden Hour

Many monumental buildings look their best in the early evening when the sun dips and the light takes on a soft golden hue.

Architectural Read

Read about Florence's icon in Ross King's *Brunelleschi's Dome: How a Renaissance Genius Reinvented Architecture.*

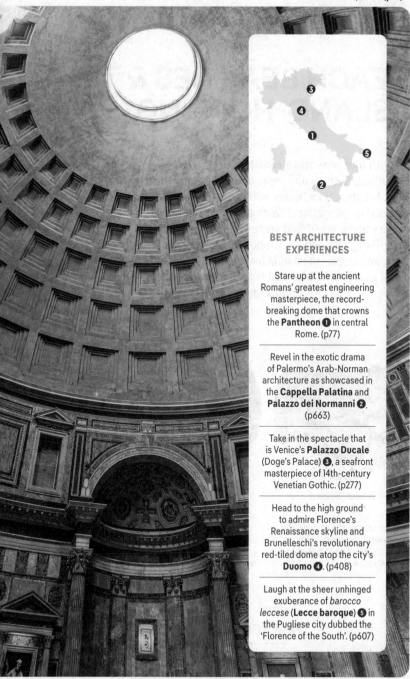

BEST ARCHITECTURE EXPERIENCES

Stare up at the ancient Romans' greatest engineering masterpiece, the record-breaking dome that crowns the **Pantheon ❶** in central Rome. (p77)

Revel in the exotic drama of Palermo's Arab-Norman architecture as showcased in the **Cappella Palatina** and **Palazzo dei Normanni ❷**. (p663)

Take in the spectacle that is Venice's **Palazzo Ducale** (Doge's Palace) ❸, a seafront masterpiece of 14th-century Venetian Gothic. (p277)

Head to the high ground to admire Florence's Renaissance skyline and Brunelleschi's revolutionary red-tiled dome atop the city's **Duomo ❹**. (p408)

Laugh at the sheer unhinged exuberance of *barocco leccese* (**Lecce baroque**) ❺ in the Pugliese city dubbed the 'Florence of the South'. (p607)

BEACH BEAUTIES & ISLAND-HOPPING

With four seas and a coastline that stretches for 7600km, Italy counts some of the Mediterranean's best beaches. So whether you're after an idyllic cove framed by plunging cliffs or a sandy strip lapped by azure waters, you'll find somewhere to suit your style. Similarly, ferry-goers can hop across the country's bays and straits to islands like Sicily and Sardinia as well as a host of lake and lagoon isles and volcanic archipelagos.

Beach Space

Beach space is often taken up by private clubs, which charge an entrance fee. To go free, search out the *spiaggia libera* (free beach).

Ferry Services

A whole fleet of ferries and hydrofoils serve Italy's islands. Services are year-round, but summer sees a surge in sailings and an increase in ticket prices.

Island Sojourns

Many islands are visited on day trips, but to get the most out of them consider spending a night or two there.

La Pelosa beach, Sardinia (p737)

BEST BEACH & ISLAND EXPERIENCES

Feast your eyes on a vision of Sardinian beach perfection at **La Pelosa ❶**, a stunning beach on an island of stunning beaches. (p737)

Boat around the bays and beaches of the **Costa degli Dei ❷** in search of the perfect swimming spot on the Calabrian coast. (p645)

Sail out to the **Spiaggia delle Due Sorelle ❸**, the pick of the beaches on Le Marche's Riviera del Conero. (p529)

Soak up the sun on the black-sand beaches of **Stromboli ❹**, the most explosive of Sicily's volcanic Aeolian Islands. (p678)

Island-hop across the **Gulf of Naples ❺**, from chic, day-trip favourite Capri to laid-back Procida and thermal Ischia, the largest and most developed island. (p566)

EGROV/SHUTTERSTOCK ©

Cappella degli Scrovegni, Padua (p347)

LESSER-KNOWN GEMS

Everyone's heard of the Colosseum and Pompeii, but the country boasts an array of cultural and natural gems that rarely make the limelight but leave a lasting impression. These range from rocky cave houses and wooded mountains to skeletal Roman ruins and Renaissance artworks.

Provincial Prospects

Away from the big cities, Italy's provincial towns and smaller centres are a rich source of hidden masterpieces and historic finds.

Alternative Sights

Go to *lonelyplanet.com/articles/ alternative-italy-5-new-places- to-discover* for a look at Italy's alternative destinations, like Puglia's Gargano Promontory and the wine-rich Langhe area of Piedmont.

BEST ALTERNATIVE EXPERIENCES

Check out an ancient theatre and amazingly preserved mosaics at **Ostia Antica ❶**. (p128)

See how Giotto revolutionised art with his fresco cycle at Padua's **Cappella degli Scrovegni ❷**. (p347)

Shiver at the thought of living in the *sassi* (cave dwellings) that riddle **Matera ❸**. (p628)

Jump into cinema history, car culture and ancient Egyptology in **Turin**'s ❹ museums. (p164)

Try to spot a brown bear in the **Parco Nazionale d'Abruzzo, Lazio e Molise ❺**. (p152)

THE WINE LIST

From aristocratic reds to rosés, crisp sparkling whites to sweet dessert wines, Italy's wine list runs the gamut with a drop for every palate. You can learn about them on guided tastings and vineyard tours or simply treat yourself to a glass or two over a long, leisurely meal or an early-evening *aperitivo*.

Regional Varieties

Each region produces its own wines. Some are household names like Piedmont's Barolo or the Veneto's prosecco, others you'll have to discover for yourself.

Wine Classifications

Italy's wines are classified: DOCG (Denominazione di Origine Controllata e Garantita; pictured); DOC (Denominazione di Origine Controllata); IGT (Indicazione Geografica Tipica); *vino da tavola* (table wine).

Vineyard Visits

Make sure to book ahead as walk-ins are not always accepted. Note also that tasting fees might be waived if you buy some wine.

BEST WINE EXPERIENCES

Discover Italy's best-loved bubbly on **La Strada del Prosecco ❶**, the country's oldest wine route in the Veneto. (p361)

Taste your way around the **Langhe hills ❷** of Piedmont, taking in Barolo and Barbaresco reds in the villages that produce them. (p173)

Meander through Tuscany's **Chianti wine country ❸**, stopping off at historic vineyards to try the local vintages. (p462)

Savour sweet Malvasia dessert wine in a family-run winery on the Aeolian island of **Salina ❹**. (p677)

Seek out the world's best white wine, the Verdicchio dei Castelli di Jesi, in the ancient wine lands of **Le Marche ❺**. (p526)

SHOP TILL YOU DROP

From fashion boutiques and flagship stores to markets, delis and artisanal workshops, Italy has shops for all tastes and budgets. Many businesses are family-owned, having been passed down through the generations, while others have grown from modest origins to become global brands known for their classic designs and quality workmanship.

What to Buy

Clothes and shoes are obvious choices, along with handmade leather goods, glassware and majolica ceramics (pictured). You could also stock up on homeware and deli treats.

Shop Hours

As a rough guide, count on 9.30am to 1pm and 3.30pm to 7.30pm Monday to Saturday. In city centres, shops often stay open at lunchtime and on Sunday mornings.

Sales

Time your trip right and pick up designer fashion for a snip of the usual price at the *saldi* (annual sales) in January and July.

BEST SHOPPING EXPERIENCES

Strut with well-heeled shoppers among the fashion boutiques of the **Quadrilatero D'Oro ❶**, Milan's top shopping district. (p234)

Take in the colours, sounds and smells of Venice's historic **Rialto Market ❷**. Get there early to catch it at its busiest. (p284)

Join the evening *passeggiata* (stroll) along **Via del Corso** and **Via dei Condotti ❸** for some swank high-end Roman shopping. (p91)

Get into the festive spirit at the Tyrolean Christmas market in the Dolomite town of **Merano ❹**.(p326)

Dive into the Dickensian throngs of people that teem around **Palermo's ❺** sprawling street markets. (p662)

CANADASTOCK/SHUTTERSTOCK ©

San Gimignano (p462)

HILL TOWNS

Italy's mountains and hills are crowned by hundreds of historic towns, many dating to ancient times. You'll find them all over the country, but they are a particular feature of central Italy where every hillside in Umbria and Le Marche seems to come with a charming medieval town of its own.

Annual Festivities

Many hilltop towns put on evocative medieval festivities during the year, often to celebrate a patron saint or commemorate a historic event.

Park & Walk

As a general rule, it pays to find a car park on the edge of the historic centre and continue exploring on foot.

BEST HILL TOWN EXPERIENCES

Bask in soul-stirring Amalfi views from **Ravello** ❶, which has seduced everyone from Wagner to Gore Vidal. (p580)

Day-trip to **San Gimignano** ❷, dubbed 'the medieval Manhattan' after its soaring centuries-old skyscrapers. (p462)

Applaud the Renaissance architecture of **Urbino**, ❸ one of many historic hill towns in Le Marche and Umbria. (p521)

Take in Unesco-listed Renaissance gardens and towering Roman ruins in **Tivoli** ❹. (p143)

Rejoice in noble Norman architecture and exquisite mosaic work in **Monreale** ❺. (p669)

23

CALL OF THE WILD

The call of the wild exerts a strong pull in Italy. From snowcapped alpine mountains to fuming southern volcanoes, from glacial lakes and salty lagoons to plunging coastlines and untamed island wilderness, Italy's landscape is a magnificent outdoor playground. There's exhilarating year-round sport to be enjoyed, or you can keep it relaxed and take to the country's back roads to luxuriate in the superlative scenery that unfurls before you at every turn.

National Parks

Italy has 25 national parks, encompassing a variety of landscapes from soaring mountains and forests to wetlands, coastal cliffs and offshore archipelagos.

Wildlife

If you're lucky, in the mountains you might catch sight of a chamois, ibex, golden eagle, peregrine falcon or even a Marsican brown bear (pictured).

Hiking Tips

The best weather for hiking is in spring (April to June) and early autumn (September). Trails are generally marked with daubed red-and-white symbols.

BEST WILDERNESS EXPERIENCES

Take in the sky-high rock spires that characterise the Dolomites on a hike around the **Tre Cime di Lavaredo ❶** in Val Pusteria. (p338)

Summit the **Gran Sasso ❷**, the Apennines' highest mountain, from the Campo Imperatore highland plain in Abruzzo. (p155)

Walk with the gods on the **Sentiero degli Dei ❸**, a thrilling coastal trail that runs along the mountains of the Amalfi Coast. (p585)

Revel in the dramatic coastal scenery that unfurls around you in Sardinia's **Parco Nazionale del Golfo di Orosei e del Gennargentu ❹**. (p729)

Learn about the myths that surround the **Monti Sibillini ❺** in Le Marche as you trek the silent slopes. (p537; pictured far left)

25

VILLAS & PALACES

Ever since ancient times, Italy's rulers have spared no expense in employing the top artists and architects of the day to design their dwellings. The result is a remarkable series of imperial palaces, royal retreats, Renaissance mansions and aristocratic villas. Many now house museums and serious art collections, while all testify to the wealth and ambition of their former owners. Understated they are most decidedly not.

The First Palace

The word 'palace' derives from Palatium, the Latin name for Rome's Palatine Hill (pictured) where Roman emperors lived in the main imperial palace.

Renaissance Showstoppers

The Renaissance was a lucrative period for builders as palaces sprang up across the country, from Vicenza and Mantua to Ferrara, Urbino (pictured) and Florence.

Gardens & Estates

Many of Italy's royal residences have vast gardens which you can sometimes visit independently of the main buildings.

BEST PALACE EXPERIENCES

Gasp at the lavish extravagance of the **Reggia di Caserta ❶**, southern Italy's epic swansong to the baroque. (p563)

Take in Vicenza's **La Rotonda ❷** and the Unesco-listed palaces designed by trail-blazing Renaissance architect Andrea Palladio. (p356)

Head to Turin's northern hinterland to visit the **Reggia di Venaria Reale ❸**, a sumptuous Savoy residence that inspired French rival Versailles. (p171)

Marvel at Mantua's Renaissance architecture, which finds monumental form in the 500-room **Palazzo Ducale** and frescoed **Palazzo Te**. **❹** (p266)

Admire the aristocratic decor of the **Palazzo Reale ❺**, the star turn in a collection of Genoese palaces known as the Palazzi dei Rolli. (p199)

REGIONS & CITIES

Find the places that tick all your boxes.

Turin & Piedmont

HISTORY AND DELIGHTS

Nestling up to the French border, Piedmont is many things to many people. Urbanites can get their fill in Turin, the region's cosmopolitan, forward-looking capital, while outdoor enthusiasts can test their mettle in the snowcapped Alps and gourmets can feast on world-class wines and decadent cuisine.

p158

Milan & the Lakes

WEALTH, CULTURE & NATURAL BEAUTY

From art galleries and design studios to medieval palaces and alpine lakes, this swath of northern Italy offers urban swagger and waterside chic. Milan is the main draw, paving the way for charming cities like Bergamo and Mantua, and the great lakes of Como, Maggiore and Garda.

p224

Italian Riviera

THE SONG OF THE SEA

Italy's Riviera, sandwiched between plunging mountains and the Ligurian Sea, boasts chic resort towns, stunning coastal scenery and salty fishing villages. At its heart, Genoa is one of Italy's great port cities, in parts cultured, aristocratic and gritty. To the east, the Cinque Terre seduces with its coastal charms.

p190

Milan & the Lakes, p224

Turin & Piedmont, p158

Italian Riviera, p190

Florence

REFRAMING THE POSTCARDS

An essential stop on every Italian itinerary, Florence is one of Europe's most venerated art cities. Its flawless Renaissance cityscape is crammed with blockbuster museums and world-renowned artworks. Beyond the Michelangelo masterpieces and Medici *palazzi*, you'll find square-side wine bars to enjoy and artisanal shops to browse.

p402

Tuscany

RED WINE, DUSTY ROADS, CASTLE-DOTTED HILLS

Ever since Renaissance artists painted the Tuscan countryside onto the map, travellers have been touring the region in search of the Italian ideal. And with good reason: it's a glorious composition of rolling hills and Chianti vineyards, medieval towns and inspiring Gothic cathedrals.

p448

The Dolomites & the Northeast

MAJESTIC MOUNTAINS, ALPINE CULTURE, FAMED VINEYARDS

Pour a glass of prosecco and toast the Triveneto, a historic area encompassing Trentino Alto-Adige, Friuli Venezia Giulia and the Veneto. Soaring across the region's north, the Dolomites present some of Italy's most spectacular scenery; at lower altitudes you can enjoy cultural riches in Verona, Vicenza and Padua.

p314

Venice

THE 'MOST SERENE' CITY OF ART

With its fairy-tale domes, Gothic facades, gondolas and romantic waterways, Venice is a city like no other. Yet for all its obvious beauty, it's still a city of secrets, a city of ethereal winter fogs and hidden gardens, sleepy *campi* (squares) and weather-worn *bacari* (bars).

p268

Bologna & Emilia-Romagna

GASTRONOMIC DELIGHTS, ` HISTORIC TREASURES

Producer of some of Italy's most celebrated foods, as well as fast cars and opera maestros, Emilia-Romagna feeds the soul and excites the appetite. From the red porticoes of medieval Bologna to mosaic-cloaked Ravenna and Rimini's brassy seafront, there's food, art and fun aplenty.

p362

Umbria & Le Marche

THE HIDDEN HEART OF ITALY

Italy's undulating centre excels in handsome hilltop towns. Chief among these are Perugia, Assisi, Urbino and Orvieto – all featuring well-preserved medieval centres and artistic treasures. Elsewhere you can hike in the brooding Monti Sibillini and soak up the sun on the Riviera del Conero's beaches.

p504

Dolomites & the Northeast, p314

Venice, p268

Bologna & milia-Romagna, p362

Florence, p402

Tuscany, p448

Umbria & Le Marche, p504

Lazio & Abruzzo, p130

ROME, p58

Southern Italy on p30

Rome

ITALY'S LEGENDARY CAPITAL

Haunting ruins, awe-inspiring art and iconic monuments combine to thrilling effect in Rome, Italy's charismatic and highly charged capital. Post-pandemic, the city is awash with travel-hungry visitors keen to carpe diem (seize the day) and live the dolce vita.

p58

Tuscany, p448

Lazio & Abruzzo

ANCIENT HISTORY & SOARING MOUNTAINS

Lazio, often overshadowed by its regional capital Rome, rarely makes it into the limelight – but with World Heritage Sites, Etruscan tombs, volcanic lakes and sandy beaches, it has a lot to brag about. To the east, the Apennine region of Abruzzo thrills with its ancient beech forests and rugged mountains.

p130

Sardinia, p708

Sardinia

WALK IN THE FOOTSTEPS OF GIANTS

There's more to Sardinia than its spectacular beaches and secluded coves. Cultured city life thrives in Cagliari and northern rival Sassari, while the wild interior opens a window onto an island spirit that finds form in prehistoric ruins, passionate festivals and splashes of modern street art.

p708

Sicily

ANCIENT RUINS & VOLCANIC ADVENTURE

Sicily's fertile volcanic landscape has combined with a history of foreign domination to create a fascinating cultural mishmash that ranges from ancient Greek temples to Norman cathedrals and baroque basilicas. Add aquamarine seas and a rich Arab-inflected cuisine, and you have all the ingredients for an unforgettable southern sojourn.

p656

Northern Italy
on p28

Umbria &
Le Marche,
p504

Puglia

TARALLI & VINO

Italy's heel is a gourmet's delight, a bastion of
old-school *cucina povera* (poor man's cuisine) and
southern hospitality. Food apart, you can admire
extravagant baroque architecture in Lecce and
weird conical-capped houses in Alberobello.
The Valle d'Itria is made for slow touring and the
Gargano provides hiking and magical sea views.

p594

Lazio & Abruzzo,
p130

OME,
p58

Naples &
Campania,
p544

Puglia,
p594

Naples & Campania

HISTORY & MYTH

With Mt Vesuvius brooding darkly on
the horizon, Naples is a high-octane
city of Dickensian backstreets and
princely palaces, soul-stirring art
and dreamy panoramas. Beyond its
boundaries, the Campania region
harbours the dramatic Amalfi Coast,
ghostly ruins at Pompeii, and spas and
sea caves on offshore islands.

p544

Calabria &
Basilicata,
p622

Calabria &
Basilicata

HISTORY AMID
SOARING MOUNTAINS

Italy's toe, rural and little known to
foreign visitors, offers an unvarnished
glimpse of life in the sun-baked south.
Tourism is largely confined to the
regions' blissful beaches and the
rocky city of Matera; venture inland
and you can explore vast tracts of
untamed mountain country in its three
national parks.

p622

Sicily,
p656

WHEN TO GO

Any time. Italy is a year-round destination that can be enjoyed as much in winter as in the busier seasons of summer, spring and autumn.

Ever since pilgrims started traipsing to Rome and classical-minded aristocrats embarked on the Grand Tour, travellers have been flocking to Italy. To follow in their footsteps, spring and autumn are the best seasons for sightseeing, touring and enjoying seasonal food. High summer means packed beaches as cities empty and holidaymakers head to the coast, while winter promises good times in the country's many ski resorts.

When planning a visit, it's also worth checking Italy's festivals programme and religious calendar. Major cultural and business events can take over even large cities, while saints' days and big religious celebrations can lead to crowds and spikes in accommodation prices.

Accommodation Lowdown

In many cities, there's no precisely defined high and low season. But as a general rule, accommodation is cheapest between November and March. On the coast, prices sky-rocket in August, so try to come in June, July or early September.

⊘ I LIVE HERE

MOUNTAIN SPORT

Denis Falconieri is a journalist and author for Lonely Planet Italia. Based in Aosta, he's a passionate hiker, climber and downhill skier. (@denisfalconieri)

I love living in the mountains throughout the year. In February and March, the ski slopes in the Valle d'Aosta are stunning and there's no shortage of opportunities for organising ski trips. For climbing and tackling the *vie ferrate*, the Dolomites have some magnificent sheer rock faces, which are at their best in June and September.

SNOW FALLS

Snow can pretty much be guaranteed in the Alps and Apennines from November to March, possibly even later. It also snows at lower altitudes, although when and how much is far less predictable.

LEFT: REDA &CO SRL/ALAMY STOCK PHOTO ©
RIGHT: KINO ALYSE/GETTY IMAGES ©

Sa Sartiglia, Oristano (p731)

Weather through the year (Rome)

JANUARY	FEBRUARY	MARCH	APRIL	MAY	JUNE
Ave. daytime max: **12°C**	Ave. daytime max: **13°C**	Ave. daytime max: **16°C**	Ave. daytime max: **19°C**	Ave. daytime max: **23°C**	Ave. daytime max: **27°C**
Days of rainfall: 7	Days of rainfall: 7	Days of rainfall: 7	Days of rainfall: 7	Days of rainfall: 6	Days of rainfall: 4

SAHARAN WIND

It's not uncommon to wake up on a spring or summer morning and find everything outside dusted in sand, particularly in Italy's south. This is thanks to the *scirocco*, a hot southerly wind that blows in from North Africa bringing sand from the Sahara Desert.

Carnivals, Processions & Palio

The run-up to Lent sees **Carnevale** festivities break out across the country. In Venice masked partygoers have a ball, while in Viareggio crowds cheer on giant papier-mâché floats. **February**

Processions take to Italy's streets to mark **Easter**. Romans flock to St Peter's Square to be blessed by the pope (p97); Florentines fire off fireworks by the Duomo (p408). **March or April**

Siena's Piazza del Campo sets the stage for the **Palio** (p454), a daredevil horse race between costumed jockeys. Each rider represents one of the city's medieval *contrade* (districts). **July and August**

Performers take to the steep streets of Spoleto for the **Festival dei Due Mondi**. For more than two weeks, the Umbrian town stages art exhibitions, opera, ballet and classical music. **June to July**

Sporting Thrills

Masquerading horse riders perform fearless equestrian acrobatics while processions march to the beat of costumed drummers at **Sa Sartiglia**, a historic carnival event held in the Sardinian town of Oristano (p731). **February**

Costumed players kick lumps out of each other during Florence's **calcio storico** (historic football match; p433), held to celebrate the city's patron saint. **June**

The late-summer skies of **Urbino** (p521) burst into colour as thousands of kites soar above the Renaissance city during the Festa dell'Aquilone. **September**

During the **Corsa degli Zingari**, hundreds of hardy runners hurtle barefoot around stony mountain paths near the small Abruzzo town of Pacentro (p153). **September**

RAINY ROME

It actually rains more in Rome than it does in London. The difference is that in Rome rain tends to fall in more predictable patterns, generally from October to February, while in London it can rain anytime.

JULY	**AUGUST**	**SEPTEMBER**	**OCTOBER**	**NOVEMBER**	**DECEMBER**
Ave. daytime max: **31°C**	Ave. daytime max: **31°C**	Ave. daytime max: **27°C**	Ave. daytime max: **22°C**	Ave. daytime max: **17°C**	Ave. daytime max: **13°C**
Days of rainfall: 3	Days of rainfall: 3	Days of rainfall: 7	Days of rainfall: 8	Days of rainfall: 9	Days of rainfall: 8

MEET THE ITALIANS

Expect passion and warmth, and discover the complexities of Italians beyond movies and stereotypes. Don't be surprised if you get your ears talked off. BENEDETTA GEDDO introduces her people

IF YOU ASK people what first pops into their heads when they think of Italians, chances are that the answer will be that we speak with our hands. And this is very much true. A conversation held without driving home each idea with the help of a well-practised hand movement – and a swear word or two – is only half a conversation.

We speak with our hands because we're passionate people. We love our cuisine, our sports, and our inalienable right to complain about anything and everything simply for complaining's sake. We love our long, golden summers – a stretch of three months each year in which it feels like everything is possible and good because it's still light outside at 9pm.

We're united by many things, including our shared love for our heritage, which we hate to see disrespected, so my heartfelt advice is to not jump in any fountains or take stones from archaeological sites. We're joined by the deep bonds that tie our families together – sometimes a blessing of community and love and sometimes a burden of obligations and expectations. And we're connected by the mark that the Catholic Church still has on our country – even though the Republic of Italy doesn't have a state religion, the influence that Catholicism has over every aspect of Italian life is almighty.

HOW MANY & HOW OLD?

Italy has a population of just over 60 million. And like many other countries, this is an ageing population, with more than half the people 45 years or older – a percentage that is only going to increase.

At the same time, I believe that few other places do regional differences like Italy. After all, Italy as we know it today is pretty young. Unification took place in 1861, and before that, it was kingdom against dukedom against the Austrian Empire against the Papal State. So we identify ourselves as Italians, yes, but always while specifying the region we come from.

It all comes back to those centuries we spent as different states and kingdoms. You'll hear a change in voice and intonation as you move up and down the country, for starters – regional Italian in Veneto has very little in common with the one in Sicily, and that's without even mentioning dialects. Bad blood sadly still lingers in the north–south divide, to the disadvantage of the south. Also several neighbouring cities still dislike each other with a passion – just ask the Tuscans. Our complicated politics is a favourite topic of complaint.

On the surface, Italy looks like a movie scene coming to life, starting from its shape as a boot in the middle of the Mediterranean. If you look behind its picturesque small towns, though, you'll find a beautiful country and people that are real and complex. And know that if we were speaking face to face, I would have accompanied my speech with a truly impressive collection of hand gestures.

I'M ITALIAN. BUT MINE IS JUST ONE STORY...

I was born and raised in Piedmont, northern Italy, where my family has lived for generations. Everything here tastes delightfully of home. The roots I have in Piedmont are strong and secure, and they only grew stronger when I returned to live here after my years abroad.

Mine is a common enough story in Italy, but it's definitely not the only one. This country has, after all, always been a place of immigration. There's a long history of Italians moving abroad during the course of the 19th and 20th centuries, and still today, really. Almost a million people have moved abroad in the last 10 years, according to the Italian National Statistics Institute, ISTAT.

And then there are the people who migrate here – ISTAT reports that around 8% of people currently living in Italy are immigrants, with the largest communities being of Romanians, Albanians, Moroccans, Chinese and Ukrainians.

LEFT: JULIAN ELLIOTT PHOTOGRAPHY/GETTY IMAGES © RIGHT: ALLSTAR PICTURE LIBRARY LTD/ALAMY STOCK PHOTO ©

View over Florence from San Miniato al Monte (p442)

GET PREPARED FOR ITALY

Useful things to load in your bag, your ears and your brain

Clothes

Smart casual Appearances matter in fashion-conscious Italy. Smart casual is the way to go when eating out in city restaurants. In summer, shorts, T-shirts and sandals are fine for sightseeing and relaxed beachside lounging. Bring a light waterproof jacket for spring and autumn, and cold-weather gear for winter.

Shoes and hats A hat can be a summer lifesaver, especially at the big archaeological sites where there's often little shade. Practical shoes are another must, as cobblestones can play havoc with heels and ankles – Pompeii in pumps is not a good idea.

Dress codes Many high-profile religious sites enforce dress codes, so if you want to get into

Manners

It's polite practice to **greet people** in shops, restaurants and bars with a '*buongiorno*' (good morning) or '*buona sera*' (good evening).

It's fine to eat pizza with your hands. Cut it onto slices, and fold the triangles lengthways.

Italians are not big on tipping. Round the bill up in pizzerias and trattorias; 5% to 10% is fine in smarter restaurants.

St Peter's Basilica or Venice's Basilica di San Marco, play it safe and cover your shoulders, torso and thighs.

📖 READ

The Leopard (Giuseppe Tomasi di Lampedusa, 1958) Historical novel evoking the social tremors that shook Sicily during Italian unification.

My Brilliant Friend (Elena Ferrante, 2012) The first of the Neapolitan Novels chronicling the friendship between two girls in postwar Naples.

SPQR: A History of Ancient Rome (Mary Beard, 2015) Celebrity classicist brings ancient Rome to life in her authoritative history.

La Bella Figura: A Field Guide to the Italian Mind (Beppe Severgnini, 2007) Italian journalist Severgnini turns his witty pen onto his countrymen.

Words

ciao (chow) is 'hi' or 'bye' to friends or family, possibly accompanied by a kiss on both cheeks.

buongiorno (bwon-jor-no) or **buona sera** (bwo-na se-ra) is a formal way of saying 'good morning' or 'good afternoon/evening'.

arrivederci (a-ree-ve-der-chee) means 'goodbye'.

per favore (per fa-vo-re) is 'please'.

grazie (gra-tsye) is 'thank you', to which the traditional response is **prego** (pre-go), 'you're welcome'.

come stai? (ko-me stai) is the informal version of 'how are you?' You could also ask **come va?** (ko-me va), 'how's it going?' More formally, you'd say **come sta?** (ko-me sta).

scusa (skoo-za) or more formally, **scusi (skoo-zi)**, is 'excuse me' when you want to attract attention. To get

past someone in a crowded space, you'd say **permesso** (per-me-so).

ecco (e-ko) is 'here you are'. It might also have an article (**lo** or **la**) attached to the end, depending on the grammatical gender of the thing being presented.

hai ragione (ai ra-jo-nay) means 'you're right'.

boh (bo) is the Italian equivalent of 'dunno'. Often accompanied by a shrug of the shoulders, it's the classic teenage response to pretty much any question.

basta (ba-sta) means 'that's enough' or 'stop'; eg when someone is pouring a drink or a market trader is piling fruit onto the scales.

un po' (oon poh) is the colloquial version of *poco*, meaning 'a bit', as in 'Would you like some wine?' **Sì, un po'.** ('Yes, a bit.')

📺 WATCH

La grande bellezza (Paolo Sorrentino, 2013) A depiction of Rome as a complex, beautiful city with a morally bankrupt heart.

Nuovo Cinema Paradiso (Giuseppe Tornatore, 1988; pictured) A coming-of-age story centred on the friendship between a boy and a cinema projectionist.

La dolce vita (Federico Fellini, 1960) Fellini's classic with Marcello Mastroianni and Anita Ekberg frolicking in the Trevi Fountain.

Call Me By Your Name (Luca Guadagnino, 2017) Timothée Chalamet adorns several northern locations in this languid love story.

🎧 LISTEN

The Three Tenors in Concert (Luciano Pavarotti, José Carreras, Plácido Domingo; 1990) The first collaborations between the three opera maestros.

Teatro d'ira: Vol. I (Måneskin; 2021) The second album by Italy's Eurovision-winning glam rockers featuring their global breakthrough hit *'Zitti e buoni'*.

La voce del padrone (Franco Battiato; 1981) The best-selling album that catapulted Italy's much-loved singer-songwriter to pop superstardom.

Sig. Brainwash – l'arte di accontentare (Fedez; 2013) Platinum-selling album by homegrown rapper, partner of social-media star Chiara Ferragni.

PAOLO GALLO/SHUTTERSTOCK ©

Spaghetti alle vongole, Naples (p550)

THE FOOD SCENE

Italy is a country that lives to eat, where food is central to social life and culinary traditions are revered with heartfelt pride.

Forget politics and football – no subject provokes passions in Italy quite like food. Everyone has an opinion on it and is willing to share that opinion, often in determined, forthright terms. Feelings run high around food.

Italy is, after all, the spiritual home of the Mediterranean diet and the birthplace of the Slow Food Movement. Yet long before Slow Food was a thing, Italian cooks had been practising what the movement preached – the use of seasonal, locally sourced ingredients. Of course, they had – and still have – access to Italy's bountiful basket of sun-kissed produce.

Italy's cuisine is famously regional and wherever you go, you'll be presented with specialities rooted in local traditions and home-grown culinary lore. But while recipes and ingredients might differ, the passion behind the pride is universal and whether you're in Palermo or Parma, there are no more exciting words to hear than '*Buon appetito*'.

The Italian Pantry

Look round an Italian kitchen and you'll typically find a selection of classic staples. There'll be pasta: *pasta secca* (dried pasta) for everyday use, and perhaps some *pasta fresca* (fresh pasta) for Sunday lunch. The bread bin will be full, too, probably with a loaf bought that same day. There'll be a bottle of olive oil and maybe some balsamic vinegar for dressing salads and seasoning dishes. You'll probably also find some

Best Italian Dishes	PIZZA MARGHERITA	TAGLIATELLE AL RAGÙ	RISOTTO ALLA MILANESE	BISTECCA ALLA FIORENTINA
	Classic pizza with tomato, mozzarella and basil.	The original spag bol: long pasta ribbons with meat sauce.	Milan's signature rice dish prepared with bone marrow and saffron.	Florence's door-stopper steak, a giant T-bone of Chianina beef.

pulses and legumes kicking around in a dark corner. Reach into the fridge and you'll come across paper wallets of thinly sliced hams, wedges of hard cheese for grating and softer cheeses for nibbling.

Regional Specialties

Of course, what type of pasta, ham or cheese you'll find will depend on where you are in the country. In Emilia-Romagna they love their egg pastas like *tagliatelle* (ribbon pasta) and tortellini (pockets of meat-stuffed pasta), while Umbrians have their *strangozzi* (a kind of rectangular spaghetti) and Puglians can't get enough of their *orecchiette* ('little ears' pasta). Similarly, there are endless variations of hams and cured meats, ranging from Parma's celebrated prosciutto to *mortadella* (pork cold cut) from Bologna and dry-salted speck from Trentino Alto-Adige. Cheese addicts will have their work cut out, too, choosing between northern *parmigiano reggiano* (Parmesan) and Gorgonzola or southern mozzarella and burrata.

Time for a Drink

For millions of Italians, a morning *caffè* (coffee) is an essential part of their daily routine. Taken standing in a bar or made at home in a *caffettiere* (moka pot), this is a shot of strong dark coffee – what non-Italians would call an espresso. Further coffees might follow later in the morning and after lunch. Cappuccino is an acceptable alternative, but only in the mornings.

To accompany meals or sip over an early-evening snack, wine is the tipple of choice. As a rule, you can't go wrong ordering a local, regional wine, be that a Barolo from Piedmont, Tuscan Chianti or Veronese Valpolicella.

DAWN DAMICO/SHUTTERSTOCK ©

FOOD & WINE FESTIVALS

Girotonno (p721) The tiny Sardinian island of San Pietro pays its respects to its prized local tuna during this June festival.

Festa delle Rose (p205) The small Ligurian town of Busalla hosts this June celebration of its roses, used to flavour liqueurs and sweeteners.

Festa te la Uliata (p599) Pugliese street food stars at this July festival in Caprarica di Lecce in the Salento.

Festival del Prosciutto di Parma (p367) Parma showcases its world-famous ham every September.

Eurochocolate (p515) Perugia's medieval centre sets the stage for the city's October homage to all things chocolate.

International White Truffle Fair (p175) Chefs, cooks and foodies flock to Alba in October to delight in the eye-wateringly expensive white truffle.

ALESSANDRO CRISTIANO/SHUTTERSTOCK ©

Barolo wine, Alba (p176)

Eurochocolate, Perugia (p515)

SPAGHETTI ALLE VONGOLE	PORCHETTA	POLENTA	CICHETI
Much-loved seafood pairing of spaghetti and clams.	Boneless pork seasoned with herbs and generally served cold.	A northern cornmeal porridge that substitutes for rice or pasta.	Venetian bar snacks, a kind of Italian tapas.

Local Specialities

Savour our selection of culinary classics and gastro challenges.

Everyday Pastas

Spaghetti aglio olio With oil, garlic and (optionally) chilli.
Spaghetti carbonara Pork lardons in a yolky egg sauce.
Pasta al pesto Mixed with a paste of basil, garlic, pine nuts and Parmesan.
Pasta e ceci An earthy marriage of pasta and chickpeas.

Street Food & Snacks

Pizza al taglio Pizza by the slice is the perfect Roman snack.
Arancini Sicilian fried-rice balls stuffed with *ragù* (meat sauce), peas and cheese.
Porchetta rolls Herbed roast pork in a crispy bread roll.
Focaccia genovese Genoa's thin focaccia brushed with olive oil and coarse salt.
Panzerotti Fried pizza pies stuffed with tomato and stringy mozzarella.

Sweet Treats

Gelato Heaven in a cone.
Cannoli Biscuity pastry tubes packed with creamy ricotta.
Sfogliatelle Flaky pastry stuffed with ricotta and candied fruit.
Tiramisu Trattoria staple consisting of coffee,

Arancini

chocolate, mascarpone and ladyfingers.
Panettone Traditional Italian Christmas cake, a sponge with candied fruit.

Offal Challenges

Il quinto quarto Roman gourmands can't get enough of 'the fifth quarter' (ie the animal's innards). Look out for *pajata* (veal intestines), *trippa* (tripe), *animelle* (sweetbreads) and *coda alla vaccinara* (oxtail).
Lampredotto In Florence, they like their cow's stomachs boiled, sliced, seasoned and served in a bread roll.
Pani ca meusa Palermo's street-food aficionados swear by these sandwiches of beef spleen and lungs dipped in boiling lard.

MEALS OF A LIFETIME

Osteria Francescana (p375) The Modena restaurant of superstar chef Massimo Bottura promises gourmet fireworks.

Enoteca Pinchiorri (p434) Enjoy refined Tuscan cuisine at this Michelin three-star restaurant in Florence.

Gagini (p666) A Renaissance art studio sets the stage for contemporary fine dining at Palermo's only Michelin-starred restaurant.

Dattilo (p644) The intense flavours of Calabria are showcased at Caterina Ceraudo's Michelin-starred *agriturismo* (farm-stay).

Trattoria al Gatto Nero (p313) Fresh-from-the-boat seafood on the Venetian lagoon island of Burano.

Bislakko Cioccoristoreria (p184) Immerse yourself in modern Piedmontese cuisine at this top Vercelli restaurant.

THE YEAR IN FOOD

SPRING

Spring brings a bumper crop of fresh vegetables. A Roman favourite is the *carciofo* (artichoke), which stars in two city dishes: *carciofo alla giudia* (deep-fried) and *carciofo alla romana* (seasoned with mint and garlic and slowly stewed).

SUMMER

Italy's markets swell with mounds of fresh produce: plump eggplants, vivid red peppers, peaches, figs, watermelons and ripe lemons from the Amalfi Coast. For seafood lovers, this is a good time for *cozze* (mussels).

AUTUMN

Autumn is accompanied by strong earthy flavours: roasted chestnuts, mushrooms, truffles. Hunting season also means a wide choice of game, like *cinghiale* (wild boar), which typically appears in stews and robust meat sauces.

WINTER

Hearty greens pair with *lenticchie* (lentils), *ceci* (chickpeas) and *fagioli* (beans) to bulk up warming winter minestrones and soups. And to keep your vitamin levels up, Sicilian blood oranges are the ideal medicine.

Restaurant terraces, Burano (p309)

SCOTTYELLOX/SHUTTERSTOCK ©

Neptune sculpture, Parco dei Mostri (p141)

THE OUTDOORS

Italy's mountainous terrain and four seas provide stunning year-round sport, from high-altitude skiing to hiking, biking and the full range of water sports.

With two mountain ranges, rivers, lakes and around 7600km of coastline, Italy is a wild outdoor playground. In winter, skiers and snowboarders sweep down slopes everywhere from the northern Alps to the southern Apennines. In the warmer months, hikers and cyclists take to the trails that snake across the country's rocky peaks and forested highlands. For fans of water sports, there are thrills and spills to be had diving in limpid azure waters, white-water river rafting and kayaking to far-flung marine grottos.

Walking & Hiking

Italy is laced with thousands of kilometres of *sentieri* (marked trails), providing everything from multi-day treks to gentle family-friendly rambles. For soul-stirring, high-altitude scenery, the Alps and Dolomites set a stunning backdrop. To the south, you'll find exhilarating walking in Abruzzo's Apennines and the Monti Sibillini in Umbria and Le Marche. Further south still, you can walk with the gods on the Amalfi Coast, enjoy stunning seascapes on the Gargano, and escape to the highlands of Calabria and Basilicata.

There's been a recent revival of interest in Italy's old pilgrimage routes. Chief among these is the Via Francigena, which passes through several regions as it runs from the Swiss border to Rome. Particularly popular are the stretches that pass through Tuscany.

To escape the worst of the summer heat and crowds, avoid August and come in spring

---

Adrenaline Sports

ROCK CLIMBING
Test your mettle on the *vie ferrate* (routes with fixed cables and anchors) of the **Brenta Dolomites** (p331).

DIVING
Plunge the depths of the Tyrrhenian Sea on a diving excursion from **Maratea** (p635) on the Basilicata coast.

SNORKELLING
The sparkling blue waters that lap **Cefalù** (p671) offer superlative snorkelling.

FAMILY ADVENTURES

Learn to tell your stalactites from your stalagmites on a guided tour of the **Frasassi Caves** (p532) in Le Marche. **The weird statues and fantastical apparitions** of Bomarzo's **Parco dei Mostri** (p141) in northern Lazio are a hit with kids and adults alike.

Enjoy a volcanic outing on the black lava slopes of **Mt Etna** (p684) or the Aeolian island of **Stromboli** (p678). **Watch out for brown bears** as you explore the highlands of the **Parco Nazionale d'Abruzzo, Lazio e Molise** (p153).

All aboard for a day of boating, bay-hopping and snorkelling off Calabria's **Costa degli Dei** (p647). **Float around the Venetian lagoon** on a boat tour with **Torcello Birdwatching** (p313), spying the local fauna and an old cemetery island.

(April to June) or in September. Tourist offices can generally provide walking information; some sell dedicated hiking maps.

Skiing & Snowboarding

Italy has some of Europe's best skiing and snowboarding. Most of the top resorts are in the northern Alps, but you'll also find smaller resorts dotted around the Apennines, particularly in the central Abruzzo region. Amazingly, you can even ski in Sicily (on Mt Etna) and Sardinia (in the eastern Gennargentu area). Facilities at the larger resorts are generally world-class, with pistes ranging from nursery slopes to challenging black runs.

The ski season runs from December to late March, but there is year-round skiing in Trentino-Alto Adige and, in Valle d'Aosta, on Mont Blanc (Monte Bianco) and the Matterhorn (Monte Cervino). January and February are generally the best, busiest and priciest months.

Cycling

Whether you're into road racing, mountain biking or cycle touring, you'll find a route to suit. Tourist offices usually provide details on trails and guided rides, and you can hire bikes in most cities and key activity spots.

In summer, many alpine ski resorts repurpose their pistes as cycling trails. For wild, white-knuckle mountain biking, the Brenta Dolomites are a perennial hot spot in Trentino-Alto Adige. In neighbouring Veneto, the Colli Euganei with its vineyards and hilltop castles is a favourite area.

Other top touring spots include Tuscany's wine-rich Chianti country and, down in Puglia, the Valle d'Itria, home to a string of handsome whitewashed towns. Offshore, further cycling opportunities await in Sicily's baroque southeastern corner and Sardinia's rugged Supramonte area.

BEST SPOTS

For the best outdoor spots and routes, see the map on p44.

NAPOLEONKA/SHUTTERSTOCK ©

Hiking, Mt Etna (p684)

KAYAKING	RAFTING	ZIP LINING	WINDSURFING
Explore hidden caves and otherwise inaccessible beaches in the **Aeolians** (p674) by sea kayak or stand-up paddleboard.	Barrel down foaming white-water rapids in the dramatic gorges of the **Raganello Canyon** (p639) in Calabria.	Fly over the medieval rooftops of hilltop Pacentro at eye-watering speeds in the **Parco Nazionale della Majella** (p154).	Ride the waters of **Lago Trasimeno** (p517), Italy's fourth-largest lake in the landlocked region of Umbria.

ACTION AREAS

Where to find Italy's best outdoor activities.

Skiing/Snowboarding

1. Sestriere, Piedmont (p172)
2. Monterosa, Piedmont & Valle d'Aosta (p187)
3. Sella Ronda, the Dolomites (p333)
4. Roccaraso, Abruzzo (p157)
5. Mt Etna, Sicily (p684)

National Parks

1. Parco Nazionale dello Stelvio (p332)
2. Parco Nazionale delle Cinque Terre (p214)
3. Parco Nazionale dell'Appennino Tosco-Emiliano (p283)
4. Parco Nazionale d'Abruzzo, Lazio e Molise (pl53)
5. Parco Nazionale del Gargano (p619)
6. Parco Nazionale dell'Aspromonte (p654)
7. Parco Nazionale del Golfo di Orosei e del Gennargentu (p728)

0   100 miles
0   200 km

44

Tyrrhenian Sea

Ionian Sea

Mediterranean Sea

Kayaking/Canoeing

1 The Aeolians, Sicily (p675)
2 Maratea, Basilicata (p635)
3 Raganello Canyon, Calabria (p639)
4 Lago Trasimeno, Umbria (p517)
5 Lago di Como (p249)

Cycling

1 Brenta Dolomites (p331)
2 Colli Euganei, the Veneto (p351)
3 Chianti area, Tuscany (p461)
4 Valle d'Itria, Puglia (p605)
5 Syracuse coast, Sicily (p687)

Walking/Hiking

1 Tre Cime, the Dolomites (p338)
2 Pescasseroli, Abruzzo (p153)
3 La Sila, Calabria (p640)
4 Lago di Como (p249)
5 Monti Sibillini, Le Marche (p537)
6 Supramonte, Sardinia (p723)
7 Via Francigena, Tuscany (p463)

45

ITINERARIES

Highlights of Italy

Allow: 10 days
Distance: 930km

From the haunting canals of Venice to the backstreets of Naples, this tour is a whistle-stop introduction to Italy's greatest hits. As you work your way down the boot you'll encounter Roman ruins, Renaissance masterpieces, baroque piazzas and mouth-watering regional cuisines.

Duomo, Florence (p408)

ROSSHELEN/SHUTTERSTOCK ©

❶ VENICE ⏱ 2 DAYS

With its achingly photogenic canals, stunning *palazzi* (palaces) and slender black gondolas, **Venice** (p268) will quickly get you in the mood. Take in must-see sights like Piazza San Marco, the mosaic-encrusted Basilica di San Marco, Palazzo Ducale and the art-laden Gallerie dell'Accademia. Scour the seafood stalls at the Rialto Market and snack on *cicheti* (Venetian tapas) over a cool glass of local prosecco.

❷ BOLOGNA ⏱ 1 DAY

Italy's culinary capital and home to Europe's oldest university, **Bologna** (p368) has a gloriously preserved medieval core. Some 20 towers loom over the red-brick centre, whose streets are lined with porticoes and crammed with delis, bars and trattorias. Check out the colossal Basilica di San Petronio, admire art in the Pinacoteca Nazionale, and chow down in the busy Quadrilatero district.

❸ FLORENCE ⏱ 2 DAYS

Two days is not long in **Florence** (p402), Italy's peerless Renaissance city, but it's enough for a breathless introduction to its signature sights: the Duomo, with its famous red-tiled dome; the Galleria degli Uffizi, home to one of the world's greatest art collections; and, of course, Michelangelo's muscular *David* in the Galleria dell'Accademia.

BBSFERRARI/SHUTTERSTOCK ©

4 PISA ⏱ 1 DAY

On day six, head west to **Pisa** (p468) to see if the Leaning Tower really does lean (spoiler: it does, a lot). The Torre Pendente is the star of a trio of medieval sights on Piazza dei Miracoli, an elegant grassy square 2km north of the train station. Alongside the Torre, you can applaud Pisa's pristine 12th-century Duomo and the stubby, cupcake-like Battistero.

5 ROME ⏱ 3 DAYS

The Eternal City where all roads lead, **Rome** (p58) has more than enough to keep you occupied for a lifetime. In three days you'll be able to visit headline sights like the Colosseum, Pantheon and Vatican Museums (home of the Sistine Chapel), while also having time to lap up the colourful street life around Campo de' Fiori and explore the atmospheric Trastevere neighbourhood.

6 NAPLES ⏱ 1 DAY

With Mt Vesuvius brooding on the horizon, **Naples** (p544) is fiery, fun and endlessly addictive. On your last day browse ancient treasures in the Museo Archeologico Nazionale, home to priceless finds from Pompeii, and gorge on the world's best pizza in any number of popular pizzerias. To really go out with a bang, enjoy a night of opera at the Teatro di San Carlo.

47

ITINERARIES

Northern Cities

Allow: 10 days
Distance: 349km

Cut a swath across northern Italy, taking in aristocratic villas and Renaissance frescoes, contemplating Shakespearian drama and sipping cult wines along the way. From Milan the road leads east, passing through a string of historic towns en route to Venice on the Adriatic coast.

❶ MILAN ⏱2 DAYS

Start in style in **Milan** (p230), Italy's fashion and finance capital. Marvel at the architectural excess of the Duomo and Leonardo da Vinci's *Last Supper* before perusing contemporary art in a former gin palace and browsing designer styles in the boutiques of the Quadrilatero d'Oro. Dine on *risotto alla milanese* and toast the road ahead with a canal-side *aperitivo* in the Navigli area.

❷ MANTUA ⏱1 DAY

Next stop is **Mantua** (p265), a prosperous Lombard town renowned for its Renaissance architecture and aristocratic palaces. Chief among these is Palazzo Ducale, the vast residence of the Gonzaga family, which ruled the city for centuries. Contemplate the palace's dazzling frescoes and compare them with the playful images that adorn Palazzo Te, a second Gonzaga palace that was often used for love trysts.

❸ VERONA ⏱2 DAYS

Dedicate the next two days to **Verona** (p352), the setting for Shakespeare's romantic tragedy *Romeo and Juliet*. Check out Juliet's fictional balcony and admire the city's Roman Arena – possibly even attending a summer opera performance. For a change of scene, modern art awaits in the Galleria d'Arte Moderna Achille Forti.

↪ *Detour:* Tour the **Valpolicella wine district** to sample its blockbuster Amarone wines. ⏱ 5 hours

④ VICENZA ⏱1DAY

Take to the streets of **Vicenza** (p356) to inspect the trail-blazing designs of 16th-century architect Andrea Palladio. His tour de force is La Rotonda, a villa on a hill overlooking the city, but you can also marvel at his work at the Teatro Olimpico and Basilica Palladiana. For different style, the baroque Palazzo Leoni Montanari has a wonderful collection of Italian art and Russian icons.

⑤ PADUA ⏱1DAY

Another stop before Venice is **Padua** (p347), a rich, dynamic university city. Its star turn, for which you'll need to book ahead, is the Cappella degli Scrovegni, a northern Sistine Chapel showcasing a celebrated cycle of frescoes by Giotto. Afterwards, you can bone up on the city's prestigious medical history at Musme and join the pilgrims at the Basilica di Sant'Antonio.

⑥ VENICE ⏱3 DAYS

Finish off with three days in **Venice** (p268). That will give you time to check out blockbuster sights such as the Basilica di San Marco and the Gallerie dell'Accademia, as well as art-rich churches and galleries like I Frari and the Peggy Guggenheim Collection. Treat yourself to a gondola tour and an *aperitivo* on Campo Santa Margherita.

ITINERARIES

A Taste of Central Italy

Allow: 7 days
Distance: 243km

Rolling hills crowned by medieval towns, verdant vineyards of the Chianti area and Italy's fourth-largest lake await. Immerse yourself in classic Renaissance scenery on this tour that meanders through southern Tuscany and neighbouring Umbria.

❶ FLORENCE ⏱ 2 DAYS

Whet your appetite for the road ahead with a couple of days in **Florence** (p402). Take in the Renaissance masterpieces of the Galleria degli Uffizi and the architectural splendours of the Duomo. Spend some time checking out the street life around Piazza della Signoria and go face to face with Michelangelo's *David*.

❷ CHIANTI AREA ⏱ 1 DAY

Dedicate day three to pottering about the vineyards and wine estates of the **Chianti area** (p461). Stop off for a tasting at Greve in Chianti, the main town in the Chianti Fiorentino (the northernmost of the two Chianti districts), before lunching on prime steak in Panzano in Chianti and admiring contemporary art at the Castello di Ama.

❸ SIENA ⏱ 1 DAY

With its medieval *palazzi* and lordly Gothic architecture, **Siena** (p454) is a sight to compare with any in Tuscany. To admire it from above, climb the Torre del Mangia, the slender tower that soars over Palazzo Pubblico and the sloping Piazza del Campo. A short walk away, Siena's 13th-century Duomo is one of Italy's greatest Gothic churches.

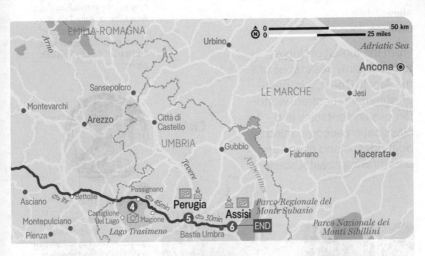

④ LAGO TRASIMENO ⏱1 DAY

After four days on the road, take a mid-trip time out at **Lago Trasimeno** (p517). The placid waters of Italy's fourth-largest lake are a soothing sight, especially if enjoyed from the medieval turrets of Castiglione del Lago, one of several laid-back towns draped along its shorelines.

⑤ PERUGIA ⏱1 DAY

Next stop is **Perugia** (p510), Umbria's regional capital and a lively student city. It's quite a climb to the hilltop centre but worth the effort as the Gothic cityscape unfurls before you. Stroll Corso Vannucci and peruse the masterpieces of the Galleria Nazionale dell'Umbria before adjourning to Piazza IV Novembre and the Cattedrale di San Lorenzo.

⑥ ASSISI ⏱1 DAY

To finish off, make the pilgrimage to **Assisi** (p510). This small cobbled town, now a major day-trip destination, is centred on the Basilica di San Francesco, a mighty church complex whose upper church shelters a celebrated fresco cycle by Giotto. Down below, the frescoed, dimly lit lower basilica leads through to St Francis' tomb.

ITINERARIES

The South Coast

Allow: 7 days
Distance: 110km

From the tumult of Naples to the dreamy seascapes of the Amalfi Coast, this 'best-of' summer tour offers world-famous ancient ruins and classical art accompanied by boat rides, island charm and breathtaking coastal scenery.

Sorrento (p582)

TRABANTOS/SHUTTERSTOCK ©

① NAPLES ⏱ 2 DAYS

Kick off with a blast of urban energy in **Naples** (p544). Feast your eyes on Pompeiian mosaics and stunning classical sculpture at the Museo Archeologico Nazionale, stop by to see the astonishing *Cristo velato* statue at the Cappella Sansevero, and tuck into to-die-for pizza in Spaccanapoli, the heart of the city's historic centre.

② POMPEII ⏱ 1 DAY

On day three catch the Circumvesuviana train and head round the bay to **Pompeii** (p560). Italy's most complete archaeological site is a unique place showcasing the remains of an entire ancient city caught in its death throes. Walk the city streets and see the world's first 'Beware of the Dog' sign as Mt Vesuvius looms menacingly on the horizon.

③ SORRENTO ⏱ 1 DAY

Continue down the coast to the sunny seaside town of **Sorrento** (p582). There are few sights here; rather, the fun is hanging out on the colourful streets, admiring the bay views and browsing the stores selling ceramics and ornate marquetry. You might also want to try some *limoncello*, a sweetly lethal liqueur made from plump local lemons.

KHD/SHUTTERSTOCK ©,

④ CAPRI ⏱ 1 DAY

Spend day five on **Capri** (p569), the most famous of the islands in the Gulf of Naples. Here you can gasp at the otherworldly blue light of the Grotta Azzurra (Blue Grotto) and poke around ancient ruins at Villa Jovis. For magnificent seascapes, take the chairlift from Anacapri to the summit of Monte Solaro, the island's highest point.

⑤ POSITANO ⏱ 1 DAY

The best way to get to **Positano** (p578), the Amalfi Coast's most Instagrammable and expensive town, is by sea. As you approach it, you'll see its steeply stacked houses cascade down the hillside in a riot of peaches, pinks and terracottas. Once on land, you can hang out on the beach and stroll its vertiginous streets lined with voguish shop displays.

⑥ AMALFI ⏱ 1 DAY

End of the road is **Amalfi** (p579), the coast's de facto capital with its striking Cattedrale di Sant'Andrea, colourful ceramic shops and busy seafront. It's not a big place so you can take your time strolling around the sun-filled piazzas.

Detour: Head up to **Ravello** to check out its ravishing gardens and the best views on the coast. ⏱ 3 hours

ITINERARIES

A Slice of Sicily

Allow: 7 days
Distance: 297km

Stretching from the black lava streets of Catania to the ancient Greek temples of Agrigento, this Sicilian tour showcases the island's spectacular baroque beauty. En route, you'll pass through a string of honey-hued towns set amid citrus and olive groves shot through with limestone cliffs and rocky canyons.

Corleone

Mazara del Vallo

Sciacca • • Ribera

Mediterranean Sea

Agrigento **6**

END

0 50 km
0 25 miles

❶ CATANIA ⏱ 2 DAYS

Overshadowed by Mt Etna, **Catania** (p680) makes an inspiring starting point. Pay homage to its distinct brand of black-and-white baroque architecture – the result of building with black lava – at the Cattedrale di Sant'Agata before soaking up the drama of La Pescheria fish market.

🔀 *Detour:* Dedicate day two to exploring the slopes of *Mt Etna*.
⏱ *1 day*

❷ SYRACUSE ⏱ 1 DAY

Birthplace of Archimedes (the mathematician of 'Eureka' fame), **Syracuse** (p687) was considered the most beautiful city in the ancient world. Still today, it's a legendary looker with a stunning central square, Piazza del Duomo, and a magnificent Duomo. Remnants of its earliest days, including a magically intact 5th-century BCE Greek theatre, can be found at the Parco Archeologico della Neapolis.

❸ NOTO ⏱ 1 DAY

Noto (p693) comes as the first of a trio of baroque towns whose beguiling looks result from rebuilds after an earthquake in 1693. Noto is the belle of the ball, boasting one of Sicily's most striking streets, Corso Vittorio Emanuele, and an eye-catching basilica, the Cattedrale di San Nicolò. Beautiful any time, the town positively glows in the early-evening sunlight.

④ MODICA ⏱1 DAY

Stick with the baroque theme in **Modica** (p694), a once-powerful medieval town set around a deep rocky gorge. Search out the Chiesa di San Giorgo in Modica Alta, the upper part of town, and join the locals for the *passeggiata* (stroll) on Corso Umberto I, perhaps snacking on a bar of the town's celebrated chocolate as you go.

⑤ RAGUSA ⏱1 DAY

Fans of the *Inspector Montalbano* hit TV series might recognise some places in **Ragusa** (p694). To find these, head to Ragusa Ibla (the historic centre) where labyrinthine lanes weave past rock-grey *palazzi* to Piazza Duomo, a frequent shooting location. From the sloping, sun-drenched square, stairs lead up to the town's signature cathedral, the Duomo di San Giorgio.

⑥ AGRIGENTO ⏱1 DAY

To finish your tour on a high, push westwards to **Agrigento** (p695), home to a series of ancient Greek temples. Pick of the bunch is the Tempio della Concordia, the headline act in the Valley of the Temples, Agrigento's sprawling archaeological park that encompasses the ruins of the ancient city of Akragas.

THE GUIDE

Chapters in this section are organised by hubs and their surrounding areas. We see the hub as your base in the destination, where you'll find unique experiences, local insights, insider tips and expert recommendations. It's also your gateway to the surrounding area, where you'll see what and how much you can do from there.

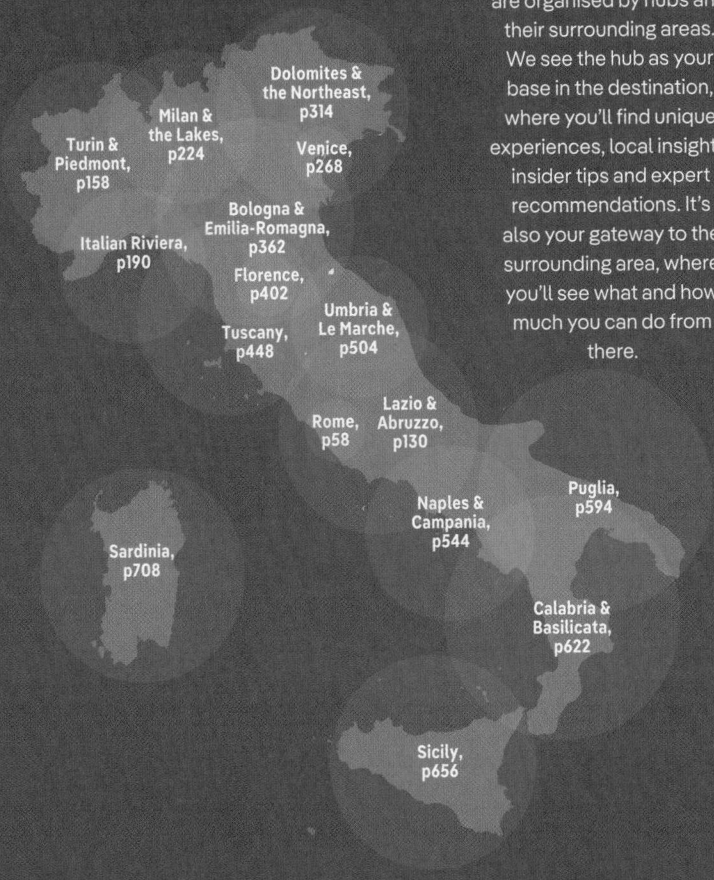

Interior of Cattedrale di Sant'Andrea, Amalfi (p579)

ROME

ITALY'S LEGENDARY CAPITAL

Post-pandemic Rome is thriving as tourism takes off again and visitors return to its historic streets and iconic monuments.

Even in this country of exquisite cities, Rome is special. Few places can rival its astonishing historical legacy and an artistic patrimony that counts some of Europe's most venerated masterpieces. Throughout its 3000-year lifespan, the city has played a starring role in many of the great upheavals of European history, first as the ancient world's *caput mundi* (world capital), and later as seat of the Catholic Church and a hotbed of artistic and architectural innovation. Mad emperors and power-hungry popes have come and gone, all leaving a trail of construction in their wake – the Colosseum, the Pantheon, the Sistine Chapel are just some of the results.

But for all its history, Rome is far from being the open-air museum it's often labelled. Italy's capital and largest city, home to 2.7 million people, is very much a modern working metropolis. So while tourists swarm to its big sights and world-class museums, everyday life plays out in the background: commuters pour in to work in government ministries, shoppers stock up at neighbourhood markets, and office colleagues lunch in old-school trattorias.

For the most part, the city copes well with the dual demands of tourism and modern civic life. But a surge in post-pandemic visitor numbers, which have been forecast to return to pre-COVID levels by 2023, is once again putting pressure on the city's ageing infrastructure and re-awakening the issue of overtourism.

Certainly, Rome can come across as chaotic. It's noisy – the sound of klaxons and buses crunching over cobblestones is something of a city soundtrack – and it's often hectic. Cars and scooters scream past, and crossing the road can become an extreme sport (tip: find a group of nuns or priests and cross with them). Yet, look closer and you'll see that most drivers are wearing their seatbelts and scooter riders generally have their helmets on. The city is not the giant free-for-all it can sometimes seem.

And that's the thing with Rome: you can spend a lifetime looking and you'll still only ever scratch the surface.

OCSKAY MARK/SHUTTERSTOCK ©

THE MAIN AREAS

MAPICS/SHUTTERSTOCK ©

St Peter's Basilica (p96)

Find Your Way

Rome is a sprawling city, but action is focused on a few central neighbourhoods that are best explored on foot. You'll probably take a wrong turn at some point but that's all part of the fun and sooner or later you'll find your way again.

PARIOLI

NOMENTANO

TIBURTINO

**Monti, Esquilino &
San Lorenzo**
p98

SAN
LORENZO

CASTRO
PRETORIO

SALARIO

ESQUILINO

🚉 Stazione
Termini

⛪ Basilica di
Santa Maria
Maggiore

SALLUSTIANO

Museo Nazionale
Romano: Palazzo
Massimo alle Terme 🏛

PINCIANO

VILLAGGIO
OLIMPICO

**Villa Borghese &
Northern Rome**
p119

VILLA BORGHESE

MONTI

🏛 Colosseum

**Tridente, Trevi &
the Quirinale**
p85

◎ Spanish
Steps

🏛 Trevi
Fountain

**Ancient
Rome**
p64

Roman Forum

FLAMINIO

FLAMINIO

Museo
Nazionale Romano:
Palazzo Altemps 🏛

◎ Pantheon

Capitoline 🏛
Museums

PRATI

Piazza ◎
Navona

Centro Storico
p73

Tiber

BORGO

**Vatican City,
Borgo & Prati**
p93

🏛 Vatican
Museums

VATICAN CITY

⛪ St Peter's
Basilica

GIANICOLO

🏛 Villa Farnesina

⛪ Basilica di Santa Maria
in Trastevere

TRIONFALE

🧭 N

0   1 km
0   0.5 miles

Trastevere & Gianicolo
p105

San Giovanni & Testaccio
p112

Southern Rome
p124

Stazione
Roma-Ostia

PIGNETO

TUSCOLANO

SAN GIOVANNI

APPIO-LATINO

CELIO

Mte
Palatino

AVENTINO

TESTACCIO

OSTIENSE

GARBATELLA

PORTUENSE

TRASTEVERE

MONTEVERDE

GIANCOLENSE

FROM THE AIRPORT

Regular trains run to Rome's main train station (Stazione Termini) from Leonardo da Vinci Airport (aka Fiumicino). Buses cover the same route but are slower. From the smaller Ciampino Airport, your best bet is to take a shuttle bus to Termini.

WALK

The best way of getting around Rome's historic centre is on foot. Distances are not great and there's really no better way of experiencing the narrow lanes than by walking. But wear comfortable shoes as the cobblestones can be murder on the feet.

METRO

The metro is quicker than surface transport, but the network is limited and only two main lines serve the centre, crossing at Termini. The metro is convenient for big sights such as the Colosseum and Vatican, but less so for the historic centre.

BUS

Buses connect with most parts of the city, but they can be slow in heavy traffic. Note also that popular routes get very crowded so be prepared to squeeze in. Limited services run through the night, when the metro is closed.

61

Plan Your Days

Kick your day off with a *cornetto* (croissant) and cappuccino before hitting the city's streets in search of artistic treasures and colourful street life.

Roman Forum (p68)

XARA KREM/SHUTTERSTOCK ©

DAY 1

Morning

● Start the day at the **Colosseum** (p66). Afterwards head to the **Palatino** (p69) to poke around ancient ruins before descending into the **Roman Forum** (p68).

Afternoon

● After lunch, climb up to Piazza del Campidoglio to admire sensational classical art in the **Capitoline Museums** (p70). Done there, enjoy great views from the **Vittoriano** (p67) before pressing on to the *centro storico* (historic centre) to explore its labyrinthine lanes and headline sights such as the **Pantheon** (p77) and **Piazza Navona** (p79).

Evening

● Round the day off in the centre, perhaps dining at **La Ciambella** (p82) before an evening coffee at **Caffè Sant'Eustachio** (p83).

YOU'LL ALSO WANT TO...

Explore Rome's neighbourhoods: go underground in the catacombs, catch a football match, swoon at the opera.

DINE ON ROMAN CUISINE

Stop by a **Testaccio** trattoria for a Roman carbonara (pasta with egg, cured pig's cheek and *pecorino*).

SHOP AT THE BOUTIQUES

Browsing independent boutiques is an essential Roman experience – **Monti** is a good place to start.

CATCH A FOOTY GAME

Cheer on Rome's footy teams – Roma or Lazio – from the towering stands of the **Stadio Olimpico**.

FROM LEFT: RARRARORRO/SHUTTERSTOCK ©, MATTEO GABRIELI/SHUTTERSTOCK ©, MIKOLAJ BARBANELL/SHUTTERSTOCK ©

DAY 2

Morning
● First up are the **Vatican Museums** (p94). Once you've blown your mind on Michelangelo's frescoes in the Sistine Chapel, complete your Vatican tour at **St Peter's Basilica** (p96).

Afternoon
● After sliced pizza at **Bonci Pizzarium** (p97), take the metro to Piazza di Spagna to check out the **Spanish Steps** (p88). From there, push on to the **Trevi Fountain** (p90). Throw your coin in then head up for sunset views on **Piazza del Quirinale** (p91).

Evening
● Spend the evening in the area around **Campo de' Fiori** (p78). Try **Open Baladin** (p84) for craft beer or **Barnum Cafe** (p83) for cocktails.

DAY 3

Morning
● Start with a trip to the **Museo e Galleria Borghese** (p122) to marvel at baroque sculpture and Renaissance masterpieces. Afterwards, take a stroll through Rome's showcase park, **Villa Borghese** (p119).

Afternoon
● In the afternoon, push on to **Piazza del Popolo** to catch a couple of Caravaggios at the **Basilica di Santa Maria del Popolo** (p91). Next, dedicate some time to browsing the shops in and around **Via del Corso** (p91).

Evening
● Over the river, picture-perfect **Trastevere** (p105) is the ideal place to spend the evening. Stroll its medieval streets and take your pick from its many bars and restaurants.

GO TO THE OPERA

Enjoy an aria at Rome's opera house, the **Teatro dell'Opera**, or see a summer performance in the ruins of the **Terme di Caracalla**.

SAMPLE THE GELATO

Search out **Otaleg** in Trastevere to try some of the finest, creamiest, most delicious gelato Rome has to offer.

LOOK THROUGH THE KEYHOLE

In the Aventino district lies a great Roman curiosity: a perfect **keyhole view** of St Peter's Basilica.

GO UNDERGROUND

Venture into the **catacombs** beneath Via Appia Antica to explore the dark underworld beneath Rome's streets.

ANCIENT ROME

EPIC RUINS OF THE IMPERIAL CITY

This is where you'll find the great ruins of the ancient city: the Colosseum, the Palatino, the forums and the Campidoglio (Capitoline Hill), the historic home of the Capitoline Museums. The area is generally busy from mid-morning until mid- to late afternoon, although in peak season it can be crowded all day.

The district has two focal points: the Colosseum to the southeast, and the Vittoriano up to the northwest. In between lie the forums, bisected by Via dei Fori Imperiali, the neighbourhood's main artery. This traffic-free road provides a wonderful free platform for surveying the ocean of ruins.

Realistically, most of the people you'll come across will be fellow visitors. But you can still find the odd glimpse of local life – joggers running circuits of the Circo Massimo, engineering students rushing to their building on the Oppian Hill, journalists waiting for the mayor outside her office on Piazza del Campidoglio.

TOP TIP

The obvious starting point for the area is the Colosseum, accessible on line B of the metro. From there you can walk to most other places, including Piazza Venezia, which is served by numerous buses. To avoid the worst crowds, visit the big sights first thing in the morning or, better still, late in the afternoon.

VOLOLIBERO/SHUTTERSTOCK ©

Mercati di Traiano Museo dei Fori Imperiali

Imperial Forums

A SEA OF SPRAWLING RUINS

The **ruins** over the road from the Roman Forum are known as the Imperial Forums. Constructed between 42 BCE and 112 CE, they were mostly buried in 1933 when Mussolini bulldozed Via dei Fori Imperiali through the area, but excavations have since unearthed much of them. The star turns are the Mercati di Traiano and the Colonna Traiana, the stunning reliefs of which depict Trajan's military victories over the Dacians.

Behind the ruins, you can see the remains of a 30m-high wall that protected the forums from the fires that frequently swept in from the nearby Suburra slums.

Mercati di Traiano Museo dei Fori Imperiali

TOWERING ANCIENT MARKETS

This striking **museum** showcases the Mercati di Traiano (Trajan's Markets), the emperor Trajan's towering 2nd-century complex, while also providing a fascinating introduction to the Imperial Forums with multimedia displays, explanatory panels and a smattering of archaeological artefacts.

Sculptures, friezes and the occasional bust are set out in rooms opening onto what was once a Great Hall. The real highlight, though, is the chance to explore the vast three-storey hemicycle, which historians believe housed the forums' administrative offices.

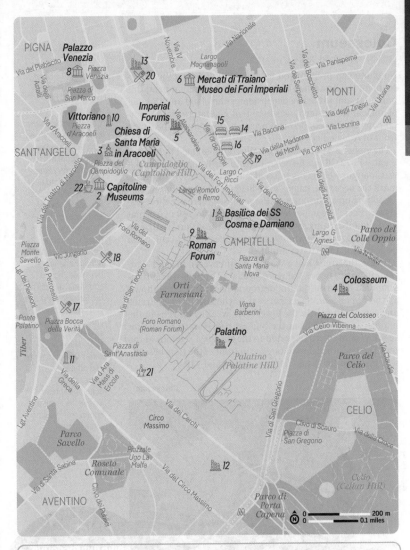

Colosseum

ROME'S FEARSOME AMPHITHEATRE

No photo can prepare you for the thrill of seeing the Colosseum for the first time. More than any other monument, this muscular amphitheatre encapsulates the blood and thunder of ancient Rome, for it was here that gladiators met in mortal combat, and condemned prisoners fought wild beasts in front of frenzied crowds.

The emperor Vespasian originally commissioned the amphitheatre in 72 CE but he never lived to see it completed and it was inaugurated by his son and successor Titus in 80 CE. To mark the occasion, games were held for 100 days and nights.

Looking up at the outer walls, you'll see there are three levels of arches. The upper level had supports for 240 masts that held a giant awning over the arena. On the ground, entrance arches, known as *vomitoria*, allowed spectators to enter and be seated in a matter of minutes.

Inside, the arena had a wooden floor covered in sand – *harena* in Latin, hence the word 'arena' – through which trapdoors led down to the underground backstage area known as the *hypogeum*. Spectators sat in the *cavea*: magistrates and senior officials in the lowest tier, wealthy citizens in the middle, and the plebs in the highest tier. Women (except for vestal virgins) were relegated to the cheapest sections at the top. The podium, a broad terrace in front of the tiers of seats, was reserved for the emperor, senators and VIPs.

TICKETS & SUPER SITES

To visit the Colosseum, you now have to pre-purchase your ticket at www.coopculture.it for a specific entry time.

The standard ticket (€16) is valid for 24 hours and covers entrance to the Colosseum, Roman Forum, Imperial Forums and Palatino. A 'Full Experience' ticket (€22) gives additional access to the Colosseum arena and underground areas as well as the so-called SUPER sites. These are a series of monuments and otherwise inaccessible buildings spread across the Roman Forum and Palatino – see https://parcocolosseo.it for further details.

Colosseum

NICOLA FORENZA/SHUTTERSTOCK ©

GOING UNDERGROUND

The Colosseum was built on land reclaimed from a lake that once formed part of the **Domus Aurea** (p100), emperor Nero's gigantic palace complex. Much of the Domus was destroyed after Nero's death, but you can still visit parts of it under the Oppian Hill.

Basilica dei SS Cosma e Damiano

BLISTERING MOSAICS IN FORUM CHURCH

Backing onto the Roman Forum, this discreet 6th-century basilica incorporates parts of the Foro di Vespasiano and Tempio di Romolo, which you can look into from the end of the nave. However, its main drawcard is its fabulous 6th-century apse mosaic depicting Peter and Paul presenting saints Cosma, Damiano, Theodorus and Pope Felix IV to Christ.

Also worth a look is the 18th-century Neapolitan *presepe* (nativity scene) in a room off the cloistered courtyard.

Basilica dei SS Cosma e Damiano

Chiesa di Santa Maria in Aracoeli

LEGENDARY HILLTOP CHURCH

Atop the Aracoeli staircase, this 6th-century Romanesque **church** marks the summit of the Capitoline Hill. Inside are several treasures, such as an impressive Cosmatesque floor and 15th-century Pinturicchio frescoes. Its chief claim to fame is a wooden baby Jesus that's thought to have healing powers, though the doll is a copy as the original was stolen in 1994.

The church sits on the site of the Roman temple to Juno Moneta and has long been associated with the nativity. According to legend, it was here that the Tiburtine Sybil told Augustus of Christ's imminent birth.

Vittoriano

MONUMENTAL ALTAR TO THE FATHERLAND

Love it or loathe it (as many Romans do), you can't ignore the Vittoriano, aka the Altare della Patria, the mountain of white marble that towers over Piazza Venezia. It was built at the turn of the 20th century to honour Italy's first king, Vittorio Emanuele II, who's immortalised in its vast equestrian statue.

The huge edifice provides the dramatic setting for the Tomb of the Unknown Soldier and, inside, the small **Museo Centrale del Risorgimento**, telling the history of Italian unification. But the real high point is the monument's summit balcony, affording 360-degree views of the city – take the panoramic **Roma dal Cielo** lift to the top.

Vittoriano

Palazzo Venezia

LANDMARK RENAISSANCE PALACE

Built between 1455 and 1464, Palazzo Venezia was the first of Rome's great Renaissance palaces. For centuries it was the embassy of the Venetian Republic – hence its name – but it's more readily associated with Mussolini, who had his office here. Today it houses the **Museo Nazionale del Palazzo Venezia** and its eclectic collection of Byzantine and early Renaissance paintings, ceramics, bronze figures, weaponry and armour.

The *palazzo* is a formidable sight with its crenellated facade, courtyard garden and monumental two-tiered cloister. Inside, check out the temporary exhibitions in Apartamento Barbo.

ABOVE: ESSEVU/SHUTTERSTOCK ©
LEFT: ARTMEDIAFACTORY/SHUTTERSTOCK ©

67

Roman Forum

RUINS OF ANCIENT ROME'S NERVE CENTRE

The Roman Forum was ancient Rome's showpiece centre, a teeming district of temples, basilicas and vibrant public spaces. Its ruins can be confusing but if you can get your imagination going, it's a wonderfully compelling experience to walk in the footsteps of so many legendary Roman figures.

Traversing the site is **Via Sacra**, the Forum's main drag. This leads to the **Tempio di Giulio Cesare** on the spot where Julius Caesar was cremated in 44 BCE. From there it's a short walk to the Curia, the seat of the original Roman Senate, and the Arco di Settimio Severo, a triumphal arch built in 203 CE to commemorate the Roman victory over the Parthians.

Nearby, eight granite columns remain from the **Tempio di Saturno**, an important temple that doubled as the state treasury. Back in the Forum's centre, look out for the three columns that survive from the Tempio di Castore e Polluce.

For a change of period, stop by the 6th-century **Chiesa di Santa Maria Antiqua**, which boasts some early Christian frescoes and one of the oldest icons in existence.

Back on the pagan trail, look out for the **Casa delle Vestali**, the home of the virgins who tended the flame in the adjoining Tempio di Vesta. Further on, you'll find the colossal Basilica di Massenzio, and beyond that, the **Arco di Tito**, which was built in 81 CE to celebrate the victories of Vespasian and Titus against rebels in Jerusalem.

VESTAL VIRGINS

Despite privilege and public acclaim, life as a vestal virgin was no bed of roses. Every year, six physically perfect patrician girls aged between six and 10 were chosen by lottery to serve Vesta, goddess of hearth and household. Once selected, they faced 30 years of chaste servitude, tending to the sacred fire in the Tempio di Vesta. If the fire went out, the priestess responsible would be flogged. More chillingly, if a priestess lost her virginity, she risked being buried alive.

Roman Forum

TILALUCIDA/SHUTTERSTOCK ©

Palatino

BIRTHPLACE OF AN EMPIRE

Sandwiched between the Roman Forum and the Circo Massimo, the **Palatine Hill** is a gorgeous expanse of evocative ruins, towering pine trees and stunning views. This is where it all began, where Romulus supposedly killed Remus and founded the city in 753 BCE, and where the ancient Roman emperors lived in palatial luxury.

The emperor Augustus lived here all his life, and successive emperors built increasingly opulent palaces – in fact, the word 'palace' is derived from the hill's Latin name, Palatium. But after Rome's decline, the area fell into disrepair, and the Middle Ages saw churches and castles built over the ruins. During the Renaissance, wealthy families had gardens laid out on the site.

Most of the Palatino as it appears today is covered by the ruins of emperor Domitian's vast complex, which served as the main imperial palace for 300 years. Divided into the **Domus Flavia** (the public part of the palace complex), **Domus Augustana** (the emperor's private quarters), and a sunken stadio, it was built in the 1st century CE. Near the Domus Augustana, the **Museo Palatino** chronicles the development of the Palatino with video presentations, models and archaeological finds.

Other highlights include the well-preserved Casa di Livia, home of Augustus' wife Livia; the frescoed Casa di Augusto, Augustus' private residence; and the Orti Farnesiani garden with a balcony that offers breathtaking views over the Roman Forum.

ROMULUS & REMUS

Rome's mythical founders were supposedly brought up on the Palatino by a shepherd, Faustulus, after a wolf saved them from death. In 2007 a cave was discovered 15m beneath the Domus Augustana that some scholars claimed was the **Lupercale**, the cave where ancient Romans believed Romulus and Remus had been suckled by the wolf.

In the southwestern part of the hill, among a series of Iron Age huts, the **Casa Romuli** is where Romulus reputedly lived in the 8th century BCE.

Domus Augustana, Palatino

HELISSA GRUNDEMANN/SHUTTERSTOCK ©

Capitoline Museums

WORLD'S OLDEST PUBLIC MUSEUMS

Housed in two stately *palazzi* (palaces) on **Piazza del Campidoglio**, the Capitoline Museums are the world's oldest public museums. They date to 1471, when Pope Sixtus IV donated a number of bronze statues to the city, forming the nucleus of what is now one of Italy's finest collections of classical sculpture. The museums' entrance is in Palazzo dei Conservatori, where you'll find the original core of the sculptural collection and the **Pinacoteca** (picture gallery), with works by many big names.

Before you head upstairs, take a moment to admire the ancient masonry in the courtyard, most notably a mammoth head, hand and foot from a 12m-high statue of Constantine.

Of the sculpture, the Etruscan Lupa Capitolina is the most famous piece, depicting a bronze wolf standing over her suckling wards, Romulus and Remus. Until recently, the wolf was thought to be a 5th-century BCE Etruscan work but carbon dating has shown it probably dates to the 1200s.

Upstairs, the picture collection boasts masterpieces aplenty. These include Pietro da Cortona's *Ratto delle Sabine* (*Rape of the Sabine Women*), and two important canvases by Caravaggio: *La buona ventura* (*The Fortune Teller*; 1595) and *San Giovanni Battista* (St John the Baptist; 1602).

Palazzo Nuovo also contains some real showstoppers. Chief among them is the *Galata morente*, a touching sculptural depiction of a dying Gaul warrior.

TREATY OF ROME

With frescoes depicting episodes from ancient Roman history and two papal statues – one of Urban VIII by Bernini and one of Innocent X by Algardi – the **Sala degli Orazi e Curiazi** provided the grand setting for one of modern Europe's key events. On 25 March 1957 the leaders of Italy, France, West Germany, Belgium, Holland and Luxembourg gathered here to sign the Treaty of Rome and establish the European Economic Community, the precursor of the European Union.

Piazza del Campidoglio

NATTAKIT JEERAPATMAITREE/SHUTTERSTOCK ©

An Ancient Lie Detector

BOCCA DELLA VERITÀ'S PHOTO OPP

For a quintessential Roman holiday snap, make a beeline for the **Bocca della Verità**. As a monument, this ancient curiosity appears fairly low-key – a bearded face carved onto a giant marble disc, possibly from an ancient fountain or manhole cover. But what makes it special is its legend. This holds that if you tell a lie with your hand in the *bocca* (mouth), the mouth will slam shut and bite your paw off. The challenge, then, is to place your hand in the mouth and smile gingerly as you tell yourself a lie.

You'll find the Bocca in the portico of the medieval **Chiesa di Santa Maria in Cosmedin**, usually at the end of a long line of waiting snappers.

Rooftop Dining & Drinking

BASK IN VIEWS OVER A DRINK

There's no better way of reminding yourself you're in Rome than enjoying an alfresco dinner or drink on a panoramic terrace. For a relaxed coffee against a backdrop of rooftops and domes, try the **Terrazza Caffarelli**, the Capitoline Museums' striking terrace cafe – you don't even need a museum ticket as you can access it from a side entrance on Piazzale Caffarelli.

Near the Bocca della Verità, the **47 Circus Roof Garden** restaurant is another scenic spot, offering stirring views of the Aventine Hill along with a menu of contemporary Mediterranean cuisine.

Easter Processions & Birthday Fun

WITNESS A HEARTFELT EASTER PROCESSION

With its evocative ruins and sky-scraping pine trees, Ancient Rome sets the stage for some of Rome's most atmospheric celebrations.

On Good Friday, you can join crowds at the Colosseum to witness the Pope lead the traditional **Via Crucis** procession. This candlelit event, which is broadcast around the world, is an important feature of Rome's heartfelt Easter celebrations.

For a more lighthearted atmosphere, Rome marks its birthday, the **Natale di Roma**, on 21 April. The programme

WHY I LOVE ANCIENT ROME

Duncan Garwood, writer

Even after more than two decades living in Rome I still get a rush every time I see the Colosseum and the great spread of the forums. More than these, though, I adore the Palatino. As well as the impressive ruins, I love the soaring pine trees and amazing views – the sight of the Roman Forum spread out beneath you really is something else. I also love the legends. If you believe it – and it's more fun if you do – this is where Romulus and Remus were saved by a wolf and founded Rome. It really is an extraordinary place.

EASTER BLESSINGS

Easter is a big deal in Rome, with events staged across the city. These culminate with the pope blessing the crowd on **St Peter's Square** (p93) at noon on Easter Sunday.

 WHERE TO STAY IN ANCIENT ROME

Residenza Maritti
Great little bolthole with 14 individually styled rooms and unforgettable views over the nearby forums. €€

Inn at the Roman Forum
Chic boutique hotel offering five-star service, a refined look, and a quiet location near the Imperial Forums. €€€

Nerva Boutique Hotel
Snug contemporary rooms await at this friendly hotel tucked away behind the forums. €€€

VIA DEI FORI IMPERIALI

Unlike the monuments that surround it, Via dei Fori Imperiali never formed part of the ancient city. In fact, it was built by Mussolini and inaugurated on 28 October 1932.

Cleaving straight through the forums, the road was built as part of a grand urban project to modernise Rome's infrastructure and improve links with the city's outlying districts. It also served a propagandistic purpose, providing Mussolini with a symbolic connection between his Fascist regime (as represented by Piazza Venezia) and the Roman Empire (as represented by the Colosseum).

To build the 900m-long road, Mussolini's bulldozers had to raze an entire Renaissance quarter, known as Alessandrino, and tarmac over much of the ancient forums.

Circo Massimo

varies each year but events and historical re-enactments are generally held around Via dei Fori Imperiali, the Campidoglio and Circo Massimo.

Later in the year, on 2 June, Italy's institutional leaders congregate on the Vittoriano and Via dei Fori Imperiali to commemorate the **Festa della Repubblica** (Republic Day) with wreath laying and a military parade.

Workout on an Ancient Racetrack

JOG AROUND THE CIRCO MASSIMO

To maintain your running routine, don your trainers and join the joggers on the **Circo Massimo**. Here you can run around what was once ancient Rome's largest chariot racetrack, a 600m circuit set inside a 250,000-seat stadium. Little remains of this vast structure apart from a small segment at the southern end, but the huge grassy basin retains its rectangular shape and there's something undeniably uplifting about exercising in the shadow of the Palatino, Rome's original birthplace.

Serious athletes take to the city's streets in late March or April for the Rome Marathon, which starts and finishes on Via dei Fori Imperiali.

 WHERE TO EAT AND DRINK IN ANCIENT ROME

Alimentari Pannella Carmela
An authentic food store ideal for picnic fare and *panini* stuffed to order at its deli counter. €

0,75
Laid-back bar on Circo Massimo favoured by a young international crowd.

Terre e Domus
Classic regional fare and a casual vibe near the landmark Colonna di Traiano. €€

CENTRO STORICO

LABYRINTHINE HISTORIC CENTRE

A tightly packed warren of cobbled alleyways, Renaissance palaces and baroque piazzas, the historic centre is the Rome many tourists come to find. Locals frequent it too, coming in to work, to take in an exhibition, or simply to unwind on a night out with friends.

The Pantheon and Piazza Navona are the headline acts, but walk around for a bit and you'll come across a host of monuments, museums and churches, many containing masterpieces by the likes of Michelangelo, Caravaggio, Bernini and Raphael.

It's not all high culture, though. The area's aristocratic *palazzi* and showpiece squares provide a wonderful backdrop for alfresco dining and late-night carousing. Between fine-dining restaurants, family-run trattorias, speakeasies and chic cocktail bars, you'll always find somewhere to suit your mood.

Bring comfortable shoes for the uneven cobbles and some good humour for those inevitable wrong turns and ever-present crowds.

TOP TIP

The best way to reach the area is by bus, to Largo di Torre Argentina. Alternatively, you can walk from Barberini or Spagna metro stations. Once in the area, you're best to explore on foot. Walking can be thirsty work, so look out for Rome's traditional drinking fountains, known locally as *nasoni* (big noses).

V_E/SHUTTERSTOCK ©

Chiesa Sant'Ignazio di Loyola

Chiesa Sant'Ignazio di Loyola

FAKE DOME & MESMERISING FRESCOES

Flanking a delightful rococo piazza, this Jesuit **church** boasts a Carlo Maderno facade and two *trompe l'œil* frescoes by Andrea Pozzo (1642–1709). One cleverly depicts a fake dome, while the other, on the nave ceiling, shows St Ignatius Loyola being welcomed into paradise by Christ and the Madonna.

For the best views of this dizzying work, stand on the small yellow spot on the nave floor. A second marble disc marks the best place to admire the dome, which is actually a flat canvas.

Galleria Doria Pamphilj

OLD MASTERS IN PRIVATE GALLERY

Hidden behind the grey exterior of Palazzo Doria Pamphilj, this wonderful **gallery** displays one of Rome's richest private art collections, with works by Raphael, Tintoretto, Titian, Caravaggio, Bernini and Velázquez, as well as several Flemish masters.

Masterpieces abound, including two early Caravaggios. The undisputed star is Velázquez' portrait of an implacable Pope Innocent X, who grumbled that the depiction was 'too real'. For a comparison, check out Gian Lorenzo Bernini's sculptural interpretation of the same subject.

The excellent free audio guide, narrated by Jonathan Pamphilj, brings the gallery alive with family anecdotes and background information.

CENTRO STORICO

Via Ulpiano
Via Triboniana
Lgt Prati
Lgt Marzio
Via di Monte Brianzo
Ponte Umberto I
Piazza Ponte Umberto I
Via dell'Orso
Via dei Portoghi
Ponte Sant'Angelo
Lgt Tor di Nona
Via G Zanardelli
Via dei Soldati

Museo Nazionale Romano: Palazzo Altemps 28

12
Basilica di Sant'Agostino 3

Ponte Vittorio Emanuele II
Lgt della Altoviti
Piazza del Coronari
Via dei Coronari
PONTE
Piazza Tor Sanguigna

Via Paola
Via del Banco di Santo Spirito
Via di Panico
21
27

Ponte Principe Amedeo
Via Acciaioli
Largo O Tassoni
Via dei Banchi Nuovi
Via Monte Giordano
Via della Pace
Via Santa Maria dell'Anima

Chiesa San Luigi Francesi 6

Via Giulia
Corso Vittorio Emanuele II
Piazza dell'Orologio
Via del Corallo
Via di Parione
Palazzo Madama 17

Via dei Banchi Vecchi
Piazza San Cesarini
Via dei Filippini
Via della Chiesa Nuova
Via del Governo Vecchio
31
PARIONE
20
Corso del Rinascimento
Piazza Sant'Eu

Via del Gonfalone
45
43
Piazza della Chiesa Nuova
Via Sora
29
Piazza Navona
Via della Cancelleria

Lgt D Sangallo
Largo L Perosi
30
Via del Pellegrino
Piazza Pasquino
Via di San Pantaleo
SANT' EUSTACHIO
Via de Sediar

Ponte G Mazzini
Via di Montoro
34
Palazzo della Cancelleria
Piazza della Cancelleria
Piazza di San Pantaleo
Piazza Sant'Andrea della Valle
Corso Vittorio Emanue

Via di Monserrato
Via dei Cappellari
14
37
1
Via dei Baullari

Via Giulia
33
Arco degli Acetari
REGOLA
Piazza Farnese
26
4
Campo de' Fiori
Piazza Vidon

Palazzo Farnese 16
Via della Corda
Via del Mascherone
Via dei Giubbonari
Via delle Grotte
35
36

18
Palazzo Spada
Via Capo di Ferro
Via Arco del Monte
Via degli Specchi
42

Lgt dei Tebaldi
Piazza Trinità Pellegrini
47

Via San Francesco di Sales
Via dei Riari
Via della Farnesina
Piazza SV Pallotti
Via dei Pettinari
39

Orto Botanico
Via della Lungara
Ponte Sisto
41
Via del Conservatorio
Via delle Zoccolette

TRASTEVERE
Lgt dei Vallati
Lgt della Farnesina

Via Garibaldi
Piazza Trilussa
Via Benedetta
Via della Scala
Piazza Benedetta
Lgt della Lungara
Lgt Raffaello Sanzio
Ponte Garibaldi

N
0 — 200 m
0 — 0.1 miles

HIGHLIGHTS
1 Arco degli Acetari
2 Basilica di Santa Maria Sopra Minerva
3 Basilica di Sant'Agostino
4 Campo de' Fiori
5 Chiesa del Gesù
6 Chiesa di San Luigi dei Francesi
7 Chiesa di Sant'Ignazio di Loyola
8 Galleria Doria Pamphilj
9 Isola Tiberina
10 Jewish Ghetto
11 Museo Nazionale Romano: Crypta Balbi
12 Museo Nazionale
Romano: Palazzo Altemps
13 Palazzo Chigi
14 Palazzo della Cancelleria
15 Palazzo di Montecitorio
16 Palazzo Farnese
17 Palazzo Madama
18 Palazzo Spada
19 Pantheon
20 Piazza Navona

SIGHTS
21 Chiostro del Bramante
22 Largo di Torre Argentina
23 Piazza della Minerva
24 Piazza della Rotonda
25 Piazza di Sant'Ignazio Loyola
26 Piazza Farnese
27 Stadio di Domiziano
28 Via dei Coronari
29 Via del Governo Vecchio
30 Via Giulia

SLEEPING
31 Eitch Borromini
32 Hotel Mimosa
33 Navona Essence

EATING
34 Barnum Cafe
35 Fatamorgana
36 Forno Roscioli
37 Grappolo D'Oro
38 La Ciambella
39 Pianostrada
40 Retrobottega
41 Rimessa Roscioli
42 Salumeria Roscioli
43 Supplizio

DRINKING & NIGHTLIFE
44 Caffè Sant'Eustachio
45 Il Goccetto
46 La Casa del Caffè Tazza d'Oro
47 Open Baladin

ENTERTAINMENT
48 Teatro Argentina

Basilica di Sant'Agostino

MARBLE MADONNA STEALS THE SHOW

The plain white facade of this early-Renaissance **church**, built in the 15th century and renovated in the late 1700s, gives no indication of the impressive art inside. Its most famous work is Caravaggio's *Madonna dei Pellegrini* (*Madonna of the Pilgrims*) but you'll also find Raphael's muscular *Profeta Isaia* (*Prophet Isaiah*) and a much-venerated Jacopo Sansovino sculpture called the *Madonna del Parto* (*Madonna of Childbirth*). Expectant mums traditionally pray to it for a safe pregnancy.

MORE CARAVAGGIOS

Caravaggio was the *enfant terrible* of Rome's 16th-century art world, shocking everyone with his wild behaviour and artistic innovations. You'll find his paintings in venues across Rome, including at the magnificent **Museo e Galleria Borghese** (p122) in Villa Borghese park.

Basilica di Santa Maria Sopra Minerva

ROME'S SOLE GOTHIC CHURCH

The much-loved *Elefantino* sculpture trumpets the presence of the Basilica di Santa Maria Sopra Minerva, Rome's only Gothic **church**. Little remains of the original 13th-century structure, and these days the main draw is a minor Michelangelo in the art-rich interior.

Inside, you'll find some superb 15th-century frescoes by Filippino Lippi and the tombs of several luminaries, including three popes and the artist Fra' Angelico. The headless body of St Catherine of Siena lies under the high altar.

Left of the altar is Michelangelo's *Cristo Risorto* (*Christ Bearing the Cross*), depicting Jesus carrying a cross while sporting some jarring bronze drapery. This wasn't actually part of the original composition and was added after the Council of Trent (1545–63) to preserve Christ's modesty.

Chiesa del Gesù

TREASURE TROVE OF BAROQUE ART

Rome's most important Jesuit **church** hosts a rich collection of baroque treasures, including a swirling vault fresco by Giovanni Battista Gaulli (aka Il Baciccia), the *Trionfo del Nome di Gesù* (*Triumph of the Name of Jesus*), and Andrea del Pozzo's bejewelled tomb of Ignatius Loyola, founder of the Jesuits. St Ignatius stayed in the church from 1544 until his death in 1556, living in rooms that you can visit to the right of the main church.

Madonna dei Pellegrini, Basilica di Sant'Agostino

Chiesa di San Luigi dei Francesi

BAROQUE HOME OF A CARAVAGGIO HAT-TRICK

Church to Rome's French community since 1589, this opulent baroque *chiesa* is home to three celebrated early Caravaggio paintings: the *Vocazione di San Matteo* (*The Calling of Saint Matthew*), the *Martirio di San Matteo* (*The Martyrdom of Saint Matthew*) and *San Matteo e l'angelo* (*Saint Matthew and the Angel*), known collectively as the St Matthew cycle. Painted between 1600 and 1602, they display their author's characteristic realism and stunning use of chiaroscuro (the bold contrast of light and dark). Also of note in the church are Domenichino's faded 17th-century frescoes of St Cecilia.

Pantheon

INFLUENTIAL MASTERPIECE OF ANCIENT ARCHITECTURE

A striking 2000-year-old temple, now a church, the Pantheon is the best preserved of Rome's ancient monuments. Built by Hadrian over Marcus Agrippa's 27 BCE temple, it has stood since around 125 CE, and while its greying, pockmarked exterior might look its age, it's still an exhilarating experience to pass through its vast bronze doors and gaze up at the largest unreinforced concrete **dome** ever built.

Hadrian's temple was dedicated to the classical gods – hence the name Pantheon, from the Greek *pan* (all) and *theos* (god) – but in 608 it was consecrated as a Christian church, and it's now officially known as the Basilica di Santa Maria ad Martyres.

Its monumental entrance portico is a massively imposing sight with 16 Corinthian columns, each 11.8m high and each made from a single block of Egyptian granite, supporting a triangular pediment. Inside, in the cavernous marble-clad interior, you'll find the tomb of the artist Raphael alongside those of kings Vittorio Emanuele II and Umberto I.

The real fascination of the Pantheon, however, lies in its massive dimensions and awe-inspiring dome, the harmonious appearance of which is due to a precisely calibrated symmetry – its diameter is exactly equal to the Pantheon's interior height of 43.4m. At its centre, the 8.7m-diameter oculus plays a vital structural role by absorbing and redistributing the dome's huge tensile forces.

THE INSCRIPTION

For centuries the Latin inscription over the entrance to the Pantheon led historians to believe that the current temple was Marcus Agrippa's original. Certainly, the wording suggests this, reading: 'M.AGRIPPA.L.F.COS. TERTIUM.FECIT' or 'Marcus Agrippa, son of Lucius, in his third consulate built this'. However, excavations in the 19th century revealed traces of an earlier temple and scholars realised that Hadrian had simply kept Agrippa's original inscription on his new temple.

Dome interior, Pantheon

TTSTUDIO/SHUTTERSTOCK ©

Campo de' Fiori

HECTIC PIAZZA
TEEMS DAY & NIGHT

Colourful and always busy, **Il Campo** is a major focus of Roman life: by day it hosts a well-known market, by night its restaurants and brassy bars swell with visitors and young locals. Its poetic name (Field of Flowers) is a reference to the meadow that stood here before the square was laid out in the mid-15th century.

Amid the square's hurly-burly, you'll see a statue of a hooded monk. This is philosopher Giordano Bruno, who was burned for heresy here in 1600.

PIT STOCK/SHUTTERSTOCK ©

Campo de' Fiori

Palazzo della Cancelleria

COLOSSAL RENAISSANCE PALACE

SISTINE FRESCOES

To see Michelangelo's frescoes in the Sistine Chapel, hotfoot it over to the **Vatican Museums** (p95) where they form the grand climax of the huge museum complex.

One of Rome's most imposing Renaissance buildings, this huge *palazzo* was built for Cardinal Raffaele Riario between 1483 and 1513. It was later acquired by the Vatican and became the seat of the Papal Chancellery. It's still Vatican property and nowadays houses various Church offices, including the Roman Rota, the Holy See's highest ecclesiastical court.

The *palazzo* also provides the location for an exhibition dedicated to Leonardo da Vinci's machine designs. If that doesn't appeal, you can always take a peek at Bramante's glorious double *loggia* or email economato@apsa.va to book a slot on a Saturday-morning guided tour.

Palazzo Farnese

EMBASSY OF REVERED FRESCOES

Home to the French embassy, this imposing Renaissance *palazzo*, one of Rome's finest, was started in 1514 by Antonio da Sangallo the Younger, continued by Michelangelo and finished by Giacomo della Porta. Inside, it features frescoes by Annibale and Agostino Carracci that are said by some to rival Michelangelo's Sistine Chapel paintings. The highlight, painted between 1597 and 1608, is the monumental ceiling fresco *Amori degli Dei* (*The Loves of the Gods*) in the Galleria dei Carracci.

Visits to the *palazzo* are by guided tour (in English, French and Italian), for which you'll need to book well in advance – see https://visite-palazzofarnese.it for details. Photo ID is required for entry.

Piazza Navona

OPEN-AIR BAROQUE SALON

With its showy fountains, baroque *palazzi* and colourful cast of street artists, hawkers, waiters and tourists, Piazza Navona is central Rome's elegant showcase square. Built over an ancient Roman stadium, it was paved over in the 15th century and for almost 300 years hosted the city's main market. Its grand centrepiece is Bernini's **Fontana dei Quattro Fiumi**, a flamboyant fountain featuring an Egyptian obelisk and muscular personifications of the rivers Nile, Ganges, Danube and Plate. Legend has it that the Nile figure is shielding his eyes to avoid looking at the nearby Chiesa di Sant'Agnese in Agone, designed by Bernini's hated rival Borromini. In truth, Bernini had completed his fountain two years before Borromini started work on the church's elaborate facade and the gesture simply indicated that the source of the Nile was unknown at the time.

The **Fontana del Moro** at the southern end of the square was designed by Giacomo della Porta in 1576. Bernini added the Moor holding a dolphin in the mid-17th century, but the surrounding Tritons are 19th-century copies. At the northern end of the piazza, the 19th-century **Fontana del Nettuno** depicts Neptune fighting with a sea monster, surrounded by sea nymphs.

The piazza's largest building is Palazzo Pamphilj, built for Pope Innocent X between 1644 and 1650, and now home to the Brazilian embassy.

Piazza Navona

STADIO DI DOMIZIANO

Like many of Rome's landmarks, Piazza Navona sits atop an ancient monument, in this case the 1st-century CE Stadio di Domiziano. This 30,000-seat **stadium**, the subterranean remains of which can be accessed from Via di Tor Sanguigna, used to host athletic meets – hence the name Navona, a corruption of the Greek word *agon*, meaning public games. Inevitably, though, it fell into disrepair and it wasn't until the 15th century that the crumbling arena was paved over and Rome's central market was transferred here from the Campidoglio.

NICOLA FORENZA/SHUTTERSTOCK ©

Museo Nazionale Romano: Crypta Balbi

DIG DEEP INTO THE PAST

The least known of the Museo Nazionale Romano's four museums, the Crypta Balbi sits over the ruins of several medieval buildings, themselves set atop the Teatro di Balbo (13 BCE). Archaeological finds illustrate the urban development of the surrounding area, while the museum's underground excavations provide an engrossing insight into Rome's multilayered past.

Isola Tiberina

Isola Tiberina

TIBER RIVER ISLAND

Rome's river island has been associated with healing since the 3rd century BCE, when the Romans built a temple here to the god of medicine, Aesculapius. Still today people come to be cured, though they now go to the Ospedale Fatebenefratelli.

The island is connected to the mainland by two bridges: the 62 BCE **Ponte Fabricio**, Rome's oldest standing bridge, which links to the Jewish Ghetto, and **Ponte Cestio**, which runs over to Trastevere.

Visible to the south are the remains of the Ponte Rotto (Broken Bridge), ancient Rome's first stone bridge, which was all but swept away in a 1598 flood.

Plaques commemorating Holocaust victims

Jewish Ghetto

HEART OF ROME'S JEWISH COMMUNITY

The Jewish Ghetto, centred on lively Via del Portico d'Ottavia, is an atmospheric quarter studded with artisans' studios, offbeat shops, kosher bakeries and popular trattorias. Crowning everything is the square dome of Rome's main synagogue.

Look out for small brass cobblestones in the road. These are plaques commemorating Rome's Holocaust victims: each plaque, placed outside victims' homes, names a person and gives the date and destination of their deportation and death.

Rome's Jewish community dates to the 2nd century BCE, making it one of Europe's oldest. Confinement to the Ghetto came in 1555 when Pope Paul IV ushered in a period of official intolerance that lasted, on and off, until the 20th century.

RIGHT: STEFANO TAMMARO/SHUTTERSTOCK © BELOW: ENNARQ/SHUTTERSTOCK ©

Museo Nazionale Romano: Palazzo Altemps

RENAISSANCE PALACE, GRIPPING CLASSICAL SCULPTURE

Just north of Piazza Navona, Palazzo Altemps is a beautiful late-15th-century *palazzo* housing the best of the Museo Nazionale Romano's formidable collection of classical sculpture. Many pieces come from the celebrated Ludovisi collection, amassed by Cardinal Ludovico Ludovisi in the 17th century.

Prize exhibits include the beautiful 5th-century *Trono Ludovisi* (*Ludovisi Throne*), a carved marble block with a central relief depicting a naked Venus (Aphrodite) being modestly plucked from the sea. In the neighbouring room, the *Ares Ludovisi*, a 2nd-century BCE representation of a young, clean-shaven Mars, owes its right foot to a Gian Lorenzo Bernini restoration in 1622.

Another affecting work is the *Galata Suicida* (*Gaul's Suicide*), a melodramatic depiction of a Gaul knifing himself to death over a dead woman.

The building itself provides an elegant backdrop, with a grand central courtyard, a finely painted loggia and frescoed rooms. These include the Sala delle Prospettive Dipinte, which was adorned with landscapes and hunting scenes for Cardinal Altemps, the rich nephew of Pope Pius IV (r 1560–65), who bought the *palazzo* in the late 16th century.

The museum also houses pieces from the Museo Nazionale Romano's Egyptian collection.

MUSEO NAZIONALE ROMANO

Palazzo Altemps is one of four museums that collectively make up the Museo Nazionale Romano. A combined ticket (€12/8), which is valid for one week, covers admission to all four sites: Palazzo Altemps, the Crypta Balbi, the Terme di Diocleziano and Palazzo Massimo alle Terme near Stazione Termini.

Trono Ludovisi, Museo Nazionale Romano: Palazzo Altemps

TAKASHI IMAGES/SHUTTERSTOCK ©

BEST RESTAURANTS

Pianostrada €€
Chic contemporary bistro with summer courtyard and a menu of creative, seasonal cuisine.

Grappolo D'Oro €€
An excellent option in the Campo de' Fiori area, serving well-executed pastas and rich desserts.

La Ciambella €€
With its light-filled interior, imaginative food and excellent location, this is a top choice near the Pantheon.

Salumeria Roscioli €€€
A celebrated deli-restaurant renowned for its classic Roman dishes and extensive wine list.

Retrobottega €€€
Regional cuisine gets a fine-dining makeover at this modern, minimalist restaurant.

The Perfect Roman Courtyard

INSTAGRAMMABLE HIDDEN YARD

For one of Rome's most picture-perfect corners, search out the **Arco degli Acetari**, just off Campo de' Fiori at Via del Pellegrino 19. Duck under the arch and you emerge onto a tiny medieval square enclosed by rusty orange houses and cascading plants. Cats and bicycles litter the cobbles, while overhead washing hangs off pretty flower-lined balconies.

Architectural Trickery

OPTICAL ILLUSION AT PALAZZO SPADA

Rome boasts several mind-bending optical illusions, including a famous *trompe l'oeil* created by the great baroque architect Francesco Borromini. Known as the **Prospettiva** (Perspective), this appears to be a lengthy colonnaded gallery leading to a hedge and a life-sized statue. In fact, the corridor is far shorter than it looks – only about 10m – and the sculpture is hip height. And look closer at that perfect-looking hedge – Borromini didn't trust the gardeners to clip a real hedge precisely enough, so he made one of stone.

The *Prospettiva* sits in **Palazzo Spada**, a fine mannerist palace with a small collection of artworks by Andrea del Sarto, Guido Reni, Guercino and Titian.

A Trio of Strolling Streets

BROWSE BOUTIQUES, BARS & PALACES

A charming street on which start your city strolling is **Via del Governo Vecchio**. To the west of Piazza Navona, this cobbled strip was once part of the papal processional route between the Basilica di San Giovanni in Laterano and St Peter's, and is now lined with bars, boutiques, independent shops and restaurants.

A short hop to the north, **Via dei Coronari** is another stroller's delight. It's famous for its antique shops but you'll now find an array of stores and casual cafes, as well as the fabulous Gelateria del Teatro at No 65–66.

To the south, **Via Giulia** is one of Rome's most charming streets, an elegant, largely car-free strip of churches, colourful Renaissance *palazzi* and discreet fashion boutiques.

 WHERE TO STAY IN THE CENTRO STORICO

Hotel Mimosa
This long-standing *pensione* makes a good base with its spacious rooms and optimal position. **€€**

Navona Essence
Snug boutique hotel with pared-down modern design and a top location in the heart of the action. **€€**

Eitch Borromini
Elegant hotel housed in a 17th-century *palazzo* designed by Borromini and overlooking Piazza Navona. **€€€**

Landmark Piazzas & Legendary Sights

WALK FROM SQUARE TO SQUARE

The *centro storico* is home to some of Rome's most prominent piazzas and several beautiful but lesser-known squares. To discover the best of them, follow this easy 1.5km walking tour.

Start off in **1 Largo di Torre Argentina**, a busy hub set around the ruins of four Republican-era temples. On the piazza's western flank, Teatro Argentina, Rome's premier theatre, sits near the spot where Julius Caesar was assassinated in 44 BCE. From there follow on to **2 Piazza della Minerva**, home of Bernini's much-loved elephant sculpture and the Basilica di Santa Maria Sopra Minerva. Next, work your way to **3 Piazza di Sant'Ignazio Loyola**, a charming square flanked by the church of the same name, and beyond that, **4 Piazza della Rotonda**, where the Pantheon needs no introduction. **5 Piazza Navona** is a short walk away.

On the other side of Corso Vittorio Emanuele II, pass through **6 Campo de' Fiori** as you stroll over to **7 Piazza Farnese**, the setting for one of Rome's great Renaissance palaces.

☕ WHERE TO GET A COFFEE IN THE CENTRO STORICO

Caffè Sant'Eustachio
Unassuming and always busy, this celebrated cafe serves some of Rome's finest coffee.

La Casa del Caffè Tazza d'Oro
Burnished, old-fashioned cafe steaming up excellent coffees a stone's throw from the Pantheon.

Barnum Cafe
A laid-back retro-cool cafe serving international breakfasts, pitch-perfect coffees and light meals.

SIGHTS WITHOUT THE CROWDS

Silvia Prosperi, tour guide, shares some of her favourite, off-the-radar sights in the *centro storico* and other central neighbourhoods. (*@afriendinrome.it*)

Crypta Balbi
This museum is essential for understanding the delicate transition from the fall of the Roman Empire to medieval Rome. Ask to visit the exedra!

Monument of Clement XIV
A masterpiece by Canova lying quietly in the Santi Apostoli church, overlooked by tourists despite being a stone's throw from the Trevi Fountain.

Chiesa di Santo Stefano Rotondo
A short way from the bustle of the Colosseum, this is a surprising church with a circular, luminous structure and Mannerist frescoes that leave no one indifferent with their realistic depiction of all sorts of martyrdom.

Chow Down on Street Food
SUPPLÌ, SLICED PIZZA & GELATO

In recent years, a trend for street food has seen quality fast-food joints spring up across town. One such, **Supplizio** (Via dei Banchi Vecchi 143), specialises in that most Roman of snacks, the *supplì* (risotto balls), with predictably delicious results.

Another Roman speciality is *pizza al taglio* (pizza by the slice). This is served in takeaways all over town but few places can top **Forno Roscioli** (Via dei Chiavari 34), a bakery selling a Babette's feast of pizzas, pastries, *supplì* and much more besides. And for dessert, just pop next door to **Fatamorgana** (Via dei Chiavari 37) for a guaranteed blast of gelato bliss.

Catch an Exhibition
MODERN ART IN A RENAISSANCE CLOISTER

Escape the tourist crowds in the backstreets around Piazza Navona by taking in an exhibition at the **Chiostro del Bramante**. This 16th-century cloister, itself a masterpiece of High Renaissance architecture, provides a terrific stage for modern-art exhibitions and cultural events. Afterwards, pop upstairs for a snack at the smart in-house cafe.

An Evening at the Theatre
DRAMA, MUSIC & DANCE

Treat yourself to an evening of drama at Rome's top theatre, **Teatro Argentina**. Founded in 1732, it stages a wide-ranging programme of classic and contemporary plays (mostly in Italian), as well as dance performances and classical music concerts. A good time to catch a performance is during the autumn **Romaeuropa** festival of theatre, opera and dance.

CHIESA DI SANTO STEFANO ROTONDO

Read more about the secluded 5th-century **Chiesa di Santo Stefano Rotondo** (p112) and its shocking interior frescoes in the San Giovanni & Testaccio section.

 WHERE TO DRINK IN THE CENTRO STORICO

Open Baladin
Stalwart of Rome's craft-beer scene with big-name beers and artisanal blends from Italian microbreweries.

Il Goccetto
Authentic, old-school *vino e olio* (wine and oil) shop complete with woody, bottle-lined interior.

Rimessa Roscioli
Aficionados adore this wine bar–restaurant that offers wine-pairing dinners, tastings, tours and classes.

TRIDENTE, TREVI & THE QUIRINALE

SIGNATURE SIGHTS & DESIGNER SHOPPING

Counting the Trevi Fountain and Spanish Steps among its A-list sights, this central area is debonair and perennially packed with tourists, shoppers and, at the weekend, excitable teenagers.

Tridente is full of old money, historic art galleries, fashionable bars and swish hotels. Designer boutiques and flagship fashion stores draw well-heeled shoppers to streets like Via dei Condotti and Via del Babuino, while department stores line Via del Corso.

In the south of the district, the Trevi Fountain stands out in a knot of dark, narrow streets. On the Quirinale Hill, Italy's presidential palace sets the tone with its august architecture, paving the way for ingeniously designed baroque churches and a profusion of masterpieces in the hallowed halls of Palazzo Barberini.

TOP TIP

You can easily walk here from the centre or take public transport: Barberini metro station (line A) is best for the Trevi and Quirinale areas, while Spagna and Flaminio (both line A) serve the Tridente. Buses also run to Piazza Barberini, Via del Tritone and Via del Corso.

ANNA PAKUTINA/SHUTTERSTOCK ©

Cerasi Chapel, Basilica di Santa Maria del Popolo

Basilica di Santa Maria del Popolo

ART-RICH RENAISSANCE CHURCH

Built to exorcise the ghost of Nero, which supposedly haunted this spot, this **basilica** is one of Rome's richest Renaissance churches. Headlining its impressive art collection are two Caravaggios: the *Conversion of St Paul* (1600–01) and the *Crucifixion of St Peter* (1601) in the 16th-century Cerasi Chapel. Other fine works include Carracci's *Assumption of the Virgin* (c 1660) and multiple frescoes by Pinturicchio.

The church's origins date to 1099 but it was subsequently made over several times, most notably by Pinturicchio, Bramante and Raphael in the late 15th and early 16th centuries. Bernini also worked on it in the 17th century.

Villa Medici

GRACEFUL RENAISSANCE VILLA

Home of the French Academy, this sumptuous Renaissance **villa** was built in 1540 and subsequently purchased by Cardinal Ferdinando de' Medici in 1576. It remained in Medici hands until 1801, when Napoleon acquired it for the Academy. Its most famous resident was Galileo, who was imprisoned here between 1630 and 1633 during his trial for heresy.

Standard admission tickets cover temporary exhibitions, or you can sign up for a guided tour and take in the sculpture-filled gardens, a frescoed garden studio and the cardinal's private apartments.

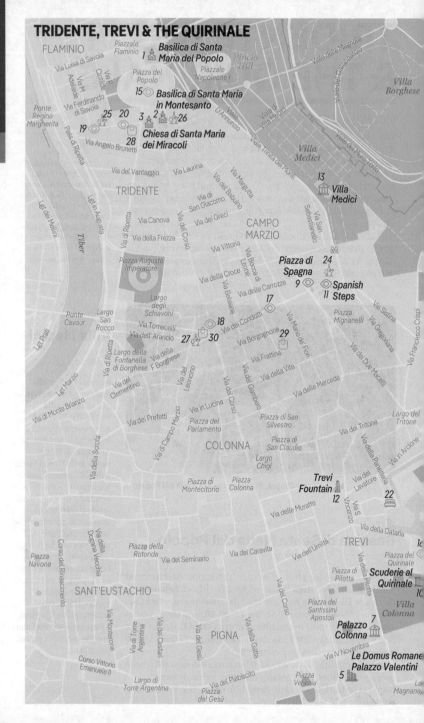

TRIDENTE, TREVI & THE QUIRINALE

FLAMINIO

Piazzale Flaminio

1 🏛 **Basilica di Santa Maria del Popolo**

Pincio Hill

Piazza del Popolo

Piazzale Napoleone I

Villa Borghese

Via Luisa di Savoia

Via M Adelaide

Via P Cicilide

Via Ferdinando di Savoia

Ponte Regina Margherita

Pass di Ripetta

Viale delle Magnolie

Viale del Castagnoleto

Viale di Villa Medici

15 ◎ **Basilica di Santa Maria in Montesanto**

Viale D'Annunzio

25 **20** **3** **2** **26** 🏛

19 ◎

28

Via Angelo Brunetti

Chiesa di Santa Maria dei Miracoli

Viale delle Magnolie

Viale di Trinità dei Monti

Villa Medici

Viale di Villa Medici

Viale del Muro Torto

Lgt dei Mellini

Tiber

Via del Vantaggio

Via Laurina

TRIDENTE

Via di Ripetta

Via Canova

Via della Frezza

Via del Corso

Via di San Giacomo

Via del Babuino

Via dei Greci

Via Vittoria

CAMPO MARZIO

Via Margutta

Via San Sebastianello

13 🏛 **Villa Medici**

Lgt in Augusta

Piazza Augusto Imperatore

Via della Croce

Via Bocca di Leone

Via Belsiana

Piazza di Spagna **24** Ⓜ

9 ◎ ◎ **Spanish Steps**

11

Piazza Mignanelli

Via Sistina

Via Gregoriana

Via Francesco Crispi

Ponte Cavour

Largo San Rocco

Largo degli Schiavoni

Via Tomacelli

Via dell' Arancio

18

27 🏛 **30**

Via delle Carrozze

17

Via dei Condotti

Via Borgognona

Via Mario de' Fiori

Via delle Carrozze

29

Via dei Due Macelli

Lgt Prati

Lgt Marzio

Via di Monte Brianzo

Via di Ripetta

Via della F. Borghese

Largo della Fontanella di Borghese

Via del Clementino

Via del Leoncino

Via dei Prefetti

Via in Lucina

Piazza del Parlamento

Via del Corso

Via del Gambero

Via della Vite

Via Frattina

Piazza di San Silvestro

Piazza di San Claudio

Via delle Mercede

Via del Tritone

Largo del Tritone

Via della Panetteria

Via in Arcione

Via della Scrofa

Via di Campo Marzio

COLONNA

Largo Chigi

Via del Tritone

Piazza di Montecitorio

Piazza Colonna

Trevi Fountain 🏛

12

Via del Lavatore

Via S Vincenzo

22 🏛

Via delle Muratte

Via della Dataria

Piazza Navona

Corso del Rinascimento

Via della Dogana Vecchia

Piazza della Rotonda

Via del Seminario

Via del Caravita

Via dell'Umiltà

TREVI

Piazza del Quirinale

1◎

SANT'EUSTACHIO

Via Monterone

Via di Torre Argentina

Via dei Cestari

Via del Gesù

Via del Caravita

Via del Corso

PIGNA

Via della Gatta

Piazza dei Santissimi Apostoli

Piazza di Pilotta

Scuderie al Quirinale 🏛

1◎

Villa Colonna

Via della Pilotta

Corso Vittorio Emanuele II

Largo di Torre Argentina

Piazza del Gesù

Via del Plebiscito

Piazza Venezia

Via IV Novembre

Palazzo Colonna 🏛

7

Le Domus Romane Palazzo Valentini

5 🏛

Lar... Magnana...

HIGHLIGHTS
1 Basilica di Santa Maria del Popolo
2 Basilica di Santa Maria in Montesanto
3 Chiesa di Santa Maria dei Miracoli
4 Chiesa di Santa Maria della Vittoria
5 Le Domus Romane di Palazzo Valentini
6 Palazzo Barberini
7 Palazzo Colonna
8 Palazzo del Quirinale
9 Piazza di Spagna
10 Scuderie al Quirinale
11 Spanish Steps
12 Trevi Fountain
13 Villa Medici

SIGHTS
14 Convento dei Cappuccini
15 Piazza del Popolo
16 Piazza del Quirinale
17 Via dei Condotti
18 Via del Corso
19 Via della Penna
20 Via dell'Oca

SLEEPING
21 La Controra
22 Palazzo Scanderbeg
23 The Radical Hotel

DRINKING & NIGHTLIFE
24 Il Palazzetto
25 Locarno Bar
26 Stravinskij Bar
27 Zuma Bar

SHOPPING
28 Bomba
29 Fausto Santini
30 Fendi

Palazzo Barberini

TREASURE-LADEN BAROQUE PALACE

This baroque palace, commissioned to celebrate the Barberini family's rise to papal power, impresses before you even start on its art collection. Many high-profile architects worked on it, including rivals Bernini and Borromini: the former contributed a square staircase, the latter a helicoidal one.

Of the masterpieces on display, don't miss Filippo Lippi's *Annunciazione e due donatori* (*Annunciation with Two Donors*) and Pietro da Cortona's ceiling fresco *Il Trionfo della Divina Provvidenza* (*The Triumph of Divine Providence*).

Other must-sees include Hans Holbein's famous portrait of Henry VIII and Raphael's *La Fornarina* (*The Baker's Girl*), thought to be a portrait of his mistress. Works by Caravaggio include *Narciso* (*Narcissus*) and the mesmerisingly horrific *Giuditta e Oloferne* (*Judith Beheading Holophernes*).

RAPHAEL'S MISTRESS

Raphael was said to have been so besotted with his mistress, the so-called Baker's Girl, that he couldn't concentrate properly on his job decorating the **Villa Farnesina** (p101) in Trastevere. He eventually got back to work with predictably brilliant results.

TODAMO/SHUTTERSTOCK ©

Borromini's staircase, Palazzo Barberini

Palazzo Colonna

ROME'S LARGEST PRIVATE PALACE

The largest private palace in Rome, Palazzo Colonna has a formal garden, multiple reception rooms and a grandiose baroque Great Hall built to honour Marcantonio II Colonna, a hero of the 1571 Battle of Lepanto.

Its opulent salons are home to major artworks, including Annibale Carracci's *Mangiafagioli* (*The Bean Eater*) and Bronzino's sensual *Venus, Cupid and a Satyr*. In the Great Hall, which was used as a set for the film *Roman Holiday*, a cannonball is lodged in the gallery's marble stairs, a reminder of the 1849 siege of Rome.

You can visit independently on Saturday mornings or join a guided tour on Friday mornings.

Palazzo del Quirinale

ITALY'S PRESIDENTIAL PALACE

This historic palace crowns the Quirinale Hill, one of Rome's original seven hills. For centuries it was a summer residence for the pope, but in 1870 it was appropriated by the Savoy royal family after Rome had been incorporated into the newly formed Kingdom of Italy. In 1946 it was taken over by the Italian head of state, the Presidente della Repubblica. Originally commissioned by Pope Gregory XIII (r 1572–85), it was built and added to over 150 years by architects including Domenico Fontana, Francesco Borromini, Gian Lorenzo Bernini and Carlo Maderno.

Guided tours (in Italian only) of its reception rooms, courtyards and gardens must be booked at least five days ahead.

The Spanish Steps

ORNAMENTAL STATEMENT STAIRCASE

Forming a decorous backdrop to **Piazza di Spagna**, this statement sweep of stairs is one of Rome's major icons and an ever-popular meeting point. Though officially named the Scalinata della Trinità dei Monti, the staircase is known to the English-speaking world as the Spanish Steps.

Piazza di Spagna takes its name from the Spanish Embassy to the Holy See, although the staircase, designed by the Italian Francesco de Sanctis, was actually built in 1725 with money bequeathed by a French diplomat. Once built, the *scalinata* quickly became a magnet for foreign visitors, particularly English travellers on the Grand Tour, leading locals to dub the area the '*ghetto degli inglesi*' (the English ghetto).

On the piazza at the foot of the 135 steps, the fountain of a sinking boat, the *Barcaccia* (1627), is believed to be by Pietro Bernini, father of the more famous Gian Lorenzo Bernini. Up above, the staircase's summit is crowned by the *Chiesa della Trinità dei Monti*, a 16th-century church notable for its sweeping city views and impressive frescoes by Daniele da Volterra.

To the southeast of Piazza di Spagna, the adjacent Piazza Mignanelli is dominated by the Colonna dell'Immacolata, built in 1857 to celebrate Pope Pius IX's declaration of the Immaculate Conception.

MOSTRA DELLE AZALEE

Crowned by the twin bell towers of the Chiesa della Trinità dei Monti, the Spanish Steps are impeccably Instagrammable. And they're in especially fine form after a €1.5 million clean-up funded by the Roman jewellery house Bulgari. To catch them at their photogenic best, try to stop by between early April and mid-May when they are decorated with hundreds of vases of blooming, brightly coloured azaleas.

Le Domus Romane di Palazzo Valentini

UNDERGROUND RUINS BROUGHT TO LIFE

Underneath the grand home of the Roma Capitale municipal authority lie the remains of several ancient Roman houses, the excavated fragments of which have been turned into a fascinating multimedia 'experience'.

Visits (book ahead) take you on a virtual tour of the dwellings, complete with sound effects, projected frescoes and glimpses of ancient life as it might have been lived in the area around the buildings. It's genuinely thrilling and great for older kids.

Spanish Steps & Chiesa della Trinità dei Monti

S74/SHUTTERSTOCK ©

89

Trevi Fountain

ROME'S FAVOURITE FOUNTAIN

Rome's most famous fountain, the **Fontana di Trevi** is a baroque extravaganza, a foaming marble and water composition filling an entire piazza.

The flamboyant ensemble, 20m wide and 26m high, was designed by Nicola Salvi in 1732 and depicts the sea-god Oceanus in a shell-shaped chariot being led by Tritons with seahorses – one wild, one docile – representing the moods of the sea. In the niche to the left of Neptune a statue represents Abundance; to the right is Salubrity. The water comes from the Aqua Virgo, a 1st-century BCE underground aqueduct, and the name Trevi refers to the *tre vie* (three roads) that converge at the fountain.

Most famously, the Trevi Fountain is where Anita Ekberg cavorted in a ballgown in Fellini's classic 1960 film, *La Dolce Vita*; apparently she wore waders under her black dress but still shivered during the winter shoot. The fountain also featured in Jean Negulesco's 1954 film *Three Coins in the Fountain*, best remembered for its theme song sung by Frank Sinatra.

The fountain gets very busy during the day, so try to visit later in the evening when it's beautifully lit and you can appreciate its foaming majesty without the hordes.

COIN TOSSING

A rite of passage for every visitor to Rome, throwing a coin into the fountain is said to ensure that one day you'll return to the Eternal City. But what happens to the estimated €3000 that's thrown in each day? It's collected daily and given to the Catholic charity Caritas, which uses it to help care for the city's homeless population and families struggling with poverty.

Trevi Fountain

R.NAGY/SHUTTERSTOCK ©

People-Watching & Window-Shopping

FLAGSHIP STORES AND FASHION BOUTIQUES

The *passeggiata* (traditional evening stroll) is a quintessential Roman custom. It's particularly colourful at weekends when families, friends and lovers take to the streets to sashay up and down, slurp on gelato, window-shop and check each other out.

A popular spot is **Via del Corso**, a largely traffic-free street lined with department stores showcasing big Italian and international brands. Leading off it, **Via dei Condotti** is Rome's top shopping strip, home to A-list designers and their swish boutiques. For chic, independent shops, search out **Via dell'Oca** and **Via della Penna**.

At the head of Via del Corso, **Piazza del Popolo** is a paradise for people-watching. Find a perch, perhaps on the steps of the twin churches that guard its entrance – the **Chiesa di Santa Maria dei Miracoli** and **Basilica di Santa Maria in Montesanto**. Alternatively, plonk yourself at the foot of the 36m-high Egyptian obelisk and watch as the world walks past.

Blockbuster Exhibitions & Smashing Sunsets

POWERHOUSE ART AND MAGICAL VIEWS

With its towering obelisk and presidential palace, **Piazza del Quirinale** provides an epic setting for blockbuster art and dreamy sunsets. You can enjoy top exhibitions at the **Scuderie al Quirinale**, a gallery housed in the palace's former stables, before basking in the last light of the day as the sun sets over St Peter's dome on the distant skyline.

Creep Yourself Out

CHILLING BONE-LINED CRYPT

Duck into the crypt of the **Convento dei Cappuccini** and you enter a strange, eerie world where everything is made of human bones. Between 1732 and 1775, the resident Capuchin monks used the bones of 3700 of their departed brothers to create a macabre *memento mori* (reminder of death) – a 30m-long passageway giving onto six crypts, each named after the type of bone used to decorate it (skulls, shin bones, pelvises etc). It's a sight that once seen is impossible to unsee.

ECSTATIC TERESA

Rome's churches boast a bewildering array of treasures. You'll never manage to take them all in, but one that should absolutely be on the list is Gian Lorenzo Bernini's *Santa Teresa trafitta dall'amore di Dio* (*Ecstasy of St Teresa*) in the **Chiesa di Santa Maria della Vittoria**. One of the great masterpieces of European baroque art, this daring and sexually charged sculpture depicts St Teresa, engulfed in the folds of a flowing cloak, floating in ecstasy as a teasing angel pierces her with a golden arrow.

It's a stunning sight, bathed in soft natural light filtering through a concealed window. Go in the afternoon for the best effect.

MORE BERNINI MAGIC

You'll find another similarly daring sculpture by Bernini, the *Beata Ludovica Albertoni* (*Blessed Ludovica Albertoni*), in the **Chiesa di San Francesco d'Assisi a Ripa Grande** (p107) in Trastevere.

 WHERE TO STAY IN TRIDENTE, TREVI & THE QUIRINALE

La Controra	**The Radical Hotel**	**Palazzo Scanderbeg**
A laid-back guesthouse offering quality hostel-style accommodation in the upmarket Via Veneto district. €	This 2nd-floor boutique hotel sports a vintage-inspired design and convenient location near Via Veneto. €€	A coin toss from the Trevi Fountain, this elegantly appointed suite hotel is housed in a 15th-century *palazzo*. €€€

BEST COCKTAIL BARS

Il Palazzetto
Negronis go hand in hand with glorious rooftop views at this terrace bar above the Spanish Steps.

Stravinskij Bar
Treat yourself to a classic cocktail in the sunny courtyard of the historic Hotel de Russie.

Zuma Bar
Dress to kill for classy cocktails at this achingly chic rooftop bar atop Fendi's flagship store.

Locarno Bar
With its courtyard terrace, the lounge bar of the art deco Hotel Locarno is a favourite spot.

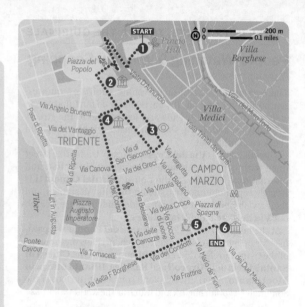

Literary Hot Spots

TRACE THE NEIGHBOURHOOD'S LITERARY HISTORY

Explore the literary haunts, both real and fictional, that speckle the streets around the Spanish Steps.

Begin your walk in the **1 Pincio Hill Gardens**, where Henry James' Daisy Miller walked with Frederick Winterbourne. Then make your way downhill to Via del Babuino and the **2 Hotel de Russie**, a favourite hang-out of the artistic avantgarde in the early 20th century.

Running parallel to Via del Babuino is **3 Via Margutta**, a picturesque cobbled street that Fellini, Picasso, Stravinsky and Puccini all called home at some point.

From there, make your way over to Via del Corso to see the **4 Casa di Goethe**, where Goethe stayed from 1786 to 1788. Continue on to Via dei Condotti and the **5 Antico Caffè Greco**, a former haunt of Casanova, Goethe, Keats, Byron and Shelley, from where it's a short hop up to Piazza di Spagna and the **6 Keats–Shelley House**, where the 25-year-old Keats died of tuberculosis in 1821.

 WHERE TO BUY ROMAN FASHION IN TRIDENTE, TREVI & THE QUIRINALE

Bomba
Sharply tailored fashions cut to classic styles and made in high-quality fabrics.

Fausto Santini
Rome's legendary shoe designer is renowned for his innovative, architecturally inspired designs.

Fendi
Ready-to-wear creations at the flagship store of a Roman fashion house.

VATICAN CITY, BORGO & PRATI

ICONIC MASTERPIECES & ARCHITECTURAL BOMBAST

Established in 1929, the Vatican City is a sovereign state – the world's smallest, with an area of 44 hectares – but in practice it's more like a city neighbourhood, albeit one with its own army (the Swiss Guards) and head of state (the pope). Nowadays, the Vatican is one of Rome's most visited areas. But with the crowds and tourist touts come priceless treasures and revered masterpieces, many of which are on show in St Peter's Basilica and the Vatican Museums, the sprawling home of the Sistine Chapel.

A short walk from St Peter's Square, Castel Sant'Angelo looms over the small Borgo district (it was once much larger, but much of it was destroyed in 1936 to make way for the monumental Via della Conciliazione). North of the Borgo, upmarket Prati is full of legal studios, and has some excellent shops, bars and restaurants.

TOP TIP

The Vatican, which can be reached by metro (line A to Ottaviano) or bus (40 or 64 from Termini), and the nearby Borgo and Prati neighbourhoods can be covered on foot. Once in the area, note that St Peter's Basilica (St Peter's Square) and the Vatican Museums (Viale Vaticano) have separate entrances.

SYLVAIN SONNET/GETTY IMAGES ©

Castel Sant'Angelo

Castel Sant'Angelo

LANDMARK RIVERSIDE CASTLE

With its chunky round keep, this castle is an instantly recognisable landmark. Built as a mausoleum for the emperor Hadrian, it was converted into a papal fortress in the 6th century. It is now the **Museo Nazionale di Castel Sant'Angelo**, with a grand collection of artworks, military memorabilia and medieval firearms. Many of these weapons were used by soldiers protecting the castle, which, thanks to a 13th-century secret passage to the Vatican (Passetto di Borgo), provided sanctuary to many popes in times of danger.

The upper floors boast elegant Renaissance interiors, including the frescoed Sala Paolina. Two storeys up, the terrace, immortalised in Puccini's opera *Tosca*, offers unforgettable city views.

St Peter's Square

THE VATICAN'S SHOWPIECE PIAZZA

Fronting St Peter's Basilica, the Vatican's central square was laid out between 1656 and 1667 to a design by Gian Lorenzo Bernini. Seen from above, it resembles a giant keyhole with two semicircular colonnades encircling a giant ellipse that straightens out to funnel believers into the basilica. Bernini described the colonnades as representing 'the motherly arms of the church'.

The scale of the piazza is dazzling: at its largest it measures 320m by 240m. There are 284 columns and, atop the colonnades, 140 saints. The 25m-high obelisk was brought to Rome from Heliopolis in Egypt.

93

HIGHLIGHTS

1 Castel Sant'Angelo
2 St Peter's Basilica
3 St Peter's Square
4 Vatican Gardens
5 Vatican Museums

SIGHTS

6 Aula delle Udienze Pontificie Paolo VI

SLEEPING

7 Hotel San Pietrino
8 Le Stanze di Orazio

EATING

9 Bonci Pizzarium
10 Fa-Bio
11 Panificio Bonci

DRINKING

12 Angelico Box Bistro

ENTERTAINMENT

13 Alexanderplatz
14 Auditorium Conciliazione
15 Fonclea Pub

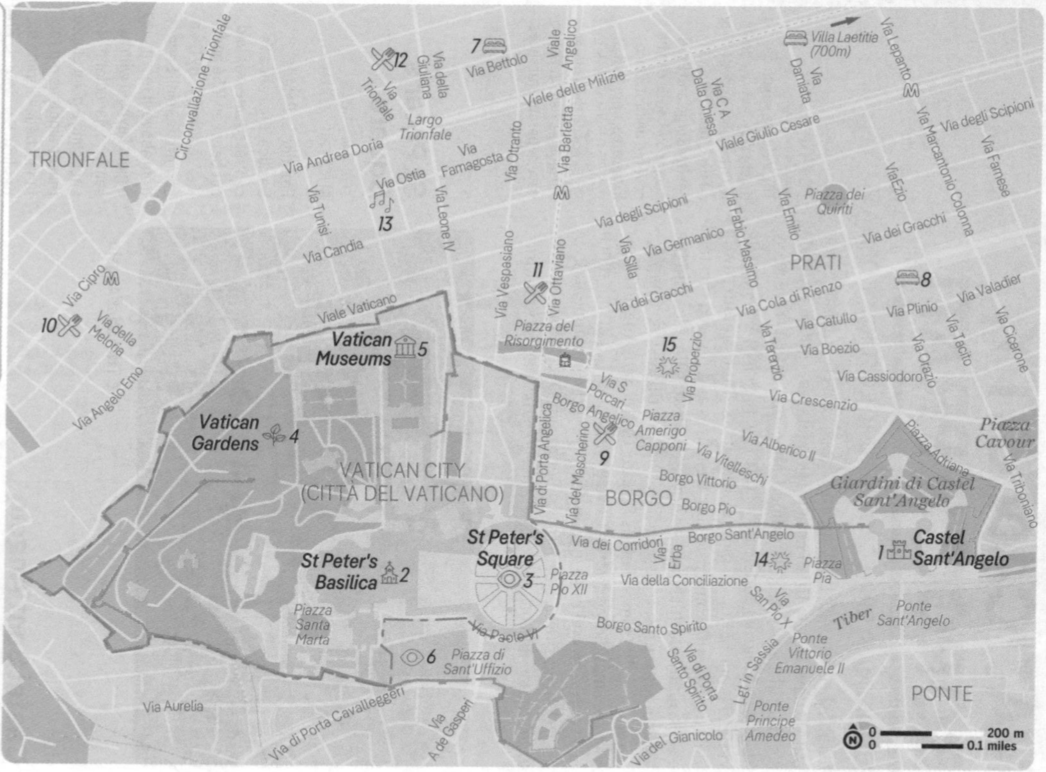

Dome of St Peter's Basilica (p96)

Vatican Museums

SISTINE CHAPEL & AWE-INSPIRING ART

Housed in the lavish halls and galleries of the Palazzo Apostolico Vaticano, the Vatican Museums contain one of the world's greatest art collections. Highlights include classical statuary in the Museo Pio-Clementino, a suite of rooms decorated by Raphael, and the Michelangelo-frescoed Sistine Chapel.

On the lower floor, the **Museo Pio-Clementino** displays some of the Vatican's finest ancient sculpture. Chief among its many treasures are the *Apollo Belvedere* and the 1st-century *Laocoön*, both in the Cortile Ottagono (Octagonal Courtyard).

From the Museo, the Simonetti staircase leads to several lengthy galleries, culminating in the extraordinary **Galleria delle Carte Geografiche** (Map Gallery). Beyond this, the **Stanze di Raffaello** (Raphael Rooms) is a suite of four chambers painted by Raphael and his students. Star of the show is Raphael's masterpiece, *La scuola di Atene* (*The School of Athens*).

From the Raphael Rooms, you pass through several further galleries before reaching the **Cappella Sistina** (Sistine Chapel), home to two of the world's most recognisable works of art – Michelangelo's ceiling frescoes (1508–12) and his *Giudizio Universale* (*Last Judgement*; 1536–41).

The 800-sq-metre ceiling design, best viewed from the east wall, centres on nine panels depicting stories from the book of Genesis. In contrast, the mesmeric *Giudizio Universale* shows Christ passing sentence over the souls of the dead.

CONCLAVE

The Sistine Chapel is where the conclave meets to elect a new pope. The rules, dating from 1274, are explicit: between 15 and 20 days after the death of a pope, the College of Cardinals (comprising all cardinals under the age of 80) is confined to the Vatican to elect a new pontiff. Four secret ballots are held each day until a two-thirds majority has been secured. News of the election is then communicated by emitting white smoke through a specially erected chimney.

Galleria delle Carte Geografiche, Vatican Museums

RED-FENIKS/SHUTTERSTOCK ©

St Peter's Basilica

THE VATICAN'S IMPERIOUS SHOWPIECE CHURCH

In a city of outstanding churches, none can hold a candle to St Peter's, Italy's largest, richest and most spectacular basilica. A monument to centuries of artistic genius, it boasts spectacular works of art, including three of Italy's most celebrated masterpieces: Michelangelo's *Pietà*, his sky-scraping dome, and Bernini's 29m-high bronze baldachin (canopy) over the papal altar.

The original St Peter's – which lies beneath the current basilica – was built in the 4th century on the site where St Peter was supposedly buried. The current church was consecrated in 1626 after a turbulent 120 years of construction.

Its immense facade, designed by Carlo Maderno, gives on to a cavernous marble interior. At the head of the right nave, you'll find Michelangelo's hauntingly beautiful *Pietà*, the only work he ever signed. A red floor disc marks the spot where Charlemagne and later Holy Roman Emperors were crowned by the pope.

Dominating the basilica's centre is Bernini's baldachin, which towers over the high altar, positioned on the site of St Peter's grave. Above, Michelangelo's dome soars to a height of 119m. This titanic cupola is supported by four stone piers named after the saints whose statues adorn their Bernini-designed niches – Longinus, Helena, Veronica and Andrew.

At the base of the Pier of St Longinus is Arnolfo di Cambio's much-loved 13th-century bronze statue of St Peter, whose right foot has been worn down by centuries of caresses.

THE SWISS GUARD

With their harlequin uniforms and lethal-looking pikes, the Swiss Guards have been the pope's bodyguards for more than 500 years.

The corps, the Vatican's de facto army, was founded by Pope Julius II in 1506. At the time, Swiss mercenaries were much in demand by Europe's constantly warring monarchs, and when a Swiss bishop suggested the pope might want to employ a permanent contingent, Julius took him up on the idea.

Baldachin, St Peter's Basilica

SANDRASWC/SHUTTERSTOCK ©

Vatican Gardens

GROTTOES, FOUNTAINS & A HELIPORT

Up to a third of the Vatican is covered by the perfectly manicured Vatican Gardens, which contain fortifications, grottoes, monuments, fountains, and the state's tiny heliport and train station. Visits are by guided tour (two hours, including a visit to the Sistine Chapel) or open-air bus (45 minutes), and should be booked well in advance. After the bus tour, you're free to visit the Vatican Museums on your own; admission is included in the ticket price.

See the Pope

ATTEND A PAPAL AUDIENCE

To see the Pope in Rome, you have three main options. Firstly, you can attend a **papal audience**. These are held on Wednesday mornings, usually in St Peter's Square but sometimes at the nearby **Aula delle Udienze Pontificie Paolo VI** (Paul VI Audience Hall). Alternatively, you can go to a **papal Mass**. Places at these services are highly sought after, particularly at Easter and Christmas, so if you know when you want to go, it pays to reserve as soon as you can. Both these options require tickets, which are free but must be booked in advance – see www.vatican.va/various/prefettura/index_en.html for details.

The third option, for which no tickets are required, is to head to St Peter's Square at noon on Sunday for the **Pope's weekly blessing**.

Catch a Gig

SWING TO JAZZ AND POP

The pope isn't the only crowd-puller in this part of Rome. Just a 15-minute walk from St Peter's Square, top Italian and international performers play to cosmopolitan music-lovers at **Alexanderplatz**, the city's most celebrated jazz club in a backstreet Prati basement.

For a change of scene, **Fonclea** is a long-standing pub venue that stages everything from blues and soul to pop, rock and doo-wop. Then there's the **Auditorium Conciliazione**, a large venue that puts on a wide range of events – classical and contemporary concerts, cabarets, dance spectacles, theatre productions, film screenings, exhibitions and conferences.

BEST TAKEAWAYS & JUICE BARS

Bonci Pizzarium €
Acclaimed takeaway serving Rome's best sliced pizza. Expect original toppings and lots of happy eaters.

Panificio Bonci €
Cornetti, bread, focaccia and pizza from celebrity baker Gabriele Bonci, founder of Pizzarium.

Fa-Bio €
Dig in to organic wraps, salads, stir-fries and fresh juices at this popular vegan-friendly joint.

Angelico Box Bistro €
juice bar, ideal for a smoothie, salad or light snack in a quiet corner of the Borgo district.

PREFER THE OPERA?

If you prefer opera to jazz, ballet to bebop, check the programme at the **Teatro dell'Opera** (p104), Rome's main opera house, or the **Terme di Caracalla** (p116), which stages outdoor concerts during the summer.

 WHERE TO STAY IN VATICAN CITY, BORGO & PRATI

Hotel San Pietrino
An old-fashioned, family-run *pensione* offering simply attired rooms within walking distance of St Peter's Basilica. **€**

Le Stanze di Orazio
A refined boutique bolthole in the elegant Prati district, a single metro stop from the Vatican. **€€**

Villa Laetitia
Boutique-style and Michelin-starred fine-dining in an art nouveau riverside villa. **€€€**

MONTI, ESQUILINO & SAN LORENZO

FROM CHIC BOUTIQUES TO ALTERNATIVE BARS

Centred on transport hub Stazione Termini, this large, cosmopolitan area can seem busy and overwhelming. But hidden among its scruffy streets are some beautiful churches, one of Rome's great art museums, and any number of cool bars and restaurants.

The Esquilino is a workaday part of town, home to a busy covered market and dozens of small shops selling mobile-phone accessories and cheap plastic goods. Down towards the Colosseum, Monti was the ancient city's notorious Suburra slum, but it's now a chic, gentrified district full of boutiques and *enoteche* (wine bars). It's a hugely popular hang-out, particularly on weekends. Studenty San Lorenzo isn't for everyone but it bursts into life in the evening as its many restaurants and bars crank into action.

TOP TIP

In the centre of the district, Stazione Termini is Rome's main transport hub. Here you can get metro B to Cavour for Monti and metro A to Vittorio Emanuele for Esquilino. For San Lorenzo, hop on tram 3 or 19. Once in the individual districts, you can cover most places on foot.

Fontana delle Naiadai, Piazza della Repubblica

Piazza della Repubblica

LANDMARK SQUARE

Flanked by 19th-century neoclassical colonnades, this landmark piazza near Stazione Termini was laid out as part of Rome's post-unification makeover. It follows the lines of the semicircular exedra (benched portico) of Diocletian's baths complex and was, in fact, originally known as Piazza Esedra. In its centre, the **Fontana delle Naiadi** provoked puritanical anger when it was unveiled in 1901. Critics objected to the nudity of the four naiads (water nymphs) who surround the central figure of Glaucus.

Museo Nazionale Romano: Terme di Diocleziano

VAST ANCIENT BATHS COMPLEX

The Terme di Diocleziano, one of ancient Rome's largest bath complexes, could accommodate up to 3000 people. Nowadays, it houses the Museo Nazionale Romano's collection of ancient inscriptions, appearing on artefacts like altars and tombstones.

Further exhibits – classical sarcophagi, carved funerary altars, sculpted animal heads – are displayed in the large 16th-century cloister. Based on drawings by Michelangelo, it was built as part of the adjacent Basilica di Santa Maria degli Angeli e dei Martiri.

On the cloister's upper floor, ancient finds chronicle the prehistory of the Latin peoples from the 11th century BCE.

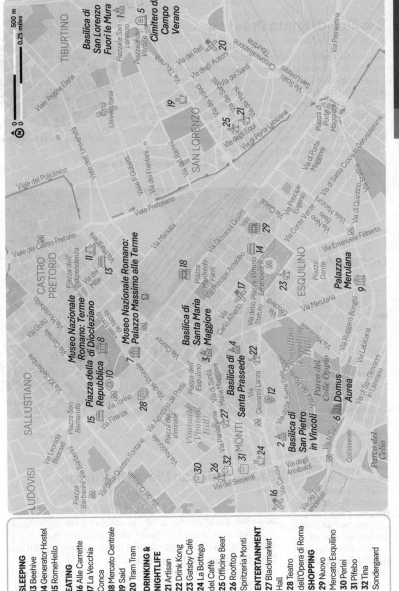

HIGHLIGHTS
1 Basilica di San Lorenzo Fuori le Mura
2 Basilica di San Pietro in Vincoli
3 Basilica di Santa Maria Maggiore
4 Basilica di Santa Prassede
5 Cimitero di Campo Verano
6 Domus Aurea
7 Museo Nazionale Romano: Palazzo Massimo alle Terme
8 Museo Nazionale Romano: Terme di Diocleziano
9 Palazzo Merulana
10 Piazza della Repubblica

SIGHTS
11 DILIT International House

ACTIVITIES, COURSES & TOURS
12 Vino Roma

SLEEPING
13 Beehive
14 Generator Hostel
15 RomeHello

EATING
16 Alte Carrette
17 La Vecchia Conca
18 Mercato Centrale
19 Said
20 Tram Tram

DRINKING & NIGHTLIFE
21 Artisan
22 Drink Kong
23 Gatsby Café
24 La Bottega del Caffè
25 Officine Beat
26 Rooftop Spritzeria Monti

ENTERTAINMENT
27 Blackmarket Hall
28 Teatro dell'Opera di Roma

SHOPPING
29 Nuovo Mercato Esquilino
30 Perlei
31 Pifebo
32 Tina Sondergaard

99

Basilica di Santa Prassede

DAZZLING BYZANTINE MOSAICS

Famous for its brilliant Byzantine mosaics, this small 9th-century church is dedicated to St Praxedes, an early Christian heroine.

The **mosaics**, which entirely cover the walls and vault, were produced by artists whom Pope Paschal I had brought in specially from Byzantium and bear all the hallmarks of their eastern creators, with bold gold backgrounds and a marked Christian symbolism. The apse mosaics depict Christ flanked by Sts Peter, Pudentiana and Zeno on the right, and Sts Paul, Praxedes and Paschal on the left.

Basilica di Santa Prassede

Further treasures await in the heavily mosaicked Cappella di San Zenone, including a piece of the column to which Christ is said to have been tied when he was flogged.

Domus Aurea

NERO'S
GOLDEN HOUSE

The Domus Aurea was Nero's vast palace complex. Built after a fire in 64 CE, it covered almost a third of the city, and was sumptuously decorated with gold and precious stones – hence its name, the **Golden House**. But such was Nero's unpopularity that after his death, successive emperors tried to raze every trace of it: most notably, Vespasian built the Colosseum on land reclaimed from the Domus' lake. Some parts survived, and you can now tour excavated sections under the Oppian Hill – booking necessary at https:// ecm.coopculture.it – and, thanks to virtual reality, see how they would have looked in their prime.

Domus Aurea

Basilica di San Pietro in Vincoli

MICHELANGELO'S MOSES AND MIRACULOUS CHAINS

Pilgrims and art lovers flock to this 5th-century basilica for two reasons: to marvel at Michelangelo's formidable *Moses* sculpture and to see the chains that are said to have bound St Peter when he was imprisoned in the Carcere Mamertino ('*in Vincoli*' means 'in Chains').

The church was built specially to house St Peter's shackles, which had been sent to Constantinople after the saint's death, but were later returned as relics. They arrived in two pieces and legend has it that when they were reunited they miraculously joined together.

Michelangelo's *Moses* forms the centrepiece of his unfinished tomb of Pope Julius II. The prophet strikes a muscular pose with well-defined biceps, a magnificent waist-length beard and two small horns.

Museo Nazionale Romano: Palazzo Massimo alle Terme

UNSUNG TROVE OF CLASSICAL ART

One of Rome's finest museums, this often-empty branch of the Museo Nazionale Romano is packed with spectacular classical art. Particularly gripping is a series of frescoes and mosaics on the 2nd floor that provides a scintillating evocation of what the interiors of grand Roman villas would have looked like.

The 2nd-floor showstopper is a room dedicated to frescoes from **Villa di Livia** (dating from 30 BCE to 20 BCE), one of the homes of Augustus' wife Livia Drusilla. These depict a paradisiacal garden full of roses, pomegranates, irises and camomile under a deep-blue, bird-filled sky. They once decorated a summer triclinium – a large living and dining area built half underground to provide shelter from the heat. Also on the 2nd floor are intricate floor mosaics and richly coloured frescoes from an aristocratic residence known as **Villa Farnesina**. A multimedia presentation gives an excellent idea of how the villa, rediscovered in Trastevere in 1879, would originally have looked.

The ground and 1st floors are devoted to sculpture. On the 1st floor, don't miss a mid-3rd-century BCE marble statue known as the *Anzio Maiden*, which depicts a young girl participating in a Dionysian ritual. On the ground floor, highlights include two 2nd-to-1st-century BCE Greek bronzes (*The Boxer* and *The Prince*) and the 4th-century BCE marble *Dying Niobid* statue.

COIN & MEDAL COLLECTION

On display in the basement (temporarily closed at the time of research), the museum's coin collection is far more absorbing than you might expect, tracing the Roman Empire's propaganda offensive through its coins. Many of the pieces, dating from around the 9th century BCE, were unearthed during work to modernise Rome in the wake of Italian unification. There's also jewellery dating back several millennia that looks as good as new.

Fresco, Villa di Livia, Palazzo Massimo alle Terme

STEFANO RAVERA/ALAMY STOCK PHOTO ©

Palazzo Merulana

MODERN ART IN STYLISH SETTING

This impressive modern-art **museum** and cultural space exhibits art sourced from the Elena and Claudio Cerasi Foundation (the Cerasi family owns the construction firm that was responsible for major building projects such as the MAXXI museum). The majority of the works on display are by Roman and Italian artists active in the first half of the 20th century, including Giacomo Balla, Giorgio De Chirico and Giuseppe Capogrossi. Additional museum perks include a spacious outdoor terrace, stylish coffee bar and excellent gift shop.

Basilica di Santa Maria Maggiore

MOSAICS SPARKLE IN PATRIARCHAL BASILICA

Crowning the Esquiline Hill, this monumental church is one of Rome's four patriarchal basilicas. It was originally built in the 5th century but has been much modified over the centuries and it's now something of an architectural hybrid.

Its grand entrance features a two-tiered baroque portico. This towering construction covers a series of glimmering 13th-century mosaics that can only really be admired by visiting the **Loggia delle Benedizioni** (€9). Rising above, the basilica's Romanesque campanile – Rome's tallest – tops out at 75m.

The cavernous interior harbours some fabulous 5th-century mosaics in the triumphal arch and nave, depicting Old Testament scenes. The central image in the apse dates from the 13th century and represents the coronation of the Virgin Mary. The nave floor is a fine example of 12th-century Cosmati paving.

At the head of the nave, an 18th-century baldachin soars over the altar, which is said to contain the relics of St Matthew and other martyrs. Steps lead down to the *confessio*, where a statue of Pope Pius IX kneels before a reliquary that is claimed to contain a fragment of Jesus' manger.

The sumptuous Cappella Sistina, last on the right, was built by Domenico Fontana in the 16th century and contains the tombs of Popes Sixtus V and Pius V. Not as lavish but more beautiful is the Cappella Sforza on the left, which was designed by Michelangelo.

MIRACULOUS SNOWFALL

According to religious lore, the Basilica di Santa Maria Maggiore was originally constructed on the spot where snow is said to have fallen in the height of summer in 358 CE. To commemorate this miraculous event, each 5 August the snowstorm is recreated with an evening light show on the piazza outside the basilica.

Mosaic, Basilica di Santa Maria Maggiore

NICOLA MESSANA PHOTOS/SHUTTERSTOCK ©

Browse the Boutiques

COOL FASHIONS IN MONTI

With its cool boutiques, indie fashions and casual cafes, Monti is perfectly set up for laid-back shopping. Kick off with a coffee at **La Bottega del Caffè** before heading up Via Bottega to browse retro-esque designs at **Tina Sondergaard** and avant-garde jewellery at **Perlei**. From the top of the street, make your way across to Via dei Serpenti, another top shopping strip, where you can rifle through vintage secondhand threads at **Pifebo**.

Hit the Markets

FOR FOOD, SPICES & ATMOSPHERE

The multicultural Esquilino neighbourhood is home to one of the capital's best-known covered markets, the **Nuovo Mercato Esquilino**. Located a block from Piazza Vittorio Emanuele, this is an authentic working market piled high with fresh fruit, veg, meat, herbs and spices.

Nearby, in Termini station, the **Mercato Centrale** is ideal for a quick bite on the hoof. A food hall housed in a vaulted 1930s hall, it's crammed with counters serving everything from *panini* and sliced pizza to ramen and sushi.

Take a Class

BRUSH UP ON ITALIAN & WINE TASTING

If you want to dig deeper into Italian culture, taking a class can be a great way of keying into local life. To brush up on your communication skills, **Dilit** *(dilit.it)* is a well-established school near Termini station that offers a range of language and cultural courses. If wine is more your thing, book a tasting at **Vino Roma** *(vinoroma.com)* in Monti. This beautifully appointed studio runs English-language tastings, dinners, tours and masterclasses, guiding both novices and aficionados in the basics of Italian vino.

Hang out in San Lorenzo

STUDENT BARS & BOHEMIAN HANG-OUTS

A short walk southeast of Termini station, San Lorenzo provides a graffiti-clad playground for left-leaning bohemians and students from the nearby Sapienza University. It's full of bars, basement clubs, cultural spaces

BEST BARS

Rooftop Spritzeria Monti
For a cool *aperitivo spritz*, book a table at this hip rooftop bar in Monti.

Blackmarket Hall
A Monti speakeasy with multiple rooms in a former monastery and eclectic vintage-style decor.

Drink Kong
Dark, moody design and bespoke cocktails at this acclaimed Monti bar.

Gatsby Café
Laid-back bar under the porticoes on the increasingly trendy Piazza Vittorio Emanuele.

Officine Beat
Inviting lounge bar good for craft beer and well-mixed cocktails in San Lorenzo.

MORE MARKET SHOPPING

Rome's largest flea market is **Porta Portese** (p111), held every Sunday in Trastevere. We've put together the inside track with tips from artisan Luigi Cigola, who has had a stall there for 17 years.

 WHERE TO STAY IN A HOSTEL IN MONTI, ESQUILINO & SAN LORENZO

Beehive	**RomeHello**	**Generator Hostel**
Small, welcoming hostel with private rooms, mixed and female-only dorms and a friendly traveller vibe. €	Big, 200-bed hostel with excellent facilities near Piazza della Repubblica. All profits go to social causes. €	Near Termini, a slick designer hostel offering bright rooms and dorms sleeping three to six. €

ALFRESCO OPERA

In July and August, the opera action moves outdoors as the Teatro dell'Opera di Roma takes its summer season to the ancient ruins of the **Terme di Caracalla** (p116).

Via del Pigneto

PIGNETO

Over the last decade or so, this former working-class district has undergone a dramatic metamorphosis to become an arty, hipster haunt. Pigneto was immortalised by film director Pier Paolo Pasolini, who used to hang out at the Necci dal 1924 cafe and shot *Accattone* (1961) here. There's a small-town feel, with low-rise houses and narrow streets daubed with graffiti and street art. Action centres on pedestrianised Via del Pigneto, scene of a morning produce market and nightly bar-revelry, but there are plenty of bars in the surrounding streets.

Get to Pigneto by metro (line C) from San Giovanni, or trams 14 or 5 from Termini.

and budget restaurants, as well as Rome's historic cemetery, the **Cimitero di Campo Verano**, and a major church, the **Basilica di San Lorenzo Fuori Le Mura**. Chocoholics can sate their cravings at **Said**, a shop-cafe in a historic chocolate factory, while craft beer and cocktail fans can get their fill at bars such as **Artisan** and **Officine Beat**.

A Night at the Opera

ROME'S PREMIER OPERA HOUSE

The Romans have long been passionate opera-goers and in the 19th century several hit operas were premiered in the city, including Rossini's *Il barbiere di Siviglia* (*The Barber of Seville*; 1816), Verdi's *Il trovatore* (*The Troubadour*; 1853) and Puccini's *Tosca* (1900), which is also set in the city. To catch a performance, the **Teatro dell'Opera di Roma** stages both opera and ballet, as well as classical music concerts, during its annual season (October to June).

WHERE TO EAT IN MONTI, ESQUILINO & SAN LORENZO

Alle Carrette
Old-school pizzeria cooking up wood-fired Roman-style pizzas on one of Monti's prettiest streets. €

La Vecchia Conca
A family-run trattoria good for traditional Roman cuisine at honest prices near Piazza Vittorio Emanuele. €€

Tram Tram
San Lorenzo stalwart specialising in classical Roman dishes and ever-popular seafood recipes from Puglia. €€

TRASTEVERE & GIANICOLO

COBBLED LANES & CARNIVAL VIBE

Trastevere is an endlessly photogenic knot of cobbled lanes, alluring piazzas and peeling, orange-hued *palazzi*. At night street sellers set up camp on its picturesque alleyways and crowds swarm to its many restaurants, bars and cafes. Its cosmopolitanism could be traced to its ancient origins as a rough outlying district populated by fishermen, freed slaves and immigrants. Its position on the wrong side of the river – the name is a derivation of *tras tevere*, meaning 'across the Tiber' – has led its inhabitants to develop a proud sense of 'other-ness', which persists to this day.

There are several excellent sights to check out while strolling around, as well as superb views to be admired from the Gianicolo Hill. This, the eighth hill of Rome, is a lovely green retreat, offering shade and a welcome change in pace.

TOP TIP

Trastevere, the narrow lanes of which are best covered on foot, is within walking distance of the *centro storico*, just across the river. Alternatively, trams 3 and 8 run down the neighbourhood's main drag, Viale Trastevere. Bus H also serves the area, connecting with Termini station.

Orto Botanico

Orto Botanico

HILLSIDE BOTANICAL GARDENS

Formerly the private grounds of Palazzo Corsini (p107), Rome's 12-hectare **botanical gardens** are a great place to unwind in a tree-shaded expanse on the Gianicolo Hill. Plants have been cultivated here since the 13th century and the current gardens contain up to 8000 species, including centuries-old trees, 400 species of orchids, and some of Europe's rarest plants.

The garden entrance is at the end of Via Corsini but be warned, there's no entrance or exit at the top of the gardens onto the Gianicolo.

Tempietto di Bramante & Chiesa di San Pietro in Montorio

MASTERPIECE OF RENAISSANCE ARCHITECTURE

Considered the first great building of the High Renaissance, Bramante's sublime **Tempietto** (Little Temple; 1508) is a perfect surprise, squeezed into the courtyard of the Chiesa di San Pietro in Montorio. It has a circular interior surrounded by 16 columns and topped by a classical frieze, elegant balustrade and dome. More than a century after Bramante completed it, Bernini added a staircase in 1628. Bernini also contributed a chapel to the adjacent church, the last resting place of Beatrice Cenci, a young Italian noblewoman who helped murder her abusive father and was publicly beheaded on Ponte Sant'Angelo in 1599.

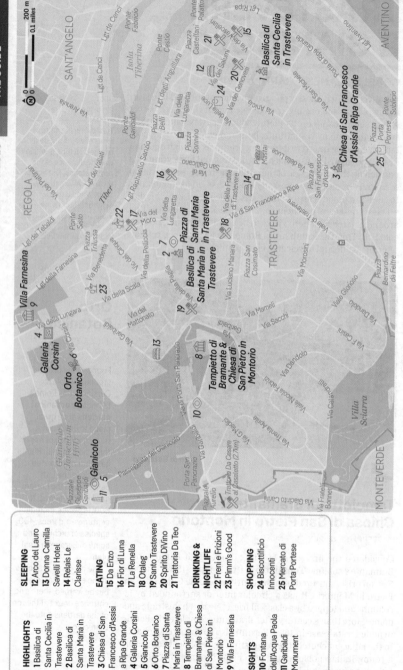

Basilica di Santa Cecilia in Trastevere

ARTISTIC GEMS IN SERENE BASILICA

This secluded basilica, fronted by a leafy courtyard and 18th-century façade, is the last resting place of Cecilia, the patron saint of music. The saint, who was supposedly martyred in a house buried beneath the current church, is represented by a sculpture under the main altar. The work of Stefano Maderno, this delicate marble statue is said to show how her miraculously preserved body looked when it was discovered in 1599 in the Catacombe di San Callisto.

The basilica's other great masterpiece is Pietro Cavallini's exquisite 13th-century fresco in the nuns' choir, showing a section of the *Last Judgement*.

Admission to the basilica is free but to visit the frescoes and underground excavations, there's a €2.50 entrance charge.

THE CATACOMBS

St Cecilia was just one of the many thousands of early Christians who were buried in the the Catacombe di San Callisto, one of three extensive catacomb networks beneath **Via Appia Antica** (p124).

Chiesa di San Francesco d'Assisi a Ripa Grande

SAINTLY HOME OF BAROQUE MASTERPIECE

Tucked away in the quieter eastern half of Trastevere, this **church** takes its name from St Francis of Assisi who is said to have stayed here in 1219. However, the main reason to visit is to admire the extraordinary Bernini sculpture of the *Beata Ludovica Albertoni (Blessed Ludovica Albertoni*; 1674). A virtuoso work of highly charged sexual ambiguity and technical brilliance – note how the marble has been transformed into flowing robes – it shows Franciscan nun Ludovica reclining in a state of religious rapture with her eyes shut, mouth open, and one hand touching her breast.

Beata Ludovica Albertoni, Chiesa di San Francesco d'Assisi

RENATA SEDMAKOVA/SHUTTERSTOCK ©

Galleria Corsini

MAJOR ART COLLECTION IN STATELY HOME

Once home to Queen Christina of Sweden, whose bedroom reputedly witnessed a steady stream of male and female lovers, the *palazzo* takes its name from the Florentine Corsini family who took it over when Lorenzo Corsini became Pope Clement XII in 1730. Nowadays, it's one of two seats of the **Gallerie Nazionali di Arte Antica** (the other is Palazzo Barberini).

Highlights of its stellar art collection include Caravaggio's *San Giovanni Battista* (*St John the Baptist*), Guido Reni's *Salome con la testa di San Giovanni Battista* (*Salome with the Head of John the Baptist*), and Fra' Angelico's Corsini Triptych, plus works by Rubens, Poussin and Van Dyck.

Note that you'll need to book online at barberinicorsini.org to visit at the weekend.

Basilica di Santa Maria in Trastevere

MOSAICS GLITTER IN ANCIENT BASILICA

Trastevere's headline **basilica** is said to be the oldest church in Rome dedicated to the Virgin Mary. It was first constructed in the early 3rd century on the spot where, according to legend, a fountain of oil miraculously sprang from the ground.

In its current form it largely dates to the 12th century when the Romanesque bell tower was added along with a glittering facade. This is decorated with a beautiful medieval mosaic depicting Mary feeding Jesus surrounded by 10 women bearing lamps. The portico came later, added by Carlo Fontana in 1702, with its balustrade topped by statues of four popes.

Inside, the main focus is the golden 12th-century mosaics. In the apse, look out for the dazzling depiction of Christ and his mother flanked by various saints and, on the far left, Pope Innocent II holding a model of the church. Beneath this are six mosaics by Pietro Cavallini (c 1291) illustrating the life of the Virgin.

Other highlight features include its 24 Roman columns, some plundered from the Terme di Caracalla; the fragments of Roman carved marbles forming an informal mosaic on the porch; the wooden ceiling designed in 1617 by Domenichino; and a spiralling Cosmati candlestick on the spot where the oil fountain is said to have sprung. The Cappella Avila is also worth a look for its stunning 17th-century dome.

FONS OLEI

To the right of the altar you'll see a marble balustrade inscribed with the words *Fons Olei*. These refer to the fountain of oil that supposedly spouted here in 38 BCE. Early Christians interpreted the miraculous gushing as a foretelling of Christ's imminent birth. Scholars, however, believe *fons olei* (oil fountain) may have been a corruption of *fons olidus* (polluted fountain), in reference to water piped into Trastevere for mock naval battles held in a local arena.

Piazza di Santa Maria in Trastevere

TRABANTOS/SHUTTERSTOCK ©

Piazza di Santa Maria in Trastevere

CENTRAL NEIGHBOURHOOD HANG-OUT

Trastevere's focal **square** is a prime people-watching spot. By day it's full of chatting locals and tourists; by night it's the domain of foreign students, young Romans and out-of-towners, all enjoying its cafes and bars. Flanking the square is Palazzo San Callisto, owned by the Holy See, and the Basilica di Santa Maria in Trastevere. The octagonal fountain in the centre, of Roman origin, was restored by Bernini in 1659 and then again by Carlo Fontana in 1692.

Villa Farnesina

RENAISSANCE VILLA WITH RAPHAEL FRESCOES

A graceful work of Renaissance architecture, this 16th-century villa is serenely and symmetrically proportioned on the outside and fantastically frescoed inside.

It was originally built for Agostino Chigi, an immensely rich banker who was famous for his lavish entertaining. It's said that after one banquet in 1518, he had the gold plates his guests had used thrown into the Tiber River as a sign of his munificence – cunningly, though, he had earlier set up nets to retrieve them. Today, the villa bears the name of the Farnese family who purchased it in 1579.

The architectural mastermind behind the villa was Baldassare Peruzzi, formerly Bramante's assistant. He also contributed to the interior decor: most notably, his frescoes in the 1st-floor Salone delle Prospettive provide a superb illusionary perspective of 16th-century Rome. His works also appear in the villa's star room, the Loggia of Galatea. This ground-floor hall is dominated by Raphael's famous depiction of the sea nymph Galatea, but also features mythological scenes by Sebastiano del Piombio.

Further Raphael works await in the next-door Loggia of Cupid and Psyche, which seethes with naked figures and muscular cupids.

RAPHAEL'S MISTRESS

It was while working at Villa Farnesina that Raphael supposedly fell in love with Margherita Luti, the daughter of a local Trastevere baker. According to the 16th-century historian Giorgio Vasari, Raphael fell for her after seeing her bathing in the Tiber. He became so infatuated that his work slowed until Agostino Chigi eventually let her into the villa. To see what she looked like, check out Raphael's painting of her, *La Fornarina*, in Palazzo Barberini (p88).

Villa Farnesina

ANNA PAKUTINA/SHUTTERSTOCK ©

BEST BAKERIES & GELATERIAS

La Renella
Historic Trastevere bakery popular for its delicious bread, biscuits and wood-fired pizza.

Biscottificio Innocenti
Homemade biscuits, bite-sized meringues and fruit tarts from a picture-perfect backstreet bakery.

Otaleg
Otaleg, or gelato backwards, regularly appears on lists of Rome's best gelaterias. Rightly so.

Fior di Luna
Natural seasonal ingredients fuel the flavoursome gelatos and sorbets at this busy little spot.

PHANT/SHUTTERSTOCK ©

Fontana dell'Acqua Paola

MORE OBSERVATION POSTS

Rome's hills and lofty monuments provide many vantage points. One of the most spectacular is the **Vittoriano** (p67), where the sky-high terrace commands 360-degree panoramas of the city and distant hills.

MORE IN TRASTEVERE & GIANICOLO

A Neighbourhood Night Out

DRINKS, DINNER & MORE DRINKS

Trastevere is one of Rome's favourite after-dark stamping grounds for foreigners and locals alike. Romans come here in droves, particularly on balmy summer nights when diners sit out on street-side restaurants and bar crowds spill onto the piazzas.

Join them by toasting the night with a cocktail at **Pimm's Good** or perhaps an *aperitivo* at perennially popular **Freni e Frizioni**. Suitably warmed up, head over to the eastern part of the neighbourhood to dine on seasonal Italian cuisine at **Spirito DiVino**. Afterwards, round things off in high style with a drink or two at **Santo Trastevere**, a fashionable bar-restaurant in a leafy corner west of Piazza Santa Maria in Trastevere.

 WHERE TO STAY IN TRASTEVERE & GIANICOLO

Arco del Lauro
On a peaceful cobbled lane, a welcoming guesthouse with low-key modern rooms. €€

Relais Le Clarisse
Central hotel offering rustic charm and rooms set around a pretty internal courtyard. €€

Donna Camilla Savelli Hotel
Classically attired hotel in a Borromini-designed baroque convent. Views and a cloistered garden add to the allure. €€€

Take a Food Tour

UNLOCK TRASTEVERE'S FOODIE SECRETS

With its centuries-old biscuit shops and bakeries, family-run trattorias and superb food purveyors, Trastevere is a fine place to indulge your culinary curiosity. A good way to do this is to join a guided food tour and get the lowdown on the neighbourhood's foodie traditions and gourmet hot spots. Reliable operators include **Casa Mia** *(https://casamiatours. com)* and **The Roman Guy** *(https://theromanguy.com)*.

Scale the Heights

VIEWS, MONUMENTS AND FILM LOCATIONS

To escape Trastevere's sometimes claustrophobic streets, the **Gianicolo** (Janiculum Hill) is a wonderful respite. Rome's highest hill, though not one of its original seven, is a superb vantage point for unforgettable views over Rome's rooftops – pro tip: get the best vistas from a spot just north of the snack stands by the **Garibaldi Monument**. This colossal bronze statue is one of many references to Italy's legendary rebel on the Gianicolo. The reason for them is that Garibaldi fought a ferocious battle here in 1849 during the struggle for Italian unification. He and a pro-unification army secured a famous victory against French troops fighting for Pope Pius IX.

More recently, the Gianicolo appeared in Paolo Sorrentino's Oscar-winning film *La grande bellezza* (*The Great Beauty*; 2013): the opening scene is set by the landmark **Fontana dell'Acqua Paola**, known locally as the Fontanone (Big Fountain).

Join the Celebrations

TRASTEVERE'S ANNUAL NEIGHBOURHOOD PARTY

To experience Trastevere in full party mode, come in the last two weeks of July for the **Festa de' Noantri** (*noantri* translates from Roman dialect as 'we others'). The neighbourhood's traditional and raucous annual festival has been drawing crowds every summer since the 16th century.

Events, accompanied by much eating, drinking and praying, are centred on two processions. The first involves a wooden effigy of the Madonna del Carmine being paraded through the streets from its home in the Chiesa di Sant'Agata to the Basilica di San Crisogono. A second, eight or nine days later, sees the Madonna loaded onto a boat and sailed home along the Tiber River.

SHOPPING TIPS FOR PORTA PORTESE

Artisans **Luigi Cigola** and **Sonia Stuppia** are the creative force behind jewellery brand Formespazio Roma *(https:// formespazioroma. it)*. Luigi gives his tips for navigating **Porta Portese**, Rome's historic flea market, where he's been selling for 17 years.

Main zones
Between Piazzale della Radio and Via Ippolito Nievo is where you'll find secondhand and vintage clothes. Via Ippolito Nievo up to Piazza Ippolito Nievo is traditionally the antiques area. A third zone around Via Porta Portese is the most commercial part, with stalls selling new clothes and everyday home stuff.

Best time for a deal
When the market opens and for the first few hours.

Bargaining
It's fundamental. You should always bargain. It's the rule.

 WHERE TO EAT ALFRESCO IN TRASTEVERE & GIANICOLO

Da Enzo	**Trattoria Da Teo**	**Trattoria Da Cesare al Casaletto**
Old-school trattoria serving staunchly traditional Roman cuisine. Expect queues and few frills. €€	Ticks all the boxes: charming piazza setting, authentic local cuisine, wisecracking waiters. €€	Amazing local food under a vine-covered arbour. Well worth the taxi ride to get there. €€

SAN GIOVANNI & TESTACCIO

TRADITIONAL TRATTORIAS & MEDIEVAL CHURCHES

San Giovanni is a largely residential quarter that fans out from its signature basilica near the Aurelian walls. Known officially as Appio Latino, the district extends along Via Appia Nuova, a major artery lined with shops, cafes and department stores.

To the east, the Celian Hill is home to Villa Celimontana, a lovely off-the-radar park where locals go to have a restorative lunchtime stroll. Further west, the leafy and pricey Aventino neighbourhood is packed with elegant Liberty-style villas and romantic views.

At the foot of the Aventino lies Testaccio, best known for its traditional Roman cuisine and disco-infused nightlife. Despite gentrification, the quarter maintains an earthy, workaday character.

TOP TIP

Southeast of the centre, this large district can be divided into two distinct areas: San Giovanni and the Celio, and to the west, Testaccio and hilltop Aventino. Both areas can be explored on foot and both can be reached by metro: line A to San Giovanni; line B to Piramide for Testaccio.

REPORT/SHUTTERSTOCK ©

Chiesa di Santo Stefano Rotondo

Chiesa di Santo Stefano Rotondo

X-RATED FRECOES

Set in its own secluded grounds, this haunting 5th-century church boasts a porticoed facade and a round, columned interior. But what really grabs your attention is its graphic wall decor – a cycle of 16th-century frescoes depicting the tortures suffered by many early Christian martyrs. Describing the paintings in 1846, Charles Dickens wrote: 'Such a panorama of horror and butchery no man could imagine in his sleep, though he were to eat a whole pig, raw, for supper.'

Basilica dei SS Quattro Coronati

BROODING MEDIEVAL BASILICA

This fortified basilica harbours some lovely 13th-century frescoes and a delightful hidden cloister. The frescoes, in the **Oratorio di San Silvestro**, depict the story of the so-called Donation of Constantine, a notorious forged document with which the emperor Constantine supposedly ceded control of Rome and the Western Roman Empire to the papacy. Further frescoes can also be enjoyed in the **Aula Gotica** (Gothic Hall), visitable by guided tour (€10; see aulagotica santiquattrocoronati.it).

The basilica, which dates from the 6th century, took on its present form in the 12th century after the original was destroyed by the Normans in 1084.

HIGHLIGHTS
1 Basilica dei SS Quattro Coronati
2 Basilica di San Clemente
3 Basilica di San Giovanni in Laterano
4 Basilica di Santa Sabina
5 Chiesa di Santo Stefano Rotondo
6 Cimitero Acattolico per gli Stranieri
7 Giardino degli Aranci
8 Monte Testaccio
9 Terme di Caracalla
10 Villa Celimontana
11 Villa del Priorato di Malta

SIGHTS
12 Mattatoio
13 Scala Santa

SLEEPING
14 Althea Inn Roof Terrace
15 Hotel Lancelot

16 Hotel Sant'Anselmo

EATING
(see 21)
Augustarello
(see 27) da Corrado al Banco 18
17 Felice a Testaccio
18 Flavio al Velavevodetto
(see 27) Food Box
(see 27) Mordi e Vai
19 Piatto Romano
20 Pizzeria Da Remo
21 Trapizzino

DRINKING & NIGHTLIFE
22 Ch 18 87
23 Coming Out
24 L'Oasi della Birra
25 Tram Depot

SHOPPING
26 Città dell'Altra Economia
27 Nuovo Mercato di Testaccio
28 Volpetti

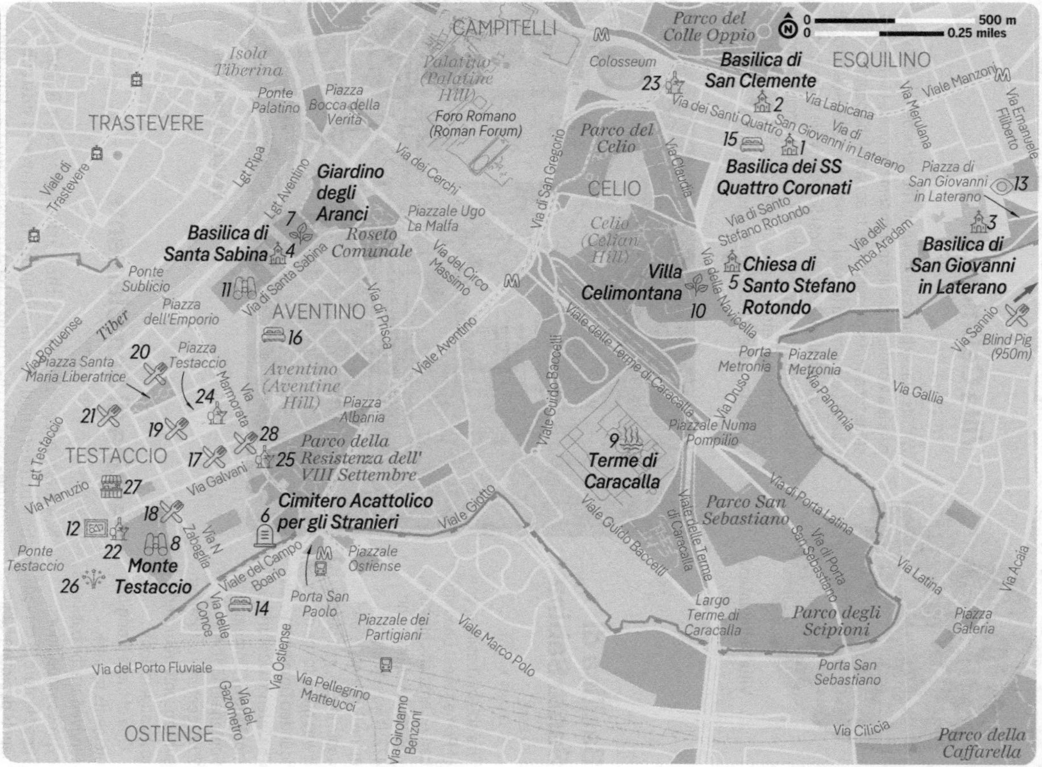

113

Villa Celimontana

Villa Celimontana

TRANQUIL PARK

With its grassy banks and colourful flower beds, this leafy park is a wonderful picnic spot. In summer, it sets the alfresco stage for a series of free concerts as part of the popular Village Celimontana festival. At its centre is a 16th-century villa housing the Italian Geographical Society, while to the south stands a 12m-plus Egyptian obelisk. Legend surrounds this ancient monument, with one story holding that the globe on top contains the ashes of the emperor Augustus.

Basilica di Santa Sabina

SERENE
AVENTINO BASILICA

This solemn basilica, one of Rome's most beautiful early-Christian churches, was founded in around 422. It was enlarged in the 9th century and again in 1216, just before it was given to the newly founded Dominican order. The interior was further modified by Domenico Fontana in 1587. A 20th-century restoration subsequently returned it to its original look.

One of the few original elements to have survived are the basilica's cypress-wood doors. These feature 18 carved panels depicting biblical events, including one of the oldest Crucifixion scenes in existence. It's quite hard to make out in the top left, but it depicts Jesus and the two thieves, although, strangely, not their crosses.

Basilica di San Clemente

Basilica di San Clemente

DESCEND INTO HISTORY

Nowhere better illustrates the various stages of Rome's turbulent past than this fascinating multilayered **church**. The ground-level 12th-century basilica sits atop a 4th-century church, which, in turn, stands over a 2nd-century pagan temple and a 1st-century Roman house. Beneath everything lie foundations dating from the Roman Republic.

Before heading underground, take a moment to admire the basilica's 12th-century apse mosaic depicting the *Trionfo della Croce* (*Triumph of the Cross*) and the frescoed Cappella di Santa Caterina.

Subterranean highlights include some faded 11th-century frescoes in the *basilica inferiore*, an ancient Roman house, and a 2nd-century temple to the pagan god Mithras. Beneath it all, you can hear the eerie sound of an underground river flowing through a Republic-era drain.

Basilica di San Giovanni in Laterano

MONUMENTAL PAPAL BASILICA

This mighty church, the oldest of the city's four papal basilicas, is Rome's official **cathedral** and the pope's seat as the Bishop of Rome. Consecrated in 324, it's revered as the *mater et caput* (mother and head) of all Catholic churches and it was the pope's main place of worship for almost 1000 years.

Over the centuries, it has been revamped several times, most notably by Francesco Borromini in the 17th century, and by Alessandro Galilei, who added the immense white facade in 1735.

The echoing, marble-clad interior owes much of its present look to Borromini, who refurbished it for the 1650 Jubilee. It's a breathtaking sight, with a golden gilt ceiling, a 15th-century mosaic floor, and a wide central nave lined with muscular 4.6m-high sculptures of the apostles.

At the head of the nave, the Gothic baldachin over the papal altar is said to contain the relics of the heads of saints Peter and Paul. In front of it, at the base of the altar, the tomb of Pope Martin V lies in the *confessio*, along with a wooden statue of St John the Baptist.

Behind the altar, the massive apse is decorated with sparkling mosaics. Parts of these date from the 4th century, but most were added in the 1800s.

Outside the church, the 13th-century cloister is a lovely, peaceful place with graceful twisted columns set around a central garden.

SCALA SANTA

Over the piazza from the basilica, you'll find another venerated site. The Scala Santa, brought to Rome by St Helena in the 4th century, is said to be the staircase Jesus walked up in Pontius Pilate's palace in Jerusalem. Pilgrims consider it sacred and climb it on their knees, saying a prayer on each of the 28 steps. At the top is the richly decorated Sancta Sanctorum (Holy of Holies), formerly the pope's private chapel.

Giardino degli Aranci

Giardino degli Aranci

ROMANTIC HILLTOP GARDEN

Officially called the **Parco Savello** but known to Romans as the Giardino degli Aranci (Orange Garden), this walled Aventino park is a romantic haven. To impress your partner, bring them here at sunset to walk amid the blooming orange trees and bask in heavenly views across to the dome of St Peter's.

Note also how the dome seems smaller from the front of the park than it does from the back, in seeming contradiction to the rules of physics.

Monte Testaccio

TESTACCIO'S NAMESAKE HILL

Rising in the heart of Testaccio, this grass-covered mount is an **artificial hill** made entirely from the fragments of smashed amphorae (*testae* in Latin, hence the area's name, Testaccio). Between the 2nd century BCE and the 3rd century CE, Testaccio was Rome's river port. Supplies of olive oil were transported here in huge terracotta amphorae, which, once emptied, were broken and the fragments stacked in a pile near the storehouses. Over time, this pile grew into a substantial 54m-high hill – Monte Testaccio.

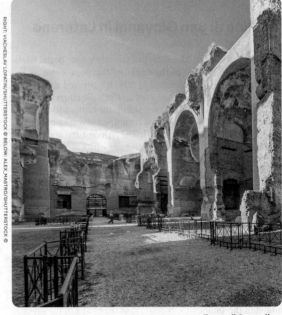

Terme di Caracalla

Cimitero Acattolico per gli Stranieri

TOMBS OF WRITERS, POETS AND PHILSOPHERS

Overlooked by Testaccio's signature pyramid, actually a 1st-century BCE tomb, Rome's 'non-Catholic' **cemetery** is a verdant oasis of peace. An air of Grand Tour romance hangs over the site, where up to 4000 people are buried. These include the Romantic poets Shelley and Keats, Italian political thinker Antonio Gramsci, and Andrea Camilleri, author of the hugely successful Inspector Montalbano books.

Among the gravestones and cypress trees, look out for the *Angelo del dolore* (*Angel of Grief*), a much-replicated 1894 sculpture that US artist William Wetmore Story created for his wife's grave.

John Keats' grave, Cimitero Acattolico per gli Stranieri

Terme di Caracalla

AWESOME RUINS OF ANCIENT BATHS

The remains of the emperor Caracalla's vast **baths** are among Rome's most awe-inspiring ruins. Inaugurated in 212 CE, the original 10-hectare site, comprising baths, gyms, libraries, shops and gardens, was used by up to 8000 people daily.

The focal point is the bathhouse, a rectangular edifice bookended by two *palestre* (gyms).

Back then, the bathhouse was centred on a *frigidarium* (cold room), where bathers would stop after the warmer *tepidarium* and dome-capped *caldarium* (hot

room). While customers enjoyed the luxurious facilities, hundreds of slaves sweated in 9.5km of tunnels below ground, operating the complex plumbing systems.

In summer, the ruins are used to stage spectacular music and ballet performances.

Through the Keyhole

CELEBRATED VIEW OF ST PETER'S

In a city of inspiring panoramas, the Aventino's famous keyhole view is one of the most unexpected. Head up to the Piazza dei Cavalieri di Malta and you'll find a pretty 18th-century piazza flanked by the ornamental facade of the **Villa del Priorato di Malta**. No view is immediately apparent, but look through the keyhole in the villa's green door and you'll see the dome of St Peter's Basilica perfectly aligned at the end of a hedge-lined avenue. The pure geometric perfection is quite astounding – though surprisingly difficult to photograph unless you're a whizz with a camera.

Food on the Hoof

FAST FOOD ROMAN-STYLE

Now occupying a modern, purpose-built site, Testaccio's **Nuovo Mercato** has long been a community hub. Still today it hums with activity as locals go about their shopping, picking, prodding and sniffing the brightly coloured produce and browsing stalls piled high with shoes, hats and clothes. Come lunchtime and the focus shifts to the market's many food stalls.

For a taste of classic, no-frills Roman street food, grab yourself a *panino con l'allesso di scottona* (bread roll filled with tender slow-cooked beef) from **Mordi e Vai** at Box 15, or a crispy *carciofo alla giudia* (deep-fried artichoke) from **Food Box** at Box 66.

For a more modern take on Roman fast food, nearby **Trapizzino** specialises in a kind of hybrid sandwich made by stuffing a cone of doughy focaccia with fillers such as *polpette al sugo* (meatballs in tomato sauce) or *pollo alla cacciatore* (stewed chicken).

And if none of that appeals, you can always pick something up at **Volpetti**, Testaccio's much-vaunted local deli.

Testaccio's Alternative Side

CONTEMPORARY ART IN DECOMMISSIONED ABATTOIR

For almost a century Testaccio was home to Rome's main slaughterhouse. The huge complex was finally decommissioned in 1975 and it has since been resurrected as a contemporary arts

BEST BARS

Tram Depot
With outdoor seating and a garden-party vibe, this Testaccio favourite is ideal for an *aperitivo*.

L'Oasi della Birra
Testaccio cellar bar renowned for its international selection of beers.

Ch 18 87
Brilliantly mixed cocktails in a discreet bar above the historic Testaccio restaurant Checchino Dal 1887.

Blind Pig
Slick San Giovanni hot spot serving expertly mixed cocktails.

Coming Out
Colosseum-side gay bar that hots up as the cocktails kick in and the karaoke comes on.

 WHERE TO EAT LIKE A ROMAN IN TESTACCIO

Pizzeria Da Remo
For the ultimate Roman pizza experience: brusque waiters, superlative fried starters, crispy wafer-thin pizzas. €

Flavio al Velavevodetto
A classic trattoria known for its earthy Roman cuisine – try the excellent carbonara. €€

Felice a Testaccio
A Testaccio stalwart with an unwavering dedication to old-school Roman dishes. €€

DISCOVER ROMAN CUISINE IN TESTACCIO

Food writer and local resident **Rachel Roddy** gives the lowdown on classic Roman cuisine and Testaccio's food scene.

Favourite dishes
I'm a big fan of *gricia* as a classic Roman pasta dish. I also like carbonara. In winter I'll often order pasta with beans (*fagioli*) or chickpeas (*ceci*). In summer, I love grilled red pepper.

Top Trattorias
Augustarello is the best place for offal. **Piatto Romano** is fantastic as well. It serves classic Roman cuisine with a personal touch.

Culinary Trend
Natural wine is happening at the moment. At the market, **da Corrado al Banco 18** is a natural wine and cheese shop where you can have a glass of wine and a plate of food for a good price.

Mattatoio

venue, the **Mattatoio**. Nowadays, the cavernous halls, themselves fine examples of 19th-century industrial architecture, stage regular exhibitions, installations and performances by established and emerging international artists.

Next door, the graffiti-clad **Città dell'Altra Economia** hosts festivals and events in the spaces that once held the animal pens.

Rock on May Day

FREE CONCERT DRAWS MEGA CROWDS

If you're an avid concert-goer, San Giovanni is the place to be on 1 May. To celebrate the *primo maggio* (1 May), tens of thousands of music fans make the pilgrimage to **Piazza di San Giovanni** for the city's free May Day concert. The festive atmosphere heats up throughout the afternoon and evening as big-name Italian stars and the occasional foreign guest entertain the jubilant crowds until well into the night.

 WHERE TO STAY IN SAN GIOVANNI & TESTACCIO

Althea Inn Roof Terrace
Excellent B&B offering modern-styled rooms, small rooftop terraces and easy access to Testaccio's many restaurants. **€**

Hotel Lancelot
A great location near the Colosseum, with striking views and super-helpful English-speaking staff. **€€**

Hotel Sant'Anselmo
A ravishing hideaway offering boutique style in an elegant villa on the Aventino Hill. **€€€**

VILLA BORGHESE & NORTHERN ROME

GREEN PARKS & CULTURAL HUBS

At its core, Villa Borghese is Rome's best-known park, counting the city zoo, several superlative museums, and a boating lake among its myriad attractions. To the northeast, Villa Ada is popular with local joggers and walkers, while Villa Torlonia, to the east, harbours a trio of low-key museums.

Parks aside, northern Rome is less crammed with traditional sights than many other parts of the city. Parioli, north of Villa Borghese, is one of Rome's most expensive areas and the root of the derogatory term '*pariolini*', used to describe designer-clad rich kids. But amid the leafy streets are a number of high-profile cultural hubs, like the Auditorium Parco della Musica, Rome's principal concert-venue; and the MAXXI contemporary art museum. The Stadio Olimpico offers culture of a more sporting kind.

TOP TIP

This sprawling swath of northern Rome extends out from Villa Borghese, central Rome's main park. This green haven is easily accessible by foot from Piazza del Popolo, or from Spagna metro station (line A). For places around Via Flaminia, Via Nomentana and Via Salaria, you'll need to take a bus or tram.

Villa Borghese

ALEXANDER DEMYANENKO/SHUTTERSTOCK ©

Villa Borghese

ROME'S CENTRAL PARK

Locals, lovers, tourists, joggers – no one can resist the lure of Rome's most celebrated park. Originally the 17th-century estate of Cardinal Scipione Borghese, it covers about 80 hectares of bosky glades, gardens and grassy banks. Among its attractions are the landscaped Giardino del Lago, complete with small boating lake; Piazza di Siena, a dusty arena used for Rome's top equestrian event in May; and a panoramic terrace on the Pincio Hill.

Bike hire is available at various points across the park.

La Galleria Nazionale

UNSUNG MODERN-ART MUSEUM

Housed in a vast belle époque palace, this modern-art gallery – known locally as **GNAM** after its full title, La Galleria Nazionale d'Arte Moderna e Contemporanea di Roma – is an unsung gem. Its superlative collection runs the gamut from neoclassical sculpture to abstract expressionism, with works by many of the most important exponents of 19th- and 20th-century art.

There are canvases by the *macchiaioli* (Italian impressionists) and futurists Boccioni and Balla, as well as sculptures by Canova and major works by Modigliani, de Chirico and Guttuso. International artists represented include Van Gogh, Cézanne, Monet, Klimt, Kandinsky, Mondrian and Man Ray.

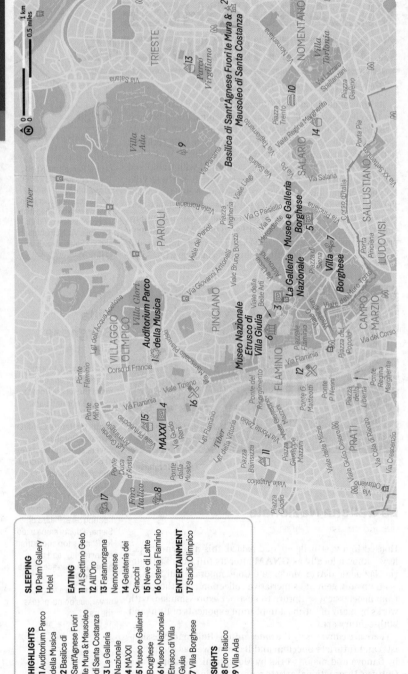

HIGHLIGHTS
1 Auditorium Parco della Musica
2 Basilica di Sant'Agnese Fuori le Mura & Mausoleo di Santa Costanza
3 La Galleria Nazionale
4 MAXXI
5 Museo e Galleria Borghese
6 Museo Nazionale Etrusco di Villa Giulia
7 Villa Borghese

SIGHTS
8 Foro Italico
9 Villa Ada

SLEEPING
10 Palm Gallery Hotel

EATING
11 Al Settimo Gelo
12 All'Oro
13 Fatamorgana Nemorense
14 Gelateria dei Gracchi
15 Neve di Latte
16 Osteria Flaminio

ENTERTAINMENT
17 Stadio Olimpico

Museo Nazionale Etrusco di Villa Giulia

ITALY'S PREMIER ETRUSCAN MUSEUM

Pope Julius III's 16th-century villa provides the charming setting for Italy's finest collection of Etruscan and pre-Roman treasures. Exhibits, many of which came from tombs in the surrounding Lazio countryside, range from bronze figurines and black bucchero tableware to temple decorations, terracotta vases and dazzling jewellery.

Must-sees include a polychrome terracotta statue of Apollo from a temple in Veio, and the 6th-century BCE *Sarcofago degli sposi* (*Sarcophagus of the Betrothed*). This astonishing work, unearthed in Cerveteri in 1881, depicts a husband and wife reclining on a stone banqueting couch.

Further finds relating to the Umbri and Latin peoples are housed in the nearby Villa Poniatowski, open on Friday afternoons.

ETRUSCAN TRAVELS

The Museo Nazionale Etrusco di Villa Giulia makes an inspiring primer for a trip to northern Lazio, where you'll find two of Italy's prize Etruscan sites: the great cemeteries of **Cerveteri** (p141) and **Tarquinia** (p140).

Auditorium Parco della Musica

ROME'S FLAGSHIP CULTURAL CENTRE

Hub of Rome's cultural scene, and home to the world-class Orchestra dell'Accademia Nazionale di Santa Cecilia, the auditorium was designed by starchitect Renzo Piano and inaugurated in 2002.

It's an audacious work of architecture consisting of three silver-grey pod-like concert halls set around a 3000-seat amphitheatre. These provide a stage for everything from classical music and jazz to lectures and film screenings.

To learn more about the complex, which also has two small museums – one displaying artefacts found during construction, and one exhibiting musical instruments – there are English-language tours on Saturday and Sunday mornings (see auditorium. com/visite_guidate.html for details).

ANNA PAKUTINA/SHUTTERSTOCK ©

Museo Nazionale Etrusco di Villa Giulia

Basilica di Sant'Agnese Fuori le Mura & Mausoleo di Santa Costanza

CATACOMBS & MAGNIFICENT MOSAICS

Although something of a hike, it's absolutely worth venturing out to this medieval church complex on Via Nomentana. Set over the catacombs where St Agnes was buried, it comprises the Basilica di Sant'Agnese Fuori le Mura and the Mausoleo di Santa Costanza, decorated by some of Christendom's oldest **mosaics**.

The basilica's star turn is its golden apse mosaic. One of the best examples of Byzantine art in Rome, this depicts St Agnes, flanked by Popes Honorius and Symmachus, standing over the signs of her martyrdom – a sword and flame.

Up from the main basilica is the mausoleum. This squat circular building has a dome supported by 12 pairs of columns and a vaulted ambulatory decorated with beautiful 4th-century mosaics.

Museo e Galleria Borghese

SENSATIONAL SCULPTURES & RENAISSANCE MASTERPIECES

Housing what's often dubbed the 'queen of all private art collections', this extraordinary **gallery** contains some of Rome's greatest treasures, including several sculptures by Gian Lorenzo Bernini and paintings by Caravaggio, Titian, Raphael and Rubens.

Things get off to an impressive start in the entrance hall, decorated with 4th-century floor mosaics and a 2nd-century *Satiro combattente* (*Fighting Satyr*). High on the wall is a bas-relief of a horse and rider falling into the void by Pietro Bernini.

The next few rooms harbour the museum's most prized sculptures. In Sala I, you'll find Antonio Canova's daring depiction of Napoleon's sister, Paolina Bonaparte Borghese, as *Venere vincitrice*. Sala III features Bernini's *Apollo e Dafne*, which captures the exact moment Daphne's hands start morphing into leaves, while Sala IV houses his great masterpiece, *Ratto di Proserpina*.

Caravaggio dominates Sala VIII. Look for his self-portrait, *Bacchino malato* (*Young Sick Bacchus*) and the much-loved *Giovane col canestro di frutta* (*Boy with a Basket of Fruit*).

Upstairs in the pinacoteca, don't miss Raphael's extraordinary *La Deposizione di Cristo* (*The Deposition*) and his *Dama con liocorno* (*Lady with a Unicorn*).

Other highlights include Lucas Cranach the Elder's *Venere e Amore che reca il favo di miele* (*Venus and Cupid Carrying the Honeycomb*) and Titian's masterwork, *Amor sacro e amor profano* (*Sacred and Profane Love*).

Ratto di Proserpina, Museo e Galleria Borghese

SILVERFOX999/SHUTTERSTOCK ©

THE COLLECTION

The museum's collection was amassed by Cardinal Scipione Borghese (1577–1633), one of the most influential figures in Rome's baroque art world. Nephew of Pope Paul V, he sponsored the greatest artists of the day, including Caravaggio, Bernini, Domenichino, Rubens and Guido Reni. Yet while he promoted the artists, he didn't always see eye to eye with them and was quite prepared to play dirty to get their works – he even had Domenichino arrested once to force him to surrender a painting.

MAXXI

CONTEMPORARY ART MUSEUM

The Zaha Hadid–designed home of the **Museo Nazionale delle Arti del XXI Secolo**, Rome's leading contemporary-art museum, makes a striking impression. The former barracks has a multilayered geometric facade and a cavernous interior full of snaking walkways and suspended staircases. Selected works from the gallery's permanent collection are on display, but the main draws are the temporary exhibitions, showcasing works by established stars and emerging artists from Italy and abroad.

A Footy Match

SPORT AT THE OLYMPIC STADIUM

Football is a Roman passion and there's no better way of experiencing it for yourself than by going to a match at the **Stadio Olimpico**. Throughout the football season (late August to May) there's a game most Sundays featuring one of the city's two Serie A teams: Roma or Lazio. If you go to a game, make sure you get it right – Roma play in red and yellow and their diehard supporters stand in the Curva Sud (South Stand); Lazio play in sky blue and their fans fill the Curva Nord (North Stand).

The stadium also hosts Italy's home games during the annual Six Nations rugby tournament (February to March), while tennis is staged at the nearby **Foro Italico** during the May Internazionali BNL d'Italia tournament.

Festival Fun

PREMIERES & PARK CONCERTS

Get into the festive spirit at **Villa Ada**, a rambling 160-hectare park that was once King Vittorio Emanuele III's private estate. From June to early August, it explodes into life as the **Villa Ada Festival** swings into action, bringing a series of energetic outdoor concerts.

For a change of scene, Rome's cinephiles roll out the red carpet for Hollywood hotshots and Italian stars during the October **Festa del Cinema di Roma**. Action is centred on the **Auditorium Parco della Musica**, but for the 10 days of the festival films are projected at venues across the city.

BEST GELATERIE

Neve di Latte
Ideally placed for the MAXXI museum; strong on classic flavours such as chocolate and pistachio.

Al Settimo Gelo
A long-standing Prati stalwart known for its creative flavours and use of carefully sourced seasonal ingredients.

Gelateria dei Gracchi
Simple flavours made the traditional way are the hallmark of this gelateria on Viale Regina Margherita.

Fatamorgana Nemorense
Near Villa Ada, Fatamorgana is a guarantee of good times – expect creative flavours and unusual combos.

OPEN-AIR CINEMA

For more summer film action, head to the **Isola Tiberina** (p80) for the Isola del Cinema festival, which sees the river island transformed into a memorable open-air cinema.

 WHERE TO STAY AND EAT IN VILLA BORGHESE & NORTHERN ROME

Palm Gallery Hotel
A Liberty-style villa decorated in eclectic style, this gorgeous hotel charms near Villa Torlonia. €€

Osteria Flaminio
Smart little restaurant on Via Flaminia cooking up seafood dishes and updated Roman classics. €€

All'Oro
Traditional regional cuisine is modernised in style at chef Riccardo di Giacinto's Michelin-starred restaurant. €€€

SOUTHERN ROME

CATACOMBS, NIGHTLIFE AND STREET ART

Southern Rome comprises several distinct districts, each with their own look and character. The most obvious drawcard is Via Appia Antica, the ancient Appian Way. This consular road cuts through pea-green countryside as it leads to romantically sited ruins and kilometres of creepy catacombs. Further out, on the coast, yet more ruins await at Ostia Antica, Rome's ancient seaport, which has been conserved almost in its entirety.

Back towards the centre, the Ostiense quarter straddles the namesake Via Ostiense. Formerly an industrial district, it has recently been reborn as one of Rome's hippest areas, home to start-ups, comms agencies, students and clubbers. Nearby Garbatella was designed as a kind of garden city to house workers from Ostiense's factories and displays an eclectic mishmash of architectural styles. The outlying EUR district is renowned for its muscular rationalist buildings housing government offices.

TOP TIP

All the places covered in this section can be reached by public transport and then explored on foot, by metro (line B) or, in Via Appia Antica's case, by bike. To get to Ostia Antica, there are regular trains from Stazione Porta San Paolo (next to Piramide metro station).

TILJAUCIDA/SHUTTERSTOCK ©

Villa dei Quintili

Villa dei Quintili

IMPRESSIVE RUINS OF OPULENT VILLA

Towering over green fields on Via Appia Antica, this 2nd-century villa is one of Rome's unsung splendours. It was the lavish home of two consuls, the Quintili brothers, but its luxurious excess was their downfall: the emperor Commodus had them both killed and seized the villa for himself, later extending it even further. The highlight of the impressive ruins is the well-preserved baths complex with a pool, *caldarium* and *frigidarium*. There's also a small museum with some good exhibits.

Catacombs

UNDERGROUND BURIAL TUNNELS

There are reckoned to be around 300km of catacombs beneath Via Appia Antica and the surrounding countryside, much of which was built by early Christians to bury their dead outside the city walls. The largest catacombs are the **Catacombe di San Callisto**. Here, in the 20km of tunnels explored to date, up to 16 popes lie buried alongside scores of martyrs and thousands of Christians. Nearby, the **Catacombe di San Sebastiano** extend beneath the 4th-century basilica of the same name, harbouring frescoes, epigraphs and three perfectly preserved mausoleums.

A third complex, the **Catacombe di Santa Domitilla**, lies west of the San Callisto catacombs. It features the remains of a 4th-century church and some exquisite wall art.

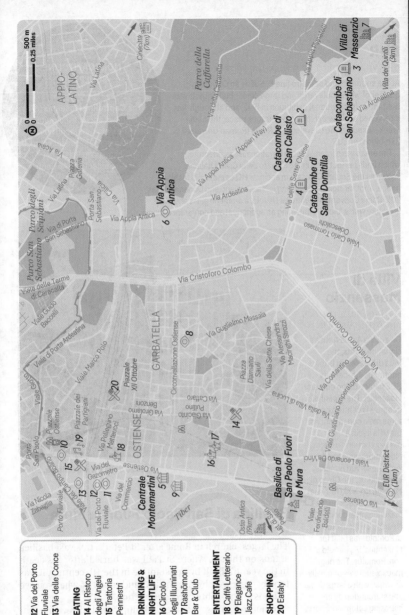

500 m
0.25 miles

HIGHLIGHTS
1 Basilica di
San Paolo
Fuori le Mura
2 Catacombe di
San Callisto
3 Catacombe di
San Sebastiano
4 Catacombe di
Santa Domitilla
5 Centrale
Montemartini
6 Via Appia Antica
7 Villa di
Massenzio

SIGHTS
8 Albergo Rosso
9 Museo
Capitoline Centrale
Montemartini
10 Ostiense
11 Via dei
Magazzini Generali

12 Via del Porto
Fluviale
13 Via delle Conce

EATING
14 Al Ristoro
degli Angeli
15 Trattoria
Pennestri

**DRINKING &
NIGHTLIFE**
16 Circolo
degli Illuminati
17 Rashòmon
Bar & Club

ENTERTAINMENT
18 Caffè Letterario
19 Elegance
Jazz Cafe

SHOPPING
20 Eataly

125

EUR

OUTLYING DISTRICT OF MODERN ARCHITECTURE

At the southern end of metro line B, EUR is an Orwellian quarter of wide boulevards and large, linear buildings. It was built for an international exhibition in 1942, and although war intervened and the exhibition never took place, the name stuck – Esposizione Universale di Roma (Roman Universal Exhibition) or EUR.

The area's main interest lies in its rationalist architecture, which finds perfect form in the Palazzo della Civiltà Italiana, known as the Square Colosseum and now HQ of the Fendi fashion house. Another signature building is Massimiliano and Doriana Fuksas' 2016 Rome Convention Centre La Nuvola, a dramatic glass and steel structure with a 'cloud' containing an auditorium and conference rooms.

MORE CAPITOLINE SCULPTURE

The **Capitoline Museums** (p70) collection of ancient sculpture is one of Rome's best, counting numerous prized pieces. To see for yourself, head up to Piazza del Campidoglio in Ancient Rome.

Villa di Massenzio

CHARIOT RACETRACK & ANCIENT MAUSOLEUM

One of Via Appia Antica's signature sights, the Villa di Massenzio is the enormous 4th-century BCE palace of the emperor Maxentius. The greenfield complex is centred on three main constructions: the villa itself, a mausoleum, and a circus. Most impressive are the well-preserved remains of the circus, the **Circo di Massenzio**, a 10,000-seat chariot racetrack built by Maxentius in around 309. Nearby, the Mausoleo di Romolo was built for Maxentius' 17-year-old son, Romulus. The huge mausoleum was originally crowned with a large dome and surrounded by an imposing colonnade, parts of which are still visible.

Palazzo della Civiltà Italiana, EUR

Basilica di San Paolo Fuori le Mura

COLOSSAL PAPAL BASILICA

The largest church in Rome after St Peter's, this vast basilica stands on the site where St Paul was buried after his death in the year 67. Built by Constantine in the 4th century, it was largely destroyed by fire in 1823 and much of what you see today is a 19th-century reconstruction.

Some treasures survived, though, including the 5th-century triumphal arch, with its heavily restored mosaics, and the Gothic marble tabernacle over the high altar. To the right of the altar, the elaborate Romanesque paschal candlestick was fashioned in the 12th century and features a grim cast of animal-headed creatures. The cloisters would be a wonderful lavender-scented refuge if they let you sit down (there are no benches or seats).

MARCO SALVINI STUDIO/SHUTTERSTOCK ©

Via Appia Antica

THE WORLD'S FIRST SUPERHIGHWAY

Via Appia Antica was the most famous of ancient Rome's consular roads. Named after consul Appius Claudius Caecus, who laid the first 90km section in 312 BCE, it was completed in 190 BCE and quickly became a key artery, linking Rome with the southern port of Brindisi.

The ancients dubbed it the *regina viarum* (queen of roads) and it's still a majestic sight: a beautiful cobbled thoroughfare flanked by stately pine trees and lush fields strewn with ruins and hidden villas.

Despite its beauty, the road has a dark history – Spartacus and 6000 of his slave rebels were crucified here in 71 BCE, and it was here that the early Christians buried their dead in 300km of underground **catacombs**. You can't visit all 300km, but three major catacombs (p124) are open for guided exploration.

Above ground, there's also plenty to take in. The **Mausoleo di Cecilia Metella** – a crenellated drum tower that started life as a 1st-century BCE tomb but was later used as a fort to collect tolls from passing traffic – is a signature sight. Nearby, you can visit the ruins of Villa di Massenzio, built by the emperor Maxentius in the 4th century. Further south, you'll find two more villas: the Capo di Bove and, 3km beyond that, Villa dei Quintili, an aristocratic villa with an opulence that led an emperor to murder.

Via Appia Antica

EXPLORE BY BIKE

The best way of exploring the Via Appia Antica is on foot or by bike. Bike hire is available at various points, including the Service Center Appia Antica *(parcoappiaantica. it)* at No 58–60. From there, you can follow the road up to the Catacombe di San Callisto and onto the *via*'s southern stretch, which has some good longer-distance rides. Maps are available at the service centre. Alternatively, you can book a guided tour by bike, on foot or by electric cart.

Centrale Montemartini

INDUSTRIAL MACHINERY & ANCIENT SCULPTURE

Housed in a former power station, this outpost of the Capitoline Museums boldly juxtaposes classical sculpture against diesel engines and steam turbines. The collection's highlights are in the echoing **Sala Macchine** (Engine Room) and **Sala Caldaia** (Boiler Room), where ancient statues strike poses around the giant machinery. Beautiful pieces include the *Fanciulla seduta* (*Seated Girl*) and *Musa Polimnia* (*Muse Polyhymnia*). There are also some exquisite Roman mosaics.

ESSEVU/SHUTTERSTOCK ©

WHERE TO CATCH A GIG

Rome-based journalist and professional speaker **Arianna Galati** shares her favourite music venues in southern Rome and elsewhere in the city.

Elegance Jazz Cafè (Southern Rome)
A format inspired by New York clubs, it's both a gourmet restaurant and live music venue, staging concerts every evening ranging from classic jazz to swing and bossa nova.

Alcazar (Trastevere)
An old cinema that has been transformed into a versatile club with a '70s vibe. It's always happily full and you can dance to well-crafted DJ sets and listen to explosive live soul and funk.

Dram Boat (Tridente, Trevi & the Quirinale)
A wooden barge on the Tiber, this is the most atmospheric place to listen to live jazz while sipping delicious cocktails.

Street Art in Ostiense

DISCOVER OSTIENSE'S COLOURFUL MURALS

Ostiense was at the forefront of the street-art trend that swept Rome in the 2010s and has more than 30 murals. Some have faded but enough survive to merit exploration.

Start in **Via delle Conce**, where a black-and-white face looks out at No 14. The work of Italian street artists Sten & Lex, this is flanked by a menacing bald gangster by French artist MTO at No 12. Nearby, on **Via dei Magazzini Generali**, a line-up of Sten & Lex portraits look onto the *Wall of Fame* by Roman JBRock.

On **Via del Porto Fluviale** you'll find a trio of well-known murals. The most talked about is artist Blu's now-faded composition of giant faces on a former air force barracks. In better nick is the five-storey *Hunting Pollution* by Milanese Iena Cruz. Further down the street, Agostino Iacuri's *Fish'n'Kids* shows a man swimming among fish.

Architecture in Garbatella

HIP NEIGHBOURHOOD WITH DISTINCT LOOK

To experience one of Rome's most idiosyncratic neighbourhoods, head to Garbatella. This colourful, and increasingly hip, district was conceived as a workers' residential quarter, but was later used to house people displaced by Fascist construction projects. Many people were moved into *alberghi suburbani* (suburban hotels) – giant housing blocks such as the landmark **Albergo Rosso**. But walk through the neighbourhood and you'll soon notice how varied it is, with its low-rise houses, communal courtyards, staircases and giant murals.

Rome's Pompeii

A FULLY PRESERVED ANCIENT TOWN

An easy train ride from Stazione Porta San Paolo, **Ostia Antica** is one of Italy's most compelling archaeological sites. The remains of ancient Rome's seaport are wonderfully complete and it's an unforgettable experience to walk around city blocks that have remained intact for thousands of years.

Ostia started life as a military camp guarding the mouth of the Tiber – hence the name, a derivation of the Latin word *ostium* (mouth). It quickly grew and by the 2nd century CE it had become a thriving port with a population of around 50,000. It started to decline after the fall of the Roman Empire and

WHERE TO GO OUT IN SOUTHERN ROME

Caffè Letterario
Cool counter-culture hang-out that's part bookshop, part gallery, part performance area and part lounge bar.

Circolo Degli Illuminati
Charge up on cocktails then cut loose to tech, house, hip-hop and chill music.

Rashōmon Bar & Club
House, techno and electronica sounds fuel the action at this post-industrial Ostiense club.

MOALLAR/SHUTTERSTOCK ©

Mosaic, Terme di Nettuno

ROME'S CINEMA CITY

In the late 1950s and early '60s, Rome was at the forefront of celebrity culture. The *dolce vita* was in full swing and Hollywood stars were regularly seen around town as they partied between shoots at **Cinecittà**. Italy's foremost film studios were founded by Mussolini in 1937 and subsequently used for many iconic films, such as Fellini's 1960 classic *La Dolce Vita* and the 1963 epic *Cleopatra*. Still today, they're in action and in recent years they've provided sets for the HBO series *Rome* and Paolo Sorrentino's *The Young Pope*.

To learn more, you can tour the studios *(https://cinecittasimostra.it)* on Via Tuscolana in the far south of the city.

was eventually abandoned. Over subsequent centuries, its ruins were buried in river silt, thus ensuring their survival.

You enter the site at **Porta Romana**, which gives onto the **Decumanus Maximus**, the city's main drag. This leads down to two highlights: the 2nd-century **Terme di Nettuno**, home to a famous mosaic of Neptune riding a seahorse chariot, and the 4000-capacity **Teatro**. The grassy area behind the theatre is the **Piazzale delle Corporazioni** (Forum of the Corporations), home to Ostia's merchant guilds.

Further down, the Forum is overlooked by the **Capitolium**, a temple dedicated to Jupiter, Juno and Minerva. Nearby, the **Thermopolium** is an ancient cafe, complete with bar and fragments of its original frescoed menu.

 WHERE TO EAT IN SOUTHERN ROME

Eataly
Food emporium near Ostiense train station offering gelato, pastries, pizza, grilled meat and craft beer. €–€€

Trattoria Pennestri
Classy trattoria good for Roman classics and updated Italian cuisine. €€

Al Ristoro degli Angeli
Savvy locals hotfoot it to this Garbatella favourite for fine pasta dishes and fresh seafood. €€

LAZIO & ABRUZZO

ANCIENT HISTORY & SOARING MOUNTAINS

Etruscan tombs and ancient Roman ruins, volcanic lakes and wild untamed mountains – Italy's little-known centre is ripe for discovery.

Lazio and Abruzzo together traverse Italy, touching the country's two seas and encompassing vast tracts of the central Apennines. This is where Italy's north meets the south, where the landscape takes on a harsher note as gentle, bosky hills give way to towering snowcapped mountains and ancient forests.

It's a part of Italy made for slow travel, for meandering along country roads to hilltop towns and remote monasteries, for hiking in national parks and dining on earthy farmhouse food. Once you're out of Rome, the pace slackens and the crowds thin, leaving you free to beat your own track.

For history buffs and treasure hunters, the area provides rich pickings: Cerveteri and Tarquinia's Etruscan tombs, magnificent Roman ruins in Tivoli, Subiaco's monasteries – these are sights to rival anything in the country. Elsewhere, Viterbo boasts a medieval centre seemingly unchanged in centuries and Sulmona sparkles amid Abruzzo's foreboding peaks.

Outdoor enthusiasts will be in their element here. Hardened hikers, skiers and mountain bikers will find plenty of challenges in Abruzzo's great national parks where wolves and bears still roam free. However, you don't have to be a seasoned thrill-seeker to enjoy the pristine wildernesses. Well-kept roads snake across the sparsely populated landscape offering scenic drives and magnificent views at every turn.

SONYWORLD/SHUTTERSTOCK ©

THE MAIN AREAS

VITERBO & ETRURIA
Lazio's Etruscan heartland. p136

TIVOLI & SOUTHERN LAZIO
Roman ruins and Unesco sites. p143

SULMONA & ABRUZZO'S NATIONAL PARKS
Thrilling mountain scenery. p150

THE GRAN SASSO
Otherworldly high country. p155

Statue of Ares, Villa Adriana (p143)

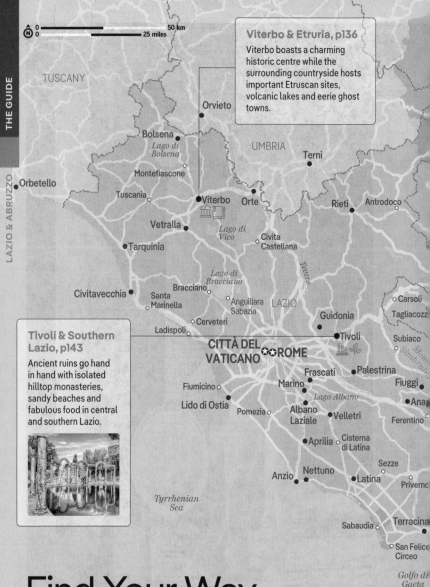

Viterbo & Etruria, p136

Viterbo boasts a charming historic centre while the surrounding countryside hosts important Etruscan sites, volcanic lakes and eerie ghost towns.

TUSCANY

Orvieto

Bolsena
Lago di Bolsena

UMBRIA

Montefiascone

Terni

Orbetello

Tuscania

Viterbo

Orte

Rieti

Antrodoco

Vetralla

Lago di Vico

Civita Castellana

Tarquinia

Lago di Bracciano

Bracciano

LAZIO

Carsoli

Tagliacozz

Civitavecchia

Santa Marinella

Anguillara Sabazia

Guidonia

Tivoli & Southern Lazio, p143

Ancient ruins go hand in hand with isolated hilltop monasteries, sandy beaches and fabulous food in central and southern Lazio.

Ladispoli

Cerveteri

CITTÀ DEL VATICANO ROME

Tivoli

Subiaco

Mon. Simbrin

Frascati

Palestrina

Fiuggi

Fiumicino

Marino

Lago Albano

Ana

Lido di Ostia

Pomezia

Albano Laziale

Velletri

Ferentino

Aprilia

Cisterna di Latina

Sezze

Anzio

Nettuno

Latina

Privern

Tyrrhenian Sea

Sabaudia

Terracina

San Felice Circeo

Golfo di Gaeta

Find Your Way

Stretching from the Mediterranean to the Adriatic, this unheralded swath of central Italy harbours some fascinating historic towns and Etruscan artefacts among its green hills, volcanic lakes and silent mountains.

Ponza

Ponza

LE MARCHE

San Benedetto del Tronto

Ascoli Piceno

Giulianova

Roseto degli Abruzzi

Teramo

Adriatic Sea

Parco Nazionale del Gran Sasso e Monti della Laga

Montesilvano

Corno Grande

Assergi

Penne

Pescara

Santo Stefano di Sessanio

Ofena

Chieti

Ortona

L'Aquila

ABRUZZO

Popoli

Monte Amaro

Guardiagrele

Lanciano

Celano

Parco Nazionale della Majella

Casoli

Vasto

Avezzano

Sulmona

Parco Nazionale d'Abruzzo, Lazio e Molise

Pescocostanzo

Roccaraso

Termoli

Pescasseroli

Agnone

Ururi

Alatri

Barrea

Sora

Monte Amaro di Opi

Isernia

MOLISE

PUGLIA

Frosinone

Campobasso

Cassino

Venafro

Bojano

Lucera

Pontecorvo

Fondi

CAMPANIA

Sperlonga Formia

Gaeta

The Gran Sasso, p155

Looming over L'Aquila, the Gran Sasso is the Apennines' highest mountain, a stark massif flanked by high plains and remote mountain villages.

Sulmona & Abruzzo's National Parks, p150

The dramatic national parks that surround the medieval town of Sulmona offer epic hiking and stunning scenery.

CAR

You'll really need a car to get the best out of Lazio and Abruzzo. You can reach most towns and villages by public transport but having your own wheels frees you to enjoy the countryside at your own pace.

BUS

If you don't have a car, the bus is generally the best way of getting around. In Lazio, Cotral has an extensive bus network with services to cities, towns and villages across the region. In Abruzzo, TUA buses serve most places.

TRAIN

Trains run to main towns such as Viterbo, Tivoli, Sulmona and L'Aquila from Rome. However, for smaller villages and more out-of-the-way towns, you'll need a bus or your own vehicle.

Plan Your Time

Lazio and Abruzzo are ideal for slow travel, with their forested peaks, laid-back towns and sandy beaches. Explore historic sights and primitive landscapes in their mountainous national parks.

MARCO RUBINO/SHUTTERSTOCK ©

Villa d'Este (p145)

If You Only Have One Day

● Head to **Tivoli** (p143) to take in the town's celebrated duo of Unesco World Heritage Sites. Start off at **Villa d'Este** (p145) up in the town's historic centre. Admire the views from the villa's terrace and its 16th-century frescoes before stepping out to scout around its exquisite terraced gardens.

● In the afternoon, take the shuttle bus to **Villa Adriana** (p143), where you can marvel at the ruins of Hadrian's vast imperial estate. When you're finished there, double back up the hill to see the day out in the **historic centre** (p145), perhaps dining at Sibilla on classic Italian cuisine and romantic views.

Seasonal highlights

There's year-round sport in Lazio and Abruzzo's natural playgrounds: skiing in winter, swimming and high-altitude hiking in summer. Spring and autumn are best for sightseeing.

JANUARY

Abruzzo's **snow-clad slopes** provide a white, winter playground for skiers and snowboarders during the annual ski season.

APRIL

Spring brings sunshine, flowers and mild temperatures, ideal for visiting big outdoor sites such as **Villa Adriana**.

MAY

As temperatures continue to rise, this is the perfect month for hearty alfresco meals in the **Castelli Romani**.

FROM LEFT TO RIGHT: GIUSEPPE NOCERA/SHUTTERSTOCK ©, VINCIBER/SHUTTERSTOCK ©STE77/SHUTTERSTOCK ©

With Three Days to Travel Around

● After a day in Tivoli (see left), set your sights eastward and make for **Subiaco** (p147), a small provincial town known for its Benedictine monasteries. On your return, treat yourself to a bumper banquet in the attractive **Castelli Romani** (p148) area southeast of Rome.

● On day three, head north to the medieval city of **Viterbo** (p136). Check out its beautifully conserved historic centre and enjoy a hearty trattoria meal. Fully sated, push on to Lazio's Etruscan heartland: take your pick between **Tarquinia** (p140) and its famous frescoed tombs, or **Cerveteri** (p141), renowned for its haunting town-sized necropolis.

If You Have More Time

● With more time, you can take to the wilds of Abruzzo for a three-day tour of its high-altitude highlights. On day one stop off at **L'Aquila** (p157) en route to **Campo Imperatore** (p157) and the **Gran Sasso** (p155). Revel in the cinematic scenery and push on to stay overnight in the mountain village of **Santo Stefano di Sessanio** (p156).

● Spend day five in **Sulmona** (p150), stocking up on *confetti* (sugared almonds) and enjoying the medieval streets. On the last day, venture into the stunning **Parco Nazionale d'Abruzzo, Lazio e Molise** (p153) by way of **Scanno** (p153) and **Pescasseroli** (p153).

JUNE

It's hot now, a good time to hit Lazio's **lakes and beaches** before the holiday crowds crash in.

JULY

Sulmona's showcase square sets the stage for medieval jousting and much costumed pomp during the **Giostra Cavalleresca**.

SEPTEMBER

Late summer is a good time to look for **bears** foraging on the higher slopes of Abruzzo's national parks.

DECEMBER

A soak in Viterbo's hot **thermal waters** provides the perfect antidote to the winter cold.

VITERBO

Viterbo

Rome

Viterbo is little-known to foreign visitors but with a well-preserved medieval centre and laid-back provincial vibe, it provides a good introduction to northern Lazio and Etruria, the land the Etruscans once called home.

Viterbo was, in fact, founded by the Etruscans before being taken over by the Romans and later developing into an important medieval centre – for a brief period in the 13th century it was actually the seat of the papacy.

It was heavily bombed in WWII but much of its walled centre survived and this attractive tangle of cobbled alleyways, towers and grey stone buildings is today in remarkably good shape. And it's in the picturesque *centro storico* (historic centre) that you'll find the city's main sights and many of its spirited bars and trattorias.

TOP TIP

Viterbo can comfortably be covered in a weekend but give yourself longer if you want to explore its verdant hinterland. Three to four days would give you enough time to enjoy the city and investigate its surrounding sights.

VITERBO'S THERMAL WATERS

Viterbo has been frequented for its hot springs since ancient times. The Romans constructed extensive baths here, and later, in the 15th century, Pope Nicholas V built himself a villa to be near the therapeutic waters. Dante even refers to a local spring in Canto XIV of the *Inferno*.

The waters, which spring from the ground at a temperature of between 40°C and 58°C, are rich in sulphur, calcium and magnesium. To have a soak yourself you can either go it alone at a wild pool or book at a thermal resort such as the **Terme dei Papi** or **Salus Terme**, both of which have excellent spa facilities.

Alfresco Carousing

RELAXED PIAZZA-SIDE DRINKING

Viterbo's atmospheric piazzas provide the perfect setting for that most quintessential of Italian experiences – the evening *aperitivo*. To partake for yourself, **Tredici Gradi Slow Bar** is straight out of central casting with tables set on picture-perfect Piazza del Gesù, a blackboard menu of ham and cheese platters, and an excellent selection of local Sangiovese wines. Nearby, **Winter Garden** is another local hot spot, good for a craft beer or cocktail overlooking the grimly named, but actually very attractive, Piazza della Morte (Piazza of Death).

A Saintly Procession

HISTORIC RELIGIOUS CELEBRATION

Every 3 September, Viterbo honours its patron saint (St Rose) by hosting one of central Italy's most physically demanding feats of religious devotion. The event, known as the **Trasporto della Macchina di Santa Rosa**, involves a team of a hundred or so bearers carrying a 5-tonne, 30m-high tower through the city's streets. Events kick off at 9pm when the city's lights are dimmed and the brightly illuminated tower is shouldered at Porta Romana. It's then carried along a 1km route, lined with thousands of spectators, to Piazza del Plebiscito and up to the Santuario di Santa Rosa.

HIGHLIGHTS
1 Necropoli di Banditaccia
2 Palazzo Farnese

SIGHTS
3 Museo Archeologico
Nazionale Tarquiniense
4 Museo Nazionale Cerite
5 Necropoli
dei Monterozzi
6 Parco dei Mostri
7 Villa Lante

**ACTIVITIES,
COURSES & TOURS**
8 Terme dei Papi

EATING
9 Lo Sfizio Del Lago
10 Pane e Olio
11 Trattoria del Moro

A COOL SUNSET STROLL

Benedetta Lomoni,
founder of Experience
Viterbo (www.
experienceviterbo.
com), a local city guide

Walk out of Porta
Faul, and start along
Via Cava, so-called
because it was literally
carved out of the rock
by the Etruscans. With
walls on both sides, it's
nice and cool, especially
in summer around
sunset. Book ahead to
have a sunset *aperitivo*
at **Podere dell'Arco
Country Charme**, a
farmhouse with its own
lavender field.

Tour the Historic Centre

GOTHIC PALACES & MEDIEVAL CHURCHES

Start in **1 Piazza San Lorenzo**, the religious nerve centre of
the medieval city. Here you'll find two of Viterbo's signature
buildings: the **2 Cattedrale di San Lorenzo** with its distinct
black-and-white bell tower, and **3 Palazzo dei Papi**. This Gothic
palace, scene of the first and longest ever papal conclave (1006
days between 1268 and 1271), was built for the popes who lived
in Viterbo from 1257 to 1281. By the *palazzo* (mansion), stairs
lead up to the arched Loggia delle Benedizione, an elegant balcony onto which the newly elected popes would emerge from
the Aula del Conclave.

WHERE TO EAT IN VITERBO

L'Archetto
Where locals take guests
for a taste of earthy, no-frills
Viterbese cooking. €

Il Gargolo Ristorantino
Lovely alfresco setting on a
lively piazza; scrumptious
pastas and creamy desserts.
€€

Al Vecchio Orologio
Updated local cuisine made
with seasonal ingredients stars
at this central hot spot. €€

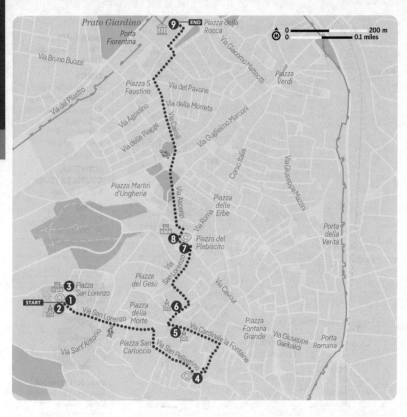

From the piazza, work your way over to the **4 Quartiere San Pellegrino**, Viterbo's oldest district. Check out its alleyways, arches, towers and grey houses, before doubling back to the **5 Chiesa del Gonfalone**, famed locally for its magical ceiling fresco (the columns at the head of the fresco follow you as you move around). Nearby, the Romanesque **6 Chiesa di Santa Maria Nova** boasts a charming cloister and a pulpit where St Thomas Aquinas preached in 1266. It's a short hop from here to **7 Piazza del Plebiscito**, Viterbo's main showcase square, where more frescoes await in **8 Palazzo dei Priori**, the Renaissance city hall.

It's a 10-minute walk up to the **9 Museo Nazionale Etrusco** where you can browse a collection of Etruscan and Roman artefacts displayed in a 14th-century fortress.

 GETTING AROUND

Viterbo, about a 90-minute drive north of Rome, can be reached by train or Cotral bus from the capital. If you drive, your best bet is to leave your car in the free car park on Via Faul and take the lift up to the historic centre. Once in the city, walking is the way to go.

Beyond Viterbo

From Etruscan tombs to Renaissance palaces, lively lakesides and silent ghost towns, the emerald-green countryside around Viterbo hides some real treasures.

Bolsena
Viterbo · Bomarzo
· Caprarola
Tarquinia
· Bracciano

A fascinating but little-publicised part of the country, Lazio's northern reaches shelter some of the region's most compelling ancient sights, popular lakeside hang-outs and haunting ghost towns. The star attractions are the World Heritage Sites of Cerveteri and Tarquinia, remarkable vestiges of the pre-Roman Etruscan civilisation. But you'll also find impressive Renaissance gardens and volcanic lakes offering summer fun and tranquil walking. Away from these holiday hot spots, you can explore the famous abandoned village of Civita di Bagnoreggio, and search out other deserted villages in Lazio's quiet, rural interior.

TOP TIP

Tourist offices in Viterbo, Tarquinia and Cerveteri are a good source of local information and transport timetables.

Fresco, Tomba dei Leopardi, Tarquinia (p140)

IMAGEBROKER/PETER SEYFFERTH CREATIVE/GETTY IMAGES ©

THE ETRUSCANS

The Etruscans dominated west central Italy from the the 8th to the 4th centuries BCE. Their territory, Etruria, was centred on a confederation of 12 city-states between the Arno and Tiber rivers.

Debate surrounds their origins: some scholars believe they migrated from Asia Minor; others maintain they were indigenous to the area. What is not disputed is that they gave rise to a sophisticated society based on agriculture, trade and mining. They were skilled architects and although little remains of their buildings, archaeologists have found evidence of aqueducts, bridges and sewers, as well as temples. In artistic terms, they were known for their jewellery and rich tomb decoration, as revealed by finds at the cemeteries of Cerveteri, Tarquinia and elsewhere.

RAGEMAX/SHUTTERSTOCK ©

Villa Lante

Top Etruscan Site

ANCIENT FRESCOES & SPECTRAL TOMBS

Take to the road to discover two of Italy's most important Etruscan sites. Some 44km southwest of Viterbo, **Tarquinia** is home to the remarkable 7th-century BCE **Necropoli dei Monterozzi**. At first sight, this greenfield cemetery doesn't look like much but once you start seeing the vivid tomb frescoes, you'll realise what all the fuss is about.

For the best paintings search out the Tomba della Leonessa; the Tomba della Caccia e della Pesca, which has some wonderful hunting and fishing scenes; the Tomba dei Leopardi; and the Tomba della Fustigazione, named after a scratchy erotic image.

Artefacts unearthed at the necropolis and in the surrounding area are also on show at Tarquinia's **Museo Archeologico Nazionale Tarquiniense**. Highlights here include the *Cavalli Alati*, a magnificent frieze of two winged horses, and the

ETRUSCAN EDUCATION

To complete your Etruscan education, make your way to Rome where Italy's finest collection of Etruscan artefacts is on show at the **Museo Nazionale Etrusco di Villa Giulia** (p121), beautifully housed in a parkside Renaissance villa.

WHERE TO EAT AND DRINK IN CERVETERI & TARQUINIA

Da Bibbo
Top restaurant in Cerveteri's historic centre serving well-executed *mare* (sea) and *terra* (land) dishes. €€

Il Cavatappi
Generous helpings of flavoursome regional food at this family-run Tarquinia restaurant. €€

Capolinea Caffè
With tables set under a medieval wall, this popular Tarquinia cafe is a fine spot for an evening aperitif. €

Mitra Tauroctono, a sculpture of the headless, handless god Mithras killing a bull.

From Tarquinia, it's 54km south to **Cerveteri** and the **Necropoli di Banditaccia**. This haunting 12-hectare necropolis is a veritable city of the dead, with streets, squares and terraces of *tumuli* (circular tombs cut into the earth and capped by turf). Some tombs, including the 6th-century BCE Tomba dei Rilievi, retain traces of painted reliefs. If you still have any energy left, you'll find more Etruscan finds, including a celebrated 1st-century BCE vase, the *Euphronios Krater*, at the **Museo Nazionale Cerite** in Cerveteri's historic centre.

Villas, Gardens & a Folly

TOUR VITERBO'S HINTERLAND

Viterbo's hinterland boasts a trio of prize Renaissance sights, each within easy striking distance of the city. In **Bagnaia**, a mere 5.5km east of town, **Villa Lante** is famous for its 16th-century mannerist gardens. Featuring monumental fountains and an ingenious water cascade, these are a favourite film location and have doubled for the Vatican Gardens in two big modern productions: Nanni Moretti's 2011 *Habemus Papam* (*We Have a Pope*) and Paolo Sorrentino's 2016 *The Young Pope*.

From Bagnaia, it's a 30-minute drive south to **Caprarola**, home to one of Lazio's most impressive Renaissance palaces. The 16th-century **Palazzo Farnese** sports a distinct pentagonal design and, inside, a remarkable columned staircase and richly frescoed rooms. Outside, its hillside gardens are strikingly beautiful.

For a change of scene, head 17km north of Viterbo to the **Parco dei Mostri in Bomarzo**. An eccentric folly conceived by **Bomarzo**'s 16th-century ruler, this is a wooded park populated by a surreal cast of sculpted ogres, dragons, giants and animals.

Volcanic Lakes

SWIMMING, WALKING & GREAT VIEWS

Splashed across northern Lazio's green landscape are several notable lakes. The largest – actually Italy's largest volcanic lake – is **Lago di Bolsena**, a 13km-long oval of water skirted by low, sandy shores. Its main centre is **Bolsena**, a pretty lakeside town where you can take a boat cruise (courtesy of Navigazione Alto Lazio), top up your tan, and enjoy great views from the 13th-century fortress that crowns the steep historic centre.

 WHERE TO EAT NEAR THE LAKES

Pane e Olio	**Lo Sfizio**	**Trattoria del Moro**
Dine on homemade pastas and locally caught perch in the shadow of Bracciano's mighty castle. €€	With a lovely summer terrace and smart modern interior, this is a top choice in Anguillara Sabazia. €€	Dine on lake fish and local staples in a thatched trattoria set above the waters of Lago di Bolsena. €€

RAPHAEL'S BOLSENA FRESCO

Bolsena's miracle is referenced in a famous painting by Raphael, the *Messa di Bolsena (Mass of Bolsena)*. This hangs in the Stanza d'Eliodoro, one of the four Raphael Rooms in the **Vatican Museums** (p95) in Rome.

Just south of Viterbo, **Lago di Vico** is much smaller and far less developed. It's a tranquil spot, lovely at sunset, with some fine walking in the surrounding beech forests.

Further south still, **Lago di Bracciano** is a favourite summer destination for weekending Romans and with its clean waters is ideal for a refreshing swim. The main town is **Bracciano**, actually a few kilometres up from the water around the 15th-century Castello Odescalchi, but most of the beach action takes place in lakeside **Anguillara Sabazia**.

Haunting Ghost Towns

ESCAPE TO LAZIO'S ABANDONED VILLAGES

A half-hour drive north of Viterbo, the small town of **Bagnoregio** harbours one of northern Lazio's most dramatic apparitions, the **Civita di Bagnoregio**, aka *il paese che muore* (the dying town). This medieval village, accessible only by footbridge, sits atop a huge stack of slowly crumbling tufa rock in the deep-cut Valle dei Calanchi. Inside its walls, you can wander the stone streets and enjoy stirring views before filling up at one of its many trattorias.

For a more intimate experience, sneak off to two other ghost towns. **Celleno**, abandoned in the 1950s, is a memorable spot with a tiny walled centre and an unexpected work of modern art. To the south, **Calcata Vecchia** lies deep in the heavily forested Treja valley. Deserted in the 1930s, it has since come back to (semi-) life thanks to a small community of artists and artisans.

GETTING AROUND

With enough patience many of the places covered in this section can be reached by Cotral bus, either from Viterbo or Rome. But to get to the more out-of-the-way places you'll definitely need your own wheels.

TIVOLI

Set astride a deep river gorge at the foot of the Tiburtini Hills, the ancient town of Tivoli is best known for its two Unesco World Heritage Sites: Villa Adriana, the sprawling estate of the Emperor Hadrian, and Villa d'Este, a Renaissance mansion famous for its landscaped gardens and lavish fountains.

These are often covered on a day trip from Rome, only 30km away, but that doesn't give you much time to take in Tivoli's other charms: its hilltop historic centre, romantic views and cascading waterfalls. Stay longer and you can enjoy these while also having time to tour central and southern Lazio.

Tivoli has hosted visitors for millennia. It was a popular summer retreat for ancient Romans and the Renaissance rich, and in the 18th and 19th centuries,it became popular with aristocrats and artists travelling through Italy on the Grand Tour.

Rome ● Tivoli

TOP TIP

Come prepared for Villa Adriana. Situated in the town's modern suburbs beneath the historic centre, it's a huge site that gets very hot in summer, so bring water, a sun hat (there's little shade) and comfortable walking shoes.

Hadrian's Villa

STUNNING ROMAN RUINS

The ruins of Hadrian's vast country estate, 5km outside of Tivoli proper, are quite magnificent. Built between 118 and 138 CE, **Villa Adriana** was one of the largest villas in the ancient world, covering around 120 hectares, about 40 of which are now open to the public. Give yourself about three hours to do the site justice.

On entering, follow the main path for about 400m to a **pavilion** where you can see a plastic model of the original villa. Much of this was designed by Hadrian himself based on buildings he'd seen around the world. For example, the **pecile**, the large pool area near the walls, was a reproduction of a building in Athens. Similarly, the **canopo** was a copy of a sanctuary in the Egyptian town of Canopus. Now one of the site's most Instagrammable spots, it features a long, narrow pool flanked by sculptural figures and headed by a monumental **nymphaeum** (shrine to the water nymph).

From the *canopo*, work your way through the remains of the **Grandi Terme** to the **Piazza d'Oro**, which bursts into colour in spring when its grassy centre fills with vivid yellow flowers.

Done there, backtrack past the **Terme con Heliocaminus** to the **Teatro Marittimo**, one of the villa's signature buildings. A circular mini-villa set in an artificial pool, this was used by Hadrian as his personal refuge.

TIVOLI'S TRAVERTINE

For thousands of years Tivoli has been quarried for its travertine. This calcareous rock's toughness and elasticity make it ideal for construction. The Romans used it on a massive scale, transporting it along Via Tiburtina and the river Aniene to supply their monumental construction projects like the Colosseum, Teatro di Marcello and Porta Maggiore. Today it's still highly sought-after, and it continues to appear in modern buildings ranging from the Getty Centre in LA to the Bank of China headquarters in Beijing.

143

SIGHTS

1 Abbazia di
Montecassino
2 Chiaia di
Luna Beach
(see 3) Monastero
di Santa Scolastica
3 Monastero di
San Benedetto

4 Museo Archeologico
Nazionale di Palestrina
5 Museo Nazionale
Etrusco di Villa Giulia
6 Palazzo Apostolico
7 Parco Nazionale
del Circeo
8 Parco Villa
Gregoriana

9 Spiaggia delle
Grotte di Nerone
10 Spiaggia di Levante
11 Spiaggia di Sabaudia
12 Tempio di Vesta
13 Villa Adriana
14 Villa Aldobrandini
15 Villa d'Este

EATING

16 Antico
Ristorante Pagnanelli
17 Gli Archi
18 La Selvotta
19 Oresteria by Ponza
(see 18) Osteria
da Angelo
20 Romolo al Porto

🍴 **WHERE TO EAT IN TIVOLI**

Bar Gelateria da Maurizio
Top spot for a coffee or gelato
on Tivoli's busy market square. €

La Fornarina
For classic pizzas, creative
pastas and meaty mains on a
handsome cobbled piazza. €€

Sibilla
Elegant restaurant serving
up classic Italian cuisine and
romantic panoramas. €€€

Renaissance Villa & Magic Gardens

FOUNTAINS, FRESCOES & GARGOYLES

Villa d'Este and its gardens are the main draw in Tivoli's hilltop centre. The villa, originally a Benedictine convent, was converted into a luxury retreat by Lucrezia Borgia's son, Cardinal Ippolito d'Este, in the late 16th century. It later provided inspiration for composer Franz Liszt, who wrote *The Fountains of the Villa d'Este* after spending time here between 1865 and 1886.

Before heading out to the gardens, take time to admire the villa's rich mannerist frescoes. Outside, the steeply terraced grounds are a glorious composition of water-spouting gargoyles, grottoes and monumental fountains. Highlights include the 130m-long **Avenue of the Hundred Fountains**, and the Bernini-designed **Fountain of the Organ**, which uses water pressure to play music through a concealed organ.

Stroll the Historic Centre

DREAMY VIEWS & CASCADING PARK

Once you've seen Tivoli's headline villas, take some time to investigate its handsome *centro storico*. An attractive walk leads down Via Campitelli to the **Casa Gotica**, a well-preserved Gothic house furnished with its own Romeo-and-Juliet balcony.

On the other side of the centre, the **Ponte Gregoriano** provides ravishing views of the 2nd-century BCE **Tempio di Vesta** and the tree-cloaked gorge beneath it. To descend into the ravine, head to the nearby **Parco Villa Gregoriana** where paths plunge down the slopes pitted with grottoes and panoramic viewing platforms, including one that looks up to a 120m-high waterfall.

MORE RENAISSANCE REVELATIONS

The countryside around Viterbo plays host to several wonderful **Renaissance sights** (p141), including a dramatic frescoed villa in Caprarola, some wonderful landscaped gardens in Bagnaia and a weird Renaissance monster park near Bomarzo.

TOP TIPS FOR THE VILLAS

Elisa Mancini, archaeologist and guide at Visite Guidate Tivoli *(www.visiteguidatetivoli.it)*, gives some tips for visiting Villa Adriana and Villa d'Este.

Best Time to Visit
I recommend seeing at least one at sunset. Villa d'Este is at its best when overflowing with flowers in spring, but even in summer its coolness is delightful. Villa Adriana is at its best mid-season (spring and autumn) and in the clear light of early morning, especially in summer.

Don't Miss
If it's open, don't miss the view from the highest terrace at Villa d'Este, accessible from the entrance courtyard. From there, you'll have a complete view of the gardens, the medieval city and the plain all the way to Rome's skyline.

GETTING AROUND

Regular trains and Cotral buses serve Tivoli from Rome. Once in town, the hilltop centre is best covered on foot. Parking can be a pain but there's a useful signposted car park on Piazzale Matteotti.

To get to Villa Adriana from the centre by public transport, take local bus 4 or 4X from Piazza Garibaldi.

Beyond Tivoli

Discover far-flung monasteries, unsung masterpieces, fabulous beaches, and glorious food in central and southern Lazio.

Tivoli

Subiaco

Frascati

Palestrina

Ariccia

Sperlonga

Extending from Rome's hinterland to Lazio's southern shoreline and far-flung eastern valleys, this area reveals natural charms and historic wonders. Chief among these are an ancient mosaic masterpiece and a trio of remote medieval monasteries founded by St Benedict. The Castelli Romani hills offer romantic lake views, aristocratic villas and a papal palace, while Lazio's southern coast provides summer fun with its long sandy beaches and idyllic waters. This being Italy, there's wonderful food and wine to be savoured at every turn, from fresh seafood in portside trattorias to much-loved meat specialities in traditional *osterias* (taverns).

TOP TIP

Spring and autumn are prime times for hitting the cultural sights, while the beaches are best in early or late summer.

Subiaco

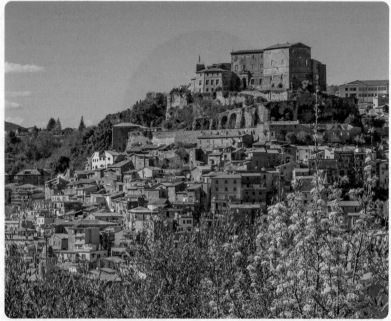

Abbazia di Montecassino

Hit the Benedictine Trail

LOFTY MEDIEVAL MONASTERIES

For a day trip off the beaten track, set your sat nav for **Subiaco**, 40km east of Tivoli. The drive will take you through a lush green landscape to the Valle dell'Aniene, harbouring two of Lazio's great medieval monasteries. The more dramatic of the two is the **Monastero di San Benedetto**, perched over the cave where St Benedict spent three years as a hermit. As well as a setting described by Petrarch as 'the edge of Paradise', it sports an interior almost entirely covered in 13th- to 15th-century frescoes.

Further down the hill, the **Monastero di Santa Scolastica** is the site of Italy's first ever printing press. It's centred on three internal cloisters, each dating from a separate period: the first from the Renaissance, the second from the 14th century, and the third from the 1200s. Lording over everything is the landmark bell tower, virtually unchanged since the 12th century.

A third Benedictine monastery, possibly for another day, lies 114km to the south. The mountaintop **Abbazia di Montecassino** was founded in the 6th century and grew to become one of the most important Christian centres in the medieval world. More recently, it was the centre of heavy fighting in WWII.

WWII BATTLES

For four months in 1944 **Montecassino** was the scene of a major battle as the Germans sought to halt the Allied push north. The mountain was key to the German defensive line and while the Abbey was itself unoccupied – although the Allies suspected it was being used as an observation point – Allied planes bombed it to rubble in February 1944. The battle dragged on, though, and it wasn't until 18 May that the German defences were finally breached.

Over on Lazio's coast, fighting was also taking place near **Anzio** following the landing of a 36,000-strong Allied force on 22 January 1944. The success of the landing proved illusory, however, and the Allies remained pinned down until May when reinforcements arrived from the south.

✕ WHERE TO EAT SEAFOOD

Oresteria by Ponza
Dine on immaculate plates of super-fresh seafood at this summery Ponza restaurant. €€

Gli Archi
A long-standing favourite in Sperlonga cooking up classic seafood salads, pastas and risottos. €€€

Romolo al Porto
Historic restaurant on the Anzio harbour-front famed for its lavish fish antipasti. €€€

BEST PHOTO OPPS

Lago Albano, Castel Gandolfo
Castel Gandolfo's hilltop centre provides the perfect platform for dreamy shots of Lago Albano.

Ponte Gregoriano, Tivoli
Position yourself on this bridge for timeless panoramas of the Tempio di Vesta overlooking a plunging green gorge.

Monastero di San Benedetto, Subiaco
The sight of this monastery grafted onto a steep wooded hillside is an unforgettable image.

Sperlonga's hilltop centre
Both a good subject and a good perch for snapping the sandy southern coast.

Lago Albano from Castel Gandolfo

A Mosaic Masterpiece

TRACK DOWN PALESTRINA'S ANCIENT MARVEL

One of the joys of travelling around Lazio is stumbling across treasures hidden in seemingly unassuming places. In **Palestrina**, a small town 25km south of Tivoli, you'll find one of the region's great ancient masterpieces. The *Mosaico Nilotico* is a breathtaking 2nd-century BCE mosaic depicting the flooding of the Nile in ancient Egypt. The star turn of the **Museo Archeologico Nazionale di Palestrina**, it dates to a period when Palestrina, then known as Praeneste, was home to a colossal hillside temple, the Santuario della Fortuna Primigenia. This has long since been built over, but you can still see its few remaining terraces in front of the museum.

Fine Food, Villas & Views

ESCAPE TO THE CASTELLI ROMANI

Forget Michelin-starred fine dining. For an authentic Lazio eating experience, make a beeline for the **Castelli Romani** area southeast of Rome. This pretty pocket of verdant hills

 WHERE TO EAT IN THE CASTELLI ROMANI

La Selvotta
Hugely popular *fraschetta* (rustic restaurant) with communal wooden tables under centuries-old chestnut trees. €

Osteria da Angelo
One of Ariccia's oldest *fraschette* serving *porchetta* and classic Castelli staples. €€

Antico Ristorante Pagnanelli
Quality seasonal food, outstanding wines and marry-me views at historic Castel Gandolfo restaurant. €€€

and volcanic lakes is loved for its country food and rustic trattorias known as *fraschette*.

You'll find *fraschette* all over but for the best, hotfoot it to **Ariccia**. This tiny town is known across Italy for its *porchetta* (boneless herbed roast pork), one of the mainstays of the classic *fraschetta* menu, along with *coppiette* (jerk-like strips of cured pork), prosciutto, marinated veggies, mozzarella, olives and crusty farmhouse bread. All served with carafes of local wine.

Of course, there's more to the Castelli than its food. In **Frascati** you can hang out in its panoramic historic centre and visit the gardens of **Villa Aldobrandini**, one of several aristocratic villas in the area. A few kilometres away in **Castel Gandolfo**, there are exquisite views over **Lago Albano** to be admired and you can tour the **Palazzo Apostolico**, the papal palace where until recently the popes spent their summers.

Cool Off at the Beach

BEACH-HOP DOWN LAZIO'S SOUTHERN COAST

When the stifling summer heat gets too much, do what the locals do and decamp to the beach. Lazio's southern coast offers rich pickings with a string of popular sandy strips around **Anzio** and, further south, a wonderfully unspoiled beach at **Sabaudia**, overlooked by the Circeo promontory, centrepiece of the **Parco Nazionale del Circeo**.

But the pick of the southern seaside towns is **Sperlonga**, a fashionable weekend hot spot equidistant between Rome and Naples. It has two beaches – the best is the **Spiaggia di Levante** to the east of the rocky promontory on which the town's historic centre sits. This tight knot of steep staircases and tiny whitewashed alleyways tops out at **Piazza della Libertà**, a dinky-sized square ringed by cafes and bars. Nearby, a belvedere commands uplifting views of the hilly coastline as it plunges southwards.

Offshore, **Ponza** and the **Isole Pontine** are another favourite summer escape. Quiet for most of the year, the archipelago buzzes in July and August as holidaymakers take to its crystalline waters and cruise around its craggy, cave-pitted coastlines.

BEST BEACHES

Spiaggia delle Grotte di Nerone, Anzio
A curved sandy strip backed by a cave-pierced rock face and the ruins of a villa built by Nero.

Spiaggia di Sabaudia
A long expanse of fine, soft sand skirted by billowing dunes capped by Mediterranean scrub.

Spiaggia di Levante, Sperlonga
Attractive crescent beach curving around the hilly coast east of Sperlonga's historic centre.

Chiaia di Luna, Ponza
Currently off-limits but still an iconic Ponza sight with its crystalline waters and sheer cliffs.

MORE NATIONAL PARKS

To the east, the mountainous region of Abruzzo offers some of central Italy's most unspoiled wilderness country, much of it protected in the region's three national parks. For heady hiking the **Parco Nazionale d'Abruzzo, Lazio e Molise** (p153) is hard to beat.

GETTING AROUND

To cover the area quickly, you'll need a car. However, with time you can get around by public transport: trains serve Tivoli and towns along the southern coast. Alternatively, Cotral buses run to most places. Year-round ferries run to the Isole Pontine from Terracina, with additional summer services from Anzio and Formia.

SULMONA

Rome ★ ● Sulmona

Overlooked by dark, brooding mountains in the Valle Peligna, Sulmona is a handsome provincial town. Founded by the Italic Peligni tribe, it went on to become a sizeable Roman town – poet Ovid was born here in 43 BCE – and, later, an important medieval centre. However, large parts of the medieval city were destroyed by an earthquake in 1706 and much of its current look results from the subsequent baroque makeover. More recently, the town has earned fame, and wealth, as Italy's best-known producer of *confetti*, a type of sugared sweet that is traditionally given to guests at Italian weddings.

Sulmona is easily covered in a day, but with good transport links, and a strategic position between Abruzzo's national parks, it makes an excellent base for exploring the region's southernmost reaches.

TOP TIP

Late July is when you'll find Sulmona decked out in finery for its great annual joust, the Giostra Cavalleresca. Costumed processions trumpet the horse riders galloping around Piazza Garibaldi in a spectacular display of equine skill.

OVID, SULMONA'S FAVOURITE SON

Ovid was born into a wealthy Sulmona family in 43 BCE. As a young man, he was packed off to Rome to study rhetoric; he soon established himself as a literary star. His great masterpiece was *Metamorphoses,* a kind of extended cover version of Greek myths culminating in homages to Caesar and Augustus. His gilded career came to a crashing halt in 8 CE when he was banished to the Black Sea. The reason why remains a mystery but Ovid himself alluded to a *carmen et error* (a poem and a mistake). He died in Tomi, in modern-day Romania, 10 years later.

Join the Passeggiata

TAKE IN THE TOP SIGHTS

A stroll along Sulmona's main drag, **Corso Ovidio**, is a favourite local pastime. Start at **Piazza Garibaldi**, the town's showcase square. Exit through the arches of the 13th-century **aqueduct** and you'll see a monumental Gothic portal. Known as the **Rotonda**, this was the entrance of the Chiesa di San Francesco della Scarpa until an earthquake in 1706 left it detached from the rest of the church.

Continuing along the *corso*, past **Piazza XX Settembre** and its statue of Ovid, leads on to the **Complesso della Santissima Annunziata**. This striking complex, founded as a hospital in 1320 and now occupied by Sulmona's Museo Civico and tourist office, displays a harmonious blend of Gothic and Renaissance architecture.

Beyond the Complesso, the **Villa Comunale** park leads down to the town's understated **Cattedrale di San Panfilo**, where the relics of hermit-turned-pope Pietro da Morrone (1215–96) are conserved in a subterranean room.

HIGHLIGHTS

1 Bosco di
Sant'Antonio
2 Cattedrale
di San Panfilo
3 Collegiata di
Santa Maria del Colle
4 Complesso
della Santissima
Annunziata
5 Gole di Sagittario
6 La Camosciara
7 Museo Confetti Pelino
8 Santuario di
Monte Tranquillo
9 Val Fondillo
10 Zipline Majella

SLEEPING

11 La Fattoria
di Morgana

EATING

12 Il Duca
degli Abruzzi

Sweet Shopping

PICK UP SOME CONFETTI

Walk down **Corso Ovidio** and you'll pass any number of shops selling what look like bouquets of brightly coloured pills. These are Sulmona's famous *confetti*. These sugar-coated almond sweets, which are traditionally given out at weddings and important celebrations, have been manufactured in town since the 1780s. To learn more, stop by the **Museo Confetti Pelino**, a small museum run by Sulmona's most famous confectioner whose *confetti* have appeared at several British royal weddings.

Confetti, Sulmona

GETTING AROUND

Sulmona is accessible by both bus and train with services from L'Aquila, Pescara and Rome. It's not a big place so you can easily get around on foot. The most convenient car park for the historic centre is the Parcheggio di Santa Chiara, which has a pedestrian exit onto Piazza Garibaldi.

Sulmona ● ● Pacentro

● Pescocostanzo

● Parco Nazionale d'Abruzzo,
Lazio e Molise

Beyond Sulmona

Stunning scenery and superlative year-round
sport await in the mountains and hilltop towns of
Abruzzo's high country.

Sulmona is surrounded by some of Abruzzo's most exciting terrain. To the southwest, the 440-sq-km Parco Nazionale d'Abruzzo, Lazio e Molise boasts swaths of beech forest and a wildlife
roll call that counts the Abruzzo chamois, Apennine wolf, lynx,
deer and, most notably, Marsican bear (the park has Italy's largest enclave of these threatened animals). East of Sulmona, the
750-sq-km Parco Nazionale della Majella is similarly dramatic
with wolves roaming its thick woods and ancient hermitages
speckled across its ominous peaks. Hiking trails crisscross both
parks and a handful of ski resorts cater to winter sports fans.

TOP TIP

The best periods for
spotting a bear are spring
(April to May) and late
summer (mid-August to
mid-September).

Hiking, Villetta Barrea

GENNARO LEONARDO/EYEEM/GETTY IMAGES ©

A Roller-Coaster Road Trip

EXHILARATING MOUNTAIN SCENERY

The slow serpentine route from **1 Sulmona** to Pescasseroli (75km; allow two hours' driving time) winds through a craggy gorge, past lakes and over a mountaintop pass into the heart of the Parco Nazionale d'Abruzzo, Lazio e Molise. The first leg leads up to Scanno, passing through the **2 Gole di Sagittario**, a rocky gorge that squeezes the road like a natural vice, and continues up past the beautiful **3 Lago di Scanno**. Stop off in **4 Scanno** to nose around its steep medieval alleyways and greystone houses, which are said to have inspired the Dutch graphic artist Escher when he passed through Abruzzo in 1928.

From Scanno, the road climbs tortuously to the **5 Passo Godi** (1630m) before it starts a long, swooping descent to **6 Villetta Barrea** at the northwestern tip of Lago di Barrea. From Villetta follow the valley floor through the lush greenery to **7 Pescasseroli**.

 WHERE TO STAY AND EAT IN THE NATIONAL PARKS

Albergo La Rua
Cosy little hotel in Pescocostanzo's centre; all stone walls and wood-beamed ceilings. €

La Fattoria di Morgana
A lovely *agriturismo*, complete with animals and farmhouse food, in the countryside beneath hilltop Opi. €€

Il Duca degli Abruzzi
Rustic charm pairs with homemade regional cuisine at this handsome hotel-restaurant in Pescasseroli. €€

Paolo Iannicca, a
hiking guide with Ecotur
(www.ecotur.org) in
Pescasseroli, outlines
his favourite places and
walks.

**The ancient beech
forest of Selva
Moricento**
The Parco Nazionale
d'Abruzzo, Lazio e
Molise is famous for its
centuries-old beech
forests. Of these, Selva
Moricento deserves
a special mention, a
hidden corner of the
park where 500-year-
old trees grow.

Creste della Rocca
A high route along the
regional border between
Lazio and Abruzzo.
Once on the ridge,
a comfortable path
unfolds from where you
can admire an extensive
view of the park.

Monte Meta (2242m)
A high-altitude itinerary
to admire the Apennine
chamois. One of the
highest peaks in
the park, this is the
undisputed kingdom
of the agile chamois,
which lives here for
most of the year.

Take to the Mountains

HIKING AROUND PESCASSEROLI

With about 150 well-marked trails, signalled by white and
red marks daubed on trees and rocks, the Parco Nazionale
d'Abruzzo, Lazio e Molise is a paradise for hikers. Routes
range from easy family jaunts to hardcore hikes over rocky
peaks and exposed highlands.

Several trails depart from La Camosciara and Val Fondillo car parks on the main SR83 road. These include a popular
3¼-hour ascent of **Monte Amaro** (1862m; Route F1) from Val
Fondillo. Note, however, that this route can only be accessed
in August with an authorised guide.

Another excellent hike leads up to the **Santuario di Monte Tranquillo** from a starting point 1km south of Pescasseroli. There's actually a gravel road through the thick woods
to the chapel, which nestles at 1600m, around 200m below its eponymous peak, but a meandering path (C3) cuts
off the corners.

Hilltop Towns

COBBLES, A CASTLE & A ZIP LINE

Adrenaline junkies should make a beeline for **Pacentro** in
the foothills of the **Parco Nazionale della Majella**. This attractive hill town, which lies largely off the main tourist circuit, is home to the **Zipline Majella** (www.ziplinemajella.
com; bookings required), central Italy's first zip line. Once
you've bombed down the wire at 80km/h and taken in Pacentro's 14th-century castle, press on southwards.

It's a relaxing drive through the **Bosco di Sant'Antonio**
wood (ideal for a picnic) to **Pescocostanzo**. This charming
town, set amid rolling meadows at 1395m, boasts a surprisingly grand historic centre that seems little changed since the
16th and 17th centuries when it was an important stop on the
Via degli Abruzzi, the main road that
linked Naples and Florence.

Check out the **Collegiata di
Santa Maria del Colle** and
Palazzo Fango, which was
designed by the great baroque
architect Cosimo Fanzago in
1624, before adjourning for a
well-earned meal, perhaps at
the **Ristorante da Paolino**.

Collegiata di Santa Maria del Colle, Pescocostanzo

GETTING AROUND

TUA buses run daily from Sumona to Scanno and
Pacentro. For Pescasseroli, Civitella Alfedena and
other villages in the Parco Nazionale d'Abruzzo,
Lazio e Molise, bus services from Sulmona require a

change at Castel del Sangro; if coming from L'Aquila
or Rome you'll need to change at Avezzano.
Realistically, having your own car makes life a
lot easier.

THE GRAN SASSO

Rome

The Gran Sasso

About 20km northeast of Abruzzo's regional capital, L'Aquila, the Gran Sasso – at 2912m, the Apennines' highest mountain – is the soaring centrepiece of the Parco Nazionale del Gran Sasso e Monti della Laga. The park, one of Italy's largest, is a harsh, often unforgiving place of sweeping vistas and rocky terrain, through which one of Europe's southernmost glaciers, the Calderone, cuts its course. Wildlife thrives in its rugged heights, which provide a habitat for wolves, chamois, kestrels and royal eagles. Back on the ground, hiking trails crisscross the park, which is studded with atmospheric castles and tough, resilient hill towns.

Approaching from the west, the small village of Fonte Cerreto is the main gateway to the Gran Sasso massif. From there a *funivia* (cable car), and a winding road, snake up to Campo Imperatore, a high windswept plateau good for summer walking and winter skiing.

TOP TIP

You can pick up a park map showing the Gran Sasso's hiking and biking trails at the small tourist information point in Fonte Cerretto. Note also that the road up to Campo Imperatore closes over the winter, typically from October to mid-May.

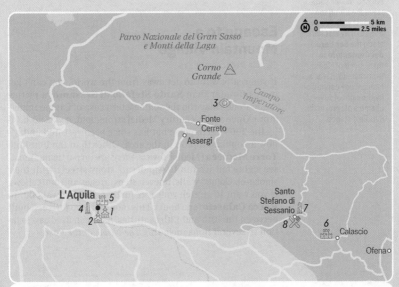

SIGHTS
1 Basilica di San Bernardino
2 Basilica di Santa Maria di Collemaggio
3 Campo Imperatore
4 Fontana delle 99 Cannelle
5 Forte Spagnolo
6 Rocca Calascio
7 Torre Medicea

SLEEPING
(see 7) Sextantio Albergo Diffuso

EATING
8 Locanda Sotto gli Archi

ENTERTAINMENT
(see 5) Auditorium del Parco

LIANEM/SHUTTERSTOCK ©

Santo Stefano di Sessanio

Escape to a Mountain Village

SILENT STONY STREETS

If you really want to get away from the world, you can't get more off-radar than **Santo Stefano di Sessanio**, a picturesque stone village on the southeastern cusp of Campo Imperatore. Once a 16th-century Medici stronghold, it was hit hard by the 2009 earthquake but has since been restored and it's now a popular stop-off in the area. Other than the 18m-high **Torre Medicea** (Medici Tower), there are no particular mustsee sights but it's fun to wander its stony streets with their smoke-blackened walls, uneven steps, arches and craft shops. If you want to stretch your legs further, you can walk out to **Rocca Calascio** (one hour). This mountaintop fortress, built between the 10th and 13th centuries, has been used as a location in several films including *The Name of the Rose*.

 WHERE TO STAY AND EAT IN THE GRAN SASSO

Hotel L'Aquila
Functional four-star offering value for money in the heart of L'Aquila's historic centre. €€

Sextantio
Has 30 rustic-chic rooms spread across the mountaintop village of Santo Stefano di Sessanio. €€

Locanda Sotto gli Archi
Earthy regional food in the arched, exposed-walled restaurant of the Sextantio hotel in Santo Stefano di Sessanio. €€

Little Tibet

EPIC MOUNTAIN SCENERY

You don't need to be a daredevil climber to get up close to the Gran Sasso. **Campo Imperatore** (2117m), a grassy highland plain known as Italy's 'Little Tibet', provides the perfect viewing platform. Whether travelling by motor or on foot, the scenery is magnificent – billowing wind-whipped grasslands overlooked by the great grey fin of the **Corno Grande** and an immense tsunami of rock.

One of the most popular hiking routes on the Campo is the *via normale* to the summit of Corno Grande. This 10km trek, graded EE (experienced hikers), departs from near the Ostello Campo Imperatore – where Mussolini was briefly imprisoned in 1943 – and takes around five to seven hours for the return trip. Another fantastic route leads along the Sentiero del Centenario to the top of Monte Brancastello (2385m). Both paths are generally clear of snow from early June to late September or early October.

Capital Sights

HISTORIC SIGHTS SHINE AGAIN

L'Aquila, Abruzzo's regional capital, is back on the travel radar. More than a decade after it was devastated by an earthquake in 2009, it has largely rebuilt itself and is now firmly open for business. It's not a big place and with the main sights concentrated in the historic centre, you can comfortably cover it in a day.

The city's signature building is the 12th-century **Basilica di Santa Maria di Collemaggio** which, with its distinctive quilt-pattern facade and Gothic rose windows, is the last resting place of hermit-pope Celestino V. On the other side of the *centro* you can admire the 15th-century **Basilica di San Bernardino** and, in a small park, L'Aquila's formidable 16th-century castle, aka the **Forte Spagnolo** (Spanish Fort). Also in the park is the **Auditorium del Parco**, a timber flat-pack concert hall designed by Renzo Piano.

To complete the city's sights, search out the **Fontana delle 99 Cannelle**, L'Aquila's erroneously named 'fountain of 99 spouts' (there are actually only 93).

BEST SKIING

Campo Imperatore
Some 13km of mainly downhill pistes in the Parco Nazionale del Gran Sasso e Monti della Laga.

Roccaraso
Abruzzo's biggest ski area has 90.5km of pistes as well as a snowpark and excellent après-ski.

Ovindoli-Monte Magnola
Well-known resort with 20km of pistes for all levels and two snowparks.

Campo Felice
A small resort south of L'Aquila with 31km of pistes and good facilities for kids.

Pescasseroli
This popular outpost has 8.5km of downhill slopes.

MORE HIKING

To tackle more of Abruzzo's mountain trails, head to the **Parco Nazionale d'Abruzzo, Lazio e Molise** (p153), where you'll find a network of trails snaking through the park's ancient woods and silent peaks.

GETTING AROUND

You can get to L'Aquila easily enough by train (via Terni to/from Rome and Pescara) or TUA bus (to/from Rome, Pescara, Sulmona). However, to travel further in the area you'll need your own wheels, even if it's only to reach the *funivia* (cable car) at Fonte Cerreto for the ride up to Campo Imperatore.

Horseriding, Barolo vineyards (p175)

TURIN & PIEDMONT

HISTORY & DELIGHTS

From mountains to hills to flatlands, Italy's second-largest region is a treasure trove of royal sights and mouthwatering cuisine.

Everything you need to know about Piedmont is in its name, which means 'at the foot of the mountains'. The Alps surround it like a crown, descending first into world-famous hills and then into the massive plain that stretches across northern Italy, shaping the region's history as it goes.

Piedmont too has always played a lead role in the making of Italy's history. It was the centre of power of the House of Savoy as it went from being a family of dukes to one of kings of Sardinia and later, kings of a unified Italy. It has also been one of the beating hearts of Italy's industrialisation. Turin, the capital of the region, still carries these legacies and you'll step right into the grandeur of this once-royal capital as you walk along its porticoes and piazzas.

There's much more to Piedmont than Turin, though. A myriad of smaller cities, towns and villages are scattered across its countryside, each holding centuries of history in their streets and churches. You'll find that life slows down among the fields, hills and mountain valleys – some might even say too much – and that there's plenty of time to take things slow, get lost and get found again. And, of course, eat and drink your fill of all that Piedmont has to offer.

ROBERTO MORABITO ITALY/SHUTTERSTOCK ©

THE MAIN AREAS

TURIN
History-rich capital.
p164

**LANGHE &
MONFERRATO**
Wineries and
medieval traditions.
p173

CUNEO & PROVINCIA
Hiking trails. p180

VERCELLI & VALSESIA
Rice fields and ski
slopes. p184

Find Your Way

Piedmont is one of Italy's largest regions, with histories that change as the landscape does. Collected here are its most significant locations, but each one of them invites you to discover even more.

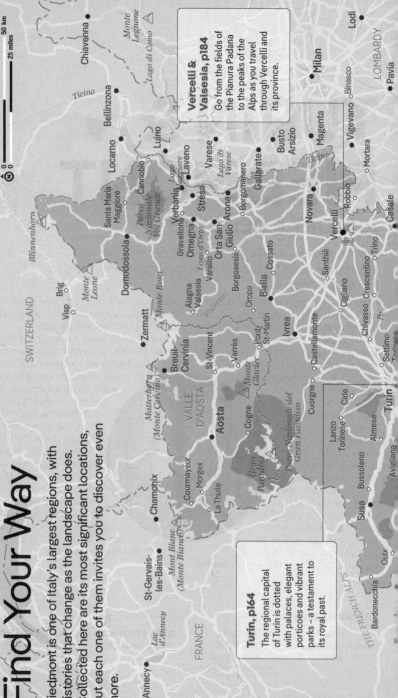

Turin, p164

The regional capital of Turin is dotted with palaces, elegant porticoes and vibrant parks – a testament to its royal past.

Vercelli & Valsesia, p184

Go from the fields of the Pianura Padana to the peaks of the Alps as you travel through Vercelli and its province.

0   50 km
0   25 miles

FROM LEFT: PAOLO GALLO/SHUTTERSTOCK ©, CLAMON/GETTY IMAGES ©

TRAIN

Moving around Piedmont's main locations via railway is relatively easy, with trains leaving Turin hourly. Delays are possible, especially with regional trains, but you'll win in both sustainability and scenery.

BUS

If you don't have a car, buses are a good way to reach the smallest locations without train stations – like hilltop villages in the Langhe and Monferrato regions. Tourist offices are your best bet for getting timetable info and tickets.

CAR

A car means freedom to explore the entire region, stopping wherever catches your fancy – be it a picturesque village or a rice mill's roadside shop. It's better to rely on public transport in big cities as parking can be tricky.

Langhe & Monferrato, p173

Rich cuisine and centuries-old traditions come alive in the winemaking hills of Piedmont.

Cuneo & Province, p180

Cuneo is the perfect base for hiking through the valleys and peaks that make up one of the region's largest provinces.

Map labels

Castegio
Giovanni
Bobbio
EMILIA-ROMAGNA
Ottone
Varzi
Rivanazzano
Tortona
Arquata Scrivia
Torriglia
Busalla
Chiavari
Borzonasca
Rapallo
Sestri
Levante
Novi Ligure
Alessandria
Acqui Terme
Ovada
Spigno
Voltri
LIGURIA
Genoa
Golfo di
Genova
Fetizzano
Nizza
Monferrato
Canelli
Arenzano
Savona
Asti
Canale
Alba
Dogliani
Finale
Ligure
Albenga
Monte
Galero
Carmagnola
Bra
La Morra
Barolo
Fossano
Mondovì
Vicoforte
Racconigi
Savigliano
Busca
Cuneo
Limone Piemonte
Punta
Marguareis
Carignano
Cavour
Saluzzo
Dronero
Borgo San
Dalmazzo
Rocca do
Abisso
Ventimiglia
Menton
MONACO
Nice
Mediterranean
Sea
Paesana
Sampeyre
Demonte
Parco Naturale delle
Alpi Marittime
Monte
Argentera
Argentina
Torre
Pellice
Monte
Chersogna
Monte
Cherso
Rocca
la Meia
Guillaumes
FRANCE
Digne-les-Bains

Plan Your Time

Even in its largest city, Piedmontese life is not particularly rushed. So take your time, whether you're sightseeing in Turin and Asti, or hiking in Cuneo and Alagna.

Palazzo Madama (p164), Turin

If You Only Do One Thing

● Explore **Turin** (p164), the city that was Italy's first national capital. It's a straight walk from Torino Porta Nuova railway station to the true heart of Turin, **Piazza Castello** (p164) with the **Palazzo Reale** (p164) and **Palazzo Madama** (p164). From there, walk under the **Via Po porticoes** (p166) until you reach **Piazza Vittorio Veneto** (p166) and the river Po.

● In the afternoon, either get lost in the elegant streets of Turin's city centre or explore one of its museums, such as the Museo Nazionale del Cinema inside the unmissable **Mole Antonelliana** (p167) or the Museo del Risorgimento headquartered at the historic **Palazzo Carignano** (p167).

Seasonal highlights

Summers and winters can be harsh in Piedmont, swinging from sweltering to chilling. Spring and autumn are the perfect seasons for being outside, exploring cities or tasting wine.

JANUARY

Layer up against the cold and take your skis or your board to the **Via Lattea ski area** slopes.

MAY

Book lovers everywhere unite – at Turin's **Salone del Libro**, a four-day event dedicated entirely to the Italian publishing world.

JUNE

Head to Nizza Monferrato for a double treat – the culinary festival **Monferrato in Tavola** and the thrilling **Barrels Race**.

ENRICOALIBERTI ITALYPHOTO/SHUTTERSTOCK ©, LUIGI BERTELLO/SHUTTERSTOCK ©, FABERI893/SHUTTERSTOCK ©

Three Days to Travel Around

● Return to Porta Nuova and head to the Monferrato hills and **Asti** (p175), where you'll arrive after an hour-long train ride. Wander through its medieval centre, from **Piazza San Secondo** (p175) to the **Cattedrale di Santa Maria Assunta** (p176), and stop for the night at **Festival delle Sagre** (p175) if you're visiting in September.

● Use your last day to reach **Vercelli** (p184), another hour-long ride from Turin, to marvel at the **Basilica di Sant'Andrea** (p185), wander through its quiet town centre and eat your fill of *panissa*, the local risotto dish (p184).

If You Have More Time

● Dedicate one or two days to the area around Turin starting from the royal residences outside the city, such as the **Reggia di Venaria Reale** (p171). If you have more time to go palace-hopping, opt for the hunting lodges in **Stupinigi** (p171) or **Racconigi** (p171). Take the train up into the Susa Valley to explore the **Sacra di San Michele** (p172), Piedmont's official symbol, picturesquely perched on top of a rock spur overlooking the town of Avigliana.

● Then add a couple more days to explore the elegant streets of **Cuneo** (p180), as well as the **valleys** (p183) that surround it if you're looking to get some hiking under your belt.

JULY

Take refuge in the mountains for a fair dose of local cuisine and entertainment at Varallo's **Alpàa** festival.

SEPTEMBER

Asti is the place to be – the **Palio** and **Festival delle Sagre** happen on the first and second weekends in September respectively.

NOVEMBER

Turin does its best to make late autumn less dreary, with the **CioccolaTò** chocolate festival and **Turin Film Festival**.

DECEMBER

Amid Christmas lights and celebrations, you're still in time to catch the end of Alba's **International White Truffle Fair**.

TURIN

More than two thousand years of history move through the streets of Turin and flow along its main river, the Po – also the primary water stream in the whole of northern Italy and the reason behind the Po valley's name. The foundations of the city were laid by the Taurini people in the 3rd century BCE, and that first settlement only grew with time, turning from the Roman colony Augusta Taurinorum in the 1st century CE into the capital of the Duchy of Savoy in the Renaissance.

Turin later became the first capital of the Kingdom of Italy after its unification in the 19th century, as well as one of the country's major economic engines from the industrial age onwards. Its centuries-long status of ducal and royal city gave Turin the look it has today – an elegant place filled with gorgeous *palazzos* (mansions), wide squares and bustling porticoes.

TOP TIP

Turin is famously 'squared', meaning that it's mostly made up of parallel, easy-to-navigate, grid-like streets. This is both because of the Romans and a Renaissance restructuring to make Turin a visual representation of the Savoys' power.

A NIGHT AT THE OPERA

Leaving Piazza Castello behind to move towards the Po river you'll encounter Turin's main theatre, the **Teatro Regio**. It originally dates back to the 18th century, but was completely rebuilt – save for its external facade – after a fire ravaged it in the 1930s. Its seasonal programmes are always full of both classical and modern plays, ballets and operas that are definitely worth advance booking. Beyond the Regio, Turin has plenty to offer for all lovers of the stage – check out what's on at **Teatro Stabile**, **Teatro Carignano** and **Teatro Gobetti** as well.

City of Dukes & Kings

PALACE-HOPPING WITH THE SAVOYS

Turin proudly presents her royal side the moment you set foot outside one of its two main train stations, **Torino Porta Nuova** and **Torino Porta Susa**, with elegant buildings that might remind you of Paris. From either one of the stations, you can easily set out on a walk that will take you right to the doorsteps of the palaces where the Savoys used to live and rule from.

Start at **Piazza Castello**, the true heart of Turin, which hosts the **Palazzo Reale**, the official royal residence. Crossing the outer and inner courtyards of the *palazzo*, you'll find yourself in the **Giardini Reali**, where you can enjoy a stroll or sit down under the shade of the trees. Another side of Piazza Castello is occupied by **Palazzo Madama**. Both palaces are museums in and of themselves, but they also often host exhibitions and events that may pique your interest. And of course, you can't have royal palaces without royal churches. Just off the side of the Palazzo Reale – not far from **Porta Palatina**, the only surviving entrance to the Roman town and part of the city's archaeological park – is

ROYAL VIBES

The **Residences of the Royal House of Savoy** (p171) spread out beyond Turin proper. From Venaria Reale to the Castello di Racconigi, all of them give an insight into life at the Italian royal court.

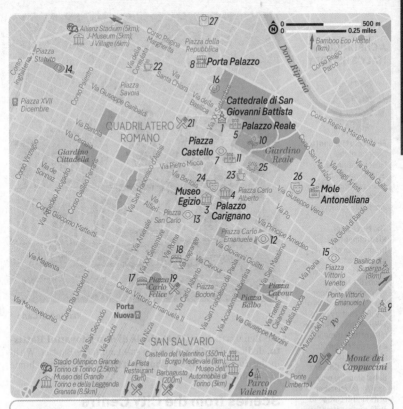

HIGHLIGHTS

1 Cattedrale di San
Giovanni Battista
2 Mole Antonelliana
3 Museo Egizio
4 Palazzo Carignano
5 Palazzo Reale
6 Parco Valentino
7 Piazza Castello
8 Porta Palazzo

SIGHTS

9 Chiesa della
Gran Madre di Dio
10 Giardino Reale

(see 2) Museo
Nazionale del Cinema
(see 4) Museo
Nazionale del
Risorgimento Italiano
11 Palazzo Madama
12 Piazza Carlo
Emanuele II
13 Piazza San Carlo
14 Piazza Statuto
15 Piazza
Vittorio Veneto
16 Porta Palatina

SLEEPING

17 Hotel Roma
e Rocca Cavour
18 Principi di Piemonte |
UNA Esperienze

EATING

19 M** Bun
(see 24) Pepino
20 PoDiCiotto
21 Poormanger
(see 24) Ristorante
Del Cambio

DRINKING

22 Caffè Al Bicerin
23 Caffè Mulassano

ENTERTAINMENT

24 Teatro Carignano
(see 26) Teatro Gobetti
25 Teatro Regio
26 Teatro Stabile

SHOPPING

27 Balon

WHERE TO EAT IN TURIN

Ristorante del Cambio
A luxury restaurant that
occupies a very special place
in Piedmont's history. €€€

Barbagusto
A typical Piedmontese *piola*
(traditional eatery) right in the
middle of Turin's nightlife hub,
San Salvario. €€

Poormanger
A menu entirely dedicated
to stuffed potatoes – with
ingredients changing
according to the season. €€

A CHRONICLE OF ITALY'S HISTORY

Ferruccio Martinotti, Director of the Museo Nazionale del Risorgimento, shares his thoughts on the museum and its incredible collection.

The **Museo del Risorgimento** is truly the museum of Italy's national history – the only one to have been dubbed '*nazionale*' ever since 1901. From the great revolutions of the 18th century up to WWI, visitors follow the birth of Italy through a vast collection of objects and locations – including the **Camera Subalpina**, the only parliament chamber of its kind in Europe to still be intact after the revolutions of 1848. The chamber is visible through a huge window, but also opens to tourists every year on 17 March – the official anniversary of the unification.

Piazza San Carlo

the Renaissance-age **Cattedrale di San Giovanni Battista**, dedicated to Turin's patron saint John the Baptist. Within the *duomo* is also the **Chapel of the Holy Shroud**, home to the Shroud of Turin.

Scenes from the City Centre

MUSEUMS, CHURCHES, SQUARES AND PORTICOES

Get lost in the atmosphere of Turin's piazzas, from shaded **Piazza Statuto** close to Porta Susa train station to gorgeous **Piazza San Carlo** with its twin churches. Take a peek at Piazza Carlo Emanuele II, which everybody refers to as Piazza Carlina, before stepping into a centre of Turin's nightlife, Piazza Vittorio Veneto. And if you're wondering how to get from one square to another, there's a very simple answer – strolling along its **porticoes**. When put together, Turin's monumental porticoes are almost 20km long, lining the streets of the city centre and allowing people to remain

WHERE TO EAT IN TURIN

M°° Bun
Classic fast food turned into typical Piedmontese, including a menu in the local dialect. €

LA PISTA Restaurant
Inside the Lingotto complex, the restaurant features a lounge bar for an exclusive experience. €€€

PoDiCiotto
Right on the shore of the Po river, this *piola* is part of a larger sports club. €

outside even when the weather isn't the nicest. And rainy days are the perfect occasions to delve into one of Turin's museums, such as **Museo Nazionale del Cinema**, located inside **Mole Antonelliana**, a skyline-defining tower so recognisable that it appears on the back of the Italian two-cent coin. Take the lift to the very top for stunning views of the entire city and the mountains surrounding it. Or head to **Museo Nazionale del Risorgimento** hosted by yet another Savoy residence, **Palazzo Carignano**, to learn about the unification of Italy. More unmissable stops that might fit into your niche interest include: **Museo Egizio**, which houses the second most important Egyptology collection in the world after the one in Cairo; and **Museo dell'Automobile**, dedicated to the history of automobiles from their invention to the modern age.

Valentino State of Mind

THE GREEN SIDE OF TURIN

There are many parks throughout Turin, but none as famous and beloved as **Parco Valentino**, just slightly off the city centre proper along the eastern shore of the Po river. It's the perfect spot to try out the *torinese* way of life and to follow the locals' example by soaking up the sun, sipping an *aperitivo*, meeting up with friends and strolling around aimlessly. Or maybe not so aimlessly – the park is filled with interesting curiosities, such as the massive **Fontana dei Mesi**, owing its name to the 12 statues that surround it, or the social media–famous **streetlamp lovers**, an installation featuring two streetlamps out on a romantic date. The most immediately recognisable sight in the whole park though is definitely **Borgo Medievale**, an accurate reconstruction of a medieval town built during the 19th century as part of a country-wide exposition. The Borgo was such a success that the plans to tear it down after the exposition were scrapped, and it's still open to visitors to this day. And if you're worried about missing out on your daily dose of royal palaces, fear not – the Savoys have left their mark here as well. They turned the whole area into a park, having bought it from local nobles in the 17th century, and they also built **Castello del Valentino**, another Unesco World Heritage residence.

LIGHT & DARK MAGIC

For all of its neoclassical elegance and royal atmosphere, Turin has also always had the reputation of being an esoteric and magical place. The entire city is thought by some to be crisscrossed by underground tunnels, known as 'alchemical caves', with the power to open doors into other dimensions. Turin is also apparently the place to search for both the philosopher's stone – hiding in one of the alchemical caves – and the Holy Grail, which may be somewhere under the church of the **Gran Madre di Dio**. **Torino Magica Tour** is the most famous way of exploring all the magical sights in the city and getting spooked by ancient legends.

MIDDLE AGES & TURIN

The Middle Ages have left their mark on Turin and its province – head out of the city to visit **Sacra di San Michele** (p172), the symbol of Piedmont.

WHERE TO SLEEP IN TURIN

Principi di Piemonte | UNA Esperienze
Right in the heart of Turin, this is the go-to destination for all luxury stays. €€€

Hotel Roma e Rocca Cavour
Family-run ever since the mid-19th century, this hotel is a comfortable stay. €€€

Bamboo Eco Hostel
Brightly coloured rooms in a hostel that places a lot of importance on sustainability. €

Two Clubs in Fair Torino

A FOOTBALL FAN'S DREAM TOUR

Two different football teams call Turin home. On the one hand, you have Torino Football Club, also known as Toro. Its matches are played at **Stadio Olimpico Grande Torino**, which also doubles as a concert venue during the off-season. You can't miss a visit to **Basilica di Superga**, perched on a hill overlooking the city and reachable by cable railway. Housing the tombs of some Savoy dukes and pre-unification kings, the basilica was also the site of one of the worst accidents in the history of Italian football – the 1949 plane crash that killed the whole of the club's team, known as 'Grande Torino' for its streak of victories. A plaque commemorates the victims, and the basilica is visited by supporters of all ages each 4 May, the anniversary of the crash. The **Museo del Grande Torino e della Leggenda Granata** collects memorabilia of the Grande Torino players to help keep their memory alive.

There's also Juventus Football Club, colloquially referred to as Juve. The club owns the **Allianz stadium**, where all of its home games are played. The stadium includes **J-Museum**, dedicated to the club's history, and it sits in the wider **J-Village area**, which features Juventus' official headquarters as well as the **J|Hotel**, meant to host Juventus supporters coming from outside the city to see their team play.

ONE CARD TO VISIT THEM ALL

Before heading out to Turin and Piedmont, you might want to check out the various offers for the **Torino+Piemonte Card**. You can choose the one, two, three or five consecutive days option for free access to the main Turin museums and exhibitions, as well as special prices on several other sights throughout the city and the region. The card can be integrated with Turin public transport for reduced fares and it's also available for young travellers, with 'Junior' prices designed for anyone under 18.

Out & About with Books & Chocolate

MARKETS, FESTIVALS & EVENTS

There are plenty of events and festivals that can make your visit to Turin that much more special. In mid-May, don't miss the **Salone del Libro**, a four-day annual event filled with book presentations, author talks and stands from pretty much every publishing house in the country. The Salone takes place at **Lingotto** and it does get quite crowded, especially over the weekend, but it's definitely worth a visit. The first weeks of June are perfect for enjoying music at **Torino Jazz Festival**, held at various clubs around the city. November also has a packed schedule. Indulge in some chocolate in the streets and piazzas of the city centre during **CioccolaTò**, from the last days of October to the first week in November, and clap for newly released films at all the major Turin cinemas at the **Torino Film Festival** in November and December.

 WHERE TO SNACK IN TURIN

Torteria Berlicabarbis
With two locations in Turin, this is the perfect place to stop for a piece of mid-afternoon cake. €

Caffè Gelateria Florio
One of the most famous gelato shops in the city, sitting under the porticoes of Via Po. €€€

Bardotto
Aperitivi and hot chocolates meet books in this cafe between Porta Nuova and Piazza Castello. €

ANTONELLO MARANGI/SHUTTERSTOCK ©

Grande Torino commemorations, Basilica di Superga

BEST NIGHTLIFE SPOTS IN TURIN

The Po riverside
Plenty of restaurants and clubs to dine and dance the night away in.

Piazza Vittorio Veneto
Elegant cafes to sip on a glass of wine or its aromatised, local version, vermouth.

Vanchiglia and Aurora
Filled with university students, the best areas to find out about the city's latest trends.

San Salvario
The place to be if you plan on wandering between clubs, cafes and *piole*.

If you can't make these events, you can still experience staples of *torinese* life at local farmers markets and fairs. Pretty much every neighbourhood has a daily farmers market, but the one at **Porta Palazzo** is one of the biggest, not only in the city but in the whole of Europe. The second Sunday of every month sees a handful of streets in the Valdocco neighbourhood turn into heaven for vintage and secondhand lovers – also known as the **Balon**, one of Turin's most famous antique markets.

GETTING AROUND

Turin is easily walkable in both sunshine and rain thanks to its porticoes, and walking is definitely the best way to explore the city centre. Its public transport system – comprising of buses and one subway line – is your best bet to move around the furthest areas of the city like Lingotto or the Allianz stadium. If you're driving into the city, you can either leave your car at one of the paid parking spots under Turin's squares, such as Piazza Carlo Felice or Piazza Vittorio Veneto, or drop it off at either of the two final subway stations (Bengasi or Fermi) and then ride the train into the city centre.

Bardonecchia   Susa   Parco La Mandria

Sestriere   Avigliana   Turin

Racconigi

Beyond Turin

The mountains surrounding Turin hold a myriad
of treasures, from abbeys and castles to some of
Italy's best slopes.

You're always aware of the mountains all around Turin, no
matter where you are in the city. So it makes sense to take
some time to wander these valleys, the natural border between
Italy and France, and a millennia-old crossroads of cultures,
languages and trades. You'll find Roman ruins, lakes, medieval abbeys perched on cliffs, and plenty of winter sports fun.
And, of course, you can't forget that the hand of the Savoys
extended well beyond the borders of Turin – traces of their
presence, mostly in the shape of castles and hunting lodges,
are many and they are all delightful to explore.

TOP TIP

Download the Trenitalia
app if you're planning to
travel by train – good for
tickets, timetables and
status updates.

Palazzina di Caccia di Stupinigi

MIKEDOTTA/SHUTTERSTOCK ©

Main hall, Palazzina di Caccia di Stupinigi

A GAME OF STAMPS

If you like to check things off on to-do lists, and you plan to dedicate quite some time to exploring the royal residences, you can fill out the **Royal Residences Passport**. Once you get your hands on one, either online or at the ticket office of each palace and castle, you can ask for a stamp to prove you've visited all the locations. It can be a fun game if you're travelling with children – but adults can definitely enjoy it too!

The Savoy Residences

MORE UNESCO WORLD HERITAGE CASTLES

Although the Turin city palaces were the main centres of power, they are not the only residences the Savoys built or acquired. The palaces, lodges and residences that formed their 'crown of delights', all around Piedmont, amount to a grand total of 16. They're part of the **Residences of the Royal House of Savoy** complex: a Unesco World Heritage Site since 1997. The most famous – and the one to visit if you can only pick one – is **Reggia di Venaria Reale**, more often identified with the name of the town in which it's located, Venaria Reale. Originally a hunting lodge that was later enlarged into a proper royal residence, its most famous feature is the breathtaking Galleria Grande – reminiscent of the Hall of Mirrors at the Palace of Versailles. The palace opens up onto the massive **Parco La Mandria**, which includes **Castello della Mandria**, a stable that King Victor Emmanuel II transformed into a private home for himself and his mistress-turned-morganatic wife Rosa. If you can dedicate more time to exploring palaces, you should also hit up **Palazzina di Caccia di Stupinigi** and **Castello di Racconigi**. The former is a hunting lodge

 **WHERE TO EAT IN VAL DI SUSA**

Ristorante 'L Fouie
Just slightly out of Bardonecchia proper, inside a restored and elegant chalet. €€

Ristorante Della Torre
Right in the Susa town centre, a perfect spot to try out local Piedmontese dishes. €€

I.GLOO Sky Bar and Food
At the bottom of the Sestriere slopes, with different features for summer and winter. €€

barely an hour away by bus from Turin's city centre. The latter – some 49 minutes by car heading south – was designed as a summer getaway from the hustle and bustle of Turin.

Up & Down Mountains

ABBEYS & SKI RESORTS

MOUNTAIN FOOD

It is a truth universally acknowledged that one of the best ways to truly get to know a place is through its food. So if you want to explore the culinary traditions and local products of the Val di Susa, you should check out the programme of **GustoValSusa** – running from May to December, it includes a wide array of events and festivals in various villages and towns throughout the valley, all featuring the best of the best of their cuisine. No matter when you're planning to visit, your chances of finding something delicious to eat are looking good.

Of the valleys that open up around Turin, you can't miss a visit to **Val di Susa**. Trains leave every half-hour from Torino Porta Nuova for either Susa or Bardonecchia, stopping at major towns along the way. You just need to decide where to hop off. Pick **Avigliana** for a stroll and a meal along its two lakes, Lago Grande and Lago Piccolo, and especially for a visit to the symbol of Piedmont – the Sacra di San Michele. Perched above Avigliana, this 13th-century abbey offers stunning views of the surrounding valleys. You can reach it by car and via hiking and climbing trails.

Further along, the small but historically significant **Susa** lends its name to the whole valley. Its location close to the natural border created by the Alps has made it a travel hub ever since Roman times, and you'll find several Roman remains, from the amphitheatre to the Arch of Augustus and the old Roman walls with their access doors, especially Porta Savoia.

If you're visiting during the cold season and want to indulge in winter sports, head to the slopes of **Bardonecchia**. At 2035m above sea level, **Sestriere** holds the title of 'highest town in Italy', and is excellent for skiing and snowboarding – the Via Lattea area is a favourite among amateurs and professionals alike, and its slopes often host alpine ski events like the World Cup.

MOUNTAIN SANCTUARIES

The peaks of Piedmont are dotted with sanctuaries that have sprung up throughout the centuries – like the **Sacro Monte di Varallo** (p164) and the **Santuario di Oropa** (p188).

GETTING AROUND

You can reach the Val di Susa using the extra-urban trains that the Servizio Ferroviario Metropolitano (Sfm for short) runs from Torino Porta Nuova to Susa and Bardonecchia. The Venaria Reale also has a dedicated shuttle bus to transport tourists to and from the palace from the city centre, with a stop right in Piazza Castello.

LANGHE & MONFERRATO

Langhe & Monferrato

Rome

The Monferrato and Langhe hills make up one of the most recognisable landscapes of the entire region of Piedmont, and one of the most beloved – by local *piemontesi* first and foremost. Very few people would say no to a weekend escape in the Langhe or a drive to Monferrato for a great meal, so you'll find that the area is always lively and populated, especially during the warmer months.

These gorgeous, vineyard-lined Piedmont hills offer you everything you could desire from a trip to Italy. Medieval towns filled with culture and traditions, delicious traditional food, amazing local wine, breathtaking views, a general vibe of slow and peaceful living – you name it, the Monferrato and Langhe hills have it. So much so that they were officially named a Unesco World Heritage Site in 2014, under the collective name of 'Vineyard Landscape of Piedmont'.

TOP TIP

The Monferrato is filled with fairy-tale-like photo opps. Try the Torre dei Contini, technically in the village of Canelli but practically in the middle of the vineyards, to feel like Rapunzel or get an *Alice in Wonderland*-type experience at the giant benches that dot the area.

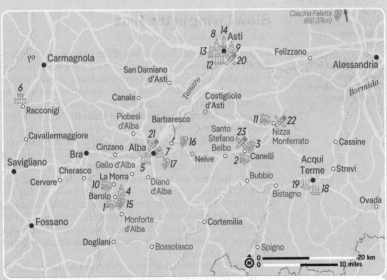

HIGHLIGHTS
1 Barolo
2 Canelli
3 Cantine Bosca
4 Cappella delle Brunate
5 Casa Marro
6 Castello di Racconigi
7 Cattedrale di San Lorenzo
8 Cattedrale di Santa Maria Assunta
9 Chiesa Collegiata di San Secondo
10 La Morra
11 Nizza Monferrato
12 Palazzo Mazzetti
(see 12) Palazzo Ottolenghi
13 Torre Rossa
14 Torre Troyana
15 WiMu

ACTIVITIES, COURSES & TOURS
16 Cantina del Glicine
17 Cascina Barac
18 Spa Lago delle Sorgenti
19 Stabilimento Nuove Terme

EATING
20 Il Cavolo a Merenda
21 La Piola
22 La Signora in Rosso
23 Osteria dei Meravigliati
(see 21) Osteria dell'Arco
(see 22) Terzo Tempo

WHY I LOVE MONFERRATO

Benedetta Geddo,
writer

The Monferrato hills have the magical ability to always make me feel at ease and at peace, whether I'm chilling on one of the big benches up on a *bricco* (hilltop) or in the middle of the chaos of the Festival delle Sagre. I love the colours and the tastes that surround me whenever I'm here, the rolling landscape and the feeling I get of truly feeling connected to my region – plus, Monferrato usually means big wine-fuelled, traditionally Piedmontese meals with friends, which are always something to look forward to.

Vineyards, La Morra

Slow Living in the Hills

TINY VILLAGES AND MASSIVE FEASTS

Strolling around the major towns of the Langhe and the Monferrato is undoubtedly great, but to get the most out of this fascinating area of Piedmont, get your own four – or two – wheels and dedicate some time to explore the villages that dot the hills.

If you're in the Monferrato, two places you definitely have to visit are **Nizza Monferrato** and **Canelli**. Nizza Monferrato – not to be confused with Nice in France, which has the same name in Italian – sits at the centre of the Barbera vineyards, ensuring that you'll never go without a tasty glass of wine during your stay. Some 15 minutes away lies Canelli, another Barbera hot spot. What makes Canelli stand out, though, is not on street level – but rather under it. The so-called 'underground cathedrals' are tunnels that have been used to store wines since the 15th century. Today, only some parts are open to visitors – book your tour through one of four wineries: Cantine Bosca, Cantina Contratto, Cantine Coppo and Cantina Gancia.

On the Langhe hills, don't miss a visit to **La Morra**, smack in the middle of Barolo lands – so much so that it even has a

---

 WHERE TO EAT IN LANGHE & MONFERRATO

Il Cavolo a Merenda
A rustic and chic interior with a menu rich in revisited Mediterranean dishes. €€

Osteria dei Meravigliati
This Canelli eatery and its beautifully frescoed ceiling are perfect for grand Piedmontese dinners. €€€

La Signora in Rosso
In the heart of Nizza Monferrato, its menu is made up of slightly revisited traditional meals. €€

multicoloured chapel dedicated to this particular wine. Speaking of **Barolo**, you really have to stop by the village it's named after – once you're there, be sure to check out the **WiMu**, a Barolo-centric museum located inside a medieval castle.

Busy Times

FESTIVALS FOR ALL FLAVOURS

There's always something special happening up and down the hills, from festivals dedicated to local delights to historical traditions dating back centuries that bring an entire city or town together. It all depends on when you're travelling, of course – the busiest months being from the start of the warm season in spring to the end of the *vendemmia* (grape harvest) in autumn. Head to Nizza Monferrato on the second weekend of June, for example, to taste local delights at the **Monferrato in Tavola** festival. If you're in Asti in September, then you have some packed days ahead of you – the first weekend of the month is dedicated to the **Palio** and all the events that precede it, like a flag-weaving exhibition on the Thursday before the actual race. Then, the second September weekend is **Festival delle Sagre** time – delegations from the surrounding villages and towns gather in Asti offering their traditional dishes. The Festival delle Sagre happens within the larger **Douja D'Or** event, one of the most important wine festivals in the country – wineries around the city open up for tastings and purchases, creating a unique atmosphere that's the perfect summer sendoff. Finally, October in Alba means one thing and one thing only – white truffle. The **International White Truffle Fair** takes place from October to December, with a whole array of events dedicated to this autumn delicacy.

The Heart of the Monferrato

A WALKING TOUR OF ASTI

Asti is exactly what pops into your head when you think of the words 'city dating back to the Roman age in the middle of the Italian wine hills'. Easily reachable by train or car, it's the perfect place to set up camp to explore the rest of the area, but not without having walked its city centre first. Start your visit in **1 Piazza San Secondo**, with the city hall and the **Collegiata di San Secondo**, Asti's patron saint. From there, step onto Asti's main street, **Corso Alfieri**. **2 Palazzo Mazzetti** – and its art gallery – and **3 Palazzo Ottolenghi** – and its Museo del Risorgimento – both look onto Corso Alfieri.

A UNIQUE RACE

Francesca Pero, a member of the Nizza Monferrato cultural association L'Erca, describes her town's unmissable event.

My favourite event happens at the beginning of June and it's a mix of tradition and cuisine – the **Barrel Race**! Local wineries compete against each other in a relay race during which the so-called *spingitori* roll barrels along the Nizza Monferrato town centre. At the end, everyone celebrates in Piazza Garibaldi, where delegations from the surrounding villages gather to cook their own local meals – all to be paired with a nice glass of Nizza DOCG.

Terzo Tempo
A modern *osteria* (tavern) in Nizza Monferrato for every Piedmontese cuisine need. €€

La Piola
The pasta with white truffle is the queen of this Alba eatery's menu. €€€

Osteria dell'Arco
Taste regional excellencies at this historic restaurant inside an inner court in Alba. €€

PALIO DI ASTI

If you visit Asti towards the end of August or the first weeks of September, you will definitely notice the colourful flags hanging around the city's streets. They're in preparation for the Palio di Asti, a **horse competition** similar to the more famous one in Siena that dates back to the Middle Ages. It sees different city neighbourhoods – as well as representatives from surrounding towns – race for victory. Asti is divided into six *rioni* (located within the oldest set of walls) and eight *borghi* (newer areas of the city). Around the cathedral, for example, you'll see a crowned black eagle on a white and blue crest, representing Rione Cattedrale.

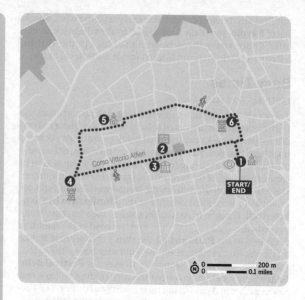

LIVING IT UP IN THE HILLS

If you time your visit to the Langhe and Monferrato right, you'll find yourself jumping from **festival** (p175) to parade to tasting until you won't even remember what 'bored' means.

No city or town in Italy would be complete without a handful of towers dating back to Roman and especially medieval times – Asti and its two towers are no exception. The first is **4 Torre Rossa**, located somewhat on the outskirts of the city centre. Take a detour to reach Piazza Cattedrale and Asti's cathedral, **5 Santa Maria Assunta** – one of the best-preserved Gothic buildings in the area, then visit the second of Asti's towers, **6 Torre Troyana**, or Torre dell'Orologio. Climbing up its almost 200 steps might not be very pleasant, but the view that awaits you is definitely worth it. Keep in mind that the tower is closed from November to March and that you can access it with the *Musei di Asti Smarticket*, a convenient option if you plan to visit more than one museum in the city.

Alba & Its Towers

THE UNOFFICIAL LANGHE CAPITAL

You'll find that it's easier to reach Alba by car if you're travelling from Asti – the trains from Turin will get you there in a little more than an hour – and once you arrive, you'll agree it was worth the journey. The city centre used to be domi-

 WHERE TO GO WINE TASTING

Cascina Faletta
In the Casale Monferrato area, this all-inclusive stop features a wine cellar and a restaurant.

Cantina del Glicine
This winery has been standing in the village of Neive, within the Langhe, ever since the 16th century.

Tenuta Baràc
The wine tour of this Alba winery is perfect for first-time tasters and experts alike.

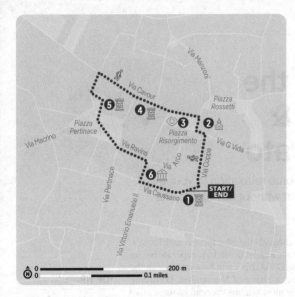

0 m 200 m
0.1 miles

FENOGLIO'S ALBA

Most people in Italy might know Alba because it appears in one of the most famous works by Italian writer Giuseppe 'Beppe' Fenoglio, an Alba native. *The 23 Days of the City of Alba* is a collection of short stories about Alba and its people during and after the liberation war of WWII, in which Fenoglio himself fought. You can trace Fenoglio's steps starting from the house in which he lived, now the headquarters of a cultural association dedicated to him – the **Centro Studi Beppe Fenoglio** – that is open for visits. Several thematic routes can then bring you to Fenoglio's places both within the city of Alba and along the surrounding hills – the team of the Centro Studi will be able to point out the best one for you.

nated by medieval towers, so much so that Alba had gained the portmanteau of Città delle Cento Torri, 'the city of a hundred towers'. Not many are left today, but there are some you can still spot. Begin at the **1 Torre di Casa Chiarlone** in Via Calissano, lowered to the same level as the nearby roofs, and meander to Alba's **2 cathedral**, dedicated to San Lorenzo, the town's patron saint. Continue your walk to **3 Piazza Risorgimento**, built on top of the old Roman settlement, and admire **4 Casa Marro** – considered one of the towers despite its name – overlooking **Piazza Pertinace**. Then get lost between Alba's two main streets, **Via Cavour** and **Via Vittorio Emanuele**, best known by the nickname 'Via Maestra'. Be sure to check out the **5 Loggia dei Mercanti** porticoes as you walk along Via Cavour, and stop once you reach number 11 on Via Vittorio Emanuele to look up at **6 Casa Fontana**, or Casa Do – a medieval house with a richly decorated facade that could intrigue you for hours.

 GETTING AROUND

Moving around by car is definitely the best way to allow yourself the freedom to explore all the hilltop villages that your heart desires, as many don't have a railway station you can rely on. Keep in mind that finding a parking spot might not always be an easy task – and avoid wearing heels as the mix of sloping streets and cobblestones can be treacherous.

Beyond the Langhe & Monferrato

Alessandria

Alba

Acqui Terme

If you want to add some relaxation to your trip, don't leave Piedmont without having tried its thermal baths.

After feasting your way through the Monferrato and Langhe hills, you might want to take a quiet break to recuperate before getting on the road again. Good thing you happen to be in the perfect place to do it. The province of Alessandria, bordering with Asti, holds one of the most famous thermal spots in all of Piedmont – the go-to destination for a whole host of spa treatments. So welcome to the Acquese – located right where Piedmont turns into Liguria, a crossroads of people and cultures ever since the Neolithic Age. The thermal baths of its main town, Acqui Terme, have been much-beloved since ancient Rome.

TOP TIP

It takes less than an hour to get to Acqui Terme from Asti by car. The trip by train is longer, with one change in Alessandria.

Thermal baths, Acqui Terme

SAVOI9774/SHUTTERSTOCK ©

STEFY MORELLI/SHUTTERSTOCK ©

Piazza della Bollente, Acqui Terme

Acqui of the Waters

SPA DAYS OLD & NEW

The town of **Acqui Terme** is synonymous throughout Piedmont with a weekend spa getaway – given it perfectly combines the benefits of its natural thermal waters with a picturesque city centre and traditional local food.

If you want to start with a stroll around the town, head to what can be considered Acqui Terme's heart, **Piazza della Bollente**. The square owns its name to the octagonal structure at its centre, La Bollente, 'the boiling one', built to surround a natural thermal spring – bringing out water at a steamy 75°C. Continue your walk by checking out what remains of the **old Roman town**, like the surviving arches of the old aqueduct over the river Bormida and the ruins of an ancient public bathhouse in Corso Bagni. You can also find the public amphitheatre around Via Scatilazzi – like many Greek and Roman theatres, it followed the natural slope of the hill to create seating space for the public. The whole Bagni neighbourhood is one of the best areas in Acqui Terme to find thermal springs, which is why there has been a steady number of spas being built, torn down and rebuilt in these streets since the Renaissance.

TREAT YOURSELF

There are a couple of ways to have all your relaxation needs met when in Acqui Terme – but first, you'll have to check whether or not the various spas and baths are open. You can do so on the website of the **Terme di Acqui group** (termediacqui. it), which manages all thermal centres in the town. Once you've done that, all that's left for you to do is decide what you want to focus on. Experience the beneficial waters of Acqui Terme for yourself at its bathhouses – for example, the – or enjoy a relaxing massage or sauna in one of its spas, such as **Lago delle Sorgenti**.

GETTING AROUND

This is still the Langhe and Monferrato area, meaning that having a car at your disposal is undoubtedly the best option to move around. If you decide to rely on the railway system, then keep in mind that getting to Acqui Terme from either Turin or Asti will require one change of train in Alessandria.

CUNEO

Cuneo

★ Rome

The province of Cuneo is known throughout Piedmont as 'la Granda', meaning 'the big one'. That's because it is one of the largest provinces, not just in Piedmont but in the whole country. It shares its borders with both France and Liguria, which means that the Mediterranean Sea is much closer than you might think – really just on the other side of the mountains – and the province offers some strikingly different landscapes and experiences. On the one hand, you have the Alps with their crisp mountain air, hearty foods and hiking trails to explore if you're out for an adventure. On the other, there are the Unesco World Heritage Langhe hills with their vineyards, picturesque small towns and indulgent lifestyle. You'll be spoiled for choice during your stay in la Granda.

TOP TIP

Remember that you're travelling through mountains here. Even if it's the middle of summer and the rest of the region is sweltering through terrible heat, always bring some form of rain protection and a sweater. Like Italian mothers say, 'you never know when you might need it'.

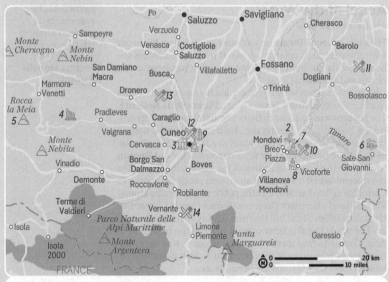

SIGHTS
1 Cattedrale di Santa Maria del Bosco e San Michele
2 Giardini del Belvedere
3 Museo Casa Galimberti
4 Narbona
5 Rocca la Meja
6 Sale San Giovanni
7 San Francesco Saverio (Chiesa della Missione)
8 Santuario di Vicoforte
9 Torre Civica
(see 2) Torre del Belvedere

EATING
10 Caffe Bertaina Osteria
11 Osteria da Gemma
12 Osteria della Chiocciola
13 Osteria Fuorimano
14 Ristorante Il Nazionale di Vernante
(see 14) Ristorante Pizzeria Cavallino

Chiesa di San Francesco Saverio

CLIMBING A DOME

Not too far from Mondovì – easily reachable by car, and doable via a train and bus combo – you can visit the **Santuario di Vicoforte**. Its defining trait, its elliptical dome, is the largest of its kind in the world. A tour will take you 60m high right to its heart, helmet and harness on, as you get up close and personal with the dome's walls. If you're not scared of heights, this is definitely the experience for you – but be sure to book in advance, as the climb is only possible during some months of the year and times vary depending on the season.

Getting Out of the City

BELVEDERES & 3D CHURCHES

If you want your stay in Cuneo to include time out of the city, look no further than **Mondovì**, less than half an hour away by train and perfect for a day trip. Start your visit in the **Mondovì Breo** neighbourhood, and don't forget to look up and study the houses' facades – Mondovì has become famous for its sundials and you'll see plenty of them on your stroll. Then board the cableway and head up to the **Mondovì Piazza** neighbourhood. You'll find yourself in **Piazza Maggiore**, with its charming frescoed or battlemeneted buildings. On one side of the square, there's the **Chiesa di San Francesco Saverio**, more commonly known as Chiesa della Missione – its interiors are definitely worth a visit. Not only do you get to see a textbook example of the *trompe l'oeil* technique – the frescoes make it appear as if there's a dome that doesn't actually exist – but you can also see the church come alive thanks to the 3D technology of the **Infinitum tour**. Before descending, don't forget to go to the **Giardini del Belvedere** for a breathtaking view of the surrounding

 WHERE TO EAT IN & AROUND CUNEO

Osteria della Chiocciola
Typical Piedmontese cuisine almost at the peak of Cuneo's 'wedge'. **€€**

Osteria Fuorimano
Located in the village of Busca, some 20 minutes out of Cuneo. **€€**

Osteria da Gemma
In the tiny village of Roddino, a VIP and celebrity stop that definitely requires booking beforehand. **€€**

Rocca la Meja

BELLA CIAO

Cuneo holds a Gold Medal of Military Valour, awarded by the Republic of Italy at the end of WWII for the efforts of the city and its people in the resistance movement. The legacy of the *partigiani* (resistance fighters) is deeply felt in Cuneo and all throughout its province as these are some of the valleys and hills where the fight for liberation was most brutal. You can trace the steps of the Resistenza in towns and villages like Boves, Dronero, San Damiano Macra, Garessio, Castellino Tanaro and Mondovì. There are also several hiking trails that can take you right along the routes that the *partigiani* travelled, like the **Sentieri della Libertà**.

TRACES OF THE PAST

The city of Alba is also particularly tied to WWII because of the literary works of its native Beppe Fenoglio, whose life you can trace at the **Centro Studi Beppe Fenoglio** (p177).

hills. And if you have a spring in your step, you can get even higher by climbing the 87 steps of the **Torre del Belvedere**.

Solemn Cuneo

UNDER PORTICOES & UP TOWERS

Cuneo stands at the intersection of two rivers, the Stura and the Gesso – when you look at it from above, this location gives the city a peculiar 'wedge' shape, which in Italian translates as '*cuneo*'. A tranquil city full of Turin-esque elegance, Cuneo is a great stop to explore the surrounding province, but the city centre also deserves a day's stroll. Start in massive **Piazza Galimberti**, dedicated to one of the heroes of the WWII Resistance, whose life you can explore at **Museo Casa Galimberti**, located on the square. If the weather is nice and the sky is clear, you can enjoy a stunning view of **Corso Nizza** with the mountains in the background; if you happen to get caught in rain, though, you can still walk around the square's convenient porticoes. Then head down **Via Roma** and stop along the way to take in some more impressive sights, such as the cathedral of **Santa Maria del**

WHERE TO EAT IN & AROUND CUNEO

Ristorante Il Nazionale di Vernante
Located in Vernante, this eatery boasts one Michelin star. €€€

Ristorante Pizzeria Cavallino
Pub atmosphere and excellent burgers at this Vernante eatery. €

Caffè Bertaina Osteria
A prime location under the porticoes of Mondovì's Piazza Maggiore. €€

Bosco. Once you reach **Largo Auffredi** be sure to look up to see **Torre Civica** – it's worth climbing on sunny days to look at the city from above, but keep in mind that it's only open during summer weekends. The little streets and alleys just off Via Roma make up the **Contrada Mondovì**, one of the most unique parts of the city centre and the way to go to find a place to eat or have a nice *aperitivo*.

Get Your Walking Shoes On

HIKING THROUGH THE GRANDA

The province of Cuneo is made for walking, and the valleys that surround the city are crisscrossed by a wide range of hiking trails that cater to all tastes and level of experience. For a relaxed start, head to the **Rocca la Meja** in Valle Stura, or take the route that will lead you all the way to the lakes of **Brignola** in Valle Maudagna. If you're travelling with children, you might enjoy the quiet **Via delle Meridiane** in Borgo San Dalmazzo. Want something a bit more difficult? Then walk through the **Monte Grosso** ring in Valle Ellero, or explore the abandoned village of **Narbona** in Valle Grana. And if winter for you means snowshoes rather than skis or a snowboard, you'll love the trek up the **Bisalta** mountain, one of the most recognisable in the area, or to the Monte **Frioland**. Let's also not forget that the province of Cuneo comes equipped with some world-class, Unesco-worthy hills – not as challenging as a mountain hike, but still packed with breathtaking sights. Like the lavender fields at **Sale San Giovanni**, which make for an amazing hike during the summer months.

Check out the **Cuneotrekking** and **AlpiCuneesi** websites for more information about each trail – including length, altitude difference and best period to hike – and suggestions for which trails may be most suitable.

MOUNTAIN SPIRIT

Juri Chiotti, owner of the Reis Cibo Libero di Montagna *agriturismo* (farm-stay accommodation), shares his memories and wishes about his native mountains.

I was raised with the memories of clean, cared-for mountains – and now I dream of living right in this corner of paradise with as little impact as possible. Under the shadow of the Monviso, whose hiking trails I suggest to everyone, there's a great desire for a change and a return to true, authentic things.

GETTING AROUND

If you're planning to spend some time hiking, a car is the best way to reach a trail's starting point, especially if it's somewhat remote. Central Cuneo is also well connected to Turin by train – a one-day tour of the city is an excellent option.

VERCELLI & VALSESIA

Vercelli & Valsesia

Rome

Vercelli and its province have what you could call a double soul – and that's because the shape of the province itself, reaching up towards the Alps, unites two very different landscapes. On the one hand, you have the Pianura Padana, or Po valley – Italy's largest flatland, stretching across its northern regions around the river Po all the way to the Adriatic Sea. The city of Vercelli itself sits in the middle of it, surrounded by fields – especially of rice, the best known local product. On the other, you have the Valsesia – an alpine valley descending from the Monte Rosa, the second tallest peak of the Alps. Two faces of the same coin, from the 'squared sea' of flooded rice fields in summer to the snowy, winter slopes of the Mont Rosa, and a bit off the most beaten tourist routes.

TOP TIP

You can't leave the vercellese area without eating its local dish, *panissa* – a risotto dish made with beans, a type of local salami and a generous dose of red wine. Hit up the Bislakko Cioccoristoreria or the Trattoria Paolino when you're in Vercelli to try it!

SUMMER NIGHTS

If you're in the area in early July, check out Varallo's **Alpàa** – a 10-day event whose highlights include markets selling everything from local delicacies to handmade items, and concerts held in the city's main square, Piazza Vittorio Emanuele II, with many Italian A-listers taking to the stage in recent years. It's also a great chance to eat your fill of typical Valsesian food as pretty much all of the valley's towns and villages cook up a storm of mountain delights.

A Mountain on Top of a Mountain

UNIQUE SIGHTS IN VARALLO

Halfway up Valsesia you'll find **Varallo**, one of the valley's two main centres. It takes around an hour to reach Varallo from Vercelli – an hour and a half if you go by bus – but there's something unique about it that deserves the trip – the **Sacro Monte**. A Sacro Monte is a particular kind of religious complex consisting of a route – of chapels, churches, altars and the like – following the natural slopes of a mountain or hill. Nine of the ones located across Piedmont and Lombardy – of which Varallo's is the oldest – were declared a Unesco World Heritage Site in 2003.

The Sacro Monte in Varallo consists of 44 chapels that host more than 800 wooden statues, telling the story of Jesus's life from the Garden of Eden to his crucifixion. Even reaching the Sacro Monte from Varallo's city centre is an experience in itself – the cableway connecting the two offers a stunning look at Varallo and the surrounding valley. Once you've come back down, you should check out the **Santuario della Madonna delle Grazie** – not too far from the cableway station. Inside, you'll find a masterpiece of Renaissance art – a massive fresco depicting the life of Jesus by Gaudenzio Ferrari, a painter native to the Varallo area who also worked extensively on the Sacro Monte.

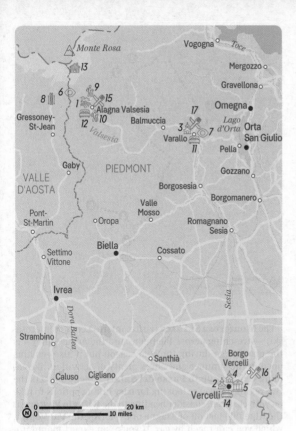

SIGHTS
1 Alagna Valsesia
2 Basilica di Sant'Andrea
3 Chiesa Santa Maria delle Grazie
4 Duomo di Sant'Eusebio
5 Museo del Tesoro del Duomo di Vercelli
6 Passo dei Salati
7 Sacro Monte di Varallo

ACTIVITIES, COURSES & TOURS
8 Monte Rosa ski area
9 Rifugio Pastore
10 Val Vogna

SLEEPING
11 Al Vicolo del Gallo
12 Alagna Mountain Resort
13 Capanna Osservatorio Regina Margherita
14 Hotel Ristorante Il Giardinetto

EATING
15 Albergo Montagna di Luce
16 Osteria Cascina dei Fiori
17 Piane Belle

At the End of the Valley

ALAGNA VALSESIA & ITS MOUNTAINS

Alagna Valsesia sits at the bottom of the Monte Rosa, the natural end point of the entire valley. It's a small town with a very tiny centre you can walk up and down in a few hours – but then again, that's not where you should look to find Alagna's highlights. The whole **Monte Rosa** area is a dream location for anyone who enjoys outdoor activities, from trekking and biking during the warm season to skiing and snowboarding in the winter months.

WHERE TO EAT IN VERCELLI & VALSESIA

Osteria Cascina dei Fiori
Traditional cuisine in the village of Borgo Vercelli, just outside of Vercelli. €€€

Piane Belle
Just slightly outside Varallo proper, it includes both set and à la carte menus. €€

Albergo Montagna di Luce
A menu rich with local dishes, and a unique location in Alagna Valsesia's hamlet Pedemonte. €€

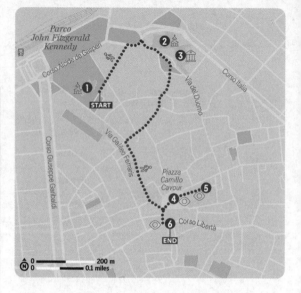

TRACING PILGRIMS' STEPS

Tiziana Grigoletto, president of the cultural association Amici della Via Francigena, recommends some of the sights along this medieval but still-beaten route.

The main activity along the **Via Francigena** consists of one-day hikes throughout the area, surrounded by rice fields that change colour depending on the different stages of rice growth. Try the historic **Tenuta Colombara** or the **Abbazia di Lucedio**, both located in the direction of Turin.

The **Monterosa Ski area** (visitmonterosa.com/monterosa-ski) – stretching across Piedmont and the Aosta Valley – is the place to go during the cold season but it also remains open in the summer and offers plenty of activities, like cabling your way up to **Passo dei Salati**, which connects the two regions. If you're looking for easy hiking options to take on with children, consider heading to the **Rifugio Pastore** at the Alpe Pile just off of Alagna or exploring the **Val Vogna**, which you can reach by car. If you're an expert mountaineer, however, look further up to the highest mountain refuge in Europe. That's the **Capanna Regina Margherita**, located over 4000m on top of Mount Rosa. There are several routes that lead there – all of them requiring significant preparation.

Cathedrals & Books

THE HIDDEN TREASURES OF VERCELLI

If you were a medieval pilgrim crossing the Alps from France, chances are one of your stops along the way would have been **Vercelli**, then a major hub along the Via Francigena connecting Canterbury to Apulia. Modern Vercelli still carries many

 WHERE TO SLEEP IN VERCELLI & VALSESIA

Il Giardinetto
A tiny hotel right in the centre of Vercelli, a few steps from the railway station. €€

Al Vicolo del Gallo
A handful of rooms located in a quiet and historic neighbourhood in Varallo. €€

MIRA Alagna Mountain Resort & SPA
For a luxurious stay with everything that the mountains can offer. €€€

traces of that past, starting from right outside the train station – the 13th-century **1 Basilica di Sant'Andrea** was one of the first examples of Gothic architecture that spread from beyond the Alps across Italy. Almost right next to it you'll find the **2 Duomo**, dedicated to the city's patron saint, Eusebio. The Duomo and its **3 museum** hold a whole array of precious artefacts, including two that are the unquestionable stars of the whole collection. The first is the massive 10th-century **crucifix** hanging within the Duomo itself, while the second is the so-called **Vercelli Book** of roughly the same period – one of the very few surviving manuscripts written in Old English, and one of only four poetic codices.

Continue your tour by going down **Via Galileo Ferraris** towards Vercelli's main square, **4 Piazza Cavour**, where the city market is held every Tuesday and Friday. You should also check out the little square just off Piazza Cavour, Piazza Palazzo Vecchio – known by locals as **5 Piazza dei Pesci** – and take some time to stroll up and down **6 Corso Libertà**, Vercelli's main avenue.

MOUNTAIN CULTURE

Around the 12th and 13th centuries, the Monte Rosa area saw the arrival and establishment of a Germanic people known as the Walser. In the years since, their culture and language have seeped into these mountains. The traditional Walser house, for example, with its wooden facade and pillars, has been reproduced thousands of times around Valsesia and you see it in every town or village you visit. You can learn more about the Walser at Alagna's own **Walser Museum**. Several locations around Alagna and the valley are also part of the 'wider' museum, with panels detailing how each site – such as a mill, an oven or a sawmill – was part of daily Walser life.

 GETTING AROUND

The best way of getting into Vercelli for a tour around the town is by train – with one stopping just a few minutes away from the town centre every hour. You can comfortably do your exploration on foot, keeping an eye out for the cobblestones in Piazza Cavour and the surrounding medieval streets. To head up into Valsesia you can rely on a car or on the single bus that travels from Vercelli to Alagna Valsesia each day, stopping at most towns and villages along the way.

Beyond Vercelli & Valsesia

Oropa
• Biella

● Vercelli

To experience even more scenes from the Piedmontese mountain life, all it takes is one slight change of valley – and climbing up towards Biella rather than Valsesia.

Biella is the textbook definition of 'small but fierce'. A relatively quiet town, its wool mills made it an economic powerhouse in the 19th century – a legacy that has been somewhat left behind today but not completely forgotten. Its elegant city centre is ideal for a tranquil day trip – but no visit can really be considered complete without moving to what's above Biella: the Santuario di Oropa. Much-beloved throughout this side of Piedmont, the sanctuary and its two churches dedicated to the Black Madonna of Oropa are an evergreen destination for a family Sunday outing – especially when you factor in the obligatory polenta stop around lunchtime at one of Oropa's historic restaurants.

TOP TIP

Reaching Biella from Vercelli is easiest with a car – the road goes pretty much straight on towards the mountains.

Santuario di Oropa

HNATENKO KOSTIANTYN/EYEEM/GETTY IMAGES ©

A Day Out in Biella and Oropa

WOOL, BANKS & MADONNAS

The historic town centre of Biella is divided into two separate areas – one above and one below. Start your visit in the *città bassa* at the **Cattedrale di Santo Stefano**, Biella's patron saint – and then continue in the surrounding streets, like **Via Italia** and **Via Duomo**, with their shops, porticoes and cobbled stones. If you're interested in fashion, check out the **Fondazione FILA Museum** – the brand was born in Biella and the town hosts an exhibition about its history and most famous pieces from the 1980s to today. When you decide it's time to move up to the *città alta*, known as **il Piazzo**, you have several options, but the most unique and fun one is the cable railway that will carry you up in minutes. Once in the Piazzo, spend some time wandering the twisty medieval streets lined with shops and cafes.

Less than 15km away from Biella you find the **Santuario di Oropa**, dedicated to the Black Virgin of Oropa. The sanctuary features two churches and a Sacro Monte, with 19 chapels in total. It's on the Unesco World Heritage list together with the one in Varallo. Before leaving the sanctuary, try *polenta concia* – polenta loaded up with different cheeses and more butter than you would find in other variants around Piedmont – at one of the local restaurants, such as **Ristorante Croce Bianca**.

FOLIAGE & VIEWS

Spreading across the mountains that surround Biella, the **Oasi Zegna** is a perfect destination – especially if you have a car – to spend time in nature, soaking in one alpine landscape after another. The best way to do so is to drive along the **Panoramica Zegna**, the road connecting Villanova Biellese to Bocchetto di Sessera, across the heart of the Oasi – plus, if your visit happens to be in autumn, you can catch some amazing foliage. And if the name rings a bell, that's because there is a connection between the Oasi Zegna and Ermenegildo Zegna of luxury clothing fame – the brand was founded in these valleys, and still operates from the Biella area.

Biella Mountains

GETTING AROUND

While there are trains connecting Vercelli and Biella – with one change in the middle – the best way to reach the town, as well as the Santuario di Oropa and the Oasi Zegna, is by car. The drive is particularly enjoyable too, especially on clear days as you'll see the mountains grow bigger and bigger on your approach.

ITALIAN RIVIERA

THE SONG OF THE SEA

The Italian Riviera is one of a kind – mountains coming to an abrupt stop and plunging into the sea, dotted by a long line of colourful cities and towns.

The region of Liguria presents itself as a half-moon, shouldered on one side by the mountains that separate it from Piedmont, and washed by the Mediterranean Sea on the other. This unique mix of natural elements has shaped the landscapes of the Italian Riviera, making them immediately recognisable.

Its beaches, alternating between sandy stretches and walls of rock that descend straight into the waves, have made it one of the country's most famous holiday destinations – the picturesque villages with handfuls of colourful houses and a delicious culinary tradition certainly help as well. Families that have been coming to Liguria for years are very faithful to their preferred town, but the entire region is ready to be explored from east to west and backwards to find what it is that you prefer best. The quiet relaxation of its westernmost towns and villages? The chic elegance of Portofino? The sights in the Cinque Terre? Or the rich history of cities like La Spezia and Savona?

At the centre of it all stands Genoa, one of the old maritime republics and one of the most important Mediterranean ports to this day – a beautifully charming place, from the *caruggi* (narrow streets) that crisscross the Porto Antico to the panoramic points that take in the whole city.

DAVE&AYIT/SHUTTERSTOCK ©

THE MAIN AREAS

GENOA	LA SPEZIA & LEVANTE	CINQUE TERRE	SAVONA & PONENTE	RIVIERA DEI FIORI
History-rich capital and main port. p196	Easternmost of the Ligurian cities and its Riviera. p206	World-famous, Unesco-worthy villages. p212	Historic city and its coast. p218	The last part of the Italian Riviera before France. p221

THE GUIDE

ITALIAN RIVIERA

OLENA ZNAK/SHUTTERSTOCK ©

Cattedrale di San Lorenzo, Genoa (p196)

Find Your Way

Liguria might seem small when you look at it on a map, but it holds a treasure trove of sights and locations to explore beyond the ones we have collected here.

PIEDMONT

Alessandria

Acqui Terme

Ova

Fossano

Cortemilia

Masone

Savona & Ponente, p218

Arrive in Savona, city of towers, fortresses and churches, then find your favourite beach on this sandy stretch of the Riviera.

Cairo
Montenotte

Millesimo

Carcare

Altare

Albissola
Marina

Vo

Arenzano

Varazze

Savona

Vado Ligure

Maritime Alps

PIEDMONT

Garessio

Punta Marguareis

Monte Galero

FRANCE

Nava

Monte Saccarello

Cima de Marte

Breil-sur-Roya

Pigna

LIGURIA

Spotorno

Noli

Varigotti

Finale Ligure

Ceriale

Loano

Borghetto San Spirito

Albenga

Alassio

Riviera di Ponente

Ligurian Sea

Cervo

Andora

San Lorenzo
al Mare

Diana Marina

Taggia

Imperia

San Remo

Arma di
Taggia

Ventimiglia

Ospedaletti

Menton

Bordighera

Riviera dei Fiori, p221

Take a breather in this last part of the Italian Riviera – one of the hubs of Italian pop culture – before reaching France.

Mediterranean Sea

192

N

0 ————— 50 km
0 ————— 25 miles

Genoa, p196

Explore Liguria's regional capital by getting lost in its *caruggi* and marvelling at the city centre's historic palaces.

La Spezia & Levante, p206

Enjoy an evening walk along La Spezia's *lungomare* (seafront promenade) and stop at the towns and villages on this side of the Riviera.

○ Bobbio

EMILIA-ROMAGNA

Arquata ○
Scrivia

○ Isola del
Cantone

○ Busalla

*Lago del
Brugneto*

Santo Stefano ○
d'Aveto

Torriglia ○

Borgo Val ○
di Taro

Pontremoli ●

Genoa ● Boccadasse

Nervi ● Recco ●

Camogli ○

Santa Margherita Ligure ●

Borzonasca ●

LIGURIA

Rapallo ●

○ Zoagli

Chiavari ●

○ Lavagna

Portofino ○

Varese ○
Ligure

Villafranca di ○
Lunigiana

*Golfo di Genova
(Gulf of Genoa)*

Sestri Levante ●

Moneglia ○

*Parco Nazionale delle
Cinque Terre*

Aulla ●

Santo Stefano ○
di Magra

Cinque Terre, p212

Step into a typical seaside village in this picture-postcard stretch of terraced coastline.

Riviera di Levante

Bonassola ○
Levento ○

Monterosso ●
al Mare

Riomaggiore ●

La Spezia ●

Sarzana ○

Lerici ○

Porto Venere ●

Isola Palmaria

Isola del Tino

Marina di ○
Carrara

CAR

Having a car means that you can move freely throughout the region, especially if you want to explore its inland towns and villages and not just stay on the coast. However, traffic and parking can be a nightmare, especially during high season.

BOAT

Exploring Liguria from the sea is definitely a way to make your trip all the more unforgettable. In almost all major cities you can find boat tours to explore that particular stretch of the Riviera – the best being the one that leaves for the Cinque Terre from La Spezia.

TRAIN

If you plan on sticking to the coast, relying on trains is a good option as *regionale* lines run through Liguria's main cities. The downside is that they can get crowded, particularly in the warmer months, and delays are always around the corner.

Plan Your Time

Liguria is not a place that inspires rushing – especially if you visit during the summer months. The heat only serves as one more reason to take everything slowly, from beach days to treks.

MAREN WINTER/SHUTTERSTOCK ©

La Spezia (p206)

If You Only Do One Thing

● If you're a city person, focus on **Genoa** (p196) and tour it all the way from its **Porto Antico** to the height of **Spianata Castelletto** – seeing the entire city spread out below you. If you're travelling with children, visit one of Europe's most famous aquariums, **Acquario di Genova** (p199).

● If you want to experience one of Liguria's most famous destinations, though, then it's the **Cinque Terre** (p212) – you can visit all five of the villages in one day, especially by train. Start from **Monterosso al Mare** (p212) or **Riomaggiore** (p216), depending on where you're staying.

Seasonal highlights

Summer rules in the Italian Riviera, with sun and crowds at an all-time high. The rest of the year, with milder weather and quieter streets, also makes for a lovely visit.

FEBRUARY

Italy comes to a standstill as Teatro Ariston's music **Festival di San Remo** goes on for five nights.

MAY

If you're in Genoa in May, visit some of the private **Rolli palaces** otherwise closed to the public.

JUNE

The streets of Sestri Levante are filled with **Andersen Premio + Festival** events, with music and theatre performances.

Five Days to Travel Around

● Visit both Genoa and the Cinque Terre, maybe dividing the latter into a couple of days so you have time to really enjoy each one – with a quick sunbathe and swim thrown in – before moving on to the next. Since you're already on the easternmost side of the region, stop at **Santa Margherita Ligure** and **Portofino** (p209) with their chic boutiques and gorgeous panoramas.

● Top off your stay by going almost all the way to the border with Tuscany and wander around the streets of **La Spezia** (p206), munching on focaccia as you go.

If You Have More Time

● As you've already seen most of the eastern side of of the region, return to Genoa and move to the other side. The first stop is **Savona** (p218), with its incredible **Fortezza del Priamàr**. From there, descend along the coast – stopping in towns like **Varazze**, **Alassio** or **Laigueglia** (p218) for a dip in the sea. Learn about the art of olive oil–making when you reach **Imperia** (p222). From there, you can either turn back towards Genoa or add a couple more days to visit **San Remo** (p223) and **Ventimiglia** (p223) at the border that separates Italy from France.

JULY	**AUGUST**	**SEPTEMBER**	**DECEMBER**
Stay in Sestri Levante to see the **Barcarolata**, a floating carnival that takes over the Baia del Silenzio.	La Spezia's neighbourhoods and surrounding villages race each other in the rowing competition called **Palio del Golfo**.	Monterosso al Mare celebrates the closing of anchovy season with salted anchovies at the **Sagra dell'Acciuga Salata**.	The hillside next to Manarola lights up with its annual **nativity scene**, a truly one-of-a-kind spectacle.

GENOA

Francesco Petrarca, 14th-century scholar and poet, famously described Genoa as La Superba, 'The Proud One' – a nickname that stuck and spread far and wide. Modern Genoa – one of the biggest cities in Italy and the country's major port – still carries the epithet with ease and a touch of melancholia for times long past. After all, it's not easy to forget almost eight centuries of being an independent republic dominating the Mediterranean. Beautifully complex and endlessly fascinating, like most port cities, Genoa is forever reminding you of its connection to the sea – you might not always see it but you'll always sense its presence, seeped into the stones that make up Genoa's elegant *palazzi* (mansions) and narrow alleys.

TOP TIP

The Genoa Tourism Office has several apps that you can download to orient yourself. Visit Genoa offers brief descriptions in Italian and English of all the city's major sights, and Palazzi dei Rolli Genova is dedicated to the Rolli palaces.

THE BEAUTY OF GENOA

Giorgia Losi, co-owner of the Trattoria dell'Acciughetta & Quelli dell'Acciughetta

Every visitor should have the experience of watching from the **Porto Antico** as Genoa comes to life with the dawn and goes to sleep with the sunset, with the scent of the sea and the hustle of the port. Genoa is a city where you can get lost in the woods in the morning, swim in the afternoon and relish in an evening *aperitivo*. My suggestion is to look around and not plan everything down to the minute, but let yourselves be carried by the moment.

A Walk Down to the Sea

FOUNTAINS, CHURCHES & COBBLED STREETS

Even though Genoa is one of the biggest cities in modern Italy, you can still easily move around its city centre on foot – especially when arriving by train at either of its two main railway stations, Piazza Principe and Brignole.

Start at **Piazza De Ferrari** with its massive bronze fountain. Once you've taken in the square and its imposing buildings, head to **Piazza Matteotti**, with **Chiesa dei Santi Ambrogio e Andrea** and **Palazzo Ducale**. Once the governing seat of the old Republic, the *palazzo* today is a magnificent location for exhibits and events. From Piazza Matteotti it's almost a straight line down to the sea, following the length of **Via San Lorenzo**. Stop at Genoa's cathedral, **Cattedrale di San Lorenzo**, with its unmissable facade painted in black and white stripes – unless there's scaffolding surrounding it for restoration works. Off Via San Lorenzo, you'll also see the typical Genovese *caruggi*, winding alleys with little sunlight and a whole lot of character. Exploring them is an adventure in and of itself, but remember that digital maps might not keep up with you as easily as they would on a main street. Once the narrow streets open up, you'll know you've reached the sea. You'll see the elevated Aurelia highway – passing through the entire Liguria coast as it connects Rome to Monaco – and beyond that, the buildings of the **Porto Antico**.

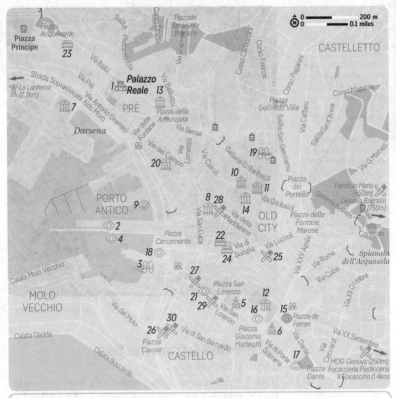

HIGHLIGHTS
1 Palazzo Reale

SIGHTS
2 Acquario
3 Bigo
4 Biosfera
5 Cattedrale di San Lorenzo
6 Chiesa del Gesù
7 Galata Museo del Mare
8 Galleria Nazionale di Palazzo Spinola
9 Il Galeone Neptune
10 Palazzo Bianco
11 Palazzo Doria-Tursi
12 Palazzo Ducale
13 Palazzo Durazzo Pallavicini
14 Palazzo Rosso
15 Piazza de Ferrari
16 Piazza Giacomo Matteotti
17 Porta Soprana
18 Porto Antico
19 Spianata Castelletto
20 Via Del Campo

SLEEPING
22 Le Nuvole
23 Ostello Bello
24 Palazzo Grillo

29 Rosso
21 Via San Lorenzo

EATING
25 Antico Forno della Casana
26 Cavour modo 21
27 Focaccia e Dintorni
28 Panificio E Grissineria Claretta Snc
29 Pizzeria Focacceria E Kebab Canneto
30 Trattoria delle Grazie

WHERE TO EAT IN GENOA

Cavour 21
Very close to Genoa's Porto Antico, this is the perfect stop to try traditional cuisine. €

Trattoria dell Grazie
Small and lively, hidden in Genoa's *caruggi* that descend down to the Porto Antico. €

MOG Genova
This eatery sits in the heart of the Mercato Orientale, Genoa's indoor farmers market. €€

YO HO HO!

As you stroll along the waterfront at the Porto Antico you might notice what looks like a pirate ship. And in fact, in some ways, it really is. Built in the 1980s as the reproduction of a 17th-century vessel, the **Neptune** was used for films and television shows for a while – including for Roman Polanski's 1986 *Pirates*. The vessel was even sailed all the way to Cannes to promote the film at that year's festival. It's now anchored in Genoa's Porto Antico as a tourist attraction – one that is particularly delightful for children going through their 'I'll be a pirate captain when I grow up' phase!

Acquario di Genova

By the Sea & from the Sea

SIGHTS ABOVE & BELOW

During the height of Genoa's power as a maritime republic, the area that we know today as the **Porto Antico** was simply the port. After a period of disuse, the Porto Antico was completely restored in the 1990s, becoming the activities-filled area that it is today. You'll immediately notice the **Bigo** – a white structure designed by architect Renzo Piano to look like the cranes used to load and unload cargo ships. One of the Bigo's 'arms' features a panoramic lift, which can take you up 40m for a breathtaking view of the city. Or you can get above street level by taking the lift inside the Eataly building.

PANORAMIC VIEWS

There are plenty of spots where you can see Genoa from above, like the **Spianata Castelletto** and the **Lanterna** (p200).

🍴 WHERE TO GET FOCACCIA IN GENOA

Focaccia e Dintorni
One of the most beloved *focaccerie* in Genoa, not too far from the Porto Antico. €

Focacceria Pasticceria Il Focaccino
The perfect focaccia stop in Genoa city centre. €

Panificio Mario
Excellent focaccia not far from Genova Brignole railway station. €

Another unmissable feature of the Porto Antico is the **Biosfera**, a sphere suspended on the water, which contains a reproduction of an Amazonian environment with its typical flora and fauna. And next to it is the **Acquario di Genova** – to which the Biosfera is connected when it comes to access and tickets. The aquarium is one of the largest in Europe and a destination loved by everyone, especially families with children. After a short walk from the aquarium along the waterfront you'll find the **Galata Museo del Mare**, a museum dedicated to the Mediterranean, its history and the art of sailing it.

Scenes of Genovese Life

SHOPPING STREETS, MUSEUMS & MUSICIANS

If you want to dedicate some time in Genoa to shopping, then check out **Via XX Settembre** – one of the main arteries that open up from Piazza De Ferrari. Covered in porticoes, it's an excellent solution for rainy days and it's also lined with beautiful buildings so don't forget to look up as you walk along! The street is crossed by an impressive **Ponte Monumentale**, which leads to the relatively small **Chiesa di Santo Stefano**. On the other side of the bridge you can deviate from Via XX Settembre to take the quieter **Via San Vincenzo** – and then take a rest on the little corner between Via San Vincenzo and Via Colombo. Yes, that Colombo. Christopher Columbus was a Genoa native, after all, and several streets bear his name – you can also visit the house in which he lived, which has of course been turned into a museum. It's located around **Piazza Dante** – itself pretty close to Piazza De Ferrari – in what feels like a small alcove that has come to us all the way from the Middle Ages, surviving the many waves of urban replanning that have changed Genoa's face over the centuries. Around Columbus' house, you can see what remains of **Porta Soprana**, a fortification that the Genovese built to defend themselves from an attack by Frederick Barbarossa that never came.

The Pride of La Superba

EXPLORING THE ROLLI PALACES

The **Rolli palaces** are without doubt a highlight of any visit to Genoa. They used to be the residences of nobles and other important people during the age of the Republic and

WATCH OUT FOR THE WINDOWS

If you look up and really take in the various facades on Genoa's residential buildings and the like, you might notice that some windows look real, but they're actually painted on in a wonderful *trompe l'oeil* effect. The reason is quite simple – it's all a matter of taxes. In the 18th century, the Genoa Republic introduced a new tax on windows to replenish its coffers, meaning that the more windows you had, the more you had to pay. So several people decided to wall up some of their windows to avoid the extra tax. You'll also find this in other spots around Liguria beyond Genoa.

Antico Forno della Casana
As you lose yourself in the maze of Genoa's *caruggi*, stop here for a bite of focaccia. €

Panificio Claretta
Focaccia with a twist as you descend down to the Porto Antico. €

Focacceria Via San Lorenzo
A quick snack just a couple of steps away from the Duomo. €

were included in lists, known as '*rolli*'. These palaces survived everything that the following centuries threw at them, and became a Unesco World Heritage Site in 2006, together with the Strade Nuove street system where most of them are located. Not all of the Rolli palaces are open to the public, but among those that are, there are three that you should definitely visit.

Start with **Palazzo Rosso** and **Palazzo Bianco**, opposite each other on Via Garibaldi and easily recognisable by the respective colours of their facades – red and white. They each house a section of the **Museo di Strada Nuova**, as does the third palace, **Palazzo Doria-Tursi**, also located on Via Garibaldi. Check out Palazzo Doria-Tursi's **Sala Paganiniana**, dedicated to a notable Genoa native, the violinist Niccolò Paganini. One of his violins – known as 'Il Cannone', 'the cannon', due to its powerful sound – is on display inside Palazzo Doria-Tursi. The palace also serves as the city hall of Genoa, so you'll see plenty of people milling around on weekdays. Other Rolli palaces open to the public are the **Palazzo Reale** and **Palazzo Spinola di Pellicceria**, which both host art galleries within their incredible interiors.

Seagull's-Eye View

GENOA FROM ABOVE

Descending down to the waterfront seems like the most natural choice whenever you're in a city like Genoa, where the sea endlessly calls to you from every street corner. But you shouldn't overlook going in the opposite direction – the higher you rise, the more breathtaking the view gets. And that's why the **Spianata Castelletto** is so beloved by locals and tourists alike – the way the city opens up under its balcony is pretty much the best of the best. To reach it you can either climb up on foot, following the streets that twist up from the city centre, or take the dedicated lift – the ticket is the same as for Genoa's other public transport. If you can't resist the siren song of the sea, though, then there's the **Lanterna** – Genoa's famous lighthouse turned iconic symbol, still fully functioning even though it was built smack in the middle of the Renaissance. Opening hours change depending on the

---

OPEN DOORS FOR EVERYBODY!

Many Rolli palaces are still private and used for the most disparate activities, meaning that they're usually closed to the public. However, that doesn't mean seeing their interiors is completely impossible – that's what the **Rolli Days** are for. Usually two times each year – around mid-May and mid-October – the city of Genoa organises a weekend where many of the Rolli palaces open their doors to visitors with guided tours. The programme of the Rolli Days is also usually rich with events, both digital and in-person.

LIGURIA IN MUSIC

Luigi Tenco is the person in whose honour San Remo holds the annual Premio Tenco, another one of the town's music events after the **Festival di San Remo** (p223).

(p223)

🛏 WHERE TO SLEEP IN GENOA

Palazzo Grillo
Incredibly close to the Porto Antico, relax and rest inside one of Genoa's famous Rolli palaces. €€€

Hotel Le Nuvole
A small and comfortable hotel located inside a historic building. €€

Ostello Bello
The Genovese headquarters of this hostel chain, with colourful vibes to spare. €

Spianata Castelletto

THE SCUOLA GENOVESE

During the 1960s, Genoa saw a new musical wave forming in its streets – the so-called *scuola genovese*, made up of singer-songwriters who are now icons of Italian music like Fabrizio De André, Gino Paoli and Luigi Tenco. You can explore their history and legacy at the museum **Via del Campo 29 rosso** – a name that all Fabrizio De Andrè listeners will recognise since it was immortalised by him in his song 'Via del Campo'.

season and weather conditions, so it's always a good idea to check ahead. The almost 200 steps are definitely worth it once you finally get to look out over the city and the sea opening up in front of it.

GETTING AROUND

You can easily walk around Genoa's city centre – but always remember to wear comfortable shoes since the streets go up and down depending on whether you're going towards the sea or away from it. Keep in mind also that some of the narrowest *caruggi* might not be well lit at night.

Beyond Genoa

Whether by the shore or on the mountains, the wider Genoa area has plenty of options for a day trip out.

Isola del
Cantone

Busalla

Acquasanta   Sant'Olcese

Vesima   Boccadasse

Genoa   Nervi

The area beyond Genoa proper is rich in activities that fully embrace what is unique about Liguria as a whole – being a very narrow strip of land where mountains and sea are impossibly close. Take a day to explore the *borghi marinari* that surround Liguria's regional capital – coastal villages where tall, brightly coloured houses pile upon each other as the sea wind beats on their windows. Or head inland, to explore the valleys that separate Liguria from Piedmont. All without forgetting to start each day with the typical Ligurian breakfast – a cup of cappuccino and some freshly baked focaccia. A break from the Italian tradition of breakfast being an exclusively sweet affair.

TOP TIP

A car is great for inland Genoa; you can get to the *borghi marinari* on foot or by public transport.

Boccadasse

SEAN PAVONE/SHUTTERSTOCK ©

Passeggiata Anita Garibaldi, Nervi

Genoa's Little Siblings

EXPLORING THE BORGHI MARINARI

Several hamlets surround Genoa. Though they are part of the city, each has its own character and can make for a perfect day excursion. Moving eastwards via bus or by walking along the *lungomare* (seafront promenade), you'll first reach **Boccadasse**, much-beloved by all *genovesi*. It is almost 4km from the city centre, though, so wear comfortable shoes and lather up with sunscreen. Once there, spend some time wandering its narrow alleys before laying down your towel at its tiny beach – or at one of the many beach clubs that dot the way from Genoa.

Further east is **Nervi**, which you can easily reach via train from Piazza Principe or Brignole – its greatest attraction is the **Passeggiata Anita Garibaldi**, a long walk where you'll be surrounded by nothing but sea and the deafening sound of cicadas. There's no beach, but you can lie on the rocks and dive into the sea at one of the equipped resorts or by carefully climbing down on your own.

On the other side of Genoa, moving westwards, is **Vesima** – another beach particularly well-loved by the locals,

BEST LIGURIAN MEALS

Focaccia
The famous Ligurian focaccia is incredibly simple to make – just take flour, water, salt and yeast. Don't forget to try out one of its many variants, such as *focaccia di Recco*, with a layer of soft cheese between two focaccia slices.

Farinata
Farinata is made with chickpea flour and is flatter and crunchier than focaccia, but still an excellent option for a lunch or a mid-afternoon snack.

Pesto (with trofie)
Made by grinding together basil leaves, pine nuts, olive oil and sometimes garlic, you can enjoy pesto on all kinds of pasta – but you'll find it most often paired with spiral-shaped *trofie*.

WHERE TO EAT OUTSIDE OF GENOA

Trattoria La Ruota
Located a few minutes from Nervi's railway station, with a wide selection of wines. €€

Matamà
A good option if you want to switch it up and indulge in some meat while in Nervi. €€

Trattoria Osvaldo
An excellent seafood stop, a few steps up from Boccadasse's beach. €€

THE PELAGOS SANCTUARY

The area of the Mediterranean Sea that opens up in front of Liguria, reaching towards the French Riviera on one side and Tuscany on the other, is part of the **Pelagos Cetacean Sanctuary** – a natural reserve aimed at protecting marine fauna that's particularly lively in this area. Several whale- and dolphin-watching tours leave daily – especially in the summer – from the Porto Antico in Genoa and take you out to the open sea for the chance of catching a glimpse of a tail flicking out from the water. Tours usually last four hours or more – of course, whether or not you'll end up seeing some of these magnificent animals in their natural habitat also comes down to luck.

FABIO LOTTI/SHUTTERSTOCK ©

Castello della Pietra

reachable by train during the summer months. Vesima also hosts the headquarters of the **Fondazione Renzo Piano**, located inside the sprawling Villa Nave.

A Trip Inland

UP & DOWN THE VALLE SCRIVIA

When the *genovesi* want to get out of the city for a weekend of rest and relaxation, many of them choose to head up into Valle Scrivia – the valley that opens up around the creek of the same name, descending from Asti and Alessandria in Piedmont towards the Mediterranean. As you leave the city behind – by car would be best – a myriad of small towns and villages appear for a day out that you wouldn't expect while holidaying in a renowned seaside location. Try **Sant'Olcese**, with the famous 18th-century **Villa Serra** and its sprawling public park. Or **Isola del Cantone**, where you can get your hiking shoes on to reach the picturesque 13th-century **Castello della Pietra** – locked between two rock spurs and seemingly having popped out of a fantasy book. The trek from Isola del Cantone isn't particularly long or difficult, though you should have the proper equipment to take

 WHERE TO EAT OUTSIDE OF GENOA

La Gabbianella e il Matto
A small eatery not far from Boccadasse's iconic bay. €€

Antica Trattoria Semino
Local cuisine located right on Busalla's main street. €€

La Morona
A typical *agriturismo* (farm-stay accommodation) in the mountains of Sant'Olcese. €€

it on. If you want to make your ascent to the castle slower and more picturesque, approach it from the hamlet of **Torre**, where the 4km-long **Sentiero dei Castellani** starts before stretching out into the woods. Finally, head to **Busalla** for a walk through its many churches and elegant villas.

Sanctuaries & Paper

THE TREASURES OF ACQUASANTA

The village of **Acquasanta** might seem like just one of many that dot the slopes leading down towards Genoa and the sea, but it holds two particular sights that make it a unique destination for a day out. The first is a trace of old artisan traditions – the **Museo della Carta di Mele**, an exhibition dedicated entirely to the art of papermaking. Its exhibition covers all steps in the process of turning old scraps of paper and natural fibres into shiny new paper – and you can also add a papermaking class at the end of your tour. Remember to book your visit in advance before arriving in Acquasanta. Once you've learned all the secrets of making paper, you can move on to the **Santuario di Nostra Signora dell'Acquasanta** – a baroque sanctuary where you can enjoy the overall quiet of this small hamlet.

The best way to reach both the Museo della Carta and the Santuario di Nostra Signora dell'Acquasanta is by car, of course, just a short half-hour drive from Genoa. You can also rely on public transport, with an equally long train ride from either one of Genoa's main stations to the Genova Acquasanta stop – both the sanctuary and the museum are within walking distance of the station.

THE VALLEY OF ROSES

The Valle Scrivia, and the village of **Busalla** in particular, are well-known for their roses. And they're not just decorative flowers here – they are actually part of the local culinary traditions. Roses are turned into rose syrup – a liquid that can be used in a thousand and one different ways, from a sweetener for one's tea to a fresh summer *aperitivo* diluted with water. The **Le Rose della Valle Scrivia** association presides over this traditional delight – and celebrates it at the annual **Festa delle Rose**, which takes place in Busalla every June.

SAILING ADVENTURES

If you want to spend more time at sea, you can visit the **Cinque Terre** (p212) by ferry or sail from Portovenere to the island of **Palmaria** (p211).

GETTING AROUND

Having a car becomes increasingly useful the further away from Genoa you get. To visit the villages of the Valle Scrivia, a car is pretty much a must-have, while you can get around using trains and buses if you stay closer to Genoa city centre – and in some cases, like Boccadasse, you can even rely on just your feet.

LA SPEZIA & LEVANTE

Of the two Rivieras into which Liguria is traditionally divided, the Riviera di Levante is the one that extends from Genoa all the way to the border with Tuscany. It boasts an air of somewhat-chic elegance when compared to its opposite, what with its star-studded destinations like Portofino and Porto Venere and its Unesco World Heritage Cinque Terre. In the end, though, both Rivieras are essentially Ligurian and you can clearly see it as you move through the Levante's towns and villages, or even just when taking a stroll along one beach or the other – this is what Liguria is all about. Mountains falling into the sea, colourful houses, clear waters and stunning cuisine.

La Spezia & Levante

Rome

TOP TIP

The seabed between Camogli and Portofino is home to the Cristo degli Abissi, a statue representing Jesus Christ lying 17m under the sea. It's a favoured sight for scuba divers but should, of course, only be taken while supervised by certified Regione Liguria guides.

SIGHTS

1 Baia del Silenzio
2 Baia delle Favole
3 Basilica Santa Maria di Nazareth
4 Biblioteca Comunale Fascie-Rossi
5 Castello Brown
6 Castello di San Giorgio
7 Chiesa del Divo Martino
8 Chiesa di San Nicolò dell'Isola
9 Giardini Pubblici
10 Museo Tecnico Navale della Spezia
11 Nostra Signora della Rosa
12 Villa Durazzo

BORIS STROUJKO/SHUTTERSTOCK ©

Baia del Silenzio

Between Two Seas

A STOP IN SESTRI LEVANTE

Halfway between Santa Margherita Ligure and La Spezia, the town of **Sestri Levante** lies quietly stretching into a small isthmus. The isthmus helps to create two separate bays, or 'two seas' as the locals have nicknamed them. On the La Spezia side you'll find the smaller and picturesque **Baia del Silenzio**, the 'bay of silence'. On the side towards Santa Margherita Ligure lies the **Baia delle Favole**, the 'bay of fairy tales' – the name is a homage to the Danish writer Hans Christian Andersen after his stay in Sestri Levante. Both include free areas as well as those equipped with facilities and resorts – keep in mind that they're very popular during the high season, so you should get there early to snag your place for the day. Once you tire of sunbathing, head back to the *lungomare* for a nice relaxing stroll, taking in both the waves and the facades of the houses that line the waterfront. Or you can explore Sestri Levante's centre, including the **Palazzo Durazzo-Pallavicini** – the town hall – and the **Palazzo Fascie Rossi**, which hosts the town's archaeological museum,

FILL YOUR DAYS IN SESTRI LEVANTE

Summer days are long in Liguria, and with plenty of things to do – Sestri Levante is no exception, so here are some events to check out if you happen to be in town.

Andersen Premio + Festival
Dedicated to the memory of Hans Christian Andersen, the Andersen Festival with its street performances and live music takes place at the beginning of June.

Barcarolata
On the last Sunday in July, a float of boats decked out in extravagant papier-mâché decorations takes over the Baia del Silenzio. At the end of the Barcarolata, there's a prize for the most creative decorations of all.

 WHERE TO EAT IN LA SPEZIA & LEVANTE

All'Inferno dal 1905
Simple traditional meals just a few steps away from the La Spezia *lungomare*. €€

Da I Gemelli
Serving up seafood and other local delights in Portofino's main square. €€€

Balin
An intimate and luxury dinner in a small restaurant on Sestri Levante's *lungomare*. €€€

ROW, ROW, ROW!

If you're in La Spezia at the beginning of August, be sure to secure a spot on the *lungomare* on the first Sunday of the month to cheer on the boats sailing by during the **Palio del Golfo** – a rowing competition between 13 *borgate* (neighbourhoods) in both La Spezia and delegations from the surrounding towns and villages. The Palio schedule is packed with events, including a nighttime parade of all *borgate* gathering to prepare for the race, a fireworks show once the Palio has been run, and a victory celebration the day immediately after.

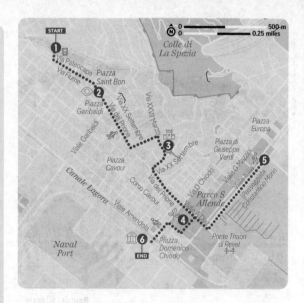

as well as the **Basilica di Santa Maria di Nazareth** and the **Chiesa di San Nicolò nell'Isola**, the oldest church in all of Sestri Levante.

Castles & a Naval Base

WALKING AROUND LA SPEZIA

La Spezia is the second biggest city in Liguria, as well as the main centre of the Riviera di Levante, so it's a great base from which to tour the many surrounding towns and villages, from Porto Venere to the Cinque Terre. And while La Spezia's city centre is relatively small, it still deserves a visit – set aside a day or an afternoon.

From its main railway station, **1 La Spezia Centrale**, head towards **2 Via Fiume** – an almost entirely pedestrianised street that brings you down to the waterfront. You can delay your descent to the sea by going up to visit **3 Castello di San Giorgio**, which hosts an archaeological museum and offers breathtaking views over the city and its ships. **4 Giardini Pubblici** is the last stop before you'll finally see the sea and the white spires of the Thaon Di Ravel bridge, leading further down the marina. The **5 Passeggiata Miorin** – whose beginning is marked by La Spezia's

---

 WHERE TO SLEEP IN LA SPEZIA & LEVANTE

Albergo delle Spezie
Near the La Spezia harbour, this hotel keeps a careful eye on sustainability. €€

La Collina degli Ulivi
Just outside the La Spezia city centre, surrounded by greenery and quiet. €€

Hotel Cenobio dei Dogi
One of the most famous hotels in Camogli for the ultimate relaxing stay. €€€

own Little Mermaid statue – is nice in the evening. Along the seafront, you'll also find the **6 Museo Tecnico Navale**, dedicated to the art of sailing and property of the Italian Navy. You'll be able to see the Navy ships at anchor beyond the museum as La Spezia is one of only three places in Italy – together with Augusta in Sicily and Taranto in Apulia – that still has an active naval base.

The Chic Side of Levante

SANTA MARGHERITA LIGURE & PORTOFINO

As you move along the Levante coast – whether by train or car – you can't miss a stop at **Santa Margherita Ligure**, one of the Riviera's summer hot spots looking right out onto the Tigullio Gulf. Its sunny *lungomare* is the perfect spot for a romantic stroll, but don't forget to dive into its town centre as well – explore with your eyes turned upwards to appreciate the decorated facades on the houses lining the streets. But watch where you're going, as the cobblestones are unforgiving. Visit Santa Margherita's main church, the **Basilica di Santa Margherita e Santuario di Nostra Signora della Rosa**, as well as **Villa Durazzo** with its beautiful gardens overlooking the sea.

It's a short bus or ferry ride from Santa Margherita Ligure to one of Liguria's most famous and elegant destinations, **Portofino** – with its small and quaint waterfront **Piazzetta Portofino** and its massive yachts hanging out in the bay. There are no fixed routes when exploring Portofino, and you'll find something to swoon over wherever your feet take you – from the polished windows of high-end shops to centuries-old sights. Don't miss out on the **Chiesa Parrocchiale del Divo Martino**, two ramps higher than the water level, and the **Castello Brown**, higher up still above the marina – reaching it is a bit of a trek, especially in hot weather, but the view at the end is stunning.

BETWEEN SANTA MARGHERITA LIGURE & PORTOFINO

If you decide to go to Portofino by bus – tickets can be purchased at ticket offices in Santa Margherita or directly on board by tapping your credit card – you'll stop at several small, idyllic beaches along the way. The most famous of these, dotting the so-called 'dolphin coast', is **Paraggi** – get here early in the day if you want to grab a spot in the sun. Paraggi is also the midway point of the hiking trails that connect Santa Margherita and Portofino, including the famous *passeggiata dei baci*.

SEASIDE CHARM

While Portofino and Santa Margherita have become synonymous with star-studded fame, **Alassio** (p218) is more than capable of holding its own with its famous Muretto – signed by wave after wave of celebrities on holiday.

GETTING AROUND

Reaching La Spezia from Genoa is incredibly easy – the trip by train only requires one change in Sestri Levante, but it might become an exercise in patience if the *regionale* lines start amassing delays.

Camogli • • • Rapallo
Zoagli • Chiavari
La Spezia
Leric
Portovenere •
Palmaria Tel

Beyond La Spezia

You're spoiled for choice with the towns and villages along the Riviera di Levante – all could be the perfect place for your dream holiday.

You can't go with the Riviera di Levante, especially if what you're looking for is sea and sun. Every single town and village dotting the Genoa–La Spezia railway line has plenty of both to offer. You could sprawl out on a different beach each day, living the typical summer routine of every seaside holiday – lying under your beach umbrella, lazy lunches and even lazier *aperitivi*, and sunsets over the sea as the day draws to a close. And let's not forget the historic little town centres, with picturesque details waiting at every corner.

TOP TIP

Moving around by car comes with its difficulties – namely traffic, especially in the high season, and almost impossible-to-find parking.

Lerici

ARKANTO/SHUTTERSTOCK ©

RENATAMACIEL/SHUTTERSTOCK ©

Castello della Dragonara, Camogli

Exploring the Riviera di Levante

FROM CAMOGLI TO LERICI

Coming down from Genoa, your first stop may be **Camogli** – with its multicoloured houses overlooking the waterfront under what used to be the watchful eye of the **Castello della Dragonara**. If you're around in mid-May, swing by the local **Sagra del Pesce**, where fish is fried in a massive pan over 3m wide. The night before the Sagra, two massive bonfires are lit on the beach for the **Festa di San Fortunato**.

As you move along the coast, you'll find **Rapallo**, **Zoagli** and **Chiavari** – stop for a swim, visit the town centre of Rapallo with its entry doors and catch sight of the lookout towers of Zoagli and the Castello di Chiavari, located not too high above the town itself. Close to the Tuscan border, there's **Lerici**, a hot spot for the summer holidays of several generations of English writers – Lord Byron, the Shelleys, Charles Dickens and Virginia Woolf, to name a few. They all passed through Lerici – Percy Shelley drowned as he was returning to Lerici from Livorno – and the town is dotted with panels collecting their thoughts and poems written as they were staring out at the **Golfo dei Poeti**, the 'gulf of the poets'. When you're in Lerici, check out its hamlet **Tellaro**, another perfect example of a *borgo marinaro*.

A PORT & ITS ISLANDS

South of La Spezia you'll find the town of **Portovenere**, which can be reached by both ferry and bus – the smallest town in the entire La Spezia province, it's a gorgeous *borgo marinaro* with narrow, brightly painted houses and a stunning sea. Once you're there you can continue by sea to reach the Cinque Terre or visit one of the islands that, together with Portovenere itself, were declared a Unesco World Heritage Site in 1997. The islands are **Palmaria**, **Tino** and **Tinetto**, with Palmaria being the closest to shore and also the only one open to visitors as Tino and Tinetto are under the direct control of the Italian Navy.

GETTING AROUND

A good way of exploring the various towns and villages that dot the coast in the province of La Spezia is by getting on one of the many boat tours that leave from its harbour – always check the timetables in advance and keep an eye on the weather, which can make your trip marvellous or cancel it altogether.

CINQUE TERRE

Cinque Terre

✪ Rome

Dotting the jagged Riviera di Levante not too far from La Spezia, these five villages and their twisty streets, brightly coloured houses and picturesque bays have gained massive popularity over the last few decades. A Unesco World Heritage Site since 1997, the Cinque Terre – consisting of Monterosso al Mare, Vernazza, Corniglia, Manarola and Riomaggiore – boast that typical Ligurian charm. Sun-baked and swept by the salt coming up from the sea, they have been an inspiration for artists of all kinds – think Pixar's *Luca*, set in what is undeniably a fictional version of the Cinque Terre.

TOP TIP

Check out the two options for the Cinque Terre Card – opt for the Trekking Card if you'll hike through the villages, and the Treno MS Card if travelling by train. Valid for one, two or three days, the card can only be used by the person whose name appears on it.

LOCAL WINES

No matter where you go in Italy, you're bound to find a local wine to accompany your meals. The Cinque Terre is no exception – the terraces all around the five villages produce the grapes that will become *Cinque Terre DOC* white wines, including the famous Sciacchetrà. Remember to take a sip of this sweet, *passito* wine – perfect for cheese platters and desserts – before you leave the Cinque Terre behind.

Beaches & Sea Gods

EXPLORING MONTEROSSO AL MARE

Monterosso al Mare – or simply **Monterosso** – is the most populated of the Cinque Terre villages and also the westernmost of the five, meaning that it's the first one you'll arrive at from Genoa. If your plan includes some time sunbathing, then Monterosso is definitely the one for you – its beach stretches out further than its neighbours, with both free and equipped areas that allow you to find space for yourself without stepping over anyone. Still, especially during the high season, it's always useful to keep in mind that the early bird really does get the worm – or the spot on the beach, in this case. Once you've soaked up your fair share of sun and waves, take a break and walk up and down the *lungomare* – which leads to something unique to see in both directions. Towards Genoa you'll find the famous **Gigante statue**, jutting out from a rock spur and dating back to the early 20th century. On the La Spezia side lies Monterosso town centre proper – take some time to wander through its streets and look up at the **Chiesa di San Giovanni Battista**, striped black and white. You can also climb up to the **Convento dei Cappuccini**, looking out onto the sea – check if there are any guided tours scheduled.

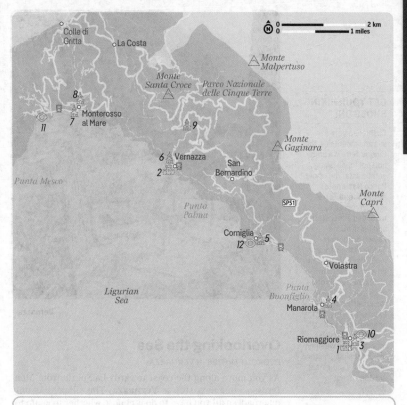

SIGHTS

1 Castello di Riomaggiore

2 Castello Doria

3 Chiesa di San Giovanni Battista

4 Chiesa di San Lorenzo

5 Chiesa di San Pietro

6 Chiesa di Santa Margherita d'Antiochia

7 Convento dei Cappuccini

8 Parrocchia di San Giovanni Battista

9 Santuario di Nostra Signora di Reggio

10 Scalinata della Valle

11 Statua del Gigante

12 Viewpoint

 WHERE TO EAT IN THE CINQUE TERRE

Kepris Pizzeria
Located in a tiny alley in Riomaggiore, serving up a huge variety of pizzas. €

Da Aristide
In a very central location in Manarola, with all kinds of fish. €€

Cappun Magru
The go-to spot to try *cappon magro*, a traditional dish made of fish and vegetables, in Manarola. €€

DUDAREV MIKHAIL/SHUTTERSTOCK ©

Vernazza

Overlooking the Sea

LOOKOUT DUTIES IN VERNAZZA

As you move along the coast towards La Spezia from Monterosso, your next stop is **Vernazza**. The village has only one road, so all you have to do is choose whether to go up towards the mountains or down towards the marina – this is common for all of the Cinque Terre, but Vernazza has made things easier by concentrating its sights down at sea level. Once you reach Vernazza's little bay, you can either stop on its free, mostly sandy beach for a dive into the waves or explore around the waterfront. The main church, **Chiesa di Santa Margherita d'Antiochia**, occupies one side of the harbour – built in brick-heavy Romanesque style, its windows open up onto the sea and make for quite a sight.

 WHERE TO EAT IN THE CINQUE TERRE

La Posada Ristorante
Featuring a quiet *belvedere*
(viewpoint) over the sea
– a good spot to rest and
recuperate in Corniglia. €€

Belforte
Its terraces are dotted along
the rock spurs that look out
over the sea in Vernazza. €€

La Cantina di Miky
A fresh seafood stop in
Monterosso, with a *belvedere*
opening up onto the sea. €€

On the opposite side of the bay from the church lies the **Castello Doria** with its lookout tower – its shape adapts to the rock spur on which it is built, making it a peculiarly irregular building. The climb up to the castle might not sound appealing if the sun is beating down, but the view you get once you reach the top is more than worth it. If you're in the mood for hiking, you can take on the 2km-long trail that leads from the train station to the **Santuario di Nostra Signora di Reggio**, where the sea peeks out from between the trees.

The Midway Point

HIGH UP IN CORNIGLIA

Corniglia is unique among the Cinque Terre in more ways than one – for starters, reaching Corniglia will mean that you're halfway through your trip, no matter which direction you're travelling in. And then, of course, there's the fact that it's the only one of the five Cinque Terre villages to not be at sea level but high up on a cliff – you'll experience a dramatic decrease in swimming time but an equal increase in breathtaking views. Because of its location, Corniglia is the only village you can't reach by ferry – once you get out of the railway station, you can either walk up to the town centre or wait for the shuttle bus running between the two. The Cinque Terre Treno MS Card is valid for the shuttle as well, but plan for some time spent queuing before you can actually get on.

Once in Corniglia proper, you can get lost in the crisscrossing narrow streets, following the scent of the sea – without being distracted by gelatos and fried fish – until you reach the **panoramic terrace** of Santa Maria. From there, you can spot the other villages on both sides as well as boats gliding by. Corniglia's **church**, dedicated to St Peter, is on the opposite side of the *belvedere* – not too far from the shuttle drop-off point.

 WHERE TO SLEEP IN THE CINQUE TERRE

Hotel Marina Piccola
This tiny Manarola hotel includes several rooms with sea-facing windows and balconies. €€€

Hotel Gianni Franzi
This tiny hotel hasromantic sea views over the Vernazza bay. €€

Albergo Hotel Porto Roca
On a vantage point above Monterosso, this luxury hotel features a pool for the ultimate relaxation. €€€

Textbook Cinque Terre

THE COLOURS OF MANAROLA

Arriving in **Manarola** from the sea is the best way to get to one of the most iconic and most photographed Cinque Terre sights – narrow, colourful houses huddling together along the waterfront and on top of rock spurs as if the whole village is moments away from tumbling into the water. And beyond the village, a panorama of terraced cultivations – especially vineyards for the famed local Sciacchetrà wine – line the entire mountainside.

The way to go about exploring the village, though, is the same whether you sail in or get off the train – start by climbing up towards Manarola's high point, marked by the **Chiesa di San Lorenzo** and its bell tower. Then take your time descending back down to the marina, with shops and eateries dotting both sides of the streets. You will find yourself returning to the waterfront and its balustrade looking out onto the sea, but make sure you also set some time aside to just get lost in the streets and alleys. A picturesque sight may be waiting behind every corner, and panoramic roads open up to lead you above the village for a stunning view across Manarola.

The Easternmost Tip

FINISHING UP IN RIOMAGGIORE

Of all the Cinque Terre villages, **Riomaggiore** is the closest to La Spezia and the border with Tuscany. Keep in mind that if you arrive by train, you'll have to take an underground tunnel to reach Riomaggiore town centre proper. Once you're there, the layout in Riomaggiore is pretty similar to that of Manarola – which makes sense, considering that the latter is technically a hamlet of Riomaggiore. The village's main road can take you down towards the marina – where you can book a boat tour on the fly or simply soak in the sun and the waves from the panoramic street that lines the waterfront. Or if you instead decide to climb up – something that is bound to happen in all of the Cinque Terre, so you'd better bring comfortable shoes even if you're not here to do any proper hiking – take the **Scalinata della Valle** and get lost in the narrow

---

CHRISTMAS LIGHTS

It's true that the Cinque Terre village shine the brightest during the warmer months and that they're the perfect location for a dream summer holiday – but the low season has some aces up its sleeve that might make a trip to the area even more special. And one of these aces is the **nativity scene** that springs up above Manarola during Christmas time. Everything, from the buildings to the people who populate the Nativity scene, is made up of thousands of lights strung up on homemade frames. It's the largest of its kind in the world, with the lights clearly visible from the sea.

 WHERE TO SNACK IN THE CINQUE TERRE

Alberto Gelateria
Located in Corniglia's main street, leading to the village's *belvedere* on the sea. €

MIVÀ
Perfect for a quick pizza and all things fried stop in Riomaggiore. €

Gelateria Il Porticciolo
Refreshing gelato located right along the waterfront in Vernazza. €

AVANT VISUAL/SHUTTERSTOCK ©

Manarola

The whole Cinque Terre area is part of the Parco Nazionale delle Cinque Terre. The national park maintains the various hiking trails that surround the five villages and preserves the sea in front of them, which is included in a protected marine area. It has a useful website – in Italian, English and French – which is worth visiting when planning your trip, as well as information points around the Cinque Terre. You'll come across one of these points as soon as you get off the train in Riomaggiore, where you can buy your Cinque Terre card as well as get your hands on any maps you may need.

alleys that lead up to the small, Romanesque-and-Gothic-mix **Chiesa di San Giovanni Battista**. Continue walking beyond the church and towards the **Castello di Riomaggiore**, easily recognisable by the clock decorating its facade, which makes for an excellent panoramic spot to look out over the whole of Riomaggiore and the other villages.

GETTING AROUND

If you have a car, it's best to leave it behind when it comes to the Cinque Terre – finding a parking spot, especially during high season, becomes an impossible task and all five villages are well connected by a transport network that consists of trains, shuttle buses and ferries.

SAVONA & PONENTE

Stretching out from the westernmost neighbourhoods of Genoa up to the border with France, the Riviera di Ponente completes the Italian Riviera and the half-moon that is Liguria. Ponente and Levante are both intimately similar in their Ligurian spirit and immensely different in their individual characteristics. You'll notice, for example, that beaches tend to be wider in Ponente – meaning that all the locations that dot the coast from Genoa to the border city of Ventimiglia are perfect destinations for families that want to spend their holidays warming up under the sun. People who have been holidaying in Liguria for half a lifetime are fierce in their support of one Riviera over the other, but don't let yourself be swayed – you need to experience both to make your Liguria trip complete.

TOP TIP

The most hassle-free way to move around the Riviera di Ponente is by train. You could also opt to use your own wheels and travel along the Aurelia highway, which passes through the entire region – finding parking, though, is a vicious task.

THE RIVIERA DELLE PALME

The coast that opens up around Savona is known as the Riviera delle Palme, and it has plenty of great spots to stop at and splay out on the beach. One of the major towns in the area is **Loano**, a particularly intriguing destination. Not only do you have the typical Ligurian multicoloured houses brightening up its town centre and a long stretch of beach to relax on, but some 20 minutes by car inland you'll also find the **Grotte di Toirano**, a cave system to explore as a break from a beach-sun-sea routine. Booking ahead and hiking shoes are mandatory.

Finale Ligure, Alassio & Everything in Between

UP & DOWN PONENTE

If you're looking for the perfect town to lay down your beach towel, then the Riviera di Ponente will leave you spoiled for choice. You could start in **Varazze**, just a few train stops away from Genoa, and its **Passeggiata Europa** bordering the sea for more than 4km. Then move on to **Albissola Marina** – known together with its neighbour Albisola Superiore as 'Albisole' – and walk along its **Lungomare degli Artisti**, paved with one mosaic after the other honouring Albissola's ceramic tradition. If you pick **Finale Ligure**, don't miss its hamlet **Varigotti**, with its colourful historic centre and long stretch of free beach.

Continue towards France to find yourself in **Alassio**, one of Ponente's most famous destinations – be sure to stop at its iconic **Muretto di Alassio**, a wall covered with ceramic tiles bearing the signatures of celebrities and other famous figures throughout history. The Muretto sprang up in the 1950s from an idea of Mario Berrino, the owner of the cafe that stands opposite it, and Ernest Hemingway, his good friend and usual patron. Finally, stop by **Laigueglia** at the end of July and beginning of August for the **Sbarco dei Saraceni**, a historical reenactment of the assault that Ottoman pirate Dragut launched on the town during the 16th century – a spectacle of music and fireworks.

SIGHTS
1 Fortezza del Priamàr
2 Grotte di Toirano
3 Muretto di Alassio
4 Pinacoteca Civica
5 Santa Maria Assunta

ACTIVITIES, COURSES & TOURS
6 Passeggiata Lungomare Europa

From Popes to Cruise Ships

TOURING SAVONA

Savona, a place of great historical significance and even greater maritime influence, is the first major city you'll encounter as you travel westwards from Genoa. Start your tour at the baroque **1 Cattedrale di Nostra Signora Assunta** in the city centre. On one side, you will find the entrance to the **2 Cappella Sistina** – and yes, it was purposefully named for the one in Rome by the pope who ordered the construction of them both. Pope Sixtus IV was born Francesco Della Rovere, the son of a powerful *savonese* family – one that produced another pope some 30-odd years later. It's because of Sixtus IV and Julius II that Savona is also sometimes known as 'the city of two popes'. Once you've finished your visit to the *duomo* and the Cappella Sistina you can wander around the Savona historic centre, up and down **3 Via Pia**, where you'll come across **4 Palazzo Gavotti** with its art gallery and ceramics museum, as well as **5 Via Paleocapa**. Head to the waterfront and turn back

WHERE TO EAT IN SAVONA & PONENTE

Osteria La Farinata
Slightly away from Savona's centre, this is the place to try *farinata* (chickpea flour flat bread). €

Nove
A Michelin-starred restaurant in a beautiful location slightly above Alassio's Muretto. €€€

Garbassu
One of Varazze's most famous spots for eating all the fried fish your heart desires. €€

WHY I LOVE THE PONENTE

Benedetta Geddo,
writer

The Riviera di Ponente has been a favoured family holiday spot ever since I was little – there are baby pictures of me smiling the biggest smile possible on the Varazze *lungomare* that have by now become legendary. That's probably why I still love it to this day – to me, the Riviera di Ponente has always meant endless, carefree summer days filled with descents to the sea and falling asleep under a beach umbrella. Even now that I'm grown up, whenever I return I always get the feeling that my life suddenly becomes uncomplicated the moment I step off the train.

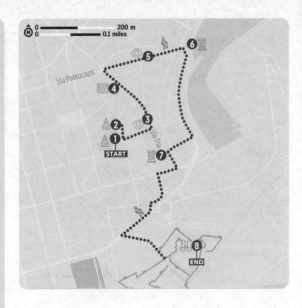

towards the city for a view of what remains of its medieval towers, the **6 Torre del Brandale** – there's also the **7 Torre Pancaldo**, standing solitary along the cruise-boarding harbour. The last stop is the formidable **8 Fortezza Priamar**, high above the city and a prime observation point – as well as the location of several museums, including Savona's archaeological museum.

GETTING AROUND

Like most major Ligurian cities, Savona is a perfect place to walk around, with everything you need to see within a reasonable distance. If you plan to stick around the coast, you won't need a car to

reach the other seaside towns either – just take the train on the Savona–Ventimiglia line and hop off at whatever destination takes your fancy.

RIVIERA DEI FIORI

Riviera di Fiori

✪ Rome

The last part of the Riviera di Ponente before Italy gives way to France is also known as the Riviera dei Fiori, the 'riviera of flowers', where – as you might be able to guess – flowers come into play quite a lot in the area's annual events and celebrations. It's mostly because of San Remo, a name that immediately brings to mind Italian music festivals, decades-long traditions, and the flowers grown in the town's several greenhouses. But Cervo, the village that is considered to be the traditional start of the Riviera dei Fiori, is also covered in cascades of flowers – a detail that perfectly links the two ends of this last stretch of the Italian Riviera.

TOP TIP

Spend some time discovering the province inland by car or scooter. Try the town of Bussana Vecchia, abandoned after a terrible earthquake in the 19th century and turned into an artist hot spot. Or Triora, theatre of a series of witch trials in the 16th century.

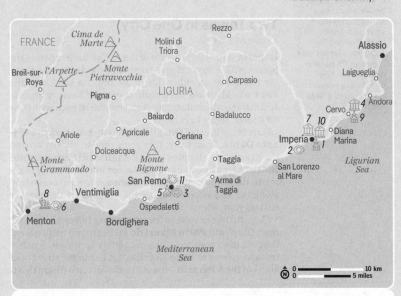

SIGHTS
1 Basilica di San Giovanni Battista
2 Borgo Paraiso
3 Casinò di Sanremo
4 Castello Clavesana – Museo Etnografico

5 Chiesa Russa Ortodossa
6 Giardini Botanici Hanbury
7 Museo dell'Olivo
8 Museo Preistorico dei Balzi Rossi e Zona Archeologica

9 San Giovanni Battista
10 Villa Glock – Museo del Clown

ENTERTAINMENT
11 Teatro Ariston

SHOPPING
(see 7) Emporio Fratelli Carli

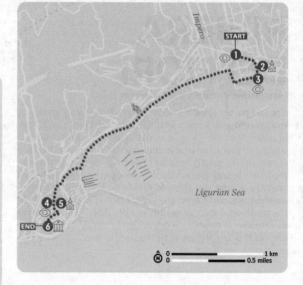

OILS & CLOWNS

If you have more time to spend in Imperia, you can go one of two ways: olive oil or clowns. In Oneglia, stop by the **Fratelli Carli** company, headquartered in the city centre, to visit its museum dedicated to the art of olive oil–making, **Museo dell'Olivo**, as well as an emporium featuring a fixed-menu restaurant. If you're not scared of clowns, head to **Villa Grock**, built by Switzerland-born artist Adrien Wettach who rose to fame in the first half of the 20th century as a juggler and comedian. His peculiar residence has been turned into a museum – check opening times before you visit.

Two Towns in One City

A TOUR OF IMPERIA

Imperia is the last province of the Italian Riviera before the border with France. It was created in the 1920s by uniting the two towns on either side of the Imperia creek, Oneglia and Porto Maurizio. Both of these parts of modern Imperia still maintain their distinct urban characters, each with their own set of sights to explore.

Start at the heart of **Oneglia**, in the city main's square **1 Piazza Dante**. From there, take some time to wander around the city centre – stopping at the **2 Basilica di San Giovanni Battista** for a look at its multicoloured interiors before heading to the harbour at **3 Calata Cuneo**, where you can stroll along the waterfront or under the porticoes if the weather isn't on your side.

Then it's time to move to the other side of Imperia – the walk from Oneglia to **Porto Maurizio** takes around half an hour, depending on your pace, or you can rely on the city's public transport. Once in Porto Maurizio, get lost in the streets and alleys of the **4 Parasio** – the old medieval town centre twist-

 WHERE TO EAT ON THE RIVIERA DEI FIORI

Osteria dell'Olio Grosso
In Imperia's Parasio neighbourhood, this tiny eatery is the spot to go for delicious seafood. €€

Ristorante Balzi Rossi
An iconic Ventimiglia eatery, looking right out onto the sea. €€€

Cafè Ariel
A great *aperitivo* stop after a long day at the beach, with one of the best views in Cervo. €€

ing up like a spiral staircase. The **5 Basilica di San Maurizio e Compagni Martiri** is impossible to miss – it's the largest church in the whole of Liguria, after all. Don't forget to stop at the **6 Logge di Santa Chiara**, a long portico with windows opening up towards the sea.

Following the Flowers

FROM CERVO TO VENTIMIGLIA

The Riviera dei Fiori's traditional starting point is **Cervo**, a beautifully picturesque town that descends down to the sea from its high point, with the **Chiesa di San Giovanni Battista** and the **Castello dei Clavesana**. The historic centre of Cervo is a maze of alleys that open up onto something new at every turn, be it a brightly coloured bench, a quick peek of the sea, or cascades of flowers that cover walls and houses during the warm season.

Another unmissable stop along the Riviera dei Fiori is **San Remo** – the very reason why this whole stretch of coast has gained this particular name. Wander around its major sights, from the **Fontana dello Zampillo** to the **Casino di Sanremo**, and be sure to steal a look at the **Chiesa di Cristo Salvatore**, built by Russian nobles and because of that, very similar in shape to Orthodox churches.

The Riviera ends at **Ventimiglia**, the last city before France. Take a stroll around its city centre but don't forget to check out the sights that lie outside it – the **Giardini Botanici Hanbury**, up on a rock spur just a 15-minute drive from Ventimiglia proper, and the **Balzi Rossi**, an archaeological site consisting of a series of caves that contained several burials and paintings. One of the caves, the **Grotta del Caviglione**, is open to visitors, depending on the weather.

FESTIVAL DI SAN REMO

To every Italian, San Remo means one thing – the Festival della Canzone Italiana, more commonly known as the **Festival di San Remo**. The festival is the country's major music competition and probably its most important media event of the year, dominating TV and radio programming for the full five nights of its running. It takes place in San Remo's **Teatro Ariston** every February – while getting a seat inside the relatively small theatre might not be the easiest of tasks, just being in San Remo while the festival is happening will mean you can breathe in the unmistakable air of Italian pop culture.

GETTING AROUND

Imperia sits right on the Savona–Ventimiglia train line. It's not as walkable as Savona or La Spezia might be, considering that it's made up of two towns grouped together, but it's not impossible either – getting around by car might be more trouble than it's worth, especially when it comes to parking. If you want to explore the Balzi Rossi archaeological site outside Ventimiglia, though, it might be worth having your own set of wheels.

R. NAGY/SHUTTERSTOCK ©

Statues, Duomo di Milano (p235)

THE MAIN AREAS

MILAN	**LAGO DI COMO**	**LAGO MAGGIORE**
Fashion, finance and design metropolis. **p230**	Grandiose villas, gardens and hiking. **p249**	Palace islands and Borromeo history. **p254**

MILAN & THE LAKES

WEALTH, CULTURE AND NATURAL BEAUTY

Meet Italy's industrious northern region, where commerce goes hand-in-hand with dreamy lakes, medieval towns and an emerging aptitude for innovation.

Tucked between the Alps and the Po river, this hardworking area of Italy's north has long been one of the country's wealthiest. It accounts for a whopping 22% of the country's total GDP and also holds one-sixth of its population, as everyone rushes north to work.

Nowhere else do you feel this more than in Milan, Italy's financial centre, where at first it seems impossible to find a *vero* (true) *milanese*. Here well-heeled locals dash to or from fashion events, design hubs, tech presentations and meetings with their can't-live-without *commercialista* (accountant). Meanwhile, Bocconi University students strategise for their future startups.

Step outside the city, though, and things slow down a notch, even though locals are still busy working in textiles, furniture, iron and steel industries. The view changes to rice fields – irrigated by a system partly designed by da Vinci – which provide the much-needed ingredient for northern Italy's beloved risotto. Quiet towns pop up bearing medieval and Renaissance treasures. But it's the glacial lakes at the seat of the Alps where everyone goes when they need to unwind. Indeed, this industrious area is also blessed with natural beauty. It's a mix of dramatic lakes, undulating foothills and the history of powerful dynasties, with one fast-paced (for Italy) city at its core.

LAGO DI GARDA
Roman ruins and a poet's home. p258

BERGAMO
Medieval centre and Venetian walls. p262

MANTUA
Palaces and the Gonzaga family. p265

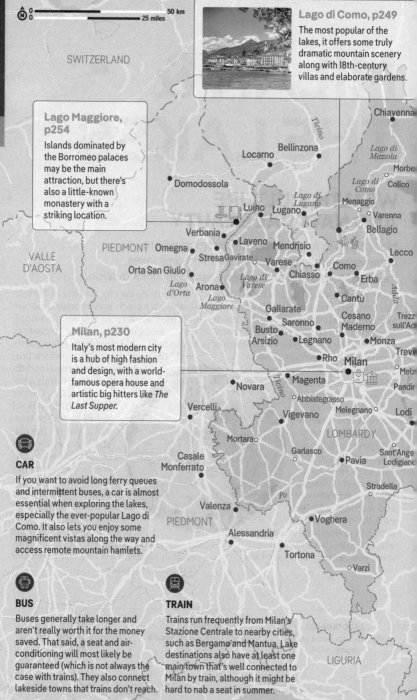

Lago di Como, p249

The most popular of the lakes, it offers some truly dramatic mountain scenery along with 18th-century villas and elaborate gardens.

Lago Maggiore, p254

Islands dominated by the Borromeo palaces may be the main attraction, but there's also a little-known monastery with a striking location.

Milan, p230

Italy's most modern city is a hub of high fashion and design, with a world-famous opera house and artistic big hitters like *The Last Supper.*

SWITZERLAND

VALLE D'AOSTA

PIEDMONT

Domodossola

Luino

Verbania

Omegna

Stresa

Orta San Giulio

Lago d'Orta

Arona

Lago Maggiore

Laveno

Gavirate

Lago di Varese

Locarno

Bellinzona

Ticino

Lago di Lugano

Lugano

Mendrisio

Varese

Chiasso

Gallarate

Saronno

Busto Arsizio

Legnano

Rho

Chiavenna

Lago di Mezzola

Morbe

Lago di Como

Colico

Menaggio

Varenna

Bellagio

Lecco

Como

Erba

Cantù

Cesano Maderno

Monza

Milan

Novara

Magenta

Ticino

Abbiategrasso

Vercelli

Vigevano

Melegnano

Mortara

Garlasco

Casale Monferrato

Valenza

PIEDMONT

Alessandria

Tortona

Po

Voghera

Pavia

LOMBARDY

Sant'Ange Lodigiano

Stradella

Varzi

Trezz sull'Ad

Trevi

Melz

Pandir

Lodi

LIGURIA

0   50 km
0   25 miles

CAR

If you want to avoid long ferry queues and intermittent buses, a car is almost essential when exploring the lakes, especially the ever-popular Lago di Como. It also lets you enjoy some magnificent vistas along the way and access remote mountain hamlets.

BUS

Buses generally take longer and aren't really worth it for the money saved. That said, a seat and air-conditioning will most likely be guaranteed (which is not always the case with trains). They also connect lakeside towns that trains don't reach.

TRAIN

Trains run frequently from Milan's Stazione Centrale to nearby cities, such as Bergamo and Mantua. Lake destinations also have at least one main town that's well connected to Milan by train, although it might be hard to nab a seat in summer.

Bergamo, p262

Ringed by 16th-century Venetian walls, the medieval Città Alta (Upper City) makes for a charming stroll into the city's past.

Lago di Garda, p258

It's home to the ruins of a Roman villa, a Unesco-protected park and the bizarre residence of poet and proto-fascist Gabriele D'Annunzio.

Mantua, p265

Protected by water on three sides, this overlooked Renaissance gem was once ruled by the Gonzagas, one of the north's powerful dynasties.

Find Your Way

This hefty slice of Italy's north is packed with lake beauty, history and culture. We've picked the places that best capture its character, radiating out from Milan, its natural heart.

FROM LEFT: FEEL GOOD STUDIO/SHUTTERSTOCK ©, RÁSTO SK/SHUTTERSTOCK ©

Plan Your Time

Wander Milan's world-class museums and fashionable haunts, getting your fill of cosmopolitan life. Break it up with Renaissance culture in the south or a dip in the glacial lakes by the mountains.

Via della Spiga (p235)

MARCOVARRO/SHUTTERSTOCK ©

Pressed for Time

● If you only manage to see one thing during your stay here, make it **Milan** (p230). The city may not have the Renaissance beauty of Florence or the history of Rome, but it makes up for that with its inimitable style and as a vision of Italy's future. Explore the high-fashion district of **Quadrilatero d'Oro** (p234), see the **Duomo** (p235) for its singular extravagance, and spare some time for what's arguably Leonardo's greatest masterpiece: **The Last Supper** (p231). While the mural painting's colours and details may have faded, the impact of seeing it in the hushed silence of the Santa Maria delle Grazie basilica certainly hasn't.

Seasonal highlights

In summer, Milan simmers, locals leave and the mosquitoes move in. Thankfully, a dip in the lakes isn't far away. In spring, the lake gardens are at their most eye-catching.

JANUARY
Stave off the cold with **winter cuisine** like steaming bowls of cassoeula (a meaty stew) and buttery polenta with braised meat.

MARCH
Nothing says **Easter** quite like chiacchiere (fried biscuits), tortelli (fried donuts) and colomba (a dove-shaped cake).

APRIL
The hundreds of exhibitions and parties happening during Milan's **Design Week** make it an exciting time to visit.

FANFO/SHUTTERSTOCK ©, OLGABOMBOLOGNA/SHUTTERSTOCK ©, PAOLO BONA/SHUTTERSTOCK ©

A Weeklong Stay

● With five to seven days up your sleeve, you can explore Milan in more detail. Maybe you can fit in a night at **the opera** (p236) or some old masters at the **Pinacoteca** (p236), plus you'll be able to spend a few days flitting around the lakes just like princesses and poets have done.

● You might have to fight off the crowds at **Lago di Como** (p249), but it'll be worth it for those dramatic views and lavish villas. Otherwise, **Lago di Maggiore's San Lorenzo** (p254) speck-like islands have equally grand palaces and are less crowded, although the lake views are a notch less impressive.

More Time to Spare

● Not only can you fit in Milan and a couple of lakes, you can also sneak in some historic towns. **Bergamo** (p262) is close enough for a short day trip and will woo you with the charm of its medieval **Città Alta** (p262) surrounded by 16th-century **Venetian walls** (p262). **Mantua** (p265) impresses with its sprawling **palaces** (p265), which tell the story of the long-reigning Gonzaga family.

● If you still have some time on your hands, visit **Lago di Garda** (p258). Wandering the **house of Gabriele D'Annunzio** (p258), the poet who inspired Mussolini's fascism, is a mind-boggling experience.

MAY	SEPTEMBER	OCTOBER	DECEMBER
Come spring, the **villa gardens** show off their best colours, with camellias, rhododendrons and azaleas in bloom.	Motor lovers won't want to miss the **Formula 1 Pirelli Italian Grand Prix** in Monza, known for its scorching speeds.	Autumn is the season for **picking chestnuts** around the lakes and eating them in all forms, from gnocchi to jam.	**Opera season** begins on Sant'Ambrogio's Day at Milan's La Scala. For fans, it's one of the year's most anticipated dates.

MILAN

Milan hits you with Italy's version of a fast-paced modern city. Home of finance, fashion and design, ever since the 2015 Expo pushed it into the limelight it's been trying hard to be a cosmopolitan melting pot more in line with cities like London and Paris.

Over the last decade two new districts – Porta Nuova and CityLife – have radically changed the city skyline. Startups have sprouted up, to the extent that the *Financial Times* declared Milan 'Italy's biggest startup hub'. Traditional trattorias have been joined by a legion of exciting locales mixing up Italian and international cuisines. Even the city's decades-long population decline seems to have been reversed with an influx of residents attracted by the new energy.

But that doesn't mean Milan has forgotten its past. It's still the same hardworking city of trade it's been since the Renaissance. And the *milanese* are as snooty but fiercely loyal (once you get to know them) as ever.

TOP TIP

It's easy to get around the centre on foot, while the metro, buses and trams are convenient for going further afield. Bike or moped are good options, but beware the stone-paved roads. Driving isn't advised – the centre is restricted (Area C) and parking is a nightmare.

BEST PLACES TO SPOT DESIGN

Triennale di Milano
Milan's first port of call for Italian design. Along with your Sottsass favourites, discover international photography, fashion and more.

Studio Museo Achille Castiglioni
Peer into the quirky mind of the great designer in the studio where he worked until his death in 2002. Visits are led by his daughter.

ADI Design Museum
Originally for industry types, but now everyone can enjoy the winning entries from the Compasso d'Oro design award in a former tram depot.

Design Week Delirium

A CITY-WIDE DESIGN FESTIVAL

Each year Design Week fever grips the entire city, turning every abandoned factory, architecture studio and neighbourhood bar into a raucous party or venue for design. But it wasn't always like this. Design Week started in the '80s with a few side events during the official Salone del Mobile, a ticketed international fair of furniture and design. Once these side events called 'Fuorisalone' (literally 'outside the Salone') eclipsed the main event, the popularity of Design Week skyrocketed. Now Airbnbs are flooded with people working in the creative industries, design enthusiasts or those just in the mood to party, from all around the world. And big brands are getting in on the action, too.

Part of the allure is the fact that Fuorisalone is free and everyone is invited. It's this all-inclusiveness that makes it unique. You could go from a large-scale Hermès installation to an exhibition by ECAL students or even a makeshift showcase of cup-holders made in someone's bedroom. Plus there's almost always a party involved. The most coveted are exclusive events thrown by design brands such as Dimoremilano, but there are plenty of events with guest DJs in (not so) secret locations for the masses.

The festival usually takes place around April or May but it changes every year, as does the line-up of showcasing brands and designers.

POGZTOS/SHUTTERSTOCK ©

The Last Supper, Basilica di Santa Maria delle Grazie

The Last Supper's Eternal Appeal

DA VINCI'S MASTERPIECE

You might want to hold your breath when standing before da Vinci's 40-sq-metre masterpiece, whether from sheer awe or because the air you're exhaling may well damage the fragile work. Having survived da Vinci's experimental technique – which caused the painting to deteriorate within 20 years of completion – along with WWII bombings and harmful restoration attempts, the fact the work remains at all is nothing short of a miracle. Now, one of its biggest threats are the visitors themselves, which is why your time here will be short (15 minutes) and involve a series of air-controlled rooms.

Housed on a wall of the refectory adjoining the **Basilica di Santa Maria delle Grazie**, *The Last Supper* still manages to astound viewers, despite being in many ways a ghostly imprint of the original. Depicting the moment when Jesus drops the bomb of his impending betrayal, the mixed reactions of his disciples rendered

LEONARDO'S LITTLE-KNOWN VINEYARD

Did you know the Renaissance man's expertise also extended into viticulture? An ardent winemaker, Leonardo Da Vinci was given a vineyard by his patron Ludovico 'Il Moro', Duke of Milan, in 1498. It sits just across the road from the Basilica di Santa Maria delle Grazie, where Leonardo was working on *The Last Supper*. While the original vineyard was destroyed during WWII, it has since been meticulously recreated with the same grape variety. These days not only can you stroll between the vines at **La Vigna di Leonardo** but you can even drink the wine, just as Leonardo might have done in days gone by.

FANCY SLEEPING AT DA VINCI'S VINEYARD?

Take a look at **Casa degli Atellani** (p236) and its 15th-century *palazzo* (mansion) restored by Piero Portaluppi. Some of the serviced apartments with furnishings by boutique Milanese brands come with views of the Basilica di Santa Maria delle Grazie.

 WHERE TO GO FOR STREET FOOD

Mercato Centrale
This artisan-led food hall capturing hearts (and stomachs) has everything from barbecued meat to empanadas. €€

De Santis
Strewn with signed photos of celebrities and football stars, De Santis is beloved for its mouthwatering *panini*. €

La Ravioleria Sarpi
Brainchild of a Chinese student and historic butcher, this tiny takeaway makes some of Milan's best dumplings. €

MILAN

Malpensa (45km)

Piazza Firenze

Via Cenisio

Cimitero Monumentale

Piazzale Lagosta Via Pola

ISOLA

Bosco Vertica 1

49

Porta Garibaldi

29 12

25

58 Via Nono

10

Via Ceresio

CHINATOWN

PORTA GARIBALDI

31

Via Piero della Francesca

Corso Sempione

Via Logarina Via L Vita Fauche

Via Giulio Cesare Procaccini

Via Monviso

Via Melchiorre Gioia

Via Bramante

Via Paolo Sarpi 43

Bastioni di Porta Nuova 26

Viale F Crispi

Bastioni di Porta Volta

Via Luigi Canonica

54

Via Francesco Ferruccio

Via Melzi d'Eril

Piazza VI Febbraio

Viale Elvezia

Piazza Repu

Via della Moscova

M

Via Canova

Arena Civica

Via Legnano

Via Soferino

Via Montebello

Piazza Sempione

Parco Sempione

24

Foro Buonaparte

Via Fatebenefratelli

Piazza Cavo

Parco Pallavicino

Via Vincenzo Monti

Via Mario Pagano

28

Viale Gadio

6 Pinacoteca di Brera

Via Pontaccio

BRERA

22

Via Brera

Sena

27 2 **Castello Sforzesco**

Via L Ariosto

Via XX Settembre

Cadorna (Stazione Nord)

Via A Manzoni

59 19 **Quadril d'O**

7

Corso C Matteo

Corso Vercelli

Via Giovanni Boccaccio

8 **The Last Supper**

Via Dante

Via Brioleto

34 13

36 53

Corso Vitt Emanuele

Lampugnano (4km)

32 16

Corso Magenta

Via Meravigli

38

Via Carducci

15

Via Orefici

M

5 3 **Duomo**

23

Via San Vittore

Via Caradosso

Via Vico

Museo del Novecento

Via Torino

Via Larga

Giar

Via Ellia

Via Paolo Giovio

Via Olona

35

Via C Correnti

Guas

Via Francesco Sforza

Parco Don Giussani

Via Edmondo de Amicis

Corso Genova

Via Molino delle Armi

Parco delle Basiliche

Corso di Porta Romana

Corso Italia

Via Santa Sofia

Via Vincenzo Foppa

Via California

ZONA TORTONA

Corso C Colombo

Viale G D'Annunzio

Corso di Porta Ticinese

Via Santa Sofia

Corso Vigentina

Via Andrea Solari

Via Standhal

Via Savona

18 37

63

60 **39**

Via S Martino

Viale Gian Galeazzo

Viale Beatrice d'Este

Darsena

20 21

11 14 57

Alzaia Naviglio Grande Via Valenza

56 61

55

Via Magolfa

Piazza XXIV Maggio

Via Pietro Teulia

Via Castelbarco

Via F Bocconi

Ripa di Porta Ticinese

NAVIGLI

Via Giovanni Segantini

Via Gottardo

Via O Tabacchi

Parco Ravizza

Viale Toscana

Viale Cassala

45

Via Giuseppe Meda

Pavia (33km)

Viale Tibaldi

Via Carlo Bazzi

Viale Liguria

Viale Liguria

HIGHLIGHTS
1 Bosco Verticale
2 Castello Sforzesco
3 Duomo
4 Fondazione Prada
5 Museo del Novecento
6 Pinacoteca di Brera
7 Quadrilatero d'Oro
8 *The Last Supper*
9 Villa Necchi Campiglio

SIGHTS
10 ADI Design Museum
11 Armani Silos
(see 8) Basilica di Santa Maria delle Grazie
12 Biblioteca degli Alberi
13 Galleria Vittorio Emanuele II
14 Gianfranco Ferré Foundation
15 L.O.V.E
16 La Vigna di Leonardo
17 Mercato Centrale
18 Museo delle Culture
19 Museo Poldi Pezzoli
20 Naviglio Grande
21 Naviglio Pavese
22 Orto Botanico di Brera
23 Palazzo Reale
24 Parco Sempione
25 Piazza Gae Aulenti
26 Porta Nuova
27 Studio Museo Achille Castiglioni
28 Triennale di Milano
29 UniCredit Tower

ACTIVITIES, COURSES & TOURS
30 I Bagni Misteriosi

SLEEPING
31 3Rooms
32 Atellani Apartments
33 Foresteria Un Posto a Milano
34 Galleria Vik
35 Ostello Bello
36 Room Mate Giulia

EATING
37 Cocciuto
38 De Santis
39 Gattullo
40 Gelsomina
41 Giolina
42 Kung Fu Bao
43 La Ravioleria Sarpi
44 Marlà
45 Nebbia
46 Onest
47 Pasticceria Sissi
48 Pavé
49 Ratanà
50 Trattoria Masuelli San Marco
51 Un Posto a Milano

DRINKING & NIGHTLIFE
52 Bar Basso
53 Camparino in Galleria
54 Dry
55 Mag Cafè
56 Pinch
57 Rocket
58 Tempio del Futuro Perduto

ENTERTAINMENT
59 Teatro alla Scala

SHOPPING
(see 31) 10 Corso Como
60 Mercato Comunale
61 Mercatone dell'Antiquariato
62 Spazio Rossana Orlandi
63 Tenoha

INFORMATION
(see 59) Teatro alla Scala Box Office

233

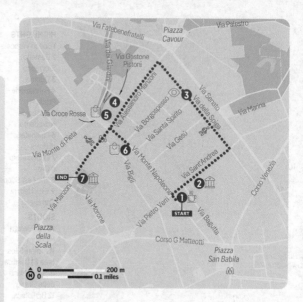

THE MAN WITHOUT SKIN

Almost everyone stops in their tracks inside the **Duomo** when they come across the gruesome sight of St Bartholomew wearing his skin like a shawl. Created in 1562 by Lombard sculptor Marco d'Agrate, the statue depicts St Bartholomew, Christ's apostle, whose penchant for converting people to the Christian faith (in particular King Polymius of Armenia and his family) aroused jealousy from religious officials. He was flayed alive, beheaded and since became a martyr. The statue also gave d'Agrate a chance to flaunt his impressive knowledge of human anatomy.

through their gestures and expressions – what da Vinci described as 'motions of the soul' – are utterly enthralling. The illusion of a 3D space created by various tricks of perspective only adds to the image's realism. Compare it to the *Crucifixion* by Giovanni Donato da Montorfano completed around the same time on the opposite wall, and you'll understand how ground-breaking the artwork really was.

Book weeks ahead during high season to guarantee yourself a spot. Guided tours are recommended for the fascinating extra detail.

Strutting the Quadrilatero d'Oro

THE HIGH-FASHION DISTRICT

Even if you don't know your Fendi from your Ferragamo, Milan's aptly named **Quadrilatero d'Oro** (Gold Quadrangle) is an eye-popping look into a world of wealth and high fashion. Just a 10-minute walk from the Duomo, this network of cobblestone streets loosely bound by Via Monte Napoleone, Via Sant'Andrea, Via Senato and Via Manzoni is packed with fashion heavyweights worth at least a morning's wander. One look at the marble facades, black-suited

 WHERE TO GET A BREAKFAST BRIOCHE

Onest
Food and coffee with a conscience is the mantra of this cafe serving up fantastically buttery pastries. €

Gattullo
Bocconi students and *sciure* (posh *milanese* women) queue for blueberry croissants at this historic pastry shop. €

Pavé
Credited for bringing cafe culture to Milan, this is the place for *brioche* (croissants) dripping with custard. €

bodyguards and flamboyant dressers will tell you, we're not in Kansas anymore.

Start at the historic **1 Pasticceria Cova**, founded in 1817 and now owned by LVMH. Enjoy a coffee and *brioche* on the inky blue banquettes. Head to **2 Palazzo Morando** down the road on Via Sant'Andrea to check out their latest fashion exhibition, before strolling down **3 Via della Spiga** to ogle over-the-top shop windows from the likes of Dolce & Gabbana. Armani's **4 Nobu**, just off Via Monte Napoleone, is the place for a sushi lunch among the well-heeled. At **5 Emporio Armani** around the corner, immerse yourself in the designer's signature understated elegance. Detour down Via Monte Napoleone to treat your feet to a pair of bespoke shoes from **6 Berluti**, an Italian shoemaker that's been in business for over a century. End the afternoon exploring the Renaissance collection of an Italian count at the eponymous **7 Museo Poldi Pezzoli**.

An Ambitious Cathedral

SIX CENTURIES IN THE MAKING

More than just an extravagant cathedral in Milan's centre, the **Duomo** is about the vision, inventiveness and tenacity of a city that brought to life the impossible. For that's what people believed when Giangaleazzo Visconti conceived of the cathedral in 1386. Canals had to be built just to bring in the enormous quantities of Candoglia marble and new technologies invented due to the cathedral's sheer size. It took 600 years to build (eat your heart out, Sagrada Família) and even became part of a Milanese expression for a never-ending task (*'Lungh 'me la fabrica del Domm'*, literally 'Long as the work on the Duomo').

Visitors will be kept busy for a good couple of hours. Crowded with 135 spires and 3400 statues including the gold-leaf-clad Madonnina, the facade and its ornate doors are densely packed. Inside there are both treasures, such as the 5m-high Trivulzio candelabrum, and peculiarities like a zodiac-laden sundial and the statue of skinless St Bartholomew. Three huge apse windows illuminate biblical scenes, while the bejewelled remains of 16th-century cardinal San Carlo sit in the crypt below.

For skyline views and a chance to admire the spires up close, climb the 150 steps to the **rooftop terraces**; you can also pay more to take the lift. Those with extra time may want to explore the archaeological area but it's hardly

WHERE TO EXPLORE FASHION

Stefano Sorci, a fashion and product consultant who lectures at Istituto Marangoni Milano, shares the best places to explore fashion. *(@stefanomilano62)*

Armani Silos
One should absolutely start at this museum by and dedicated to the immense work of Giorgio Armani.

Gianfranco Ferré Foundation
A beautiful space dedicated to the most productive years of one of Italy's most prolific designers. You can research all of his work, even the years when Gianfranco was creative director of Christian Dior. By appointment only.

Fondazione Prada
Not focused specifically on fashion but very linked to it. The Prada Osservatorio is also nice and convenient to visit – it's above the Galleria Vittorio Emanuele II.

Marlà
They'll leave you with a creamy moustache, but the airy *maritozzi* (cream-filled buns) are worth it. €

Pasticceria Sissi
Fashionable folk come for signature *brioche* with honey and sit in the vine-covered courtyard. €

Gelsomina
Choose from *cannoli siciliani* (ricotta-filled pastry shells) and other sugary wonders beneath the glass counter. €

HISTORY, HAUTE COUTURE & BULL'S BALLS

With its triumphal arch and glass canopy, it's easy to see how **Galleria Vittorio Emanuele II** broke the mould of shopping arcades. Built in 1867 and named after the king who unified Italy, it soon became a meeting point for locals, earning the nickname Salotto di Milano (Drawing Room of Milan).

Inside is a mix of genteel cafes and haute couture. Historic spots include Biffi restaurant, here since the Galleria's opening, and the first Prada shop with its original 'Fratelli Prada' (Prada Brothers) sign. Don't miss the curious tradition of spinning with your heel on the balls (now a worn-down hole) of the mosaic bull – legend has it this will bring you luck.

LOOKING FOR SOMETHING MORE CONTEMPORARY?

Fondazione Prada (p239) is the city hub for thought-provoking artworks by the likes of Damien Hirst. Its younger sibling **Prada Osservatorio** (p235) is smaller, but also centrally located and worth checking out.

essential. Skip the audio guide and download the identical app at a fraction of the price.

La Scala Like a Local

OPERA HOUSE ON A BUDGET

It's where Maria Callas made her debut, Verdi triumphed and Toscanini established his legacy as a virtuoso conductor. Sitting in the crimson and gilt boxes of **Teatro alla Scala** among the *milanese* dressed to impress is one of those moments you won't soon forget. And while tickets may usually set you back by around €200, there's a little-known way to get them for under €15 like locals do – provided you have the patience.

Arrive before 1pm on the day of the performance with some ID in tow and register at the **Teatro alla Scala box office**, a five-minute walk from the Duomo. Then go down the adjacent Via Filodrammatici where you'll spot someone sitting in a plastic chair. Leave your name with them and return at 5.30pm to pay and collect your ticket (only one ticket is allowed per person).

As you might have guessed, these seats are quite literally far from the best ones in the house. Located in the highest galleries, you'll either be forced to stand (if you're in the second row) or crane your neck (from the first row) just to put a face to those angelic voices. Plus you'll enter from a discreet side door instead of the sumptuous main entrance. But you'll still get to revel in the butterflies-inducing energy of a performance at La Scala – at an unbeatable price.

Immersion in the Old Masters

PINACOTECA DI BRERA'S MASTERPIECES

You can thank Napoleon for this gallery and its impressive collection amassed by the French army. Upstairs from the city's celebrated art school, the **Pinacoteca di Brera**'s 38 rooms wind around the 1st floor of Palazzo Brera, taking you from Lombard frescoes from the Middle Ages to 19th-century Italian stalwarts. You might notice a religious theme emerging, as many works were confiscated from churches during the time of the Kingdom of Italy.

While the collection may not be vast – you can see it in less than two hours – it's certainly brimming with masterpieces, with ample works by Caravaggio, Tintoretto and the Bellini brothers. Standouts include

WHERE TO STAY IN MILAN

Galleria Vik
Lofty views of the Galleria and 89 artist-designed suites make this a sought-after address. €€€

Room Mate Giulia
By hotshot designer Patricia Urquiola, this hotel is unbeatable in terms of good looks and location. €€€

Atellani Apartments
Home to Leonardo's Vineyard, this 15th-century *palazzo* has apartments restored by Milan's own Portaluppi. €€€

Pinacoteca di Brera

THE SECRET GARDEN IN PALAZZO BRERA

Down a hall echoing with the chatter of students, you'll see the entrance to a rambling garden that fulfils all childhood yearnings for a secret garden. Originally a place where the Humiliati monks used to meditate in the 14th century, the **Orto Botanico di Brera** was officially established as a botanical garden by Empress Maria Theresa of Austria in 1774. Brimming with medicinal and rare plants, along with two gingko trees that are around 250 years old, the garden continues to be a place for learning, just as it was during the mansion's former life as a Jesuit college.

Mantegna's *Lamentation of Christ*, which shows with brutal realism the death of Jesus while also providing a fantastic lesson in foreshortening. *The Kiss* by Francesco Hayez is arguably the artist's best-known work and worth gazing at for its still potent sense of romance and patriotism. There's also some Picasso and Braque thrown in to whet your appetite for the Pinacoteca's modern collection, to be housed in the long-awaited Palazzo Citterio.

The standard ticket has been replaced with the Brera-CARD, which lets you visit unlimited times for three consecutive months. Otherwise, for just €3 from 6pm on the third Thursday of the month, you can see all the masterpieces against a background of live music, from quartets to solo piano.

Where Aperitivo Was Born

MILANESE PRE-DINNER DRINKS

Italy's answer to happy hour has become so popular you can find it all over the country, but Milan is where its winning modern-day formula was born. Made famous by the historic Camparino bar in the Galleria Vittorio

GOT A TASTE FOR MILANESE TRADITION?

Discover the delights of **Milanese cuisine** (p242), from *risotto alla milanese* (saffron and bone marrow risotto) to *cotoletta* (breaded veal), and find out some of the best places to dig in to these dishes.

Ostello Bello
Cheap-and-cheerful rooms, *aperitivi* and karaoke sessions make this the most inviting hostel in town. €

3Rooms
Kick back in a Marcel Breuer chaise longue amid designer furnishings at fashionable Corso Como 10. €€€

Foresteria Un Posto a Milano
Dating back to 1695, this inner-city farmhouse has four simply furnished rooms in a bucolic setting. €€

WHERE TO GO FOR INSPIRATION

Ilaz, an artist based between Milan and New York, tells us where she goes for inspiration. (@ilazzz___)

In Milan big names have made the history of this city, creating something timeless. The permanent collection of **Triennale di Milano** (p230) is superlative, full of iconic pieces. The Triennale has also become very active from the point of view of experimental theatre since Romeo Castellucci has become the director. I love the theatre of Castellucci, which can't even be defined as theatre in the purest sense of the word. I also like to go to the **Teatro alla Scala** (p236) and when I have the opportunity, the fashion shows, where you sometimes find fantastic scenography.

Bar Basso

Emanuele II, and believed to have been invented as early as the 1920s, the humble *aperitivo* (pre-dinner drink) is more than a social pastime: it's a Milanese tradition.

It usually goes from 6pm to 9pm and lets you enjoy an array of nibbles for the price of a cocktail. While traditionally the drink of choice involves Aperol, Campari and vermouth, these days any cocktail will suffice. The accompanying snacks range anywhere from olives and chips to curated small plates or sometimes an all-out buffet, thus catapulting *aperitivo* to *apericena*, a hearty near-substitute for dinner.

Almost every bar has its own version of *aperitivo*, but at **Bar Basso** it comes with a slice of city history. This place invented the Negroni Sbagliato (substituting prosecco for gin), which is served in a giant goblet with a hunk of ice, exactly as it was in the 1970s. Other excellent options include **Bagni Misteriosi** for its garden poolside setting, **Un Posto a Milano** at the urban farmhouse Cascina Cuccagna, **Camparino** for the art nouveau surrounds, and **Tenoha** for its fusion of Japanese and Italian style. Canalside *aperitivo* in the Navigli area is also a classic.

 WHERE TO FIND ART IN MILAN

Pirelli HangarBicocca
This former locomotive factory houses Anselm Kiefer's concrete towers and provocative temporary exhibitions.

Fondazione Prada
Revamped to Prada's vision, this stylish former distillery has works by Damien Hirst and Carsten Höller.

Museo del Novecento
From futurism to Arte Povera, this museum proves Italy's contribution to the arts goes well beyond the Renaissance.

Milan's Modern Side

GLIMPSING A GREENER FUTURE

While only a six-minute train ride from the centre, **Porta Nuova** seems light years ahead of the rest of the city, if not the country. Instead of classic *case di ringhiera* (traditional Milanese houses), shiny skyscrapers dominate the cityscape along with modern green spaces. It's the result of one of the most significant regeneration projects in Italy's history, which saw the transformation of 290,000 sq metres of abandoned industrial space by some of the biggest names in international architecture into what's become a symbol for the city's greener future.

Designed by the Argentine architect César Pelli, **Piazza Gae Aulenti** is the beating heart of the neighbourhood. Elevated 6m above street level, it puts a progressive spin on the humble piazza, with solar panels and a pool of water that cascades down two floors, blocking out traffic noise while creating a system of natural ventilation and light. Ringed by buildings, the most impressive is the needle-tipped **Uni-Credit Tower**, Italy's tallest building and also certified for its sustainable design. From there it's a two-minute walk to contemporary park **Biblioteca degli Alberi** and Stefano Boeri's **Bosco Verticale** (Vertical Forest), two high-rise apartments that seem to be disappearing under 700 trees and 20,000 plants said to absorb 30 metric tons of carbon dioxide every year.

Contemporary Art Meets Prada Style

PRADA'S ART AND CULTURE COMPLEX

Formerly a century-old gin distillery, this sprawling 19,000-sq-metre complex in south Milan has been given the Prada touch. What that means exactly is 'A Haunted House' clad in dazzling 24-carat gold leaf, lashings of aluminium foam and a 60m-high white concrete tower, not to mention a '50s-style bar designed by filmmaker Wes Anderson. Conceived of by Miuccia Prada and hubby Patrizio Bertelli, and designed by Pritzker Prize–winning architect Rem Koolhaas, **Fondazione Prada** is the slick industrial home of contemporary art, film and multidisciplinary projects that often seek to probe our perceptions of modern life.

You could easily lose a whole afternoon here. Along with Prada's permanent collection, which includes fly-focused works by Damien Hirst, Carsten Höller's giant rotating

A DIVISIVE FINGER

It's impossible to ignore the 11m-tall white marble hand with amputated fingers, which appears to be giving the middle finger to the Milan stock exchange. Entitled **L.O.V.E.** – an acronym for *Libertà, Odio, Vendetta, Eternità* (Liberty, Hate, Revenge, Eternity) – but commonly referred to as *Il Dito* (*The Finger*), it's a divisive artwork by Milan-based artist Maurizio Cattelan who is infamous for his provocative pieces. It was inaugurated in 2010 during the financial crisis and placed in front of the fascist-era stock exchange building, so both the timing and placement of the sculpture appear loaded with meaning. Many have interpreted the work as a statement against financial institutions that have become the new fascism. The artist, however, is keeping mum.

Palazzo Reale
Crowd-pulling exhibitions often come to stay in this lofty former residence of Napoleon and King Ferdinand I.

Museo delle Culture
This renovated former industrial plant is home to an impressive ethnographic collection and blockbuster exhibitions.

Museo Poldi Pezzoli
Gian Giacomo Poldi Pezzoli's mansion-turned-museum has Renaissance masterpieces and a Dante-inspired room.

mushrooms and an underground grotto, it has regular temporary exhibitions likely to shock, thrill and maybe even disturb you. Views stretching over the city and the nearby abandoned train tracks can also be enjoyed from the 6th-floor restaurant **Torre**, which (as you might have guessed) has a focus on art. Pieces by the likes of Jeff Koons are hanging on the walls along with plates designed by established artists. This attention to detail hasn't escaped the refined menu of Italian cuisine.

A 1930s Villa of Dreams
WHERE RATIONALISM MEETS GLAMOUR

Milan's star architect Piero Portaluppi was given carte blanche by high-flying industrialists Nedda and Gigina Necchi and Gigina's husband Angelo Campiglio to create the home of their dreams. The result was a severe yet glamorous villa unlike anything upper-class Milan had ever seen. While it had a pool, tennis court and technology considered cutting edge for its time, what made it really stand out was Portaluppi's signature rationalist style.

Touring the many rooms of **Villa Necchi Campiglio** will give you a taste of 1930s high society, particularly as you explore Nedda's wardrobe complete with a custom-made Dior scarf. It also allows you to you appreciate Portaluppi's obsessive attention to detail, noticeable in the geometric radiator covers and even the tableware. Diehard fans of the architect might be miffed by Tomaso Buzzi's renovations to soften the Portaluppi look, only a few years after the house was completed. And while it's easy to get engrossed in the architectural detail, spare a look for artworks by Adolfo Wildt and Italian futurists like Giorgio de Chirico, which blend effortlessly with the house.

Nestled in a street lined with lavish mansions, Villa Necchi Campiglio is a 10-minute walk from San Babila. Opt for a guided tour as there's much to learn about this socialite trio, their royal guests and the work of one meticulous Milanese architect.

The City's Last Canals
EXPLORING THE NAVIGLI

Many don't realise that Milan could have been like Venice. The city was once laced with waterways that da Vinci himself had a hand in developing during medieval times. Sadly, in the 1930s the fascist regime decided to close them (another thing to blame on

WHERE TO EAT PIZZA IN MILAN

Cocciuto
Skip the poke because Cocciuto is synonymous with thick Naples-style pizza, oozing with fresh, quality toppings. €€

Dry
In this slick bar, the pairing of gourmet pizza and elaborate cocktails proves irresistible to Milan's pretty people. €€

Giolina
Decked out in vintage books, brass chandeliers and traditional tiles, it's a cosy place for Naples-style pizza. €€

Navigli
Naviglio Grande

WHY I LOVE MILAN

Stephanie Ong, writer

I could wax lyrical endlessly about Milan. I love that it's so international but at the same time small enough that you run into familiar people constantly. And nothing is further than a 20-minute bike ride. Some people adore the Renaissance, but give me Milan's rationalist architecture, with its sharp geometric lines, any time of day. I love *aperitivo* along the canal. I love the way the *milanese* like to dress up and how black is always elegant. I love that dinner at 8pm is considered early. I love the loyalty and unfailing generosity of the *milanese*.

Mussolini) for supposed hygiene reasons and to accommodate the increasing number of cars. Now you can stop for a drink on the **Naviglio Grande** and **Naviglio Pavese**, the city's most photogenic corner, and imagine what might have been.

Both canals are lined with bars, cafes and restaurants that thrum with activity day and night (some well into the night). Naviglio Grande has established itself as the place for *aperitivo* and on Saturday nights it can feel like the whole city, plus tourists and out-of-town teenagers, are here. Head to **Mag Cafe** and **Pinch** where the cocktails are above par. Mosquito repellent is essential during summer. On the last Sunday of the month the Naviglio Grande also hosts the **Mercatone dell'Antiquariato**, an antiques market where you can get preloved treasures like Alvar Aalto chairs or a mid-century lamp. And if you're looking for a different view of the canals, hire a bike and do some picturesque pedalling past small villages and old *cascine* (farmhouses).

FOR ARCHITECTURE ENTHUSIASTS

Milan's modern skyscrapers and sustainable new developments, which include a tower overflowing with plant life, can be found in the aptly named **Porta Nuova** (p239) area. It's a giant leap from the city's rationalist architecture and *case di ringhiera* (traditional Milanese houses).

WHERE TO GO CLUBBING IN MILAN

Tempio del Futuro Perduto
Started by disenchanted youths, this cultural centre with dystopian vibes is the place for electronica nights.

Plastic
A club with a star-studded history. Join the ranks of Keith Haring, a regular at the former location.

Rocket
Young clubbers come to twerk, trap and pump their fists to techno at this dependable Navigli locale.

MILAN'S ANSWER TO SOHO

Somewhat gritty, multicultural and touted as the new LGBTIQ+ area, **NoLo (North of Loreto)** is a side of Milan far from its manicured veneer. Running loosely from Loreto north to the Martesana, it's a place where Chinese takeaways and neon-lit kebab joints meet hip drinking haunts like **GhePensiMI** and **NoLoSo**, an LGBTIQ-friendly bar with an '80s vibe. On Saturday nights a rough-and-ready crowd gathers around Piazza Morbegno, drinking at bars like the all-female **Caffineria** or playing ping-pong on the public tables. Explore the rowdy nightlife scene, try international eateries like **Kungfu Bao** or fuss-free dining at the **Mercato Comunale**, and savour pastries at **Fòla**.

REDA &CO SRL/ALAMY STOCK PHOTO ©

Cotoletta, **Trattoria del Nuovo Macello**

The Satisfaction of Milanese Cooking

ITALY'S UNSUNG CUISINE

In a land famed for its gastronomy, Milanese cuisine often gets elbowed out by crowd-pleasing favourites like the ever-present Neapolitan pizza. But miss it and you forgo sampling one of the unsung heroes of Italian cuisine. Fabulously buttery and meat-heavy, Milanese food is not for the faint-hearted, but it is deeply satisfying, especially when the weather turns cold.

The golden *risotto alla milanese* is the city's signature dish. It combines the delicate flavour of saffron with a meaty broth, arborio rice and (not so) healthy lashings of butter and Parmesan. **Ratanà** has one of the best in town. The dish is perfectly paired with *osso bucco* (literally 'bone with a hole'). Made of slow-cooked veal shanks, the oozy bone marrow is the most prized part of the dish.

Schnitzel fans may also be surprised to learn that this crumbed cutlet might have originated here as *cotoletta*. Many variations can be found around town, from flat and boneless to thick and juicy, but all should

THIRSTY FOR MORE APERITIVO SPOTS?

Find out more about how **aperitivo** (p237) began and discover standout places to enjoy it, including a poolside setting, an urban farmhouse and a bar that invented the Negroni Sbagliato, the city's signature drink.

 WHERE TO BROWSE CONCEPT SHOPS

Tenoha
Slurp ramen, buy a nifty bento box and maybe even see some art at this concept store from Tokyo.

10 Corso Como
A microcosm of on-point brands, it has a fashion store, gallery space, design bookshop, digs and dining.

Spazio Rossana Orlandi
This design showroom, shop and gallery is curated by the keen (sunglass-wearing) eye of Rossana Orlandi.

be fried in butter to be authentic. **Trattoria del Nuovo Macello** does an excellent version, which is thick, crusty and lightly pink inside. Otherwise, you can't go wrong at **Trattoria Masuelli San Marco**, run by the same family since 1921. Trust them to introduce you to the Milanese kitchen – although the fried brains aren't for everyone.

Where the Mighty Used to Rule

THE SFORZAS' RENAISSANCE CASTLE

Powerful medieval and Renaissance dynasties have ruled the roost from **Castello Sforzesco**, the dusty-red brick castle in the city's northwest. First it was the Viscontis, who built the original fortress, then the Sforzas, who turned it into a residence fit for a king (or duke, as the case may be). Da Vinci, Bramante and Bramantino were brought in to beautify it with frescoes; da Vinci also had a hand in the design of the castle's defences. Today it houses several museums where you can spend an afternoon.

If you don't have time to see them all, the most interesting is the **Museo d'Arte Antica** (Museum of Ancient Art) for its frescoed ducal rooms – unfortunately the Sala delle Asse, where Leonardo left his mark, is closed for restoration with no date given for its completion. The unfinished *Pietà Rondanini* by Michelangelo, in the **Museo Pietà Rondanini**, is a short stop and a fascinating look at the artist's last work at the ripe old age of 88. In the **Pinacoteca** you'll find a Mantegna masterpiece, the sombre *Trivulzio Madonna*. There's also the **Museo dei Mobile**, whose furniture collection goes from a 15th-century wedding chest to Ettore Sottsass' wildly sculptural cabinet.

Complete your visit with a stroll in the adjacent **Parco Sempione**, former ducal hunting grounds that are now the city's main green lungs.

WHERE TO EAT & DRINK

Luca Scanni, co-owner of Pavé (p234) and a born-and-bred *milanese*, tells us about the city's food scene and his favourite places to eat and drink. *(@noozieman)*

Milan is in super evolution. And what's exciting is that a lot of younger people are opening new places replacing an older style, which is something my friends and I did with Pavé back in 2014. My favourite places include **Nebbia**, which was opened by young people with a passion for food; **Birrificio Lambrate**, one of the first places in Milan to do something with beer and a unique place to meet; and **Trattoria San Filippo Neri**, a *circolo* (social club) that offers simple Milanese dishes at honest prices.

GETTING AROUND

The metro is a convenient way of getting around. Trams and buses are a tad slow but cover anywhere the trains miss. Buses 90, 91 and 92 are infamous for being the worst in town, so take care if you're riding them alone at night. It's easy to receive tickets by phone – just send the message 'ATM' to the number 48444. Otherwise buy them at the station or from tobacconists and newsstands.

Getting around by bike or moped lets you slip through the congested traffic. Both have on-street share options such as BikeMi and Cityscoot. Driving isn't worth the hassle due to the heavy traffic, near-impossible parking and Area C, which restricts access to the city centre. If you do dare drive, street parking is colour-coded: yellow is for residents, blue is paid and the mythical white is free.

Taxis don't meet the demand of the city, especially during events such as Fashion Week. This means you're unlikely to hail one off the street; look for a taxi rank or call to book.

Varese

Monza

Milan

Brescia

Pavia

Beyond Milan

Renaissance treasures, stretches of rice fields
and a more relaxed energy emerge in the area
surrounding Milan.

The green expanse beyond Milan is absorbing for those with
the patience to look. Monza has been attracting royalty since
the wife of a Lombard king chose it for her summer residence
in the 6th century. Its Villa Reale was inhabited by illustrious figures, from Napoleon's stepson to the King of Savoy.
Towards the Po river, student-happy Pavia was the seat of
the Visconti court from 1365 to 1413 and holds vainglorious
reminders of the family's wealth. Further-flung Brescia has
the longest history, 3200 years to be exact. It used to be the
Roman town of Brixia and its ancient ruins are in surprisingly good condition.

TOP TIP

Trains from Milan's
Stazione Centrale run
frequently to the region's
hubs. Most places can be
reached in under an hour.

Villa Reale

POSZTOS/SHUTTERSTOCK ©

Formula 1 race, Autodromo Nazionale Monza

A Regal Summer Palace

HOME OF THE HABSBURGS AND SAVOYS

A 35-minute train ride from Milan, this colossal U-shaped villa stands proudly on the south end of Monza's 295-hectare walled park. Built between 1777 and 1780, the neoclassical **Villa Reale** was commissioned by the Empress Maria Theresa of Austria as a summer residence for her 14th child, Archduke Ferdinand of Austria. Modelled after Vienna's Schönbrunn Palace (their 'other' royal residence), its facade is surprisingly restrained as the Habsburgs didn't want to flaunt their wealth in an Austrian-occupied country.

The interiors, however, are a different story. Further embellished in the century that followed by Napoleon's stepson and the King and Queen of Savoy, the palace is decked out in glittering chandeliers, golden boiserie, tapestries, lacquered wood furniture and marble floors. Too bad Vittorio Emanuele III closed it in 1900, following the assassination of his father the King of Savoy at a sporting event in Monza. Left to languish, the palace was restored and opened to the public in 2014.

FULL THROTTLE ON THE MONZA CIRCUIT

For Grand Prix lovers, Monza's 5.8km race track, the **Autodromo Nazionale Monza**, needs no introduction. One of the oldest tracks in Europe, it was built in 1922 and is known for its blistering high speeds, long straights, fast curves and the woody setting of Monza's monster-sized park. Many flock here for its glitzy Formula 1 race days, but you can also visit for a spin in a grand tourer or Formula 1 or Formula 3 single-seaters. There are also track days, when racing enthusiasts can take to the circuit in their own car, and a go-karting area where kids (over the age of six) and adults can indulge in their need for speed.

✂ WHERE TO EAT IN MONZA

L'Albero dei Gelati
One of Italy's best gelaterie, with fluffy ice cream made from natural ingredients provided by handpicked farmers. €

Osteria del Cavolo
A tad twee, with mint-green tablecloths and fake flowers, but the Lombard dishes are excellent. €€

Forno del Mastro
By a former baker from Milan's Davide Longoni, it does exceptional slabs of pizza with a crunchy base. €

LOOKING FOR ANCIENT BRIXIA

Down the road from Santa Giulia lies the **Brixia Parco Archeologico,** which has some of the best-preserved Roman ruins in Italy. Dating back to a time when Brescia was the Roman town of Brixia, it's made up of three parts that can be visited in an hour or less. The **Santuario Repubblicano** was built in the 1st century CE and impresses with its frescoes in vivid colours. The **Templo Capitolino** was where the devout would come to worship Jupiter, Juno and Minerva. Built in 73 CE, it has the original marble flooring and a bronze *Winged Victory* statue found here in 1826. There's also a Roman **theatre,** but it's sadly in worse shape than the rest.

Santa Giulia museum

Dedicate an hour or two to the 28 rooms – including the **royal apartments** of King Umberto I and his wife Margherita, a 100-seat theatre and a richly decorated chapel – and the orderly English-style **gardens** brimming with over 4000 rose varieties.

The Forgotten Unesco Sight

ROMAN RUINS, CHURCHES AND RELICS

RUMINATING ON THE ROMANS

Delve deeper into Roman history at the **Grotte di Catullo** (p259) in Lago di Garda. These tumble-down remains of a luxury Roman villa from the 1st century CE give you an inkling of life on the lake a very long time ago.

Only in Italy, a country that boasts the highest number of Unesco sites, would a place like the **Santa Giulia** museum fall off the tourist radar – which is good news for you. After a 35-minute train ride from Milan, hours can be spent wandering through this massive ex-monastery packed with 12,000 objects documenting Brescia's history from the 3rd millennium BCE to the Renaissance. Containing several other buildings and riddled with Roman statues, fragmented mosaics, tombstones, sarcophagi and Corinthian capitals, it can be a tad overwhelming – in which case you might want to skip to the key attractions.

✂ WHERE TO EAT IN BRESCIA

La Vineria
This restaurant and wine bar does fantastic regional cuisine, like *casoncelli* pasta with braised meat. €€

Belvedere 030
During summer months locals flock to the city's castle, where you can eat from food trucks in the open air. €

Vivace
Geothermal heating, a wine 'theatre' and artistic cuisine are the ingredients of standout contemporary dining. €€€

The most notable are two **Roman townhouses:** Domus di Dioniso (named for its mosaic depicting Dionysius, god of wine) and the Domus delle Fontane, named after its (missing) fountains. From raised walkways you can admire their still beautiful coloured mosaics and fresco fragments.

The Romanesque church **Santa Maria in Solario**, which is covered in frescoes, is also impressive, but the real treasure here is the glass-encased Cross of Desiderius, blinged-up with 212 gems set in hammered metal. In the church's lower chamber you can see the precious Lipsanoteca, an embellished ivory box containing holy relics. The cavernous church of **San Salvatore** also has some of the best preserved frescoes from the Early Middle Ages while the Coro delle Monache (Nun's Choir) houses the elaborate Martinengo mausoleum.

Villa Panza's American Collection

CONTEMPORARY ART IN 18TH-CENTURY SURROUNDS

An hour's drive northwest of Milan, this 18th-century villa is the unlikely venue for a stellar collection of contemporary American art. And yet when looking down a vaulted corridor with aged parquet, blazing in Dan Flavin's neon lights, the contrast undeniably works.

Built atop the Biumio hill in Varese, **Villa Panza** was conceived in 1755 as a summer playtime residence for Marquis Paolo Antonio Menafoglio. Fast-forward a couple of centuries, through several titled owners and renovations done by Luigi Canonica and Piero Portaluppi, and you reach Count Giuseppe Panza who started amassing the collection in 1956. He also invited artists to transform the shed and stables in the villa.

Now its sumptuous rooms decorated with Renaissance furnishings and scattered with African and pre-Columbian artefacts are the harmonious backdrop for minimalist works that play with light, colour and space. Artworks include monochrome canvases by Phil Sims, a frameless window in a white room by Robert Irwin and the numerous light installations of Dan Flavin. The Italian garden is similarly dotted with art and offers lovely glimpses of Varese below.

A visit should take a couple of hours. If you're feeling hungry, the **Luce** restaurant makes for a refined dining spot with garden views. The villa is closed on Mondays.

SPIRITUAL TREK WITHOUT THE CROWDS

Nestled on a hilltop north of Varese, the **Sacro Monte di Varese** is a Unesco World Heritage Site that remains blissfully uncrowded. One of the nine Sacri Monti (Sacred Mountains) of Piedmont and Lombardy, it was conceived in the 17th century.

Wend your way up the mountain along a 2km-long cobblestone path dotted with 14 chapels (which represent the mysteries of the Rosary) and blessed with picture-perfect views. The final stop is the Santuario di Santa Maria del Monte. It should take less than two hours. At the top the village of **Santa Maria del Monte**, with its winding alleys and stone walls, is a pretty place for a drink with views.

WHERE TO EAT IN VARESE

Buosi
Denis Buosi's cafe is home to chocolate in all forms, along with delectable pastries. €

Ristorante Pinocchio 1826
Headed by ex-MasterChef participant Davide Aviano and noted for its sophisticated Italian cuisine. €€€

La Piedigrotta
A cult pizza place in the town centre – even Liam Gallagher is said to have sung its praises. €

BEST DINING IN PAVIA

Amare €€
Feast on fresh prawns and Sicilian scampi from Milan's fish market, just five minutes from the Certosa.

Alvolo Cibi di Strada €
Dig into gourmet *panini* with mouthwatering combos like Tuscan bacon with anchovies and roasted peppers.

Osteria della Madonna €€
This rustic *locale* does hearty Pavese dishes, like pasta and beans, a stone's throw from the cathedral.

A Duke's Final Resting Place

THE VISCONTI MONASTERY

Ten kilometres north of Pavia and an hour's train ride from Milan, the **Certosa di Pavia** is by no means a modest monastery. Its church facade brims with reliefs depicting the life of Christ and the glittering career of Gian Galeazzo Visconti (first duke of Milan), along with inlaid marble, statues and spires. This inclination for extravagance comes as little surprise, seeing as it was worked on by some of the same architects as Milan's Duomo. It was suitably grandiose for Gian Galeazzo Visconti, who commissioned it as the resting place for him and his family. Started in 1396 and completed almost a century later, it's an unusual mix of Gothic and Renaissance styles.

Pay your respects to said duke in a less-than-sombre tiered tomb in the south transept. Across in the north transept lies middle-aged Ludovico il Moro Sforza and his young wife Beatrice D'Este, in a monument that bears their sculpted sleeping likenesses. The triptych in the sacristy, carved in wood, hippo teeth and turtle bones, is an intricate highlight. Don't forget to look for the painted friars peeking from the *trompe l'œil* windows by the central nave. It will take a couple of hours to see everything.

The Certosa is closed on Mondays and between 11.30am and 2.30pm. Entry is by donation. Monks lead the tours in Italian.

A TASTE FOR EXCESS

Visit Milan's **Duomo** (p235) to take a look at what inspired the excessive style of the Certosa di Pavia. Some of the same architects worked on both buildings even though the Certosa was finished centuries earlier.

GETTING AROUND

Trains are without a doubt the easiest way of getting from Milan to smaller towns and regional hubs. They run regularly from Milan's Stazione Centrale. Buying 1st-class tickets will sometimes guarantee you air-conditioning and a more pleasant trip, but not always. Buses are much slower and often the difference in price is negligible; they also run less frequently. Driving a car comes with some intense traffic jams during August as this is the time most locals flee Milan. Additionally, in some towns you won't be able to drive through the centre because they are traffic-limited zones (check the signs). Parking can be harder to come by in summer, but is nonetheless not too difficult. Remember when it comes to on-street parking: yellow is for residents only, blue is paid, and white is the jackpot (free).

LAGO DI COMO

● Lago di Como

✪ Rome

This wishbone-shaped lake in the shadow of the snowcapped Alps has long held the world in its thrall. Virgil sang its praises while Shelley wrote, 'This lake exceeds anything I ever beheld in beauty'. And since Roman times, when it was a wealthy trade centre, it's been the summer residence of the affluent – a tradition it continues even now (hello Clooney).

In the 18th and 19th centuries the became renowned for its silk industry (its textile industry is still big today) and many villas were built beautifying its shores. Como's popularity took a slight hit, though, when Mussolini was captured and shot there in 1945.

Today Como teems with people in summer and is a hub of chic hotels and eateries. Bellagio, with its stone staircases and rhododendron-filled gardens, is the lake's most picturesque location, while quieter Varenna still rivals the rest for good looks.

TOP TIP

In summer, consider skipping the ferries from main towns like Como, where queues can be up to an hour long. It's better to drive although there are some tight turns and narrow roads along the lake. Finding parking in popular areas is also a challenge.

Elegant Villas of the Elite

BELLE ÉPOQUE VILLAS AND GARDENS

Swanning around the illustrious former country estates of various nobility, cardinals, politicians and even an avid explorer is part of the allure of any trip to Lake Como. Admire the extravagance of villas decked out in marble staircases and crystal chandeliers, and the audacity of gardens brimming with rare fauna and flora from around the globe. Each villa will take at least a couple of hours if not a leisurely afternoon, especially if you want to relax in the gardens and soak up those lakeside views.

Jutting out from the Lenno hamlet like a secluded paradise, **Villa del Balbianello** exudes cinematic appeal – understandable given that it appeared in both *Casino Royale* and *Attack of the Clones*. A guided tour of this 18th-century villa is one of the most coveted experiences on the lake (you'll have to book a week in advance to be guaranteed a spot), which also introduces you to the life of Guido Monzino, the villa's last owner. An explorer and mountaineer, he left behind many mementoes from his travels, including a snow sled from an expedition to the North Pole. The villa can be accessed by a 1km path from the main square along the lake shore. You can also take a taxi boat from Lenno.

Villa Carlotta sits on top of a terraced garden on the Tremezzo shoreline. Named after a Prussian princess, it's known for the rich art collection left by its second owner

CRUISING THE WATERS

There's no better way to experience the lake than from the water. Taking a ferry from one town to the next is just the tip of the iceberg. You can also go on a luxury boat tour, or if you're looking for the flexibility of exploring at your own pace, captaining your own boat is a surprisingly easy affair. No licence is needed for boats with smaller motors (40hp), and in most cases all you need is ID and a cash deposit.

If you're looking for something more active, water activities abound. Stand-up paddleboarding, wakeboarding, kayaking, water- and jet skiing are all readily available. Kayak tours will also take you paddling to all the main sights.

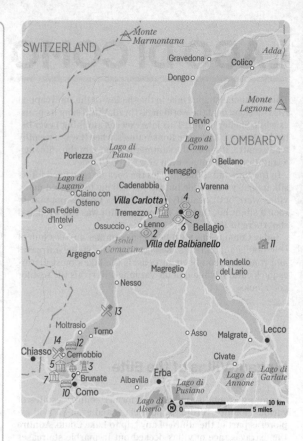

Giovanni Battista Sommariva, whose passion for art was second only to his political ambition. Works by Francesco Hayez, Antonio Canova and Bertel Thorvaldsen pop up throughout the villa. The enormous gardens alone will take 45 minutes to an hour of your time, leading you from a bamboo forest with 25 species to a lush setting filled with ferns and palms from Australia. Come spring and the garden breaks out in blooming rhododendrons, azaleas and camellias.

Across from Villa Carlotta on the Bellagio shoreline, the neoclassical **Villa Melzi** has an English-style garden, scattered

 WHERE TO EAT ON LAGO DI COMO

Beretta il Fornaio
Fluffy *nuvole* (literally 'clouds'), are this Como bakery's sweets of choice. €

Ristorante Materia
Splurge on Michelin-star cuisine in Cernobbio with innovative dishes like marrow and saffron dessert. €€€

Da Luciano Bottega e Caffè
This family-run cafe-cum-butcher's in Laglio has lakeside views and top-quality meat dishes. €€

BEN PETCHARAPIRACHT/SHUTTERSTOCK ©

Villa del Balbianello (p249)

FUNICULAR RIDE FROM THE 1800S

The weathered wood and brick entrance is the first clue that you'll be boarding a **cable railway** dating back to 1893. Connecting Como with the quiet village of Brunate, which sits 715m high on a hill, the funicular takes several minutes as it trundles up, giving you plenty of time to enjoy the panoramic views of the lake and mountains.

From the top you can walk 25 minutes uphill to the **Faro Voltiano** (lighthouse in San Maurizio), dedicated to Como-born pioneering scientist Alessandro Volta. Muster the energy for the 143 spiralling steps to the top of the 29m-high tower, and you'll be rewarded with views said to extend as far as the golden Madonnina of Milan's Duomo on a clear day.

THE GUIDE

MILAN & THE LAKES

with statues that include Egyptian-style lions and the neo-classical Dante and Beatrice; the latter is said to have inspired the music of Liszt. A meander through the garden will take you to a grotto, a maple-lined Japanese pond, and an area with more than 250 camellias that harks back to a time when camellia rivalry was a 'thing' among elite lakeside dwellers. Nearby **Villa Serbelloni**, which sits on top of the Bellagio promontory, delivers sweeping views of both the Como and Lecco side of the lake, as you stroll 18km of paths lined with manicured hedges, olive trees and geometric flower beds.

The Lake's Undeniable Pearl

BELLAGIO'S NATURAL BEAUTY

At the crux of the lake's inverted Y, **Bellagio** is quite simply gorgeous. Flanked on both sides by silky waters and lined with villas, dark cypress groves, oleanders and lime trees, it's not known as the 'pearl' of the lake for nothing. Perhaps Flaubert said it best when visiting Bellagio in 1845: 'One could live and

 WHERE TO HAVE DRINKS ON LAGO DI COMO

Fresco Cocktail Shop
Let owner and mixologist Andrea Attanasio whip you up a cocktail zinging with fresh flavours. Located in Como.

Cava Turacciolo
In a cavernous Bellagio cellar, the 300-strong wine selection is complemented by heaped plates of cold cuts.

Hemingway
In the style of a Cuban gentleman's club, this is the place to sip Hemingway's favourite cocktails in Como.

KILOMETRE OF KNOWLEDGE

In a town busting with tourists, the 1km-long pedestrian path known as the **Chilometro della Conoscenza** (Kilometre of Knowledge) manages to keep itself off the beaten track. Connecting three villas on Como's western shore, it's a tranquil 45-minute stroll that begins at **Villa Olmo**, passes through **Villa del Grumello** and ends in **Villa Sucota**. Along the way you'll wander through wooded areas, past 19th-century greenhouses and the quaint Celesia chapel, while getting your fill of camera-worthy lake views. Entrance is free and it's open from 9am to 5pm Sunday to Friday, from April to October.

ARKANTO/SHUTTERSTOCK ©

Bellagio

MORE ON LAGO DI COMO'S VILLAS

Find out more about Villa Melzi and Villa Serbelloni and take a look at the many other sumptuous **villas** (p249) on the lake's shores. Villa Balbianello is the silver-screen favourite.

die here'. And even though some things have changed since Flaubert's time (he'd probably agree there are too many tourists), an afternoon on its shores has to be done.

From the port, wander up the stoney stairs of Salita Serbelloni, stopping to peruse the wine and silk shops. At Via Garibaldi, if you turn right and walk for 10 minutes you'll hit Punta Spartivento, the northernmost tip of the town where there's a swath of green and some pretty views. You'll pass the town's brick Romanesque church on the way, which is worth ducking into for its stark simplicity. But the real stars of Bellagio are its **villa gardens** (the villas themselves are not open to the public), which also provide a nice respite from the crowds. Villa Serbelloni's (p251) park is perched atop the promontory with some expansive views, whereas Villa Melzi's (p250) lakeside garden brims with exotic plants, giant rhododendrons and azaleas.

 WHERE TO STAY ON LAGO DI COMO

Posta Design Hotel
In central Como, this boutique hotel has chic neutral-toned rooms and a pumping street-level bistro. €€

Villa D'Este
Glimpse aristocratic extravagance from a bygone era in this 16th-century Cernobbio villa turned five-star hotel. €€€

Ostello Bello
Bright rooms, cheerful staff, a garden nook and oodles of activities make this Como hostel a budget winner. €

Sights Set on the Summit

HIKING TRAILS AND EPIC VIEWS

Lake Como's dreamy mountainscape is more than just for looking at, and several days can be spent exploring its many valleys and peaks. A dense network of well-trodden routes exist, connecting villages to rocky summits and *rifugi* (mountain shelters), where you can not only get a hearty hot meal, but also stay the night with basic amenities. Best of all, with the aquamarine waters below and snow-clad mountains in the far distance, there's no shortage of impressive views.

The most famous mountains in the area are part of the Grigna massif and sit on the Lecco side of the lake. The **Grigna Settentrionale** (aka Grignone) is the highest at 2410m, while to the southwest stands the smaller **Grigna Meridionale** (aka Grignetta), which is dominated by stoney spires and towers that seem deliberately made for climbing; one even has a bell that you can ring when you make it to the top. Both mountains are laced with trails for hikers of all levels. If you want to make it to the Grignone summit, it will take you around 3½ hours one way; park around the Rifugio Cainallo before heading up. At the top, rest your weary legs at the **Rifugio Brioschi**. Soaring panoramic views more than make up for the somewhat frill-less accommodation.

A MEMORABLE MOMENT

Alberto Trombetta, an alpine guide born in Como who founded outdoor activity service Lake Como Adventures (@ *lakecomoadventures*), shares his most memorable moment on the lake.

Seeing the sunset at **Rifugio Brioschi** is unforgettable. It's on top of one of the highest peaks in Lake Como, the Grignone. It's a long walk to get there and the area is quite wild. I take clients here sometimes to stay overnight. What makes it unique is you get to see the whole lake beneath your feet. The place is really spectacular. And there are hardly any tourists because you can't do it in a day. It's a deeper experience of the lake.

GETTING AROUND

The ferry system is extensive but a tad confusing because of the many options. The slow ferries operate two routes, Como–Colico and Lecco–Bellagio (only in summer), making multiple stops along the way. Fast hydrofoils and large ferries (which can carry vehicles) connect main hubs such as Como, Bellagio, Varenna and Menaggio. Keep in mind that, while ferries are a scenic way of getting around, from main towns like Como ticket queues can be up to an hour long. Consider taking the bus, which is less crowded and air-conditioned, although it runs less frequently (around five times a day depending on the destination).

Driving a car can be great for those who aren't put off by the idea of tight turns and narrow roads that get clogged by bulky buses. If you want to avoid traffic congestion, head there early and leave after dinner when day-trippers have gone home.

LAGO MAGGIORE

Lago Maggiore

Rome

Snaking its way through gentle hills to the seat of the Swiss Alps, Lago Maggiore is Italy's longest lake. Churchill spent his honeymoon on its shores, Hemingway convalesced here, and both left gushing about its beauty. Additionally, from the Middle Ages aristocratic families such as the Viscontis, Sforzas, Borromeos and Habsburgs fought over it, leaving behind villas and castles you can now admire.

Its history is marred only by the Lago Maggiore massacres of WWII, when Jewish families were executed and thrown into the lake by the Nazis. And more recently in 2021, when a tragic cable-car crash left Italy reeling.

Stresa is the place to revel in its bygone decadence, a quick boat ride from the enchanting Borromean Islands. Bustling Verbania, the biggest town on the lake, is a good place to base yourself, whereas fairy-tale-like Cannobio makes for a quieter stay at Switzerland's border.

TOP TIP

It's less busy than Lake Como, so having your own transport isn't as necessary. Ferries regularly cruise between most shoreside towns, and ticket queues are manageable. You only really need a car if you're planning on exploring inland and the mountains.

MORE FROM THE BORROMEOS

The stark, towering **Rocca di Angera** was bought by the Borromeos from the Viscontis back in 1449. Along with 13th-century frescoes, it houses the priceless (and creepy) family doll collection spread over 12 rooms in the Museo della Bambola. Arrive by ferry from Arona, and it's a 1.5km walk. The **Parco Pallavicino** was bought in 2017 by Prince Vitaliano Borromeo (yep, the family is still going strong). The neoclassical villa is closed to the public, but the extensive gardens and a zoo with over 50 species can be accessed with a ticket.

From Rocks to Aristocratic Residences

THE BORROMEO PALACE ISLANDS

What's not to envy about the Borromeo family? They had wealth (they were bankers), power (they were high-ranking cardinals), and in the 16th century they created their own corner of paradise on Lake Maggiore, with these tiny islands a quick boat ride from Stresa.

Isola Madre is the biggest of the islands and is dominated by the palace, where you can peek into the Borromeo family's private life. The stairs are lined with portraits of the Borromeos' distinguished members and the rooms are decorated with plush furnishings from their various residences. Mannequins in servant's livery pop up occasionally to surprise the unsuspecting. The sunny Venetian Room, decorated as a pergola intertwined with plants, and a room dedicated to a puppet stage, give you the sense of a charmed domestic life. But it's the 8-hectare garden that's the real showstopper. An array of flashy looking pheasants and peacocks roam the grounds steeped in palm trees, cacti, camellias and a 160-year-old cypress tree.

Isola Bella shows the family at their most ambitious. Before Carlo III Borromeo transformed the island and named it for his *bella* (beautiful) wife, it was just a craggy rock inhabited by a few fishermen. But it was Vitaliano VI who turned it into the baroque vision of opulence we see today.

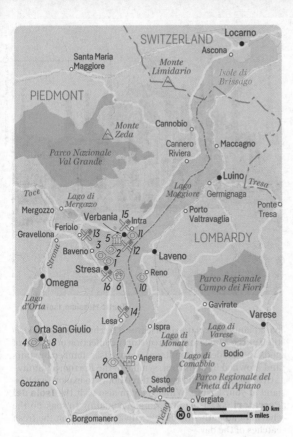

The palace has more than 20 rooms for you to wander through. Along with the ornate Sala del Trono (Throne Room) and the Sala delle Regine (Queens' Room), standouts include the Galleria Berthier, which is lined floor-to-ceiling with gilt-edged paintings from the likes of Raphael and Titian. The biggest surprise, though, is the downstairs **Grotto**. Decorated in rough stones and stucco ornaments of nymphs and mermaids, the cavernous chambers look like a place Neptune might call home.

The 10-tiered garden overflows with exotic flowers and plants, such as a centuries-old camphor tree and giant rhu-

 WHERE TO EAT AROUND LAGO MAGGIORE

Ristorante Il Vicoletto
Try creamed lake fish, ricotta-filled ravioli and Piedmontese favourites in this unassuming Stresa restaurant. €€

Il Rapanello
Nab a lakeside table in Lesa to gorge on fish soup, followed by pasta cooked in the remaining sauce. €€

Fiore di Latte Pizzeria
Try authentic Neapolitan pizza dripping with fresh quality ingredients by this husband-and-wife team in Feriolo. €

FRANCESCO BONINO/SHUTTERSTOCK ©

Teatro Massimo, Isola Bella

There's something altogether unnerving about coming across the 35m-tall statue at **Sacro Monte di San Carlo** in the quiet lakeside town of Arona, the birthplace of San Carlo Borromeo (1538–84) who was a cardinal, archbishop of Milan and also a verified saint. It was his cousin Cardinal Federico Borromeo who decided to build this monument in his memory. It's accompanied by a church and three chapels, a slight downgrade from the originally projected 15 chapels. Completed in 1698, it's said to have inspired New York's Statue of Liberty. Climb inside and peer through the saint's eyes and nostrils for some lovely views.

barb plants with plate-sized leaves. The cherry on the cake is the **Teatro Massimo**, a three-storey confection of statues of gods and goddesses, fountains and obelisks, flanked by stairs and crowned by a unicorn, symbol of the Borromeo family.

Give yourself a solid two to three hours to explore each island at your leisure. While you can also visit the **Isola dei Pescatori** (aka Isola Superiore), it's mainly to soak up the charm of an authentic fishing village and dine on the fresh catches of the day.

A Scottish Captain's Exotic Garden

VILLA TARANTO'S ENGLISH GARDEN

Villa Taranto's Normandy-style mansion is closed to the public, not that anyone is asking. They're too busy exploring the rambling 16-hectare garden created by Neil McEacharn, the Scottish captain who wanted an English-style garden that would remind him of his native land (only with more exotic plant life). He bought the estate in 1931 from Marquise Sant'Elia after spotting it in an advertisement in *The Times*, then set to work on its 30-year transformation. This involved creating an 8km network of pipes to pump water from the

 WHERE TO HAVE DRINKS AROUND LAGO MAGGIORE

La Casera
This deli-bistro in Verbania is a shrine to cheese (ripened in their own cellar) and Piedmontese wines.

AC Picchia Bar
Tucked away in Verbania's Villa Giulia, the lush garden and lake view make this bar a scenic drink stop.

Sky Bar
Sip martinis while gazing out at the Borromean Islands from the chic 7th floor of Hotel La Palma in Stresa.

lake and large-scale excavations to dig out an artificial valley. Twenty thousand plant species later, and it's considered one of Europe's finest botanic gardens. It's at its most eye-catching in spring when fuchsia and scarlet rhododendrons, azaleas and tulips jostle for your attention. It also has some of the biggest specimens of South American water lilies.

The garden is open from March to November. The villa has its very own dock, which makes it easy to get to by ferry. Otherwise it's a 20-minute walk from central Pallanza. While you're in Pallanza, you might want to make a stop at the **Museo del Paesaggio**, a 17th-century *palazzo* that's home to the distinct impressionist sculptures by prince and artist Paolo Troubetzkoy.

Monastery on a Cliff Face

A HERMIT, FRESCOES AND VIEWS

Hanging off a rocky cliff face on Lago Maggiore's southeast shore, the centuries-old hermitage of **Santa Caterina del Sasso** is an awesome sight seemingly stuck in another time. Legend has it that it all started with shipwrecked merchant Alberto Besozzi who, after being 'saved' by the holy martyr Catherine of Alexandria in Egypt, renounced his life of wealth for that of a cave-dwelling hermit. He's responsible for the site's first structure, a small chapel dedicated to St Catherine built around the 13th century. His remains also happen to be displayed here in a creepy manikin encased in glass, which doubles as a donation receptacle.

Over the centuries various structures were tacked on to Besozzi's chapel and embellished. Now you can spend an hour wandering through hushed porticoes, a presbytery, chapels and an arbour with, unsurprisingly, spectacular views. There are also plenty of frescoes to marvel and ponder over, including a bizarre series from the 16th century depicting the Danse Macabre (Dance of Death), where a jovial skeleton (death) appears before a cheating merchant and a lustful couple.

Approach by ferry for the most dramatic views. From the dock you'll need to climb up the 80 steps from the entrance; otherwise take the 268 scenic steps down from the car park or pay €1 to take the lift dug into rock.

DETOUR TO LAGO D'ORTA

Leave the crowds behind in the forested shores and medieval towns of Lago d'Orta, shy sister to Lago Maggiore. Just a 35-minute drive from Stresa, the village of **Orta San Giulio** is considered the lake's jewel. Aside from the charm of its tangled laneways, its hilltop is scattered with 20 chapels that make up the **Sacro Monte di Orta**. Wandering from one to the other and marvelling at the lake below is a peaceful way to while away the afternoon. Meanwhile, in front of Orta San Giulio's main square the minuscule island of **San Giulio** beckons across the waters, with its handful of streets where life ebbs at a leisurely pace.

GETTING AROUND

There are regular car and passenger ferries along with fast hydrofoils, which make it fairly easy to get around. Services include those connecting Arona and Stresa, and Verbania and Pallanza. If you're planning on spending a full day zipping to and from the islands, consider getting the Libera Circolazione (Free Movement) ticket, which lets you hop on and off the ferries all day; the ticket expires when you return to the island you started from.

The area is well connected by trains along the west bank to Stresa but less so along the east shore, where you'll have to take a combination of buses and trains to reach your destination. Driving a car around Lago Maggiore is also fairly easy and gives you the freedom of detouring to Lago d'Orta. There's a regular car ferry service between Intra and Laveno.

LAGO DI GARDA

● Lago di Garda

✪ Rome

This ladle-shaped lake has a literary pedigree that's hard to match. German poet Goethe made it his home, DH Lawrence finished his novel *Sons and Lovers* here, while Ezra Pound urged James Joyce to visit. Sensitive thinkers are seduced by the mild Mediterranean climate of Italy's biggest lake and its shores spilling with olive groves and lemon trees. But they're not the only ones.

The Roman ruling class built their summer villas here and Renaissance noble families picked up the habit. Mussolini also chose the lake's west bank as the headquarters for his doomed Italian Social Republic. Additionally, many wanted to claim it as their own. In the 13th century it was the seat of power struggles between the Della Scala and Visconti families and the Republic of Venice.

Sirmione, on a skinny and picturesque peninsula, is the main draw and swarms with tourists during summer. Gardone Riviera appeals for its belle époque charm.

TOP TIP

Skip the sporadic buses and slow ferry rides and hire a car, especially if you want to visit more than a couple of towns. Keep in mind that parking in popular areas is scarce and check before entering town centres as they might be limited-traffic zones.

(DON'T) DRIVE LIKE BOND

If you've seen the opening chase scene of *Quantum of Solace*, **Strada della Forra** might seem familiar – that is, if you dare pry your eyes from the road to look around. Climbing its way from the lake to 414m-high Tremosine sul Garda, the route is a sweat-inducing 6km of hairpin bends, narrow tunnels and zigzags along rocky cliff faces. Winston Churchill described it as the eighth wonder of the world. From the lake, follow the SP38 detour that goes up Via Benaco. In high season you can only drive uphill due to congestion. It's for skilled drivers only – and don't follow Bond's example; take it easy to enjoy those heart-pounding views.

The Strange World of Gabriele D'Annunzio

HOME OF A PROTO-FASCIST POET

Poet, war hero and womaniser, Gabriele D'Annunzio also has the dubious honour of inspiring Mussolini's brand of Italian fascism. **Il Vittoriale degli Italiani** is the place he lived and died in and designed to enshrine his war-time heroics. Mussolini's government foot the bill, preferring to keep D'Annunzio dabbling in home renovations rather than politics. From the looks of it, D'Annunzio was happy to oblige. Walking through his home, you soon suspect the man was as excessive and bizarre as the buildings themselves.

His home includes a Roman-style amphitheatre, a museum of his military successes, a real-life battleship and his grandiose mausoleum. The Priory (his main residence) reveals much about the man. Dimly lit (his eyes were light-sensitive), it's cluttered with leather-clad books, busts and animal statues. Details such as a low-hanging beam that forces visitors to bow before entering his study are telling. So is a wall inscription reading, 'As there are five fingers on a hand, there are only five mortal sins' – apparently, lust and greed weren't sins to D'Annunzio. Especially unnerving is the Leper's Room with its bed resembling both a coffin and cradle, where he intended to be laid after death.

You could spend ages digging through the **Priory** alone, but two hours in D'Annunzio's strange world is enough for most. The estate is a 20-minute bus ride east of Salò.

HIGHLIGHTS
1 Grotte di Catullo
2 Il Vittoriale
degli Italiani

SIGHTS
3 Parco Archeologico
Rocca di Manerba
4 Strada della Forra

**ACTIVITIES,
COURSES & TOURS**
(see 1) Aquaria
Thermal SPA
5 La Strada del Ponale

SLEEPING
6 Meet Garda
Lake Hostel
7 Restel de Fer
8 Villa Arcadio

EATING
9 Bruschetteria Nose
10 Lido 84
(see 2) Osteria
Antico Brolo
11 Osteria dell'Orologio
12 Ristorante Capriccio
13 Trattoria Il Riolet

**DRINKING
& NIGHTLIFE**
14 Ponale
Alto Belvedere

Ruins of a Roman Villa

A NOBLE 1ST-CENTURY CE HOME

On the tip of the Sirmione peninsula with views of the lake on three sides, it's easy to imagine how the teetering arches, crumbling walls (some reaching heights of over 13m) and broken corridors were once part of an enormous Roman villa. Believed to have been owned by an aristocratic family from Verona, the **Grotte di Catullo** dates back as far as the 1st century CE – which shows just how long Lago di Garda has been home to prime real estate.

FOR MOUNTAIN LOVERS

Lago di Garda also happens to be a hotspot for **hiking and climbing** (p260). The Grigna massif, in particular, has numerous trails for all levels coupled with tranquil views of the lake below.

 WHERE TO STAY ON LAGO DI GARDA

Villa Arcadio
Surrounded by olive groves, this former monastery above Salò is the place for a quiet, elegant stay. €€€

Restel de Fer
Expect a warm welcome at this family-run *locale* in Riva del Garda with tasteful rooms and home cooking. €€

Meet Garda Lake Hostel
Rooms are a tad stark but the friendly vibe and chill-out zones make up for it. Located in Peschiera del Garda. €

WHERE TO DINE

Riccardo Camanini,
chef and part-owner
of Michelin-starred
restaurant Lido 84
(*@ristorantelido84*) in
Gardone Riviera, shares
his favourite places
to eat around Lago di
Garda.

**Osteria
dell'Orologio, Salò**
For the homemade
pasta dishes and the
style and warmth of a
true Italian welcome
from the owner Alberto.

**Trattoria Il Riolet,
Gardone Riviera**
For the breathtaking
view of the lake, as well
as the goodness of the
food on offer, without
unnecessary frills but
extremely rich in both
substance and taste.

**Ristorante Capriccio,
Manerba del Garda**
To give yourself a nice
treat where you always
feel at home.

GORILLAIMAGES/SHUTTERSTOCK ©

Mountain biking, Lago di Garda

It's spread over 2 hectares, so if you want to go in depth you can spend over an hour wandering from the 'swimming pool' to various rooms such as the 'Hall of Giants' reconstructing the villa in your mind. There's also a museum that contains fragments of mosaics and household tools unearthed during the excavations, which paint a picture of life in the Roman villa. Don't forget to bring your swimming suit as the ticket lets you access a rocky secluded beach in the northwest; follow the music from the bar on the beach.

And for those scratching their head over the distinctly non-grotto nature of this Grotto, it was given this name in the 15th century when early discoverers mistook the remains for natural caves.

Hiking the Rocca di Manerba
NATURE AND FORTRESS RUINS

This little-known **rocky promontory** packs a surprisingly big punch. A rocky spur poking out of Lago di Garda's southwest coast, this is where the goddess Minerva had her

WHERE TO EAT ON LAGO DI GARDA

Lido 84
Dining here is a rare pleasure –
it's ranked in the world's top 10
and Michelin-starred to boot.
In Gardone Riviera. €€€

Osteria Antico Brolo
Classic Italian dishes with artful
touches in a Gardone Riviera
osteria (tavern) brimming with
old-world charm. €€€

Bruschetteria Nose
This temple to bruschetta
offers 13 tasty toppings, such
as ricotta and sausage. In
Desenzano del Garda. €

temple for obvious reasons – it's a natural paradise. Carpeted in feather grass, dogtooth violets and wild orchids, and roamed by butterflies and kestrels, it's little surprise that the park is also Unesco-protected.

There are 17 **trails** that will take you on two- to three-hour-long explorations of the park's fauna and flora. Otherwise, those short on time can take the steep 15-minute walk from the car park to the medieval fortress on its summit. Not only will you enjoy panoramic views of the lake, but you won't have to share them with scores of tourists.

There's an **archaeological museum** for those interested in delving into the history of the area, with ancient artefacts from the Mesolithic to the medieval periods. The area is also dotted with tucked-away beaches (which happen to attract the odd nudist), where you can cool off after a hike.

The Cliff-Hugging Strada del Ponale

HISTORIC WALKING ROUTE

Snaking along cliff faces and ducking into tunnels carved into rock, the 10km-long **Strada del Ponale** is a historic route for cyclists and hikers looking for incredible lake views – without too much effort. Built in the 19th century, it was once the only route connecting Riva del Garda with Valle di Ledro. Abandoned in the '90s, it was reopened in 2004 by popular demand, but this time without the cars.

The route is unpaved but nonetheless is relatively easy with gentle inclines. Begin in Riva del Garda near the port and the hydroelectric plant. From there, follow the sign for Via del Ponale. And if you're not up for the entire route or just feel like a break, stop at the **Ponale Alto Belvedere**, where you can enjoy a drink on the outdoor terrace accompanied by sublime views. If you do decide to go the whole way, bring your swimming suit and you can finish up with a dip in Lago di Ledro.

SOAKING IN THERMAL WATERS

Since the 1890s **Sirmione** locals have been enjoying the benefits of these naturally warm sulphurous waters, said to heal everything from dermatological problems to hearing (yes, you heard correctly). Now you can too, in the **Aquaria Thermal SPA**, where relaxing curative options abound. Soak away your tension in the thermal pools, or have them pound away on 'paths' flanked by water jets. Slap on some thermal mud and re-emerge with skin that's tingling, red and baby-soft. There's also a freshwater infinity pool if you want to relax and just let your gaze run uninterrupted from the sky to the sea.

GETTING AROUND

Lago di Garda is Italy's largest lake and distances are considerable. The extensive ferry system is not the fastest way to get around. It's better to take the ferry for shorter distances, from Salò to Sirmione or Toscolano-Maderno. Buses are somewhat faster and run regularly, but driving a car is by far fastest and most convenient. The only downside is that the streets are likely to be congested in summer and you might not be able to access some town centres, which are traffic-restricted at certain hours. Parking in crowded Sirmione is also no mean feat. That said, roads going up to the mountains offer some spectacular scenery, if you're able for the narrow roads. Car ferries also run between Toscolano-Maderno and Torri del Benaco, and Limone sul Garda and Malcesine (depending on the season).

BERGAMO

Bergamo

Rome

Bergamo may have been hard hit by the coronavirus in 2020, but by all appearances it's put this tragedy behind it. Its textile mills, cement and electrical manufacturers are busy making up for lost time, as are its resolute citizens. Moreover, with its views of the mountains and its medieval architecture, this is still the city that Frank Lloyd Wright was once stunned by.

Set at the foothills of the Bergamasque Alps, it was the seat of a Lombard duchy before being ruled by the Milanese Visconti family and then ceded to the Republic of Venice. Its 16th-century Venetian city walls date back to a time when power struggles between northern states called for greater fortification.

Bergamo is divided into two parts: the Città Alta (Upper City) represents its past, and the Città Bassa (Lower City) its future. The lower part is modern and industrious, while the upper part is all old-world beauty.

TOP TIP

The Città Alta is small enough to be tackled on foot, but to get there from the Città Bassa you'll have to either take a funicular or bus, or walk 10 minutes up the stairs and steep path. Queues for the funicular can be long in summer, so get there early.

BEST PLACES TO DINE WITH CITTÀ ALTA VIEWS

Roof Garden €€€
Floor-to-ceiling windows provide stunning eyefuls of the Citta Altà, while the modern Italian cuisine always satisfies.

Antica Trattoria La Colombina €€
Dine on standout local dishes, including bacon-filled *casoncelli alla bergamasca*, at reasonable prices.

Baretto di San Vigilio €€
'Beppe del Baretto' runs this restaurant that boasts terrace views and low-lit romance.

A Count's Treasured Art Collection

ACCADEMIA CARRARA'S ITALIAN MASTERS

When Count Giacomo Carrara's art collection became too big for his own abode, he decided to have a neoclassical mansion built east of the city walls specifically to house it (as you do). And so the **Accademia Carrara** was born in 1794. Since then, various individuals (from senators to art historians) have contributed to its collection of Italian art from the 15th to the 19th centuries, with major works from Mantegna, Pisanello, Hayez, Rubens, Raphael, Titian and Canaletto.

It's spread across two floors, and a visit shouldn't take more than an hour or two. Highlights include Mantegna's moody Madonna and Child against a black background and Raphael's day-dreaming St Sebastian, painted before the artist was 20. The *Ricordo di un dolore (Memory of a Pain)* by Giuseppe Pellizza da Volpedo, which the artist painted after his younger sister died of tuberculosis, is also quietly moving, while a set of bronze-hued tarot cards from the 15th century is a quirky addition. The gallery is a 15-minute walk down from the Città Alta.

Meandering the Medieval Old Town

VENETIAN WALLS AND CITTÀ ALTA

Start at **1 Porta San Giacomo**, an imposing gate on the Unesco World Heritage–listed Venetian walls. Marvel at the view of the Città Bassa far below and these 6km defensive walls that

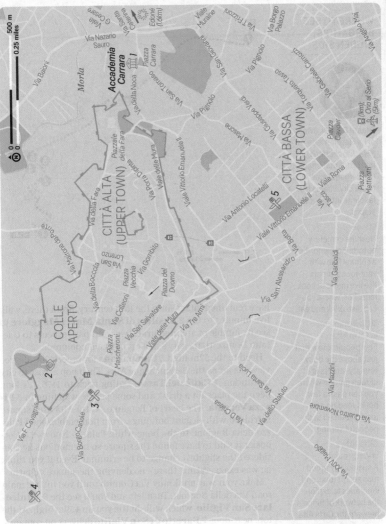

HIGHLIGHTS
1 Accademia
Carrara

SIGHTS
2 Orto Botanico

EATING
3 Antica Trattoria
La Colombina
6 Baretto di San
Vigilio
5 Ristorante Roof
Garden

Accademia Carrara 1

CITTÀ ALTA (UPPER TOWN)

Piazzale della Fara

Piazza Vecchia

Piazza del Duomo

Piazza Mascheroni

COLLE APERTO

CITTÀ BASSA (LOWER TOWN)

Piazza Cavour

Piazza Matteotti

5

THE GUIDE

MILAN & THE LAKES

Città Alta funicular (p264)

KYNA STUDIO/SHUTTERSTOCK ©

263

WHERE TO SEE BERGAMO'S HIDDEN SIDE

Gianni Danesi, owner of La Fiaschetteria (@la_fiaschetteria), a bar-bistro that brings the Bergamasque Alps to the city, shares his favourite little-known places.

Edoné
Near the cemetery outside Bergamo, it's a cultural hub with year-round events like live music or book launches, where you can also drink and eat.

Orto Botanico in Città Alta
Few people know that just above the busy touristy streets is a hidden garden where you can pass a few hours reading and losing yourself in the peaceful setting.

Città Alta's underground
A speleology group runs secret tours and itineraries to explore the network of tunnels beneath the Città Alta.

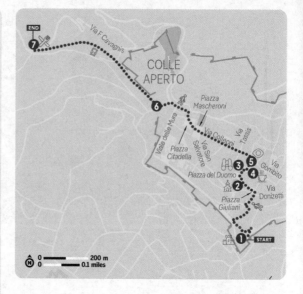

have remained intact since the 16th century. From there, walk five minutes to the **2 Basilica di Santa Maria Maggiore** to see its jumble of architectural styles and pay respects to Gaetano Donizetti, the city's most prominent composer.

Head to the 52m-high **3 Campanone** for breezy 360-degree views as far as the Bergamasque Alps. Then pop across to city institution **4 Caffè del Tasso**. Dating back to 1476, it's long been the place for a drink and some people-watching in **5 Piazza Vecchia**. The heart of Bergamo's Città Alta, this square is fringed with elegant buildings, from lion-emblazoned Palazzo della Ragione to the bone-white Palazzo Nuovo. Le Corbusier is said to have found the square so harmonious he considered the slightest change to be criminal. Even if you think he was exaggerating, there's no denying the square's charm.

Make your way up skinny Via Gomito until you hit the main road Via della Boccola. Turn left and you'll see the **6 Funicolare San Vigilio**, which will shuttle you up 459m high. At the top, next-door **7 Baretto di San Vigilio** delivers on romantic views and refined traditional cuisine.

 GETTING AROUND

You can get to most sights in Bergamo by using a combination of bus, funicular and your feet. Bus 1 connects the train station with the funicular to Città Alta and Colle Aperto, where the funicular to San Vigilio departs. Tickets cost €1.30 and last 75 minutes; buy them at newsstands, tobacconists, train and funicular stations. A car isn't really necessary as regular trains from Milan will whisk you here in around an hour. If you do happen to drive, remember to keep an eye out for the ZTL (Zona a Traffico Limitato) signs, which indicate areas where traffic is limited, such as the historic centre of the Città Alta.

MANTUA

Mantua

Rome

Voted Italian City of Culture in 2016 and part of the European Region of Gastronomy in 2017, Mantua has a lot to brag about. And yet, you'd never guess from the number of tourists (which is no bad thing).

It was first ruled by the Bonacolsi family, but people tend to forget them in the face of the Gonzagas, who left their indelible mark on the city over an almost four-century reign. Made up of vicious despots, horse-loving dukes and one saint, thankfully a lot of them had excellent taste in the fine arts. They prettied the city with palaces and artistic works that have made Mantua a Renaissance treasure – and it has changed less than you might imagine. It's not called La Bella Addormentata (The Sleeping Beauty) without reason and its population of around 48,000 hasn't changed much since the 1500s. That said, the city is slowly evolving, spurred on by the Mantova Hub regeneration project.

TOP TIP

The city is packed with cycle lanes, making it a pleasure to bike around. There's a scenic path along the lake lined with trees and a route that takes you all the way to Peschiera in Lago di Garda. The city centre is pretty compact and manageable on foot.

The Gonzagas' Colossal Palace

FRESCOES AND FAMILY HISTORY

The Gonzaga family were a shrewd lot. Not only did they manage to elevate themselves from landowners to dukes, bishops and cardinals, but for almost 400 years they controlled Mantua. And the **Palazzo Ducale**, a massive 35,000-sq-metre 'city-palace', was their home. It's made up of three parts: the Corte Vecchia, the Corte Nuova and the Castello di San Giorgio with a courtyard garden (Giardino dei Semplici). You can easily lose an entire afternoon wandering through its elaborate rooms adorned with frescoes and trimmed in golden boiserie.

The **Camera degli Sposi** (Bridal Chamber), completed in 1474 by Andrea Mantegna, is the palace's crowning glory and where Ludovico II liked to impress visiting nobles and ambassadors. Considered a masterpiece of *trompe l'œil*, the walls are painted with columns and brocaded curtains appearing to open onto a stage of court scenes where three generations of Gonzagas are the princely protagonists. Look carefully and you can also see Mantegna's face, cheekily painted into the garland on the right side of the door. Meanwhile, heaven peeks out from the hole in the ceiling, complete with chunky cherubs depicted from not-so-flattering angles.

Other highlights include the Sala di Troia, decked out in tumultuous Trojan war scenes suitable for Federico II's council chamber; the Sala dello Zodiaco with its constellation-packed

FLOATING DOWN THE MINCIO

As part of Mantua's 12th-century defence strategy, the town was surrounded by artificial lakes formed by the Mincio river. While one dried up in the 18th century, a boat ride through the remaining three – Superior, Middle and Inferior – is an idyllic way to get to know the area. Not only does it give you another view on the glorious Gonzaga estates, but you'll also get to explore the **Parco del Mincio**, a protected natural reserve made up of marshy wetlands where you can spot floating white water lilies and pink-hued lotus flowers along with roaming herons and loons.

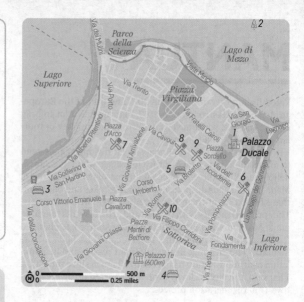

WHERE TO DINE IN MANTUA

Il Cigno €€€
This elegant family-run restaurant is the place to to tuck into *tortelli di zucca* (pumpkin-stuffed pasta).

Osteria delle Quattro Tette €
Sit elbow-to-elbow with locals chowing down on tasty tripe or pasta in this no-frills *osteria*.

Fragoletta Antica Osteria €€
A favourite of Casanova, this homey restaurant dating back 250 years serves classic Mantuan dishes.

ceiling; and the Sala del Pisanello, with its fragmented frescoes of chivalric knights.

A Palace of Desire

THE GONZAGAS' PALAZZO TE

Federico II Gonzaga gave painter and architect Giulio Romano a free hand when it came to creating the pleasure palace of his dreams, where he could escape for trysts with his mistress Isabella Boschetti. And Romano did not fail. Considered the architect's greatest work, **Palazzo Te** embodies Romano's playful mannerist imaginings, where 'slipping' triglyphs beneath the roof are seen as architectural witticisms.

The cheeky mood continues in the palace interiors, also designed by Romano, particularly in the **Camera dei Giganti** (Room of the Giants) where an almost cartoon-like scene unravels. Here Jupiter hurls thunderbolts at grotesque giants daring to ascend Olympus. It's painted across the walls and ceiling in one continuous scene, so the viewer is placed at its centre and, like the giants, overwhelmed by the chaos.

 WHERE TO STAY IN MANTUA

Scaravelli: Residenza
Part of the Scaravelli empire, it has sleek, centrally located rooms and apartments in glacial white. **€€**

Casa dei Gonzaga
Rooms are somewhat tired-looking but quiet and clean, and air-conditioning is a plus. Near the train station. **€**

Palazzo Valenti Gonzaga
Feel like nobility in this 16th-century *palazzo* adorned with frescoes and white marble statues. **€€**

Camera dei Giganti, Palazzo Te

BEST FOR LOCAL SPECIALITIES

Panificio Pavesi
This unassuming bakery in the city centre turns out wonderfully crumbly *sbrisolona* (a nutty, biscuit-like cake).

Salumeria Giovanni Bacchi
Crammed with local cheeses and cured meats, this deli also has bucketfuls of *mostarde mantovana* (spicy candied fruit).

But the palace is best summed up by the **Camera di Amore e Psiche** (Room of Cupid and Psyche), with its wedding banquet scene, attended by scantily clad gods, satyrs, nymphs and even an elephant. On the wall a golden inscription proclaims the villa as a place for 'honest leisure' (wink, wink) after taxing government duties. Finally, spare a look at the **Sala dei Cavalli** with its life-size painted horses, if nothing else to remind you of the Gonzagas' obsession with them. With all this juicy detail to absorb, a visit will take at least two hours.

GETTING AROUND

Due to its compact size, Mantua is easy to negotiate on foot. The city also has plenty of bicycle lanes, making it convenient to get around by bike. You can either rent a bike or use the on-street bike-sharing system. APAM buses run through the city centre, departing every 15 minutes, and can be used to get to outlying areas. If you do happen to drive a car, keep in mind you won't be able to access the city centre, but it shouldn't be much trouble to park. There's plenty of on-street paid parking by the lake.

VENICE

THE 'MOST SERENE' CITY OF ART

Reports of Venice's demise have been greatly exaggerated. But it's up to us to keep it that way.

First things first: Venice isn't dead. It's not impossibly crowded, either, despite what you might have heard. At least not if you want to see Venice the city, as opposed to Venice the tourist attraction. The latter comprises just Piazza San Marco and the Rialto Bridge – on busy days, over 100,000 people cram around here.

Though spectacular, those two sites aren't the real Venice. You'll find it in the labyrinthine alleyways crisscrossing the 118 islands that make up the city. Venice is churches hung with some of the world's greatest art. It's *cicheti* (bar snacks) washed down with an *ombra* (glass) of wine (see p276). It's staggeringly beautiful *palazzi* reflecting in the water, as a shoal of fish flits past.

MAPMAN/SHUTTERSTOCK ©

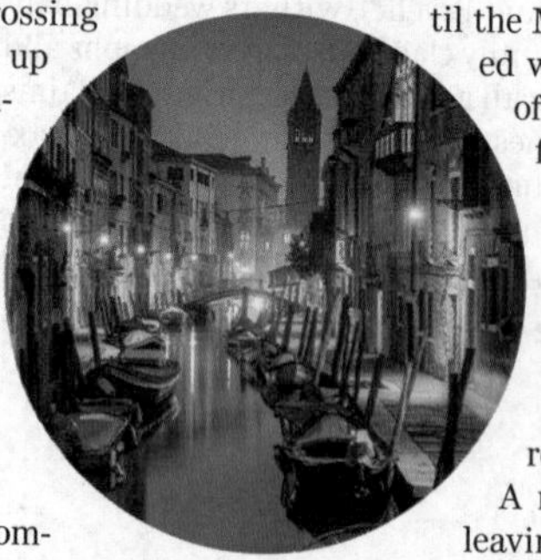

This has always been a complex place. Its 1100 years as La Serenissima ('The Most Serene', Venetian Republic) saw it produce world-class art and welcome residents and traders from around the world. But it also used that art as propaganda to push its image as a divinely appointed empire. In reality, Venice often conquered by force; it looted ruthlessly from abroad (even the bones of St Mark were stolen from Alexandria); and foreign residents, particularly Jews and Arabs, were confined to strictly delineated neighbourhoods. As its power waned in the 18th century, it dropped its weapons and embraced tourism. Three centuries on, little has changed.

This formidable city epitomises both resilience and resistance. It dealt with *acqua alta* (high tide) flooding for 1200 years, until the MOSE flood barriers started working in 2020. It staved off invaders for 1100 years before Napoleon came knocking, ending the Republic in 1797. And still Venetians hold on – just. The last 70 years have seen a 70% drop in population; in 2022 the number of residents fell below 50,000.

A major reason people are leaving is the lack of affordable housing. You can help Venetians by staying in a hotel or B&B rather than a rental. Another is lack of non-tourism jobs. Buying from artisans instead of souvenir shops helps keep ancient trades alive.

Venice is famously precarious, but it's not dead. It's our responsibility to keep it in good health.

THE MAIN AREAS

SAN MARCO
Bombastic and breathtaking. p274

SAN POLO & SANTA CROCE
A thousand-year-old market. p280

DORSODURO
Art and waterside walks. p266

CANNAREGIO
Nightlife and Jewish history. p292

ALPIN/GETTY IMAGES ©

San Giorgio Maggiore (p307) from the Piazzetta di San Marco

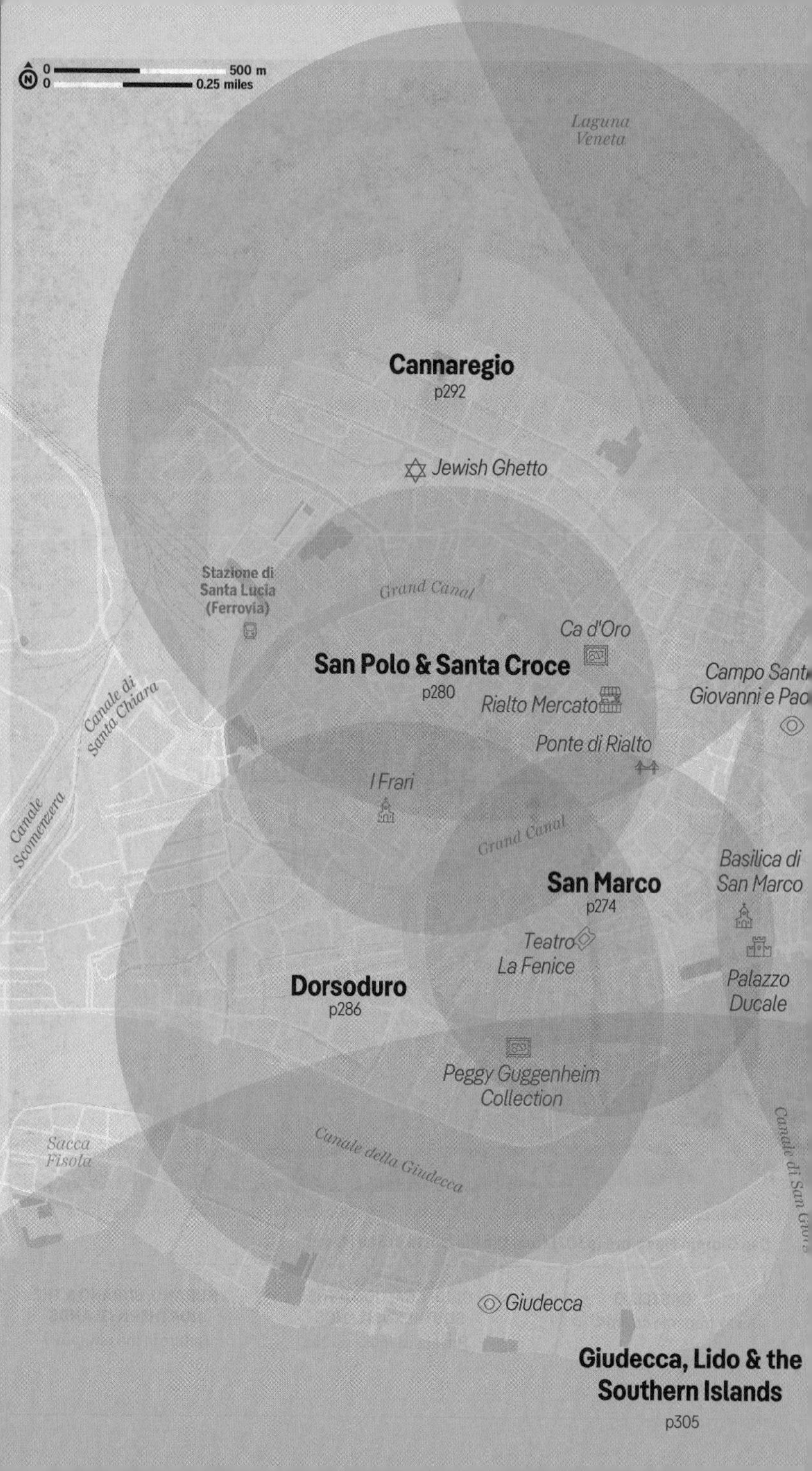

0   500 m
0   0.25 miles

Laguna Veneta

Cannaregio
p292

✡ Jewish Ghetto

Stazione di
Santa Lucia
(Ferrovia)

Grand Canal

Ca d'Oro

San Polo & Santa Croce
p280

Canale di Santa Chiara

Rialto Mercato

Campo Santo
Giovanni e Pao

Canale Scomenzera

Ponte di Rialto

I Frari

Grand Canal

San Marco
p274

Basilica di
San Marco

Teatro
La Fenice

Dorsoduro
p286

Palazzo
Ducale

Peggy Guggenheim
Collection

Sacca Fisola

Canale della Giudecca

Canale di San Gio

◎ Giudecca

Giudecca, Lido & the
Southern Islands
p305

Sacca
Serenella

Canale
Serenella

MURANO

Museo del
Vetro

*Canal di
Murano*

Burano
(5.25km)

**Murano, Burano &
the Northern Islands**
p309

Cimitero di
San Michele

*Isola di
San Michele*

FROM THE AIRPORT

The most spectacular way in from Marco Polo airport is by Alilaguna ferry, which chugs through the north lagoon and around the city. Otherwise, coaches drop you at Piazzale Roma (the main bus station) in 20 minutes. From there, hop on a *vaporetto*.

WALK

The easiest, and often quickest, way to get around the city centre is on foot – you can reach most of our picks in around 20 minutes from Rialto. There's normally one main drag in each *sestiere*, either heading to Piazza San Marco or to the Rialto Bridge.

VAPORETTO

These waterbuses are Venice's only form of public transport (apart from real buses on the islands of Lido and Pellestrina). The most beautiful way to get around, they chug down the Grand Canal and around the outside of the centre.

Castello
p299

*Darsena
Grande*

TRAGHETTO

Need to cross from one side of the Grand Canal to the other? These are just the ticket – gondolas repurposed as public shuttles, which paddle back and forth. They're a great taster of for the real gondola experience, too.

*Bacino di
San Marco*

Sant'Elena

*Darsena di
Sant'Elena*

San Giorgio
Maggiore

Find Your Way

Venice is famously shaped like a fish, swimming towards the mainland, with the Giudecca an eel wiggling under its belly. The Grand Canal swishes through the middle in an inverted-S shape, emptying into St Mark's Basin. The centre has six *sestieri* (districts): Cannaregio, Santa Croce, San Polo, Dorsoduro, San Marco and Castello.

*Laguna
Veneta*

Plan Your Days

Sail down the Grand Canal, saunter along the Zattere waterfront, and head out into the lagoon – as well as taking in Venice's historical big hitters.

Vaporetto, **Grand Canal (p294)**

MATTEO COLOMBO/GETTY IMAGES ©

DAY 1

Morning

● Take *vaporetto* 1 down the **Grand Canal** (p294), and get off at Rialto Mercato. Potter about the ancient **market** (p284) then head west, to the gargantuan **Frari church** (p282) and the **Scuola Grande di San Rocco** (p282), Tintoretto's version of the Sistine Chapel.

Afternoon

● Wander down the **Zattere** (p288) for your first sight of San Marco from the water. Take the *traghetto* across from Punta della Dogana to arrive at **Piazza San Marco** (p276). Marvel at the iconic **Basilica** (p278), and afterwards explore the **Palazzo Ducale** (p277) till closing time.

Evening

● Wind down on Piazza San Marco with a bang – with a slap-up meal at Michelin-starred **Quadri** (p279).

YOU'LL ALSO WANT TO...

See iconic art, hit the islands of the lagoon, and explore the lesser-told stories of Venice – those of immigrants and outcasts.

HAVE AN ART ATTACK

The **Gallerie dell'Accademia** is a repository of Venice's greatest Renaissance artists from Titian to Tintoretto.

SKIRT THE ARSENALE

Now an event space, this enormous former **shipyard** dominating Castello gives an idea of La Serenissima's power.

TAKE A DIP

The 12km sandbar that is the **Lido** has some of the Adriatic's best beaches, plus the time-capsule village of **Malamocco**.

LUCAMATO/SHUTTERSTOCK ©, ANDERSPHOTO/SHUTTERSTOCK ©, INGUS KRUKLITIS/SHUTTERSTOCK ©

DAY 2

Morning
● Get your modern-art fix at the world-class **Peggy Guggenheim Collection** (p288), then stroll through Dorsoduro to Longhena-designed **Ca' Rezzonico** (p286) to see how lavish La Serenissima life was, grabbing gifts from artisan **Paolo Olbi** (p290) nearby.

Afternoon
● Take the *vaporetto* up to Cannaregio to admire the glorious **Ca' d'Oro** (p294), Venice's most heartfelt museum. From there, head further north to the **Jewish Ghetto** (p295) for a guided tour of Venice's unsettling Jewish history.

Evening
● Skip dinner and fill up on *cicheti* at the bars along the **Fondamenta degli Ormesini** (p295).

DAY 3

Morning
● Get a fuller understanding of life in La Serenissima at the fantastically informative **Fondazione Querini Stampalia** (p301). Then walk to Fondamente Nove and catch the *vaporetto* to Murano's **Museo del Vetro** (p312) to learn all about the art of glass-blowing.

Afternoon
● Hop back on the *vaporetto* to Torcello, to see where Venice began. Gasp at the glittering mosaics at the **Basilica di Santa Maria Assunta** (p311), then hop over to neighbouring Burano for a trip into the lagoon with fisherman **Andrea Rossi** (p313).

Evening
● Stay on for a lagoon-hauled dinner at **Trattoria al Gatto Nero** (p313), and drink in the peace of Burano once the crowds have departed.

EAT MEATBALLS
Historic *bacaro* (tavern) **Alla Vedova** in Cannaregio is legendary for its huge meatballs, which you order individually.

EXPLORE A PRIVATE ISLAND
The island of **San Giorgio Maggiore** has everything from a show-stopper church to art in the sprawling parkland.

LIVE VENICE'S MULTICULTURALISM
The **Scuola di San Giorgio degli Schiavoni** tells the history of one of Venice's many immigrant communities.

SEE A QUARANTINE ISLAND
The **Lazzaretto Nuovo** was where arrivals were once sent to self-isolate for 40 days – the world's first quarantine.

SAN MARCO

THE SEAT OF POWER

For many, Venice *is* San Marco. This *sestiere* has the best views of all: overlooking St Mark's Basin, with the long Riva degli Schiavoni waterfront – which unfurls into neighbouring Castello – providing one of the world's most beautiful walkways. One of the city's oldest areas, San Marco is a warren of twisting alleyways that spill out into Piazza San Marco. In the days of La Serenissima, when people arrived by sea, it was a more impressive entrance: the Palazzo Ducale (Doge's Palace) rising from the lagoon, with Basilica di San Marco in the background and its soaring Campanile (bell tower) marking the entrance to the square. Yet there's more to San Marco than its piazza: churches and bell towers fill the *campi* (squares), while extravagant *palazzi* (mansions) line the Grand Canal. Around the Rialto Bridge, at the northernmost tip, is the most touristy part of town – but even here, a block or two off the main drag, you'll find pockets of quiet.

TOP TIP

The Grand Canal curls around San Marco in an elongated C shape. The Rialto Bridge and Piazza San Marco top and tail the eastern edge. The main tourist artery follows the shape of the Grand Canal through the district from the Rialto to Campo Santo Stefano, then turns east to reach the Piazza. Vaporetti ply the same route.

Teatro La Fenice

VIVIDA PHOTO PC/SHUTTERSTOCK ©

Teatro La Fenice

REBORN FROM THE FLAMES

In 1996 Venice's famous **opera house** burned down; but true to its name ('The Phoenix'), it was rebuilt eight years later. Audio-guide tours get you into the outré auditorium, but the best way to experience La Fenice is by going to a performance. The season is in full swing from January to July and September to October.

Museo Correr

LA SERENISSIMA'S HISTORY

This museum sprawls across most of the Procuratie Nuove and the Napoleonic Wing with its whistle-stop tour through Venetian history (plan for two hours). Don't miss the nearly 50cm-high platform shoes worn by 15th- and 16th-century women, or Jacopo de' Barbari's Venetie MD: a bird's-eye view of the city from 1500, which shows how little has changed. The Correr shares the building with the Museo Archeologico and the Sansovino-designed library, Biblioteca Marciana. Then there are the Sale Reali: royal rooms, created after the Republic's fall. In 2022, 11 rooms used by the Bonapartes, Habsburgs and the Savoy family of Italian royals opened, taking the total to 20.

A BROKEN MARRIAGE

Napoleon destroyed the last *bucintoro* – the Doge's extravagant ship with which he 'married' the sea each year. Some remnants are in the Museo Correr; others are in the **Museo Storico Navale** (p299).

Map Labels

CASTELLO

Campo Santa Maria Formosa

Rio del Vin

Rio di Palazzo della Paglia

Salizzada San Lio

C A Bale

C S Antonio

C de Specchieri

C dei Preti

Piazzetta dei Leoni

Basilica di San Marco 1

Campanile 2

Palazzo Ducale 6

Piazzetta San Marco

Marzaria del Orologio

Chiubica

Piazza San Marco

Museo Correr 3

Negozio Olivetti 5

Giardini Ex Reali 13

Canale di San Marco

C Vallaresso

C Frezzaria

Rio Orseolo

Fond Orseolo

C dei Fabbri

Rio dei Scoacamini

C dei Fuseri

Rio dei Barcaroli

Rio della Fava

Ponte di Rialto

Campo San Bartolomeo

Rio di San Salvador

Campo San Salvador

Campo San Luca

C del Carbon

C Goldoni

Riva del Carbon

Rialto

San Silvestro

San Salvador

Museo Fortuny 4

Rio dei San Luca

Campo Manin

Rio Tera Patarian

Rio Tera de la Mandola

Campo San Angelo

Sant'Angelo

Rio di San Luca

C del Avvocati

C dei Frati

C Caffettieri

C de Verona

Rio de la Verona

Campo San Fantin

Teatro La Fenice 8

Rio de la Veste

C del Cristo

Campo San Moisè

Campo di San Moisè

C de 13 Martiri

Fond del Forteghetto

C del Traghetto

C Larga XXII Marzo

Rio de le Veste

C del Traghetto

C de Ostreghe

Campo Traghetto

Santa Maria del Giglio

Campo San Maurizio

Rio di San Maurizio

Rio del Santissimo

C del Spezier

Campo Santo Stefano

Campo di San Vidal

Rio di San Vidal

Ponte dell'Accademia

Campo dell'Accademia

DORSODURO

Campo de la Salute

SAN POLO

Rio della Madoneta

Campo San Polo

Rio di San Polo

Rio della Frua

San Tomà

C Mocenigo Cà Vecchia

C de Carrozze

Campo San Samuele

San Samuele

Grand Canal

9 Calle

17 Rio

18 Piazzetta del Orologio

21

16

7

20

15

10

22

19

12

11

14

200 m
0.1 miles

N

Basilica di San Marco (p278)

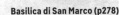

PAOLO GALLO/SHUTTERSTOCK ©

275

Piazza San Marco

ITALY'S ICONIC SQUARE

Napoleon put it best: the 'drawing room of Europe' was how he described **Piazza San Marco**, overlooking St Mark's Basin. That's an understatement: from the 12th century, when the square was created, this has been a place to gather for people from across the globe – whether to trade, as they did in the past; to have their palms read and fortunes told, once Venice started drawing in tourists; or simply, as now, to nurse a drink at one of the historic cafes.

With the undulating domes of the Basilica di San Marco (p278) surrounded by porticoed buildings on three sides, the symmetry is dazzling. The two long sides, the Procuratie Vecchie and Procuratie Nuove, were built for the 'Procurators' – think civil servants – of San Marco in the 16th and 17th centuries, while the shorter far end of the square was added by Napoleon to connect the two 'wings'. Today, the Museo Correr and Archaeological Museum occupy the Procuratie Nuove and Ala Napoleonica, while in 2022 the top floor of the Procuratie Vecchie opened to the public.

The 99m **Campanile**, or bell tower – the city's tallest building – has a viewing platform for bird's-eye views; you can also climb the five storeys of the **Torre dell'Orologio** (Clock Tower) on guided tours. You could spend a day sightseeing, so take a breather at one of the historic cafes. **Florian** is the most famous; **Quadri** is run by the Veneto's Michelin-starred Alajmo brothers.

A SHADY PRACTICE

To accompany your *cicheti* – Venice's famous bite-size bar snacks – you'll probably want an *ombra*: a small(ish) glass of house wine. The word means 'shadow' or 'shade'. Why? Back in the days of the Republic, the square was filled with stalls, and workers and visitors needed boozy fuel. The wine sellers set up under the Campanile, in the *ombra* (shade), to stop their wares from overheating, moving their stalls throughout the day to follow the bell tower's shadow.

Piazza San Marco

Palazzo Ducale

THE ART-FILLED SEAT OF POWER

No building epitomises Venice more than the **Doge's Palace** – not only because of its waterfront location and its symbolism (this was the Republic's seat of power for around 900 years), but because of its looks. The current palace was built in the 1300s, and is the zenith of the Florid Gothic or Venetian Gothic style, which swiped ideas from both Byzantine and Islamic architecture, then gussied it up with bright colours and extra detail like that pink-and-white facade of concentric diamond patterns.

Inside, it's a dizzying collection of politicians' rooms, works of art each more spectacular than the next, and, of course, the **Ponte dei Sospiri**, or Bridge of Sighs – named, supposedly, for the groans of the prisoners who were walked through here to the jails below (tip: it's better from the outside). The scale can be overwhelming, so decide what you want from your visit – to understand the highly complex system of Venetian rule, to see the artworks by the likes of Veronese, Titian and Tintoretto, or simply to wander.

The centerpiece is the behemoth **Sala del Maggior Consiglio** (Great Council Hall). Today, it's dominated by Tintoretto's *Paradiso*, thought to be the largest canvas painting in the world. Around 25m long and containing 500 swirling figures, it was commissioned in 1577 and was Tintoretto's last work – he was helped by his son Domenico.

Palazzo Ducale

FRANCESCO BONINO/SHUTTERSTOCK ©

BEHIND THE SCENES

For a more intimate view of the usually crowded Doge's Palace, book an **Itinerario Segreto** – guided tours of the 'secret' spaces of the building, including labyrinthine offices for penpushers, archive rooms, a torture chamber, rooftop prison cells, and the attic above the Sala del Maggior Consiglio, a veritable puzzle of beams and trusses holding up the picture-clad ceiling. You then visit the rest of the palace alone.

Negozio Olivetti

MODERN STYLE HIDING IN PLAIN VIEW

Amid the pomp of the Piazza, you'll miss this sliver of modernity at first glance. That was the aim of Venetian architect Carlo Scarpa, who transformed a cramped unit of the Procuratie Vecchie into a **showroom** for Olivetti typewriters in 1957 by turning it into a glass-fronted window onto the square. The airy, open-plan interior has a mosaic floor reflecting lagoon colours and a 'floating' staircase up to the plinths where the typewriters were kept. It's a quick break from the Piazza's bombast.

SKOVALSKY/SHUTTERSTOCK ©

Basilica di San Marco

Museo Fortuny

THE FASHION KING

Spanish-born designer Mariano Fortuny ruled the early-20th-century fashion world with his daring Delphos dress, made from super-fine pleated silk that clung to every curve. He was also an artistic and architectural polymath who revolutionised theatre lighting. This 15th-century *palazzo* – sagging and crumbling in just the right way, west of the Rialto – was the home and workshop of Mariano and his wife, dressmaker Henriette Negrin. Closed after damage from the 2019 flood, it reopened in 2022 with a new layout that's more of a **museum** than the low-lit, slightly chaotic home it was before. While it's lost atmosphere, it's still worth an hour.

Basilica di San Marco

ALL THAT GLITTERS IS GOLD

The heart of Piazza San Marco is the spectacular **St Mark's Basilica**. Venice always has to be different – when this church was built in the 11th century, it meant nicking the style and much of the materials from Constantinople. The Venetians enriched that Byzantine model to make their city the blingiest place on the planet. Outside and in, it's an eye-popping jumble of riches. The floor has nearly 3000 sq metres of mosaics made from precious stones, such as serpentine and porphyry, brought from Greece, Turkey and Egypt. The walls and domes glitter with gold mosaics, installed between the 13th and 18th centuries. Behind the altar is the **Pala d'Oro**, a Byzantine altarpiece of pure gold, studded with over 2000 jewels looted by Venetians during the 1300s and 1400s, and covered with figures of saints and angels. Upstairs is the **Loggia dei Cavalli**, the outdoor balcony overlooking the Piazza. Its four prancing horses are reproductions – the originals, ancient bronzes stolen from Constantinople in 1204, are in the attached museum.

CHRISTOPHE BOISVIEUX/SHUTTERSTOCK ©

Pala d'Oro, Basilica di San Marco

IACOMINO FRIMAGES/SHUTTERSTOCK ©

Scala Contarini del Bovolo

MORE IN SAN MARCO

Beyond the Piazza

SECRET GARDENS AND MODERNIST MARVELS

Sitting in Piazza San Marco is banned, but you can take a pew in the **Giardini Reali**, gardens laid out by Napoleon beneath the Procuratie Nuove. Back in the square, the top floor of the **Procuratie Vecchie** is now a refugee charity's HQ, offering public access to the exhibition *A World of Potential* – worth a visit to see the space revamped by David Chipperfield.

The main route west of San Marco takes in several churches. First up is **Chiesa di San Moisè**, its bombastic baroque facade a stark contrast to the brutalist-looking 1949 Bauer Hotel beside it (a rare modernist building). The next one, **Chiesa di Santa Maria del Giglio**, is famous for having Venice's only work by Rubens – a busty *Madonna and Child* – though more interesting are the 17th-century maps of towns conquered by La Serenissima carved into the facade, including Zadar, Split and Corfu. Nearby, the barn-like **Chiesa di Santo Stefano** has a tiny Museum of Sacred Art, including works by Vivarini, Tintoretto, and sculptors Pietro Lombardo and Canova.

En route to Rialto, dip off the main drag to climb the **Scala Contarini del Bovolo**, a fairy-tale Gothic spiral staircase.

 WHERE TO HAVE DRINKS WITH A VIEW IN SAN MARCO

Quadri
Historic cafe with a Michelin-starred restaurant above and peerless views of the piazza.

Ombra del Leone
The canalside bar of La Biennale di Venezia's HQ faces the Punta della Dogana art gallery.

Bar Longhi
The Gritti Palace hotel's bar has Pietro Longhi paintings and a terrace over the Grand Canal.

SAN POLO & SANTA CROCE

WHERE HISTORY COMES ALIVE

After most visitors see Piazza San Marco, they want to see Rialto. They usually mean the white bridge straddling the Grand Canal; but to Venetians, Rialto is the area on the San Polo side with a 1000-year-old market. *Rivo alto* (high bank) was one of the first places settled in the lagoon. That history is still visible in the streets – a labyrinth of narrow alleyways and jumbled houses, with walkways underneath the 1st floors of *palazzi*, dead ends and so many offshoots that it feels like you're in a 'Choose Your Own Adventure' book. History here is fun and bawdy – the Ponte delle Tette, or Bridge of Tits, once signalled the red-light district.

Rialto occupies the *sestiere* of San Polo, which – along with Santa Croce to the northwest – comprises the inner twist of land in the city centre. Stately Santa Croce is home to museums galore, while San Polo offers knockout churches, *palazzi* and repositories of art to explore. These are two of the best *sestieri* to get lost in – every street you take is a surprise, with villas and lush gardens lurking behind high walls.

TOP TIP

It's easy to get off the beaten track here, but the main drags get you to the main sites. Santa Croce offers a fast route in and out of town: Piazzale Roma (the bus station) is here, and the Ponte degli Scalzi leads right from the railway station into the *sestiere*. *Vaporetti* 1 and 2 go from Piazzale Roma to Rialto.

MISTERVLAD/SHUTTERSTOCK ©

Ponte di Rialto

Ponte di Rialto

ITALY'S ICONIC BRIDGE

Venice's iconic **bridge** doesn't technically belong to a *sestiere*, straddling the Grand Canal with one foot in San Marco and the other in San Polo. This was the canal's key crossing, between business-centre Rialto and the political hub of San Marco – in fact, until 1854, it was the only bridge across the entire Grand Canal. In 1524 it was decided to build a bridge worthy of its location, instead of the wooden structures that had existed before. The result is this wedding-cake affair of white Istrian stone, constructed between 1588 and 1591 by Antonio da Ponte. Most of the shops on the bridge are tourist traps – save your money for the artisans elsewhere.

Campiello dei Meloni

ARTISANS
OLD AND NEW

The main route from Rialto through San Polo is full of tourist traps, but two brilliant artisans are in this blink-and-you'll-miss-it 'square'. Paolo Pelosin, of Il Pavone, is a maestro of paper-marbling – or ebru, as it's known in Turkey, where it originated. In his workshop he marbles stationery, photo albums, pencils and even earrings. Next door, at Dila, Laura Bollato and her nephew Sebastiano make Venice souvenirs with a difference – everything, from mugs to T-shirts and pencil cases, is cat-themed and drawn by hand. Their muses, of course, are their own cats.

HIGHLIGHTS
1 Ca' Pesaro
2 Campiello dei Meloni
3 Chiesa di San Giacomo dall'Orio
4 Chiesa di San Giacomo di Rialto
5 I Frari
6 Il Pavone di Paolo Pelosin
7 Palazzo Mocenigo
8 Ponte di Rialto
9 Rialto Market
10 Scuola Grande di San Rocco

SIGHTS
11 Calle de la Donzella
12 Calle del Megio
13 Campo Erbaria
14 Campo Rialto Novo
15 Campo San Polo
16 Chiesa di San Polo
17 Chiesa di San Stae

(see 18) Fondaco dei Turchi
18 Museo di Storia Naturale di Venezia

SLEEPING
19 Albergo Casa Peron
20 Cima Rosa
21 Hotel San Cassiano

EATING
22 Pasticceria Rizzardini

DRINKING & NIGHTLIFE
23 All'Arco
24 Banco Giro
25 Cantina Do Spade
26 Da Lollo

SHOPPING
27 Dila
28 Process Collettivo

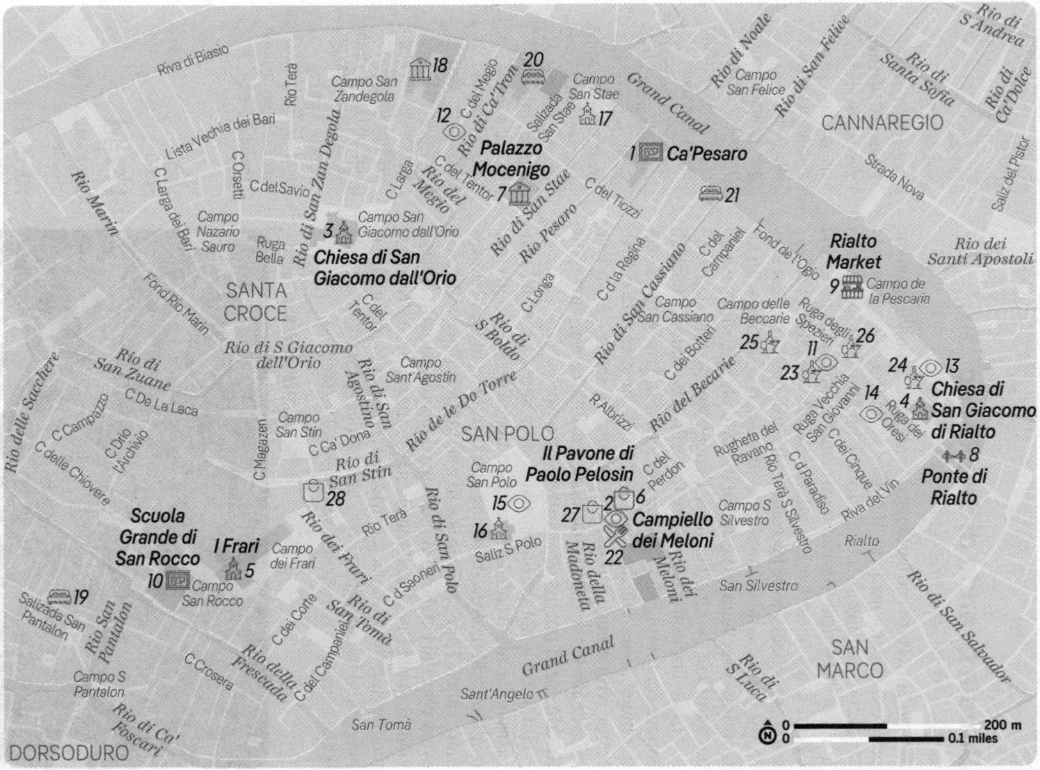

Scuola Grande di San Rocco

TESTAMENT TO VENETIAN RESILIENCE

Jacopo Tintoretto revolutionised Venetian art, building on the progress already made by the likes of Bellini, Giorgione and Titian, but dialling up the colours and making every painting a flurry of movement. His canvases dominate the city, but behind I Frari is his finest work of all: the **Scuola Grande** (Venice's *scuole*, or schools, were lay communities) dedicated to San Rocco, the patron saint of the plague-stricken, is plastered with his paintings to celebrate the end of the 1576 plague, which wiped out a third of the city. The more than 60 works start at ground level, but dazzle upstairs where the ceiling is inlaid with lavish frames containing Old Testament scenes, and the walls depict the life of Jesus. Off the main hall is the smaller Sala dell'Albergo, with a huge, full-of-life *Crucifixion* scene – a work so spectacularly theatrical that not even 19th-century art critic Ruskin dared put his observations into words.

Tintoretto is not the only artist at work here – below his canvases in the main hall are Francesco Pianta's esoteric carvings of allegorical figures, including one that looks like a highwayman, called *The Spy*. This is still a significant place in Venice: every year the Patriarch comes to say Mass (originally, it was a visit from the Doge), and the plaque on the grand staircase remembering the 1576 plague, which 'started in March and was longer and harsher than ever', hits harder since 2020. Outside is the church of San Rocco, with more Tintorettos.

Scuola Grande di San Rocco

DREAMER COMPANY/SHUTTERSTOCK ©

DOING (GOOD) TIME

Opposite I Frari is **Process Collettivo**, the shopfront of an initiative that sees inmates in Venice's jails trained and given employment throughout their sentences (and often after). This shop, supported by US artist Mark Bradford, sells toiletries, and chic bags and accessories from recycled PVC. Another initiative, **Banco Lotto n.10** (near the Scuola di San Giorgio in Castello), makes exquisite, vintage-style womenswear, often using precious silks and fabrics from Venetian companies Rubelli, Fortuny and Bevilacqua. All proceeds go back into the initiatives.

I Frari

GARGANTUAN GOTHIC CHURCH

This church is as impressive as its full name, **Basilica di Santa Maria Gloriosa dei Frari**. The altarpiece by Titian, depicting the Assumption of Mary, has inspired artists from Raphael to the 21st century. There are works by everyone from Bellini to Donatello, plus the eye-popping tomb of Canova. It was designed by the artist himself, sculpted by his pupils, and contains his heart.

Interior, Palazzo Mocenigo

Chiesa di San Giacomo dall'Orio

A PATCHWORK CHURCH

The Romanesque **San Giacomo dall'Orio** church should be a mess – founded in the 800s, then nipped and tucked throughout the centuries. Instead, it's an atmospheric jumble of the ages, with a wooden ceiling shaped like a ship's keel, gilded arches, a pine-green marble column and medieval carvings of various saints. Not to mention paintings by the likes of Veronese, Palma il Giovane and Paolo Veneziano whose 14th-century crucifix hangs above the altar.

Waistcoats, Centro Studi di Storia del Tessuto e del Costume

Palazzo Mocenigo

HOW THE OTHER HALF LIVED

The *portego* (1st-floor entrance hall) of this great multipurpose **museum** is worth the ticket price alone. Mainly, it's a view of how patrician families like the Mocenigos used to live. The damask-clad walls – the 17th-century building is also part of the Centro Studi di Storia del Tessuto e del Costume, a fashion and textiles archive – are covered with paintings of former doges and other eminent family members; Burano lace tablecloths and Murano glass chandeliers grace the rooms; and one floor features a mosaic of the family coats of arms. There's also a small but interesting display about perfume.

Ca' Pesaro

A GIFT TO STRUGGLING ARTISTS

When Countess Felicita Bevilacqua La Masa donated this grandest of Grand Canal mansions to the city in 1899, she stipulated that it should be a place for young artists to work and exhibit. In 1902 it became Venice's contemporary **art gallery**. By 1910, when futurist Umberto Boccioni held his first solo exhibition here, Ca' Pesaro's 'summer camps' were already an alternative to the Biennale. That means the surprisingly small collection is heavily Italian-focused, but there are also works by Bonnard, Chagall, Klimt and Rodin, plus local surprises, like the Van Gogh–like Umberto Moggioli, part of the post-impressionist 'Burano school'. Swap the rather uncomfortable Museum of Oriental Art for a drink at its canalside bar.

Rialto Mercato

A THOUSAND-YEAR-OLD MARKET

'What news on the Rialto?', Shakespeare asked in *The Merchant of Venice*. Today's news is somewhat different – what used to be the business centre for the Republic is now a top tourist site. Having said that, the **market** still exists, and the alleyways are still rammed with *bacari* (taverns) serving *cicheti* and *ombre* to people from all over the world. But instead of rich textiles, spices and jewels, the ever-dwindling *mercato* – founded in the 11th century – has retained only its fish, fruit and vegetable sections; and instead of those foreigners being traders, they're now tourists. With the decline in residents, it's hard for the stalls to break even, so try to buy something, like local veg from the island of Sant'Erasmo, or minuscule shrimps from the lagoon.

At the foot of the bridge sits the **Chiesa di San Giacomo di Rialto**, or San Giacometto. Legend dictates the church was founded in 421, along with the city. Although that's been disproven (the Venice creation myth was propaganda), we do know that it was rejigged around the time the market was founded. Next to it was the Bancogiro, a public bank founded in 1524 – the name is now used by a bar in the nearby **Campo Erberia**, the former fruit and veg market turned Grand Canal bar strip. Enjoy getting lost around here – this is the oldest part of Venice, as the alleyways attest.

ANDAR PAR BACARI

That's Venetian for 'tavern-hopping'. Here are some of Rialto's best.

Do Spade €
There's been a tavern here since 1488; today it's known for its spicy meatballs.

All'Arco €
Serving *cicheti* for more than a century, with a vast array that changes by the minute.

Bancogiro €€
Gourmet and inventive *cicheti* overlooking the Grand Canal. Go for the seafood, fresh from the market.

Da Lollo €
Just behind the market; the real draw here are the fist-deep *tramezzini* (sandwiches).

Fish stall, Rialto Mercato

FLEGERE/SHUTTERSTOCK ©

San Polo's Former Bullring

PARK LIFE, VENETIAN-STYLE

Campo San Polo is Venice's second-largest square, after San Marco, and there's a reason it's round: it used to be a bullring during the Republic of Venice. With trees shading scarlet benches, it's the perfect place to sit and enjoy a cake from historic **Pasticceria Rizzardini**, a minute's walk away. The 9th-century **Chiesa di San Polo**, in the corner, isn't the prettiest, but it has a humdinger of an artwork by Giandomenico Tiepolo, the son of the more famous Giambattista: a cycle of the *Stations of the Cross*.

Canalside in Santa Croce

INSIDE THE GRAND CANAL GEMS

Elegant Santa Croce has a string of big hitters along the Grand Canal. Tourists sunbathe outside the baroque **Chiesa di San Stae**, but enter the church to find some of the kookiest art in town, from saints being blinded by Jesus' light, to the stag St Eustace (San Stae) was hunting when he converted. A short walk north – you need to retreat a couple of blocks from the water, then go back out – is the mesmerising **Fondaco dei Turchi,** the former headquarters of the Turkish and Arabic traders. The striking double layer of porticoes – peak Italo-Byzantine architecture – is best seen from a *vaporetto*, though note that the building was almost completely reconstructed in the 1800s. Today it's full of stuffed animals as it houses the freaky **Museo di Storia Naturale** (Natural History Museum).

WHERE TO STAY IN SAN POLO AND SANTA CROCE

Hotel San Cassiano
Gorgeous little hotel on the Grand Canal in Ca' Favretto, the former home of 1800s painter Giacomo Favretto. €€

Cima Rosa
Five-room B&B run by an American-Italian couple, with soothing modern rooms and a private courtyard. €€€

Albergo Casa Pero
Super-simple guesthouse, an easy walk from Piazzale Roma bordering Dorsoduro and San Pantalon. €

DORSODURO

THE 'HARD BACK' WITH WORLD-CLASS ART

San Marco has its Piazza and San Polo has Rialto, but Dorsoduro has two Venice icons: the wooden Ponte dell'Accademia, and (more importantly) the church of Santa Maria della Salute. Dorsoduro means 'hard back' – in the early days, this was the most solid terrain to build on. Today, it's still the spine of the city, the Zattere waterfront forming the sleek belly of Venice's 'fish', and the land tapering into a pencil-thin point where canal meets lagoon.

The area between the Gallerie dell'Accademia and the Peggy Guggenheim Collection, the two most popular attractions, is slightly chichi. But there are other sides to Dorsoduro: the northern part is lively thanks to the Ca' Foscari University. Further west, Dorsoduro stills into near-silence, with just the sound of gently swishing canals towards the Chiesa di San Nicolò dei Mendicoli. Completing the *sestiere*, the Zattere is where all Dorsoduro comes together: walking, jogging, or just sitting on stone benches.

TOP TIP

Dorsoduro is relatively easy to navigate, with the near-straight Zattere and an obvious route along the Grand Canal side, topped and tailed by Ca' Foscari University and Punta della Dogana. *Vaporetto* 1 calls at Ca' Rezzonico and Santa Maria della Salute; others run along the Zattere towards San Marco.

JACZHOU 2015/GETTY IMAGES ©

Basilica di Santa Maria della Salute

Ca' Rezzonico

THE SWAGGERING 1700S

A monumental marble staircase sets the tone for the **Museo del Settecento Veneziano**, or Museum of 18th-Century Venice. The Baldassare Longhena-designed *palazzo*, once home to poet Robert Browning, is a worthy repository for the city's most outré furniture and artworks: chairs carved as human figures, gilded humans swishing swords from ceiling-height picture frames, and plenty of paintings, from Tiepolo's Throne Room ceiling masterpiece to Canaletto's *View of the Grand Canal*. Don't miss the Longhi Room, wall-to-wall with Pietro Longhi's portraits of everyday life – from a cup of hot chocolate to the rhinoceros that visited the city for the 1751 Carnevale.

Basilica di Santa Maria della Salute

INSIDE AN ICON

You already know this **church** from centuries of images: the big, white blancmange of a building at the mouth of the Grand Canal. Built by Baldassare Longhena as a thanks to the Madonna for returning Venice to good health (salute) after the 1630 plague, it's also a subtle tribute to motherhood – to spur on women to recreate the third of the population that was lost. Highlights include Titian's Descent of the Holy Ghost, the icon over the baroque altar (brought from Crete), and the view from the cupola, which opened for visits in 2022 (warning: there are 150 steps).

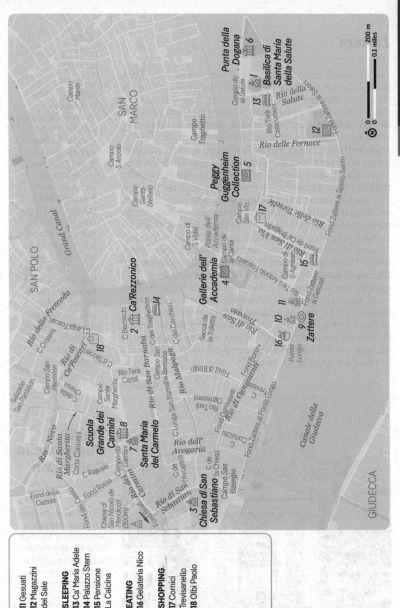

Zattere

VENICE IN MINIATURE

The Riva degli Schiavoni is Venice's best-known waterfront, but it can never equal the sheer joy you get walking along the ever-sunny **Zattere**. Skirting the southern edge of Dorsoduro, this is 1.5km of waterfront beauty. Walking from San Basilio, its western point, to Punta della Dogana, there are stonking views of Giudecca island, the Euganean Hills on the mainland and, as you near the end, of San Marco. There's action – seagulls swaggering along the waterfront, boats chugging along the wide Giudecca Canal, water sloshing at your feet and old ladies walking their tiny dogs. Along the way are churches, galleries and Venice's best ice-cream parlour, **Gelateria Nico**. Spend half an hour watching the world go by from its terrace cantilevered over the water, and you'll taste heaven – in the shape of its signature Gianduiotto (hazelnut-chocolate ice cream with whipped cream).

Essential Zattere stops: the **Gesuati** church, halfway down, where Tiepolo and Tintoretto lurk within; the deconsecrated **Chiesa di Santa Maria della Visitazione** next door, if it's open for an exhibition (the reflection of the water dances on its roof); and the, a cavernous salt warehouse that's now an exhibition space for the **Fondazione Vedova**, converted by Renzo Piano for his friend, the late Venetian artist Emilio Vedova. By the time you reach Punta della Dogana, with San Marco on one side and San Giorgio Maggiore island on the other, you'll be breathless from all the beauty.

OLD BUILDINGS, MODERN ART

On the other side of the Punta della Dogana area, a 17th-century customs house is now the **Punta della Dogana gallery**, part of the Pinault Collection. Owner François Pinault also owns **Palazzo Grassi** in San Marco, the last mansion to be built on the Grand Canal before the Republic fell. In Santa Croce, the Ca' Corner della Regina has become **Fondazione Prada**. All have regular exhibitions and are worth visiting for the architecture even if you're not keen on modern art.

Gesuati

ARK NEYMAN/SHUTTERSTOCK ®

Peggy Guggenheim Collection

MODERN ART IN MS G'S HOME

Palazzo Venier dei Leoni is an unfinished palace, with a single storey built in the 18th century before the Venier family ran out of cash. Arts doyenne Guggenheim moved in in 1949, bringing her world-class **collection of modern art**. Today you can walk through her former home gawking at works by up to 200 artists including Picasso, Chagall and Max Ernst, and exit via her dogs' graves in the garden.

Scuola Grande dei Carmini

On the western edge of Campo Santa Margherita is this little gilded **scuola** (religious confraternity) and the neighbouring church, **Santa Maria del Carmelo**. The Gothic church is a grander version of Mendicoli, with gilded wooden saints straddling the huge arches and an altarpiece by Lorenzo Lotto where the countryside is the star, not saints. The *scuola* packs in as much as its far bigger siblings (think San Rocco), with a staircase clad in stucco cherubs and mermaids, and a ceiling by Tiepolo.

Madonna statue, Chiesa di Santa Maria del Carmelo

Chiesa di San Nicolò dei Mendicoli

MAGICAL, GLITTERING CHURCH

In the far west of Dorsoduro, this glorious little **church** is said to have been founded in the 7th century (the current structure dates back to the 12th) and named after the *mendicoli* (beggars) it once sheltered. The simple brick facade belies the wonderland – gold-tipped columns prop up wooden arches, also gilded and fitted with life-size carvings of saints. Framed paintings by Veronese's pupils cling to the ceiling, while a high screen separates the altar from the congregation, carvings of the Crucifixion perched on top looking like a stage set. With the gold glittering in the soft light, it's truly magical.

Chiesa di San Sebastiano

Chiesa di San Sebastiano

VERONESE'S SISTINE CHAPEL

San Sebastiano is to Veronese fans what San Rocco is to Tintoretto lovers: a whole **church** decorated by the great painter, in less-trammelled western Dorsoduro. In 1542 the resident monks raised money to build six new chapels, just so Veronese could work his magic on them. Today, this is his Sistine Chapel – the walls frescoed with prophets and sibyls, the roof telling the story of Esther, and those chapels, each with a painting, from the grey-skinned *Crucifixion* to the colour-popping *Martyrdom of St Sebastian*. Even the organ is painted. Veronese is buried here – to the right of the organ, a memorial bust of the painter looks down at you as you survey his work.

Gallerie dell'Accademia

WORLD-CLASS VENETIAN ART

If you think Venice has a lot of churches now, you should know that during La Serenissima days, there were even more – it was Napoleon who closed some, destroyed others, and nicked their most precious works of art. Many of these have made it back to Venice, where this **gallery** has collated one of Italy's most important art collections. It's focused almost entirely on Venetian artists, but why not, when they start with Paolo Veneziano, continue with Carpaccio, Mantegna and Bellini, then blossom into the works by Veronese, Titian and Tintoretto before finishing with Canova? The gallery also introduces you to artists you may not have heard of, like Giorgione. He died of the plague at the age of 36, but not before creating *La Vecchia*, a photo-precise portrait of an old woman (thought to be his mother), and the mysterious *Tempest*, a breastfeeding woman being watched by a man in the countryside as lightning flashes. Its meaning, even 500 years on, is one of art's great mysteries.

That's not to say everything here was created in Venice. There's a set of four Hieronymous Bosch panels, *Visions of the Afterlife*, which includes a scene of souls floating through a dark tunnel towards the light – so contemporary that it looks out of place in the gallery. Other highlights include Titian's fragile last work, *Pietà*, and Tintoretto's *Creation of the Animals*, where the sea pulses with marine life and birds crowd the air.

Feast in the House of Levi by Veronese, Gallerie dell'Accademia

HERCULES MILAS/ALAMY STOCK PHOTO ©

DORSODURO'S ARTISANS

Artists and artisans go hand in hand in Venice. Two of Dorsoduro's best are Paolo Olbi and the Trevisanello family. Near the Accademia, at **Cornici Trevisanello**, the latter – father Aldo has handed over to children Filippo and Silvia – craft beautiful picture and photo frames, from simple made-to-measure ones (past clients include Picasso) to gorgeous inlaid wood and mirror-specked frames. Eighty-something **Paolo Olbi** crafts pretty journals, folders and albums, covered with Venetian and Byzantine-style prints, made in the Armenian community's nearby *palazzo*.

MORE IN DORSODURO

A San Pantalon to Salute Stroll

BRIDGES FOR FIGHTING, PASTRIES FOR EATING

Crossing into Dorsoduro from San Rocco, you hit the lively Calle San Pantalon. Have a pastry at **1 Tonolo**, then head south via **2 Acqua Marea** – a shop that debuted selling rain boots but switched to chic city shoes. Further down, past **3 Mamafè** – a Pugliese bakery for *pasticiotto* pastries and *pucce* (bread rolls, toasted and filled) – is the **4 Chiesa di San Pantalon**. The ceiling was painted across 40 canvases by Gianantonio Fiumani, making it the world's largest work of its kind. Cross the bridge (note the 2019 Banksy on your right, featuring a child refugee holding a flare) to **5 Campo Santa Margherita**. This large, bar-lined square is the student nightlife hub.

From here, the route to Santa Maria della Salute crosses the **6 Ponte dei Pugni** (Bridge of Fists), built for staged fights. Past Campo San Barnaba, you'll reach **7 Libreria La Toletta**, the city's oldest bookshop, with a huge range of English-language books about Venice. Stop for a drink at **8 Centurion Palace**, a five-star hotel with tables cantilevered over the canal. At Salute, the **9 Pinacoteca Manfrediana** is the Venice Patriarch's Diocesan Museum. It's tiny, without big-hitter art, but the inscriptions in the courtyard taken from destroyed churches are interesting.

ARTISTIC DORSODURO

Giovanni Pelizzato owns Libreria La Toletta, founded by his grandfather in 1933. Born off Campo San Barnaba, he knows Dorsoduro as an inspirational place.

This is the *sestiere* of artists, poets and writers. So let's head to the Zattere: to **Pensione La Calcina**, where John Ruskin (author of *The Stones of Venice*) stayed. The terrace in front of it used to be the historic Al Cucciolo gelateria. As a child I often saw the elderly Alberto Moravia there, sipping coffee while he read a book or the paper. Cross the bridge and you're on the **Fondamenta degli Incurabili** – that's the Italian title of Russian poet Joseph Brodsky's masterpiece *Watermark*, a unique tribute to Venice.

🛏 **WHERE TO STAY IN DORSODURO**

Ca' Maria Adele
Small but perfectly formed hotel, across a small canal from the Santa Maria della Salute church. €€€

La Calcina
Ruskin wrote much of *The Stones of Venice* during his stay here on the Zattere, overlooking Giudecca. €€

Palazzo Stern
Next to Ca' Rezzonico, this former family home is now a four-star hotel with an idyllic garden on the Grand Canal. €€

CANNAREGIO

STATELY HOMES & GRAND CANALS

If you're arriving by train, Cannaregio will be your introduction to Venice. It's the second-largest *sestiere*, which means that if you're walking from the station to San Marco, it might seem like one long, souvenir-shop-lined street. But it's far more than a thoroughfare, as you'll realise if you stray even a block off the main drag.

Today, most Venetians live in Cannaregio, so it's full of local bakers, newsagents and ironmongers – as well as great places for *cicheti* and an *ombra* of wine. The student population gives it an energy that isn't always apparent in other parts of the city.

Perhaps even more so than the other *sestieri*, Cannaregio feels like a place of extremes. On one side of the main drag is the Grand Canal, with some of the most elegant *palazzi* in town, like Ca' Vendramin Calergi and the luscious Ca' d'Oro. On the other side, quiet residential areas unfurl along wide canals. There's a peace and an airiness you won't find elsewhere in Venice.

TOP TIP

Cannaregio is probably the easiest *sestiere* to navigate, as its streets are straighter, and its main drag runs right from the station to the Rialto. By *vaporetto*, take the Grand Canal routes or head north to the lagoon to catch the round-city services. Boats for the lagoon leave from Fondamente Nove.

RENATA SEDMAKOVA/SHUTTERSTOCK ©

Ceiling fresco, Chiesa di Sant'Alvise

Chiesa di Sant'Alvise

OFF THE MAP, HEAD IN THE CLOUDS

Reach for the sky at this teeny **church** (dating back to 1388) with an unassuming, bare brick exterior. Inside, its extraordinary 17th-century *trompe l'œil* ceiling features grand balustrades and fluted columns that wiggle up to an azure heaven, where chubby cherubs dandle amid the clouds. Back at ground level, look for the three laceratingly realistic Tiepolos: *Flagellation, Crown of Thorns* and *Road to Calvary*. In the far north of Cannaregio, this is a rarely visited area and all the more peaceful for it.

Chiesa di Santa Maria dei Miracoli

THE ULTIMATE FLORENCE–VENICE COLLABORATION

Wedged between a *campo* (square) and a canal is this tiny jewel of a **church** clad entirely in precious marble, inside and out. Surprisingly sober, it's the pinnacle of Renaissance architecture in Venice, completed by Pietro and Tullio Lombardo in 1489 and mixing clean Florentine geometry with that swaggering Venetian love of colour. The ceiling panels feature Pier Maria Pennacchi's portraits of saints and prophets dressed as Venetians.

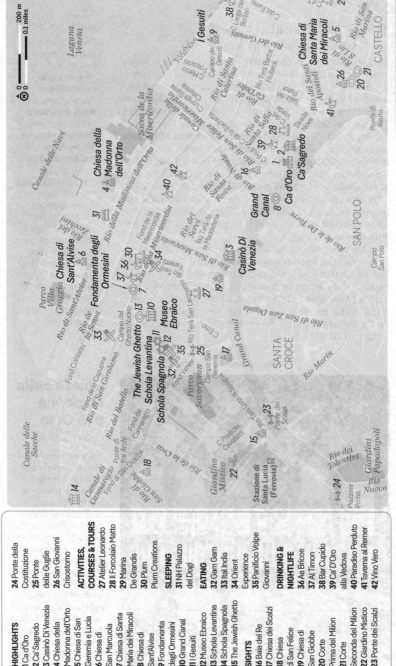

The Grand Canal

THE WORLD'S MOST LAVISH WATERWAY

Snaking through the city centre, the Grand Canal is almost a *sestiere* in itself, of course – but most people's first view of it will be in Cannaregio. The lavish *palazzi* that line it were designed to be seen from the water, so hop on a *vaporetto* to see them in style. The full canal cruise takes 45 minutes.

On the Cannaregio stretch, down to the Rialto Bridge, you'll see huge churches like **San Geremia** and **San Marcuola**; landmarks including the elaborate Ca' Vendramin Calergi, now the posh **Casinò di Venezia**, and lush **Ca' Sagredo**, a 15th-century mansion turned hotel; and semi-hidden spots (make a note to return to **Taverna al Remer**, a waterside bar).

Perhaps most glorious of all is the mesmerising **Ca' d'Oro** (p296), looking like a mini Doge's Palace. Its subtle pink, grey and eau-de-nil stone and multi-toned columns shift colour with the changing light.

On the other side of this top stretch, Santa Croce and San Polo reveal the **Fondaco dei Turchi** (p285; the old HQ for Middle Eastern and European Muslim merchants – the Venetian word *fontego*, or *fondaco* in Italian, is derived from Arabic); **San Stae** (p285) church, the location for the final scene in cult horror film *Don't Look Now*; and the bombastic **Ca' Pesaro** (p283), before the Rialto market and bridge come into view.

Grand Canal from the Ca' d'Oro (p296)

WHERE TO CROSS

Despite being nearly 4km long, Venice has just four bridges: the **Ponte della Costituzione** at Piazzale Roma; the **Ponte degli Scalzi** by the train station; the **Rialto**, of course; and the **Ponte dell'Accademia**, connecting San Marco and Dorsoduro. Nowhere near? Hop on the *vaporetto* 1, which darts from side to side, or get a *traghetto* (the large gondolas shuttling people across). There are five points, from Santa Sofia (near Ca' d'Oro) in the north to Punta della Dogana at the mouth of the canal.

Chiesa della Madonna dell'Orto

BIG-HITTING ART

This great barn of a Gothic **church** used to be best known for a 'miraculous' statue of the Madonna, but today it's more famous as the parish church of Tintoretto. The Renaissance artist created 10 huge canvases for it, including *Presentation of the Virgin* and *Last Judgement*. He and his artist children, Domenico and Marietta, are buried here; other works by Cima da Conegliano, Titian and Palma il Giovane make this one of the city's best churches for art.

Fondamenta della Misericordia

Fondamenta degli Ormesini

CANALSIDE CICHETI

Cannaregio's wide canals are perfect for laying out tables and chairs, and the stretch of the Fondamenta degli Ormesini and Fondamenta della Misericordia north of the Ghetto is now Venice's premier bar strip. Our top picks: **Ae Bricoe** for cicheti, **Al Timon** (where you can drink on a boat) and **Paradiso Perduto** for its wine list.

THE MAN WHO SAVED THE JEWS

Venice's Jewish community was about 1000-strong when WWII broke out. The fact that only 246 people were sent to concentration camps is down to one doctor: **Giuseppe Jona**. When German occupiers asked him for a list of Jews, Jona destroyed all identifying documents and then killed himself, rather than risk betraying them under torture. A wing of Venice's hospital, his old place of work, is dedicated to Jona, as well as a plaque in the Campo del Ghetto Novo.

The Jewish Ghetto

A HISTORY OF OUTSIDERS

'Ghetto' comes from the Venetian *ghèto*, or foundry – which is what this area off the Cannaregio Canal was until medieval times. Then abandoned, it was the least desirable part of town when it was assigned to the Jews in 1516, when they were first allowed to live in Venice rather than come from the mainland to work as money-lenders (the only job they were permitted to have). Originally spanning one tiny island, the area was expanded in 1541 and 1633 – though it was still highly restricted, hence the eight-storey 'skyscrapers' – and residents were gated in at night under curfew. Apart from a brief, French-dictated break in 1797, they were confined here until Italy unified in 1866.

The Ghetto's five synagogues, built from 1528 to 1575, served different communities. Three are currently closed for restoration, along with the small Museo Ebraico, but guided tours visit the lavish **Schola Levantina** and **Schola Spagnola**, both revamped by Baldassare Longhena in the 1600s and filled with sumptuous carvings and marble. Spend a few hours taking in the area's atmosphere.

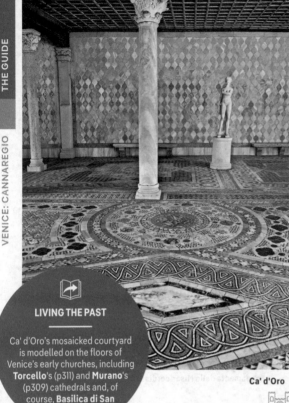

HERACLES KRITIKOS/SHUTTERSTOCK ©

I Gesuiti

TOP-TO-TOE MARBLE

At first glance, it looks like this **church** just off the Fondamente Nove has been hung from top to bottom in lavish Venetian damasks. In fact, it's better – the 18th-century rococo church is entirely clad in marble, intricately inlaid to form paisley-style 'wall hangings', a 'carpet' rolling down from the altar, and even frilly, tasselled 'drapes' bunched around the pulpit.

LIVING THE PAST

Ca' d'Oro's mosaicked courtyard is modelled on the floors of Venice's early churches, including **Torcello**'s (p311) and **Murano**'s (p309) cathedrals and, of course, **Basilica di San Marco** (p278).

Ca' d'Oro

Ca' d'Oro

A LABOUR OF LOVE

This is the ultimate love letter to Venice: a lavish 15th-century Grand Canal *palazzo*, rescued from ruin and turned into a gallery by Baron Giorgio Franchetti. Franchetti – who bought the florid, Gothic '**Golden House**' in 1894 – was a hands-on owner, sourcing individual chunks of marble to create the mosaic flooring in the courtyard, and filling the *palazzo* with art, much of which he rescued after it had been ripped from churches by Napoleon. Highlights include Mantegna's *St Sebastian*, and five faded frescoes by Titian that once graced the facade of the Fondaco dei Tedeschi (the German trading HQ at Rialto); but Franchetti also collected works by lesser-known artists, like Gian Cristoforo Romano's 15th-century bust of a young boy. There are peerless views of the Grand Canal, overlooking the Rialto market, from the two balconies. Franchetti committed suicide in 1922, four years before his museum opened; his ashes rest beneath an ancient porphyry column in the courtyard, as Ca d'Oro's eternal custodian. Stay a few hours.

WORLD ON YOUR PLATE

Surprisingly, as Venice used to be one of Europe's most cosmopolitan cities, there's a lack of non-Italian restaurants these days. Three excellent ones are in Cannaregio. **Ital India** serves halal Indian food on the Fondamenta degli Ormesini bar strip. In the Ghetto, Israeli restaurant **Gam Gam** excels at veggie dishes (its nine-plate antipasto is exceptional). And then there's the super-affordable **Orient Experience**, serving dishes from Syria, Iraq, Bangladesh and Afghanistan. Afghan filmmaker Hamed Ahmadi opened the restaurant to tell the stories of (and give work to) fellow refugees.

Ponte delle Guglie

MORE IN CANNAREGIO

A Canalside Ramble in Cannaregio

CANNAREGIO'S MANY VILLAGES

Cannaregio's sheer variation gives it the feel of a series of villages, which makes this a *sestiere* for walking. Start by dipping off the main drag at the **Ponte delle Guglie** – the wide, gargoyle-hung bridge that crosses the Cannaregio Canal, perhaps the second-busiest artery in the city centre. Walk up past the fresh-fish stall set up on the canalside. At **Gam Gam** (p296), which marks the entrance to the Ghetto, you can see where the gate that closed the Jews in at night was located until 1866. Just beyond it, pop into **Panificio Volpe** for some traditional Jewish pastries, then come back out onto the canal and continue past the grand *palazzi*.

Cross the next bridge, Tre Archi, to arrive at the **Chiesa di San Giobbe**. It's a fascinating taste of Tuscany, with sober Renaissance styling by Pietro Lombardo. The ceiling of one chapel is encrusted with ceramics by the Della Robbia brothers. Back across the bridge, continue up to the modern estate on the lagoon-front, **Baia del Re**. Built as social

GREEN LUNGS

Where San Marco and San Polo are tightly wound warrens, Cannaregio is a more stately area of wide canals and walkways, and stand-alone *palazzi* rather than ones squashed together. That means there's room for gardens, too. A particularly beautiful one belongs to the **NH Palazzo dei Dogi** hotel – buy a drink at the bar and ask to go for a wander. Another is the **Giardino Mistico**, or 'Mystic Garden', behind the Chiesa dei Scalzi by the train station. Book a tour with the Wigwam Club Giardini Storici Venezia to see more gardens that are closed to the public.

WHERE TO DRINK IN CANNAREGIO

Ae Bricoe
Excellent *cicheti* (bar snacks) and a Venetian clientele at a hole-in-the-wall run by three siblings.

Vino Vero
Natural wines are on the menu at this bar, which is a cut above its rowdy surroundings.

Bar Cupido
Friendly staff and well-priced wine by the glass with waterside tables on Fondamente Nove – a great lunch spot.

CANNAREGIO'S BEST ARTISANS

Valeria Duflot, co-founder of Venezia Autentica *(@venezia autentica)* and Overtourism Solution, knows that artisans not only keep centuries-old traditions going, but they help keep the city alive. These are her favourites.

Marina De Grandis
Bookbinder Marina designs, cuts and sews high-quality leather notebooks, bags, wallets, and restores valuable old books.

Plum Plum Creations
Arianna Sautariello's artisanal prints create unique memories of Venice while introducing you to ancient techniques.

Il Forcolaio Matto
Piero Dri crafts traditional wooden oars and oarlocks, key to the survival of Venetian rowing; they also make beautiful design elements.

Atelier Leonardo
Brothers Stefano and Ferruccio Leonardo craft jewellery from vintage and modern Murano glass beads.

housing in the 1930s, it's a rare glimpse of modern architecture in Venice, and the lagoon views from the pine-shaded benches are a delight. From here, head east along the San Girolamo Canal, and you'll find yourself on the **Fondamenta degli Ormesini** (p295) in time for a drink.

The Road to Rialto

EVEN THE SUPERMARKETS ARE MAGICAL

The main route from the train station to the Rialto can be packed, but among all the souvenir shops and touristy bars you'll come across some real gems. By the station, the **Chiesa dei Scalzi** has a ridiculously flamboyant baroque interior drenched in marble. Short-sighted folk may want to drop into **Chiesa dei San Geremia e Lucia**, where the body of St Lucy (the patron saint of eye health) is kept, before continuing to **Chiesa di San Marcuola**, home to an early Tintoretto – it's fascinating recognising his style, even though it's less pronounced than in his later works.

At the nearby **Teatro Italia**, a neo-Gothic theatre-turned-cinema-turned-supermarket, the aisles sit beneath lavish frescoes and the deli counter takes up the old stage – stock up on snacks here, as you can't exit without a receipt. If you'd prefer a bar, there's **Ca' d'Oro alla Vedova**, a historical tavern that serves wine by the jug and makes the best meatballs in town. Nearby, another Tintoretto lurks in the canalside **Chiesa di San Felice**: St Demetrius wearing brilliant scarlet leggings.

The narrowing street and growing crowds signal you're approaching Rialto. At the church of San Giovanni Cristosomo, dip left to the **Corte Prima del Milion** and **Corte Seconda del Milion**. These two connected courtyards are said to be where Marco Polo lived.

WHERE TO DRINK IN CANNAREGIO

Il Santo Bevitore
Beer fans will dig the 20-odd craft beers on tap; others might prefer the homemade, lagoon-distilled gin.

Cantina Aziende Agricole
Outdoor seating aplenty makes this friendly bar a great alternative to the nearby Fondamenta degli Ormesini.

Torrefazione Cannaregio
Who needs alcohol when you have an artisan coffee roaster? Try the granita (crushed ice made with coffee) in summer.

CASTELLO

OPEN SPACES AND LIVING HISTORY

Venice's largest *sestiere* is the 'tail' of the fish – and what a tail. It's often overlooked by visitors, who don't realise that it nibbles at the heels of Cannaregio and San Marco. In fact, heading east from Piazza San Marco, once you pass the Doge's Palace you're already in Castello. It shares the Fondamente Nove with Cannaregio.

Though less ostentatious than San Marco, Castello still has big hitters, like its first-rate museums just a few minutes' walk from the Piazza. The Riva degli Schiavoni has to be one of the world's most beautiful waterfronts. The northern side is larger than life – hangar-like places of worship, a spectacular hospital with a gilded *scuola*, and the Arsenale dwarfing the houses around it.

You'll be mingling with locals in Castello's bars and shops – Via Garibaldi , is the closest Venice gets to a real main street. To the east lie the Giardini Pubblici, the principal Biennale premises, and Sant'Elena further beyond.

TOP TIP

Castello is big, and the best (and most beautiful) way to navigate it is by the *rive* (waterfront walkways) that lead east from San Marco, detouring north to sightsee. The *vaporetti* 4.1 and 4.2 loop the district, travelling up the *rive*, around the island of San Pietro di Castello and west towards Fondamente Nove.

LIUDMILA ERMOLENKO/SHUTTERSTOCK ©

Museo Storico Navale

Museo Storico Navale

AT ONE WITH THE SEA

A **Naval History Museum** might not sound like a riot, but this one, connected to the Arsenale, has some brilliant stuff spread across its five floors: massive 16th-century ship lanterns, fearsome weaponry, folk-art paintings by sailors convinced the Madonna saved them from drowning in the 1500s and 1600s, and whopping figureheads and sculptures once attached to Venice's ships – which gives you an idea of just how gargantuan the boats were. Peggy Guggenheim's gilded gondola sits on the 4th floor.

Palazzo Grimani

HAUNTED BY THE PAST

Horror fans will know this as the location for the chilling denouement of *Don't Look Now*, and it's a fittingly offbeat **museum**. A Renaissance *palazzo* abandoned after the demise of the Grimani family, it was falling apart by 1973 when Donald Sutherland was filming here; even now it's hauntingly hollow – and curiously intimate You'll find empty spaces with fresco fragments on the walls, and the odd Tintoretto hanging unframed. Don't miss the Tribune room, filled to the gills with Roman sculptures, and the Sala a Fogliami's ceiling painted with birds swooping around plants including maize and tobacco from the New World.

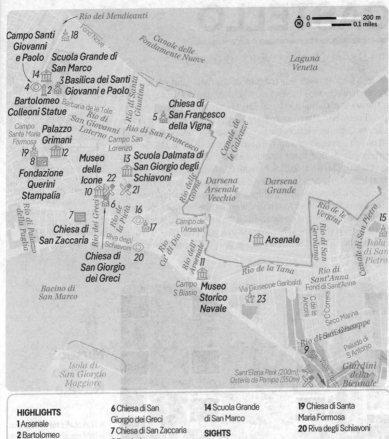

Fondazione Querini Stampalia

AN ARTISTIC JEWEL FOR THE COMMUNITY

Ten minutes from Piazza San Marco, this is one of Venice's most exciting spaces: a museum, gallery, library, archive and modernist garden, all in a 16th-century *palazzo* left to the city in 1868 by Count Giovanni Querini Stampalia, who stipulated that his home must be accessible to all. Today, you'll find students taking breaks on the cutesy bridge that separates it from Campo Santa Maria Formosa, or sitting in the cafe garden designed by Carlo Scarpa as part of his groundbreaking ground-floor wing. You'll need a few hours here.

Since 2018 the 3rd floor has housed the art collection of a local bank, including works by Tintoretto, Tiepolo and Canaletto – though the real draw is the collection of eight bronze bas-reliefs by Arturo Martini, showing the horrors of WWI. One floor down is the main **museum**. In 2022 the information panels were overhauled, putting the world-class art into context and elevating this into one of the most fascinating places in Venice. Paintings of a couple by Palma il Vecchio are accompanied by information about Venetian arranged marriages; a room of homoerotic art reveals how one gay member of the Querini Stampalia family was jailed for seven years. One work that needs no explanation is Bellini's *Presentation at the Temple*, sitting on a simple easel designed by Scarpa. His wing and garden downstairs blend modernism with Japanese influences creating an open-to-the-elements space, the canal lapping at the floor.

VENICE'S MODERN ARCHITECT

Venetian-born architect **Carlo Scarpa** (1906–78) made his buildings blend in with the city's historical architecture, rather than compete with it. Instead of using doors and barriers to keep floodwater out, he designed open spaces that allowed it to flow in and easily out. He was also artistic director of **Venini** (p312) glassworkers, where his designs are still on sale, but his main work is the **Negozio Olivetti** (p277).

Tesa 105

MATTHIAS SCHOLZ/ALAMY STOCK PHOTO ©

Arsenale

THE SHIPYARD WHERE THE MAGIC HAPPENED

Forget the Doge's Palace; La Serenissima's power hinged on what this gargantuan **shipyard** could produce (it's said that the assembly line could roll out a galleon in three days). Back then, the Arsenale was so chaotic that Dante placed it in his Hell; now, it's a peaceful oasis, and host to events like the Biennale. You can get a glimpse through the 15th-century gateway at the southern entrance or on a walkway alongside its northern wall. There, you can usually enter one of the warehouses to access the cafe Tesa 105, or the inner waterfront if there's no event on.

Chiesa di San Giorgio del Greci

Chiesa di San Zaccaria

PERMA-FLOODED CRYPT

East of the Doge's Palace, **San Zaccaria** is more of a gallery than a church – you can't see the walls for the paintings, their frames slotted side by side, including a whopping *Sacra Conversazione* by Bellini and an early Tintoretto. But the real draw lies behind the door in the right-hand nave: traces of the churches here since the 9th century. There are snatches of mosaic flooring, remnants of 15th-century frescoes, and the crypt (usually part-flooded) where eight doges are buried.

Chiesa di San Giorgio dei Greci

A COMMUNITY FOR 600 YEARS

Venice's Greek community swelled after the fall of Constantinople (and the end of the Byzantine Empire) in 1453. In 1561, east of San Zaccaria, they consecrated this church – **St George of the Greeks** – which still glitters with Byzantine and Renaissance icons. Next door is the **Museo delle Icone**, a superb collection of nearly 100 icons, from an almond-eyed Byzantine Madonna to an 18th-century depiction of Noah's Ark, complete with camels and unicorns. Don't miss the 1514-dated letter from the doge giving permission to the community to build a church, and the 14th-century illuminated manuscript in Greek and Arabic, telling the story of Alexander the Great.

TOP LEFT: JORGE SANCHEZ/SHUTTERSTOCK © BOTTOM RIGHT: BARABANSCHIKOW ALEXANDER/SHUTTERSTOCK ©

Chiesa di San Zaccaria

Scuola Dalmata di San Giorgio degli Schiavoni

CARPACCIO'S MASTERPIECE

Named after the Slavic population who founded the **Scuola Dalmata** (Dalmatian School) in 1451, this jewellery box of a building contains a cycle of paintings to rival San Rocco's. Vittore Carpaccio was called on to decorate the small *scuola*. His nine-painting cycle of the lives of Sts George, Tryphon and Jerome is an explosion of detail, from the parrot pecking at a flower in one scene, to the crescent-shaped vessel in the painting of St Augustine (a copy of the real one, which is displayed in a cabinet). The most famous work, *St George and the Dragon*, was away for restoration at the time of writing, with a copy in situ.

Campo Santi Giovanni e Paolo

Chiesa di San Francesco della Vigna

A MYTHICAL SPOT

While it's somewhat out of the way today, tradition has this Franciscan **church** as one of Venice's most important points: it was supposedly the place where St Mark docked during a storm and was told that his body would end up in Venice (more of that dubious creation myth). Designed by Jacopo Sansovino and with a facade by Palladio, it's a big-hitter church with an attached cloister. Inside are extravagantly carved chapels, plus two standout depictions of *Madonna and Child* – one by Bellini, and the other, from 1455, on a flower-wreathed throne by Antonio da Negroponte.

Campo Santi Giovanni e Paolo

CASTELLO'S ANSWER TO SAN MARCO

Castello's main square is a much more peaceful affair than Piazza San Marco, with cafes, a canal and monumental buildings. First to catch your eye is the blinding white facade of the **Scuola Grande di San Marco**, now the city hospital. Enter past the bas-reliefs of lions on the Pietro Lombardo–designed facade and up a grand staircase by Renaissance architect Codussi, to find the Sala Capitolare (the main room of the *scuola*) with a deliriously gilded, coffered ceiling and paintings by Domenico Tintoretto (Jacopo's son) telling the story of St Mark. On the canal side of the hospital is the **Chiesa di San Lazzaro dei Mendicanti**, containing Tintoretto's *St Ursula* and a haunting *Crucifixion* by Veronese. Back in the square is the vast, Gothic **Basilica dei Santi Giovanni e Paolo**, a mass of elaborate tombs and memorials with a roll call of great artists within its chapels and altarpieces: Veronese, Bellini, Lorenzo Lotto and Cima da Conegliano. Don't miss Andrea Verroccio's **equestrian statue of Bartolomeo Colleoni** in the square.

Cloister, Chiesa di San Francesco della Vigna

CASTELLO'S HIDDEN HIGHLIGHTS

Originally from Senegal, **Moulaye Niang** is the first non-Venetian maestro of Murano glass techniques. His jewellery (*@collection muranero*) combines Venetian and African bead traditions.

I came to Venice while living in Paris, and saw this place that was neither city nor countryside – a middle way. The sounds are really particular – without the noise of cars you hear the bells, the footsteps, the languages.

I'm from southern Senegal and I miss its green, so **Sant'Elena**'s park is a gift. Next to it is **San Pietro di Castello**, which is the real Venice – not at all touristy. Then there's **Campo della Bràgora**, which is like a village – people wave out of the windows, and greet you in the street.

A Waterfront Walk to Sant'Elena

ICONIC LAGOON VIEWS

The waterside walk from San Marco up to the tip of Sant'Elena is a classic Venice experience. Head east from the Doge's Palace on the **Riva degli Schiavoni**. This promenade takes you to Venice's far eastern edge, the water lapping at your feet. All those famous views of St Mark's Basin are from here. You might want to stop for a drink at **El Rèfolo** bar on lively Via Garibaldi, which veers 'inland' just after the Arsenale. You'll also pass the **Giardini Pubblici** – one of Europe's first public parks when it was opened by Napoleon in 1812, and today the home of the Biennale. Continue up the waterfront to reach the pine-shaded park at **Sant'Elena**.

Church-Hopping in Castello

WORSHIP-WORTHY INTERIORS

Leave the waterfront to hit Castello's churches. First up: the Late Gothic **Chiesa di San Giovanni in Bràgora**, where composer Antonio Vivaldi was baptised. Behind the altar is a *Baptism of Christ* by Cima da Conegliano, with the jagged Dolomites rising up behind the cherubs in the clouds. Further 'inland' is **Chiesa di Santa Maria Formosa**, a sterling example of Codussi's clean-lined Renaissance architecture in Venice. It's home to (almost certainly) the city's only altarpiece by a woman, Giulia Lama. Finally, the island of **San Pietro di Castello** is dominated by the eponymous church. This used to be the religious centre of Venice, hence the grand Palladio facade. Don't miss the 'throne of St Peter' – a bishop's seat made from a stolen Arabic headstone, inscribed with verses from the Koran.

Vivaldi bust, Chiesa di San Giovanni in Bràgora

AJBORGES/SHUTTERSTOCK ©

 WHERE TO EAT IN CASTELLO

Osteria da Pampo
Lagoon seafood with a Genoese touch at this friendly restaurant in Sant'Elena. €

Trattoria da Remigio
A local favourite for seafood-swirled dishes, from lagoon-netted shrimp to spider-crab-laced gnocchi. €€

Ristorante Local
Traditional lagoon ingredients turned into a Michelin-starred tasting menu; near San Zaccaria church. €€€

GIUDECCA, LIDO & THE SOUTHERN ISLANDS

TRAVELLING THROUGH TIME

The eel-shaped island wriggling beneath Venice's 'fish', peaceful Giudecca is the perfect place to watch the sun set over the city from one of its waterfront bars. The other big hitter of the southern islands is the Lido – an 11km sandbar that, with neighbouring Pellestrina, forms a barrier between the Adriatic and the lagoon. In between, tiny islands double as time capsules: flowers blossom as they have for centuries and dinky settlements recall pre-powerhouse Venice.

The Lido is Venice's beach resort and, with its turn-of-the-century buildings, a place to escape reality (while embracing the modern cars and buses). To feel really remote, head back towards town. The lagoon between Lido and Giudecca is a liminal space of monasteries, sublime art and painful history. Sliding between San Giorgio Maggiore, San Lazzaro and San Servolo islands makes for a perfect summer day.

TOP TIP

It's worth getting a *vaporetto* pass if you're island-hopping – especially as you'll likely need to go back and forth from San Zaccaria, instead of travelling island to island. Giudecca is walkable but (at 3.7km) long. To save time, *vaporetti* run its full length.

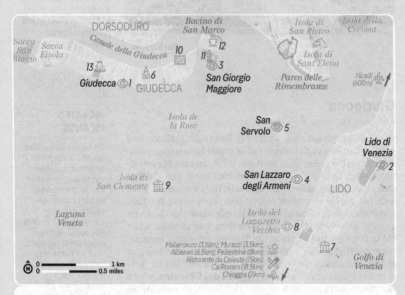

HIGHLIGHTS
1 Giudecca
2 Lido di Venezia
3 San Giorgio Maggiore
4 San Lazzaro degli Armeni

5 San Servolo

SIGHTS
6 Chiesa del Santissimo Redentore
7 Hotel Excelsior
8 Lazzaretto Vecchio

9 San Clemente
10 Tre Oci
11 Vatican Chapels

DRINKING & NIGHTLIFE
12 San Giorgio Cafe

SHOPPING
13 Artigiani del Chiostro

TRAVELSCAPES/ALAMY STOCK PHOTO ©

San Servolo

San Servolo

FROM MENTAL ASYLUM
TO ART EXHIBITIONS

Today, San Servolo's lush, sculpture-filled gardens make it an oasis squaring off against San Marco. Look a little closer at those sculptures, though, and you'll get a hint of the anguish that once consumed this island as one of Venice's two mental hospitals. A small **museum** details the traumatic history, but a walk around tells the story better. Those gardens are deliberately high-walled, and the asylum's long corridors are usually filled with exhibitions – the island today is an event space and international university.

Giudecca

ARTISANS AND MONKS

Spend an afternoon walking the full length of Giudecca, and you'll get an idea of its history: one of grand Renaissance monasteries and working-class heritage. While lacking big attractions, other than Palladio's **Redentore** church and the **Tre Oci** photography gallery, it's a wonderfully disjointed place with old warehouses lying empty, boatyards facing the Lido and the odd flash of the gardens that once made this the green heart of Venice. Monks stride by on their way to Mass, while old ladies rush to be first at the Thursday-morning organic-vegetable stall at the female jail. Around Palanca, there's a glut of bars and restaurants overlooking the Zattere. But the jewel in Giudecca's crown is the **Artigiani del Chiostro**, where 12 artisans work in a 15th-century cloister. Don't miss Mistero Buffo masks, or Stefano Morasso, a Murano-glass *maestro* who blows modern glasses, vases and jewellery as you watch.

ISOLATED ISLANDS

On the smaller southern islands, Venice feels within reach, almost swimmable; yet wait an hour for the *vaporetto* on San Lazzaro, and you'll start feeling claustrophobic. Today's glorious isolation was once used to segregate. From the **Lazzaretto Vecchio** (the world's first quarantine island, born of the 14th-century plague) to **San Clemente** (an asylum turned luxury hotel), this is where immigrants, those with infectious diseases and the mentally ill were offloaded. The last lagoon asylum closed in 1992.

San Giorgio Maggiore

San Lazzaro degli Armeni

KNOW YOURSELF
THROUGH OTHERS

The *vaporetto* sign in Armenian – the only one in a foreign language in Venice – is the first hint you're somewhere special. This island, given to Armenian monk Mekhitar in 1717, is one of the last remaining in-situ communities from the cosmopolitan days of La Serenissima. You can't know yourself until you know other cultures, was Mekhitar's motto, and over the past 300 years the island's **monastery** has built an eclectic collection of items from around the world, from Europe's best-preserved Egyptian mummy to the world's oldest copper dagger. It's also a repository of precarious Armenian heritage, with the world's largest collection of Armenian manuscripts.

San Giorgio Maggiore

ART-FILLED OASIS

Just across the water from Piazza San Marco is this Venice in miniature, with a knockout Palladian **basilica** and a *campanile* (bell tower) to rival St Mark's. In 982 CE the Republic gifted the island to Benedictine monks, who are responsible for the church and attached monastery, as well as the art inside, including five Tintorettos. Ad-hoc tours of off-limits areas are often possible – ask at the *campanile* ticket office, though not before you've taken the lift up 60m for showstopper lagoon views.

Today, the island belongs to the Fondazione Giorgio Cini, a cultural foundation. Much of it is an oasis of parkland, dotted with artistic and architectural installations with audio-guide tours. Don't miss the **Vatican Chapels** – 11 meditation spaces constructed by the likes of Terunobu Fujimori in a waterside glade of Aleppo pines. Monastery tours take in a Palladian cloister and the Manica Lunga (the old monks' dormitory, now library), while the **San Giorgio Café** serves lagoon-sourced fish.

INTERESTED IN BOOKBINDING?

There was once a printing press on San Lazzaro degli Armeni, too. Today, bookbinder **Paolo Olbi** (p290) does his printing in the Armenian community's Dorsoduro *palazzo*.

Pellestrina

WILDLIFE AND WILD LIFE

Both long, skinny sandbars, Lido and Pellestrina seal the bulk of the lagoon from the Adriatic. But while Lido is all about fun, Pellestrina is an idyllic fishing **island** (try the best the lagoon has to offer at **Ristorante da Celeste**). **Ca' Roman**, at its southern tip, is a dune-rumpled nature reserve, home to migratory birds. Between here and Pellestrina village, the island thins to the Murazzi flood barrier and nothing else.

TOP RIGHT: CLIMBER 1959/SHUTTERSTOCK © BOTTOM LEFT: STEVANZZ/SHUTTERSTOCK ©

Pellestrina

Chioggia

A MINI VENICE – WITH CARS

A sublime day trip takes you from the Lido to Chioggia, the southernmost **town** in the lagoon, via Bus 11 that connects with ferries to hop between the islands. Becoming rapidly more popular, Chioggia resembles a mini Venice, with its canal-cut streets – only it has cars, lots of fishing boats and is firmly in the 21st century. Part of the Venetian territory, it has plenty of history left, from the lion over the fortress-like entrance gate to San Domenico church, with a Carpaccio painting of St Paul browned by centuries of candle smoke.

Chioggia

Lido di Venezia

BEACHSIDE PLEASURE PALACE

Who doesn't love the **Lido**? This is a place dedicated to pleasure: days on the beach (choose any of the private ones, or head to the small public beach at the western end), brisk walks along the Adriatic and, of course, the Venice Film Festival, which brings the glamour each September. You can dine in the art deco restaurant at Italy's oldest commercial airport, the dinky Nicelli; see how Venice used to look at the ancient village of Malamocco; and enjoy the wild beach at Alberoni, on the southern tip. From there, you can walk back towards the Hotel Excelsior (film festival central) via the **Murazzi** – the 18th-century flood barrier in blinding white Istrian stone, the Adriatic foaming at your feet.

MURANO, BURANO & THE NORTHERN ISLANDS

WHERE NATURE AND HISTORY COLLIDE

While the south lagoon is manicured, the north is a wilder place. It's the oldest part of the lagoon – despite the creation myth of the Veneti tribe fleeing from barbarian invasion in the 5th century, the northern islands were already inhabited in ancient times. By the 5th and 6th centuries, Torcello was a key Adriatic port and Burano a fishing community; in the 7th century the bishop of mainland Altinum transferred to Torcello; and in 1291 glassmakers from Venice were moved en masse to Murano to avoid burning down the city centre.

Today, the north lagoon is one of the most popular places to visit in Venice. Burano and Murano are usually uncomfortably busy; lines for the *vaporetto* can be hundreds-deep. Spend some time on the lagoon itself, an otherworldly place of still waters, mudflats, rare birds, and history at every turn.

TOP TIP

Regular *vaporetti* leave for the northern islands from Fondamente Nove in Cannaregio. *Vaporetto* 12 ticks off Murano, Mazzorbo, Burano and (depending on the time of day) Torcello, though boats are often full when they reach Murano. It's under 10 minutes from Cannaregio to Murano, or 45 minutes to Burano.

Vineyard, Mazzorbo

IN VINO VERITAS

The lagoon has always been self-sufficient – and that includes wine. The golden Dorona grape, beloved by doges, was rescued from near-extinction by the local Bisol family – today they grow it on **Mazzorbo**, the island next to Burano, and serve their Venusa wine at their Michelin-starred restaurant, **Venissa**. On Sant'Erasmo, the island next to Lazzaretto Nuovo that is still full of farms, **Orto di Venezia** offers tastings of their Malvasia-based wine – even chef Alain Ducasse is a fan.

Cimitero di San Michele

FLOATING CEMETERY

Few cemeteries can match San Michele for its setting. Hovering between Cannaregio and Murano, **San Michele** has views of the city, lagoon, and the Dolomites in the distance. It was originally a monastery, but when La Serenissima fell, Napoleon turned the island into a cemetery. There's a startlingly modern section designed by David Chipperfield, who oversaw the recent renovation of the Procuratie Vecchie (p276). The most interesting part is the Protestant area, where the likes of Igor Stravinsky, Sergei Diaghilev and Ezra Pound are buried, alongside tourists who died here – like Sarah Drake and her daughter Janet, who drowned in a steamer boat disaster while returning from the Lido in 1914.

MARIAMASLOVA/SHUTTERSTOCK ©

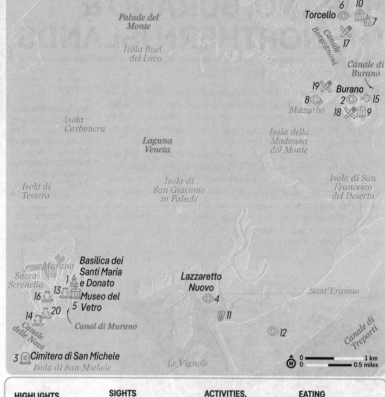

Palude del
Monte

Isola Buel
del Lovo

Torcello 6 10
7

Canale
Borgognoni

17

Canale di
Burano

Isola
Carboncra

Laguna
Veneta

19 Burano

8 2 15

Mazzorbo 18 9

Isola della
Madonna
del Monte

Isola di
Tessera

Isola di
San Giacomo
in Palude

Isola di San
Francesco
del Deserto

Murano
Sacca
Serenella

Basilica dei
Santi Maria
e Donato

1

13 Museo del
16 5 Vetro
14 20

Lazzaretto
Nuovo

4

Sant'Erasmo

11

Canal di Murano

12

Canale
delle Navi

Canale di
Treporti

3 Cimitero di San Michele
Isola di San Michele

Le Vignole

0 — 1 km
0 — 0.5 miles

HIGHLIGHTS	SIGHTS	ACTIVITIES, COURSES & TOURS	EATING
1 Basilica dei Santi Maria e Donato	7 Basilica di Santa Maria Assunta	13 De Biasi	17 Taverna Tipica Veneziana
2 Burano	8 Mazzorbo	14 Lucevetro	18 Trattoria al Gatto Nero
3 Cimitero di San Michele	9 Museo del Merletto	15 Pesca Burano	19 Venissa
4 Lazzaretto Nuovo	10 Museo di Torcello	16 Wave Murano Glass	
5 Museo del Vetro	11 Orto di Venezia		SHOPPING
6 Torcello	12 Sant'Erasmo		20 Venini

Lazzaretto Nuovo

QUARANTINE ISLAND

This **island** east of Murano became Venice's second quarantine island in 1468. While the 'old' one, Lazzaretto Vecchio near San Lazzaro, was for people who were already sick with plague, this was where any traders or sailors coming from outbreak ports were isolated for 40 days. Goods were smoked and disinfected with vinegar in the **Tezon Grande**, the vast, open-air warehouse in the middle, which still has graffiti of ships and signatures. Guided tours run from May to October.

Lazzaretto Nuovo

Torcello

WHERE VENICE BEGAN

With its unspoiled fields, wild footpaths and fewer than 20 residents, **Torcello** today is one of the most bucolic places in the entire lagoon. But 1500 years ago, it was a different story. This was Venice before Venice even existed – the first island to be settled in the lagoon, and the society that proved living on water was not only possible but profitable.

Eventually the harbour silted up, the inhabitants moved south to create Venice, and Torcello became a home for monasteries and churches during the medieval period before they crumbled, leaving just two churches. Today, the campanile of **Basilica di Santa Maria Assunta** dominates the north lagoon. Its interior glitters with astonishing Byzantine-style mosaics: an 11th-century *Madonna and Child* with saints above the altar, all almond-eyed and floating in gold, and the *Last Judgement* across the entire back wall, its six vivid layers ripping from heaven to hell. The floor is a precursor of San Marco and Murano's Santi Maria e Donato (p312), with geometric mosaics formed with precious marbles from all over the world.

Outside, the **Museo di Torcello** gathers ancient Roman, Etruscan, Greek and Egyptian finds from the lagoon area, and tells the story of the island's former churches. Take the paths round the back of the church to wander through meadows studded with the odd ruined wall, and stop at **Taverna Tipica Veneziana**, an affordable buffet of lagoon dishes set in a peaceful garden.

Museo di Torcello

FAR LEFT: MARK EDWARD SMITH/GETTY IMAGES; RIGHT: © ALIAKSANDR ANTANOVICH/SHUTTERSTOCK ©

WHY I LOVE THE NORTH LAGOON

Julia Buckley, writer

Venice can be visually overwhelming, so to reset I hop on the *vaporetto* to Burano for a long lunch at **Gatto Nero** (p313), and a quiet walk around the island – from the south waterfront, the lagoon is usually glassy still, and you can see Venice (and Castello, where I live) across the water. The liminal north lagoon sparks an inner stillness – and hopping in a boat to float past a flock of pink flamingos, you feel like you're in Tanzania, not Italy.

XSMIRNOVX/SHUTTERSTOCK ©

Marble 'carpet', Basilica dei Santi Maria e Donato

Museo del Vetro

A HISTORY OF GLASS

These days **Murano** is synonymous with glass, but in the frescoed **Palazzo Giustinian** you'll learn that it was discovered and perfected in the Middle East – and it was Venice's medieval trading ties with Syria that allowed it to copy the techniques so proficiently that Murano helped spark the decline in Islamic glass production. This fascinating **museum** starts with ancient exhibits from Palestine, Syria, Greece and the Balkans, then shows how Murano's 15th-century glassworkers took things to another level by inventing clear glass. By the Renaissance period, the *muranesi* were inventing ways to swirl colours and layer patterns so complicated that several techniques were lost until the 1800s, when a financial crash meant glassworkers needed to look to the past to find a way forward. Temporary exhibitions prop up the exceptional eight-room permanent collection.

Basilica dei Santi Maria e Donato

A MINI SAN MARCO

Look down, and you could be in the Basilica di San Marco. Murano's **cathedral** has an extraordinary 12th-century marble 'carpet' of swirling geometric shapes, mosaic peacocks, gryphons, snails and – our favourites – two 'in love' crickets gazing at a flower. Look up for the Torcello-style gold mosaic of the Madonna in the apse (in restoration at the time of writing, due to be finished in 2023), and don't miss the glass crucifix by 1970s maestro Ermanno Nason on your way out.

WHERE TO BUY GLASS

Wave Murano Glass
A team of 10 young artisans with a modern take on ancient traditions. They also offer furnace tours and even glass-blowing lessons.

Lucevetro
Cecilia Cenedese designs her products, and island *maestri* make them for her.

Venini
The first company to make glass high art sells designs by the likes of Carlo Scarpa and Ron Arad.

De Biasi
Artisans designing their own jewellery, picture frames and even chopsticks.

Burano

GATEWAY TO THE WILDERNESS

Pretty **Burano** with its multi-coloured cottages is a top Venetian draw, but there's more to the island than being photogenic. This is the oldest community of the lagoon – the *buranelli* have been fishing here since Roman times, and helped feed Torcello in its boom-town days. When Torcello died out, Burano continued – and its distance from Venice (now a 45-minute *vaporetto* ride, back then about a four-hour paddle) kept its culture intact.

Today, most visitors do a quick circuit, but to appreciate Burano takes at least a day. Start with a trip into the near-pristine lagoon with fifth-generation fisherman **Andrea Rossi**. He and fishing partner Michele Vitturi of **Torcello Birdwatching** take visitors out in their boat, cutting through the *barene* – the mudflats and salt marshes on which Venice was built – and swishing across centimetres-shallow channels in search of rare ibis birds and elegant flamingos. It's a view of the lagoon as it once was.

Taste Andrea and Michele's daily haul at **Trattoria al Gatto Nero**, a superb restaurant run by the Bovo family since 1965. They serve rigorously local seafood caught by the islanders – don't leave without trying the *risotto di gò*, or goby fish.

Afterwards, head to the **Museo del Merletto**, which tells the story of the island's traditional lace industry, originally driven by poverty. The pieces are detailed works of art, dating from the 16th century – and if you're lucky, in the last room you'll catch some of Burano's last *merlettaie* at work.

THE LAGOON'S LAST MOECANTI

One of the lagoon's most prized dishes is *moeche* or crabs, caught just when they've shed their shells. It's a highly skilled job to net them within a 10-hour window – *moecanti* can tell a crab on the turn at a glance – and it's also a dying art. *Buranello* Domenico Rossi of **Pesca Burano** is one of just 30 left in the lagoon. His family have been *moecanti* since La Serenissima times; to preserve the heritage, he takes visitors out on his *bragozzo* boat to see how it's done.

Burano

MIKEDOTTA/SHUTTERSTOCK ©

DANIEL GARRIDO/GETTY IMAGES ©

Lago di Carezza (p325)

THE MAIN AREAS

BOLZANO
South Tyrolean culture, mountain gateway. p320

TRENTO
Glasses of bubbly, frescoed palaces. p327

BRESSANONE
Fairy-tale architecture, trendy cafes. p335

TRIESTE
Cultural crossroads, neoclassical waterfront. p340

DOLOMITES & THE NORTHEAST

MAJESTIC MOUNTAINS, ALPINE CULTURE, FAMED VINEYARDS

The northern regions of Trentino-Alto Adige (Südtirol), Friuli Venezia Giulia and the Veneto are a year-round wonderland framed by the imposing peaks of the Dolomites.

These once Austro-Hungarian holdouts – known collectively as 'Triveneto' in Italian – are Italy at its most distinctive, a wild 180-degree turn from what most think of as quintessentially Italian. Trains run with Swiss precision, and pizza, pasta and vestiges of the Roman Empire are no longer the stars of the show. The jagged peaks of the Dolomites span the semi-autonomous regions of Trentino and Alto Adige or Südtirol (jutting into neighbouring Veneto), where German is often the mother tongue, kitchens of distinction serve hearty, Austrian-influenced mountain cuisine, apple orchards replace olive groves and the minority Ladin people offer distinct cultural perspectives to already divergent surrounds. Europeans flock here in winter for highly hospitable resorts, sublime natural settings and extensive, well-coordinated ski networks (in summer, skis are swapped out for mountain bikes and hiking boots).

At lower elevations, cultural complexities characterise the small, little-visited region of Friuli Venezia Giulia, tucked away on the country's borders with Austria and Slovenia. Immediately southwest, the Veneto beckons, highlighted by the city-states Venice annexed in the 15th century: Padua (Padova), Vicenza, Verona. It's all chased with some of Italy's finest wines – storybook vineyards canvasing the region produce Amarone (the Veneto's Valpolicella), Lagrein (Alto Adige), Trento DOC (Trentino) and prosecco (the Veneto). *Willkommen in Italia!*

BUTTERFLY MEDIA/GETTY IMAGES ©

VERONA
Roman coliseum and pretty piazzas. p352

PADUA
Masterpiece frescoes, place of pilgrimage. p347

TREVISO
Scenic canals, authentic Veneto vivacity. p358

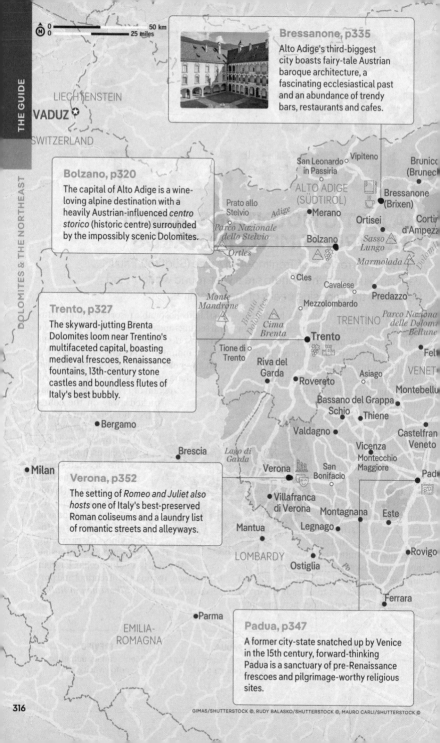

Bressanone, p335

Alto Adige's third-biggest city boasts fairy-tale Austrian baroque architecture, a fascinating ecclesiastical past and an abundance of trendy bars, restaurants and cafes.

Bolzano, p320

The capital of Alto Adige is a wine-loving alpine destination with a heavily Austrian-influenced *centro storico* (historic centre) surrounded by the impossibly scenic Dolomites.

Trento, p327

The skyward-jutting Brenta Dolomites loom near Trentino's multifaceted capital, boasting medieval frescoes, Renaissance fountains, 13th-century stone castles and boundless flutes of Italy's best bubbly.

Verona, p352

The setting of *Romeo and Juliet* also hosts one of Italy's best-preserved Roman coliseums and a laundry list of romantic streets and alleyways.

Padua, p347

A former city-state snatched up by Venice in the 15th century, forward-thinking Padua is a sanctuary of pre-Renaissance frescoes and pilgrimage-worthy religious sites.

Map labels:

LIECHTENSTEIN
VADUZ
SWITZERLAND

0 — 50 km
0 — 25 miles

San Leonardo in Passiria
Vipiteno
Brunico (Brunec)
ALTO ADIGE (SÜDTIROL)
Bressanone (Brixen)
Prato allo Stelvio
Adige
Merano
Ortisei
Cortina d'Ampezzo
Parco Nazionale dello Stelvio
Bolzano
Sasso Lungo
Dolomi
Ortles
Marmolada
Cles
Cavalese
Predazzo
Monte Mandrone
Mezzolombardo
TRENTINO
Parco Naziona delle Dolom Bellune
Brenta Dolomites
Cima Brenta
Trento
Fel
Tione di Trento
VENET
Riva del Garda
Asiago
Montebellu
Rovereto
Bassano del Grappa
Schio
Thiene
Castelfran Veneto
Bergamo
Valdagno
Vicenza
Montecchio Maggiore
Brescia
Lago di Garda
Verona
San Bonifacio
Pad
Milan
Villafranca di Verona
Montagnana
Este
Mantua
Legnago
Rovigo
LOMBARDY
Ostiglia
Po
Ferrara
Parma
EMILIA-ROMAGNA

Find Your Way

The Dolomites and the northeast encompasses the regions of Trentino-Alto Adige (Südtirol), Friuli Venezia Giulia and the Veneto (minus metropolitan Venice), a huge swath of northern Italy. Our picks reflect the region's natural travel hubs.

CAR

Nowhere in Italy is having your own set of wheels going to enhance your experience as much as in the Dolomites, whose towns, villages and valleys are all best explored by car.

BUS

SAD Trasporto Locale and Trentino Trasporti buses link major villages throughout the mountains from Bolzano and Trento, respectively. Trieste, Grado, Udine and Gorizia (in Friuli Venezia Giulia) and Padua, Verona and Vicenza (in the Veneto) all offer bus services.

TRAIN

Geographic barriers obviously hinder widespread train travel in the Dolomites, though Bressanone, Bolzano (with connections to Merano), Trento and Rovereto are serviced en route to Verona. Frequent train service connects major cities in Friuli and the Veneto.

Treviso, p358

Uncrowded and undervalued, Treviso's pretty canals, narrow cobbled streets and frescoed churches have earned it the nickname 'Little Venice'.

Trieste, p340

A collision of cultures defines Friuli Venezia Giulia's waterfront capital, which harbours a deep devotion to literature, coffee and its pronounced multi-personality.

Plan Your Time

The Dolomites and the northeast offer majestic alpine peaks, Unesco-listed art and architecture and Austrian-influenced mountain cuisine chased by some of Italy's finest wines.

Bolzano (p320)

Just a Few Days

● Northeast Italy isn't a hurried destination, but this four-day round trip hits Unesco-listed highlights against a backdrop of a month's worth of mountain scenery. Set out from **Bolzano** (p320) after a day taking in the Südtirol capital including the spectacular **Funivia del Renon** (p321), stopping for another outrageously scenic cable-car ride to **Alpe di siusi** (p333). Don't miss lunch at **Ristorante Durnwald** (p338) en route to **Padua** (p347), where you'll be wowed by Giotto's masterpiece frescoes inside the **Cappella degli Scrovegni** (p347) the next day.

● Spend day four in **Verona** (p352) – the 1st-century CE Roman Arena stands as remarkably preserved as Rome's version – before returning to Bolzano.

Seasonal highlights

The Dolomites shine seasonally (winter and summer); many places – and ski lifts – shut in October and May. Lower elevations offer year-round pleasures.

JANUARY
Alta Badia's **Sommelier on the Slopes** and the **Dolomiti Balloon Festival** near Dobbiaco kick off winter festivities in the Dolomites.

FEBRUARY
It's **peak-season powder** on the world-famous slopes of the Sella Ronda. Uncrowded runs await in the Carnic and Giulie Alps.

JUNE
Feste Vigiliane fills Trento with merry-making; the spectacular **Arena di Verona Festival** wows opera fans till September.

MATTEO FES/SHUTTERSTOCK ©, EVA BOCEK/SHUTTERSTOCK ©, NICK_NICK/SHUTTERSTOCK ©

A Two-Week Tour

● Settle into the Alto Adige valley of your choice and day-trip: meet Ötzi the Iceman at **Museo Archeologico dell'Alto Adige** in **Bolzano (p320)**; float away in the therapeutic waters in **Merano (p325)**; feast on schnitzel and strudel in the wonderful **Val Pusteria (p334)**; and explore the scenic **Alpe di siusi (p333)** with the commanding peaks of **Parco Naturale Sciliar-Catinaccio** (p324) as a backdrop – don't miss wonderful alpine cuisine at **Gostner Schwaige** (p324) while you're there!

● Spend the second week cherry-picking your way through Veneto's top cities – **Verona** (p352), **Padua** (p347), **Vicenza** (p356) and **Treviso** (p358) – chasing them with world-class wines in **Valpolicella** (p355) or the Unesco-listed **Prosecco Hills** (p361).

A Month Around the Mountains

● Explore the Dolomites properly: ski the **Sella Ronda** (p333), a 40km circumnavigation of the Gruppo di Sella range linked by cable cars and chairlifts; leisurely enjoy the culture and cuisine of Ladinia around **Val di Fassa** (p333), **Val Gardena** (p333) and **Val Badia** (p339); and spoil yourself on fine dining and incredible hiking in the Brenta Dolomites around **Madonna di Campiglio** (p331). Toast with some of Italy's finest bubbly in **Trento** (p327) before moving southeast across the Veneto, stopping at Unesco World Heritage Sites in **Verona** (p352), **Vicenza** (p356) and **Padua** (p347). Pause for exquisite mosaics and under-visited Roman ruins in **Aquileia** (p344) before winding down in eclectic **Trieste** (p340).

JULY

Discover high-altitude **walking trails** and mountain huts in the Brenta Dolomites and Cortina d'Ampezzo.

AUGUST

The Veneto **cycling season** runs between July and August – all trains offer special coaches to transport bikes.

SEPTEMBER

Annual **grape harvests** lure oenophiles to the wonderful vineyards of Valpolicella, Il Collio and the Prosecco Hills.

DECEMBER

Tyrolean **Christmas markets** create winter wonderlands in Bolzano, Merano and Bressanone; **ski season** kicks off across the Dolomites.

BOLZANO

Bolzano (Bozen), the provincial capital of South Tyrol, is anything but provincial. Once a stop on the coach route between Italy and the flourishing Austro-Hungarian Empire, this small city is worldly and engaged, a long-time conduit between cultures that has more recently become home to Europe's first trilingual university. A stage-set-pretty backdrop of grassy, rotund hills sets off rows of pastel-painted townhouses, while bicycles ply riverside paths and wooden market stalls are laid out with alpine cheese, speck (cured ham) and dark, seeded loaves. German may be the first language of 95% of the region, but Bolzano is an anomaly. Today its Italian-speaking majority – a legacy of Mussolini's brutal Italianisation program of the 1920s and the more recent siren call of education and employment opportunities – looks both north and south for inspiration. Being *bolzanino* means possessing unmistakable Germanic-level efficiency and promptness, but taking comfort in *La Dolce Vita* slowness come *aperitivo* time.

TOP TIP

A German-style beer is never far, but Bolzano is fundamentally a wine-drinking town. The iconic wines of the area – like Lagrein, Schiava and Gewürztraminer – are enthusiastically appreciated. Do indulge.

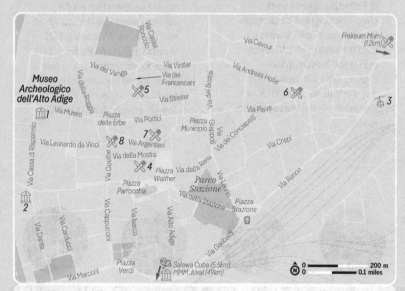

HIGHLIGHTS
1 Museo Archeologico dell'Alto Adige

Sights
2 Museion

ACTIVITIES, COURSES & TOURS
3 Funivia del Renon

EATING
4 Campo Franz
5 Franziskaner Stuben

6 Löwengrube
7 Restaurant 37
8 Vögele

DRINKING & NIGHTLIFE
9 Batzen Häusl
10 Lisa Wine Boutique

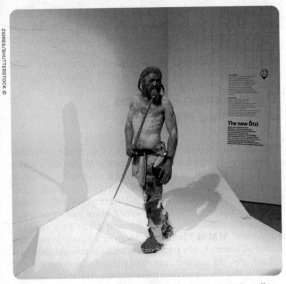

ZIGRES/SHUTTERSTOCK ©

Ötzi, Museo Archeologico dell'Alto Adige

The Iceman Cometh

PONDERING PRE-HISTORIC MURDER IN BOLZANO

If you have visited archaeological museums in other parts of Italy, you've probably had your fill of Etruscan pottery and Roman busts – but Bolzano presents an altogether different, wildly fascinating experience. The star of the **Museo Archeologico dell'Alto Adige** is Ötzi the Iceman, with almost the entire museum being given over to the Copper Age mummy. The 5000-year-old Ötzi, whose name is a cross between the Tibetan word Yeti (meaning 'abominable snowman'), and the Ötztal Alps, where the mummy was found murdered.

Not only is Ötzi the oldest wet mummy (meaning individual cells remained hydrated enough for extensive research) ever found, he's also one of the world's oldest unsolved murder cases (the flint arrow that killed him can be seen via X-ray). His remarkably preserved remains, kept in a temperature-controlled 'igloo' room, can be viewed through a small window (peer closely enough and you can make out faint tattoos on his legs). But you'll want to set aside an hour to peruse the enthralling contents of his prehistoric gear (think *CSI* meets *2001: A Space Odyssey*).

WHAT TO SEE AND DO IN BOLZANO

Funivia del Renon
The 12-minute ride over the Renon (Ritten) plateau to Soprabolzano (Oberbozen) is nothing short of spectacular.

Museion
Bolzano's four-storey contemporary art space housed in a huge multifaceted glass cube.

Salewa Cube
Italy's largest indoor-climbing centre. There are over 2000 sq metres of climbing surface and 180 different routes.

BEST STUBEN

Point your palate to Bolzano's *stuben*, traditional, wood-panelled social gathering establishments.

Vögele €€
Outstanding *canederli* (Tyrolean dumplings) and *Erdäpfel* (fried potato tartlet), expertly paired with local wines.

Restaurant 37 €€
Trendy *stube* excelling at top-tier alpine fusion on an alfresco rooftop with views to match.

Franziskaner Stuben €€
Tyrolean specialities – roasted alpine ox in Lagrein sauce, venison carpaccio – above a medieval cellar.

Löwengrube €€€
Bolzano's oldest *stube*, with a neo-Gothic wine cellar and foundations from the 1200s.

Vögele

Ötzi died dressed in a bearskin cap stitched with animal tendons and ligaments, and shoes fashioned from deer hide and lime-tree string netting. He carried a birchbark container with burning embers insulated by maple leaves, a hazelwood-framed backpack, and a one-of-a-kind trapezoidal axe with a 99.7% pure-copper blade. Most shocking of all? The copper is Tuscan.

The Mountain Museums of Reinhold Messner

DRAMATIC ARCHITECTURE, UNORTHODOX MUSEUMS

South Tyrolean renegade mountaineer, explorer and author Reinhold Messner, the first climber to ascend Mt Everest without supplemental oxygen in 1978, summoned a flair for the dramatic when crafting his own legacy in the form of six incredible mountain museums across the region. All but two (MMM Ortles and MMM Juval) can be reached on some form of public transport.

Bolzano's imposing Castel Firmiano (945 CE) is the centrepiece of **MMM Firmiano**, Messner's flagship museum. Based on humankind's relationship with the mountains across all cultures, the architecture itself suggests the experience of shifting altitudes, and requires visitors to traverse hundreds of stairs and mesh walkways over two hours or so. **MMM Ortles**, 91km west of Bolzano in Solda, is located – quite literally – inside a hill and articulates the theme of 'ice' with artistically presented exhibits on glaciers, ice climbing and Pole expeditions, all at 1900m. **MMM Juval**, 44km northwest of Bolzano in Vinschgau, occupies the medieval Juval Castle (Messner's private home) and features fine-art paintings of the world's holy mountains. To the east, 85km from Bolzano, **MMM Ripa** documents the cultures of mountain peoples on four continents from Brunico's 13th-century hilltop castle. **MMM Corones**, the most architecturally thrilling and spectacularly sited, literally hangs off the 2275m summit of Kronplatz high above Val Pusteria. Lastly, **MMM Dolomites** offers panoramic views across the Dolomites from its perch at 2181m on Monte Rite in Cadore (the Veneto).

GETTING AROUND

Bolzano's *centro storico* is small, so navigating on two feet or two wheels is optimal. Three cable cars – San Genesio, Renon and Colle – serve surrounding villages at higher altitudes. Public transport serves attractions further afield such as MMM Firmiano and Salewa Cube.

Merano

Val Gardena

Bolzano · Alpe di Siusi

Val di Fassa

Beyond Bolzano

Merano's Habsburg-era spas and bygone-time promenades beckon decelerated holidaymakers, while the incalculably gorgeous Dolomites summon lovers of the great outdoors.

East of the Adige river from Bolzano, the jagged peaks of the Dolomites dominate the landscape, dotted with immensely picturesque valleys, storybook vineyards, hearty alpine kitchens and an incredible arsenal of outdoor diversion (hiking, biking, skiing).

This is God's country and it boasts few rivals. The former Habsburg-era spa town (and Tyrolean capital) of Merano feels like a world away from Bolzano despite its location just 34km northeast. Awash in leafy boulevards, birdsong, oleanders and cacti, the town was once a summer playground and wellness destination for Austrian royalty. Botanical gardens and tree-fringed promenades trace the Passer river and surround the town's intact medieval core.

Castelrotto (p324)

TOP TIP

Most hotel bookings in Alto Adige net you a free tourist card that includes transport within the South Tyrolean Transportation Network.

FELIX LIPOV/SHUTTERSTOCK ©

WHY I LOVE ALTO ADIGE (SÜDTIROL)

Kevin Raub, writer

No region in Italy is as abruptly distinctive from its surrounds as Alto Adige is from the rest of the country. Given the semi-autonomous region was actually part of the Austro-Hungarian Empire as recently as 1919, the distinguishing qualities of this fairly-tale landscape should come as no surprise, yet revelation and wonder remain its calling cards. Postcard-perfect chalets, vine-strewn hillsides, dramatic alpine peaks, hearty Austrian-influenced meals – its personality couldn't be less similar to the Italy of most people's imaginations. Discovery remains alive and well here.

Mountain High, Valley Low

A DRIVE IN THE DOLOMITES

This 120km clockwise trip from Bolzano encircles Parco Naturale Sciliar-Catinaccio via Alpe di Siusi, Val Gardena, the Sella Pass into Trentino and Val di Fassa before returning to Bolzano. It can be done in three hours in a straight shot, but you'll want to stop and smell the mountain air a bit over a few days. Outrageous Dolomite views, hearty alpine cuisine, Ladin culture and outdoor distractions in spades await.

Follow the Adige river east along SS12 out of Bolzano towards Alpe di Siusi. Explore the villages that dot the valleys – including **1 Castelrotto** (Kastelruth), **2 Fiè allo Sciliar** (Völs am Schlern) and **3 Siusi allo Sciliar** (Seis am Schlern) – signposted by postcard-perfect onion-domed churches. Take the **4 Seiser Alm Aerial Cableway** (the road up is closed to most motorists for much of the year) up to Europe's largest plateau for views of the towering Sciliar massif and Crayola-green pastures teeming with incredible hiking, biking and skiing. A farm-to-table lunch at **5 Gostner Schwaige**, reached via a 20-minute walk from Compaccio, is mandatory.

 WHERE TO SLEEP IN THE DOLOMITES

Hotel Heubad
Indulge in outstanding views and typically Tyrolean hay baths at this lovely Fiè allo Sciliar hotel. €€

Hotel Waldrast
Stylish boutique hotel in Siusi; Sciliar looms large over the pool, spa, outdoor whirlpool tub and sauna. €€

Agritur Weiss
Highly recommended dairy farmstay on a mountainside above Vigo di Fassa with 360-degree views. €€

Continue east past countless picturesque timber barns, the beautiful Val Gardena and incredible views of Sasso Lungo (3181m) and Gruppo del Sella, which follow you as you turn south over the 2218m Sella Pass (you can practically kiss Sasso Lungo from here). At the top, you'll cross over into Trentino. After descending into Canazei, the Ladin sausage cooks at **6 Wurstelstand Pippotto** await at their roadside stall next to a raging stream near the bus station. Their *currywursts* are a Canazei institution, catering to ravenous skiers all winter and famished hikers all summer.

As you head west along SS48 around into Val di Fassa, Trentino's only Ladin-speaking valley, you are surrounded. The stirring peaks of the Gruppo del Sella to the north, the Catinaccio to the west and the Marmolada (3343m) to the southeast frame a near-360-degree ring of flawless mountain views. Brush up on Ladin culture at **7 Museo Ladin de Fascia** in the village of Vigo di Fassa, full of beautiful wood carvings, quotidian objects and exhibits on family life plus furniture-, bread- and cheese-making.

Here the road continues west on SS241; you'll cross back into South Tyrol and pass a majestic relic of a bygone era, the **8 Residence Grand Hotel Carezza** – the first structure above 1630m to have electricity when it was built in 1894. Empress Elisabeth of Austria and Queen of Hungary holed up here for a little mountain R&R in 1897. From the tiny but colourful **9 Lago di Carezza** (Karersee), outstanding views of the Latemar range (2842m) dwarf the horizon and alpine pine forest dominates the landscape along the southern portion of the trip. As the drive winds down, you'll encounter a series of tunnels from which you'll emerge with a view of perfectly framed, vineyard-strewn hillsides. You're back in Bolzano – time for wine!

Habsburg Hideaway

MANICURED GARDENS, THERAPEUTIC WATERS

The modern spa town of **Merano** (Meran), a 40-minute train ride from Bolzano, has more in common with Salzburg than Siena, with its colourful Habsburg architecture amid lush surrounds and a river running through it. Once a summer playground for Sissi – Empress Elisabeth of Austria – and an impressive list of literary and scientific glitterati, it boasts 80 hectares of parks and gardens and 30km of promenades.

In fact, the promenade or *passeggiata* (evening stroll) has long been a Merano institution. In town, the

MONUMENTAL MASSIF

Some of the Dolomites' most dramatic landscapes call the 7291-hectare **Parco Naturale Sciliar-Catinaccio** home. The formidable Sciliar (Schlern) massif between Siusi, Tires and Fiè allo Sciliar is one of the region's most iconic mountains and, when viewed from the pastureland of Alpe di Siusi, appears like a granite tsunami tumbling over Europe's largest plateau. The nearby Catinaccio massif takes its German name, Rosengarten, from its pink-shaded glow at sunset (due to the presence of mineral dolomite). Hiking and biking through the park's pine forests, pastureland and lakes is expectedly popular.

LOOKING FOR LADINIA?

Five valleys in the Dolomites, known as **Ladinia** (p339), are majority Ladin-speaking and offer fascinating insight into this minority group whose culture, gastronomy and language form a small but profound part of South Tyrol culture.

Gasthof zu Tschotsch
Family-run inn off the beaten path between Fiè allo Sciliar and Castelrotto; destination-worthy restaurant. €

Chalet Gerard
Spectacularly set lodge, started by award-winning skier Gerard Mussner, between Val Gardena and Passo Gardena. €€€

Alpina Dolomites
High-style luxe lodge fit for a high-altitude plateau; a wood, stone and glass confection of contemporary cool. €€€

IT'S CHRISTMAS TIME IN SÜDTIROL

It's not only snowcapped peaks that draw gaggles of tourists to Trentino-Alto Adige in winter. This is **Christmas market** territory, too! And while Italy can't compete with the likes of Germany and Austria, Merano's annual Weihnachtsmarkt gives it a go. The mulled wine flows freely and the scent of roasting chestnuts fills the air from late November through Epiphany (6 January). Merano is one of the five original South Tyrolean Christmas markets along with Bolzano, Bressanone, Brunico and Vipiteno. Not to be outdone, Trentino's Mercatini di Natale in Trento and Rango round out the region's best.

LORENZA62/SHUTTERSTOCK ©

Schloss Trauttmansdorff Gardens

Winterpromenade (700m) and Sommerpromenade (900m) follow centrally located walking paths on either side of the pretty Passer river. Give yourself 30 minutes to stroll both.

The 3km Sissiweg traces the route that Empress Elisabeth herself once trod from downtown Merano to her summer home at **Trauttmansdorff Castle**. Over the course of 45 minutes or so, you'll get a glimpse of some of Merano's most refined neighbourhoods, passing a series of villas, privately owned castles, parks and gardens on your way up the hill to Merano's principal attraction, the 12-hectare Schloss Trauttmansdorff Gardens. Exotic cacti and palms, fruit trees and vines, beds of lilies, irises and tulips all cascade down the hillside surrounding the mid-19th-century castle where Sissi spent the odd summer. People spend all day at these wonderful botanical gardens, but a few hours should suffice. Afterwards, rest your weary hoofers at the 13 indoor pools (plus 12 outdoor in summer) at **Therme Meran**, Merano's showcase thermal baths. Pssst...bring your own towel!

GETTING AROUND

It goes without saying that having a car in the Dolomites is near-essential, but towns, villages and ski resorts are well connected in South

Tyrol by SAD and Silbernagl buses and Trentino Trasporti in Trentino. Merano is made for walking.

TRENTO

Trento

Rome

Unlike many Italian cities, Trentino's underrated capital isn't as easy to pin down. Its patchwork of Italianness is diverse and long-winded, but essentially noncommittal to any one genre of Italy's greatest hits. It's Roman in origin – Trento's centrepiece fountain pays tribute to its foundations as the ancient city of Tridentum, named after the Roman god Neptune – but home to a furious collage that counts a dozen historical eras intermingling seamlessly among stone castles, shady porticoes and signature medieval frescoes. Although this historical potluck leaves no doubt you're in Italy, Trento's Austrian personality stands up to be counted, too: apple strudel is ubiquitous and Austrian baroque architecture not uncommon. In a way, Trento's experience as a consummate host goes back centuries: the ecumenical Council of Trent convened here in the 16th century during the tumultuous years of the Counter-Reformation, dishing out far-reaching condemnations to uppity Protestants.

TOP TIP

For a bird's-eye view of Trento and the surrounding mountains, take the Funivia Sardagna to Monte Sardagna (600m), where you can enjoy a panoramic view of Trento from above – best admired over an *aperitivo* at Trento Alta Bistrot.

Trentino's Magnificent Museums

ART, SCIENCE AND STRIKING ARCHITECTURE

Two of Italy's most important museums in their respective genres call the Trento area home, both housed within world-class architectural structures that are at once an evocative compliment and in striking contrast to their surroundings.

In Trento's Quartiere delle Albere district, Renzo Piano's stunning modernist **Museo delle Scienze** (MUSE) cleverly echoes the surrounding mountain summits and anchors Trento's most innovative and sustainable (LEED Gold-certified) residential district. Highlights of the very family-friendly museum include a truly amazing collection of suspended taxidermy; the fabulous Maxi Ooh! experiential kids' area; and a fascinating interactive terrestrial sphere connected to the National Oceanic and Atmospheric Administration (NOAA). Entries here are limited to three hours.

In Venetian-influenced Rovereto, 25km south of Trento, Swiss architect Mario Botta's four-storey, 12,000-sq-metre steel, glass and marble behemoth, **Museo di Arte Moderna e Contemporanea Rovereto** (MART), houses some of Italy's most important modern art. Mountain light from a soaring cupola matching the circumference of Rome's Pantheon gently fills the central atrium, which leads to a formidable collection of avant-garde and futurism-focused 20th-century Italian art. Masterpieces by Umberto Boccioni, Giorgio de Chirico, Fortunato Depero and Carlo Carrà – including the superb *Le figlie di Loth* – highlight the exquisitely curated permanent collection (give yourself two hours). End the visit at the museum's Michelin-starred Alfio

ESCAPE FROM TRENTO

Alessandra Stelzer, the second-generation co-owner of Maso Martis winery (@masomartis)

Living in Trentino is a real blessing! We have the opportunity to do lots of outdoor sports in all seasons and enjoy breathtaking views. On weekends I love to cycle to cool mountain lakes, my favourite being the **Laghi di Lamar**, where I can have a restorative swim. Or take treks to huts like the **Rifugio Maranza**, where I can eat local products in good company and with a great glass of wine.

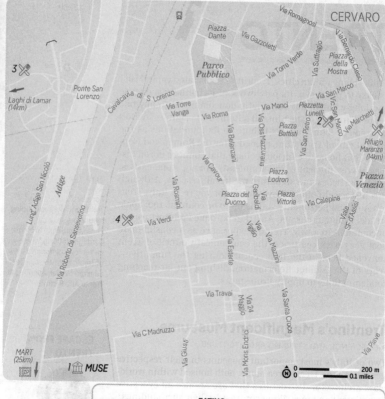

CERVARO

HIGHLIGHTS	EATING	
1 MUSE	2 Il Cappello	3 Il Libertino
		5 Pizzeria da Albert

PURSUING VINEYARDS?

The Veneto's **Valpolicella wine region** (p355), 145km south of Bolzano, is home to some of northern Italy's most sought-after vineyards. Its highly prized Amarone is one of the world's most coveted red wines.

Ghezzi Bistrot, whose furnishings are a museum of Italian design in and of themselves.

Trento on Two Feet

FRESCOED PALACES, URBAN LEGENDS

A two-hour walk through Trento's *centro storico* is a laundry list of Italo-superlatives – an ancient castle, medieval palaces with fading frescoes, a Romanesque cathedral

WHERE TO EAT IN TRENTO

Il Cappello
Small but exceptional menu of Trentino-Tyrolean standouts, including an incredible rabbit *ragù*. Top choice. €€

Pizzeria da Albert
Gourmet pizza often calling on local products (speck, 100% Alto Adige mozzarella), 400m east of the cathedral. €

Il Libertino
Wood-panelled restaurant just east of the Adige river; think venison, chestnuts, radicchio, boar sausage and river trout. €€

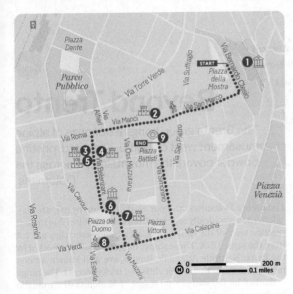

START

END

TRENTINO'S BUBBLY

The geoclimatic conditions in the foothills between 200m to 900m surrounding Trento are fertile grounds for the region's prized bubbly, **Trento DOC** – the first Italian appellation to be reserved exclusively for sparkling wine made by the bottle-fermentation method (better known as Champagne's *Méthode traditionnelle*). The 64 Trento DOC wineries produce white and rosé sparkling wines using only Trentino grapes (chardonnay and pinot noir are the stars; pinot blanc and pinot meunier are used more sparingly). Widespread flutes of the straw-yellow and pink wines add a contagious sparkle to Trento's *aperitivo* scene; outside the city, numerous wineries welcome guests for tastings and tours.

– with a bit of Fascist monumentalism and a mythical murder to keep intrigue level high. Set off from the medieval-Renaissance 1 **Castello del Buonconsiglio**, whose showpiece Torre Aquila is adorned with a 14th-century 'months of the year' fresco cycle depicting May garden parties, the wine harvest and a medieval snowball fight.

Most people pay no attention to the two controversial stone medallions by sculptor Francesco Oradini on the facade of the Renaissance 2 **Palazzo Salvadori** on Via Manci. Look closely on the left: it gruesomely depicts the ritualistic murder of a child, a tall tale awash with overt anti-Semitism. Continue along the regal Via Belenzani, where the frescoed 3 **Palazzo Geremia**, 4 **Palazzo Thun** and 5 **Palazzo Quetta Alberti-Colico** all once hosted Council of Trent guests. At Piazza del Duomo, with its centrepiece late-baroque fountain dedicated to Neptune, the vibrant Renaissance frescoes of 6 **Case Cazuffi-Rella** depict moral guidance; and 7 **Palazzo Pretorio**, home to Trento's prince-bishops before they moved into the castle, attaches to the 8 **Cattedrale di San Vigilio**, which sits on top of the remains of a 4th-century temple. Finish at the wildly out-of-place Fascist entry portal above 9 **Galleria Legionari Trentini**. Mussolini's name has been razed from his quote: 'The Italian people created the Empire with their blood and will fertilise it with their labour and defend it against anyone with their arms.'

GETTING AROUND

Trento's *centro storico* highlights are easily reached on foot. For Trento DOC wineries and attractions further afield, car hire is recommended.

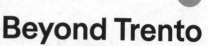

Val Pusteria
Val Gardena
Alta Badia
Madonna di
Campiglio
Val di Fassa
Pinzolo
Trento

Beyond Trento

The Brenta group brings a bonanza of alpine
amusement west of Trento; eastward, pristine
powder covers the mountaintops across the
Dolomites.

The Brenta Dolomites, an hour west of Trento by car, are considered geographically separate from the Dolomites due to their
position west of the Adige. Geologically, however, they are cut
from the same DNA. These sharp, majestic peaks, protected by
the Parco Naturale Adamello Brenta, are well known among
mountaineers for their sheer cliffs and tricky ascents. The range
is flanked by the swanky ski resort of Madonna di Campiglio
on the western side and the high plateau of Altopiano della Paganella closer to the capital. Northeast of Trento, Val di Fassa, with 120km of downhill and cross-country runs, kicks off
a chain of fresh Dolomite powder extending all the way to the
Veneto's Cortina d'Ampezzo.

TOP TIP

Nudge your hotel for your
Trentino Guest Card, a
region-wide digital tourist
card that nets free public
transport, among other
benefits.

Madonna di Campiglio ski resort

ANSHARPHOTO/SHUTTERSTOCK ©

Hiking, Via Ferrata delle Bocchette

High Adventures in the Brenta Dolomites

OUTDOOR ESCAPADES, GOURMET EATS

The dramatic peaks of the Brenta Dolomites are like an army of skyward-jutting rocky outcrops lying in wait. On their eastern side, less than an hour's drive from Trento, the cinematic 40km-long, 12km-wide chain is obscured by the Altopiano della Paganella, a high plateau with gorgeous alpine-jade waters (Lake Molveno). To the north and densely forested west, scenic Val di Non, Val di Sole and Val di Pejo hide the secret as well. The wiggly S421, S237, S239 and S42 linking them all make for some scenic driving, but it's not until the popular resort of **Madonna di Campiglio** – the ideal (albeit expensive) base for attacking the Brenta Dolomites – that the group's eight peaks above 3000m announce their presence. The region is one of Europe's top outdoor playgrounds, offering first-rate climbing, trekking and mountain biking in summer (plus world-class skiing and snowboarding in winter).

The Holy Grail for average outdoor enthusiasts is the **Via Ferrata delle Bocchette**, a world-famous *via ferrata* (trail

AN OLYMPIAN'S VIEWPOINT

Alberto Maffei (@ *alberto_maffei)* is a professional snowboarder and 2018 Winter Olympics participant from Madonna di Campiglio. His perfect day in the Brenta Dolomites goes something like this:

I live in one of the most beautiful and magical places in the world. Whenever I return home after a trip, I can't wait to wake up in the morning and get on the snowy slopes. I take the first Spinale gondola at 8.30am to reach the highest area of Campiglio, **Grostè**, and spend the entire day turning and jumping on the slopes of **Ursula Snowpark**! Once I'm down, I catch some rest at home before heading into Campiglio and enjoying a good pizza at the **Pizzeria al Pappagallo** and a beer with friends at **Home Stube**.

 WHERE TO SLEEP IN THE BRENTA DOLOMITES

Agriturismo Florandonole
Modern farmstay in Fai della Paganella; liberal use of local-wood furniture and crisp goose-down duvets. €€

Chalet Fogajard
Rooms evoke a craft ethos from another era at this six-room, sustainably focused chalet outside Campiglio. €€€

Pimont Alpine Chalet
In near-isolation between Pinzolo and Campiglio, this alpine-chic chalet oozes idyllic mountain retreat. €€€

PARCO NAZIONALE DELLO STELVIO

Italy's largest **national park** (in fact, the largest in the Alps), Parco Nazionale dello Stelvio (Nationalpark Stilfser Joch), clocks in at 1346 sq km and protects precious real estate across 24 municipalities, spilling over into the neighbouring region of Lombardy and rubbing up against Switzerland's Parco Nazionale Svizzero. The park is divided into three separately administered sectors: Trentino to the south, the South Tyrol sector to the north and Lombardy to the west. The park lures walkers who come for the extensive network of well-organised mountain huts (14 in total) and marked trails.

GIACOMO BONA/SHUTTERSTOCK ©

Rifugio Alimonta

IN PURSUIT OF POWDER?

The **Dolomites**, east of Trento and Bolzano, are home to the largest ski area in the world, unravelling across at least 12 ski resorts and more than 1200km of slopes.

with permanent cables and ladders) drawing legions of expert and amateur rock climbers alike. From Campiglio, it takes about 4½ hours to hike to **Rifugio Alimonta**, the closest mountain hut to Bocchette Centrali. Take a bus to **Vallesinella waterfall**, ascend through a spruce forest and stop for lunch at **Rifugio Brentei** before tackling the last uphill stretch to Rifugio Alimonta, your base for the night. Don't miss the *enrosadira*, a natural phenomenon happening at sunset in the Dolomites, when the rocks take on a pink-orange hue.

Set off first thing in the morning to maximise your chances of clear views. The start of the route is only half an hour from Alimonta via a rill, which may require the use of crampons. Five ladders take you onto the panoramic ledges – the second is the most scenic one, a horseshoe-shaped path with views of **Campanile Basso** (2883m), the most iconic peak in the Brenta Dolomites. The route is as easy as *vie ferrate* go, but there are some exposed sections with huge drops to the side. It takes three to four hours to complete the *via ferrata*, plus a further hour to reach Rifugio Brentei, where you can rest and hike back to Campiglio.

 WHERE TO DRINK IN THE BRENTA DOLOMITES

Home Stube
Cosy bar/restaurant skewing younger and sportier; Campiglio's snow brass come for burgers, beers and cocktails.

1550 Birrificio Alpino
Campiglio's only craft brewery is takeaway only, but local-centric brews fly out the door.

Bar Suisse
On the main square, this old-school lodge is Campiglio's iconic see-and-be-seen *aperitivo* hot spot.

For less heart-stopping adventures, the circular **Giro dei Rifugi** trek takes some of the Brenta group's most famous *rifugi* (mountain huts) – **Casinei**, **Tuckett** and **Brentei** – over the course of a medium-difficulty, 15.5km ramble (figure about six hours). The views of **Crozzon di Brenta** (3135m) are astounding. Got wheels? The intermediate-level **Malga Fevri** mountain-bike tour runs downhill from **Monte Spinale** (2100m) to Campiglio; it takes about 45 minutes. On a clear day, the 360-degree panorama from Spinale (reached via gondola from Campiglio) frames the best of the Brenta group plus the Adamello-Presanella and Ortles-Cevedale groups.

Between adventures, refueling around Campiglio and **Pinzolo** is a foodie's dream. For a combined population of just 4000 inhabitants, the villages count two Michelin-starred restaurants – **Stube Hermitage** and **Gallo Cedrone** – and four more (**Semola Fina**, **Grual**, **Due Pini** and **Mildas**) that probably should be. Dig in! Calorie burn is not an issue.

Get Piste!

SOARING SUMMITS, SACRED SLOPES

Europeans flock to the jagged peaks of the Dolomites in winter – their extensive, well-coordinated ski networks, highly hospitable resorts and sublime natural settings offer powder hounds some of the world's best downhill and cross-country skiing and snowboarding. You can embrace it all on this multi-day, greatest-hits run northeast across the best slopes of Trentino-Alto Adige.

Variety lures skiers to the Ladin-speaking **Val di Fassa**, with 120km of downhill and cross-country runs as well as challenging alpine tours and the world-famous **Sella Ronda** ski circuit. **Canazei**, 102km northeast of Trento, is the main hub. The Gruppo del Sella is approached from **Passo Pordoi**, where a cable car travels to almost 3000m. The best approach to the Catinaccio group is from **Vigo di Fassa**, 11km southwest of Canazei; a cable car climbs to 2000m, dropping you off near the cheerful mountain hut **Baita Checco**. Fassa is also the nexus of Italy's cross-country skiing scene. **Moena** plays host to the sport's most illustrious mass-participation race, the annual **Marcialonga**.

The Sella Ronda circuit connects Val di Fassa with **Val Gardena** and **Alpe di siusi**, where you can ski the longest slope in Südtirol. Appropriately named **La Longia**, this 10km run from Mount Seceda to **Ortisei** features a 1273m elevation gain across everything from wide slopes to a narrower canyon and a frozen waterfall. Elsewhere, the gentle slopes of Alpe di Siusi

THE ULTIMATE SKI PASS

For those in pursuit of powder, **Dolomiti Superski** is the ultimate prize on northeast Italy's slopes, created in 1974 in order to issue a common ski pass among member resorts. Today, that ski pass – offered in single-day, multi-day and season formats – gives you access to 450 lifts and some 1200km of ski runs, spread over 16 ski areas and 12 resorts in the Dolomites. Plan de Corones (Kronplatz), Alta Badia, Cortina d'Ampezzo, Val di Fassa, Val di Femme and Alpe di Siusi (Seiser Alm), among others, highlight the long list of network ski resorts; snowparks and night skiing are available as well.

 WHERE TO APRÈS-SKI IN THE DOLOMITES

K1
Kronplatz pizzeria and night club at the valley lift terminal at Reischach; Südtirol's biggest après-ski.

Chalet Tofane
The Socrepes lift practically lands on the terrace of this contemporary hot spot above gorgeous Cortina d'Ampezzo.

L'Murin
Alta Badia favourite inside a converted Corvara barn; in summer it flips into a craft brewery.

AROUND THE SLOPES IN A DAY

The **Sella Ronda**, a 40km circumnavigation of the Gruppo di Sella range (3151m, at Piz Boé) – linked by various cable cars and chairlifts – is one of the Alps' iconic ski routes. The tour takes in four passes and their surrounding valleys – the Val Gardena, Val Badia, Arabba (in the Veneto) and Val di Fassa – all of them steeped in the region's unique Ladin heritage. Kicking off from Selva ski resort (1565m), experienced skiers can complete the clockwise (orange) or anticlockwise (green) route in a day. In summer, the same trails are utilised by mountain bikers and there's a hop-on, hop-off bus for walkers.

SEEKING WINTER WONDERLANDS?

Cortina d'Ampezzo isn't the only see-and-be-seen ski resort in the Dolomites. West of Trento, in the Brenta Dolomites, **Madonna di Campiglio** (p331) is home to Skiarea Campiglio, 156km of Trentino's most fashionable slopes.

make a perfect training ground for beginners and young families. Sella Ronda is directly accessed from the picturesque village of **Selva**.

High above the **Val Pusteria**, 90km northeast of Val Gardena the short way round, 119km of ski runs await across 476 hectares at **Plan de Corones** (Kronplatz), one of the Dolomites' world-class ski resorts. Set off from the flat plateau of the 2275m Mount Kronplatz, where you'll be greeted with an astonishing 360-degree view of the Dolomites. Advanced skiers are in for a high-adrenaline jolt, too: Plan de Corones boasts five black slopes, known collectively as the **Black Five**.

The ski-bus shuttle runs every 20 minutes from the **Piculin** cable-car station to **Sponata** (Sompunt), connecting **Alta Badia** – another Dolomites winter wonderland (and Sella Ronda branch) – with Plan de Corones. Movimënt manages numerous 'snow fun' parks within the 130km of slopes here, including **Alta Badia Snowpark**, along with the legendary Gran Risa where the Skiing World Cup giant slalom race has taken place since 1985.

In Alta Badia, you can go as far east as **Armentarola** on skis; from there a minibus connects with the **Falzarego Pass**, where a Dolomiti Superski pass allows you to set off again on skis to **Cinque Torri** (Bai de Dones). Don't miss the **Great War Ski Tour**, an 80km itinerary taking in the area's most famous peaks along with gun emplacements, trenches, shelters and forts of the WWI 'open-air museum'. From Cinque Torri, you can further connect to **Son dei Prade** in the Veneto's **Cortina d'Ampezzo** on the new two-way **Cortina Skyline** (a 15-minute gondola ride). Fabulous Cortina, the stomping ground of supermodels, snow bunnies and assorted Italian *winterrati*, will host the 2026 Olympic and Paralympic Games. It features a whopping 13 black slopes, including the legendary **Staunies** black mogul run, which starts at 3000m. *Buona fortuna!*

GETTING AROUND

The ski valleys themselves are often walkable, but renting a car will give you the freedom to resort-hop across the region (you can also ski between some of them). The Brenta Dolomites, though well served by Trentino Trasporti buses, are no exception – get yourself some wheels.

BRESSANONE

Bressanone

Rome

Sitting scenically at the confluence of the Isarco (Eisack) and Rienza (Rienz) rivers, Bressanone (Brixen) is the oldest city in Alto Adige and the third-biggest behind Bolzano and Merano. Dating to 901, its prettily perfect Altstadt (old town) teeters just a smidgeon on the right side of the edge between authentic and alpine kitsch. It might be the picture of small-town calm, but it has a grand ecclesiastical past and a lively, cultured side. Spectacular baroque architecture is set against a beguiling alpine backdrop, a stately piazza leads into a tight medieval core, and pretty paths trace the fast-moving Isarco river.

The *bressanonesi* – over 70% German-speaking – flood the city's trendy cafes, where the signature drink, the Hugo (a *spritz* of prosecco, elderflower, lemon and mint), free-flows alongside excellent local wines and often modern takes on traditional Tyrolean cuisine.

There's stellar hiking in summer, spectacular views and powder on Mount Plose in winter, and a distinct air of cool year-round.

TOP TIP

Bressanone is famed for its drinking water – dubbed 'Blue Gold' – which is drawn direct from nearby mountain springs. The city has set up a system for refilling reusable drinking bottles. Look for the 'Refill Your Bottle' signs on fountains around the city.

Break from Tradition in Brixen

TRENDY EATERIES, PICTURESQUE ARCHITECTURE

Bressanone's trendy cafes, restaurants and wine bars are the perfect antidote for anyone who can't bear the thought of another plate of *canederli* (bread dumplings) served in another dining room that's a tad too alpine-for-dummies. This lively, progressive city is unwilling to rely on alpine kitsch as its overriding architectural principle.

That's not to say the city isn't bubbling over with culture, arts, history and tradition – the lofty two-spired baroque **Dom** (cathedral) dominates the postcard-perfect main square, and the immaculately preserved **Hofburg**, or Bishop's Palace, is one of South Tyrol's finest examples of Renaissance architecture. In fact, Bressanone's entire Altstadt, along with neighbouring Stufels, is a cavalcade of 15th-century arcades, colourful medieval buildings, and baroque and Renaissance accents. But Bressanone boasts a trendy side behind those quaint facades.

Pop into *enoteca* (wine bar) **Vitis**, where oak and steel elements cleverly evoke the barrels, concrete and steel prevalent in the surrounding vineyards. The wine shop, bar and restaurant hybrid's interior terrace or minimalist tasting room are wonderful spots to indulge in the wares of Italy's northernmost wine-growing region. At **Decantei**, contemporary Tyrolean cuisine is served in stunning 13th-century quarters made over by Pedevilla Architects.

HIGH-PRICED SNAPS

The **Chiesetta di San Giovanni in Ranui**, located just east of the village of Santa Maddalena di Funes in the idyllic **Val di Funes**, 21km southeast of Bressanone, is one of the most endearing symbols – and iconic photo ops – of these mountains. But photographing this teensy onion-steepled baroque church (built in 1744), sitting alone in a meadow below the gargantuan spiky peaks of the Odle group, now costs €4 – a direct result of the Instagram effect. Electrified fencing, strategically placed farm equipment and 24-hour paid parking (unheard of in rural Italy) deter those who want to circumvent the pay turnstile, installed in 2019.

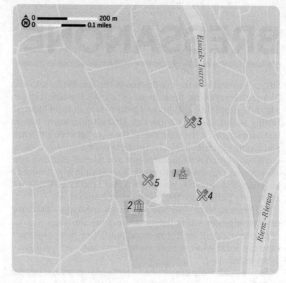

SIGHTS
1 Dom
2 Hofburg

EATING
3 Alter Schlachthof
4 Decantei
5 Vitis

Dom (p335)

Liberal use of larch wood inside and stone pine in the interior patio induce high-attitude vibes in modernist ways. On the edge of the historic centre, **Alter Schlachthof** (an 1850s slaughterhouse) is now a stylish brewpub that wouldn't be out of place in lower Manhattan. Join the hip and cultured *bressanonesi* over venison burgers and fantastic fries chased with tasty Weizens, Helles and pale ales.

GETTING AROUND

Bressanone's Altstadt is wonderfully walkable. Biking is also popular for getting around town.

Bressanone   Val Badia

Val Gardena

Val di Fassa

Parco Naturale delle
Dolomiti di Sesto

Beyond Bressanone

Quintessentially Tyrolean Brunico is the gateway
to the traditional Val Pusteria and coveted
Dolomites peaks of Tre Cime.

TOP TIP

If you're heading into
the mountains outside
Bressanone, ditch the
plastic – it's banned on
Mount Plose.

Running from the junction of the Valle Isarco at Bressanone
to San Candido (Innichen) in the far east, the narrow, verdant
Val Pusteria (Pustertal), 45 minutes east of Bressanone by car,
is profoundly Tyrolean and almost entirely German-speaking.
Brunico (Bruneck), 35km east of Bressanone, is the main hub
in the region; its principal historic drag, Stadtgasse, is one of
the region's prettiest and warrants far more than a passing
glance. Dobbiaco (Toblach), where Gustav Mahler once holed
up and wrote his troubled but ultimately life-affirming *Ninth
Symphony*, is the jumping-off point for the ethereal Parco Naturale delle Dolomiti di Sesto, home of the much-photographed
Tre Cime di Lavaredo ('Three Peaks' or, in German, Drei Zinnen) – iconic across the entirety of the Alps.

Ćiastel de Tor (p339)

DAN74/SHUTTERSTOCK ©

SHAITH/SHUTTERSTOCK ©

Tre Cime di Lavaredo

Chasing Tre Cime

TRIPLET PEAKS, OUTSTANDING EATS

Iconic photo ops in the Dolomites are as commonplace as hands in the cookie jar. There comes a certain point after a few days of travelling in the region where you come to the realisation that you simply can't stop and take a picture of everything. But the luminous **Tre Cime di Lavaredo**? That's a picture that must be taken.

Tre Cime di Lavaredo (Drei Zinnen) is the money shot in the Dolomites. These dramatic triplet peaks – **Cima Grande** (2999m), **Cima Occidentale** (2973m) and **Cima Piccola** (2857m) – emit a kaleidoscopic interplay of colour depending on the time of day and, depending on the weather, pristinely reflect off a small lake near the **Malga Langalm** mountain hut: Instagram jackpot!

To reach these epic peaks inside **Parco Naturale delle Dolomiti di Sesto**, drive the summer and early-autumn toll road (cars €30; or pre-book the summer shuttle bus from Dobbiaco) to **Rifugio Auronzo** (2320m), 7.5km northeast of Lago Misurina. From here, the Tre Cime di Lavaredo Circuit is one of the top hikes in the Dolomites. Give yourself four hours for

 WHERE TO SLEEP AND EAT IN VAL PUSTERIA

Niedermairhof
A wonderful, family-run B&B meets boutique hotel set in a rambling 13th-century farmhouse just outside Brunico. €€

Acherer Patisserie & Blumen
A Vienna apprenticeship led to strudel and Sachertorte at this landmark Brunico *pasticceria* maybe being the region's best. €

AlpINN
Triple-starred Michelin chef aside, the views from this glass-walled restaurant cantilevered over Kronplatz are unforgettable. €€€

the 9.7km jaunt (best between late June and mid-October). Follow trail 105 and behold the view from **Rifugio Locatelli**.

That was a lot of work, though, wasn't it? Next time just drive to the **Vista Panoramica Tre Cime Lavaredo** between the village of Dobbiaco and Lago di Landro for a distant – but no doubt magnificent – view of these mammoth peaks.

Livin' la Vita Ladin!

LADIN KITCHENS, CULTURALLY UNIQUE VALLEYS

The Dolomites are home to five valleys collectively known as **Ladinia**. **Val di Fassa** in Trentino, **Val Gardena** and **Val Badia** in South Tyrol, and **Cortina d'Ampezzo** and **Fodom** in the Veneto. According to Val Gardena locals, to be Ladin is a way of feeling. Growing up speaking the language – which is not a dialect of Italian but a separate language descended directly from Vulgar Latin and preserved for centuries by the geographical isolation of these high mountain valleys – means Ladin people don't feel Italian, or South Tyrolean, but Ladin.

Experience Ladin history and culture for yourself in a number of folk museums across the region. The best of the three is **Museum Ladin**, which covers the breadth of Ladin culture. It's cinematically set in the 13th-century Ćiastel de Tor in San Martino in Badia. At **Museum de Gherdëina** in Val Gardena and **Museo Ladin de Fascia** in Val di Fassa's Vigo di Fassa, wooden toys, sculptures and woodcarvings are highlights.

But the Ladin kitchen, with its particular emphasis on game, wild greens and herbs, is the true highlight. Point your palate to **Fana Ladina** in San Vigilio di Marebbe, where ancient Ladin culinary traditions have been kept alive inside a revamped 17th-century farmhouse for a half-century. Don't miss heritage Ladin dishes at **Prè de Costa**, the Crazzolara family's farm-to-table destination restaurant; and reinvigorated alpine-Ladin cuisine in cosy environs at the unwaveringly local-centric **Restaurant Ladinia**, both in Val Badia. *Bun apetit!*

EUROPE'S HIGHEST MICROBREWERY

High above the Ladinia stronghold of San Vigilio di Marebbe in Val Badia, something special sits at 2050m – Europe's highest microbrewery. At **Rifugio Lavarella**, a two-hour hike into Parco Naturale di Fanes-Sennes-Braies from the trailhead near Pederü Berggasthaus in San Vigilio, Hungarian beer sommelier and brewer Gábor Sogorka brews four beers on the premises – an unfiltered lager, a Dunkel (dark lager), a Weizenbier (Bavarian-style wheat) and an IPA – fiercely adhering to the Reinheitsgebot (German Beer Purity Law) of 1516 along the way. After an exhilarating hike in one of Europe's most stunning regions, few things go down as satisfyingly as these cold beers.

 GETTING AROUND

Ladinia's five valleys are spread out across Trentino, South Tyrol and the Veneto. As is usually the case across mountain ranges, your own wheels will significantly broaden opportunities for making the most of the region.

TRIESTE

● Trieste

✪ Rome

Talk with a *triestino* and they'll describe their hometown as both everything and nothing: on one hand a historic cross-roads and critical port of the Habsburg Empire; and, on the other, a transient point where three cultures – Austro-Hungarian, Italian and Balkan (mainly Serbian and Slovenian) – collide in the middle of nowhere, with liberal sprinkles of Jewish, Hellenic and Germanic influences thrown in for good measure. As such, Trieste preserves its own unique border-town culture and retains a fascinating air of fluidity encapsulated in the Triestine dialect, a strange mélange of Italian, Austrian German, Croatian and Greek.

Trieste's easy-on-the-eyes waterfront is lined with portentous neoclassical architecture on a par with London's, although its view across the blazing-blue bay is considerably finer. It is this view, plus the marina chock-full of sleek white yachts, the city lidos, the long, sandy beaches and the vineyard-draped hinterland of the Karst Plateau that hold the real magic of Trieste.

TOP TIP

If you want to eat well and save some dosh, head to a Triestine buffet. These legacies of Trieste's Austro-Hungarian past aren't all-you-can-eat affairs but more like delis with home-cooked meals for under €10. Pork – baked, boiled, cured, stuffed into a sausage or fried – is the star attraction.

MAXIMILIAN'S MIRAMARE

Sitting on a rocky outcrop 7km from Trieste, **Castello di Miramare** is the city's elegiac bookend, the fanciful neo-Gothic home of the hapless Archduke Maximilian of Austria. Its decor reflects Maximilian's wanderlust and various obsessions of the imperial age: a bedroom modelled on his cabin on the SMS *Novara*, on which he and wife Carlota departed Miramare to Mexico in 1864; ornate Far East–themed salons, a silk-lined throne room and exquisite wood panelling across numerous walls and ceilings. Upstairs, a suite of rooms used by military hero the Duke of Aosta in the 1930s is also intact, furnished in the Italian rationalist style.

The Free Territory of Trieste

DUELLING PERSONALITIES, MULTICULTURAL CROSSROADS

James Joyce famously wrote, 'When the soul of a man is born in this country there are nets flung at it to hold it back from flight. You talk to me of nationality, language, religion. I shall try to fly by those nets.' Trieste was his destination.

The multiple personalities of the city's freethinking history are patently evident. Pay attention to Trieste's main square, **Piazza dell'Unità d'Italia**. Where is the *duomo* (cathedral)? There isn't one – a rarity in Italy for any square, let alone the main square. That's not to say religion hasn't flourished here, however. Visit the Byzantine-style Serbian Orthodox **Chiesa di Santo Spiridione**, juxtaposed with the neoclassical 1842 Catholic **Chiesa di Sant'Antonio Taumaturgo**, both of which appear to be duelling for domination of the **Canal Grande**. There's the imposing and richly decorated neoclassical **Synagogue** as well, one of Italy's most beautiful and most important. For sustenance, there are spicy Serbian sandwiches at **Rustiko**, Venetian-leaning seafood at wonderful restaurants like **L'Osteria Salvagente** or juicy baked ham with fresh grated *kren* (horseradish), *capuzi* (sauerkraut) and *senape* (mustard) at Austro-Hungarian holdout buffets like **Da Siora Rosa**.

Trieste's port-driven wealth is evident at the extraordinary house-museum **Museo Revoltella**, home to an incredible art collection amassed by wealthy timber magnate Pasquale

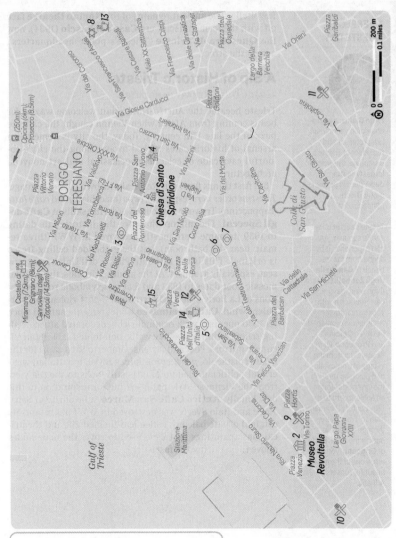

HIGHLIGHTS
1 Chiesa di
Santo Spiridione
2 Museo Revoltella

SIGHTS
3 Canal
Grande di Trieste
4 Chiesa di
Sant'Antonio
Taumaturgo
5 Piazza
dell'Unità d'Italia
6 Questura
di Trieste
(Casa del Fascio)
7 Roman Theatre
8 Synagogue

EATING
9 Da Siora Rosa
10 L'Osteria
Salvagente
11 Rustiko
12 Urbanis

**DRINKING &
NIGHTLIFE**
19 Antico Caffè
San Marco
20 Caffè degli
Specchi
21 Caffè
Tommaseo

Canal Grande

FILIPPO FERRARO/SHUTTERSTOCK ©

Revoltella. The ancient remains of the **Roman theatre** face off with the former fascist-era **Casa del Fascio** (1934), now the **Questura di Trieste** (Trieste's police headquarters), across the street.

A Sip of Historic Trieste

REGAL CAFES, LITERARY HANGOUTS

Trieste became the Austro-Hungarian welcome wagon for beans coming from Africa when Vienna caught the caffeine buzz in the late 17th century. Today, the city is home to an arsenal of historic cafes tucked away among the city's colourful cavalcade of eclectic, neoclassical and art nouveau architecture.

But first things first: Trieste speaks its own coffee language. *Triestini* order *nero* (espresso), *capo* (macchiato) and *caffe latte* (cappuccino). Try your new coffee-ordering skills at **Caffè degli Specchi**. The mirrors that give this historic cafe dating to 1839 its name were mostly destroyed in WWI (three remain near the bathroom), but the embedded ceiling fresco is original. This is the ultimate Piazza dell'Unità front-row seat, especially at sunset. At the modern Urbanis, the original mosaic floor dates to 1832 and features symbolic representations of La Bora – the Mediterranean's most violent and turbulent wind. **Caffè Tommaseo** is virtually unchanged since its 1830 opening, with original richly decorated stucco ceiling reliefs, primrose-yellow walls, lion-footed tables and Viennese mirrors. Poet and novelist Umberto Saba came for the gelato (pistachio, *per favore*); James Joyce, too! Italian writer and politician Claudio Magris still looks to the sea view from the Viennese-style patio seating for inspiration to this day. Finally, **Antico Caffè San Marco**, a favourite of Saba, Joyce and Italo Svevo, was destroyed in WWI but retains its original ornate balcony, coffee-leaf-themed gilt and theatrical mask paintings that were used to cover the male nudes above them during the fascist era.

GETTING AROUND

Trieste's historic centre is easily navigated on foot.

Dolegna del
Collio

San Floriano
del Collio

Cormòns

Aquileia

Trieste

Beyond Trieste

The wonderful border-straddling Il Collio wine region near Slovenia and the fascinating Roman ruins of Aquileia await within earshot of Trieste.

Friuli Venezia Giulia's marshy, lagoon-filled Adriatic coastline around the bygone-era seaside resort of Grado (home to Europe's northernmost sandy beaches) and La Costiera Triestina – the 20km Strada Costiera (coastal road) heading north out of town bookended by two Habsburg castles – are easy draws for quick, sun-kissed getaways. But a bounty of shockingly under-visited highlights await a bit further afield. Some of Italy's finest white wines are produced in the Il Collio DOC wine region, a picture-perfect Italo-Slovenian Eden of border-fluid vineyards and cross-cultural cuisine that feels like a discovery, just 60km north of Trieste. And Aquileia, 50 minutes northwest of Trieste by car, is where some of Europe's most prized Roman ruins sit equally untrampled by the masses.

TOP TIP

The FVG Card nets free civic-museum admissions, transport benefits and discounts in the region's shops, spas, beaches and parks.

Basilica di Santa Maria Assunta, Aquileia (p344)

PAOLO NOVELLO/SHUTTERSTOCK ©

343

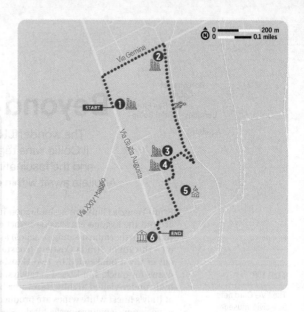

START

END

PERFECT PAIRINGS

Winemaker **Ilaria Felluga** works the grapes at Marco Felluga family cellars in Gradisca d'Isonzo and Russiz Superiore in Capriva del Friuli. (*@ilariafelluga*)

I live in Capriva del Friuli. Our rolling hills have been cultivating vineyards for more than 2600 years, so I am going to tell you about my favourite places where you can combine high enology with good food. **Osteria La Preda** (Cormòns) is a place surrounded by greenery with reinvented local dishes where you can have excellent aperitifs and also buy typical products directly from the source. **Trattoria Alla Luna** (Gorizia) is another place in my heart, where you savour the Friulian tradition in every course and, above all, drink it!

Adventures in Aquileia

ROMAN RUINS, EXTRAORDINARY MOSAICS

Italy on a bad day can be relentlessly stunning but at its best, it's simply not of this earth. That sums up the extraordinary moment you walk into the criminally under-visited **Basilica di Santa Maria Assunta** in Aquileia. The charming rural town, a 1¼-hour bus ride from Trieste, was conferred with Unesco World Heritage listing in 1998 and is home to one of the most complete, unexcavated Roman sites in Europe. One thousand years separate the incredible 4th-century mosaic floor (with 760 sq metres, one of the world's largest intact Christian-themed mosaics) and the mid-14th-century wooden ceiling. This spectacular example of antiquity-era handiwork – the animals, the symbolism, the colours – is simply mind-blowing.

It features astonishingly vivid episodes from the story of Jonah and the whale, and exacting depictions of lagoon wildlife and other symbolistic characters intended to convey the message of Christianity. And that's before you even reach the basilica's two crypts. The 9th-century Cripta degli Affreschi (Crypt of Frescoes) is adorned with faded 12th-century frescoes depicting the trials and tribulations of saints, while the

WHERE TO SLEEP AND EAT IN IL COLLIO

Venica & Venica Wine Resort
Six smart rooms and two apartments above cellars that produce one of Italy's most famous sauvignon blancs. €€

L'Argine a Vencò
Antonia Klugmann's Michelin-starred restaurant in an off-the-beaten-track mill in the Friuli countryside. €€€

La Subida
A landmark family-run inn, restaurant (and more affordable *osteria*) with border-crossing dishes and ingredients. €€€

Cripta degli Scavi (Excavations Crypt) reveals more mosaic floors in varying states of preservation.

The basilica is hardly the only jaw-dropping moment on this half-day exploration of Aquileia. Start at the open-air **1 Foro Romano** along Via Giulia Augusta – this was the north–south Cardo Maximus that connected Norico (now Austria) with the Roman port at Grado when the city was founded in 181 BCE to protect the Empire from barbarian invasion. Mussolini, eager to spotlight the Roman origins of a territory that was part of the Austro-Hungarian Empire until 1918, restored many columns with red bricks. Head north then east on Via Gemina to the entrance to the **2 Porto Fluviale**, where a walking path known as Via Sacra follows what was once the west bank of the Roman river port to the basilica. Small decorative ruins line the path – don't miss the first one on the left, a working Roman sundial.

Before you reach the basilica, two astonishing dwellings await in what was once an *insula* (Roman city block). **3 Domus di Tito Macro** is one of the largest Roman homes ever found in northern Italy (reservations in advance recommended). Not only notable for its size (1700 sq metres!), it contains a complete representation of every room in a typical Roman home. The home has been painstakingly reconstructed, complete with terracotta shutters and a new roof. Head into the 5th-century **4 Domus e Palazzo Episcopale**, or Bishop's House, to get a vivid sense of the archaeological layering that has taken place over the centuries. You can clearly view the 1st-century bottom level as well as the 4th-century middle level, where richly detailed mosaics of grape bunches, fruit baskets, fish, birds and more are splendidly preserved and surpassed only by what awaits in your next stop, the **5 basilica**.

To see the archaeological bounty excavated from the site, finish at the **6 National Archaeological Museum of Aquileia**, one of the oldest of its kind in Italy. It features monumental sculptures, artefacts and treasures that played a role in civic and religious life.

Il Collio Calling

CROSS-BORDER VINEYARDS, FRIULIAN KITCHENS

Ask for a local wine at **Osteria La Subida**, and you might get an Italian-produced 2012 Ronco del Tasssi Malvasia or a 2018 Burja Zelen from Slovenia. *Benvenuti a Il Collio!* This cross-border wine region, equidistant from the Austrian Alps and the Adriatic Sea, has a sunny, breezy microclimate that conspires with the marlstone soil to produce grapes of aston-

ROADS LESS TRAVELLED

Friuli Venezia Giulia ranks 15th out of Italy's 20 regions by tourism arrivals, so many of its treasures – like Aquileia – are unknown, comparably speaking. Take **Cividale del Friuli**, 15km east of the FVG culinary capital of Udine, for example. Here the well-preserved chapel of Tempietto Longobardo houses the only surviving example of Lombard architecture and artwork in Europe. Dating to the 8th century, it features a detour-worthy assemblage of rare frescoes as well as unusually naturalistic stucco work whose luminous whiteness is accented by the dark wood choir stalls.

 WHERE TO SLEEP AROUND AQUILEIA

Belvedere Pineta Camping Village	**Albergo Alla Spiaggia**	**Ostello Domus Augusta**
Huge campsite (plus bungalows and apartments) in a fragrant pine forest near Grado. €	Grado accommodation in a modernist building wedged between a pedestrian zone, historic centre and beach. €€	Spotless institutional hostel; 92 bunks, 28 private rooms. Popular with cyclists pedalling between Salzburg and Grado. €

THE WILD CARNIC ALPS

Stretching as far west as the Veneto Dolomites and as far north as the border with Austria, **Carnia** is intrinsically Friulian – the language is widely spoken here in lieu of Italian – and named after its original Celtic inhabitants, the Carnics. Geographically, it contains the western and central parts of the Carnic Alps and presents down-to-earth ski areas, wild and beautiful walking country and curious, pristinely rustic villages. A good base is **Sappada** (Plodn in dialect), voted one of the most beautiful villages in Italy and the winner of a sustainability award in 2019 – a picture-postcard alpine village set on a sunny slope surrounded by dramatic Dolomitic peaks.

LUCIANO MORTULA - LGM/SHUTTERSTOCK ©

Vineyards, Il Colio

LOOKING FOR MORE MOSAICS?

The Unesco World Heritage-listed town of **Ravenna** (p396) in Emilia-Romagna is home to a cavalcade of Early Christian mosaic artwork.

ishing fragrance and minerality, yielding some of the finest DOC-accredited white wines in Italy. With its idyllic vine-covered hillsides, excellent restaurants and smart farmhouse accommodation, it's a superb place to kick back and a fascinating destination as-yet-untapped by mass tourism.

The Italian share of the border-straddling region focuses on the charming hamlets of **San Floriano del Collio**, **Cormòns** and **Dolegna del Collio**. After exploring 300 local wines by the glass at **Enoteca di Cormòns** in the mini Habsburg town of Cormòns, head into these hills. At **Russiz Superiore**, hotshot 6th-generation winemaker Ilaria Felluga produces the award-winning Collio Bianco; the extraordinary cellar packed with decades-old bottles covered in crusts of dust is worth the trip alone. **Gradis'ciutta**, the first and biggest organic winery in Il Collio, produces a fine Metodo Classico Spumante using grapes split 50/50 between Italian and Slovenian vineyards. Both wineries offer superb accommodation: seven classically appointed rooms with views of Slovenia at Russiz; and 12 modern offerings with original wood-beamed ceilings and rescued armoires from a revamped 16th-century country villa at Gradis'ciutta.

GETTING AROUND

As is the case with most wine regions, exploring Il Collio requires a car. Vehicles are a burden in compact Grado (bikes are well suited), and Aquileia is a 10-minute bus ride from the island.

PADUA

● Padua

❀ Rome

Though less than an hour from Venice, Padua (Padova in Italian) seems a world away with its medieval marketplaces, fascist-era facades and hip student population. As a medieval city-state and home to Italy's second-oldest university, Padua challenged both Venice and Verona for regional hegemony. A series of 14th-century fresco cycles recall this golden age – including Giotto's blockbuster Cappella degli Scrovegni (part of a Unesco World Heritage Site), Menabuoi's heavenly gathering in the baptistry and Titian's St Anthony in the Scoletta del Santo. For centuries, Padua and Verona fought for dominance over the Veneto plains, but Venice finally occupied Padua permanently in 1405.

As a strategic military-industrial centre, Padua became a parade ground for Mussolini speeches, an Allied bombing target and a secret Italian Resistance hub (at its university). Even today, Padua remains an important industrial city – its industrial zone employs some 50,000 people – a dynamic university town and an important pilgrimage centre.

TOP TIP

From April to November (and other select days throughout the year), you can book double the normally allotted time inside Padua's Cappella degli Scrovegni as part of the Unesco World Heritage Site's night-visit program between 7pm and 10pm.

Divinity Humanised

MASTERPIECE FRESCOES, DIVINE REVELATIONS

The Vatican's Sistine Chapel hogs all the headlines, but Padua's version – a striking cycle of frescoes inside the **Cappella degli Scrovegni** painted by Giotto 200 years earlier – helped spawn an unprecedented age of enlightenment known as the Renaissance. Prior to Giotto's vibrant fresco cycle, medieval churchgoers had been accustomed to blank stares from enthroned saints. Giotto introduced biblical figures as human characters in recognisable settings, changing not only how people saw themselves – no longer lowly vassals but vessels for the divine – but revolutionising the art world as well.

Visiting Giotto's unprecedented work, unsuspectingly housed inside a modest chapel you might not otherwise give a second glance, requires pre-booking. Arrive at least 15 to 30 minutes before your tour starts, or an hour before if you want to get around the **Musei Civici agli Eremitani** beforehand.

Giotto's moving, modern approach holds no less power of captivation today than on its 1305 unveiling. Telling the story of Christ from Annunciation to Ascension in impressively large and comprehensive detail, its chromatic vibrancy remains stirringly whole. Giotto also used unusual techniques such as impasto, building paint up into 3D forms. You'll get 15 to 20 minutes in the chapel itself – nowhere near enough, but sufficient to bear witness to one of the most important masterpieces of Western art come to life under Giotto's starry sky.

ST ANTHONY OF PADUA

Padua's gigantic **Basilica di Sant'Antonio** draws pilgrims the world over as the burial place of St Anthony of Padua (1193–1231), a Portuguese priest and friar of the Franciscan order who was canonised less than one year after his death. The church incorporates rising Byzantine domes atop a Gothic brick structure crammed with Renaissance treasures. Behind the high altar, nine radiating chapels punctuate a broad ambulatory homing in on the Cappella delle Reliquie (Relics Chapel), where the relics of St Anthony reside.

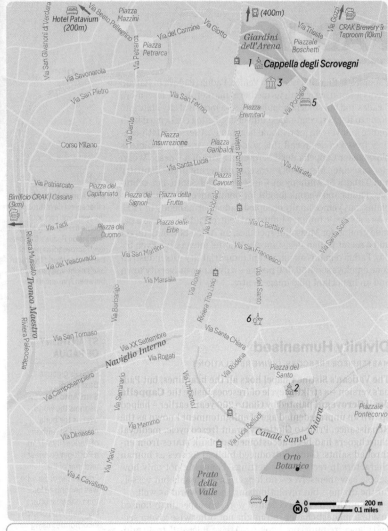

HIGHLIGHTS	**SIGHTS**	**SLEEPING**	**DRINKING**
1 Cappella degli Scrovegni	2 Basilica di Sant'Antonio	4 Hotel al Prato	**& NIGHTLIFE**
	3 Musei Civici agli Eremitani	5 Scrovegni Room & Breakfast	6 Enoteca da Severino

 WHERE TO SLEEP IN PADUA

Scrovegni Room & Breakfast
Contemporary furniture under beamed or frescoed ceilings at this lovely B&B a stone's throw from the Scrovegni Chapel. €

Hotel al Prato
Modern hotel with artistic leanings located just off Italy's largest piazza, Prato della Valle. Quiet and comfortable. €

Hotel Patavium
Classically furnished boutique hotel with wide beds, flat-screen TVs, modern bathrooms and a private garden. €€

The Craft of CRAK

CRAFT BEER, DESTINATION TAPROOMS

Italy's position as an Old World wine vanguard is certainly unshakable, but the country isn't exactly barren of brews, either. It has both its own signature style (Italian Pils – a German-inspired Pilsner dry-hopped with European hops) and is considered the world's best at another (grape ales – high-fermentation ales flavoured with grape musts). Craft-beer connoisseurs, or *nerds della birra* as the Italians say, will be pleased to know the country's top craft brewery, **Birrificio CRAK**, calls Padua home.

In rural Campodarsego, 15km north of Padua's Prato della Valle square, **CRAK TapRoom** awaits in a 1950s warehouse converted into an American West Coast–style brewery and massive summer beer garden complete with cornhole, fairy-lit picnic tables and vintage lawn furniture. Italy's best IPAs, double IPAs, barrel-aged stouts and grape ales run 24 taps deep here. Closer to the city, CRAK's fantastic **Casana** bar features 30 taps best enjoyed on the masterly crafted garden picnic tables at this revamped 1900s farmhouse 3km west of central Padua. Drinking at either means immersing yourself in the country's top craft-beer experience while embellishing the often hop-forward handiwork of brewer Marco Ruffa, whose mantra is focused on freshness. And don't be surprised if they hand you something from the tap list in a can – CRAK believes certain brews are freshest without the aid of glassware. Resistance is futile – these hops don't lie.

PADUA PERFECTION

Padua-born and raised street artist **Joys** has painted across the world. Here he shares a perfect Padua evening. (@joys_ead)

For those who are often travelling for work, 'home' becomes any place to stay temporarily. This is why when I am in Padua, after closing the door of my atelier, I choose to unwind in places and venues where I feel at home. First and foremost, **Enoteca da Severino**, the oldest in Padua, just a stone's throw from Via del Santo and Palazzo Bo. The vast selection of wines combined with the intimate and quaint setting allows you to disconnect while exchanging chats with friends and perfect strangers, too.

MORE UNESCO?

Want to see more of Italy's newest Unesco World Heritage Sites? Bologna's **medieval porticoes** (p368), which line the Emilia-Romagna capital across 62km, were inaugurated in 2021 along with Padua's 14th-century fresco cycles.

GETTING AROUND

The preferred method of transport for the *padovani* is two wheels. GoodBike Padua is a bike-sharing scheme with 25 stations dotted around the city.

Padua

Colli Euganei

Beyond Padua

Fortified medieval walls, castles and thermal hot springs – adventures in the Euganean Hills begin barely outside Padua's city limits.

Just a few minutes southwest of Padua by car begins a verdant landscape of gentle cone-shaped reliefs shaped by 40 million years of volcanic activity. These hills, sitting in clear anomaly surrounded by the characteristically flat Po valley, top out at the 601m-high Monte Venda 30km southwest of Padua. Some 18,694 hectares are protected as part of the Parco Regionale dei Colli Euganei, next to the Roman-era spa towns of Abano Terme, Montegrotto Terme, Galzignano Terme and Battaglia Terme. Beyond the therapeutic thermal springs, these hills are dotted with scenic medieval stone villages, misty vineyards producing Fior d'Arancio DOCG Moscato, and several small towns totally overshadowed by their remarkably preserved fortified walls dating to the Middle Ages.

TOP TIP

Villa dei Vescovi, one of the Veneto's best-preserved pre-Palladio Renaissance villas, has two bookable apartments overlooking the Euganean Hills.

Defensive walls, Montagnana

FEDELE FERRARA/SHUTTERSTOCK ©

Castles in the Colli

MEDIEVAL WALLS, HILLTOP FORTRESSES

The **Colli Euganei** (Euganean Hills) hide Roman-era spa towns, misty vineyards, hilltop medieval castles and, most impressively, a series of extremely well preserved walled towns. It's a popular mountain biking and cycling destination (check out the 63km Anello dei Colli Euganei from Monselice to Lozzo Atestino), but hilltop-hopping by car makes for a great day out, too.

Closest to Padua, the modern pools and balneo-mud therapies at **Hotel Mioni Pezzato & SPA** in Roman-era Abano Terme are perfect for a relaxing and rejuvenating day in the hills. As you approach the tiny hilltop enclave of Monselice, the remarkable medieval castle within its boundaries remains mostly unseen. The **Castello di Monselice** has worn many shirts over the centuries, its oldest portions dating to the 11th century as a stately home before evolving into a defensive tower and a Venetian villa in the 16th century. In **Este**, only the Guelph-merloned 1km-long castle walls remain of the once formidable Castello Carrarese di Este (1050), now encasing wonderful public gardens and the **Museo Nazionale Atestino**. Housed in a handsome 16th-century *palazzo*, Este's notable archaeological museum contains around 65,000 objects, among them pre-Roman and Roman artefacts from the region. Finally, **Montagnana**, whose magnificent 2km medieval defensive walls pack a lot of head-snapping wow on approach. With its *palazzi*-saturated piazza, it's the region's best for wandering. A Slow Food meal at Hostaria San Benedetto, one of the region's best restaurants, makes for a fitting finale.

IF YOU LOVE A GOOD MEDIEVAL WALL...

The city of **Ferrara** (p384) in Emilia-Romagna is home to some of Italy's most impressive city fortifications. Only Lucca (Tuscany) and Bergamo (Lombardy) can claim a more complete – albeit shorter – set of walls than Ferrara.

 GETTING AROUND

You can reach the area by bus from Padua, and trains serve all towns except Arquà Petrarca, but to really enjoy things here you'll need a hire car.

VERONA

Best known for its Shakespeare associations, Verona attracts a multinational gaggle of tourists to its pretty piazzas and knot of lanes, most in search of Romeo, Juliet and all that. But beyond the Renaissance romance, Verona is a bustling city whose centre is dominated by a mammoth, remarkably well preserved 1st-century CE amphitheatre, the venue for the city's annual summer opera festival. Add to that countless churches, a couple of architecturally fascinating bridges over the Adige, regional wine and food from the Veneto hinterland and some impressive art, and Verona shapes up as one of northern Italy's most attractive cities. Monuments and architecture in the city's Unesco-protected core offer stunning opportunities to travel back in time through classical antiquity, medieval and Renaissance periods; yet you'll find no shortage of contemporary distractions, from cutting-edge cocktail bars to extraordinary modern art. Shake off the star-crossed silliness and revel in the real Verona: a historic beauty that needed no Shakespearean introduction.

TOP TIP

The VeronaCard, available in 24- or 48-hour versions, nets you all sorts of discounts on city attractions, but its true value becomes immediately apparent when you see the line at the Arena di Verona ticket counter: it allows you to skip the line.

VERONA VERITÀ

Alice Roncali owns Verona's best craft-beer pub, Maratonda, in Veronetta. (@alice_beerland)

I recommend starting your morning with a *risino* (shortcrust pastry filled with rice and custard) at **Pasticceria Flego** and a nice walk to **Castel San Pietro** where you can see the best view of the city from above; nearby there's the archaeological museum of **Teatro Romano**. The perfect day in Verona ends with an Americano *aperitivo* at **Archivio** and a tasty plate of *bigoli* with donkey *ragù* at **Osteria al Duca**.

A Night at the Opera

WORLD-CLASS OPERA, ROMAN RUINS

Built of pink-tinged marble in the 1st century CE, Verona's **Roman Arena** survived a 12th-century earthquake to become the city's legendary open-air opera house, with seating for 30,000 people. It dominates Verona's Piazza Bra and elicits audible gasps at first sight. It's one of Italy's most astounding buildings and one of the world's best-preserved ancient structures. And nothing of the incredible inside is visible from outside. Pass through the dingy ancient corridors, wide enough to drive a gladiator's chariot, to re-emerge into the massive, sunlit stone arena, with at least 50 levels of seating rising from the mammoth, oval showground (note the amphitheatre is completely open so this is not a great place to visit in the rain).

In fact, it's difficult to call the eighth-biggest amphitheatre in the Roman Empire (which predates the Colosseum in Rome) a ruin at all – it's still in use. While visits are possible year-round, it's at its best during the summer **Arena di Verona Festival**. Around 14,000 music lovers pack the Roman Arena on summer nights during the world's biggest open-air lyrical music event, which draws international stars. Performances usually start at 9pm. No need to spring for top-end tickets – the numbered stone steps are fine. Rent a cushion and prepare for an unforgettable evening with Verdi's *Aida*, *Nabucco*, *La Traviata* or Puccini's *Turandot*, among others.

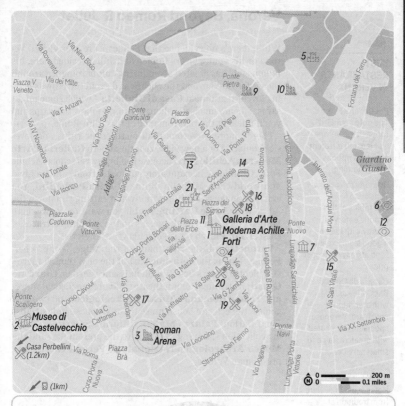

HIGHLIGHTS

1 Galleria d'Arte Moderna Achille Forti
2 Museo di Castelvecchio
3 Roman Arena

SIGHTS

4 Casa di Giulietta

5 Castel San Pietro
6 Giardino Giusti
7 Museo Archeologico Nazionale di Verona
8 Palazzo Maffei
9 Ponte Pietra
10 Teatro Romano
11 Torre dei Lamberti
12 Veronetta

SLEEPING

13 Corte delle Pigne
14 Due Torri Hotel

EATING

15 Café Carducci
16 Hostaria La Vecchia Fontanina
17 Locanda 4 Cuochi

18 Osteria al Duca
19 Osteria da Ugo
20 Pasticceria Flego

DRINKING & NIGHTLIFE

21 Archivio

◎ **WHAT TO SEE IN VERONA**

Torre dei Lamberti
This 84m-high 12th-century watchtower provides panoramic views; it's reached by the late-Gothic Scala della Ragione.

Museo di Castelvecchio
Cangrande II's massive 1350s fortress (restored by Carlo Scarpa), with medieval, Renaissance and modern art.

Ponte Pietra
Two of this ancient bridge's arches date from the Roman Republican era; postcard-ready views of the city and river.

Verona, Beyond Romeo & Juliet

FASCINATING MUSEUMS, RENAISSANCE GARDENS

While there's no evidence that Shakespeare ever visited Verona or his young lovers Romeo and Juliet resided here, his famous tale has created an enduring cult of romance around the city. To get beyond the clichés and avoid the crowds leaving lovelorn graffiti at **Casa di Giulietta** – which some might say is...ahem...much ado about nothing – follow these tips and you'll unearth the real romance of this mini-Rome.

There's more to Verona than picturesque ruins and lovesick couples. For a new view, visit the superb **Galleria d'Arte Moderna Achille Forti** bequeathed by Jewish scholar Achille Forti. Or indulge in exquisitely curated mixology at Archivio and world-class Michelin dining at **Casa Perbellini**. You can even make a thrilling white-water rafting run down the Adige with **Adige Rafting**. And if you want to know where Verona's teen lovers really go, it's up to the hilltop terraces of **Castel San Pietro** for spectacular sunset views.

Veronetta, on the right bank of the Adige, is the 'other' Verona. This is the authentic part of the city, though there's still plenty to see: a beautiful Renaissance garden, **Giardino Giusti**; a striking Roman theatre and archaeological museum, **Teatro Romano e Museo Archeologico**; and two new gems – the eclectic house-museum of Veronese industrialist Luigi Carlon, **Palazzo Maffei**, featuring an extraordinary art collection spanning antiquity to the present day, and the **Museo Archeologico Nazionale di Verona** chronicling pre-Roman Verona.

FOR CULTURE CONNOISSEURS

Art, architecture and literature enthusiasts might consider a detour 108km south of Verona to **Ferrara** (p384), one of Italy's most important Renaissance hubs. The city was a stomping ground for some of the era's most important artistic and intellectual elite.

GETTING AROUND

Most of Verona's sights are easily reached on foot, including those on the other side of the river, such as Giardini Giusti or Castel San Pietro (the latter can also be reached by funicular).

Valpolicella   Vicenza

Verona

Beyond Verona

Pre-Roman vineyards overflowing with rich
Amarone reds await in the vicinity of Verona.

The 'valley of many cellars', from which Valpolicella gets its
name, has been in the business of wine production since the
ancient Greeks introduced their *passito* technique (the use of
partially dried grapes) to create the blockbuster flavours we
still enjoy in the region's Amarone and Recioto wines. Situated in the foothills of Monte Lessini, about 20 minutes or so by
car north and northwest of Verona, the valleys benefit from
a happy microclimate created by the enormous body of Lake
Garda to the west and cooling breezes from the Alps to the
north. Vicenza, on the other hand, lies 57km east, and features
an arsenal of Unesco World Heritage–listed villas and buildings designed by legendary Renaissance architect Palladio.

The Vines of Valpolicella

STORYBOOK VINEYARDS, WORLD-CLASS WINES

The juice flow in the Veneto's famed Valpolicella wine region
predates the Roman Empire. Not only that, but Amarone isn't
the first wine to achieve legendary status in the area – Roman
poets and historians held the Rhaetian wine (Vino Retico) that
was produced in the hills around Verona in similar mythical
regard. Put simply: this is the good stuff.

This 57km counterclockwise round trip from **Verona**
takes in some of the most exquisite Valpolicella wines, not
all Amarone: sweet, full-bodied Recioto, lighter Valpolicella Classico Superiore and Superiore Ripasso (considered the poor man's Amarone) are all exquisite. Tastings/
tours generally run €20 to €80 (best to pre-book). The lovely
1 Villa Mosconi Bertani is housed in a historic walled estate
on 22 hectares, with English-style gardens, lakes, orchards
and Guyot vineyards to explore. **2 Giuseppe Quintarelli**
put the Valpolicella region on the world wine map and their
extraordinary, limited-production Amarone is a Holy Grail
for serious oenophiles.

Family-run **3 Damoli** is distinctly more down to earth. Friendly Lara Damoli pours their excellent-value Checo Amarone (€38)

Giuseppe Quintarelli
wine

PALLADIO'S MASTERPIECE

No matter how you look at it, all roads lead to **La Rotunda**. This villa, located 2.5km southeast of Vicenza's Piazza dei Signori, is a showstopper: the namesake dome caps a square base, with identical colonnaded facades on all four sides. This is one of Palladio's most admired creations, inspiring variations across Europe and the USA, including Thomas Jefferson's Monticello. Inside, the circular central hall is covered from the walls to the soaring cupola with *trompe l'œil* frescoes. The villa is surrounded by grassy farmland dotted with bucolic bales of hay in summer, a scene that only adds to the pastoral picturesqueness of it all.

while explaining the family history of cultivating wines in Negrar since 1623. Showstopper 4 **Allegrini** holds wine tastings in the remarkable 16th-century Villa della Torre in Fumane. Finally, history pervades at 5 **Serego Alighieri**. Pietro Alighieri, son of Italy's great medieval poet Dante, acquired the grand Casal dei Ronchi villa in 1353 – and 21 generations of descendants of the Supreme Poet have lived here since. Tours are well worth it just to hear the fascinating story.

A City of Palladian Proportions

PALLADIAN ARCHITECTURE, JAW-DROPPING THEATRE

Padovano Renaissance architect Andrea Palladio transformed the history of European architecture after a stint studying ruins in Rome in the 1540s led him back to his adopted city of **Vicenza**, where the autodidact began creating his extraordinary buildings. A tour de force of sophistication and rustic simplicity, reverent classicism and bold innovation, his genius would turn Vicenza (a 25-minute train ride from Verona) into one grand Unesco World Heritage Site.

For the full Unesco route, pick up the Palladian Itinerary from IAT Vicenza, the city tourism office next to the Teatro Olimpico. Instead, this greatest-hits walking tour starts in

---

 WHERE TO SLEEP AND EAT IN VALPOLICELLA

Porta delle Torre
Two great-value, modern country-style rooms in the charming stone village of San Giorgio. €

La Caminella
Pretty B&B in San Pietro in Cariano, housed in an old stone structure once used for drying tobacco leaves. €€

Enoteca della Valpolicella
This ancient farmhouse is Fumane's gastronome focal point; outstanding local wines, produce-driven cuisine. €€

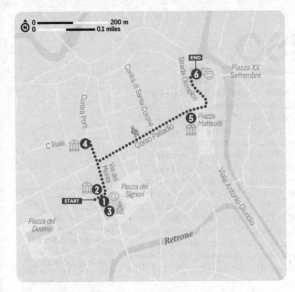

Carlo Meroni, owner/winemaker at the Meroni Wine Estate in Sant'Ambrogio di Valpolicella. (@meroni.carlo)

I would make a short drive up to the town of **San Giorgio** and visit the Romanesque Pieve di San Giorgio, then probably stick around and have an *aperitivo* at **Bistro del Borgo**, which has a beautiful terrace with stunning views of Lake Garda and Valpolicella. For lunch, I would go to **Dalla Rosa Alda**. My favourite dish here? Homemade tagliatelle by the owner's grandmother… don't miss out on this! Alternatively, if it's cloudy, I would go to Spirito Wine Boutique, which is my usual hang-out for a good glass of wine!

1 Piazza dei Signori, home to two amazing face-to-face Palladian buildings: the salmon-toned, mid-16th century **2 Loggia del Capitaniato** (closed to the public), and the grand **3 Basilica Palladiana**, with its triumphant double order of loggias (added by Palladio to the existing 15th-century *palazzo*) and enormous copper dome reminiscent of the hull of a ship. Pop in the frescoed halls of the **4 Palladio Museum** for context before heading to **5 Palazzo Chiericati** (1550), one of Palladio's finest buildings and home to Vicenza's worthwhile civic art museum since 1855. Catty-corner to the northeast, a fitting end both literally and figuratively: **6 Teatro Olimpico**, a Renaissance marvel that stands as Palladio's last hurrah before his death in 1580. Vincenzo Scamozzi finished the elliptical theatre after Palladio's passing, adding a stage set modelled on the ancient Greek city of Thebes, with streets built in steep perspective to give the illusion of a city sprawling towards a distant horizon.

STILL THIRSTY?

The Dolomites and the northeast pack in an extraordinary portfolio of incredible wine regions. Consider the **Prosecco Hills** (p361), 184km northeast of Valpolicella, for further enological pursuits.

GETTING AROUND

Wheels will enrich visiting Verona's wine country (or call Pagus Wine Tours). Vicenza is very walkable, though Palladio's villas dot the countryside.

TREVISO

Treviso is often dubbed 'Little Venice' for its picturesque canals and waterways, but unlike its far more famous neighbour to the south, the city is not inundated – its pretty canals often sneak up on you, announcing their presence with an air of demure subtlety. The city, 41km north of Venice, has everything you could want from a mid-sized Veneto city: medieval city walls, lots of pretty canals, narrow cobbled streets and frescoed churches. It's an easy-going, authentic piece of Veneto veritas that was founded – if legends are to be believed – by the Celtic-Oriental Taurisci (though Romans granted its town charter in 49 BCE). Treviso is home to a bevy of well-known Italian brands (Benetton, Sisley, Geox, Diadora, De'Longhi and Pinarello) and has quietly become an arts hotbed. For a taste of authentic Veneto life while keeping your distance from the throngs of tourists, Treviso delivers. Oh, and tiramisu was invented here.

TOP TIP

Museums in Italy are traditionally closed on Mondays, but Treviso's Museo Collezione Salce is open on weekends only (Friday to Sunday). Plan accordingly – you don't want to miss this fascinating collection of retro Italian advertising posters.

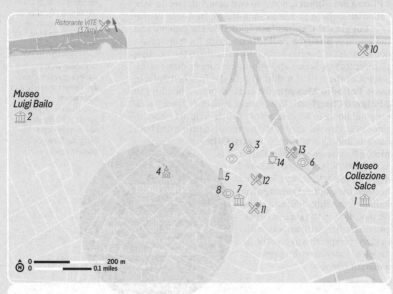

HIGHLIGHTS
1 Museo Collezione Salce
2 Museo Luigi Bailo

SIGHTS
3 Canale dei Buranelli
4 Duomo
5 Fontana delle Tette
6 Isola della Pescheria
7 Palazzo dei Trecento
8 Piazza dei Signori
9 Piazza San Vito

EATING
10 Antica Osteria Al Botegon
11 Hostaria dai Naneti
12 Le Beccherie
13 Osteria Muscoli

DRINKING & NIGHTLIFE
14 Camelia Bakery

The City of Arte & Acqua

SCENIC CANALS, WORLD-CLASS ART

Picturesque canals intersperse arcaded streets lined with fresco-painted *palazzi* in Treviso's medieval walled centre, offering lovely watery views punctuated by weeping willows and water wheels. Most of the waterways are east of Treviso's main square, **Piazza dei Signori**, behind which you'll find the curious **Fontana delle Tette** in the loggia of the **Palazzo dei Trecento**. From the breasts of the 16th-century naked female torso shoots potable water today (hilariously, folks do drink from them!) but wine once flowed from this sumptuous pair. The romantic **Canale dei Buranelli** was used by women doing the laundry right up until WWII. The small bridge off **Piazza San Vito** is a requisite photo op. Treviso's fish market sits picturesquely surrounded by waters on **Isola della Pesceria**, connected by an iron bridge to the surrounding mainland – a charming spot for *aperitivo* and *cicheti* (Venetian tapas) at **Osteria Muscoli**.

Art lovers will find plenty of distractions among the waterways. **Museo Collezione Salce** is a graphic-arts treasure trove of globally important Italian advertising posters donated to the state in 1962. **Museo Luigi Bailo** houses a stunningly good 20th-century art collection. When you're done exploring, go and get yourself a serving of the original tiramisu, which according to a notarial deed with the Accademia Italiana della Cucina, first appeared on the menu at **Le Beccherie** in 1972.

WEEKENDS IN TREVISO

Federico Sbrissa, Chief Marketing Officer for Treviso-born cycling brand Pinarello. (*@federicosbrissa*)

Nothing is better during the weekend in Treviso than a morning walk along Il Calmaggiore from the **Duomo** to Piazza dei Signori, then down to the fish market with a stop for breakfast at **Camelia Bakery**. In the evening, try a *spritz* at **Antica Osteria Al Botegon** or **Hostaria dai Naneti** – known for *ombra de vin* (wine and freshly made sandwiches). A new restaurant for dinner just opened a few minutes outside Treviso next to our office, too: **Ristorante VITE** in Villorba.

Calmaggiore

GETTING AROUND

Wandering aimlessly here on foot is a delight, discovering on your own the quaint canals that drift among centuries-old villas and Venetian architecture.

Valdobbiadene   Conegliano

Treviso

Beyond Treviso

The wildly picturesque Unesco-listed Prosecco Hills around Conegliano and Valdobbiadene emerge less than 40km north of Treviso.

Easy trips heading north out of Treviso include the panoramic hilltop town of Asolo (33km northeast) and the monumental Sacrario Militare mausoleum at Monte Grappa (73km northeast), but it's the cinematic prosecco wine region around Conegliano and Valdobbiadene, 40 minutes north of Treviso by car, that is the toast of the Veneto. Here in the foothills of the Alps, vineyards that produce one of Italy's most famed white wines are dramatically draped across steep terraced hillsides using a chequerboard landscaping technique in place since the 17th century. Over 300 years later, in 2019, Le Colline del Prosecco (Prosecco Hills) became one of Italy's three newest Unesco World Heritage Sites. Brace yourself for a travel trifecta: storybook vineyards, fine wine and excellent Veneto cuisine.

TOP TIP

Exported prosecco is usually Extra Dry or Brut, but don't miss Col Fondo (unfiltered), Tranquillo (non-sparkling) and top-of-the-line Cartizze while here.

Vineyards, Valdobbiadene

FRANCESCO RICCARDO IACOMINO/GETTY IMAGES ©

Prosecco, per Favore!

VINE-DRAPED HILLSIDES, GLASSES OF BUBBLY

As the Alps begin to concede to lower altitudes in the foothills around the Veneto towns of Conegliano and Valdobbiadene, one of Italy's most beautiful wine regions announces itself with startling effect: waves of diving hillsides known as 'hogback' hills (*ciglioni* in Italian) awash in grassy terraces harbouring Crayola-green vineyards unravel across the countryside. Welcome to the Le Colline del Prosecco (Prosecco Hills).

La Strada del Prosecco (Prosecco Road) is Italy's oldest wine route and covers 120 producers between Conegliano and Valdobbiadene. Servo Suo is the award-winning prosecco produced by the Faganello family at **Colsaliz** in Refrontolo. Tastings are free – enjoy the terrace view with a glass of their intense-tasting wine. Nearby, prosecco counts for half of **Toffoli's** 16 varieties; their modern techniques create prosecco with an intense apple, pear and lemon nose (tastings start at €15). At **Bisol1542** in the hills of Valdobbiadene, 21 generations of Bisols have been striving to produce the best prosecco in the world since 1542. Their signature labels are the award-winning Cartizze Dry and Jeio Brut. If you're lucky, they'll let you taste them in the atmospheric underground cellar.

Don't miss **Antica Osteria Al Forno** in Refrontolo, where blue-collar townsfolk partake in refined glasses of DOCG prosecco which run just €3 a pop, before retreating to the outstanding restaurant for faultless Veneto cuisine.

PROSECCO 101

Prosecco is a dry, crisp white wine made in spumante (bubbly), frizzante (sparkling) and still varieties with at least 85% Glera grapes (the remaining 15% coming from varietals such as Verdiso, Bianchetta Trevigiana, Perera, chardonnay, pinot bianco, pinot grigio and pinot noir). In 2009 Conegliano's prosecco was promoted to DOCG (guaranteed-quality) status, Italy's highest oenological distinction. In 2019 the entire region was crowned a Unesco World Heritage Site, joining the ranks of Pantelleria (Sicily), Langhe-Roero and Monferrato (Piedmont) as Italy's only three wine regions with this coveted distinction.

ANOTHER ROUND?

Italy's Trento DOC appellation, the country's first to be reserved exclusively for sparkling wine made by the bottle-fermentation method, sits in the foothills surrounding **Trento** (p327), 134km east of the Prosecco Hills.

GETTING AROUND

Four wheels are essential for touring the vineyards of the Prosecco Hills.

BOLOGNA & EMILIA-ROMAGNA

GASTRONOMIC DELIGHTS, HISTORIC TREASURES

Italy's culinary cradle is a blessed heartland of rich pastas, centuries-old art and architecture, and modern, high-speed supercars – Emilia-Romagna thrives in the contrast.

Emilia-Romagna boasts some of Italy's most hospitable people, some of its most productive land and some of its fastest vehicles. Since antiquity, the verdant Po lowlands have sown enough agricultural riches to feed a nation and finance an unending line of lavish products: luxury cars, regal *palazzi* (mansions), Romanesque churches, prosperous towns and a gigantic operatic legacy (Verdi and Pavarotti, no less). Both historically and in modern times, the region has attracted masterful minds – intellectuals flock to the University of Bologna as they have since the oldest continually operating university in the world set up shop in 1088, engineers help Motor Valley's luxury sports cars continue to set new standards in speed and design, and agronomists focus on Emilia-Romagna's groundbreaking agricultural practices.

But unlike its provincial neighbours north and south, Emilia-Romagna is home to no dominant tourist hot spot. Rather, it offers a treasure trove of oft-neglected destinations – vibrant Bologna with its photogenic porticoes, Ravenna with its dazzling mosaics, posh Parma and Rimini, the Roman frontier town turned beach resort – bound by an undeniable overriding theme: food! Emilia-Romagna is home to an enviable pedigree of some of the country's most famous gastronomic triumphs. Whether you seek authentic *ragù* in Bologna, *parmigiano reggiano* cheese in Parma or a seat at one of the world's most famous restaurants in Modena, Emilia-Romagna is an unbeatable place to eat.

INQUARIBILE VIAGGIATORE/SHUTTERSTOCK ©

THE MAIN AREAS

Portico, Bologna (p372)

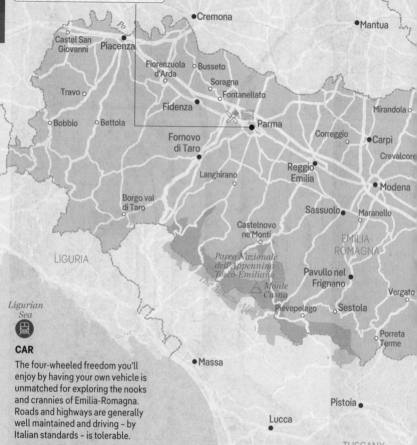

Parma, p368

With iconic gastronomy, spectacular religious sights and a rich and historic devotion to opera, posh Parma stocks a trifecta of Italian greatness within its *centro storico* (historic centre).

Ferrara, p384

One of Emilia-Romagna's most prominent unsung heroes, bike-addicted Ferrara is a small and manageable living museum of both the medieval and Renaissance eras.

CAR

The four-wheeled freedom you'll enjoy by having your own vehicle is unmatched for exploring the nooks and crannies of Emilia-Romagna. Roads and highways are generally well maintained and driving – by Italian standards – is tolerable.

BUS

Buses are particularly useful in the Apennines around Parco Nazionale dell' Appennino Tosco-Emiliano and Castelnovo ne' Monti (and to a certain extent, Brisighella). Elsewhere they certainly exist, but most people opt for the train.

TRAIN

Trains are Italy's most popular mode of transport and Emilia-Romagna is no exception. Bologna, Ferrara, Modena, Parma, Ravenna and Rimini (along with Reggio Emilia) are all serviced by both high-speed train and regional trains.

Find Your Way

Emilia-Romagna is Italy's sixth-largest region by area, inserted between a series of natural wonders – the Po Delta, the Apennine mountains and the Adriatic Sea. Our selections exemplify the region's greatest hits.

Ravenna, p396

Another of the region's criminally under-visited gems, Ravenna offers some of the world's most beautiful Early Christian mosaic art and a wonderful, less crowded seaside.

Bologna, p368

Emilia-Romagna's capital is one of Italy's best cities to eat, a vibrant medieval city and intellectual and political powerhouse lined with immensely pretty, Unesco-listed porticoes.

Rimini, p390

A wildly popular Adriatic seaside resort with a fascinating ancient core, Rimini shines both as a sun-soaked holiday destination and a cultural attaché for the Roman Empire.

VENETO

Po

Copparo

Ferrara

Cento

an Giovanni
Persiceto

Comacchio

Porto
Garibaldi

Argenta

Bologna

Conselice

Marina di
Ravenna

asso
Marconi

Lugo

Russi

Ravenna

Imola

Faenza

Cervia

Brisighella

Bellaria

Forlì

Igea Marina

Adriatic Sea

Cesena

Savignano sul
Rubicone

Rimini

*Parco Nazionale delle
Foreste Casentinesi,
Monte Falterona
e Campigna*

SAN
MARINO

Riccione

Cattolica

*Monte
Falterona*

SAN
MARINO

Pesaro

Bagno di
Romagna

LE MARCHE

Florence

UMBRIA

0 50 km
0 25 miles

365

Plan Your Time

Emilia-Romagna warrants pumping the brakes a bit. From the Apennines to the Adriatic, famed gastronomy, celebrated supercars, and Unesco-listed art and architecture await.

Basilica di San Vitale, Ravenna (p396)

VISUAL INTERMEZZO/SHUTTERSTOCK ©

If You Only Do One Thing

● Marvel at the intricate beauty of Italy's most gorgeous mosaics in **Ravenna** (p396). Spend the morning gazing at the rich greens, brilliant golds and deep blues of the mosaics bathed in soft sunlight inside **Basilica di San Vitale** (p396), ogle Ravenna's oldest mosaics at **Mausoleo di Galla Placidia** (p398), and try to tear your eyes away from the 26 white-robed mosaic martyrs dating from from the year 560 CE inside **Basilica di Sant'Apollinare Nuovo** (p398).

● Lunch on the region's famed cuisine at **Cucina del Condominio** and spend the afternoon on the beach or exploring **Museo Arcivescovile** (p398) and **Battistero Neoniano** (p399). End the day with craft beers at **Darsenale** (p396).

Seasonal highlights

Spring and autumn bring ideal temperatures for alfresco dining, mountain hikes or beach lazing. Avoid August – many bars, restaurants and shops close (Rimini notwithstanding).

MARCH
Bologna shows signs of life as it breaks out of its tortellini-fuelled winter slumber; spring colours illuminate the **Po Delta** sunrises and sunsets.

APRIL
Motor Valley buzzes with motorsport aficionados when Formula 1's **Emilia Romagna Grand Prix** usually rides in to nearby Imola.

MAY
Brisighella's short but sweet artichoke season lures foodies. The **Sagra del Carciofo Moretto** festival celebrates this unique local delicacy.

A Few Days to Play With

● Hit the ground running in **Bologna** (p368), where a cavalcade of Italy's most famous dishes await. Between meals, enjoy the medieval centre, including its Unesco-listed porticoes, the captivating **Casa di Lucio Dalla** (p372), the labyrinthine **Basilica di Santo Stefano** (p368) and the intimate **San Colombano – Collezione Tagliavini** (p372) museum of musical instruments. It's an easy train ride to **Modena** (p375) for one of Italy's best-preserved Romanesque cathedrals. Next, **Motor Valley** (p376) beckons: car lovers can't miss the factory tours and museums at **Maserati** (p376) and **Museo Enzo Ferrari** (p376) in town and **Museo Ferrari** (p376) in nearby Maranello. Finish off admiring the captivating Early Christian mosaics in **Ravenna** (p396).

A Week to See It All

● Begin based in **Bologna** (p368), strolling under the graceful porticoes and indulging in fabled gastronomy between short train rides through the region. Rev your engines among the world's most iconic supercars in **Motor Valley** (p376) around Bologna and **Modena** (p375). In **Parma** (p377), pamper yourself with an early-evening aperitivo among spectacular religious sights and world-renowned ham and cheese. Cycle around the muscular medieval walls of Renaissance beauty **Ferrara** (p384). Marvel at the gorgeous mosaics in **Ravenna** (p396), with a detour to gaze at the pristinely preserved medieval village of **Brisighella** (p401) from castle-topped mountains. Cap things off by discovering Roman treasures and beachside pleasures in **Rimini** (p390).

JUNE	JULY	SEPTEMBER	OCTOBER
Sotto le Stelle del Cinema – evening films shown on Europe's largest projection – packs Piazza Maggiore in Bologna for 50 nights.	Toasty temperatures make for perfect **beach weather** in Ravenna and Rimini before August brings high prices and crowded sands.	While Parma celebrates the **Festival del Prosciutto di Parma**, hikers make their way to Parco Nazionale dell'Appennino Tosco-Emiliano.	The **Tour-tlen** festival sees two dozen local chefs reinterpreting tortellini; **white-truffle season** begins in Savigno.

BOLOGNA

Bologna

Rome

Fusing haughty elegance with down-to-earth grit in one beautifully colonnaded medieval grid, Bologna is a city of two intriguing halves. One side is a hard-working, high-tech city located in the super-rich Po valley, where suave operagoers waltz out of regal theatres and into some of the nation's finest restaurants. The other is a bolshie, politically edgy city that hosts the world's oldest university and is famous for its graffiti-embellished piazzas filled with mildly inebriated students swapping Gothic fashion tips.

No wonder Bologna has earned so many historical monikers. La Grassa (The Fat One) celebrates a rich food legacy (*ragù*... erm...*bolognese* sauce was first concocted here). La Dotta (The Learned One) doffs a cap to the city university founded in 1088. La Rossa (The Red One) alludes to the ubiquity of the medieval terracotta buildings adorned with miles of porticoes, as well as the city's long-standing penchant for left-wing politics.

TOP TIP

Head up the newly opened 13th-century clock tower at Palazzo Comunale instead of the overcrowded Torre degli Asinelli. It's less busy, way easier to climb and offers a better view. The ticket includes entrance to the Collezioni Comunali d'Arte.

WHY I LOVE BOLOGNA

Kevin Raub, writer

Bologna was the first Italian city I ever visited back in 2007 and today it's home. It's very easy to sing the praises of its gastronomic landscape, its musical history, its medieval architecture or the forward-thinking vibrancy that comes with being home to the oldest continually operating university in the world, but why I love it is simpler. Bologna is big enough, but not too big. Bologna is touristy, but not too touristy. Bologna's dining, nightlife and cultural scenes offer plenty, but not too much. Bologna is just right.

A Medieval Marvel

LEANING TOWERS, MEDIEVAL PALAZZI

The foundations of Bologna's forward-thinking ethos, cultural greatness and left-leaning politics were laid in the Middle Ages. Home to the world's oldest continually operating university, founded in 1088, the city welcomed great medieval minds from far and wide – Dante, Copernicus, Petrarch – and prosperity followed.

On this day tour, all roads lead to pivotal 13th-century **Piazza Maggiore** dominated by **Basilica di San Petronio**, Europe's sixth-largest church. On the western flank is **Palazzo Comunale** (Palazzo d'Accursio), home to the Bologna city council since 1336 and the **Collezioni Comunali d'Arte**, a collection of 13th- to 19th-century paintings, sculptures and furniture. Head up the attached 13th-century clock tower for panoramic views of the city, including the symbol of Bologna: the leaning 97.2m-high **Torre degli Asinelli** and its shorter, off-limits neighbour, **Torre Garisenda**, which sit side-by-side 450m east of the main square along Via Rizzoli. During the Middles Ages, over 100 towers kissed the sky within the city walls – only 22 survive today. The climb up Asinelli, booked via the Bologna Welcome tourism office, is not for the faint of heart. Finally, there's **Basilica di Santo Stefano**, Bologna's most unique religious site, a labyrinth of interlocking ecclesiastical structures dating back to the 11th century whose architecture incorporates Romanesque, Lombard and even ancient Roman elements.

Wind down with a glass of whatever is pouring at divey **Osteria del Sole** in the city's medieval market area – a notorious wine bar at it since 1465.

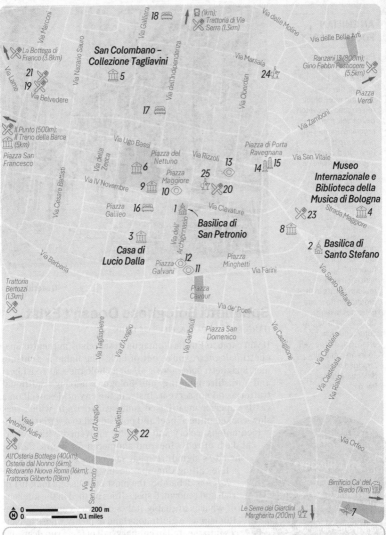

AN EMILIAN FOOD ODYSSEY

Emilia-Romagna's best and most popular guided food tour is a one-day deep dive into three of the region's most coveted delicacies: *parmigiano reggiano* (Parmesan), *prosciutto di Parma* (dry-cured Parma ham) and *aceto balsamico* (balsamic vinegar). These fascinating (and delicious) tours generally visit a *caseificio* (dairy); an *acetaia*, where balsamic vinegar is produced and aged; and a *prosciuttificio* (prosciutto producer), with each stop featuring visits to the production floor and generous tastings. Despite the latter, an outrageous lunch is often included as well. Tours are generally arranged out of Bologna, Modena and Parma.

VIVIDA PHOTO PC/SHUTTERSTOCK ©

Quadrilatero

STILL HUNGRY?

Head to **Parma** (p377), another of Emilia-Romagna's wondrous culinary landscapes and home to *parmigiano reggiano* (Parmesan) and *prosciutto di Parma* DOP, two more of the region's world-renowned specialities.

Spaghetti Bolognese Doesn't Exist

HAND-ROLLED PASTA, PILES OF PORK

If you came to Emilia-Romagna in search of 'authentic' spaghetti *bolognese*, you're out of luck. The name is a misnomer. Spaghetti *bolognese* is about as Bolognese as roast beef and Yorkshire pudding, and Bologna's fiercely traditional trattorias do not serve it. Instead, the city prides itself on a vastly superior meat-based sauce called *ragù*, which sees slow-cooked minced beef and pork added to a *soffritto* (sautéed onions, celery and carrots), enlivened with a liberal dash of red wine, and simmered for hours. Calling the city's signature meat sauce 'spaghetti *bolognese*' is like calling Champagne 'fizzy wine'.

Ragù is debatably the most famous of a long list of rich and renowned specialities birthed in the kitchens of what is arguably Italy's culinary capital, Emilia-Romagna – a gluttonous land of plenty whose inductees into the Italian culinary hall of fame run deep and wide and tall. Lasagne, tortellini, *mortadella*, *gramigna con salsiccia* (pasta with sausage *ragù*), *passatelli* (pasta made with breadcrumbs, eggs and Parmesan) and

WHERE TO DRINK IN BOLOGNA

Ruggine
Locally driven craft mixology near Piazza Maggiore: housemade shrubs, Venetian aperitifs, Romagnan brandies.

Caffè Rubik
Bohemian pop-art coffee bar; the Amaro selection is the city's best.

Le Serre dei Giardini Margherita
One of Bologna's best alfresco drinking dens in the formerly abandoned city greenhouses.

cotoletta alla bolognese (fried veal cutlet topped with prosciutto and Parmesan) all hail from here. Naturally, Bologna is a wonderful place to eat.

At last count, Bologna's city centre was home to a head-spinning 700-plus restaurants and, while you can't really go wrong at any of them, a more insidery culinary adventure awaits just outside the city's historic gates. At **Trattoria Bertozzi** locals in the know, food experts from far and wide, and Bologna FC super fans gather to indulge in authentic local specialities. The antics of loud and brash partners Alessandro (kitchen) and Fabio (wine, socialising) only up the ante on this authentic Bolognese experience. Make this your first meal in Bologna.

The next morning, walk off the calories around the city's old food market, a squared grid of narrow lanes just off the southeast corner of Piazza Maggiore known as the **Quadrilatero**. Follow your senses as you navigate a parade of freshly shaped tortelloni stuffed with ricotta, mountains of thinly sliced *mortadella* and buckets of slow-cooked *ragù*. For a deeper dive into local kitchens, get cooking with **Cesarine**, a national private cooking class network born in Bologna offering wonderful opportunities to learn the city's signature dishes inside the homes of local culinarians.

For a truly authentic Bolognese experience, it's well worth renting a car and heading into the surrounding hillsides, known as the *colli bolognesi*. Fiercely local trattorias pepper the landscape, often with pastoral views across the surrounding countryside (and Bologna in the distance). At travel-worthy destination restaurants like **Nuova Roma**, **Osteria dal Nonno** and **Trattoria Gilberto**, locals devour platters of *mortadella*, *prosciutto di Parma* DOP, local *salume* and farmstead cheeses sandwiched between *crescentine* (fried squares of dough) and *tigelle* (baked round bread) – with nary a tourist in sight!

The Sound of Music

EXTINCT INSTRUMENTS, SURPRISING ARTEFACTS

Bologna's status as a world-renowned culinary destination is no secret; a little lesser-known detail about the city is its exceptional musical pedigree both past and present. In addition to an outstanding contemporary music scene (Bologna's finest include legendary singer-songwriter Lucio Dalla, groundbreaking Italian hip-hop act Sangue Misto and current chart-topper Cesare Cremonini), the city was crowned a Unesco Creative City of Music in 2006.

A DAY OFF IN BOLOGNA

Daniele Bendanti is the chef at Bologna's Oltre, one of the city's top modern trattorias. Here he shares his day off in the city. (@d.bendanti)

I can't miss a great breakfast at **Gino Fabbri Pasticcere** in La Caramella, a bit outside Bologna but worth it. I take a nice walk at **Giardini Margherita**, the city park that raised me. I eat something from Alessandro, my meat supplier at **Macelleria Agnoletto & Bignami**, and stop for two glasses of wine at the **Osteria del Sole**, where time seems to stand still. Towards evening, I cuddle up with a nice plate of *tagliatelle* at **All'Osteria Bottega**, where I worked as a chef for five years and to which I'm very attached.

 WHERE TO GO FOR MODERN MEALS IN BOLOGNA

Oltre	**Bottega di Franco**	**Ahimè**
Oltre (Beyond) bucks tradition with creative nightly specials, but doesn't forgo outstanding modern takes on classics. €€€	Book way ahead for this highly recommended restaurant inside a kitsch-filled farmhouse; modern takes on tradition. €€€	Michelin experience in daily changing small bites; try the mind-blowing Japanese mustard greens pesto. €€

Between meals, music fans should plan half a day for two fantastic museums. Head to **Museo Internazionale e Biblioteca della Musica di Bologna** inside Palazzo Sanguinetti and wander in awe of one of the most astonishing collections of musical artefacts in the world, including extinct instruments (cornets, chromatic harps, lutes, trumpet marine etc) and documents (manuals, sheets, notes, scores etc) curated from the lifelong collection of Giambattista Martini, considered a human Wikipedia of musical history. This humble friar single-handedly assembled the world's first encyclopedia of ancient musical knowledge with no money and no resources in the mid-18th century and is considered the father of maestros. Then head over to **San Colombano – Collezione Tagliavini**, where Chilean ancient music history specialist Catalina Vicens oversees a wonderful collection of over 80 musical instruments amassed by the late organist Luigi Tagliavini. Many of the assembled harpsichords, pianos and oboes date from the 1500s and, even more surprisingly, are still in full working order – ask Catalina to play them for you!

The Porticoes of Bologna

INNOVATIVE ARCHITECTURE, MEDIEVAL COLONNADES

Bologna's signature porticoes – lavished with Unesco World Heritage status in 2021 – began appearing in the 12th and 13th centuries to expand commercial and artisan activities and, eventually, to combat population growth due to an influx of students at the University of Bologna. By building roofs over the sidewalks, the city could extend space in the buildings above without building new structures. Today, Bologna's 62km of porticoes come in several incarnations: medieval wooden porticoes over buildings, Gothic and Renaissance porticoes integrated into buildings, 14th-century *beccadelli* (semi-porticoes without columns) and 19th-century porticoes featuring court architecture. They reach as high as nearly 10m, as narrow as 97cm and as long as 4km (the world's longest, Portico di San Luca, featuring some 664 arches).

Take a few hours and wander on the lookout for highlights: beautiful fossils trapped in the Veronese red stone used for Piazza Maggiore's **Portico del Pavaglione**, the city's most iconic; **Portico Via Farini**, featuring the vibrant 19th-century frescoes of Gaetano Lodi; the terracotta busts peering at passers-by along **Portico Palazzo Bolognini** in Piazza Santo Stefano. In the residential district of Barca, the

WHERE TO EAT TRADITIONAL IN BOLOGNA

Trattoria da Amerigo
Emilia-Romagna's best restaurant, a Michelin-starred trattoria in Savigno (30km west of Bologna). Casual, rustic. €€€

Trattoria di Via Serra
Flavio and Tommaso bridge classic Emilian and hilltop twists at this unassuming Bolognina trattoria. €€

Osteria al 15
Rustic, off-the-beaten-path *osteria* (tavern) that retains an air of Bolognese authenticity. €€

Portico Via Farini

snaking, 600m-long reinforced concrete edifice known as **Il Treno** represents the lone contemporary portico, an icon of postwar urbanism.

Reserve ahead for a meal at **All'Osteria Bottega** to enjoy the city's best Petroniana-style veal cutlets (topped with *prosciutto di Parma* and *parmigiano reggiano*) and other Slow Food delights under the **Portico Santa Caterina**.

BOLOGNA'S BEST BOUTIQUE HOTELS

Casa Isolani €
Good-value rooms, many with original details like terracotta ceilings and period furnishings, in two meticulously renovated historic residences with epic Bologna views.

Hotel Metropolitan €€
Top design choice; the 42-room Met mixes functionality with handsome modern furnishings and superior rooms upstairs surrounding a small courtyard with olive trees.

Grand Hotel Majestic €€€
Bologna's lone five-star choice, originally an 18th-century archiepiscopal seminary. Since 1912 its classic luxury has been appreciated by Sinatra, Princess Di and others.

GETTING AROUND

Bologna is compact – nearly all of the main sights are within walking distance of each other. Otherwise, TPER runs an efficient bus system.

Sant'Agata
Bolognese
Modena ● ● Argelato
San Cesario ● Bologna
sul Panaro

Beyond Bologna

World-renowned luxury sports cars are produced around Bologna and Modena, the latter also home to legendary cuisine and opera singers.

TOP TIP

Motor Valley factory tours must be booked in advance and they generally don't take place on weekends. Plan accordingly.

On the plains of the Po, just 43km west of Bologna, lies one of the nation's great gastronomic centres. Modena is the creative force behind real balsamic vinegar, giant tortellini stuffed with tantalising fillings, and sparkling Lambrusco wine. It boasts backstreets crammed with some of the best restaurants no one's heard of, and one, Osteria Francescana, that everybody's heard of – it was the first Italian restaurant to conquer the coveted 'World's 50 Best Restaurants' list. Modena shares another equally lauded legacy with Bologna: cars. Some of the fastest supercars in existence, including Ferrari, Maserati, Pagani, Lamborghini and Ducati, are forged here.

Mercato Albinelli, Modena

MASSIMO PARISI/SHUTTERSTOCK ©

Torre Ghirlandina, Modena (p376)

Made in Modena

CULINARY TRIUMPHS, ROMANESQUE ARCHITECTURE

If you're reading this after arriving in Modena (a half-hour train ride from Bologna) and you haven't already secured a reservation at superstar chef Massimo Bottura's fabled 12-table restaurant **Osteria Francescana**, you're probably out of luck. Unless, of course, you're staying at his wonderful countryside villa, **Casa Maria Luigia**, 7km east of Modena – the only route to a guaranteed reservation. But despite Bottura's reimagined Emilian fare being nearly single-handedly responsible for Modena's upgraded status on the Italian beaten path, this wonderful medieval city is an exercise in slow tourism. Ease up on the throttle, loosen your belt and let Modena captivate you for a day.

Start your day much like Bottura – with a wander through **Mercato Albinelli**, Emilia-Romagna's best covered food market, 200m south of the Unesco World Heritage–listed **Piazza Grande**. Here Modena's celebrated **Duomo** combines the austerity of the Dark Ages with throwback traditions from the Romans in Italy's finest example of a Romanesque church. Rising behind the cathedral is the early-13th-century

PAVAROTTI'S MODENA

Legendary tenor Luciano Pavarotti hailed from Modena and lived out his final years in a modest home prettily perched in the Modenese countryside 8.5km southeast of the city. Self-guided audio tours (40 minutes) in nine languages take visitors through **Casa Museo Luciano Pavarotti**, which was turned into a museum in 2015. Highlights of the tour include access to private areas like his bedroom and bathroom, his buttery-yellow kitchen and to personal letters from Frank Sinatra, Bono and Princess Di. Outside the **Teatro Comunale Luciano Pavarotti** in town, a life-sized bronze statue of Pavarotti was erected in 2017 (at the corner of Via Carlo Goldoni and Corso Canal Grande).

✄ WHERE TO EAT IN MODENA

Gelataria Bloom
The region's best gelato; its farm-to-table philosophy sees collaborations with farmers specialising in ancient fruits. €

Ristorante da Danilo
Modena's most outstanding dish – spinach-stuffed tortelloni with bacon cream sauce – is perfection here. €

Trattoria Ermes
Ermes died in 2022, but his legendary trattoria lives on. Outstanding takes on Emilian cuisine. €

Emilia-Romagna's Formula 1 raceway at **Imola**, 40km southeast of Bologna, is perhaps most widely known for tragedy – it was here at **Autodromo Enzo e Dino Ferrari** that F1 legend Ayrton Senna lost his life in 1994. The anti-clockwise raceway hosted the San Marino Grand Prix between 1981 and 2006; and returned to the F1 circuit in 2020 with the Emilia-Romagna Grand Prix. Today, it's worth a visit for self-drives in a Ferrari or Lamborghini, shuttle tours that let you walk on the track, and to catch a glimpse of the track's resident feline, **Formulino** (@Formulinotheking).

Formula 1 Raceway, Imola

87m **Torre Ghirlandina**, also part of the Unesco site. **Palazzo Ducale**, the baroque masterpiece that dominates the northeast end of Modena's historic centre, houses Italy's most prestigious military academy but worthwhile tours can be booked via the city's tourism office, Modenatur.

Walk off newly added calories browsing some of the region's best shops, including artisanal leather goods at **La Vacchetta Grassa** and Traditional Balsamic Vinegar of Modena DOP – worth its weight in gold at **La Consorteria 1966**.

Get Your Motor Runnin'!

LUXURY SUPERCARS, ITALIAN DESIGN

It hardly takes a car enthusiast to be wowed by the dizzying displays of history, high performance and stunning Italian design in the museums of Motor Valley, spread between the provinces of Bologna and Modena less than 45 minutes' drive from the cities. It takes a few days to see them all – there are no duds here.

In Bologna, **Museo Ducati** takes visitors on the top-end motorcycle brand's journey from vacuum tube and condenser beginnings to superbike. Ferrari offers a double dose of pilgrimage-worthy collections: the world-class **Museo Ferrari** at Maranello headquarters cradles the world's largest collection of Ferraris, while **Museo Enzo Ferrari** in Modena celebrates memorabilia of the founder. Lamborghini also splits inventories: **Mudetec** in Sant'Agata Bolognese is the showcase gallery focusing on history and innovation, while Argelato's **Museo Ferrucio Lamborghini** is a mesmerising 9000 sq metres of family heirlooms: helicopters, tractors and legendary cars.

For car buffs looking for the Holy Grail of supercar fandom, factory tours await. Peeking behind the curtain on a production-line tour at **Automobili Lamborghini** in Sant'Agata Bolognese is a hypnotic glimpse into a fantastically oiled machine. Deep dives into hand-built engines and the new MC20 production line dazzle at **Maserati** in Modena. But **Museo Horacio Pagani** in San Cesario sul Panaro, which produces just 40 supercars per year, is the stuff of motorsport dreams. Each piece of €1.3 to €2.5 million motorised fine art is astonishingly assembled by hand – seeing the action up close and personal is as good as it gets for connoisseurs.

GETTING AROUND

Walking and cycling are preferred methods of transport in Modena, but you'll want wheels to fully embrace Motor Valley.

PARMA

Parma

Rome

If reincarnation ever becomes an option, pray you come back as a *parmense*. Where else can you cycle to work through streets virtually devoid of cars, lunch on fresh-from-the-attic prosciutto and aged *parmigiano reggiano*, quaff crisp Lambrusco wine in art nouveau cafes, and spend sultry summer evenings listening to classical music in architecturally dramatic opera houses?

Starting from its position as one of Italy's most prosperous cities, Parma has every right to feel smug. This city helped give rise to a world-renowned composer called Verdi, an incalculably influential conductor named Toscanini, and enough ham and cheese to start a deli chain. The historic sights of the city and its surrounds, most notably the stunning baptistry from 1196 and Magnifico Pier Maria Rossi's impressive Castello di Torrechiara, are often touted as archetypes of Italian architecture.

Though the city is Emilia-Romagna's second-largest, locals joke that it's little more than a sizeable village, at once both regal and rustic.

TOP TIP

If you've come for *parmigiano reggiano* (Parmesan), you've come to the right place! The traditional version, made from Holstein cow milk, is everywhere, but look out for the rarer Vacche Rosse version, made from the milk of Reggio's red cows.

Parma from the Inside Out

DRAMATIC ART, STORYBOOK ARCHITECTURE

From its historic core and out to the countryside, Parma offers a protean pedigree for the quintessential Italian experience over a day or two. Begin at the stately **Piazza del Duomo**, where the *duomo* of the **Cattedrale di Santa Maria Assunta** (Lombard-Romanesque facade, baroque interiors) is decorated with Antonio da Correggio's *Assunzione della Vergine* (*Assumption of the Virgin*), a kaleidoscopic swirl of cherubs and whirling angels. The attached 63m-tall bell tower is topped by a replica gilded angel (the original, struck by lightning in 2009, resides at the piazza's **Museo Diocesano**). The octagonal pink-marble **Battistero**, one of the most important such structures in Italy, is richly coloured with 13th-century Byzantine frescoes and contains a fascinating set of figures representing the months, seasons and signs of the zodiac. Half a kilometre east of Piazza del Duomo, the monumental **Palazzo della Pilotta** houses the **Galleria Nazionale**, **Museo Archeologico Nazionale** and **Teatro Farnese**. The latter, the complex's highlight, is a rebuilt Renaissance theatre made almost entirely out of wood.

One of Emilia-Romagna's most storybook castles, **Castello di Torrechiara**, rises from the countryside 20km south of Piazza del Duomo. Built between 1448 and 1460, its five massive, extraordinarily preserved square towers highlight one of the most important examples of Italian castle

DINING IN PARMA

Maria Anedda, a *parmense* chef, culinary consultant and once-participant in *Top Chef Italia*.
(@maria.anedda)

Parma...the Unesco Creative City of Gastronomy. From local products to culinary art, it's all about food. Stop at **Ó Bistrot** for a classy breakfast in elegant surroundings. Have a quick lunch at **Pepén** as all the locals love to do. Don't miss a gelato at **La Gelateria**. Head down to **Via Farini** for some drinks, street food and bustling life. You can easily move out of town for a peaceful dinner in the countryside at **Ristorante Romani**.

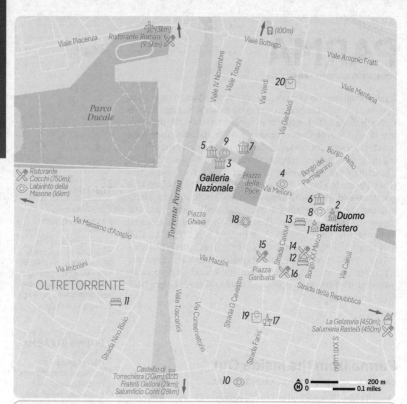

 WHERE TO SLEEP IN PARMA

B&B Pio
Location, comfort and hospitality come together at this B&B whose owner has a passion for local food and wine. €

Al Ducale
Giovanni is a consummate host at this Oltretorrente choice, popular with composers, actors and singers. €

Palazzo dalla Rosa Prati
Kick back like Marie Antoinette in regal digs right next to Parma's cathedral. €€€

Teatro Regio

OPERA IN PARMA

Parma is one of Italy's storied places to see live opera. Though it's not as immediately recognisable as La Scala (Milan) or La Fenice (Venice), the city's **Teatro Regio** is a top-notch venue for world-class performances. Inaugurated in 1829 at the request of Napoleon's wife, Duchess Maria Luigia of Habsburg-Lorraine, the neoclassical venue features interiors embellished with gilded stucco and a painted ceiling (and curtain) by Giovan Battista Borghesi. The best time of year to go is during the internationally renowned **Festival Verdi**, which takes place annually in late September and early October.

architecture. Its stunning interior fresco, Benedetto Bembo's *Camera d'Oro*, is Italy's only medieval painting glorifying courtly love between two royals to survive in its entirety.

In Pursuit of Prosciutto

SACRED CHARCUTERIE, FINE WINES

Along with Bologna and Modena, Parma forms an Emilian culinary triumvirate from which some of the most legendary Italian gifts to world gastronomy hail. Parma, however, is the only one whose culinary landscape has achieved Unesco status. Numerous speciality food shops (known as *salumerias*) around the city centre feature hocks of ham hanging from the rafters, each aged for a minimum of 400 days to 36 months. This is the coveted *prosciutto di Parma* (Parma ham), a hallmark of this Unesco Creative City of Gastronomy.

To sample the goods, head to **Salumeria Garibaldi**, a bountiful delicatessen dating to 1829, with dangling sausages, shelves of Lambrusco wines, slabs

LOOKING FOR RENAISSANCE DRAMA?

Teatro Farnese was inspired by Andrea Palladio's stunning **Teatro Olimpico** (p357) in Vicenza (Veneto). Along with Teatro all'Antica in Sabbioneta (Lombardy), these are Italy's only surviving theatres from the Renaissance (though Farnese was mostly destroyed in WWII).

 WHERE TO EAT IN PARMA

Pepèn
Prepare to battle the throngs of locals for a bite of Parma's most famous *panini*. €

Borgo 20
Consistently innovative bistro taking Km0 DOC products to new heights. The Parmesan-laced risotto is memorable. €€

Ristorante Cocchi
Behold this traditional Parmigiano experience untainted by the city's influx of culinary tourism. €€

CORREGGIO'S INAUGURAL COMMISSION

Renaissance master painter Antonio da Correggio's first artistic commission in Parma was closed off to the public for two centuries, but today the **Camera di San Paolo** inside the restored former monastery of the same name is welcoming visitors. The fresco, inside the private vault apartment of the monastery's 1520 abbess, is an illusionistic painting simulating a pergola opening to the sky. Considered a masterpiece of Italian High Renaissance art, it features 16 segments, each with an oval *trompe l'œil* opening revealing playfully posed *putti* (cherubs) with dogs, bows and arrows, hunting gear and trophies.

FEELING PECKISH?

You've come to the right region! Emilia-Romagna is Italy's gastronomic overachiever. To devour more of the region's famed specialities, head to the capital **Bologna** (p368), where layers of lasagne and tables of tortellini await!

of Parma ham and wheel upon wheel of *parmigiano reggiano* just steps from the train station, or the Strada della Republica location of **Salumeria Rastelli**. Both can set you up with charcuterie boards best washed down with local wines from the Colli di Parma. To pick up picnic provisions, **La Prosciutteria**, Silvano Romani's temple of swine, is one of Parma's absolute best for cured meats. For a more old-school bar atmosphere, **Enoteca Fontana** is a fantastic spot to mingle with locals over exquisitely curated wines and *taglieri di salumi* (charcuterie boards).

For a deeper dive into the art of prosciutto, many producers open their doors to visitors. Two of the best around Parma are **Salumificio Conti** and **Fratelli Galloni** (28km and 21km south of Parma, respectively), the latter pairing prosciutto with fine countryside views.

Lost in the Labyrinth

EXTRAORDINARY ART, A LEGACY LABYRINTH

The opening of the world's largest maze in 2015 fulfilled a lifetime dream of publisher and art collector Franco Maria Ricci, who published what many considered to be the most beautiful art magazine in the world, *FMR*, from 1982 to 2004. The soft-cover quarterly publication was more or less the prototype for the modern coffee-table book, paving the way for Taschen and others. Ricci passed away in 2020, the year before *FMR* resumed publishing. His 7-hectare bamboo **Labirinto della Masone** in Fontanellato, 17km west of Parma in the countryside, is perhaps Emilia-Romagna's quirkiest unmissable attraction. Unfortunately, you'll need personal transport to reach the park (a taxi from central Parma is around €20). Kids and adults alike love getting lost en route to an interior courtyard – set aside an hour – which includes two luxury suites (€500 per night).

In addition to the maze, Ricci's extraordinary personal art collection, amassed over 50 years, includes myriad Napoleonic busts, mannerist works, paintings spanning the 16th to 19th centuries, original illustrations of Luigi Serafini's *Codex Seraphinianus*, a wooden model of Milan's Duomo, countless *FMR* magazine covers, and a thoroughly fascinating room devoted to morbid 17th-century still-life vanitas.

GETTING AROUND

You won't need a car to visit Parma's most notable attractions within the *centro storico*, but getting out into the surrounding countryside will be far more efficient with a car (though TEP buses do reach some locations).

Beyond Parma

Verdi country – the stomping ground of famed composer Guiseppe Verdi – and the Apennine mountains beckon not far from Parma.

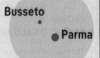

During the 'golden age of opera' in the second half of the 19th century, only Wagner came close to emulating Giuseppe Verdi, Italy's operatic genius who was born in the tiny village of Roncole Verdi, 38km northwest of Parma, back in 1813. Today, you can discover his extraordinary legacy starting in the town of Busseto (35km northwest of Parma), a pleasant place imbued with history and endowed with some good cafes and restaurants.

Parma also makes for a decent base to set off for Parco Nazionale dell'Appennino Tosco-Emiliano, one of Italy's newer national parks. It can be reached from the village of Castelnovo ne' Monti, 58km southeast of Parma in Reggio Emilia province.

TOP TIP

From Castelnovo ne' Monti, you can walk or taxi 3km to Parco Nazionale dell'Appennino Tosco-Emiliano's surreal Pietra di Bismantova.

Pietra di Bismantova (p383)

GIORGIO MORARA/SHUTTERSTOCK ©

©IMAS/SHUTTERSTOCK ®

Teatro Verdi

MICHELIN-STARRED SALUME

The only cold cut more coveted than *prosciutto di Parma* in these parts is the region's famed *culatello di Zibello*, a protected designation of origin (PDO) *salume* with origins around Busseto. The one-star Michelin **Antica Corte Pallavicina**, 7.5km southwest of Busseto, is a detour-worthy hotel/restaurant where this regional delicacy reigns supreme. Here, 5000 of the world's very best *salumi* hang alongside name cards of their owners (King Charles III, Monaco's Prince Albert II) inside a 14th-century castle often enveloped in cinematic Po river fog. Best advice: go hog wild here on top-of-the-line *culatello di suico nero di Parma* (made from the free-range black pigs) and thank us later.

Of Music & Masterpieces

STATELY VILLAS AND OPERAS

Names don't get any more grandiose in the opera world than Italian composer Guiseppe Verdi. Over a half-decade career, he composed more than 25 operas, many of which remain the most widely produced in the world today, including *Rigoletto, La Traviata, Aida* and *Otello*. A day-long visit to Verdi country, a 40-minute train ride from Parma, is an unmissable excursion for fans of the genre but Verdi's weight and might will be of equal interest to music fans, history buffs and Italophiles alike.

Start off in the centre of Busseto at **Teatro Verdi**. This tiny (but stately and gorgeous) theatre on the aptly named Piazza Verdi was built in 1868, although Verdi himself initially dismissed the idea. It opened with a performance of his masterpiece *Rigoletto*. Don't miss the opportunity to see a Verdi opera here during the annual **Festival Verdi** in October. Also in town is the **Museo Nazionale Giuseppe Verdi**, a fine country mansion turned museum that cleverly maps out the story of Verdi's life through paintings, music and audio guides.

 WHERE TO SLEEP AND EAT IN BUSSETO

I Due Foscari
Twenty old-fashioned rooms with simple wooden accents along with a restaurant and a *cantina* (winery). €

Salsamenteria Storica e Verdiana Baratta
A storied Busseto hot spot for charcuterie and cheese plates chased with local wines. €

Trattoria Vernizzi
A few kilometres east of Busseto, this lost-in-time trattoria offers a verbal menu of rustic local specialities. €

But it was Verdi's 56-room villa, located a few kilometres northwest of town, where Italy's greatest composer made the magic happen. He lived and worked at **Villa Verdi** from 1851 onwards and literally willed it to remain the same as he left it, with a fascinating array of furniture, personal artefacts and art, just as it was the day he passed away in 1901.

Adventures in the Apennines

MOUNTAIN ADVENTURES, DRAMATIC INSELBERGS

In the late 1980s Italy had half a dozen national parks. Today it has 25. One of the newer additions is **Parco Nazionale dell'Appennino Tosco-Emiliano**, a 260-sq-km parcel of land that straddles the border between Tuscany and Emilia-Romagna. Running along the spine of the Apennine mountains, the park is notable for its hiking potential, extensive beech forests and small population of wolves. In 2015 it achieved Unesco's Man and Biosphere Reserve status.

While more often associated with Reggio Emilia rather than Parma, the jumping-off point for the park, the village of **Castelnovo ne' Monti**, is just a 1¼-hour drive from Parma, making it a sensible expedition for outdoor enthusiasts from there as well. The park offers a wealth of hiking and climbing options, including at least seven or so organised Club Alpino Italiano paths. Day-hikers can scale the highlight of the region, the imposing **Pietra di Bismantova** (1047m), a stark limestone outcrop visible for miles around – it's popular with climbers and weekend walkers. The Italian Alpine Club has carved a 5km loop up and back from Piazzale Dante (the parking lot in front of Foresteria San Benedetto), about 4km south of Castelnovo ne' Monti. The striking mountain was alluded to as a stepping stone to purgatory in Dante Alighieri's *Divina Commedia*.

APPENINE HIKES

Of the Parco Nazionale dell'Appennino Tosco-Emiliano's many majestic peaks, the highest is **Monte Cusna** (2121m), easily scalable from the village of Civago, near the Tuscan border, on a path (*sentiero* No 605) that passes the region's best mountain hut, the **Rifugio Cesare Battisti**. The *rifugio* sits alongside one of Italy's great long-distance walking trails: the three-week, 375km-long **Grande Escursione Appenninica (GEA)**, which bisects the park in five stages from Passo della Forbici (near the *rifugio*) up to its termination point just outside the park's northwest corner in Montelungo. Sections of the GEA can be done as day walks.

 GETTING AROUND

Trains (change in Fidenza) and buses reach Busseto from Parma, but you'll need a car to explore the Apennines.

FERRARA

Ferrara

Rome

A heavyweight Renaissance art city peppered with colossal palaces and still ringed by its intact medieval walls, Ferrara jumps out at you like an absconded Casanova (he once stayed here) on the route between Bologna and Venice. But, like any city situated close to La Serenissima ('The Most Serene', ie the Venetian Republic), it is serially overlooked, despite its Unesco World Heritage status. As a result, Venice avoiders will find Ferrara's bike-friendly streets and frozen-in-time *palazzi* relatively unexplored and deliciously tranquil.

Historically, Ferrara was the domain of the powerful Este clan, rivals to Florence's Medic, who endowed the city with its signature building – a huge castle complete with moat slap-bang in the city centre. Ferrara suffered damage from bombing raids during WWII, but its historical core remains intact. Of particular interest is the former Jewish ghetto, the region's largest and oldest, which prevailed from 1627 until 1859.

TOP TIP

For a lesser-seen view of Ferrara's main square, Piazza Trento Trieste, head into the Libraccio bookshop inside Palazzo di San Crispino. From the 1st floor, you can admire a beautiful view of the south side of the Duomo and Palazzo Municipale.

A TALE OF TWO CITIES

Ferrara is famed for its position as a Renaissance stomping ground of the artistic and intellectual elite, but its wonderfully preserved medieval old town, south of Castello Estense, is something to see in its own right. You can't miss the stunning **Loggia dei Merciai** along Piazza Trento Trieste, but deeper into the notably more clustered district, a wealth of Middle Age might reveals itself. Don't miss **Via delle Volte**, which features numerous elevated passages (known as *volte* or vaults) that connected merchants' houses (on the south side) to their warehouses (on the north side).

Treasures of Corso Ercole I d'Este

RENAISSANCE PALAZZI, TITANIC CASTLES

Ferrara's historical importance is intrinsically linked with the Renaissance – intellectuals and artists of all ilk flocked here in the 15th and 16th centuries. The works of artists such as Piero della Francesca, Jacopo Bellini and Andrea Mantegna adorn the palaces of the House of Este, the dynasty responsible for flipping Ferrara into a city of international esteem. Today, the Biagio Rossetti–designed **Corso Ercole I d'Este**, the pivotal artery of Ferrara's Erculean Addition, is considered a masterpiece of Renaissance urban planning and is a part of the Unesco World Heritage–listed city centre.

The Corso begins from the dominating **Castello Estense**. Complete with a moat and drawbridge, the towering castle was commissioned by Nicolò II d'Este in 1385 (it's due to close in 2023 for multi-year renovations). Follow the Corso 500m north to **Quadrivio degli Angeli**, where a treasure trove of richly decorated Renaissance architecture intersects: the **Palazzo Turchi di Bagno**, **Palazzo Prosperi-Sacrati**, **Palazzo Strozzi Bevilacqua** and **Palazzo dei Diamanti**. Inside the latter, **Pinacoteca Nazionale**

 WHERE TO STAY IN FERRARA

Le Stanze di Torcicoda	Alchimia B&B	Albergo Annunziata
Four rooms in a late-14th-century *cassero* (medieval house) down a crooked lane in Ferrara's old Jewish quarter. €	Classy B&B occupying a remodelled 15th-century home with a spacious backyard. Six rooms, three apartments. €€	Six of the sharp modernist rooms at this top-notch 27-room four-star offer direct views of Castello Estense. €€

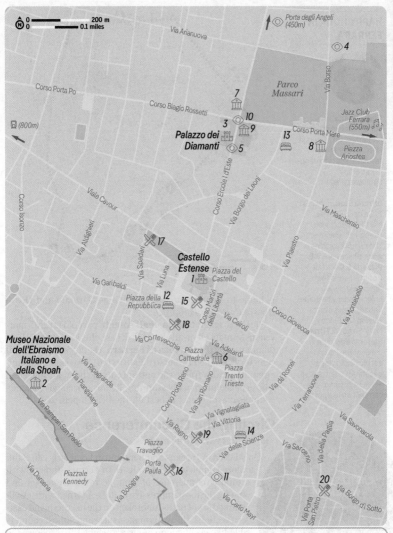

HIGHLIGHTS
1 Castello Estense
2 Museo Nazionale dell'Ebraismo Italiano e della Shoah
3 Palazzo dei Diamanti

SIGHTS
4 Certosa di Ferrara
5 Corso Ercole I d'Este

6 Loggia dei Merciai
7 Palazzo Prosperi-Sacrati
8 Palazzo Strozzi Bevilacqua
9 Palazzo Turchi di Bagno
(see 3) Pinacoteca Nazionale

10 Quadrivio degli Angeli
11 Via delle Volte

SLEEPING
12 Albergo Annunziata
13 Alchimia B&B
14 Le Stanze di Torcicoda

EATING
15 Birraria Giori
16 Me Pizzeria & Cocktail Room
17 Take Eat Easy
18 Tiffany Ristorantino
19 Trattoria da Noemi
20 Trattoria le Nuvole

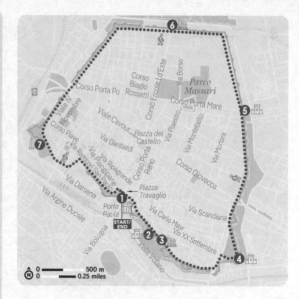

CASTLES CALLING YOUR NAME?

Head to Parma, whose **Castello di Torrechiara** (p377) is often held up as one of Italy's archetypical examples of citadel architecture.

is home to Renaissance riches such as Garofalo and Dosso Dossi's *Costabili Polyptych*.

The Corso ends at **Porta degli Angeli**, part of Ferrara's marvellously intact city wall – one block east, this stretch is entirely dominated by the **Certosa di Ferrara**, the city's monumental cemetery designed by Borso d'Este in 1461. Two snaking, semi-circular arcades frame the entrance to the open-air museum, whose peaceful, visually stunning Renaissance-style grounds count as one of Ferrara's best off-the-beaten-path gems.

Circling the Circumference

ANCIENT CITY WALLS BY BIKE

Only Lucca in Tuscany and Bergamo in Lombardy can claim a more complete set of walls than Ferrara, though with a total circumference of 9km, Ferrara's are longer and among the most impressive in Italy. Adorned with a well-marked set of paths, unbroken on the northern and eastern sections, the walls make a pleasant, almost countryside-like cycling loop along a greenbelt that follows the path of the former moat.

Begin and end at **1 Porta Paola** in the southwest of the city. A small museum here chronicles the history of Ferrara's walls. The **2 Baluardo di San Pietro** is visible, its spade-

WHERE TO EAT IN FERRARA

Take Eat Easy
Fantastic gourmet street-food stand doing traditional with occasional twists. Craft beer and wine. Reserve ahead! €

Trattoria da Noemi
Book ahead for some of the city's best *cappellacci di zucca* (pumpkin-stuffed pasta), grilled meats and macaroni pie. €€

Trattoria le Nuvole
Crafty-chic seafood superstar lit by candlelight tucked away in the medieval quarter. €€€

shaped fortification once considered the most innovative defence system in Europe. **3 Porta di San Pietro** marks the entryway into the oldest part of Ferrara, where a Byzantine military encampment marking the city's beginnings once stood to fend off the Lombards. North of **4 Baluardo della Montagna**, the path becomes more park-like, with groomed shrubbery, benches and well-maintained green spaces. You'll pass over two *doccili*, small channels added during the Renaissance to carry sewage out of the city. North of **5 Torrione di San Giovanni**, you'll ride on the tree-lined earthen wall just west of the original fortification added during the Erculean Addition as a second line of defence. Don't miss **6 Porta degli Angeli**, which has been closed since 1598 when the Este clan left Ferrara for good. The city's southwest corner was once dominated by a huge pentagonal fortress, Cittadella di Paolo V, demolished in 1859 – only a few external walls and a modest **7 Statue of Pope Paolo V** remain today.

A Moment in MEIS

POIGNANT ITALIAN-JEWISH HISTORY

Like Berlin's Memorial to the Murdered Jews of Europe or Atlanta's National Center for Civil and Human Rights, Ferrara's **Museo Nazionale dell'Ebraismo Italiano e della Shoah** (MEIS; National Museum of Italian Judaism and the Shoah) shakes you to your core. Born by an Italian parliamentary decree to create a National Holocaust Museum, MEIS opened in 2017 in the renovated buildings of Ferrara's 1900s prison. By 2025 the last works connecting all the buildings via five brise-soleil solar panels of diffused light bearing inscriptions from the five books of the Torah should be completed – a remarkable modern architectural twist to the otherwise historic setting.

The museum chronicles 2200 years of Italian-Jewish history (Italy was once the cradle of Jewish culture in Europe and it has the oldest active Jewish community in the Western world) via audio-visually stunning exhibitions lifted from the perspective of Jewish-Roman historian Josephus Flavius. In the permanent exhibition, don't miss the **Holy Arc** dating to 1472, an extraordinarily detailed 1st-century **statue of Titus** once buried under Pompeii, vibrant **Renaissance paintings** by Andrea Mantegna, and the 24-minute film *Through the Eyes of Italian Jews*, which adds mesmerising context. A haunting new exhibition, *1938: Humanity Denied*, accounts for fascist Italy's racism laws told through the eyes of two families – one Jewish, the other not. The 45-minute, six-room multimedia experience is distressing but intensely important. For reasons all wrong, it's impossible to not feel alive here.

A TOWER OF JAZZ

There are few places in the solar system more cinematic than this extraordinary and intimate house of swing and syncopation occupying the restored Renaissance defence tower of San Giovanni dating to 1493. Considered one of Europe's top jazz venues, **Jazz Club Ferrara** draws ace talent from around the world – especially the USA and Brazil – and seeing a show here is a privilege indeed. Go on a Sunday, when entrance is free and a €5 glass of wine nets you a buffet dinner with a world-class jazz soundtrack. The season runs from late September to late April. Always reserve – it holds but a paltry 150 people.

LIKE WANDERING THE WALLS?

Italy's walled towns always make for dramatic touring – check out further examples in Veneto's **Euganean Hills** (p288) outside Padua, an easy 75km or so detour north of Ferrara.

GETTING AROUND

Ferrara's city centre is compact and walkable, but if you want to move like a local, get in the saddle and join the hundreds of other pedallers in one of Italy's most cycle-friendly cities. The tourist office at Castello Estense can provide info on the region's well-developed network of bike routes.

Ferrara

Comacchio

Beyond Ferrara

Italy's greatest river empties into the Adriatic Sea at the biodiverse Po Delta, 50km or so east of Ferrara.

TOP TIP

Fans of wild beaches should seek out the sands of Riserva Statale Sacca di Bellocchio III, 13km south of Comacchio.

The Po Delta is one of Europe's largest wetlands – protected in the Unesco-recognised Parco del Delta del Po – often doused in an eerie fog, especially in winter. The wetlands are notable for their birdlife – 300 species have been registered here. The flat terrain not only attracts birders, but nature enthusiasts and cyclists alike. A network of paths offer day trips and long-distance cycling excursions. The delta's main centre, Comacchio, is a picturesque fishing village of canals and brick bridges, a wealth of seafood restaurants and a fascinating museum. The unique setting of the entire region has historically served as one of Italy's most popular feature film locations.

Abbazia di Pomposa

ANDREW MAYOVSKYY/SHUTTERSTOCK ©

The Mighty Po Delta

PROTECTED WETLANDS, SHIPWRECK MUSEUMS

A labyrinthine unravelling of Italy's longest river commences in the Po Delta, where tributaries of the Po river have crafted a wealth of waterways for nature enthusiasts to explore over a day. The Unesco-recognised **Parco del Delta del Po** encompasses one of Europe's largest wetlands and a pair of alluring lagoons, the Valli di Comacchio and Valle Bertuzzi. With more than 300 bird species nesting or passing through the area, it's a paradise for ornithologists. In late April and early May every second year, **Comacchio** (45 minutes by car from Ferrara) hosts the **International Po Delta Birdwatching Fair**, the largest event of its kind in Europe.

Due to the flat terrain, cycling is particularly popular and a network of paths has developed, many of them on raised dykes. Of note is the 46km route linking the freshwater lagoons of Argenta to their saltwater equivalents in Comacchio. Nearly two-hour boat tours on Comacchio's lagoon depart from Stazione Foce, 4km south of the village twice daily – a must for birders and those who'd like insight into delta living (you'll visit a typical fisherman's house).

Po Delta Tourism is the go-to agency for excursions in the area, including sunset hikes to the **Saline di Comacchio**. This experience puts you in the right place at the right time: among Europe's northernmost flamingo colony (and Italy's second-biggest, after Sardinia) in the limited-access Comacchio saltworks as the sun sets in a spectacular show of pink-hued hullabaloo.

BEST SIGHTS IN THE PO DELTA

Museo Delta Antico
The showstopper of this beautifully laid-out museum in Comacchio is the intriguing cargo of a Roman merchant shipwreck, sunk between 19 and 12 BCE.

Manifattura dei Marinati
Dedicated to Comacchio's traditional eel-fishing industry; pop in to see skewered eels and anchovies marinating in traditional vats of salt and vinegar from September to December.

Abbazia di Pomposa
One of Italy's oldest Benedictine endowments, about 20km north of Comacchio. The musical scale was reputedly invented here, and in the 11th century it was one of Italy's foremost cultural centres.

GETTING AROUND

Comacchio itself is tiny and easily walkable. You'll likely come by car and want to explore the delta by bike and/or boat upon arrival.

RIMINI

Rimini

Rome

Roman relics, jam-packed beaches, hedonistic nightclubs and the memory of film director and native son Federico Fellini make sometimes awkward bedfellows in seaside Rimini. Although there's been a settlement here for over 2000 years, Rimini's coast was just sand dunes until 1843, when the first bathing establishments took root next to the ebbing Adriatic. The beach huts gradually morphed into a megaresort that was sequestered by a huge nightclub scene in the 1990s.

Though this seaside resort harbours an interesting history, fascinating Roman ruins, Fellini-esque movie memorabilia and decent food culture, 95% of Rimini's visitors come for its long, boisterous, sometimes tacky beachfront. Changes over the last decade have drastically improved the latter, however, including a new, design-driven seafront promenade (Parco del Mare), a new €92-million rapid transit system connecting the train station with beaches all the way to Riccione (Metromare), and at least 30km of new bike paths.

TOP TIP

If you don't want to pay for the convenience of a *bagno* (beach club) in Rimini, look for a *spiaggia libera* (free beach) at Lido San Giuliano (a small section near the Darsena marina) or the area next to the old port in front of the panoramic Ferris wheel.

ICONIC SLEEPS

Impossible to miss just off the beach in Marina Centro (next to Parco Federico Fellini), the **Grand Hotel** is an imposing art nouveau bastion dating to 1908 that radiates *La Dolce Vita*. Fellini was transfixed as a child, only to grow up and become a fixture at this symbol of opulence on the Adriatic. His words in *Fare un film (Making a Film)* say it all: 'Murders, kidnappings, nights of mad love, blackmail, suicides, the garden of torture, the goddess Kali: everything happened at the Grand Hotel.' Today, the Grand is as much a monument as a place to stay.

The Cinematic Adriatic

FOLLOWING FELLINI'S FOOTSTEPS

Though Italian cinematic maestro Federico Fellini spun his neorealistic dreamscapes – an artistic style that came to be known as Felliniesque – from Rome, it was his hometown of Rimini that most heavily influenced the creation of the idiosyncratic tales that became his signature style. His 1973 semi-autobiographical masterpiece *Amarcord*, which chronicles daily life in Borgo San Giuliano in 1930s fascist Italy, was Fellini's love letter to Rimini.

The famed director and screenwriter was born on Via Dardanelli in Marina Centro, just a few hundred metres from the **Grand Hotel**, in 1920. Today, **Parco Federico Fellini** commemorates his childhood stomping grounds. Fellini-centric sights in Rimini include **Fontana della Pigna** in Piazza Cavour and **Piazza Tre Martiri** (both immortalised in *Amarcord*), while murals depicting his works and characters pepper Borgo San Giuliano. But two sights stand above all others.

The splendid **Cinema Fulgor** in the *centro storico* was the theatre of Fellini's youth. Renovated according to original renderings of Oscar-winning set designer and Fellini protégé Dante Ferretti, the striking, art deco–esque marriage of red velvet and ornate, gold-leafed accents, reopened as a working cinema on Fellini's birthday in January 2018. The new **Museo Fellini**, inaugurated in 2021, mainly occupies the Renaissance Castel Sismondo, but also the restored

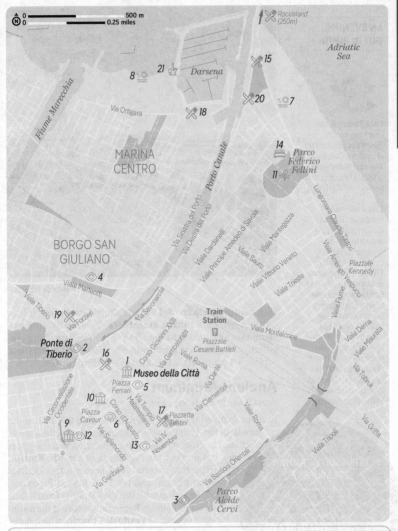

HIGHLIGHTS

1 Museo della Città
2 Ponte di Tiberio

SIGHTS

3 Arco di Augusto
4 Borgo San Giuliano
(see 10) Cinema Fulgor
5 Domus del Chirurgo

6 Fontana Della Pigna
7 Le Milton Beach
8 Lido San Giuliano
9 Museo Fellini
10 Palazzo del Fulgor
11 Parco
   Federico Fellini
12 Piazza Malatesta
13 Piazza Tre Martiri

SLEEPING

14 Grand Hotel

EATING

15 Avamposto
16 Il Pescatore
   del Canevone
17 Io e Simone

18 La Petite
   Langoustine
19 Osteria De Borg
20 Strampalato

**DRINKING
& NIGHTLIFE**

21 Darsena Sunset Bar

AN EVENING OUT IN RIMINI

Luca Zamagni, the heart and soul of Rimini's contemporary art gallery, Galleria Zamagni (*@zamagni_arte*). He fills us in on a perfect night in Rimini.

Take a walk to rediscover Roman Rimini following the *decumanus* (east–west Roman street) between **Ponte di Tiberio** and the **Arco di Augusto**. Dine at **La Petite Langoustine** overlooking Rimini's Darsena where the flavours of the sea meet those of the land. Spend a night in the fascinating setting of the **Grand Hotel**, the symbol of *La Dolce Vita* and the place of Fellini's imagination.

IN PURSUIT OF ROMAN TREASURES?

One of Emilia-Romagna's most fascinating Roman attractions is Comacchio's **Museo Delta Antico** (p389), home to the intriguing cargo of a Roman merchant shipwreck, sunk between 19 and 12 BCE.

Ponte di Tiberio

18th-century **Palazzo del Fulgor** along with dramatic new outdoor spaces in **Piazza Malatesta**. This captivating museum takes visitors into the films of Fellini, provoking cinematic grandeur with innovative audio-visual effects and replica set props. It's like a dream – Fellini's dream.

Ancient Ariminum

ROMAN ARCHES, BRIDGES AND ARTEFACTS

Romans founded the *colonia* of Ariminum in 268 BCE at the mouth of the Ariminus river (known today as the Marecchia). The city was a key communication and transport hub and marked the beginning of the **Via Emilia**, the important arterial road between the Adriatic coast (at Rimini) and the Po valley (at Piacenza), which linked up with the Via Flaminia from Rome.

Start your half-day Roman adventure at the astonishing five-arched **Ponte di Tiberio**, which dates from 21 CE. In Roman times it marked the start of the Via Emilia. These days, the bridge still connects Rimini's centre to the old fishing quarter of **Borgo San Giuliano** and rests on its original foundations,

 HAPPY-HOUR HOT SPOTS IN RIMINI

Avamposto
Fascist-designed 1930s naval association HQ turned hip sunset hot spot. Next to Rimini's Ferris wheel.

Rockisland
Long-standing destination bar-restaurant on the tip of Rimini's pier. Dramatic sunsets.

Darsena Sunset Bar
Reserve a prime spot in advance at this trendy cocktail bar hidden away in Rimini's marina (Darsena).

ALEX.UGALEK/SHUTTERSTOCK ©

an ingenious construction of wooden stilts (cars were only banned in 2020!). It's particularly atmospheric at night. Continue deeper into the *centro storico* and duck into the **Museo della Città**, whose bounty of Roman artefacts includes splendid mosaics and a rare and exquisite representation of fish rendered in coloured glass. It's also home to the world's largest collection of Roman surgical instruments, recovered next door at the **Domus del Chirurgo**, a must-see excavation of three Roman homes – including dear old doc. End your tour at the triumphant **Arco di Augusto**, the oldest of its kind in northern Italy. Commissioned by Emperor Augustus in 27 BCE, it was once the end point of the ancient Via Flaminia.

The Riviera Romagnola

SUN-KISSED SANDS, PINE-BACKED BEACHES

There's no denying that Italy's most storied beaches await further south in Sardinia, Puglia and Campania, but the coast of Romagna – cleverly christened the Riviera Romagnola – isn't without its charms. Stretching for 110km from the northern end of Ravenna province (Casalborsetti) to the southern end of Rimini (Cattolica), there's a patch of sand for everyone.

If you're looking for beach resorts, urban infrastructure and more of a party atmosphere, Rimini is ground zero – its 15km of beaches are like a slice of California in Italy. For navigational purposes, beaches are numbered (from one to 150 heading south, one to 75 heading north, divided by a five-beach supersized area known as **Lido San Giuliano** between Porto Canale and the Marecchia river). Beach clubs, known as *bagni*, maintain a designated area and provide services and items for a fee, such as lounge chairs, changing rooms and sun umbrellas.

As a quick primer, Nos 5 and 14 are sporty (with foot volley and volleyball, respectively), surfers hang out at No 8, **Milton Beach Cafe** at No 5 is more posh, No 26 is the party beach, and Nos 1 to 50 are where the locals hang out. The *bagni* are generally open from 7am to 7pm Easter through September.

The beaches of Ravenna are more low-key and less developed. Beach clubs exist, but on a smaller scale. Northern beaches such as **Punta Marina**, **Lido di Dante** and **Casalborsetti** are backed by beautiful pine forest, a unique and serene backdrop compared to Rimini's clamorous hotel development.

BEST RESTAURANTS IN RIMINI

Il Pescatore del Canevone €€
Contemporary, family-run seafooder; the daily changing chalkboard menu features a dozen or so faultlessly fresh choices.

Io e Simone €€
A super friendly, family-run affair in *centro storico* that's rooted in tradition but unafraid to experiment. Wonderful courtyard.

Osteria de Borg €€
Top choice in Borgo San Giuliano; simple, honest traditional food made with local ingredients. Heavily favoured for massive steaks.

Strampalato €
Family-friendly, non-touristy spot for decent burgers, pizza and fried seafood. Near Ponte di Tiberio and on the beach in Marina Centro.

GETTING AROUND

Rimini's Roman ruins and Fellini sights are walkable. However, you'll want a bike for all the beach-hopping you're likely to do – the city has 150km of bike paths. Bike Park Rimini is a convenient source for bike and e-bike rentals.

Rimini

SAN MARINO ✪

Beyond Rimini

Of the planet's 195 independent countries, San Marino is the fifth-smallest and – arguably – the most curious.

TOP TIP

For direct access to the Città di San Marino *funivia* (cable car), park at Parcheggio 11 in Borgo Maggiore.

Tiny San Marino's existence is something of an enigma. It is the sole survivor of Italy's once powerful city-state network, a landlocked micronation that's clung on long after the kingdoms of Genoa and Venice folded. Still it endures, secure in its status as the world's oldest surviving sovereign state and oldest republic (since 301 CE). At 61 sq km, it's larger than many outsiders imagine, being made up of nine municipalities each hosting its own settlement. The largest 'town' is Dogana (on the bus route from Italy), a place 99.9% of the two million annual visitors skip in transit to its Unesco-listed capital, Città di San Marino.

Torre Guaita, Città di San Marino

DUCHY/SHUTTERSTOCK ©

The View from San Marino

CITY-STATES, COMMANDING VISTAS

The rocky Apennine outcrop of Monte Titano rises 739m above sea level and can be seen from miles away. Getting to the top – that is, arriving in **Città di San Marino**, the Unesco-listed capital – is half the fun. You'll need to either leg it up or take the easy way out: the panoramic cable car from Borgo Maggiore, an hour's bus ride from Rimini. Once at the top, the reasons for this side trip southeast of Rimini's coast become immediately clear: it's undeniably gorgeous up here. Città di San Marino is gifted with spectacular views.

Head first to the **Ufficio del Turismo** (tourism office) to get your passport stamped with a San Marino visa for €5 (cash only). Begin your exploring from Piazza della Libertà; ever popular in the summer is the hourly **changing of the guard**. The neo-Gothic **Palazzo Pubblico** – San Marino's official seat of government – overlooks the piazza with its late-19th-century battlements, corbels and camera-friendly clock tower. Don't miss the two castles that bookend the city. The 13th-century **Torre Cesta** dominates the skyline while the older, larger **Torre Guaita** dates to the 11th century and was a prison as recently as 1975. The art, history, furniture and cultural objects on display at San Marino's best museum, **Museo di Stato**, are also worth exploring. Close things out over a bounty of local San Marino provisions at **Giuletti Km0**, toasting to the uptick in your 'countries visited' list.

SANT'ARCANGELO UNDERGROUND

At first glance, the idyllic medieval Romagnan *borgo* of Sant'Arcangelo is just that: a wonderfully cinematic village that ticks all the boxes. Ancient castle? Check. Photogenic alleyways? Check. Wonderful restaurants specialising in the renowned regional cuisine? Obviously. But a mysterious parallel city lurks underfoot. An ancient patchwork of galleries and tunnels carved from the sandstone and clay below harbour secret escape routes, old granaries and at least 150 caves. This cloaked labyrinth's construction date and purpose remain a mystery, though there are theories. Visits are by guided tour only; contact **Pro Loco Santarcangelo** (*iatsantarcangelo. com*).

SEEKING CITY-STATES?

Well, you're in luck – San Marino isn't Italy's only country within a country. In fact, the world's smallest country is also here: the **Vatican** (p93), surrounded by Rome.

GETTING AROUND

Città di San Marino's walkable *centro storico* is reached on foot or by cable car from numerous car parks in Borgo Maggiore.

RAVENNA

Ravenna

Rome

For mosaic lovers, Ravenna is an earthly paradise. Spread out over several churches and baptisteries around town is one of the world's most dazzling collections of Early Christian mosaic artwork, enshrined since 1996 on Unesco's World Heritage list. Wandering through the unassuming town centre today, you'd never imagine that for a three-century span beginning in 402 CE Ravenna served as the capital of the Western Roman Empire, chief city of the Ostrogoth Kingdom of Italy and nexus of a powerful Byzantine exarchate.

During this prolonged golden age, while the rest of the Italian peninsula flailed in the wake of barbarian invasions, Ravenna became a fertile art studio for skilled craftsmen, who covered the city's terracotta brick churches in heart-rendingly beautiful mosaics. Ravenna was momentous as inspiration for Dante Alighieri's greatest work, *Divina Commedia*; and romantic toff Lord Byron added further weight to Ravenna's literary credentials when he spent two years here in the early 19th century.

TOP TIP

As state monuments have free admission on the first Sunday of the month, you can visit three of Ravenna's Unesco World Heritage Sites (Battistero degli Ariani, Basilica di Sant'Apollinare in Classe and the Mausoleo di Teodorico) for free if you plan accordingly.

DOCKS & BOCKS

The 1200-sq-metre **Darsenale** brewpub and beer garden is Emilia-Romagna's most ambitious craft-beer undertaking. Local brewery Birra Bizantina flipped this long-abandoned warehouse along Ravenna's neglected docklands into a hophead playground in 2019, firmly planting itself as the anchor of the revitalising Darsena district. You'll find 16 taps and two hand pumps of core, rotating, special-edition and guest beers along with a menu of *pala*-style (rectangular) pizza, burgers etc. Also at the docks, **S Club** serves trendy cocktails on its terrace while **DarsenaPopUp** is a sport, culture and leisure hub fashioned from shipping containers.

Ravenna's Marvellous Mosaics

DAZZLING BASILICAS AND BAPTISTRIES

When Dante Alighieri arrived in Ravenna in the early 14th century, he was wowed by the city's famed mosaics, once describing them as a 'symphony of colour'. Indeed, the city's brilliant 4th- to 6th-century gold, emerald and sapphire masterpieces will leave you struggling for adjectives over the two days it takes to see them.

Six of Ravenna's mosaic-related Unesco sights form a triangle within the city centre and are easily accessed on foot on a 2km walk (the other two, **Mausoleo di Teodorico** and **Basilica di Sant'Apollinare in Classe**, are located 1.5km east and 5.7km south of the centre, respectively). Pre-booking is required online (ravennamosaici.it) or at L'Opera di Religione della Diocesi di Ravenna Ticket Office near San Vitale (seeing all eight sights runs €23.50).

Start at **1 Basilica di San Vitale**, where the lucid mosaics that adorn the altar of this ancient church consecrated in 547 by Archbishop Massimiano invoke a sharp intake of breath in most visitors. The mosaics on the side and end walls inside the church represent scenes from the Old Testament: to the left, Abraham prepares to sacrifice Isaac in the presence of three angels, while the mosaic on the right portrays the death of Abel and the offering of Melchizedek. Inside the chancel, two magnificent mosaics depict the Byzantine emperor Justinian with San Massimiano and a particularly solemn and expressive Empress Theodora, who was his consort.

SIGHTS
1 Basilica di San Francesco
2 Casa Alighieri (see 5) Chiostri Francescani (Old Franciscan Cloisters)
3 Dante Mural
4 Giardini Pubblici
5 Museo Dante
6 Museo TAMO
7 Quadrarco di Braccioforte
8 Tomba di Dante
9 Zona del Silenzio

SLEEPING
10 Ai Giardini di San Vitale
11 Albergo Cappello
12 M Club Deluxe

EATING
13 Chalet Ravenna
14 Darsena PopUp
15 Mercato Coperto

ACTIVITIES, TOURS & COURSES
16 Koko Mosaico

Basilica di San Vitale

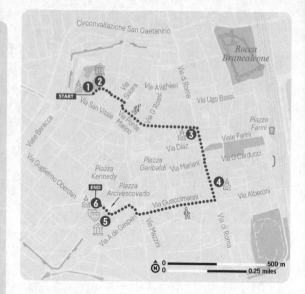

Next door, the small but equally incandescent **2 Mausoleo di Galla Placidia** was constructed for Galla Placidia, the half-sister of Emperor Honorius, who initiated the construction of many of Ravenna's grandest buildings. The mosaics here are the oldest in Ravenna, probably dating from around 430 CE.

Make your way to **3 Battistero degli Ariani** and admire the breathtaking dome mosaic, depicting the baptism of Christ encircled by the 12 apostles, which was completed over a period of years beginning in the 5th century. At nearby **4 Basilica di Sant'Apollinare Nuovo**, it's almost impossible to take your eyes off the 26 white-robed martyrs heading towards Christ with his apostles on the right (south) wall.

Continue on to **5 Museo Arcivescovile** on the 2nd floor of the Archiepiscopal Palace. It hides two not-to-be-missed exhibits: an exquisite ivory throne carved for Emperor Maximilian by Byzantine craftsmen in the 6th century (the surviving detail on the 27 engraved panels is astounding) and a stunning collection of mosaics in the 5th-century chapel of

WHERE TO SLEEP IN RAVENNA

Ai Giardini di San Vitale
Family-run B&B with simple rooms and jungly back gardens located near Basilica di San Vitale. €

M Club Deluxe
Converted family home with ancient beamed ceilings, historic bric-a-brac and luxurious furnishings. €

Albergo Cappello
Central, intimate boutique hotel with Murano glass chandeliers, original 15th-century frescoes and coffered ceilings. €€

San Andrea, which has been cleverly incorporated into the museum's plush modern interior.

Finish off at neighbouring **6 Battistero Neoniano**, Ravenna's oldest intact building, constructed over the site of a former Roman bathing complex in the late 4th century. The mosaics, which thematically depict Christ being baptised by St John the Baptist in the River Jordan, were added at the end of the 5th century.

Life & Death in Exile

TRACING DANTE'S LEGACY

Dante Alighieri was exiled from Florence in 1302 for being on the wrong side of a political battle between the Black (pro-Papacy) and White Guelphs (anti-Papacy). After a few years of wanderings, the greatest Italian poet of all time made his way to Ravenna on the invitation of Prince Guido Novello da Polenta in 1316. Dante spent five years living with the Polentas – the finishing touches on the *Divina Commedia* were written here – until his death in 1321.

Ravenna offers Dantephiles a lot to work with for a day. Numerous sites associated with the poet are centred around the **Zona del Silenzio** (Area of Silence) in the historic centre. **Tomba di Dante** (Dante's Tomb), built between 1780 and 1782 and still partly maintained by the city of Florence as an act of penance, and the contemplative **Quadrarco di Braccioforte** (Braccioforte Courtyard) behind it are essential stops; the latter features an earthen mound marking the spot where Dante's remains were preserved during WWII. Next door, **Museo Dante** brings the poet's life and work to life in an interactive space set around the charming **Old Franciscan Cloisters**. The **Basilica di San Francesco**, where Dante's funeral was held, and **Casa Alighieri** (closed to the public), where he lived, are steps away.

For modern art inspired by Dante, don't miss the exhibit of 21 thematic works commissioned from great Italian artists in the 1960s at **Museo TAMO** and Brazilian street artist Kobra's **Dante Mural** on Via Pasolini.

MERCATO COPERTO

Ravenna's historic **covered market** dates to 1922 in its current incarnation, but this wonderful gourmet food and dining hall, reopened in 2019 after years of restoration, has roots dating back to the 9th century. Today, the undeniably cool bastion of culinary arts features numerous locally focused restaurants, bars, cafes and bakeries (among other gastronomic endeavours). Inside, famed Italian architect Paolo Lucchetta and interior designers Beatrice Bassi and Leonardo Spadoni call on Edison lighting inside suspended wooden bird cages, a see-through escalator and bygone-era-evoking art and antiques to instil a sense of industrial-chic time travel. The alfresco seating along its exterior is one of Ravenna's best spots for an adult beverage and some people-watching.

GETTING AROUND

Ravenna is wonderfully foot- and bike-friendly (the white paths through the streets have become unofficial bike paths; pedestrians stick to either side). All but one of its Unesco World Heritage Sites (Basilica di Sant'Apollinare in Classe) are reachable on foot.

Ravenna

Brisighella

Beyond Ravenna

Seaside charm, 35km of coastline backed by wonderful pine forests, and a stunning medieval village await in Ravenna province.

TOP TIP

The Moretto artichoke season is mid-April to mid-May only. That's the time to visit Brisighella.

When the *ravennati* need a city break, it's a mere 8km east to the nearest beach, Punta Marina, which marks the midway point of Ravenna's pretty coastline. Cervia, built on an empire of salt and characterised by its enchanting port canal, sits 25km south. Brisighella, 54km west of Ravenna, is Romagna's storybook medieval village, set on the slopes of the Tosco-Romagna Apennines and cradled by pastoral green hills peppered with vineyards and olive plantations. Brisighella is defined by its trio of iconic hilltop structures – La Rocca (The Rock), La Torre (The Tower) and Il Monticino – which overlook the sunset-hued rooftops of one of Italy's most picturesque *borghi* (villages).

Torre dell'Orologio, Brisighella

ERMESS/SHUTTERSTOCK ©

Il Borgo Bello

STORYBOOK MEDIEVAL VILLAGE

Shhhhhh! A 55-minute drive from Ravenna, beautiful **Brisighella** is Emilia-Romagna's fairy-tale secret, tucked away in the picturesque **Valle del Lamone** just 14km northeast of the Tuscan border, where its castle-topped hillsides, rolling olive groves and stunning medieval architecture harbour all the beauty of its southern neighbour without any of the fuss and fanfare.

Begin your day-long explorations here along the remarkable **Via degli Asini**, a low-slung, wood-beamed, delightfully uneven medieval walkway dating to 1290 that sits hidden behind a colourful patchwork of warped homes right through the middle of the *borgo*.

From here, 400 steps invite a climb above town, where Brisighella's iconic hilltop structures stand sentinel over the village. Maghinardo Pagani's **Torre dell'Orologio** (clock tower), erected in 1850, and the **Rocca di Brisighella** are connected by an 800m walking path. The views from the latter – a medieval fortress constructed by the Manfredi family (Lords of Faenza) in 1310 and later expanded by Venetians between 1503 and 1506 – are the reason you have come to Brisighella. **Santuario del Monticino**, an isolated chapel built in 1758, sits on a neighbouring hilltop surrounded by cypress trees.

Brisighella is famed Italy-wide for its exquisite DOP olive oil as well as its unique Moretto artichoke, a tiny, thorny and very tasty variety that only grows in the Valle del Lamone. Don't leave town without trying both!

CERVIA & THE PORTI CANALE ROMAGNOLI

An empire of white gold built the charming seaside resort of Cervia (it was originally constructed as a salt worker housing commune on the order of Pope Innocenzo XII in 1697). Today, Cervia's famed sweet salt is a sought-after artisanal product, and its historic salt warehouses have been turned into bars, restaurants and museums such as the fascinating **MUSA** salt museum and the trendy **Darsena del Sale**. Cervia's port canal is lined with atmospheric bars and restaurants. **Cesenatico**, Cervia's southern neighbour, also features a pretty port canal – this one surveyed by Italian know-it-all Leonardo da Vinci in 1502.

GETTING AROUND

Though Ravenna's coastline and inland towns are well served by public transport, a car hire will certainly enhance your experience.

FLORENCE

INSPIRING BEYOND THE OBVIOUS

Medieval towers and art-filled palaces attract millions each year, but the 'cradle of the Renaissance' cliché conceals a cosmopolitan character worth discovering.

Between the 14th and the 17th centuries, painters, sculptors and architects at the top of their game were attracted to Florence by the ruling class's renewed interest towards classical arts and philosophy, transforming the city into the glorious epicentre of a cultural rebirth defined by a shift towards humanism in much of Europe. The body of masterpieces produced during the artistic golden age known as the Renaissance will overwhelm anyone who tries to tick them off a list, but ask Florentines what makes them proud of their city and you'll likely hear a diverse set of answers.

Some will mention the role of Florence in shaping the Italian language and collective culture, thanks to the work of the city's Divine Poet Dante Alighieri, but due to influential institutions such as the Accademia della Crusca, a public organisation devoted to the study of linguistics since the 16th century, or the Gabinetto Vieusseux, a library of European literature that favoured the exchange of progressive ideas in the 19th century, attracting the likes of Stendhal,

Fyodor Dostoevsky, Mark Twain and Aldous Huxley.

Others will tell you about the world's first catwalk, organised on 12 February, 1951 by entrepreneur Giovanni Battista Giorgini in Oltrarno's Villa Torrigiani, an event that turned local tailors' workshops into internationally sought-after brands, and led to high-end fashion events such as today's celebrated Pitti Immagine. Or there's the still hotly debated origins of the gelato, whose invention is contested between the alchemist Cosimo Ruggeri and the architect Bernardo Buontalenti.

And that's just scratching the surface. With so many layers to dig through, any attempt at exhausting the place is doomed to fail. At times, Florence's global fame seems to fit a bit too tightly to the rather small city and its residents of less than 400,000. Perhaps its heritage is not there to simply be gazed at, but to be listened to and inspired by, day after day.

GABRIELE MALTINTI/SHUTTERSTOCK ©

THE MAIN AREAS

PIAZZA DEL DUOMO & PIAZZA DELLA SIGNORIA
Home of Brunelleschi's iconic dome. **p408**

SANTA MARIA NOVELLA
Not just a transport hub. **p418**

SAN LORENZO & SAN MARCO
Shopping and food in a lively market atmosphere. **p423**

DAVE Z/SHUTTERSTOCK ©

Aerial view of Florence

SANTA CROCE & SANT'AMBROGIO
Museums, churches and nightlife. **p429**

SAN FREDIANO & SANTO SPIRITO
Creative hub with many *aperitivo* spots. **p435**

SAN NICCOLÒ, BOBOLI & PIAZZA PITTI
Elegant gardens and great views. **p442**

0 500 m
0 0.25 miles

**San Lorenzo &
San Marco**
p423

SAN MARCO

🏛 Galleria dell'Accademia

SAN LORENZO

LE CURE

SAN
JACOPINO

FROM THE AIRPORT

Florence's Peretola Airport is directly connected to the city centre by the T2 tram, found on the left side of the arrivals hall. The tram runs every few minutes to the Santa Maria Novella (SMN) train station (€1.50).

WALK

There is no better way to explore Florence than by foot. Much of the city is flat and closed to car traffic – walking through its narrow alleys is an experience in itself.

TRAIN

The Santa Maria Novella station, 10 minutes' walk from Piazza del Duomo, is Florence's main transport hub. There are regional trains to most destinations in Tuscany, while high-speed Le Frecce and Italo trains reach the major cities in Italy, including Milan, Bologna, Rome and Naples.

TRAM

Florence has two relatively new tram lines, T1 and T2, which run to the airport and to the Villa Costanza coach station. Tickets cost €1.50 and can be purchased at the automatic machines found at each stop.

PIGNONE

MONTICELLI

BELLOSGUARDO

Santa Maria Novella
p418

Suppose museo
Museum

Basilica di Santa
Maria Novella

Arno

SAN FREDIANO

SANT'AMBROGIO

**Santa Croce &
Sant'Ambrogio**
p429

SANTA
CROCE

Cattedrale di Santa
Maria del Fiore

**Piazza del Duomo &
Piazza della Signoria**
p408

Palazzo Vecchio

Uffizi

Ponte
Vecchio

Ponte
Santa
Trinità

SANTO
SPIRITO

**San Frediano &
Santo Spirito**
p435

OLTRARNO

SAN NICCOLÒ

MONTE
ALLE
CROCI

**San Niccolò, Boboli
& Piazza Pitti**
p442

Find Your Way

Despite the huge number of artistic and architectural attractions it houses, Florence is a relatively small city. The historic centre is best explored on foot – you can cross the city in less than an hour and then climb up one of the surrounding hills for exceptional views of its red rooftops.

Plan Your Days

Contemporary art, Renaissance architecture, traditional street food and postcard-worthy views can all be found near each other in the Tuscan capital. Plan carefully or go with the flow – either way, surprises await.

Piazza del Duomo (p408)

DAY 1

Morning
● Avoid queues and crowds by starting your visit to the **Cattedrale di Santa Maria del Fiore (Duomo)** (p408). Get your blood flowing by climbing the 414 steps of the campanile, then learn about the history of the building at the **Museo dell'Opera del Duomo** (p410).

Afternoon
● Taste local flavours in the vibrant **Mercato Centrale** (p423), then head to **Palazzo Vecchio** (p413) and join a 'secret passages' tour to discover the hidden secrets of Florence's centre of power, before entering the mesmerising Salone dei Cinquecento.

Evening
● Cross Ponte Vecchio and head for the outdoor dining in charming **Santo Spirito** (p435).

YOU'LL ALSO WANT TO...

Spend a day visiting the arts scene, exploring markets and artisanal shops, sipping a Negroni or Chianti before dinner.

EAT A STUFFED SCHIACCIATA
The Florentine sandwich par excellence, the **schiacciata** is sold on Via de' Neri and in many other corners of the city.

DISCOVER MICHEL-ANGELO'S LEGACY
From the glorious **David** to the **Cappelle Medicee**, many are the gifts left by one of Florence's most revered artists.

LISTEN TO EXPERIMENTAL JAZZ
Catch a live music gig at **Sala Vanni**, a concert hall hidden in a section of the Basilica di Santa Maria del Carmine.

DAY 2

Morning

● Start the day with delicious raw vegan patisseries at the **Cortese Café 900** (p418), and while you're there peek at the 20th-century works housed in the **Museo Novecento** (p418). Continue your contemporary-art-themed morning by checking out an exhibition at **Palazzo Strozzi** (p412).

Afternoon

● Stop for a well-deserved lunch at the **Cibreo** (p432), then step into the **Street Levels Gallery** (p420) to discover the masters of the Florentine urban-art scene.

Evening

● Conclude your post-Renaissance art tour at the **Collezione Roberto Casamonti** (p410), then step onto **Ponte Santa Trinità** (p435) to see **Ponte Vecchio** (p413) turn red as the sun sets.

DAY 3

Morning

● After a morning espresso, get yourself into the majestic **Palazzo Pitti museums** (p445) – tickets are half-price before 9am! If weather allows, spend the rest of your morning roaming the monumental **Giardino di Boboli** (p444), and climb up to **Forte di Belvedere** (p444) to see the city from above.

Afternoon

● Enter the **Giardino Bardini** (p444) for a late lunch outdoors at **La Loggetta di Villa Bardini** (p444) overlooking the Duomo.

Evening

● Exit the park to reach San Niccolò, where eclectic artists such as **Alessandro Dari** and **CLET Studio** have their workshops, and reward yourself with an *aperitivo* at **Rifrullo** (p447).

VISIT MORE CHURCHES

Churches like the **Basilica di Santa Maria Novella** and the **Basilica di Santa Croce** hold invaluable works of art.

CRUISE THE ARNO

See the city from a unique perspective by hopping on a wooden boat with the legendary **renaioli** boatmen.

SIP ON A NEGRONI

Strong and bitter, the century-old **Negroni cocktail** is a Florentine invention best enjoyed in historical cafes such as Rivoire.

SHOP AT ARTISANAL BOTTEGAS

Handmade frames, mosaics, ceramics, leather goods and jewellery – hunt for treasures in **Santo Spirito**.

PIAZZA DEL DUOMO & PIAZZA DELLA SIGNORIA

HOME OF BRUNELLESCHI'S ICONIC DOME

The bustling Via dei Calzaiuoli – the city's main drag – connects Piazza del Duomo with Piazza della Signoria, cutting through the heart of the city dominated by some of the most imposing symbols of the Renaissance: the Cattedrale di Santa Maria del Fiore, the towering Palazzo Vecchio, functioning as the city's centre of power for the past 700 years, and the Uffizi Gallery, with its vast collection of artworks produced by some of the world's greatest.

The concentration of art, history and architecture in such a small area can feel overwhelming – you could spend days roaming through solemn palaces, museum halls and religious structures without uncovering all the secrets this fragment of Florence hides. Rather than rushing, stop and look around you – what you'll see are a good deal of reasons to come back.

TOP TIP

From the Santa Maria Novella train station, you can walk to Piazza del Duomo in about 10 minutes. From there take Via dei Calzaiuoli to reach Piazza della Signoria, where you'll find both Palazzo Vecchio and the Uffizi.

MISTERVLAD/SHUTTERSTOCK ©

Battistero di San Giovanni & Cattedrale di Santa Maria del Fiore

Cattedrale di Santa Maria del Fiore

MAJESTIC CATHEDRAL TOPPED BY BRUNELLESCHI'S DOME

The **Santa Maria del Fiore Cathedral (Duomo)** is the unchallenged Florence icon at the heart of the city. It was built over 140 years on the remains of the ancient Santa Reparata church, believed to have been erected to celebrate the victory of the Roman and Florentine army over the Ostrogoths in the early 5th century. Its terracotta-tiled dome designed by Filippo Brunelleschi inspires awe from both the exterior and interior, where Giorgio Vasari's and Federico Zuccari's *Last Judgement* (1572–79) can be admired as you climb the 463 steps leading to the rooftop.

Battistero di San Giovanni

FLORENTINE ROMANESQUE ARCHITECTURE

Overshadowed by the nearby cathedral, the **baptistery** dedicated to St John the Baptist is often neglected by travellers lining up to enter its more visually striking neighbour. It shouldn't be – the octagonal-shaped structure is one of the best examples of the Florentine Romanesque architectural style. It hides Byzantine-inspired 13th-century mosaics by Cimabue, Coppo di Marcovaldo and Meliore behind its three monumental doors, which were designed by Andrea Pisano and Lorenzo Ghiberti (now substituted with copies to preserve the originals, exhibited in the nearby Museo dell'Opera del Duomo).

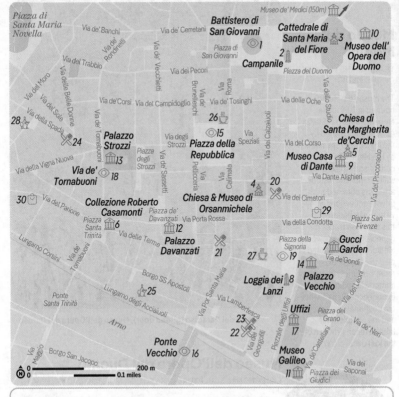

Piazza di Santa Maria Novella

Museo de' Medici (150m)

Battistero di San Giovanni 1

Piazza di San Giovanni

Cattedrale di Santa Maria del Fiore 3

Museo dell' Opera del Duomo 10

Campanile 2

Piazza del Duomo

Chiesa di Santa Margherita de'Cerchi 5

Museo Casa di Dante 9

26

15

Piazza della Repubblica

Palazzo Strozzi 13

Via de' Tornabuoni 18

28

24

30

Collezione Roberto Casamonti 6

12

Palazzo Davanzati 21

Chiesa & Museo di Orsanmichele 4

20

29

Gucci Garden 7

27

19

14

Loggia dei Lanzi 8

Palazzo Vecchio 14

25

Uffizi 17

23

22

Ponte Vecchio 16

Museo Galileo 11

Arno

N
0 — 200 m
0 — 0.1 miles

HIGHLIGHTS

1 Battistero di San Giovanni
2 Campanile
3 Cattedrale di Santa Maria del Fiore
4 Chiesa & Museo di Orsanmichele
5 Chiesa di Santa Margherita de'Cerchi

6 Collezione Roberto Casamonti
7 Gucci Garden
8 Loggia dei Lanzi
9 Museo Casa di Dante
10 Museo dell'Opera del Duomo
11 Museo Galileo
12 Palazzo Davanzati

13 Palazzo Strozzi
14 Palazzo Vecchio
15 Piazza della Repubblica
16 Ponte Vecchio
17 Uffizi
18 Via de' Tornabuoni

EATING

20 I Due Fratellini

21 Il Trippaio del Porcellino
22 'Ino
23 Ora d'Aria
24 Trattoria Marione

SHOPPING

29 Dr Alessandro Bizzarri
30 Riccardo Luci

TTPHOTO/SHUTTERSTOCK ©

Giotto's campanile

Giotto's Campanile

BELL TOWER OFFERING INCREDIBLE VIEWS

The 84.7m-tall **bell tower** of the Santa Maria del Fiore Cathedral was begun by Giotto in 1334 and completed by Andrea Pisano and Francesco Talenti after his death in 1337. Reflecting the cathedral's Gothic style and colour palette, the campanile encloses a narrow staircase leading to the platform Talenti added in 1359 – climb the 414 steps for unmatched views of Brunelleschi's dome and the surrounding red rooftops.

409

Museo de' Medici

TRACING THE HISTORY OF THE MEDICI

The Museo de' Medici opened in 2019 in the elegant Palazzo di Sforza Almeni, once owned by the Medici and still marked by the Medici-Toledo coat of arms affixed to its wall. Combining historical artefacts obtained from private collections with virtual installations, this **museum** traces the genealogy of the powerful Medici family, who ruled over the city for over three centuries, through immersive audiovisual experiences, Renaissance-era costumes, documents and the world's most faithful reconstruction of the lost ducal crown.

TOP RIGHT: CACIO MURILO/SHUTTERSTOCK © BOTTOM LEFT: MITZO/SHUTTERSTOCK ©

Porta del Paradiso (gilded door), Museo dell'Opera del Duomo

Museo dell'Opera del Duomo

EXCEPTIONAL SCULPTURE COLLECTION & HISTORICAL ARTEFACTS

The neo-Gothic facade of the Santa Maria del Fiore Cathedral is relatively recent – architect Emilio de Fabris designed it in the late 19th century, after it had been left unfinished for centuries. A reproduction of the facade's original 1296 design by Arnolfo di Cambio is found today inside this **museum**. The three massive, gilded doors that once led into the baptistery are exhibited here, along with 750 other artworks spread across 28 rooms, including works by Donatello and Michelangelo. The museum also features an educational section where you can learn gold-leaf decoration, pottery glazing and mosaic making (see stazioneutopia.com for workshops).

Museo dell'Opera del Duomo

Collezione Roberto Casamonti

PRIVATE CONTEMPORARY ART COLLECTION

For a break from Renaissance art make a detour to the Roberto Casamonti Collection, housed inside the Palazzo Bartolini Salimbeni. As one of Italy's richest modern and contemporary art collections on exhibit, the **gallery** spans

most of the 20th century, featuring works by Maurizio Cattelan, Le Corbusier and Joan Miró. The building itself has an interesting story. Look up above the entrance and you'll notice a band of poppies decorating the facade: legend has it that a

member of the Bartolini family increased his wealth by drugging his competitors in the textile trade with opium before a wool auction. Following his plan's success he decided to make poppies his family icon, to remind everyone of his cleverness.

The Uffizi

MEDIEVAL AND RENAISSANCE ART GALLERY

When the Uffizi was originally commissioned by the first Grand Duke of Tuscany Cosimo I de' Medici, its purpose was to provide office space for the Florentine government judiciary. Legendary court architect Giorgio Vasari took on the project, replacing the medieval architecture of the time with a modern but classically inspired symmetrical structure locked within Piazza della Signoria and the Arno river. The gradual transformation from functional space into one of the world's most precious art collections is much owed to Cosimo's introverted son Francesco I, who decided in 1581 to turn the top floor of the Uffizi into a **gallery** filled with paintings, statues and precious objects. The space was increasingly filled with art until eventually, in 1769, it opened to the public. Today the gallery traces the evolution of art during the Middle Ages and the Renaissance. With paintings from the likes of Giotto, Botticelli, Leonardo, Lippi, Raffaello and Caravaggio, it's difficult to pinpoint a single highlight. Starting from the First Corridor adorned with mesmerising grotesques, each room offers a visual journey that can hardly get more fulfilling. Newly opened sections of the museum include a room dedicated to previously unseen 16th-century works by Florentine and Venetian artists such as Tiziano, Rosso Fiorentino and Andrea del Sarto, and the outstanding **Terrazzo delle Carte Geografiche**, a room filled with 16th-century maps reopened to the public after 20 years of renovation.

The Uffizi

CORRIDOIO VASARIANO

The Florentine art world has long awaited the reopening of Giorgio Vasari's Corridoio Vasariano – the 760m-long **elevated passageway** connecting Palazzo Vecchio with Palazzo Pitti, commissioned by Grand Duke Cosimo I in 1565 and closed for renovations since 2016. The reopening of the not-so-secret tunnel connecting the ruling class's residence with the governmental offices was planned for late 2022. It was announced that the hefty €45 ticket will give access to a one-of-a-kind experience that will include panoramic views, historical documentation and world-class art. Visit uffizi.it/en/corridoio-vasariano for updates.

TRABANTOS/SHUTTERSTOCK ©

Palazzo Strozzi

CONTEMPORARY ART EXHIBITIONS

The imposing stone fort commissioned in the 15th century by powerful banker Filippo Strozzi is located between fashionable Via de' Tornabuoni and Piazza Strozzi, connected by the elegant inner courtyard designed by Benedetto da Maiano. The **palace** hosts rotating contemporary art shows – depending on when you're in Florence you might encounter exhibitions of the likes of Jeff Koons' steel balloons, NFT screenings or Marina Abramović's performances.

Loggia dei Lanzi

Loggia dei Lanzi

OPEN-AIR SCULPTURE GALLERY

One of the few free Renaissance art exhibitions in Florence sits in front of the entrance of Palazzo Vecchio, in the **open-air sculpture museum** Loggia dei Lanzi, the 14th-century covered terrace originally built to host public meetings in Piazza della Signoria. The best-known of the 11 statues overlooking the square are Benvenuto Cellini's grim *Perseus* (1554), depicting the Greek demigod holding up the freshly decapitated head of Medusa, and Giambologna's *Abduction of the Sabine Women* (1583), a representation of the myth according to which the Romans kidnapped women from regions surrounding Rome to keep the city population growing.

Courtyard, Palazzo Strozzi

Palazzo Davanzati

RESIDENTIAL PALACE OF THE RENAISSANCE NOBILITY

Having reopened in September 2022 after months of renovation works, the palace once inhabited by the Davizzi, one of the wealthiest families of 14th-century Florence, offers a glimpse into the lifestyle of the elite during the late Middle Ages and the Renaissance. Also known as the **Museo della Casa Fiorentina Antica** (Museum of the Ancient Florentine House), the building was bought in 1578 by the Davanzati family, whose coat of arms still hangs above the entrance. There are study rooms, tapestry-decorated bedrooms, kitchens and lavatories furnished as though they're stuck in time. The 1st-floor Sala dei Pappagalli and the 3rd-floor Camera delle Impannate remain among the best-preserved examples of Renaissance interior design.

Palazzo Vecchio & Salone dei Cinquecento

TOWN HALL ADORNED WITH GIORGIO VASARI'S ART

For over seven centuries, the **'old palace'** has housed the seat of the local government and today it continues to function as Florence's town hall. The fortification, constructed above the remains of an ancient Roman theatre, was designed by Arnolfo di Cambio in 1299 but gradually expanded over time, following the tastes and ideas of changing rulers. The marvellous courtyard was designed by architect Michelozzo in 1453 and decorated by Giorgio Vasari in 1553 for the wedding of Joan of Austria and Francesco I de' Medici, and welcomes those who enter the palace. But the true highlight is the astonishing, 1250-sq-metre **Salone dei Cinquecento**, originally commissioned by preacher Giacomo Savonarola to gather a 500-member, citizen-led governing body he established after the brief ousting of the Medici.

In 1504 Michelangelo's *David* was placed in front of the palace's main gate (where a 20th-century copy now stands) and in 1540 the first Grand Duke of Tuscany, Cosimo I, moved in with his court. During this era the Salone was adorned with the grandiose Giorgio Vasari paintings we see today. At the centre of the coffered ceiling is *L'Apoteosi di Cosimo I* (1565), a godly portrait of the Grand Duke, and on the walls are huge depictions of two important wars won by the Florentine army: on the west is the battle against the Pisans (fought between 1495 and 1509) and on the eastern side is the conquest of Siena (1553–75).

Salone del Cinquecento

RED-FENIKS/SHUTTERSTOCK ©

PONTE VECCHIO

An icon of Florence's urban landscape since 1345, the triple-arched **'old bridge'** survived a Nazi bombing in 1945 and the massive flood that hit the city in 1966. It features 48 mismatching jewellery stores perched on its sides – it was Grand Duke Ferdinando I who ordered the *beccai* (butchers) who formerly worked here to abandon the bridge in 1593 and leave space for goldsmiths, as he couldn't stand the smell of rotting meat. Despite the exclusive nature of the businesses operating on the Ponte Vecchio since those involved in 'vile arts' were evicted, its cobblestones get justifiably crowded year-round. Come for a stroll in the evening to see resident street musician Claudio Spadi performing around the monument to sculptor Benvenuto Cellini.

SECRET PASSAGES

Many sections of Palazzo Vecchio are invisible to those who access the structure through its main entrance. Discover the palace's hidden wonders by joining a **'secret passages' tour** (p416).

Gucci Garden

FINE-DINING
RESTAURANT AND
FASHION MUSEUM

The 14th-century Tribunale della Mercanzia houses the colourful Gucci Garden, a multifunctional space run by the Florentine fashion powerhouse. Spread across three floors, it comprises an inviting **boutique**, the Gucci Giardino **cocktail bar** and the **Osteria** run by superstar chef Massimo Bottura. There's also a museum tracing the history of the brand launched by Guccio Gucci in 1921, showing the evolution of the company's stylistic choices through hundreds of rare historical pieces.

TOP RIGHT: DIRECTPHOTO COLLECTION/ALAMY STOCK PHOTO © BOTTOM LEFT: VVOE/SHUTTERSTOCK ©

Gucci Garden restaurant

Museo Galileo

MODERN SCIENCE MUSEUM

Sundial,
Piazza dei Giudici

In Piazza dei Giudici, on the banks of the Arno, is a monumental sundial, which allows the measurement of time through shadows projected on the pavement. Here you can enter a modern **museum** that will entertain children and adults alike thanks to its interactive exhibition of scientific instruments. Over 1000 tools collected since the Medicean era are available to view – explore the halls of the museum to see the telescopes used by Galileo Galilei to discover the moons of Jupiter and continue on to see the macabre shrine where the scientist's middle finger is kept intact.

Chiesa & Museo di Orsanmichele

ART-FILLED CHURCH

The **Orsanmichele Church** may initially appear odd compared to Florence's other religious structures. Its cubic shape and unassuming entrance might not produce the expected spiritual vibe, but it is exactly the unusual architecture and history that make it worth visiting. Originally built as a grain storehouse in 1337, it became a place of worship in the 15th century to protect the Florentine guilds. Wool traders, bankers, silk weavers, skinners and judges all chipped in to decorate the church with statues of their patron saints, positioned in the 14 tabernacles found outside and created by renowned artists like Donatello, Ghiberti and Giambologna. Inside is the magnificent tabernacle by Andrea Orcagna (1349–59), positioned between biblical frescoes, twisted columns and intricate stained-glass windows.

Chiesa di Santa Margherita de' Cerchi

DANTE'S CHURCH

It is in this unassuming **church** in Via Santa Margherita that Dante is believed to have had his first encounter with Beatrice Portinari, the wife of Simone de' Bardi, who is said to have inspired one of the *Divine Comedy*'s central characters. A plaque indicates Beatrice's tomb, although her remains are likely buried in Santa Croce with her husband's. Heartbroken visitors come to this symbol of unrequited love to leave wishful notes.

Piazza della Repubblica

Piazza della Repubblica

HISTORICAL SQUARE WITH ELEGANT CAFES

The ancient heart of Florence is found in this lively **piazza**, where the city's main Roman forum once stood. During the Middle Ages it transformed into the main market square and later housed the ghetto established for the city's Jewish community by Cosimo I. Few traces are left of its early history today, as the municipality decided to rebuild the area after the proclamation of Florence as the capital of a newly united Italy in the late 19th century. The reconstructed piazza became surrounded by stately mansions, luxurious hotels and elegant cafes such as Caffè Le Giubbe Rosse, Caffè Paszkowski and Caffè Gilli, which attracted artists and intellectuals.

Dante bust outside Museo Casa di Dante

Museo Casa di Dante

HISTORICAL MUSEUM OF MEDIEVAL HISTORY

Few neighbourhoods in the city have preserved their medieval character as well as the area between Borgo degli Albizi and Via della Condotta. It's here that Dante Alighieri, Florence's best-known man of letters, grew up and refined his craft, shaping the modern Italian language.

This **museum** educates visitors about the customs and habits of pre-Renaissance Florence. It displays a variety of objects and clothing from the 1300s next to documents recounting some of the era's defining events, including the Battle of Campaldino in which Dante took part. Despite

its name, the museum is not the place where Dante grew up, but rather a tribute to the great poet, which helps place his work into context.

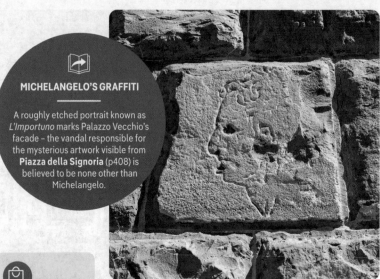

MICHELANGELO'S GRAFFITI

A roughly etched portrait known as *L'Importuno* marks Palazzo Vecchio's facade – the vandal responsible for the mysterious artwork visible from **Piazza della Signoria** (p408) is believed to be none other than Michelangelo.

L'Importuno, Palazzo Vecchio

BEST ARTISANAL SHOPPING

Riccardo Luci
Stationery enthusiasts will love this store in Via del Parione, where Riccardo Luci makes marbled-paper notebooks and crafts.

Dr Alessandro Bizzarri
Make your own fragrances with rare herbs and essential oils in what seems like the workshop of an alchemist of a past epoch.

MORE IN PIAZZA DEL DUOMO & PIAZZA DELLA SIGNORIA

Palace Secrets

DISCOVERING THE PALACE'S HIDDEN PASSAGEWAYS

Throughout its seven-century-long history, **Palazzo Vecchio** has amassed a vast number of mysteries – if only those walls could talk. From the mythical encounter between Renaissance masters Leonardo da Vinci and Michelangelo Buonarroti, who were commissioned to design two large frescoes for the Salone dei Cinquecento but never completed the project, to the public hanging from the palace's windows of Jacopo and Francesco Pazzi, who sought to bring down the Medici through the murder of Giuliano and Lorenzo, endless are the events involving Palazzo Vecchio that changed the course of the city's history.

Joining one of the excellent guided tours by **Mus.e** through the secret rooms and passageways of the palace will allow you to gain deeper insight into the personality of those who inhabited it. Enter via a barely visible door in Via della Ninna and find yourself climbing the narrow stone staircase carved into the thick medieval wall commissioned by Gualtieri of Brienne, Duke of Athens and ruler of Florence (1342–43), until

✄ WHERE TO EAT IN PIAZZA DEL DUOMO & PIAZZA DELLA SIGNORIA

I Due Fratellini
A hole-in-the-wall sandwich bar serving dozens of scrumptious *panini*, always served with wine on the side. €

Il Trippaio del Porcellino
A street-food icon serving *trippa* and *lampredotto* from a stall in Piazza del Mercato Nuovo. €

'Ino
Short for '*panino*'. Choose your own fillings or ask Alessandro for a recommendation. €

you'll reach one of the most intriguing spaces of Palazzo Vecchio – Francesco I's **studiolo**.

Grand Duke Francesco I de' Medici was more interested in alchemy than politics. He loved to retire in solitude to experiment with art and chemistry, and constructed his windowless *studiolo* – a hidden chamber of wonders designed by Giorgio Vasari and filled with paintings representing the four elements – to do exactly that. Directly connected via a door opening behind a canvas is the *studiolo* of Cosimo I (Francesco's father), an equally astonishing space that went forgotten during the Lorraine rule and was only rediscovered in 1908.

The Medici's *studioli* lead directly to the majestic **Salone dei Cinquecento** which, on this tour, can be observed from above rather than below. Enter the dark room to understand how Vasari's wooden truss system continued to work, supporting both the 1200-sq-metre roof and the many huge paintings visible from one of the city's most elegant halls.

The Art of the Aperitivo

THE INVENTION OF THE NEGRONI

Ask any serious cocktail bar around the world for a Negroni and you'll be served the same ice-filled tumbler with equal parts gin, Campari and sweet vermouth. For over a century this vigorous red drink has been made in much the same way. The addition of the Negroni to the list of successful Italian exports is owed to one Florentine man, the adventurous Count Camillo Negroni. In 1919 he entered his favourite bar – the now closed Caffè Casoni – and conducted his habitual *aperitivo* ritual with a twist, asking his bartender to substitute the soda of his usual Americano cocktail with a measure of gin. A few sips were enough for Count Negroni to declare the bitter concoction a triumph of mixology.

Legend has it that the count was extremely jealous of his invention, but keeping the drink a secret became difficult as he drank up to 20 a day. Negroni's 'modified Americano' quickly became the trendiest of drinks among the Florentine elite. Though not for everyone, the Negroni has stood the test of time, becoming a classic that continues to inspire modern variations.

The uninitiated should start their *aperitivo* journey in one of the city's historic bars, like **Caffè Rivoire** in Piazza della Signoria or **Caffè Gilli**, where bartender Luca Picchi – author of many books on the history of the Negroni – has been mixing drinks for decades. The newly opened **Manifattura**, near Palazzo Strozzi, keeps it traditional – every drink on the menu is mixed with Italian spirits only. And if bitterness is your thing, keep it going at the 1920s-inspired **Bitter Bar** after dinner – but please, stop before your 20th Negroni...

DECOLONISING THE RENAISSANCE

Edson Manuel, an Angolan museum mediator working for the Amir Project, points us to three places showing traces of enslaved Africans in Renaissance Florence.

Cappella Sassetti, Chiesa di Santa Trinità
The central scene of Ghirlandaio's fresco shows an enslaved African girl standing behind Francesco's daughters.

Cappella dei Magi, Palazzo Medici Riccardi
Represented in Benozzo Gozzoli's *Cavalcata dei Magi*, a young man appears with African features holding a bow in his hand. Scholars believe he may have been an Ethiopian slave.

Istituto degli Innocenti
The Institute's archives contain the earliest documents (dated 1461) describing the purchase in Lisbon of black slaves destined for Tuscany.

Amblé
Vintage furniture and unique interior-design choices, plus juices and light bites. Great lunch stop between sights. €€

Trattoria Marione
Rustic ambience and a menu filled with Tuscan classics – you can't go wrong. €€

Ora d'Aria
Right behind the Uffizi, here you'll find a creative menu that's ideal for anyone looking for something refined. €€€

SANTA MARIA NOVELLA

NOT JUST A TRANSPORT HUB

The Santa Maria Novella neighbourhood is often perceived as an extension of the eponymous train station. Trains to every corner of Italy depart Giovanni Michelucci's Fascist-era railway hub and, at first glance, anonymous hotels and fast-food joints seem to serve only travellers in a rush to get elsewhere.

But exit the station's immediate surroundings and you'll see this eclectic neighbourhood has evolved to cater for its diverse population of long-time residents, immigrants, Polimoda fashion students, and attendees of the many events hosted by the Fortezza da Basso, a huge exhibition space and home to the Mostra Internazionale dell'Artigianato (International Crafts Fair) held each April.

The main sights revolve around the beautiful Basilica di Santa Maria Novella – the core of the neighbourhood – but walk beyond the piazza and you'll quickly come across historic bakeries, whose owners have guarded their family recipes for decades, alongside spice shops, art galleries and multilingual bookstores.

TOP TIP

Santa Maria Novella is well positioned for accessing most sights in the city. In a few minutes you can walk to the Mercato Centrale in San Lorenzo, Piazza del Duomo and the Arno river. And if you feel like wandering further away, trams and train are at your disposal.

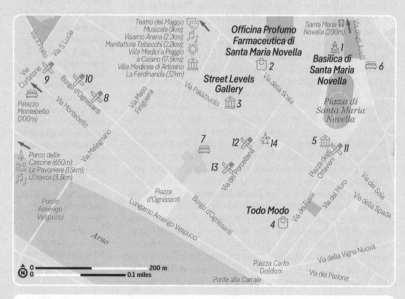

Basilica di Santa Maria Novella

MAJESTIC CHURCH FILLED WITH RENAISSANCE ART

Founded by the Dominican monastic community in the late 13th century, the **Santa Maria Novella** is one of Florence's most precious religious structures, standing right by the busy central station. The basilica's symmetrical, green-and-white marble facade is owed to wool merchant Giovanni Rucellai, whose name can still be read in the inscription above the oculus. In the 1450s Rucellai commissioned the young architect Leon Battista Alberti with the completion of the church, which had its front wall left bare. Alberti's awe-inspiring architectural achievement took the Gothic style to a new level, echoing Florentine Romanesque designs and adding intricate geometrical patterns. The interior is an unmissable showcase of works by some of the Renaissance greats – Giotto, Masaccio, Brunelleschi and Ghirlandaio all contributed to making the basilica a timeless gallery of inestimable worth. If one work was to be selected as the highlight it would be Filippino Lippi's visually striking **Cappella di Filippo Strozzi**, frescoed to represent a series of events that marked the lives of St Philip and John the Evangelist.

MUSEO NOVECENTO & CORTESE CAFÉ 900

Opened in 2014, right in front of the Basilica di Santa Maria Novella, this **museum** houses a wide collection of 20th-century artworks, in three floors previously belonging to the San Paolo Hospital. The permanent exhibition includes works by Giorgio Morandi, Lucio Fontana, Marino Marini, Carlo Levi and a vast body of works by Florentine painter Ottone Rosai. The adjoining **cafe** is a worthy stop too – the **Cortese Café 900** is Florence's first raw patisserie, serving cakes, cookies, pralines and gelato made sans flour, milk, eggs, yeast or sugar.

Basilica di Santa Maria Novella

TODAMO/SHUTTERSTOCK ©

Street Levels Gallery

URBAN ART GALLERY

Opened in 2016, Street Levels Gallery is Florence's first art space dedicated to **urban art**. The pioneering gallery in Via Palazzuolo showcases works by the elusive Florentine street-artist community, including Clet's famous ironically altered street signs, Ache77 magnetic portraits and Guerrilla Spam's fun, politically charged posters. The gallery aptly extends beyond its walls, and is often involved in public-art installations and events dedicated to the diverse facets of the contemporary urban art world. Check what's on at www.streetlevelsgallery. com.

TOP RIGHT: BUSA PHOTOGRAPHY/GETTY IMAGES © BOTTOM LEFT: SIMONA FLAMIGNI/SHUTTERSTOCK ©

Parco delle Cascine

Bottles, Officina Profumo Farmaceutica di Santa Maria Novella

Todo Modo

WELCOMING BOOKSHOP WITH CAFE

A little flag marks the unassuming entrance of bookshop Todo Modo, a neighbourhood favourite. Don't be deceived by the small room visible from the front door – walk through and around the corner you'll find a quaint, wood-furnished **cafe** where you can enjoy your world literature with a glass of wine or a plate of *testaroli al pesto* before continuing your city explorations.

Todo Modo occasionally organises English-language story-telling nights when guests are invited behind the mic to test their oratory skills in the store's little theatre.

Officina Profumo Farmaceutica di Santa Maria Novella

OLDEST PHARMACY IN THE WORLD, APPARENTLY

Part museum, part (pricey) **apothecary**, the Officina Profumo Farmaceutica di Santa Maria Novella is one of the oldest continuously operating pharmacies in Europe. Its origins can be traced back to 1221, when the Dominican monks from the nearby Basilica di Santa Maria Novella began cultivating herbs to make healing balms and ointments. The current pharmacy opened its doors to the public in 1612, when it began specialising in fragrances and perfumes for the Florentine elite and the travelling nobility of the time. Enter the scented hall via the floral doorway and awaken your senses as you roam past the walnut furniture brimming with artisanal colognes.

The Transformation of Florence's Green Lung

CHANGING TUNES IN THE CASCINE PARK

For years, the infamous **Parco delle Cascine** (Cascine Park) used to be the beating heart of Florence's nightlife and transgressions. Removed from the city centre and distant from residential areas, the 160-hectare grounds bordering the Arno came alive after dark, when thousands arrived to dance under the influence of house and techno beats. International DJs made frequent appearances in the glamorous, neon-lit halls of legendary clubs such as Central Park and Meccanò, but prostitution, drugs and drink-driving crashes featured in the local press more often than the big electronic-music performers.

In 2011 the council approved a redevelopment project that aimed to give the Cascine a new life. The clubs shut down permanently and were demolished shortly after, erasing once and for all the history of Florentine nightlife culture. Florence's biggest park caters to a different type of crowd today, and while music remains central to its identity, much has changed compared to over a decade ago.

Teatro del Maggio Musicale

In 2014 the Teatro del Maggio Musicale officially opened to the public, replacing the former **city theatre**, the now-demolished Teatro Comunale in Corso Italia. Hosting a variety of opera and classical-music performances year-round (see the full programme at maggiofiorentino.com), the structure boasts a 1890-seat opera hall, a 1000-seat auditorium for orchestral concerts and an academy for young talent. It takes its name from the Maggio Musicale Fiorentino, an important music festival running from April to June, held since 1933 but rooted in ancient springtime celebrations.

Manifattura Tabacchi

Located 500m from the park's greenery is the Manifattura Tabacchi complex, a 1930s Rationalist structure built when the state, who owned the monopoly on tobacco production, decided it needed a new manufacturing plant. Designed by Pier Luigi Nervi, the complex that once employed 1400 people to produce cigars and cigarettes has been converted into a **multifunctional space** that houses co-working areas, pop-up shops, cafes, exhibition spaces and a brewery.

BEST CAFES & BAKERIES IN SANTA MARIA NOVELLA

Cioccolateria Ballerini
An institution of Borgo Ognissanti, baking fresh, crunchy *schiacciata* (flat bread made with olive oil) daily plus a variety of sweets you will not be able to resist.

Café Pasticceria Gamberini
Recently opened but inspired by past traditions, Gamberini has great coffee, pastries and old-school atmosphere.

Bar Pasticceria Piccioli
A breakfast favourite among locals, who come back daily for pistachio or chocolate-filled *cornetti* (croissants) and cappuccinos.

Manifattura Tabacchi

WHERE TO EAT IN SANTA MARIA NOVELLA

Ostaria dei Centopoveri
A daily-changing two-course meal and wine costs only €11 at this old-style *osteria*, which gets packed at lunchtime. €

La Boite
A little wood-panelled wine bar on Piazza San Paolino serves great charcuterie boards and *schiacciata* sandwiches. €

Trattoria 13 Gobbi
You'll keep talking about their legendary rigatoni with tomato and buffalo mozzarella for days after leaving. €€

Le Pavoniere

This **public swimming pool** is hidden from sight due to the park's lush vegetation. Inside, however, is an exclusive space that comes alive during summer and features an elegant restaurant and a cocktail bar.

Ultravox and the Amphitheatre

Nestled near the western end of the park, steps away from the statue of Fyodor Dostoevsky (donated to the city by the Russian Embassy for the 200th anniversary of the author's birth), is an amphitheatre embedded in nature that becomes an **open-air concert space** during summer. During the Ultravox food and music festival (ultravoxfirenze.it), local and international acts play in this hidden oasis most days between June and August.

Visarno Arena & Firenze Rocks

Since the summer of 2015 the **Visarno Hippodrome** has been hosting Florence's largest music events, including concerts by David Gilmour, Sting, Guns N' Roses and many more. From 2017 the racetrack became the home of the Firenze Rocks festival, a four-day event that's featured artists of the likes of Ed Sheeran, Metallica, Green Day and the Red Hot Chili Peppers.

TUESDAY MARKET

The largest and least touristy **market** in the city takes place on the banks of the Arno every Tuesday morning, from approximately 8am to 2pm. Stretching for 1km between the Cascine's two pedestrian bridges, this is the kind of place where locals shop. Secondhand clothing, basic necessities, fresh produce, flowers and artisanal delicacies are what people come here to hunt for.

Dostoevsky in Florence

Why is there a statue of Fyodor Dostoevsky in the middle of Cascine Park? The author lived in Florence between 1868 and 1869, as shown on the plaque by his former residence in **Piazza Pitti** (p442).

 WHERE TO SLEEP IN SANTA MARIA NOVELLA

New Generation Hostel
Well located in Borgo Ognissanti and offering soft beds, big lockers, free wi-fi and an elegant courtyard. €

Garibaldi Blu
Designer hotel facing Piazza Santa Maria Novella, with spacious rooms and friendly service. €€

Palazzo Montebello
A luxurious property hidden in plain sight on a quiet street just steps away from the river. €€

SAN LORENZO & SAN MARCO

SHOPPING & FOOD IN A LIVELY MARKET ATMOSPHERE

Loud and lively, the area surrounding central Florence's largest market is an exciting mix of flavours, languages, and artistic treasures carefully preserved behind thick palace walls. The unassuming Palazzo Medici Riccardi is where the Medicis began their conquest of the city's institutions that led to 300 years of hegemony. San Lorenzo remains closely tied to the past – the Medici's family church still dominates the area with its unfinished facade.

But San Lorenzo and San Marco are also transforming: with gentrification increasingly pushing locals to the city's outskirts, fruit and vegetable vendors have been largely substituted with traders of nicely packaged artisanal items and mass-produced souvenirs. Finding authenticity may have become more difficult in recent times, but this area rewards those who dig deeper.

TOP TIP

San Lorenzo is located minutes away from both Santa Maria Novella and Piazza del Duomo. Walk north from the market through Via Cavour to get to Piazza San Marco, the heart of the San Marco neighbourhood.

EQROY/SHUTTERSTOCK ©

Mercato Centrale

Mercato Centrale

MODERN FOOD MARKET SELLING DELICACIES

Florence's **Central Market** has two entirely different souls that coexist in the same building. On the ground floor, the historic stalls have sold fruit, vegetables, meats and fish since 1874, while in the modern, 3000-sq-metre hall on the top floor, local and international restaurants, *enotecas* (wine bars) and food artisans offer specialities at the large shared tables surrounding a bar island. There are charcuterie boards, pizza, dumplings and vegan burgers – order from any stall and sit where you like. Want to learn some tricks of the trade? Sign up for a cooking course at the Lorenzo de' Medici Cooking School (cucinaldm. com) inside the market and make your own pasta.

Mercato di San Lorenzo

OPEN-AIR MARKET

The outdoor section of the city's central market – surrounding the Mercato Centrale almost entirely – is dedicated predominantly to **clothing and accessories**. For centuries, Florence and other Tuscan cities located by the Arno have taken advantage of their direct access to water to tan leather, and the material is still the main product hanging from the market's stalls. Belt, handbag, notebook and coat vendors line up one after the other, making San Lorenzo an ideal place for gift shopping (although the goods' quality can be dubious). Feel free to haggle.

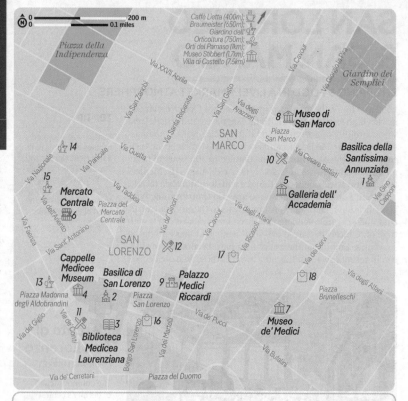

Museo di San Marco

NATIONAL MUSEUM WITH WORKS BY FRA' ANGELICO

Museo di San Marco

Adjoining the San Marco Basilica, the Museo di San Marco may not receive the crowds of other museums in Florence, but its collection of **Renaissance artworks** can definitely compete with more famous galleries for elegance and worth. The protagonist here is undoubtedly Fra' Angelico, the religious painter previously known as Il Beato Angelico, who was made a saint by Pope John Paul II in 1984. Behind Michelozzo's Chiostro di Sant'Antonio you'll find the Sala dell'Ospizio dei Pellegrini, with Fra' Angelico's luminous *Deposizione dalla Croce* (1432), which Giorgio Vasari described as looking as if it'd been painted by a saint or an angel, and the *Giudizio Universale* (1431).

Biblioteca Medicea Laurenziana

ONE OF THE WORLD'S MOST IMPORTANT MANUSCRIPT COLLECTIONS

Inside the Basilica di San Lorenzo is another structure designed by Michelangelo – the Biblioteca Medicea Laurenziana. The **library** holds over 11,000 manuscripts, 1681 original 16th-century books and the largest collection of Egyptian papyri in Italy. It's a testament to the cultural shift towards humanism started by Cosimo the Elder, the first ruler to understand the importance of a classical education for the flourishing of society.

TOP RIGHT: SILVERFOX999/SHUTTERSTOCK © BOTTOM LEFT: FELIX LIPOV/SHUTTERSTOCK ©

Basilica di San Lorenzo

Tomb of Giuliano de Medici, Cappelle Medicee

Basilica di San Lorenzo

THE MEDICI'S BRUNELLESCHI-DESIGNED FAMILY CHURCH

Built on the foundations of a 4th-century church, the harmonious **San Lorenzo Basilica** was drastically transformed during the 15th century when the Medici declared it their family church and mausoleum, and funded its monumental expansion. In 1425 Brunelleschi provided a new design to Cosimo the Elder, whose tomb is in the crypt, but the facade's renovation was commissioned to Michelangelo in 1516 by Pope Leo X. Michelangelo's Carrara marble project never took off, and the basilica has kept its bare look to this day. Still, in the main nave there are some exceptional artworks, like Filippo Lippi's *Annunciazione Martelli* (1440) and Donatello's *Pulpito della Resurrezione* (1460).

Cappelle Medicee

MICHELANGELO'S ARCHITECTURAL MASTERPIECE

While Michelangelo never completed the basilica's facade, the artist's architectural abilities can be admired in San Lorenzo's Sagrestia Nuova. It's now part of the **Cappelle Medicee Museum**, where prominent Medici family members are buried, including

Lorenzo the Magnificent and his brother Giuliano. Erected between 1520 and 1534, the new sacristy is a sculptural wonder, with symmetrical marble arches, pillars, balustrades and frames adorned with monumental sculptures, whose details are

elevated by two sources of natural light, which Michelangelo viewed as an essential design element. There are two separate entrances – and tickets – for the Basilica di San Lorenzo and the Cappelle Medicee Museum.

Palazzo Medici Riccardi

THE MEDICI'S FIRST RESIDENCE

Any Medici-inspired tour of Florence should start at the Palazzo Medici Riccardi, their first official residence. Get to Via Cavour, steps from the Duomo, and enter the **palace** via the elegant Cortile di Michelozzo, named after the building's architect. A staircase in the courtyard leads to the centrepiece – Cappella dei Magi, the mesmerising private family chapel vividly frescoed by Benozzo Gozzoli (1459). Continue to reach the Luca Giordano Gallery, a baroque mirror-filled hall where you can admire the stunning Apoteosi dei Medici (1685).

Apoteosi dei Medici, Luca Giordano, Palazzo Medici Riccardi

Basilica della Santissima Annunziata

MARIAN BAROQUE CHURCH

In existence since the 11th century, the Marian **Santissima Annunziata Basilica** took its current baroque character after centuries of transformation. Beyond the arched facade designed by the Medici's court architect Michelozzo is the antechamber – the Chiostrino dei Voti – where biblical scenes frescoed by mannerist greats such as Pontormo and Andrea del Sarto welcome you. It's hard to spot the masterpieces hanging inside the church's 12 chapels but it's worth navigating the interior's darkness for a close look at the *Glorious Virgin during the Annunciation*, a legendary painting started by Friar Bartolomeo in the 13th century and said to have been completed by angels when the artist fell asleep.

Basilica della Santissima Annunziata

Galleria dell'Accademia

SCULPTURE GALLERY, HOME OF MICHELANGELO'S DAVID

Home of the city's most iconic statue – Michelangelo's original *David*, created from a single block of marble when the legendary artist was only 26 – this **gallery** is worth the queue, not just to praise the glorious 5.17m-tall masterpiece up close, but also to examine the collection of unfinished figures trapped in massive white marble blocks that surround Florence's most famous piece of art. Enter via the Sala del Colosso, where you'll find the plaster model of Giambologna's *Rape of the Sabines* (1580) surrounded by paintings from Uccello, Lippi, Ghirlandaio and Botticelli, then complete your tour in the hall dedicated to 17th- and 18th-century artful musical instruments.

Green Escapes

FLORENCE'S LESSER-KNOWN GARDENS

The area north of San Marco doesn't get nearly as many visitors as the central neighbourhoods – and that's exactly why you should consider going there. Some of the lesser-known city parks climb up the hills surrounding the city centre, offering well-deserved respite from the crowds as well as great views of the red rooftops that surround the Duomo.

Extending from the 19th-century Giacomo Roster Tepidarium *(societatoscanaorticultura.it)* is the **Giardino dell'Orticoltura**, founded in 1859 by the Tuscan Society of Horticulture as an experimental space for the cultivation of rare and exotic flora. The association still organises one of the city's largest flower markets in the park during the last week of April, and the tepidarium is regularly used for art exhibitions and cultural events.

From the Giardino dell'Orticoltura you can climb up to the artsy **Orti del Parnaso**, where a huge, colourful sculpture of a snake (or is it a dragon?) crawls down a staircase that leads to one of the least photographed yet most satisfying views of the city. Further up the road are the lush, cypress-dotted gardens surrounding Villa Fabbricotti, a luxurious residence dating back to 1894, whose prestigious guests have included Queen Victoria and Elisa Bonaparte, sister of Napoleon.

And if all the climbing and exploring makes you thirsty, stop by at **Caffè Lietta**, near Piazza della Libertà, for a fresh juice and a sweet treat on your way back to the city centre.

BEST CRAFT BEER IN SAN LORENZO & SAN MARCO

Mostodolce
Great selection of internationally inspired beers: try their Belgian-style Martellina with a wood-fired pizza.

PanicAle
Right by the Mercato Centrale, this little bar serves craft brews and cocktails.

Braumeister
In Via Madonna della Tosse, with a cool pub atmosphere, great food and an ever-changing selection of tap brews.

Alibi
Small pub in Via Faenza with local and international beers on tap.

A Villa of Wonders

FREDERICK STIBBERT'S MIND-BLOWING ART COLLECTION

The elegant halls of the beautiful Villa di Montughi would be worth visiting empty, but the odd, surprising collection of objects amassed by Anglo-Italian collector and entrepreneur Frederick Stibbert over the course of the 19th century will reawaken your curiosity, even if you've already had your fair share of Florentine museum roaming.

Removed from typical art trails, the **Museo Stibbert** features over 50,000 artefacts from different eras, with the core of the collection being a vast array of weapons gathered from different corners of the globe. The villa's halls house a parade of 16th- and 17th-century armour from Italy, Germany, Turkey and India, plus the largest body of

Museo Stibbert

 WHERE TO EAT IN SAN LORENZO & SAN MARCO

All'Antico Vinaio
Florence's best-known sandwich shop has opened in Piazza San Marco – come for the *schiacciata* minus the queues. €

La Ménagère
Open all day from brunch to dinner, this restaurant attracts those ready to splurge on an aesthetically pleasing meal. €€

Konnubio
Dimly lit, romantic atmosphere and a creative menu filled with experimental flavour combinations. €€€

THE GUIDE

FLORENCE: SAN LORENZO & SAN MARCO

FLORENCE'S HIDDEN GARDENS

Lorenzo Dal Piaz, born and raised in Florence, has worked in the tourism industry in Italy and abroad for many years.

You'll be surprised to find out how many gardens are hidden near Via Cavour, giving a touch of fresh air and quietness to the neighbourhood. The most special green space is no doubt **Orti Dipinti**, an urban garden built to inspire the community to connect with nature, despite living in the heart of the city. I'm always amazed by the amount of projects going on there, ready to capture your imagination. You can participate in community events or pick herbs to bring home and cook, in exchange for a donation.

Orti Dipinti

ancient Japanese weaponry outside of Japan, including katana swords that belonged to the last group of samurais.

There is more than weapons – over the course of his life, the wealthy Stibbert collected paintings by the likes of Sandro Botticelli, Luca Giordano, Alessandro Allori, Pieter Brueghel the Younger and many other greats, all currently on display in the mesmerising rooms of his opulent former residence.

 WHERE TO SHOP IN SAN LORENZO & SAN MARCO

Scarpelli Mosaici
One of the few remaining families keeping the art of mosaic-making alive, in their beautiful atelier in Via Ricasoli.

Red Light Rock Shop
Walk down the staircase of this underground T-shirt and accessories store to travel back to your goth years.

Street Doing
Unique and carefully selected vintage finds spanning most of the 20th century.

SANTA CROCE & SANT'AMBROGIO

MUSEUMS, CHURCHES AND NIGHTLIFE

The historic neighbourhood of Santa Croce can be a much different place depending on whether you come here during the day or at night. Before dinnertime you can immerse yourself in the artistic legacy of the Renaissance's pioneers; after dark you'll find students hopping from karaoke bar to sticky pub. The area is dedicated to keeping local traditions alive, evident in its many street-food joints, fine-dining restaurants and carefully restored historic architecture.

Sant'Ambrogio is often left off short-term visitors' radars, but the neighbourhood locked between the grandiose synagogue, Piazza Beccaria and Santa Croce deserves a place on the map, if only for the chance to interact with the many Florentines who spend long, wine-soaked summer evenings in its bar-dotted piazzas.

TOP TIP

Via dei Benci and Via Ghibellina are Santa Croce's main drags, linking it to Ponte alle Grazie and the city centre. Sant'Ambrogio starts from the eastern edge of Via Pietrapiana. Both areas are easily reached on foot from both the Duomo and Piazza della Signoria.

Tomb of Michelangelo, Basilica di Santa Croce

Basilica di Santa Croce

IMPOSING CHURCH WITH THOUSANDS OF ARTWORKS

Interior and exterior stand in sharp contrast in the Franciscan **Santa Croce Basilica**, one of the city's most important religious buildings. Looking up at the neo-Gothic facade dominating the piazza you'll notice a Star of David positioned in the tympanum above the oculus – a symbol left behind by the Jewish architect Niccolò Matas, who completed the marble exterior in 1863. The austere, low-lit interior is notable for its collection of tombs – Michelangelo, Galileo, Ghiberti and Machiavelli are buried here. But prominent dead people aren't the sole draw – surrounding Agnolo Gaddi's grand fresco *Leggenda della Croce* are nearly 4000 artworks by the likes of Giotto, Brunelleschi and Donatello.

Casa Buonarroti

MUSEUM HOUSED IN MICHELANGELO'S RESIDENCE

This often-deserted Via Ghibellina **museum**, housed in an apartment purchased by Michelangelo Buonarroti in the early 16th century, was expanded and transformed by his heirs in the following century. Michelangelo and his family owned various properties in Florence and spent only a brief time here before moving to Rome permanently in 1534. Still, the museum hosts two bas-reliefs produced by the unchallenged Renaissance master in his teenage years, the *Madonna della Scala* (1491) and the *Battaglia dei Centauri* (1492), next to the art collection acquired by Michelangelo Buonarroti the Younger (1568–1647), the artist's grandnephew.

429

HIGHLIGHTS
1 Basilica di Santa Croce
2 Casa Buonarroti
3 Cibrèo Ristorante
4 Cibrèo Trattoria
5 Contempo Records
6 Le Murate
7 Locale
8 Mercato di Sant'Ambrogio
9 Museo del Bargello
10 Synagogue & Jewish Museum of Florence

SIGHTS
11 Piazza di Santa Croce

EATING
12 All'Antico Vinaio

(see 17) Budellino
13 Drogheria
14 Enoteca Pinchiorri
15 Gelateria dei Neri
(see 12) La Fettunta
16 La Giostra
17 La Prosciutteria
(see 12) La Schiacciata
18 Le Vespe Café
19 L'Ortone
20 Melaleuca

DRINKING & NIGHTLIFE
21 Base V Juicery
22 Bitter Bar
23 Ditta Artigianale
24 Eby's
25 Rex Café

Museo del Bargello

THE WORLD'S LARGEST COLLECTION OF RENAISSANCE SCULPTURES

The towering 1255 fortification on Via del Proconsolo was originally built as the residence of the *podestà*, the city's highest judiciary, but was transformed into a prison in the 15th century before becoming Italy's first national **museum** in 1865. Today the Museo del Bargello houses the world's vastest collection of Renaissance sculpture. Donatello's long-haired bronze *David* (c 1440) stands on Goliath's head under the vaulted ceiling of the Hall of Donatello, next to an earlier marble version of the biblical figure (1408) and the *San Giorgio* statue (1415–18). But there's more than Donatellos – the Sala Michelangelo houses Buonarroti's *Bacco* (1497), the unfinished *David-Apollo* (1530) and Benvenuto Cellini's *Narciso* (1548–65).

Great Synagogue of Florence

MONUMENTAL PLACE OF WORSHIP AND JEWISH MUSEUM

From any high point in the city you'll be able to spot the turquoise copper dome of Florence's synagogue, the home of the local Israelite community near the Sant'Ambrogio neighbourhood. The Moorish-style structure known as **Tempio Maggiore** was designed by architects Mariano Falcini, Marco Treves and Vincenco Micheli in the late 19th century, following the unification of Italy and the subsequent razing of the ghetto near Piazza della Repubblica. Inside, polychrome stained-glass windows, marble-enriched floors and intricate chandeliers adorn a low-lit space. Walk to the end of the nave to closely inspect the mosaic-clad Aron framed in a theatrical canopy, then climb to the upper floors to visit the **museum**, tracing the history of the Jewish community in Florence.

Locale

CREATIVE COCKTAIL BAR AND RESTAURANT

Nominated in the World's 50 Best Bars list, Locale has conquered the Florentine cocktail scene since opening in 2015. Hidden inside the historic Palazzo Concini, the **cocktail bar** faces a lush vertical garden with a tropical feel. The experimental cocktail menu changes seasonally and the sophisticated ambience attracts a fashionable, international crowd.

Le Murate

Le Murate

LITERARY CAFE IN A FORMER PRISON

Nowadays Le Murate is a **creative space** dedicated to the celebration of contemporary culture through reading, exhibitions, screenings and live music, but the monumental complex hasn't always been a fun gathering spot. For over 150 years, Le Murate was a prison – famous figures such as anarchist philosopher Errico Malatesta, antifascist author Carlo Levi and political activist Alcide de Gasperi have all been guests of the panopticon structure. After its closure in 1984 it was left abandoned until 2001, when a long renovation process guided by starchitect Renzo Piano began to give Le Murate new life.

Contempo Records

RECORD STORE

Rock fans will love this dark store brimming with **vinyl records** from all music eras, tucked among gelaterias and sandwich shops on busy Via de' Neri. Contempo Records seems to have managed to maintain its '70s character throughout the years and continues to offer customers a rich selection of rare Italian and international albums to browse through for hours on end – and you might get headbanging to the loud metal music played day in, day out.

Mercato di Sant'Ambrogio

Mercato di Sant'Ambrogio

LIVELY MARKET AND STREET-FOOD DESTINATION

If you're looking for a genuine market atmosphere away from too-tourist-friendly San Lorenzo's, head to Sant'Ambrogio and enter the oldest functioning **market** in the city. Running since 1873, this quintessential Florentine destination is great for people-watching, filling up on local produce or stopping for lunch at one of the stalls serving freshly baked *schiacciata*, *lampredotto* and plates of steaming pasta. The Mercato di Sant'Ambrogio is open every day apart from Sunday, from 7am to 2pm.

Aperitivo,
Cibrèo Trattoria

Cibrèo Trattoria

TRADITIONAL CUISINE WITH AN ARTISTIC TOUCH

It would be an understatement to define Cibrèo as simply a restaurant. The brainchild of Fabio Picchi, the late restaurateur turned TV star who opened Sant'Ambrogio's most iconic eatery back in 1979, Cibrèo has evolved from traditional trattoria to a cultural experience with multiple souls. You can visit the welcoming **Cibrèo Trattoria**, also known as Il Cibreino, where generous portions and a no-fuss attitude feed local regulars, or the more formal **Cibrèo Ristorante** for a refined take on Tuscan cuisine. (And there's also the 'Tosco-Eastern' Ciblèo, a surprising 16-seat fusion restaurant blending local and Asian cooking techniques, the Cibrèo Caffè and its sweet treats, and the Teatro del Sale, with a Tuscan buffet and live theatre.)

Street-Food Delights

FLAVOURS BEYOND THE OBVIOUS

A disorderly queue stretches out on Via de' Neri most days of the year, clogging up the street traffic – it's the people waiting to get the famed stuffed *schiacciata* sandwich from **All'Antico Vinaio**, Florence's best-known street-food joint and obligatory stop for many who visit the city. The shop sells Tuscany's traditional flat bread – whose name literally means 'pressed', referring to the act of pressing down the dough with one's fingers before baking it – with a variety of tasty fillings, from *prosciutto crudo* (cured ham) to *pecorino* cream and sundried tomatoes. All'Antico Vinaio has grown into a street-food empire, with half a dozen shops scattered around Italy and pop-up venues in New York and Los Angeles. Travellers not caught up in FOMO, however, may ask whether waiting half an hour for a sandwich is actually worth it. The answer is simple: Via de' Neri is filled with opportunities elsewhere to taste equally delicious quick bites rooted in the Tuscan culinary tradition.

The aptly named **La Schiacciata**, for instance, serves salty sandwiches brimming with cold cuts, cheeses, vegetables and home-made sauces next to **La Fettunta**, where you can sit and feast on pastas, cured-meat boards, steaks and more. Down the road are **La Prosciutteria** and **Budellino**, two other great options for takeaway eats, both hot and cold and always served with a generous dose of red wine on the side. **Ditta Artigianale** paved the way for speciality coffee to reach Florence – if you're in need of a caffeine kick after stocking up on carbs, that's where you should stop. Did someone say dessert? **Gelateria dei Neri** means artisanal gelato, but if you're looking for something on the healthier side opt for a nutritious smoothie at **Base V Juicery**.

BEST NIGHTLIFE IN SANTA CROCE & SANT'AMBROGIO

Eby's
A Florentine icon, Eby's has been serving creative shots from this hole in the wall for decades.

Rex
Behind thick black curtains is a fun yet sophisticated cocktail bar attracting a mixed crowd until late.

Bitter Bar
Speakeasy vibes and well-researched flavour combinations make this lounge in Via di Mezzo a great place for a nightcap.

A Violent Affair

THE CALCIO STORICO TOURNAMENT

Turn up in **Piazza di Santa Croce** on 24 June and you'll find a much different environment than the typically empty square leading up to the neo-Gothic basilica. On this date, Florence celebrates its patron saint John the Baptist, but the reason why 4000 people cheer from the bleachers of a temporary sand arena, surrounded by ambulances, is far from religious.

The final match of the *calcio storico* tournament is one of the city's most awaited events of the year. Institutionalised

LACKING PATIENCE?

If you want to get a taste of All'Antico Vinaio's revered *schiacciata* without having to stand in line, try their recently opened **Piazza San Marco shop** (p427).

WHERE TO EAT IN SANTA CROCE & SANT'AMBROGIO

Melaleuca	**Le Vespe Café**	**Drogheria**
Stop for breakfast, brunch or lunch and fill up on fresh pastries and coffee prepared with an Australian touch. €€	Friendly brunch spot in Via Ghibellina, ideal for a healthy break between sights. €€	For an alternative to pasta, pizza and steaks, try the massive burgers here – you won't be disappointed. €€

VOVA POMORTZEFF/ALAMY STOCK PHOTO ©

Calcio storico **ceremony, Piazza di Santa Croce (p433)**

WHY I LOVE SANTA CROCE

Angelo Zinna, writer

Florence's city centre can feel a bit too orderly at times, but Santa Croce hits differently. This part of the city changes abruptly as night comes – while its stately piazza draws all the attention during the day, the low-key bars found in the neighbourhood's alleys come to life after dark, disrupting the usual sight-to-sight flow of people and allowing for unexpected events and encounters to happen. Plus, it's the only place to get a slice of pizza in the middle of the night.

in 1530 when Florentine neighbourhoods organised a soccer game to prove their fearlessness in front of the invading troops of Charles V (an ally of the Medici family who wanted to re-establish control over the city), the reenactment of that glorious Renaissance tournament has been ongoing since 1930.

The uninitiated may be horror-struck by the brutality of *calcio storico*. Bare-knuckle punches, kicks and tackles are all acceptable strategies to score a '*caccia*' (hunt) by carrying the ball into the opponents' net at the end of the field. Elements of rugby, wrestling and soccer combine in the game that's played on a 100m by 50m *sabbione* (sand arena). The competing teams, with 27 players each, represent Florence's four historical districts – Santa Maria Novella's Rossi (Reds), Santa Croce's Azzurri (Blues), Santo Spirito's Bianchi (Whites) and San Giovanni's Verdi (Greens).

Despite hospital runs being the norm year after year, this legendary tournament, consisting of two semifinals and one final, continues to sell out, with crowds coming to see their district's *calcianti* fight each other for 50 minutes in scorching summer heat. No prize apart from glory is awarded to the winners of the final, an event rooted in Florentine folklore – clearly, keeping tradition alive is worth spilling blood for.

WHERE TO EAT IN SANTA CROCE & SANT'AMBROGIO

L'Ortone
A beautifully designed space serving traditional dishes with a twist. €€

La Giostra
A favourite among celebrities, who come here for the rustic-chic decor, excellent food and huge wine list. €€€

Enoteca Pinchiorri
One of Italy's most prestigious restaurants, three-Michelin-starred Enoteca Pinchiorri serves works of art. €€€

SAN FREDIANO & SANTO SPIRITO

CREATIVE HUB WITH MANY APERITIVO SPOTS

Until the early 2000s craftspeople set up shop in the Oltrarno, attracted by its vicinity to the city centre and the cheap rent, but since the 2010s, the once working-class area comprising San Frediano and Santo Spirito has radically transformed to cater for the growing population of international residents and visitors. The neighbourhoods have opened up to contemporary art galleries, hip cocktail bars and quirky restaurants, drawing waves of travellers seeking to experience a different facet of the city's identity.

Despite their evident contradictions, San Frediano and Santo Spirito are among the most exciting neighbourhoods in Florence to visit today. Though rough around the edges, these are places where ideas continue to rapidly change the urban landscape.

TOP TIP

San Frediano and Santo Spirito are adjacent neighbourhoods divided by Via dei Serragli and spread for approximately 1km kilometre along the Arno river. From the city centre you can cross Ponte Santa Trinità, Ponte alla Carraia or Ponte Amerigo Vespucci to get here.

ALBERTO PIZZOLI/AFP/GETTY IMAGES ©

Michelangelo's crucifix, Basilica di Santo Spirito

Santo Spirito's Secret

MICHELANGELO AND AN ART DISCOVERY

The centrepiece of the Basilica di Santo Spirito is a little-known wooden **crucifix** that has long kept art historians debating. The slender figure attributed to Michelangelo, who lived and studied anatomy in the church when he was 17, was known through Giorgio Vasari's writings but deemed lost in the 18th century following the French occupation. It wasn't until 1964 that the crucifix gained recognition, after German researcher Margrit Lisner claimed that it had never left its original location. According to Lisner, a bad paint job had made Michelangelo's early masterpiece unrecognisable; while scholars were initially doubtful, further analysis in 1999 supported the theory.

Basilica di Santo Spirito

RENAISSANCE ART AND ARCHITECTURE

Begun in 1444, the grand **Santo Spirito Basilica** was the last project Florence's master architect Filippo Brunelleschi worked on before his death in 1446. When seen from the outdoor seating area of one of the piazza's many bars, the minimalist, cream-coloured facade might not look impressive enough to make you get up and leave your *spritz*, but inside the church you'll find exceptional frescoes including Filippino Lippi's *Pala Nerli* (1485–88) and Alessandro Allori's *Cristo e l'Adultera* (1577) nestled amid *pietra serena* columns adorned with Corinthian capitals.

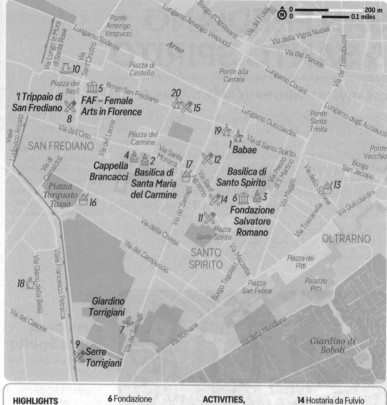

Fondazione Salvatore Romano

LITTLE-KNOWN SCULPTURE MUSEUM

MICHELANGELO'S YOUTH

Learn more about Michelangelo's early life by visiting the **Casa Buonarroti museum** (p429) in Santa Croce.

Overshadowed by the world-renowned museums on the other side of the Arno, the Fondazione Salvatore Romano, an **art collection** housed in the Augustinian complex of Santo Spirito, is often unnoticed by short-term visitors despite being one of the city's great treasures. Located inside the former refectory of the 14th-century church featuring Andrea Orcagna's 1365 Gothic masterpiece *La Crocifissione e l'Ultima Cena*, the museum is home to some invaluable sculptures. These include Jacopo della Quercia's *Madonna con Bambino* (1400–38) and a fragment of Donatello's *San Massimo* bas-relief (1443–53), which Neapolitan antiquarian Salvatore Romano (1875–1955) gathered over the course of his life.

Cappella Brancacci

RENAISSANCE FRESCOES

In 1771 a huge fire destroyed much of San Frediano's **Basilica di Santa Maria del Carmine**, an important religious structure dating back to the 13th century. Miraculously, one of the few sections to survive was also one of Florence's most precious collections of art pieces. The Renaissance treasure known as Cappella Brancacci, commissioned by wealthy merchant Felice Brancacci in 1424, features a series of frescoes by revolutionary artists Masaccio and Masolino da Panicale (completed by Filippino Lippi half a century later), which adorn the chapel's interiors around the rare 1268 panel *Madonna del Popolo*. Recently restored, the cycle of 14 paintings recounting the life of St Peter represents a defining shift towards realism in Renaissance art through their refined use of perspective and the chiaroscuro technique, which Masaccio and Masolino da Panicale pioneered. The **chapel**, whose entrance is found on the right side of the church's doors, is closed between Tuesday and Thursday. Only 30 people can enter at the same time.

SALA VANNI

One section of the Basilica di Santa Maria del Carmine is currently dedicated to a more contemporary form of art – **experimental jazz** music. The Sala Vanni, a hall decorated by the 1645 fresco *Cena di Cristo in casa del Fariseo* by Giovanni Battista Vanni, is managed by the Musicus Concentus association, which organises regular concerts featuring local and international acts in the 195-seat space. Past performers have included Sonic Youth's guitarist Lee Ranaldo and Radiohead's drummer Philip Selway. See the calendar of events at musicusconcentus.com.

Cappella Brancacci

ANNA PAKUTINA/SHUTTERSTOCK ©

Babae Wine Window

HISTORICAL DRINKING CUSTOMS

In the 17th century many wine traders began selling wine from literal holes in the wall to avoid direct contact with customers, as the plague was spreading around the city. **Babae** – located right on Via Santo Spirito, a street loved by seekers of unique and unusual interior design items – is a cafe that features one of the last remaining functioning *buchette del vino* (wine windows) in Florence. Ring the leaf-shaped bell to order your tipple of choice, which will be handed over to you via the small aperture.

TOP RIGHT: ECE CHIANUCCI/SHUTTERSTOCK © BOTTOM LEFT: IMARZI/SHUTTERSTOCK ©

Babae wine window

FAF – Female Arts in Florence

CONTEMPORARY ART GALLERY

Near the western end of Borgo San Frediano is an inviting, continuously transforming shop window. Female Arts in Florence, a new **art project** created by women for women, has been run with enthusiasm by curator Giulia Castagnoli since late 2019. It's a contemporary art gallery, artisanal studio and co-working space hosting cultural events to celebrate the work of women from around the world. Jewellery, painting, printmaking and pottery come together here, with artists and artisans welcome to bring their own ideas. Visitors can join one of the many workshops organised year-round. See the links on Instagram *(@femaleartsinflorence)* for the full programme of events.

Lampredotto

'l Trippaio di San Frediano

BUDGET STREET FOOD

Few traditional dishes leave foreign visitors as perplexed as the infamous **lampredotto**, a quintessentially Florentine dish made by cooking one of the four sections of the cow's stomach, the abomasum, in broth before covering it in a garlic and parsley green sauce. 'l Trippaio di San Frediano serves succulent *lampredotto* sandwiches and many other local favourites (including tripe, tongue and *peposo* beef stew) from a fixed street stand in Piazza dei Nerli every day at lunchtime. Join in with neighbourhood residents on their meal break and take a look at the ever-changing menu or ask for a recommendation to sample some of Tuscany's all-time classics.

Giardino Torrigiani & Serre Torrigiani

GREEN ESCAPES AND ROMANTIC GARDENS

Hiding in plain sight between the Basilica di Santa Maria del Carmine and the 14th-century city gate Porta Romana is Europe's largest private garden built within a historic urban centre. Designed by landscape architects Luigi de Cambray Digny and Gaetano Baccani during Romanticism's peak period in the early 18th century, the monumental **Giardino Torrigiani** covers nearly 7 hectares and contains a vast collection of secular flora, citrus trees and exotic herbs originating from different corners of the globe. The beautifully curated property, owned by the Torrigiani Malaspina and Torrigiani di Santa Cristina families, can be visited only by booking a private tour (email info@giardinotorrigiani.it), available in both Italian and English (from €25 per person) and run by the welcoming Tommaso Torrigiani, who'll enthusiastically tell you all about the masonic symbolism surrounding the 1824 three-storey tower at the centre of the park. The section of the garden known as **Serre Torrigiani** *(serretorrigiani.it)* has been transformed into a picturesque cocktail bar and romantic open-air restaurants serving a wide range of refined dishes prepared with herbs grown in the property's greenhouses.

IL CONVENTINO

Culture and nature combine in another Oltrarno favourite, the recently opened Il Conventino. Launched in 2019, the **complex** located in Via Giano della Bella 20 organises public readings, live music and yoga classes, all as part of the regeneration project of the historic Chiostro Del Vecchio Conventino, a long-neglected century-old convent turned artisan hub. The laptop-friendly cafe and bookshop welcomes students and remote workers with great coffee and craft beers in a chilled space with a rustic touch, while the idyllic courtyard offers a refreshing break from city wanderings.

Ruin, Giardino Torrigiani

VLADIMIR SAZONOV/SHUTTERSTOCK ©

Ponte Vecchio

BEST GELATO IN OLTRARNO

Sbrino
One of the best gelaterias in town, near Piazza Santo Spirito, with vegan options. There are also alcoholic granitas in summer.

Gelateria della Passera
The scoops are on the small side, but the gelato is great and the flavours unique.

La Sorbettiera
A bit out of the way, this Piazza Tasso artisanal gelateria is worth the walk. Try the *cioccolato fondente* (dark chocolate).

MORE IN SAN FREDIANO & SANTO SPIRITO

The City at Water Level

THE ARNO ON A BARCHETTO

The history of Florence is closely tied to the city's relationship with the **Arno**, Italy's fourth-longest river, which stretches for 241km from Mt Falterona to the Tyrrhenian Sea. It was to gain access to this water course that, in 59 BCE, the legions of Julius Caesar founded Florentia, the last among the Roman colonies in the Arno Valley, and built the wooden bridge that would become the progenitor of the **Ponte Vecchio**. And it was thanks to the abundant water resources of the river that during the Middle Ages, despite its unfavourable position, the city became one of the richest in the region, through the work of textile merchants and manufacturers who built mills and infrastructure for mass dyeing, felting and drying of fabrics.

The Arno was also directly responsible for the urban expansion of Florence, providing essential building materials for the construction of the city's famed architecture. For centuries,

WHERE TO EAT & DRINK IN SAN FREDIANO & SANTO SPIRITO

#RAW
Specialising in dishes made with (mostly) uncooked ingredients, with vegan and gluten-free burgers, ramen and pizza. €€

La Cité
Study, work, eat or drink amid oddly mixed vintage furniture and books at this all-time Borgo San Frediano classic. €

MAD Souls & Spirits
Its craft cocktails and welcoming atmosphere make MAD a safe late-night choice. €€

renaioli boatmen cruised the waters on small boats known as *barchetti*, extracting sand and gravel from the riverbed to sell it to masons busy erecting the structures that still define Florence's skyline. Horse-drawn *barrocci* (carts) filled with the Arno's precious soil travelled from the shore to construction sites in the city until the first half of the 20th century, when modern technologies supplanted the *renaioli*'s long shovels, quickly ensuring sand extraction became a dying profession.

While the *renaioli* no longer carry out their original mission, their story lives on thanks to three Florentine friends who, in 1995, decided to restore a series of ancient *barchetti* and get back on the river. Today the **Renaioli Association** (*renaioli.it*) organises boat cruises (from May to October), guiding the wooden vessels with traditional long barges under the Ponte Vecchio and the Corridoio Vasariano, allowing visitors to see the city from an alternative perspective.

Make Your Own David

CLAY SCULPTURE WORKSHOPS

Museums such as the Bargello, the Galleria dell'Accademia, the Uffizi and Palazzo Pitti are filled with iconic sculptures that have come to form the core of Florence's artistic heritage, but few are the workshops that continue to keep alive the craft of turning rock and soil into realistic figures.

One of them is **Galleria Romanelli**, found near the western end of Borgo San Frediano, steps away from the 14th-century city gate. Push the glass door and enter a showroom filled to the brim with white, monumental figures inspired by classical compositions – equestrian statues sit next to busts of Roman emperors and reproductions of famous fight scenes.

Originally a small church, the space was converted into an art studio in 1829 by Lorenzo Bartolini, the former sculptor of the Bonaparte family whose neoclassical masterpieces can be admired in the Uffizi, the Galleria dell'Accademia and the Basilica di Santa Croce. Upon the master's death, his student Pasquale Romanelli took over the studio, and since then six generations of the Romanelli family have carved marble and clay here.

Next to working on international commissions, Galleria Romanelli offers the opportunity to test your skills at clay sculpting. In the shorter three-hour sessions for beginners (starting at €99), Raffaello Romanelli guides students through the basic concepts of sculpting clay with the objective of producing a section – usually the nose or an eye – of Michelangelo's famous David. Longer courses are also available for the particularly inspired.

THE OTHER SIDE OF FLORENCE

Lilith, long-time San Frediano resident, runs L'Ornitorinco, an independent bookshop and cultural hub in the neighbourhood.

The reason I love San Frediano? Because it was the first place that made me feel at home. Florence is one of the most beautiful cities in the world, but sometimes it can be difficult to handle as an outsider. San Frediano makes you feel welcome anytime. Everyone knows and greets each other, the greengrocer down the street calls you by your name and knows what you like best. Here you get the whole package: the wonders of Florence and the warmth of a small town. I couldn't have chosen a better place for me and my small bookstore.

Il Santino
A few tables, tasty bites, an endless wine list and a small crowd of regulars spilling onto the sidewalk. €€

Hostaria da Fulvio
Opening up directly onto the street, da Fulvio blends refined decor with great pastas, seafood and desserts. €€

Cuculia
A charming, artistic vibe and a great combination of typically Italian flavours with international ingredients. €€

SAN NICCOLÒ, BOBOLI & PIAZZA PITTI

ELEGANT GARDENS AND GREAT VIEWS

It's no coincidence the area extending from San Niccolò is so different from the rest. Until the mid-19th century, much of Florence still preserved its medieval architecture, with high stone walls separating the city from its surroundings, despite having lost their defensive purpose. Following the naming of Florence as the newly unified Italy's capital in 1865, local authorities thought it necessary to propel the city into modernity.

The redevelopment of this part of the city was commissioned to architect Giuseppe Poggi, who tore down the ancient walls to create the *viali* (wide roads encircling the city). The cherry on top of the cake was Piazzale Michelangelo, a terrace in one of the highest spots in the city, offering a perfectly framed view of Florence.

TOP TIP

Piazza Pitti is easily reached on foot by crossing the Ponte Vecchio. To walk up to Piazzale Michelangelo and San Miniato al Monte, head to San Niccolò then climb up via the Rampe del Poggi in about 15 minutes. Or take bus 12 from Lungarno Soderini or bus 13 from Santa Maria Novella.

ALEX_MASTRO/SHUTTERSTOCK ©

View of Florence from Piazzale Michelangelo

Michelangelo's Panoramic Terrace

CITY WALK AND PHOTO-WORTHY SUNSET VIEWS

Legend has it that 18 oxen were required to bring the bronze copy of the *David* to **Piazzale Michelangelo** in 1873. Since then, Florence's most iconic sculpture hasn't stopped gazing over the Arno slithering through the city. You'll likely do the same, as the panoramic terrace, easily reached by a 10-minute uphill hike from Porta San Niccolò, offers one of the most privileged sunset views over Florence's red rooftops. Walk up the Rampe del Poggi staircase, where an artificial waterfall flows down through a series of grottoes to San Niccolò's fountain.

Basilica di San Miniato al Monte

FLORENTINE ROMANESQUE ARCHITECTURE

Steps away from Piazzale Michelangelo is the **San Miniato al Monte Basilica**, founded by Holy Roman Emperor Henry II in the early 11th century. Clad with white Carrara marble and green Pisan marble, its facade is one of the most prominent examples of Florentine Romanesque architecture – a style that would come to define the city's urban landscape in the following centuries. The barely lit interior houses the 1448 Cappella del Crocefisso, an intricately sculpted ciborium designed by the Medici's own architect Michelozzo, assisted by Agnolo Gaddi and Luca della Robbia.

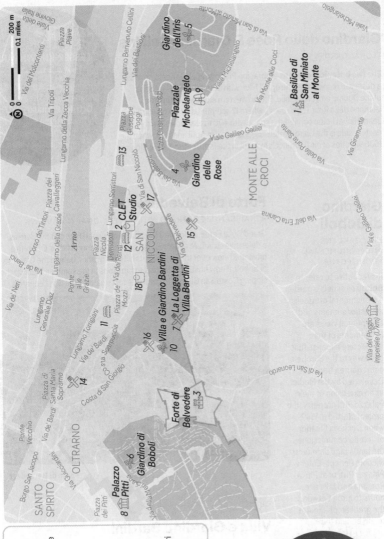

HIGHLIGHTS
1 Basilica di San Miniato al Monte
2 CLET Studio
3 Forte di Belvedere
4 Giardino delle Rose
5 Giardino dell'Iris
6 Giardino di Boboli
7 La Loggetta di Villa Bardini
8 Palazzo Pitti
9 Piazzale Michelangelo
10 Villa e Giardino Bardini

SLEEPING
11 Fuor d'Arno
12 Hotel Silla
13 Serristori Palace

EATING
14 De'Bardi
15 La Beppa Fioraia
16 La Leggenda dei Frati
17 Rifrullo

SHOPPING
18 Alessandro Dari

Basilica di San Miniato al Monte

FLORIAN AUGUSTIN/SHUTTERSTOCK ©

Giardino delle Rose & Giardino dell'Iris

FLORAL GARDENS

The two **botanical gardens** embracing Piazzale Michelangelo provide a deserved respite after the uphill hike, with equally satisfying views of the Duomo and campanile. On the western slope you'll find the Giardino delle Rose (open daily), where 12 sculptures by Belgian artist Jean-Michel Folon cohabit the space with 400 rose species. On the eastern side is the Giardino dell'Iris, open only in April and May, when the 1500 varieties of iris (Florence's symbol in the 13th century) are in bloom.

LESSER-KNOWN PARKS

Looking for an alternative to the famous parks? The little-known **Orti del Parnaso** (p427), on the northern edge of the city, offers equally spectacular views.

Giardino di Boboli

CITY GARDENS AND MONUMENTAL ARCHITECTURE

It's reductive to refer to **Boboli** as simply a garden – monumental grottoes, majestic fountains and exceptional views are all elements of the 45-hectare expanse that gave way to the European court garden tradition. Developed by the Medici as an extension of their Palazzo Pitti property, the project started in 1549, when Duchess Eleanor of Toledo commissioned the landscape architect Niccolò Pericoli. Enter via Palazzo Pitti or at Porta Romana and take a few hours to stroll between the great amphitheatre found behind the palace to the park's most intriguing sights. These include Bernardo Buontalenti's intricate grotto and the Museo delle Porcellane, located inside the neoclassical Palazzina del Cavaliere on the upper side of the garden. A Palazzo Pitti and Boboli Gardens combined ticket is available for €22.

Forte di Belvedere

RENAISSANCE FORTRESS WITH EXCEPTIONAL CITY VIEWS

Grand Duke Ferdinando I de' Medici commissioned Fort di Belvedere as a defensive structure to protect the city from enemy attacks. Offering a privileged view over the city from its hillside location behind the Giardino di Boboli, it now hosts rotating **art exhibitions** in the summer. Walk up the sloping Costa San Giorgio to get to the fort's gate on Via San Leonardo.

KAVALENKAVA/SHUTTERSTOCK ©

Forte di Belvedere

Villa e Giardino Bardini

CITY GARDENS, HISTORICAL VILLA AND VIEWS

An Italian-style garden sits next to an English garden and an agricultural park in the 4-hectare property surrounding **Villa Bardini**, the former residence of antique collector Stefano Bardini. One of Florence's most charming corners, the **Bardini Garden** is best enjoyed during springtime when the many varieties of flowers are in full bloom. Reach the park via Costa San Giorgio and stroll through the labyrinthine routes between citrus trees, fountains and sculptures all the way to **La Loggetta di Villa Bardini**, where cold drinks come with a side of wonderful Duomo views. Make sure you visit the interior of the villa as well to see the works of painter Pietro Annigoni (1910–88).

Palazzo Pitti

GRANDIOSE ARCHITECTURE AND ART MUSEUMS

Commissioned to architect Filippo Brunelleschi by Florentine banker Luca Pitti around 1440, Palazzo Pitti, the most imposing building of the Oltrarno area, has been the residence of the ruling class since the mid-16th century, when Cosimo I de' Medici's wife Eleanor of Toledo decided to move here from Palazzo Vecchio, hoping that leaving the city centre's crowds behind would benefit her declining health. Shortly after the Medici chose the palace as their new official residence, expanding the structure and transforming it into the grandiose horseshoe-shaped building we see today. The palace, which after the Medici's decline in 1737 became home to the Habsburg-Lorraine dynasty, houses invaluable paintings, sculptures and historical artefacts.

The palace's **museums** are comprised of the Palatine Gallery and the Imperial and Royal Apartments, the Treasury of the Grand Dukes (formerly known as the Museo degli Argenti), the Museum of Costume and Fashion, the Gallery of Modern Art and the new Museum of Russian Icons, the vastest collection of Russian icon art outside the historical region of Ruthenia. The visually striking 'planet rooms' are among the Palatine Gallery's highlights, together with the largest collection of Raphael's portraits. While the number of artworks can be overwhelming, don't skip the Treasury of the Grand Dukes, the former summer apartments of the Medici family, where magnificent *trompe l'œil* frescoes by Giovanni da San Giovanni await.

Palazzo Pitti

LITERARY PLAQUES AROUND PIAZZA PITTI

Many are the great writers who've made Piazza Pitti and its surroundings their home over the centuries, as the **marble plaques** dotting the square remind the most attentive of passersby. Look up and you'll learn that Carlo Levi wrote *Christ Stopped at Eboli* in Annamaria Ichino's Piazza Pitti 14 apartment between 1943 and 1945. Fyodor Dostoevsky is said to have completed *The Idiot* in 1868–69 just steps away. In nearby Piazza San Felice, another sign pays tribute to British poet Elizabeth Barrett Browning, who lived in Florence between 1847 and 1861.

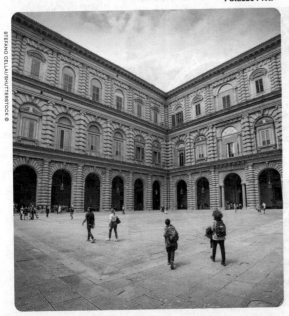

STEFANO CELLAI/SHUTTERSTOCK ©

CLET Studio

URBAN ART GALLERY

As you walk through the streets of Florence, you may notice that some of the traffic signs have a slightly odd design. For instance, the white band of the red 'no trespassing' sign could appear hugged by a loving policeman and one-way signs may become Cupid's arrows piercing a heart. Such decorations are not the result of the authorities' sense of humour, but of street artist Clet Abrahams – better known simply as **Clet** – who, over the past two decades, has kept busy transforming road signage in Florence and many other cities worldwide.

Born in Brittany, Clet moved to the Tuscan capital in 2005 and has since devoted himself to adorning the city furniture with stickers meant to make you think twice about the meaning of symbols often taken for granted. The now-iconic works blend ironic statements with political commentary, and while controversy is not new to the French artist, most Florentines appreciate Clet's playful twist on the urban landscape. With some exceptions, Clet's works are regularly removed by the authorities – his *L'Uomo Comune*, an iron statue of a man stepping into the void, hanging from Ponte alle Grazie, led to a €10,000 fine due to the lack of authorisation. But reproductions of the artist's work can be admired in his San Niccolò studio in Via dell'Olmo 8r, where stickers, T-shirts and limited-edition street signs are available for purchase.

ALESSANDRO DARI GIOIELLI

While Clet is known for transforming cities, steps away from his studio you'll find the workshop of an artisan who works on a much smaller scale. Master of Goldsmith Arts Alessandro Dari exhibits his tiny, wearable sculptures in the eerie atmosphere of his personal **gallery** in San Niccolò. Enter the magical atmosphere of this low-lit space to admire incredible handcrafted rings, bracelets, earrings and necklaces inspired by medieval symbolism and fantasy worlds.

Clet street art

The Medici Beyond Florence

VISIT THE UNESCO-LISTED VILLE MEDICEE

Palazzo Pitti might have been the most imposing residence in Florence, but the Medici's living spaces extended well beyond the palace's 32,000 sq metres. Built between the 15th and 17th centuries, the 12 villas and two ornamental gardens scattered around the Tuscan countryside that were built as leisure destinations by the Medici family were added to the Unesco World Heritage list in 2013, as innovative examples of architecture embedded in nature.

Unlike the fortifications erected during the Middle Ages, the **Ville Medicee** *(villegiardinimedicei.it)* were not designed to affirm the rulers' power, but rather to escape from it – these 'villas of idleness' were spaces where one could forget about politics and dedicate entire days to literature, the arts, and to rest. Closest to Florence are the **Villa di Castello**, with its elegant Italian gardens still intact after centuries – Botticelli's *The Birth of Venus* was originally commissioned to adorn this residence – and the **Villa del Poggio Imperiale**, a 10-minute drive from Piazzale Michelangelo.

The Medicis took their holidays away from Florence as well. Two impressive pieces of architecture that once belonged to the family are the symmetrical **Villa Medici di Poggio a Caiano**, designed by Giuliano da Sangallo for Lorenzo the Magnificent and containing a cycle of frescoes by Pontormo, Andrea del Sarto, Franciabigio and Alessandro Allori, and the **Villa Medicea di Artimino La Ferdinanda**, created by Bernardo Buontalenti for Ferdinando I in 1596.

BEST RESTAURANTS & CAFES IN SAN NICCOLÒ, BOBOLI & PIAZZA PITTI

Rifrullo €€
Right in the middle of San Niccolò, Rifrullo is great for breakfast, *aperitivi* and dinner.

La Beppa Fioraia €€
The inviting garden setting and relaxed atmosphere make La Beppa Fioraia a spring and summer favourite.

La Leggenda dei Frati €€€
Nestled in the Bardini Garden's greenery, this award-winning restaurant serves creatively concocted modern Tuscan dishes.

De'Bardi €€€
This high-end restaurant and cocktail bar comes to life in a beautifully refurbished Renaissance building.

THE GUIDE

FLORENCE: SAN NICCOLÒ, BOBOLI & PIAZZA PITTI

La Beppa Fioraia

 WHERE TO STAY IN SAN NICCOLÒ, BOBOLI & PIAZZA PITTI

Fuor d'Arno
This cosy B&B has rooms inspired by different cities from around the globe. €€

Hotel Silla
Welcoming staff, large rooms and generous breakfasts, located close to the city centre and Piazzale Michelangelo. €€

Serristori Palace
Quiet studio apartments and a little terrace with great views of the Duomo and the National Library. €€

TUSCANY

ICONIC CITIES AND WINE LANDS BETWEEN MOUNTAINS AND SEA

Vineyard-covered hills, sandy beaches and lush forested parks surround Unesco-listed cities dedicated to keeping centuries-old traditions alive.

Fortified palaces and ancient *case-torri*, the tower houses erected by wealthy pre-Renaissance families, define the skylines of cities like Siena, San Gimignano and Volterra, as do the stone-built bell towers of Gothic and Romanesque churches continuously visited by long-distance pilgrims for nearly a millennium. But charming urban areas are only part of a picture that no camera will be able to fully capture. Hills furnished with perfectly lined cypress trees, vineyards and olive groves in areas such as the Val d'Orcia World Heritage Site and the protected Chianti Classico region pay testimony to centuries of human attempts to shape nature and thrive off its precious fruits. Exiting cities through the twisting roads that gently cut the countryside, however, means exploring beyond the visually striking. Take in the relaxing Mediterranean atmosphere along the Etruscan Coast, walk the legendary Via Francigena or climb to the mountainous lands of Casentino and Garfagnana – the further you keep going, the more diverse Tuscany gets.

SOFIA GARAVANO/SHUTTERSTOCK ©

THE MAIN AREAS

SIENA	PISA	LUCCA
Artistic wonders and architectural masterpieces. p454	Home of the Leaning Tower. p468	Medieval charm and wild nature. p474

RASTO SK/SHUTTERSTOCK ©

Siena (p454)

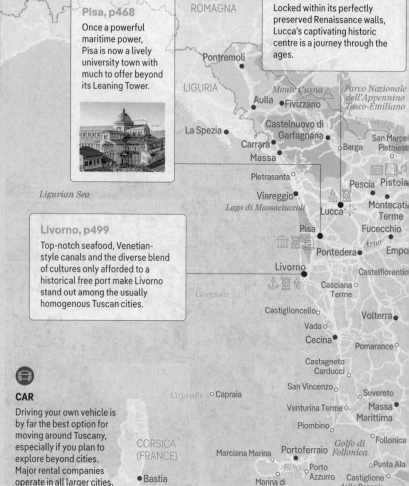

Pisa, p468

Once a powerful maritime power, Pisa is now a lively university town with much to offer beyond its Leaning Tower.

Lucca, p474

Locked within its perfectly preserved Renaissance walls, Lucca's captivating historic centre is a journey through the ages.

Livorno, p499

Top-notch seafood, Venetian-style canals and the diverse blend of cultures only afforded to a historical free port make Livorno stand out among the usually homogenous Tuscan cities.

N 0 — 50 km
0 — 25 miles

Ligurian Sea

EMILIA-ROMAGNA

LIGURIA

Pontremoli

Aulla • Fivizzano

Monte Cusna

Parco Nazionale dell'Appennino Tosco-Emiliano

Castelnuovo di Garfagnana

La Spezia •

Carrara •

Massa •

Pietrasanta

San Marce
Barga   Pistoiese

Viareggio •

Lago di Massaciuccoli

Lucca

Pescia   Pistoia

Montecati
Terme

Pisa

Pontedera •

Fucecchio

Arno   Empo

Livorno

Castelfiorentin

Casciana
Terme

Gorgona

Castiglioncello

Volterra •

Vada

Cecina •

Pomarance

Castagneto
Carducci

Capraia   Capraia

San Vincenzo

Venturina Terme

Suvereto

Massa
Marittima

CORSICA
(FRANCE)

• Bastia

Piombino

Marciana Marina

Portoferraio

Elba   Porto
Azzurro

Marina di
Campo

*Golfo di
Follonica*

Follonica

Punta Ala

Castiglione
della Pescaia

Marina di
Grosseto

Pianosa

CAR

Driving your own vehicle is by far the best option for moving around Tuscany, especially if you plan to explore beyond cities. Major rental companies operate in all larger cities, with Pisa and Florence being the main hubs.

BUS

Local buses reach the smaller urban areas located outside the rail network, but are few and often far between. Travelling by bus is doable but slow, and requires some planning.

TRAIN

Most cities, such as Pisa, Lucca, Pistoia, Siena, Grosseto and Arezzo, are well connected by rail – you can easily get to these by regional train from Florence. There's no need to book tickets in advance.

Montecristo

Giglio

Campese   Gig
Por

*Tyrrhenian
Sea*

Find Your Way

Good road and rail networks connect all major cities in Tuscany; however, the more remote corners of the region can be tricky to reach with public transport. When driving, be especially careful on narrow mountain roads.

Pistoia, p480

Charming Pistoia doesn't see as many visitors as it deserves, but its history and architecture make it a worthwhile trip.

Arezzo, p486

The backdrop of Roberto Benigni's film *Life is Beautiful*, offering world-class yet crowd-free art and architecture.

Siena, p454

An important city-state, Siena flourished in the 13th century and continues to maintain its medieval character through marvellous architecture and historic events.

Grosseto, p492

Maremma's main city doesn't have a long list of sights, but it's a good base for exploring the Parco Regionale della Maremma and the Etruscan sites Roselle and Vetulonia.

Plan Your Time

Take it slowly and enjoy Tuscany's delights one toast at a time, shifting from family-run farmhouses to dramatic fortresses, wine-centric countryside and relaxed seaside towns.

Piazza del Campo, Siena (p454)

If You Only Do One Thing

● Head straight to **Siena** (p454) to discover the art and architecture of the medieval republic, starting from one of Tuscany's best-known city squares – the semicircular **Piazza del Campo** (p454), composed of nine slices in reference to the days when the city was ruled by the Government of the Nine. Enter the **Palazzo Pubblico** (p454) and roam the halls of the treasure-filled Museo Civico, before moving to Piazza del Duomo to admire the astonishing **Duomo** (p457) that even the Florentines envy, before getting lost among the artworks housed inside the former hospital of **Santa Maria della Scala** (p458).

Seasonal highlights

Avoid winter, ideally, if you want to make the most of your Tuscany trip; wait until spring for long, sunny days to start exploring. It shouldn't be difficult – the cold, wet season is typically short.

MAY

As days get warmer and the weather clearer, the Casentino opens up with endless opportunities for **hiking**.

JUNE

Arezzo's **Giostra del Saracino** has its first run on the second-last Saturday of the month, bringing the Middle Ages back to town.

JULY

The **Lucca Summer Festival** draws crowds to the city's main square for a series of live concerts.

Three Days to Travel Around

● After a few hours in Livorno, take the ancient Via Aurelia all the way south to Piombino, and hop on an hour-long ferry to **Elba** (p502). Here, time slows down, with over a hundred beaches to gambol between and plentiful sunshine from April to October.

● Hire a car and spend a few days exploring along the precipitous mountain roads, with panoramic views over neighbouring Corsica. At 224 sq km, Elba has different corners that offer something for all tastes: wild windswept cliffs, sandy coves, azure waters and charming harbours abound, with a healthy dose of Napoleonic history in the biggest port town, **Portoferraio** (p502).

If You Have More Time

● Jump in your rental car in Pisa and follow the road north of Lucca to explore the hamlets of the **Serchio Valley** (p477) on the way to the mountainous Garfagnana region.

● Get ready to tackle one of the many hiking trails of the **Apuan Alps** (p478) available around the Lago di Vagli. As you return to lower ground make a detour to **Pistoia** (p480), one of Tuscany's underrated art cities, then head back towards Pisa, stopping at the charming city of **Lucca** (p474) to admire its medieval architecture from the height of its well-preserved defensive walls.

AUGUST
The **Palio** horse race (also held in July) is Siena's most awaited event – the entire city stops to see the different districts compete.

SEPTEMBER
Livorno hosts the festival **Cacciucco Pride** each September in honour of its iconic fish soup, with street feasts, live music and culinary events.

OCTOBER
The **Eroica** cycling race starts at 4.30am on the first Sunday of October, with over 7000 cyclists competing in vintage gear.

NOVEMBER
As the white-truffle season reaches its end, San Miniato hosts the important **Mostra Mercato Nazionale del Tartufo Bianco**.

SIENA

Many of the most powerful Italian city-states that emerged from the Middle Ages drew their wealth from water. Republics such as Pisa or Venice made their fortunes thanks to fearless navies that roamed the Mediterranean in search of valuable goods to trade and lands to conquer, while Florence grew rapidly thanks to its textile industry, which depended on the Arno river for both the production and transport of wool. Siena – nestled on three hills located between the Crete Senesi and the Val d'Elsa area – didn't have such an advantage. Unlike other major medieval powers, it could not rely on access to water, yet it flourished during the 13th century, developing a political system that would guarantee a period of peace prolonged enough to allow for the development of one of Italy's most influential universities and one of Europe's richest art collections, which has lasted to this day.

TOP TIP

The city is split into three *terzi* – the historical areas set on the three hills Siena is built on – known as Città, San Martino and Camollia, which are divided into 17 *contrade*, the districts still playing a key role in the identity of each Siena native.

THE PALIO

The Palio **horse race** takes place in Piazza del Campo on 2 July and 16 August, but the four days leading up to it are filled with centuries-old rituals, such as the decoration of each neighbourhood with its team's colours, the ceremonious draw for the assignment of horses to each team, and the blessing of the horses in local churches. A historic parade runs through the city on race day, preceding the entrance of the *fantini* (jockeys) representing Siena's *contrade* (city districts) and their Sardinian Anglo-Arab horses onto the piazza. Riding bareback, the jockeys must complete three laps of Piazza del Campo to win, with wild celebrations held in the winner's *contrade* the night following the race.

Discovering Piazza del Campo

SIENA'S MAIN SQUARE

The striking amphitheatre that is **Piazza del Campo** – often simply referred to as **il Campo** – is the starting point for every visit to the city. Siena's shell-shaped, sloping, red-bricked central square, admired for its unique geometry and well-preserved medieval architecture, has functioned as the centre of politics and social life for over seven centuries. Existing in its earliest form since the late 12th century, Piazza del Campo went from market square to being the fulcrum of Siena's civic life with the construction of the **Palazzo Pubblico**. This grandiose Gothic palace occupies most of the square's southern side and was built to symbolise the power of the Sienese independent republic, then ruled by the Government of the Nine.

With the exception of some renovation work done between the 17th and 19th centuries – including the refurbishment of the stately **Palazzo Sansedoni** and **Palazzo d'Elci** – the core structure of the square dates back to Siena's golden age, in which art and architecture flourished during a rare period of relative peace in the city's history, from the 1260s to the 1348 arrival of the Black Death. During this time the government released a series of guidelines that architects working on the development of the piazza's buildings were obliged to follow in order to maintain a coherent urban aesthetic – no balconies were allowed and all windows had to be either double- or triple-arched in line with the Gothic tastes of the era, for instance. Despite

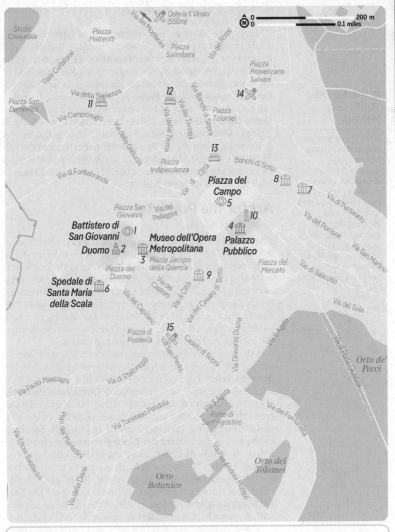

HIGHLIGHTS
1 Battistero
di San Giovanni
2 Duomo
(see 4) Museo Civico
3 Museo dell'Opera
Metropolitana

4 Palazzo Pubblico
5 Piazza del Campo
6 Pinacoteca Nazionale
7 Spedale di Santa
Maria della Scala

SIGHTS
8 Logge del Papa

9 Museo delle
Tavolette di Biccherne
10 Palazzo Chigi
Saracini
11 Torre del Mangia

SLEEPING
12 Albergo Bernini

13 Antica
Residenza Cicogna
14 B&B Il Corso

EATING
15 Il Cavaliere Errante
16 Osteria
Boccon del Prete

the changes, il Campo has managed to maintain its harmonious look largely intact.

Measuring 333m in circumference and split into nine slices, in reference to the nine members of the Republic's ruling class, the square hosts the **Mercato del Campo** (*mercato nelcampo.it*), inspired by the medieval market once held in the same space, each December. However, it is most famous for being the home of the **Palio**, Siena's most awaited event of the year. An 1869 copy of Jacopo della Quercia's monumental **Fonte Gaia** (1419) sits on the northern edge of the square. A statue of Venus once topped the fountain, but religious leaders destroyed it following the Black Death, believing that the epidemic was a result of worshipping pagan deities – the statue's fragments are said to have been buried in Florentine lands to wish the enemy an equal misfortune.

Art for the Powerful

ANCIENT PROPAGANDA

Flanked by the 88m-tall **Torre del Mangia** is Siena's most iconic building, the **Palazzo Pubblico**, among the most glorious examples of civil Gothic architecture in the country. A symbol of the once-powerful independent republic and originally intended as the seat of the Government of the Nine, it was completed in various stages between 1288 and 1342, and further expanded in 1680. It still houses the city hall, though its municipal activities are far less interesting than the incredible art collection the palace boasts.

At the time of its construction, the most celebrated Sienese artists were hired to decorate the halls of what is now the **Museo Civico**. Located on the 1st floor of the Palazzo Pubblico and accessible via the photogenic **Cortile del Podestà**, the museum's exhibition is not chronological. Start in the picture gallery containing artworks produced between the 16th and 18th centuries, then continue via the **Loggia dei Nove** to the 19th-century **Sala del Risorgimento** and reach the marvellous **Sala di Balìa**, featuring Martino Bartolomeo's *Sixteen Virtues* fresco and Spinello Aretino's detailed cycle *Storie di Alessandro III*, both completed in the early 1400s.

Continue through the **chapel** and you'll soon reach the **Sala del Mappamondo**, the former seat of the republic's council, with frescoes by Simone Martini, whose *Maestà* (1312) was intended to demonstrate the devotion of the Sienese towards the Holy Mary, renewed every year through during the Palio. It is in the **Sala della Pace**, however, that the centrepiece of the Museo Civico is found.

CLIMBING THE TORRE DEL MANGIA

Siena's most famous **tower** takes its name from bell ringer Giovanni di Balduccio, nicknamed *mangia guadagni* ('money eater') for his unhealthy spending habits. Reaching the top of the tower (tickets €10) requires you to climb 400 steps – an effort that will be rewarded by one of the best views of the city.

 WHERE TO STAY IN SIENA

Albergo Bernini
This 10-room family-run hotel at the northern end of the city centre makes for a cosy stay, with beautiful terrace views. €€

B&B Il Corso
Warm atmosphere with a rustic touch just a couple of minutes from Piazza del Campo and Siena's main sights. €€

Antica Residenza Cicogna
As its name suggests, this hotel has Middle Ages origins, though its amenities have been elegantly updated since then. €

Ambrogio Lorenzetti's *Effetti del Buon Governo in Città* and *Effetti del Buon Governo in Campagna* (1337–39) form a unique political manifesto, which differ greatly from the religious artworks found elsewhere. They were intended to influence the rulers of the republic by showing the results of a good government in both the city and the countryside – a thriving society of joyful dancers, artisans trading goods and people hunting and collecting produce. And if the message wasn't clear enough, opposite the fresco you can see the *Effetti del Cattivo Governo*, the effects of a bad government.

Awe-Inspiring Duomo

THE LEGACY OF SIENA'S CATHEDRAL

Blending elements of Romanesque and Gothic styles, the intricate facade of Siena's **cathedral** dominates the piazza that has functioned as the core of the city's religious life since the Middle Ages. Originally established in 1179, the cathedral dedicated to the Assumption of Mary has changed and expanded over subsequent centuries, becoming a sight that astonishes no matter how many other Tuscan churches you may already have seen.

The facade took nearly 600 years to complete. For over a decade starting in 1287 Giovanni Pisano worked on the lower part, composed of three monumental doors topped by Gothic tympana, but he never completed his polychrome marble gem, leaving the city for Pisa in 1296. The statues of prophets and apostles dating back to Pisano's age have now been placed in the nearby **Museo dell'Opera del Duomo** and substituted with copies. The rose window was added in 1288, but construction on the upper section didn't begin until 1376, when Giovanni di Cecco took it on, inspired by Orvieto Cathedral. The mosaics, created by Augusto Castellani, were added only in the late 19th century.

The facade is only part of the masterpiece – enter and you'll immediately notice the striking black-and-white pillars leading to the starred vaults of the ceiling, but look down to admire the exceptional **floor**, made of 56 panels composing an elaborate, large-scale mosaic. Representing scenes from the Old Testament, the marble compositions were produced between the 14th and 19th centuries by up to 40 different artists – all Sienese apart from Pinturicchio.

Among the other artworks adorning the church are Gian Lorenzo Bernini's sculptures *Santi Girolamo* and *Maria Maddalena* (1661–63), located in the Baroque **Cappella della Madonna del Voto**, and the octagonal Carrara-marble **pulpit**, sculpted by Nicola Pisano with the assistance of his son Giovanni and Arnolfo di Cambio between 1266 and 1268.

BELOW THE DUOMO

What is commonly referred to as the **'crypt'** was in fact a welcome centre for pilgrims travelling on the Via Francigena, who would enter the rooms found below the cathedral to admire the 13th-century cycle of biblical frescoes decorating the walls. These hidden rooms were rediscovered only in 1999 – the artworks' vibrant colours had been greatly preserved thanks to the lack of exposure to sunlight and are now a key part of Siena's medieval heritage.

Duomo di Siena

WHERE TO EAT IN SIENA

Osteria Il Vinaio
By Porta Camollia, informal Il Vinaio has a changing selection of local cheeses, cured meats and freshly made meals. €

Il Cavaliere Errante
Siena's comfort-food destination, serving pizzas, pastas, antipasti and generous amounts of house wine. €

Boccon del Prete
The exposed-brick and vaulted ceilings make for a rustic feel, but the handmade pasta will make you forget the decor. €€

PICCOLOMINI'S LEGACY

Born in nearby Pienza, Enea Silvio Bartolomeo Piccolomini – better known as Pope Pius II – was one of the most influential figures of the Sienese Renaissance. In 1462 he commissioned the **Logge del Papa**, near the Chiesa di San Martino, and lived in the **Palazzo Chigi Saracini**, now home to a fine art museum run by the Accademia Musicale Chigiana. After his death the pope's heirs erected the imposing Palazzo Piccolomini, which now houses the impressive **Museo delle Tavolette di Biccherne**, a collection of 105 painted tablets used as covers for the accounting files of the local magistrate between the 13th and 17th centuries.

PIENZA

The true masterpiece of Enea Silvio Bartolomeo Piccolomini was the 'ideal city' of **Pienza** (p465), in the Val d'Orcia.

The cathedral is also home to the **Piccolomini Library**, built around 1495 to preserve the vast collection of manuscripts of Enea Silvio Bartolomeo Piccolomini (Pope Pius II). In the left nave are frescoes attributed to Pinturicchio representing scenes from the life of Pope Pius II, and the precious *Altare Piccolomini* by Andrea Bregno (1481–85), which includes four niche statues produced by Michelangelo between 1501 and 1504.

Treasures Beyond the Cathedral

THE MUSEUMS OF PIAZZA DEL DUOMO AND SURROUNDS

The astounding beauty of Siena's Duomo often means that its surroundings go unnoticed. It shouldn't be so – medieval and Renaissance treasures hide all around. In front of the cathedral's entrance is the **Spedale di Santa Maria della Scala**, a 10th-century hospital and orphanage that continued to assist those in need until 1980, when it was converted from polyclinic to museum. Collecting donations since at least 1090 – as the earliest documents show – Santa Maria della Scala became an incredibly wealthy organisation that gathered and funded a vast artistic legacy.

The monumental building includes the 13th-century **Chiesa della Santissima Annunziata**, the **Pellegrinaio** (the pilgrim's hall frescoed in the mid-15th century by Sienese artists like Il Vecchietta and Domenico di Bartolo), Jacopo della Quercia's original **Fonte Gaia**, and the **Museo Archeologico Nazionale**, which traces the history of Siena's archaeological discoveries.

To the east of the Duomo, in Piazza Jacopo della Quercia, is the **Museo dell'Opera Metropolitana**, built on a space originally meant to be an expansion of the cathedral itself (the unfinished Duomo Nuovo). The museum houses 13th-century artworks previously belonging to the Duomo, such as the fine marble figures sculpted by Giovanni Pisano that once adorned the church's facade, Duccio di Buoninsegna's high-altar masterpiece *Maestà*, and works by Donatello, Ambrogio Lorenzetti and Domenico Beccafumi.

After climbing the 130 steps to reach the museum's **Facciatone**, offering one of the best views of Siena, return to ground level and visit the **Battistero di San Giovanni**, behind the Duomo. Behind its marble facade, this 14th-century church hides some of the most important frescoes of the Sienese Renaissance, including paintings by Il Vecchietta and an intricately sculpted baptismal font produced by Jacopo della Quercia, Donatello and Lorenzo Ghiberti.

GETTING AROUND

Siena is easily reached by public transport from Florence. Buses are slightly faster than trains, taking just over an hour from Florence's Santa Maria Novella station. Siena's entire city centre is closed to private cars. Minibuses known as 'Pollicino' run regularly through Siena's narrow streets, but the city's core is small enough that walking is the best way to get around. Even cycling can be difficult due to the steep climbs found in some areas. The train station is located to the north, easily reached from the escalators near Porta Camollia.

Beyond Siena

Otherworldly landscapes, medieval military strongholds and mythical abbeys surprise those who wander outside the city borders.

San Gimignano
Monteriggioni
Siena
Asciano
Buonconvento
Pienza
Montalcino

Few places are considered as quintessentially Tuscan as the cypress-lined roads embracing the hilly Val d'Orcia landscape. Dreamy farmhouses and stone-built hamlets surrounded by hay bales, sunflowers and vineyards are part of the enchanting composition that has formed the backdrop of numerous Hollywood movies, including Anthony Minghella's *The English Patient* (1996) and Ridley Scott's *Gladiator* (2000), and led to the area entering the list of Unesco World Heritage Sites in 2004. But Siena's surroundings offer more than landscapes – once-impenetrable fortifications are a reminder of the long history of conflict between the Sienese and the Florentine powers, while the Chianti region, Montalcino and Montepulciano offer endless opportunities to indulge.

TOP TIP

Siena's surroundings are best visited by car, although you can reach Monteriggioni by foot in a day, following 20km of the Via Francigena pilgrim route.

Val d'Orcia

PETER ZELEI IMAGES/GETTY IMAGES ©

MARCO SARACCO/SHUTTERSTOCK ©

Abbazia di San Galgano

MUSEO CIVICO E DIOCESANO D'ARTE SACRA DI SAN GALGANO

To learn more about the history of San Galgano, visit the Museo Civico e Diocesano d'Arte Sacra di San Galgano in nearby Chiusdino. This space housed inside the historic **Palazzo Taddei** showcases a small collection of works depicting San Galgano, obtained from chapels and churches that once dotted the surrounding countryside. Entrance to the museum is included in the abbey's ticket (€5).

A Gothic Wonder

EXPLORING THE LEGENDARY
ROOFLESS ABBEY AND ITS HERMITAGE

A 35-minute drive from Siena takes you to one of central Tuscany's most impressive pieces of religious architecture, eminently emerging from the hilly countryside. Spiritual inclinations are not necessary to admire the roofless **Abbazia di San Galgano**, one of Tuscany's earliest Gothic churches that was built by Cistercian monks some 800 years ago.

The abbey is located below the hill housing the circular, Romanesque-style **Eremo di Montesiepi**, a 12th-century chapel established to honour knight Galgano Guidotti (1148–81), who, following an appearance to him by Archangel Michael, chose to renounce his worldly possessions and violent past to retire in solitude in this remote corner of the region. Adorned with 14th-century frescoes by Sienese painter Ambrogio Lorenzetti, the chapel is built around a sword piercing a rock – this is believed to be Galgano's own weapon, symbolically left there as a gesture proving the warrior's willingness to give up arms. Tuscany's own Excalibur is visible in front of the altar protected by a shrine.

 WHERE TO EAT NEAR SAN GALGANO

Ristorante Antico Tempio
A warm, rustic atmosphere and great Tuscan cuisine, located opposite the abbey (with prices on the high end as a result). €€

Salendo Wine Bar
Local wines, *aperitivi* and light bites prepared amid the lush vegetation of Montesiepi, right behind the hermitage. €€

Trattoria sull'Albero
The luxurious restaurant of the Borgo San Pietro resort has great views and farm-to-table fare cooked to perfection. €€€

A short hike connects the Eremo with the Abbazia di San Galgano, a 1500-sq-metre structure whose construction started in 1218 to cater for the growing flow of pilgrims reaching the area, attracted by Galgano's myth. The project would take seven decades to complete, but the monks decided to abandon the abbey in the 15th century. In 1786 lightning struck the abbey's bell tower, which collapsed on the roof, destroying it. Entering the roofless church today is a hard-to-match spectacle. Three naves compose the interior, with pointed arcades forming two galleries on the sides and a large, 12-petalled central rosette opening on the facade – all covered by nothing other than the sky.

A Heroic Cycling Trip

FOLLOWING THE EROICA'S ROUTE ON TWO WHEELS

Leave the asphalt behind and set out to explore the white roads of the Sienese Chianti on two wheels, following the legendary Eroica route. The first edition of the **Eroica race** *(eroica.cc)* took place in 1997 – back then only 92 participants accepted the challenge of covering over 3700m of elevation gain on vintage bikes along the Chianti's dirt roads. Stretching out for 209km, the circular itinerary starting and ending in **Gaiole in Chianti** now gathers over 7000 cyclists on the first Sunday of October to compete in one of the world's most enthralling amateur races. Anyone who dares is allowed to sign up, as long as they ride – wearing vintage clothing – on a steel-frame old-school racing bike.

The official race typically takes on average 15 hours to complete, but you can ride the Eroica year-round at your own pace without having to compete or wear a quirky vintage hat. The full loop runs on public roads through the picturesque Crete Senesi area and the Unesco-listed Val d'Orcia, via Siena, Montalcino, Buonconvento and Asciano, before returning to the Chianti area. Alternatively, shorter routes ranging from 46km to 135km can also be done. Traditional and electric bicycles are available for rent in Gaiole in Chianti at **Tuscany Bicycle** *(tuscanybicycle.com)* or **Biciclettaio** *(bicyclesinchianti.com)*.

A Taste of Chianti

THE BIRTHPLACE OF MODERN CHIANTI

As you'll likely gather, there is no shortage of castles in central Tuscany. But the **Castello di Brolio**, south of Gaiole in Chianti, is worthy of special mention – this place has defined what it means to produce Chianti Classico.

 WHERE TO EAT IN GAIOLE IN CHIANTI

Lo Sfizio
Family-run restaurant that makes simplicity its strength, with great pizza to fuel you before the long cycle ahead. €

Taverna Le Cose Buone
Its name, meaning 'the good stuff', couldn't be more apt for this traditional trattoria cooking up classic Tuscan delights. €€

La Gorgia Vino & Cucina
Traditional flavours combine creatively to create exquisite, seasonally changing dishes, always served with a smile. €€

EVERYTHING RETRO

Fans of vintage cycling gear will want to stop at **La Bottega** *(bottegagaiole.it)* in Gaiole in Chianti. Every detail of this store breathes old-school vibes – find clothing, accessories and bike parts to get ready for your next athletic endeavour.

The neo-Gothic red-brick structure derives its form from an 1835 refurbishment of the castle, owned by the Ricasoli family since 1141 and originally built as a Florentine defensive outpost bordering the Sienese territory. It was here that Baron Bettino Ricasoli (1809–80) developed the recipe for the modern-day Chianti, following years of experimentation with different grape varieties. Until the late 19th century, local wines were made predominantly by fermenting Sangiovese grapes only. Baron Ricasoli began blending different grape varieties until he found the perfect formula – 70% Sangiovese, 20% Canaiolo, 10% Malvasia. The 'Vino di Brolio' was awarded its first gold medal at the International Exhibition in Paris in 1867, setting the standard for Chianti production, which would become strictly regulated a century later.

Tours of the castle (starting from €30; bookings required) include a visit to the Cappella di San Jacopo, where the members of the Ricasoli family are buried, the small weaponry museum and a tasting session of Ricasoli's current production.

ANTINORI NEL CHIANTI CLASSICO

One of the most famous **wineries** in the Chianti are the futuristic Antinori nel Chianti Classico, 6km south of San Casciano. The Antinori family has been involved in winemaking for over 600 years, ever since Giovanni di Piero Antinori joined the Arte Fiorentina dei Vinattieri (Florentine Winemakers' Guild) in 1385, but you wouldn't know from the cutting-edge architecture of their headquarters, developed in 2012 by Archea Associati. Nearly invisible when seen from a distance, the structure emerges from two horizontal slits in the vineyards and also sits below ground, allowing the wine to rest at naturally constant temperatures year-round.

Medieval San Gimignano

EXPLORING THE MANHATTAN OF THE MIDDLE AGES

With a thousand years of history to tell, the Unesco World Heritage city of San Gimignano is an astonishing testimony of life in the Middle Ages, so well preserved as to become both the ideal magnet for mass tourism and an easy victim of travel writers' clichés. Still, no matter how numb to the charms of medieval hilltop towns you may be, San Gimignano proves that experience can go well beyond expectations.

Two concentric rings of defensive walls, dating to the 10th and 13th centuries, embrace the inner-city core formed by ancient stately palaces, Romanesque churches and *case-torri* (tower houses) reaching up to 54m in height. Start your medieval tour by entering the city via **Porta San Giovanni**, completed in 1262, and walk by the artisanal stores of **Via San Giovanni** to quickly reach the triangular **Piazza della Cisterna**, named after the 13th-century cistern found at its centre. From here you'll be able to admire two sets of twin towers peeking above the rooftops, the **Torri dei Salvucci** and the **Torri degli Ardinghelli**, which take their name from the competing Guelphs and Ghibellines, who built them to reach 52m in height but were later punished for their hubris and forced to shorten them. Nearby is the **Chiesa di San Lorenzo in Ponte**, a 13th-century church housing the *Madonna col Bambino in Gloria* fresco.

In the 13th century – the city's golden age – San Gimignano's skyline counted 72 towers built by influential families

  WHERE TO STAY (IN CASTLES) IN THE CHIANTI AREA

Castello di Cafaggio
Picture-perfect property close to Florence, with uniquely furnished rooms, a pool and enviable surroundings. €€

Castello di Gabbiano
A dreamy fortress with four circular towers north of Greve. Come for the atmosphere, stay for the property's wine. €€€

COMO Castello Del Nero
This 12th-century castle turned luxury hotel has over 300 hectares of vineyard-covered hills, plus a spa. €€€

Piazza della Cisterna, San Gimignano

CANADASTOCK/SHUTTERSTOCK ©

SAN GIMIGNANO 1300

While the city has managed to keep much of its medieval character intact over the centuries, it would be untrue to say that nothing has changed. To learn how San Gimignano used to look in its golden age enter the **museum** San Gimignano 1300. It houses a handmade ceramic 1:100 scale reproduction of the city as it stood in the 14th century, allowing visitors to picture what the Via Francigena pilgrims saw when they reached San Gimignano after weeks on the road.

of traders, bankers and politicians. Only 14 of these towers have survived to this day, the taller being the **Torre Grossa**, standing in **Piazza del Duomo**, the city's main square. Below the Torre Grossa you'll find the **Palazzo Comunale**, the municipal palace Dante visited in 1299 as a Guelph ambassador, which is now home to some of the most precious medieval art pieces in the city. Here you'll be able to admire the cycle of frescoes by Lippo Memmi and Azzo di Masetto.

A Three-Day Pilgrim Walk

CROSSING CENTRAL TUSCANY AT A SLOW PACE

A great way to explore the surroundings of San Gimignano is by walking a section of the **Via Francigena**, the ancient pilgrim route running from Canterbury to Rome and eventually Jerusalem. An ideal three-day itinerary through central Tuscany begins in San Miniato, easily reached by train from Florence or Pisa, making your first stop approximately six hours later in **Gambassi Terme**, passing by the stone-built **Pieve di Santa Maria Assunta a Chianni**.

After recharging your batteries at the **Terme di Gambassi** *(termedigambassi.com)*, an easy three-hour hike through

 WHERE TO EAT IN SAN GIMIGNANO

Gelateria Dondoli
Dondoli is the reason many travel to San Gimignano. Try their signature Crema di Santa Fina to understand why. €

Echoes Bruschetteria
As the name suggests, Echoes specialises in *bruschette*, which are huge, tasty and overflowing with a variety of toppings. €€

Perucà
Vaulted ceilings, exposed brick, dark-wood furniture – you know the drill. Loyal to old Tuscan recipes, Perucà is a safe bet. €€

VIA FRANCIGENA BY BIKE

The majority of the Via Francigena can be done by mountain bike; however, some sections can be difficult to cycle through due to uneven ground and steep ascents, especially if you're bikepacking with heavy luggage. The blue-and-white markings show alternative routes meant for cyclists. Maps and GPS tracks are available at viafrancigena.bike.

STEVANZZ/SHUTTERSTOCK ©

Hilltop fortification, Monteriggioni

vineyards and olive trees will lead to towering San Gimignano. From here one of the most picturesque sections of the Via Francigena begins: the 31km stretch leading to **Monteriggioni** travels by the enchanting **Abbazia di Santa Maria Assunta a Conèo** and the **Chiesa di San Martino**, before reaching the gates of the hilltop fortification. If time allows, continue all the way to Siena (and why not Rome, and Bari and the Holy Land...?).

Note that the Via Francigena is best done during late springtime, when there's likely to be sunshine and the temperatures are still bearable. Guesthouses, *agriturismi* (farm stay accommodation), campgrounds and hotels are available along the way, with prices starting at about €30 per night. You will also find pilgrim hostels, churches and guesthouses that offer accommodation in exchange for a donation. Maps and detailed itineraries are available at regione.toscana.it/via-francigena and viefrancigene.org.

 WHERE TO SLEEP ON THE VIA FRANCIGENA

Le Finestre del Seminario
A Via Francigena favourite offering spacious private rooms in the 17th-century Seminario Vescovile di San Miniato. €

Ostello Sigerico
Welcoming hostel in Gambassi Terme adjoining a church, ideal for recharging after a long walk from San Miniato. €

B&B Il Cipresso
A very small, family-run B&B located 3.5km away from the historic fortress of Monteriggioni. €

Pienza's Utopian Architecture

INSIDE THE VISION OF PICCOLOMINI

Nestled in the cypress-dotted landscapes of the Val d'Orcia Unesco World Heritage Site, Pienza is not your usual *borgo* (medieval hamlet) in the Tuscan countryside. Built from scratch during the late 15th century following the utopian vision of Enea Silvio Bartolomeo Piccolomini, a humanist who became Pope Pius II in 1458, Pienza was created to be the 'ideal city' of the Renaissance.

Completed in only three years between 1459 and 1462 by Bernardo Rossellino, the finely carved travertine facades, Ionic stone columns and opulent palaces that compose Pienza's historic heart are compressed into the small area surrounding **Piazza Pio II**, steps away from the hamlet's gate at **Porta al Murello**. The striking **Cattedrale dell'Assunta**, flanked by the slender white bell tower, dominates the square. Look up to see the coat of arms of the Piccolomini family embedded in the tympanum; look down to notice the grid formed by travertine stripes on the square – twice a year the church's shadow fills the piazza's nine rectangles exactly, marking the spring and autumn equinoxes. The solemn interior showcases part of Piccolomini's personal art collection, including works by Sienese greats such as Il Vecchietta and Giovanni di Paolo. More art is found in the 11 halls of the **Museo Diocesano**, housed inside Palazzo Borgia (or Palazzo Vescovile), the palace Pope Pius II donated to Cardinal Borgia that now exhibits a collection of 14th-century Sienese paintings next to rare tapestries, goldwork and sacred vestments dating to the Middle Ages. Facing the cathedral is **Palazzo Piccolomini**, the former residence of the Pope, hiding an elegant Italian garden opening up to a beautiful view of the Monte Amiata.

A Landscape Photographer's Dream

SCENIC ROADS AND CYPRESS-DOTTED HILLS

You will encounter completely different scenery depending on when you decide to visit the **Val d'Orcia**. The bright green hills turn golden as spring withdraws to make room for the hot summer; colours get warmer with the arrival of autumn, and some winter days might even offer the awe-inspiring spectacle that is the Val d'Orcia covered in snow.

While spring and early summer tend to be the preferred seasons for most visitors, any time makes for a great tour of the iconic landscapes of the region, especially if you're seeking to return home with some photographic memories. Get

TASTING PIENZA'S CELEBRATED PECORINO

Matured for at least 90 days in oak barrels previously used to age wine, Pienza's *pecorino* cheese is a must try, especially after a long journey on Val d'Orcia's twisting roads. Made from sheep's milk, the food product Pienza is most proud of comes in many different varieties and is best enjoyed over an indulgent plate of *pici* – the strictly hand-rolled pasta believed (by locals, at least) to be spaghetti's ancestor. *Pici* and *pecorino* can be enjoyed in most restaurants around town, but no celebration of the barrique-aged cheese beats the **Fiera del Cacio** – Pienza's cheese festival, held in early September. During this event the whole town gathers around Piazza Pio II to cheer on its historic neighbourhoods competing in the Palio del Cacio Fuso, a traditional game where participants roll wheels of cheese around a wooden spindle placed in the middle of the square.

 **WHERE TO EAT IN PIENZA**

La Taverna del Pecorino	Marusco e Maria	Trattoria Latte di Luna
For a tasting of all the varieties of Pienza's *pecorino* cheese, stop at this little place and order a lavish, flavourful tray. €€	Different interpretations of Pienza's cheese are served with locally produced wines in their richly stocked wine store. €€	With a romantic atmosphere in the heart of the historic centre, this is a great spot to try genuine Val d'Orcia cuisine. €€

up early for the best lighting and head to one of Tuscany's most photographed roads, found on the way to **Monticchiello**, one of Val d'Orcia's best-preserved medieval hamlets. Near Pienza, not far from the ancient **Pieve di Corsignano**, you'll also find the wheat fields Russell Crowe walked through in the final scenes of the movie *Gladiator*.

On the way to charming San Quirico d'Orcia, make a detour to the picturesque **Cappella della Madonna di Vitaleta**, a tiny chapel hugged by cypresses and loved by wedding photographers. For more cypress shooting, continue for about 5km past San Quirico d'Orcia along the SR2 road and you'll soon come across what is perhaps the most photographed group of trees in all of Italy. Known as the **Cipressi di San Quirico d'Orcia**, the trees have been planted to form an orderly circle in the middle of an isolated hill, making for a visually striking composition of shapes and shadows. When golden hour strikes, park by the road (aptly named Cypress Avenue) leading to the **Agriturismo Poggio Covili** for a framing of the perfectly lined double row of conical-shaped trees.

Montalcino & its Brunello

WORLD-CLASS WINE TASTINGS

An irregular fortress dating back to 1361 appears from the distance as you start climbing the hill to Montalcino's historic centre. Carrying the Medici's coat of arms – the famous six-ball emblem – the defensive structure with its angular towers is one of the most imposing in central Tuscany. It's not because of medieval architecture, however, that most people reach this little town of 5000. Montalcino is most famous for its Brunello, one of the world's most sought-after wines, whose rarest vintages sell for thousands of euros.

Compared to other Italian wines, the history of the **Brunello di Montalcino** is relatively recent, as you'll be able to learn if you visit the newly opened **Tempio del Brunello** interactive museum, found inside the Sant'Agostino complex in the heart of the city. The fame of this wine is much owed to the Biondi Santi family, who began diversifying their winemaking in the late 1800s, experimenting with different ageing processes and selected grapes. Today, Brunello production is strictly regulated – only local Sangiovese grapes can be used and the wine, which can only be released on the market five years after harvest, has to age a minimum of two years in oak.

Tasting opportunities abound both inside and outside the fortress. Montalcino's castle houses the **Enoteca la Fortezza di Montalcino**, a great place to start your Brunello jour-

---

THE NOBLE WINE OF MONTEPULCIANO

Perched at 600m altitude, Montepulciano houses an impressive collection of Renaissance architecture, although its attractiveness is not set in stone – the city is best known for its **Vino Nobile**, whose production dates to as early as 789. Montepulciano's 'noble wine' is made predominantly with Sangiovese grapes and aged for a minimum of two years (of which at least one is in wood).

Cantina Ercolani is a great place to start learning about Montepulciano's wine culture – the store features an 'Underground City' museum showing barrel-filled ancient cellars below the city's historic palaces. Outside the city walls, the winery **Avignonesi** offers an excellent wine-tasting experience.

 WHERE TO EAT AROUND THE VAL D'ORCIA

Dopolavoro La Foce
You'll be spoiled for choice on the welcoming terrace of the Dopolavoro La Foce, a gourmet lunch spot. €€

Osteria di Porta al Cassero
This family-run restaurant in Montalcino preserves deep-rooted traditions and serves all the Val d'Orcia classics. €€

Trattoria Toscana al Vecchio Forno
Comfort food in a friendly yet refined setting in the greenery of San Quirico d'Orcia. €€

JAZZ & WINE

Each year in mid-July, Montalcino's fortress becomes an open-air concert hall hosting the **Jazz & Wine Festival** *(jazzandwine montalcino.it)*, a highly awaited week-long music event where the inebriating sounds produced by Italian and international jazz acts are paired with some of Italy's finest wines.

Cappella della Madonna di Vitaleta

ney and learn all about the local wine varieties. The vineyard-covered area surrounding the town is home to dozens of wineries, ranging from small, family-run operations to established brands with global reach. Stop by at the little **NostraVita**, where great wine produced in limited quantities comes with a side of rotating art exhibitions, or visit the historic winery **Ciacci Piccolomini D'Aragona**, which has been making exceptional vino from its Castelnuovo dell'Abate palace since the 17th century. If your thirst is yet to be quenched, continue for a vertical tasting of six Brunello di Montalcino vintages at the **Casato Prime Donne**, the first Italian winery run exclusively by women, founded by local entrepreneur Donatella Cinelli Colombini.

GETTING AROUND

Driving is a great way to explore the hilly region surrounding Siena, especially if you are planning to take advantage of the many landscape photo opportunities found in the Val d'Orcia countryside. Trains run frequently to Florence crossing the Chianti region and to Buonconvento, while buses connect the city to the smaller hamlets. If you're looking for a more active way to explore the region, you can rent a bike in Siena and cycle around the countryside. There are several bike paths that traverse the hills and valleys of around the urban centre.

PISA

The symbolic strength of the Leaning Tower (*Torre Penden-te*) is so powerful that visitors often reduce Pisa just to its world-famous architectural mistake, leaving the city behind after a quick stop below the landmark. There's no denying that the Unesco-listed Piazza dei Miracoli is a sight to behold, but beyond the marble wonders that continue to inspire the production of souvenirs of questionable taste, Pisa is first and foremost a place where ideas are shared and culture is made. While up to 50% of the city was bombed and destroyed during WWII, traces of Pisa's important contribution to Tuscany's art and science heritage are still visible and worth diving into. Once a maritime powerhouse that massively enriched itself and influenced trade routes across the Mediterranean, Pisa is now a prestigious research hub that attracts a large student population to its universities, as demonstrated by the lively atmosphere you'll encounter in its centre.

Pisa

★ Rome

TOP TIP

For a bird's-eye view of the city and its major monuments, step onto its 11m-tall walls, built between 1154 and 1161. Running from Torre Nuova, by Piazza dei Miracoli, to Torre di Legno, near the Lungarno, the Mura di Pisa walkway (tickets €5) extends for approximately 3km.

SOLVING THE TILT

After its completion in 1370, Pisa's famous **bell tower** continued to slowly tilt southward for over six centuries. Only in the 1990s did engineers find a solution for stabilising its foundation through a technique known as 'controlled sub-excavation', which involved the removal of small quantities of soil from beneath the north side of the structure. Over the past three decades the tower has straightened by as much as 4cm, and is now tilted by 'only' 3.97 degrees. It's currently considered as stable as it has ever been.

A Piazza of Miracles

THE LEANING TOWER AND ITS SURROUNDINGS

Beyond one of Italy's oldest examples of preserved **city walls** stretches a green carpet housing one of Tuscany's most iconic squares, the record-smashing **Piazza dei Miracoli**. Most visitors come to this monumental open-air museum (tickets €27) to see the world's best-known architectural mishap, but it's worth extending your stay beyond the customary selfie to discover the white-marble masterpieces of this Unesco World Heritage Site.

The Romanesque **Cattedrale di Santa Maria Assunta** (Duomo) is the centrepiece of the square. Its construction began in 1063 after the Pisan army returned victorious from Sicily with six ships filled with valuable materials. The 56m **leaning tower** was conceived in 1173 as an essential addition to the cathedral, but after five years of work (and four floors already built), architects realised that the tower was leaning northwards and halted the project. It would take engineers two centuries to figure out how to deal with the soft soil under the bell tower's foundation and complete the 14.5-tonne structure; their attempts resulted in the tower then starting to tilt southward. Today you can climb its 251 steps amid columns and arches to reach the eighth floor for a splendid, panoramic view of the city.

From the top you'll be able to admire the circular **Battistero di San Giovanni**, the world's largest baptistery, whose Gothic-Romanesque architecture houses a refined marble pulpit. Enter the Battistero to experience the acoustic effects produced by the double dome (live demonstrations every 30 minutes), then continue to the monumental **Camposanto**, Pisa's most

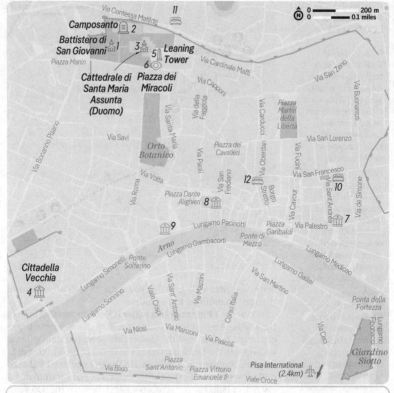

HIGHLIGHTS
1 Battistero di San Giovanni
2 Camposanto
3 Cattedrale di Santa Maria Assunta
4 City walls
5 Leaning Tower
6 Piazza dei Miracoli

SIGHTS
7 Galileo's House
8 Palazzo della Sapienza
9 Palazzo Reale

SLEEPING
10 B&B Camilla
11 Hostel Pisa Tower
12 Rinascimento B&B

important cemetery, featuring frescoes by Buonamico Buffalmacco, Taddeo Gaddi and Benozzo Gozzoli.

Non-Leaning Architecture

A WALKING TOUR OFF THE BEATEN TRACK

It's a common mistake to make a quick stop under the Leaning Tower and then continue onwards to other Tuscan destinations. Don't take Pisa for granted – its compact yet lively

 WHERE TO STAY IN PISA

Hostel Pisa Tower
A budget option steps away from the leaning tower. Friendly staff, clean dorms, but bring your own padlock. €

B&B Camilla
Minutes away from Borgo Stretto; at this lovely B&B no detail goes unchecked. €€

Rinascimento B&B
Modern amenities hidden inside a medieval tower house. €€€

IN GALILEO'S FOOTSTEPS

Galileo's House
Galileo Galilei was born on 15 February 1564, in what is today Via Giusti. A plaque marking his birth can be found outside Casa Ammannati, in the Sant'Andrea neighbourhood.

Palazzo della Sapienza
In this elegant university building Galileo taught mathematics and conducted much of the research that formed his treatise *Sidereus Nuncius*.

Palazzo Reale
The tower of the 16th-century palace commissioned by Francesco I de' Medici – now a museum exhibiting the Medici's tapestries and furnishings – was used by Galileo to observe the night skies with his telescope.

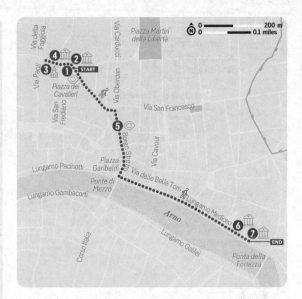

MUSEO GALILEO

To learn more about Galileo Galilei's life and work, check out the **Museo Galileo** (p414) in Florence.

historic centre will surprise you with its rich architectural heritage spanning a millennium.

Start at the **1 Piazza dei Cavalieri** (Knight's Square), built in the Middle Ages on the remains of a Roman-era forum. It was converted by Cosimo I de' Medici (whose statue stands in the square) into the headquarters of the Order of the Knights of St Stephen. Nearby you'll find Giorgio Vasari's opulent **2 Palazzo della Carovana**, adorned with sculptures and sgraffito imagery rich in Renaissance symbolism. Steps away is the 900-year-old, stone-built **3 Chiesa di San Sisto**, a classic example of the Pisan Romanesque style whose sand-coloured, bare exterior is dotted with Islamic majolicas, and the 17th-century **4 Palazzo dell'Orologio**, also built following Vasari's design.

Walk south through the charming **5 Borgo Stretto** and you'll reach the romantic Lungarno Mediceo stretching along the Arno. In a matter of minutes you'll find yourself under the art-filled **6 Palazzo Medici** (tickets €5), an 11th-century *casa-torre* (tower house) converted into a palace and purchased by the Medici in 1441 – it hosts illustrious figures like Lorenzo the Magnificent and Charles VIII of France. Nearby is the **7 Museo di San Matteo**, Pisa's main public art institution, where you'll find vast numbers of medieval and early-Renaissance artworks, including paintings by Taddeo Gaddi, Ghirlandaio, Masaccio and Fra' Angelico.

GETTING AROUND

Served by many low-cost airlines, Galileo Galilei airport is linked to the city centre via the Pisa Mover monorail, which takes a matter of minutes. From Pisa's central railway station, about three regional trains per hour run to

Florence and one train per hour goes to Lucca. When visiting from Florence by train, get off at Pisa San Rossore station (rather than Pisa Centrale), to reach Piazza dei Miracoli on foot.

Beyond Pisa

Sea, mountains, contemporary art and top-notch food – nature and culture become one in Pisa's surroundings, where queue-free experiences reward those who travel at a slow pace.

Pisa

San Miniato

Pontedera

Volterra

The area surrounding the Arno river's mouth has long been revered for its lush vegetation, seen as both a resource and an oasis. In the 16th century the Medici set up a large estate along the coast, which is still home to thriving fauna and forms the core of a 230-sq-km reserve waiting to be explored on foot or by two wheels. But it's by reaching the small hilltop towns scattered across the province that you'll gain access to a perfectly balanced combination of idyllic landscapes, ancient history, memorable flavours and surprising art, both historical and contemporary. Whichever direction you choose to take, be ready to be surprised.

TOP TIP

Trains to San Miniato, Lucca and Viareggio depart from Pisa's central station. If you plan to leave the cities and explore the countryside, however, a car is needed.

Volterra (p472)

KIRK FISHER/SHUTTERSTOCK ©

Tasting Tuscany's White Gold

HUNTING FOR TRUFFLES

Right between Pisa and Florence is the medieval hilltop town of **San Miniato** – a place of culinary wonders marked by the **Torre Federico II**, which you'll spot as soon as you reach the town's vicinity by train or by car. San Miniato's highly prized *tuber magnatum pico* (white truffle) is the reason so many come here between September and December, but the rest of the year will make your mouth water just as much.

While white truffles grow in autumn, different varieties of the precious tuber are found year-round in the calcareous slopes surrounding San Miniato. Don't plan on digging in the ground on your own – only experienced, certified *tartufai* (truffle hunters) can search the forests with their dogs for truffles, which are typically found near oaks, poplars and hazels. The largest truffle ever recorded – a massive 2.5kg tuber donated to US President Dwight D Eisenhower – was found in San Miniato in 1954, as the statue to *tartufaio* Arturo Gallerini and his dog Parigi in Viale XXIV Maggio testifies.

During the last three weekends of November, charming San Miniato hosts the **Mostra Mercato Nazionale del Tartufo Bianco**, a much-awaited event where freshly hunted truffles of all kinds and sizes are cooked, smelled, tasted or auctioned to visitors, traders, restaurateurs and enthusiasts. And if eating them is not enough, you can book a truffle-hunting session with one of the local *tartufai*, during which you'll be able to closely follow trained dogs and their owners through the forests as they uncover nature's treasures. **Truffle in Tuscany**, run by long-time truffle hunter Massimo Cucchiara, and the **Barbialla Nuova** *(barbialla.it)* biodynamic farm, located in nearby Montaione, offer regular tours followed by tasting sessions during the white-truffle season.

Volterra Across the Ages

A WALK THROUGH THE CITY'S HISTORY

Etruscan, Roman, medieval and Renaissance elements combine to form the urban core of ancient **Volterra**, the awe-inspiring city whose early development was due to the wealth of natural resources found in its vicinity. Etruscans mined silver, copper and lead from the nearby **Colline Metallifere** in the 5th century BCE, but it was the salt (essential for food preservation in pre-industrial societies) extracted from Volterra's basins that made the city a dominant commercial power in the region.

 WHERE TO SLEEP IN SAN MINIATO

Le Mammole
A lovely, family-run B&B fully immersed in nature. €€

Agriturismo Marrucola
This bucolic stay has a swimming pool and generous meals. €€

Relais Sassa al Sole
Luxurious resort embraced by vineyards, 6km from San Miniato's centre. €€€

A chronological tour of Volterra's historic sites starts at the outskirts of the city centre. Volterra's Etruscan roots crop up above ground in the **Parco Archeologico Enrico Fiumi**, where remnants of two temples dating back to the 3rd and 2nd centuries BCE can still be seen. An even better place to learn about the early days of the city is the **Museo Etrusco Mario Guarnacci**, one of Italy's most important collections of Etruscan artefacts. Archaeological findings – including the impressive collection of over 600 funerary urns – are spread across three floors in the **Palazzo Desideri Tanbassi**. A step forward in time leads to the Roman Amphitheatre, believed to have been built at the end of the 1st century CE. Rediscovered by local archaeologist Enrico Fiumi in the 1950s, the structure was once able to hold nearly 2000 spectators. Climb atop the **Mura del Mandorlo** for a panoramic view of the site.

As you enter the city centre you'll notice that the imprint is clearly medieval. **Piazza dei Priori** marks Volterra's heart, overshadowed by the imposing Palazzo dei Priori, Tuscany's oldest municipal palace, built between 1208 and 1254. Steps away is the ever-present **Duomo**: Volterra's main church, built in 1120, may not look like much from the outside, but its interior hides 15 chapels adorned with frescoes and monuments by artists of the likes of Giovanni della Robbia, Benozzo Gozzoli and Pieter de Witte. Dominating the skyline is the **Fortezza Medicea**, the most impressive remnant of the Renaissance. It's divided into two sections – the Rocca Vecchia, constructed in 1343, and the Rocca Nuova, completed in 1475. The latter section was built under the orders of Lorenzo the Magnificent after Volterra fell under Florentine rule, and has been used as a prison since then. Unfortunately, the fortress is not accessible to visitors.

MASTERS OF ALABASTER

Besides its archaeological wonders, Volterra is well known for its artisanal heritage. Since Etruscan times alabaster carving has played a key role in shaping the city's character, and continues to do so today, as you can learn at the **Ecomuseo dell'Alabastro**. Many workshops dotting the city centre keep the tradition alive and make Volterra a great destination for those seeking unparalleled crafts. To find one-of-a-kind artworks visit Alab'Arte, Romano Bianchi, or Alabastri Pecchioni if unique musical instruments are what you're looking for.

Alabaster carving, Volterra

GETTING AROUND

By picking up a rental car at Pisa airport upon your arrival, you'll be able to go beyond the most famous sites of northwestern Tuscany and visit many of the lesser known corners of this part of the region – from coastal towns to mountain villages. San Miniato, Pontedera, and Florence are connected by a direct rail line, and can be easily reached from Pisa's Stazione Centrale.

LUCCA

Lucca

Rome

As one of the Tuscan cities that has best preserved its historic character, enchanting Lucca is a spectacle worth discovering, layer after layer. Hiding behind its monumental Renaissance walls is a city that blends Roman roots with an aristocratic disposition, made up of stately places, richly adorned villas and grandiose marble churches connected by cobblestoned alleys.

Ruled by powerful families of merchants and bankers for most of the past millennium, Lucca had its golden age between the 11th and 14th centuries, when the silk trade and its privileged position on the Via Francigena brought massive wealth to the city's traders, leading to the construction of tower houses and fortifications that still mark the city's skyline. Unlike other major cities in Tuscany, Lucca managed to largely maintain its independence until the turn of the 19th century, never falling under Florentine domination. Today, exploring the heritage of this city-state is a stimulating adventure through the remnants of past epochs.

TOP TIP

Lucca is known as the 'city of a hundred churches'. While not exactly 100, the many churches found within the historic walls tell the story of the noble family that founded both their construction and the artistic treasures found inside.

Monumental Walls & Medieval Towers

SEEING THE CITY FROM ABOVE

LUCCA COMICS & GAMES

Europe's largest **comics and gaming festival** takes place in Lucca's historic heart each October. Cosplayers and comics fans from all over the country attend a wide variety of exhibitions, events and open-air markets. See the full programme at lucca comicsandgames.com.

Lucca's 12m-tall walls are also its green lungs, surrounding the urban core with lime, plane and oak trees and other lush flora. The **Mura di Lucca** are some of Europe's best preserved fortifications, which have remained intact since their construction between 1513 and 1650. A 4km pathway connecting the 11 bastions, built to defend the city in case of attack, offers the opportunity for a pleasant *passeggiata* (stroll) with panoramic views of the city's medieval rooftops and towers. Any excess of *tordelli lucchesi* (the local pasta specialty) or Colline Lucchesi wine can be sweated off on Saturday mornings when the free Mura di Lucca 5km Parkrun *(parkrun.it/muradilucca)* takes place, starting at 9am from Piazzale Vittorio Emanuele.

For even better views you can climb the **Torre Guinigi**, one of the last remaining medieval towers still standing in the city, once belonging to Lucca's most powerful family. Take the 230 steps leading to the top of the 45m brick tower crowned with five century-old oaks. If you're craving more 360-degree views, head over to the tallest structure in the city, the 50m **Torre del'Ore**, where a clock dating to 1390 (but refurbished in 1754) sits just below the rooftop, which you'll reach after climbing 207 steps.

Walking Through 2000 Years of History

TAKE A LOOK AROUND

A walk across Lucca's historic centre is a journey through time. Start at the **1 Porta San Pietro** gate near the train station and you'll soon reach the relatively recent **2 Piazza Napoleone**, also

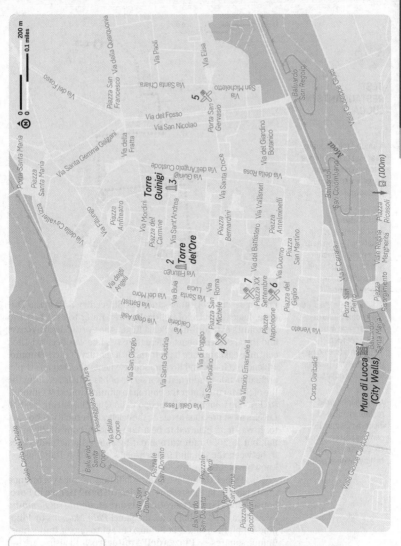

HIGHLIGHTS
1 Mura di Lucca
(City Walls)
2 Torre del'Ore
3 Torre Guinigi

EATING
4 Buca di
Sant'Antonio
5 Gli Orti
di Via Elisa
6 Il Giglio
7 Nanda's

Torre Guinigi

FABIO MICHELE CAPELLI/SHUTTERSTOCK ©

Nanda's €
A lunch-time favourite near Piazza Napoleone offering great vegan burgers, sandwiches, pastas and cakes.

Buca di Sant'Antonio €€
As welcoming as it is traditional – stop here for a plate of fresh, handmade pasta and a glass of Colline Lucchesi wine.

Gli Orti di Via Elisa €€
A seasonal menu of dishes made with locally sourced ingredients (including great gourmet pizzas), served in a cosy spot.

Il Giglio €€€
A Michelin-starred restaurant located inside an elegant 18th-century palace, with a six-course vegetarian tasting menu available.

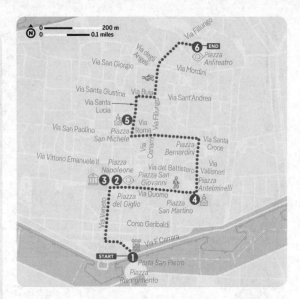

known as Piazza Grande, and the 16th-century **3 Palazzo Ducale**, Lucca's centre of political power. Enter to visit Lorenzo Nottolini's extraordinary Scala Regia, the Cortile degli Svizzeri and the art-filled rooms where the city's fate was decided, then continue east and step back to the 11th century at the **4 Duomo**.

Blending Gothic and Romanesque elements, the Duomo's triple-arched facade is adorned by a series of bas-reliefs retelling the life of St Martin. Enter the church to admire works by Tintoretto, Fra' Bartolomeo and Jacopo della Quercia, sitting next to Lucca's most precious artefact, the celebrated crucifix Volto Santo. It was long believed to be a 12th-century copy of the original, but in 2020 radiocarbon dating showed it actually dates to between the 7th and 9th centuries, making it Italy's oldest known wood sculpture.

Still, it's not the oldest thing you'll find in Lucca. Continue north, passing by the striking **5 Chiesa di San Michele in Foro**, housing the glazed terracotta sculpture *Madonna col Bambino* by Andrea della Robbia and the panel *Pala Magrini* by Filippino Lippi, then take Via Fillungo to get to one of Italy's most unique squares – **6 Piazza dell'Anfiteatro**. Still visible are the remains of the 2nd-century Roman amphitheatre. Take a seat in one of the cafe terraces in the square and reward yourself with a vino after your trip back through time.

GETTING AROUND

Lucca's railway station is located in Piazza Ricasoli, steps away from Porta San Pietro. Lucca connects to Florence, Viareggio and Pisa, making it easy to plan day trips to art cities and the beaches of the Versilian coast. The historic centre of Lucca is not accessible by car (unless you are a resident with a special permit). If you are driving your own vehicle you can reach Lucca via the A11 highway, then park your car outside the walls (parking €2/hour).

Carrara

Parco Naturale
delle Alpi Apuane

Pietrasanta

Viareggio   Lucca

THE GUIDE

TUSCANY

Beyond Lucca

Trendy and relaxed or rural and wild. As you exit
Lucca to explore its surroundings, choose your
direction wisely – two entirely different worlds
await.

Lucca's province extends northwest of the city, encompassing
quaint medieval villages as well as glamorous beach towns
where over-the-top hotels and fashionable nightclubs attract
VIP crowds in summer. Drive through twisting roads to discover the hamlets and landscapes of the Serchio Valley, with stone-built architecture, deep canyons and lush forests stretching all
the way to the majestic Apuan Alps, where Carrara marble has
been extracted since Roman times. And after a dose of wilderness, head east towards Pistoia, to admire some of the region's
most intriguing medieval architecture without the crowds. Be
ready to experience Tuscany from an unexpected perspective.

TOP TIP

Lucca is connected by
rail to Viareggio and
Pietrasanta. There's
also a slow historic train
between Lucca to Aulla,
although the area is best
explored by car.

Isola Santa (p478)

THREE TOP TRAILS IN THE APUAN ALPS

Alberto Pellegrinetti, from Garfagnana Dream, recommends three of his favourite hikes. (*@garfagnanadream.it*)

Puntato–Col di Favilla
Starting from Tre Fiumi, this beginners' hike is surrounded by beautiful peaks, like Mt Sumbra and Pizzo delle Saetta. You can also see Mt Corchia's north face and Mt Freddone's crest.

Sentiero della Libertà
At the foot of the Panie complex, this loop trail, marked by historical sights, offers spectacular views of the Uomo Morto (Dead Man) formation. Start from Piglionico and descend towards Colle a Panestra, site of WWII trenches.

Rifugio Orto di Donna
The highest hut in Val Serenaia is the base camp to tackle Mt Pisanino, the tallest peak of the chain. All routes here are for experienced hikers only and professional equipment is essential.

ESSEVU/GETTY IMAGES ©

Castelnuovo di Garfagnana

Hiking the Apuan Alps

THE RUGGED CRESTS OF GARFAGNANA'S MOUNTAINS

The **Parco Naturale delle Alpi Apuane** is crisscrossed by a seemingly endless network of trails winding through untamed peaks and landscapes. Sweating for the views is not essential – drive to the idyllic **Isola Santa** for fairy-tale scenery or rent a pedal boat on the Lago di Gramolazzo and enjoy the mountains without having to pull on your boots. But if hiking is your thing, here you'll be spoiled for choice.

Set off from **Castelnuovo di Garfagnana** and head to the artificial **Lago di Vagli**, covering the submerged village of Fabbriche di Careggine (a Tuscan Atlantis abandoned in 1947). Then reach the **Campocatino** oasis where a light, 30-minute trek leads to the **Eremo di San Viviano**, a fascinating sanctuary located at 1090m altitude, emerging from the face of **Monte Roccandagia**.

Those looking for a more intense hike should aim for the peak of the **Pania della Croce**. Following trail numbers 7 and 126 (managed by the CAI; the Italian Alpine Club) from Piglionico, in approximately one hour you'll reach the **Rifugio Rossi** hut below the **Uomo Morto** – a rock formation

---

 WHERE TO SLEEP IN GARFAGNANA

Il Pradicciolo
A homely *agriturismo* where welcoming Silvia delights every visitor with homemade chestnut bread, jams and wine. €€

Agriturismo Ai Frati
Set in the 15th-century Convento di San Francesco, this farmhouse is only minutes by car from Castelnuovo. €€

Agriturismo La Palazzina
Just outside Castelnuovo proper, this farmhouse may be a bit dated but is still a great choice for a restful weekend. €€

vaguely recalling the profile of a dead man's face. From here a steep ascent leads to the 1859m-high mountaintop and its cross, where you'll be able to admire the whole Apuan Alps region and the coast, before heading back down on the other side for a bucolic late lunch at the **Rifugio del Freo** and concluding the loop back to Piglionico.

And if hiking is not enough, the Apuan Alps offer great climbing opportunities for experienced mountaineers. The Oppio–Colnaghi route on **Monte Pizzo d'Uccello** (1781m) is one of the best known in the area thanks to its 800m vertical wall, while the **Le Rocchette**, near Molazzana, is more suited to beginners.

The Art of Sculpting Marble

CARRARA'S MARBLE HERITAGE

Everything here is marble. From the black-and-white cladding of **Piazza Alberica** standing in sharp contrast to the colourful facades of the surrounding buildings, to the Romanesque exterior of the **Cattedrale di Sant'Andrea**, to the neoclassical Teatro degli Animosi and Kenneth Davis' floating ball sculpture at the **Piazza D'Armi**, Carrara's history has been defined by the presence of the precious material in the nearby mountains.

To understand the long-lasting – but far from unproblematic – relationship between Carrara and its marble, head out of the centre to reach the **Cava Museo Fantiscritti** (open March to November), where you'll be able to step into the lunar landscape of a marble quarry and learn about the harsh reality for workers who used to extract the massive blocks of white gold from the mountains.

While marble today is mostly extracted for architectural projects and the cosmetics industry, it has been used by sculptors to produce art since Roman times. In Villa Fabbricotti, the **CARMI Museum** tells about the life and work of one of history's best-known marble connoisseurs – Michelangelo Buonarroti. Through physical and digital reproductions of his work and historical documents, the museum's six thematic rooms trace the Renaissance artist's bond with Carrara.

The city is also home to one of Italy's most important art academies, the **Accademia di Belle Arti**, founded in 1769 by Princess Maria Teresa Cybo-Malaspina and still located in her former residence, the **Palazzo Cybo-Malaspina**. Inside, you can find one of the most important plaster-cast collections in the world, with over 300 works by famous artists such as Antonio Canova and Lorenzo Bartolini.

HIKING AROUND THE MARBLE QUARRIES

Start your hike from **Colonnata**, a tiny hamlet on the outskirts of Carrara known for the production of its traditional *lardo* (marble-cured fatback), and follow the red-and-white markers of route 195 all the way to Cima d'Uomo and Foce Luccica. The trail passes through a centuries-old *via di lizza*, an old track used by quarry workers to slide marble blocks down to the valley on wooden beams. It then continues through **Vergheto** before climbing back up to **Cima Gioia** via route 196. Cima Gioia has been a landmark since 2017, when Brazilian street artist Eduardo Kobra produced a multicoloured 10m-tall painting of Michelangelo's *David*, overlooking the Cava Gualtiero Corsi.

GETTING AROUND

Most seaside towns of the Versilia region can be easily reached by train from Lucca, although at times you might have to change trains in Viareggio, the main transport hub on this section of the coast. The Serchio Valley, north of the city, makes for a great road trip leading to the mountainous Garfagnana - the best way of getting around is with your own vehicle.

PISTOIA

Pistoia

Rome

Proclaimed the Italian Capital of Culture in 2017, Pistoia presents itself more timidly than other Tuscan art cities to visitors who reach its historic centre. A short walk separates the train station from the old town, whose charm remains overlooked by mass tourism, making roaming the city's quiet streets and buildings an even more pleasant experience.

Founded in the 2nd century BCE, the city was initially a military outpost for Roman troops who were fighting against the Ligurians. Over the centuries, Pistoia grew to become an independent municipality before falling under Florentine dominance in 1401. With its political importance decreasing, the city became an influential centre of the arts – music, poetry, theatre and painting funded by noble families shaped Pistoia's culture and continue to be core elements of the city's character to this day.

TOP TIP

About 7km east of Pistoia is the Fattoria di Celle, the farm hosting the permanent Gori Collection (goricoll. it), an environmental art exhibition surrounding a grandiose 15th-century villa. It's open May to September (book ahead).

PISTOIA BLUES FESTIVAL

For a week in July each year, Pistoia's Piazza del Duomo becomes one of Tuscany's most important music stages, hosting Italian and international acts. Past editions of the Pistoia Blues Festival, running since 1980, have welcomed artists of the calibre of Santana, Frank Zappa and Miles Davis. Check the full programme of future festivals at pistoiablues.com.

Pistoia Underground

ANCIENT TUNNELS BELOW THE CITY'S SURFACE

During the mid-14th century, Pistoia's former hospital, known as Spedale del Ceppo, played a key role in slowing down the black plague epidemic that struck the city and its surroundings. Founded in 1277, the institute functioned as a hospital for over seven centuries.

With a new hospital built in 2013, the Spedale del Ceppo – recognisable by its elegant loggia embellished with five ceramic medallions attributed to Giovanni della Robbia – was turned into the **Museo dello Spedale del Ceppo**, detailing the history of the structure through documents and a collection of past surgical instruments. The museum also includes the 17th-century Teatrino Anatomico, a tiny 'theatre' where students learnt anatomy through cadaver dissection.

It is under the former hospital, however, that much of Pistoia's history can be understood. The underground museum **Pistoia Sotterranea** (irsapt.it/it/pistoia-sotterranea) is formed by a 650m network of tunnels originally carved by the dried river Brana. By joining a guided tour run by the Historical and Archaeological Research Institute (IRSA), you'll be able to see the evolution of Pistoia's urban plan, observe remains found during a recent renovation of the tunnels, and learn that the hospital once used the river running below its surface as a dump for its waste – a fact that will make you grateful for modern hygiene procedures, considering that the water ran from the hospital to the public washhouses used by residents.

HIGHLIGHTS
1 Museo dello Spedale del Ceppo
2 Pistoia Sotteranea

SLEEPING
3 Casa Rowe B&B
4 Palazzo 42
5 Palazzo Puccini

EATING
6 Locanda del Capitano del Popolo
7 Osteria dell'Abbondanza
8 Vitium

Discovering Pistoia's Landmarks

ART & ARCHITECTURE WITHOUT THE CROWDS

Romanesque architecture defines much of Pistoia's medieval core, as proven by the striped 1 **Chiesa di San Giovanni Fuorcivitas**, completed in the 13th century, which you'll encounter as you enter the city from its southern edge. The distinctive facade stands in contrast with the obscure interior, which houses Taddeo Gaddi's precious *Polittico* (1355). Around the corner is the little 2 **Piazza della Sala**, Pistoia's market square, built around Cecchino di Giorgio's 1453 well.

Piazza della Sala comes to life every morning when fruit and vegetable stands crowd the square, but a larger market is held on Wednesday and Saturday in Pistoia's main square, 3 **Piazza del Duomo**, where you'll also find the city's main sights. These include the solemn 4 **Cattedrale di San Zeno**, housing the masterful *Altare d'Argento di San Giacomo* (a silver sculpture completed between the 13th and 15th centuries by some the greatest goldsmiths of the time), the museum 5 **Antico Palazzo dei Vescovi**, with its 7.9m by 2.7m *Arazzo Millefiori* tapestry, and the Gothic 6 **Battistero di San Giovanni**, designed by Andrea Pisano and built

---

 WHERE TO SLEEP IN PISTOIA

Casa Rowe B&B
There's a comfortable, quiet and warm atmosphere at this B&B in Via Antonio Gramsci. €€

Palazzo Puccini
Step back into the past by staying in this historic *palazzo* with high ceilings and frescoed walls. €€

Palazzo 42
This early-20th-century residence in the heart of Pistoia has a boutique feel and friendly service. €€

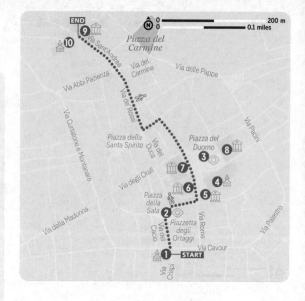

BEST RESTAURANTS IN PISTOIA

Vitium €
Locally inspired light bites and a large selection of wines make Vitium a perfect *aperitivo* spot near Piazza del Duomo.

Locanda del Capitano del Popolo €€
The eclectic decor doesn't distract from the delicious meals at this authentic trattoria in Via di Stracceria.

Osteria dell'Abbondanza €€
A place that sticks to its promise – abundant portions of Tuscan classics, with dishes inspired by the 'poor' cuisine of the past.

between 1303 and 1361 by combining white Carrara marble and 'serpentine' green Prato marble.

Next to finely adorned religious structures, two stately palaces stand on opposite sides of the square – the 1367 **7 Palazzo Pretorio**, housing the city court, and the **8 Palazzo del Comune**, home of the local government and of Marino Marini's Miracolo sculpture. Leave Piazza del Duomo behind and continue north. In front of the contemporary-art museum at **9 Palazzo Fabroni**, you'll find one of Pistoia's most revered artefacts, hidden behind the unassuming Romanesque facade of the **10 Chiesa di Sant'Andrea**. The intricately carved pulpit by Giovanni Pisano (1298–1301) is one of the masterpieces of medieval sculpture, telling stories of Christ's life through five panels standing on seven porphyry columns.

GETTING AROUND

The city of Pistoia is one of the easiest day trips to plan from Florence. Multiple trains depart every day from Florence's Santa Maria Novella station, arriving in Pistoia in approximately 50 minutes. Pistoia's train station is a 10-minute walk away from the city's centre, where you'll be able to navigate the sights independently. Those visiting by car can reach the city by taking the Pistoia exit on the A11 highway and then follow the signs to Pistoia Centro. If you are planning any outdoorsy trips, from Pistoia you can easily reach the Apennines by following the SS66 road north - just check the weather conditions if you are travelling in winter, as snow may occur.

Beyond Pistoia

Diverse and intriguing, Pistoia's surroundings pack much more than you'd expect.

Pistoia

Prato

Vinci

Heading away from Pistoia you could find yourself in tiny, remote Apennines towns, charming hamlets surrounded by vineyard-covered hills or historic cities. By heading north, you'll encounter the Montagna Pistoiese area, with Abetone being a favourite local skiing destination. West, on the way to Lucca, is exclusive Montecatini Terme, which has been attracting well-heeled tourists with its spas and luxury hotels, and Collodi, home to Pinocchio Park. East of Pistoia sits industrious Prato – a city with the third-largest Chinese community in Europe (after London and Paris) and an artistic legacy that, despite its worth, few make the effort to come and see. Finally, drive south to re-enter the province of Florence and stop at the birthplace of one of Tuscany's most revered historic figures – Leonardo da Vinci.

TOP TIP

Prato is easily reached by train from Pistoia (12 minutes). Buses run regularly to smaller towns in the area, although your own vehicle will make things much easier.

Cattedrale di Santo Stefano, Prato (p485)

MATTEO BRACALI/SHUTTERSTOCK ©

STEVANZZ/SHUTTERSTOCK ©

Vinci

CELEBRAZIONI LEONARDIANE

One of the most heartfelt events in the town of Vinci takes place on the anniversary of Leonardo da Vinci's birth, on 15 April 1452. On **Leonardo Day**, theatrical performances, film screenings, markets, workshops and special exhibitions honour Vinci's most famous citizen.

Inside the Mind of a Genius

LEONARDO DA VINCI'S BIRTHPLACE

It was in the little town of **Vinci**, 24km south of Pistoia, that the great Leonardo da Vinci was born. Painter, scientist, engineer and inventor, Leonardo's collection of achievements in entirely different disciplines has earned him the often-overused title of icon of the Renaissance. The **Museo Leonardiano** is a distributed museum split across three buildings that include the house where Leonardo da Vinci was born in 1452 (which includes a life-sized holographic representation of the great man), a space dedicated to Leonardo's career as a painter in Villa del Ferrale, and the inventions museum, showcasing a vast collection of machines built following Leonardo's designs. This last exhibition space, found inside the Castello dei Conti Guidi, is also the largest, and contains Leonardo's innovations in the fields of construction, textile production, military equipment and aviation. Before you leave, make sure you climb up the castle's terrace, for an amazing 360-degree view of Vinci's rolling hills.

 WHERE TO EAT IN VINCI

La Bottega di Nonno Mario
A recently opened family-run pizza place in the heart of Vinci. Great for both lunch and dinner. €

La Beccheria
This warm and welcoming traditional trattoria prepares massive charcuterie boards with accompanying local wines. €€

Caffè del Castello
Known for its legendary *bruschette*, this is an ideal spot for a quick lunch on the way to Leonardo's museum. €€

Old & New Art

CONTRASTS IN TUSCANY'S SECOND CITY

Prato, the second-largest Tuscan city by population, is only 15 minutes' drive from Pistoia and less than 30 minutes from Florence, though it doesn't see many visitors. A city that's been growing relentlessly since the mid-1800s thanks to its textile industry (there are over 7000 factories here), Prato is also an important cultural hub where the old blends with the new.

The **Castello dell'Imperatore**, the only example of Swabian architecture in central Italy, dating back to 1240, emerges staunchly from the heart of Prato's historic core, although it is Piazza del Comune that marks the medieval centre of the city. Here you'll find the towering, 12th-century **Palazzo Pretorio**, former centre of political power and now the most important museum in the city. It houses over 3000 artworks, including masterpieces such as Agnolo Gaddi's *Madonna col Bambino* (1392–95), Pietro di Miniato's *Incoronazione della Vergine e i Santi Mattia e Matteo* (1412–13) and Alessandro Allori's *Miracolo del Grano* (1603).

The nearby 13th-century **Cattedrale di Santo Stefano**, built in the Romanesque style of the era over a previous church, is the city's main religious structure. On the right-hand corner of the facade you'll notice the famous *Pergamo del Sacro Cingolo* (1434–38), the semicircular pulpit created by Michelozzo and Donatello, then you can enter to admire works by Agnolo Gaddi, Paolo Uccello and Giovanni Pisano, and Fra' Filippo Lippi's early-Renaissance cycle of frescoes found behind the altar, praised by both Michelangelo and Vasari.

In contrast to the preserved artworks of centuries past are the exhibitions at the brilliant **Centro Pecci**, Prato's futuristic contemporary-art centre, which hosts rotating shows featuring internationally acclaimed visual and performing artists under its distinctive golden roof. It's located 3km from the city centre (check what's on at centropecci.it).

BEST RESTAURANTS IN PRATO

Tonio €€
Top-notch seafood dishes have been served in this unassuming, family-run restaurant since the 1950s.

Osteria su Santa Trinita €€
Homemade comfort food served under elegant painted vaults, with a wide offering of local wines to pair.

Pepe Nero €€€
Chef Mirko Giannoni prepares refined revisitations of classic Tuscan dishes in his award-winning restaurant in Via Adriano Zarini.

GETTING AROUND

Reaching Prato takes under 15 minutes from Pistoia by train, making for an excellent day trip into one of the lesser visited historic cities of Tuscany. Florence is easily reached as well with public transport, but to reach smaller centres and the Apennines in the north a car is essential.

AREZZO

Arezzo

Rome

Nestled between four valleys – the Valtiberina, Valdarno, Valdichiana and Casentino – Tuscany's fourth city by population has evolved over the centuries from Etruscan trading post to influential political and artistic centre, showing traces of overlapping eras in its cinematic historic centre. During the 11th century Arezzo established itself as a flourishing independent republic, a city-state whose commitment to the Ghibelline cause would lead to continuous clashes with Guelph Florence. On 11 June 1289, Arezzo experienced a major defeat during the Battle of Campaldino – a conflict with over 10,000 soldiers on each side, including none other than a young Dante Alighieri – and a century later, in 1384, the city was ultimately subjugated by the Florentines. The most enduring symbols of the Florentine era are from the 16th century – the works by Piero della Francesca and legendary architect Giorgio Vasari survived the WWII bombing of the city and remain some of the most valued treasures of historic Arezzo today.

TOP TIP

Arezzo is easily reached from Florence's Santa Maria Novella station by train in about an hour. A train linking Arezzo with the main Casentino settlements runs regularly, but you'll need a car to reach remote corners of the mountainous area.

WHY I LOVE AREZZO

Angelo Zinna, writer

Arezzo is one of my favourite cities to visit from Florence. An often half-empty train leads directly to the city, which, despite its historic architecture, has managed to keep its small-town atmosphere intact, offering a sense of discovery that other hyper-photographed centres seem to have lost. Catching the **Fiera Antiquaria** is especially cool – you never know what odd object you might return home with.

Life is Beautiful in Arezzo

LA VITA È BELLA'S FILM LOCATIONS

Roberto Benigni's 1997 film *La Vita è Bella* (*Life is Beautiful*) is one of the most acclaimed movies to emerge from the Italian contemporary film scene, winner of three Academy Awards and nine David di Donatello Awards. It tells the story of Guido Orefice, a Jewish man, played by Benigni himself, who moves to the city in search of work during the Fascist era and is later sent to a concentration camp with his son Giosuè. *La Vita è Bella* has left a mark in Italy's collective memory through the many iconic scenes filmed in Arezzo, and you can visit their locations.

In the film, Guido cycles through **Piazza della Badia**, crossing paths with Dora, the teacher he loves (played by Nicoletta Braschi). Connecting Piazza della Badia with **Piazza Grande** – another recurring backdrop of the movie – are Via Cavour and Corso Italia. Via Cavour is home to the now-closed **Caffè dei Costanti**, an old-school cafe that is seen in the film denying entry to Jewish people. Corso Italia leads to the imposing **Cattedrale dei Santi Pietro e Donato**, Arezzo's cathedral (with stained-glass windows by Guillaume de Marcillat and Andrea della Robbia's glazed terracotta sculptures), outside which Benigni drove the 1934 Fiat 508 Balilla Torpedo car to impress Dora, before laying a red carpet across the cathedral's staircase to avoid her stepping into puddles.

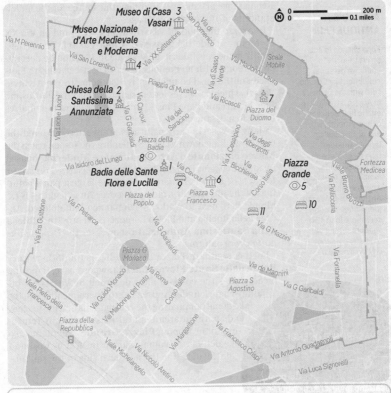

In Giorgio Vasari's Footsteps

FOLLOWING A RENAISSANCE GREAT

Painter, architect, sculptor and author, Giorgio Vasari was born in Arezzo in 1511. He is a defining figure of Tuscany's art heritage, and often considered the initiator of art history as a field of study thanks to his literary magnum opus *The Lives* – his collection of biographies of some of the greatest

 WHERE TO STAY IN AREZZO

Palazzo dei Bostoli
A few simple rooms in a (refurbished) 13th-century building ideally positioned for exploring the city. €€

La Corte del Re
In the heart of the city, these old-charm apartments with tall ceilings and dark-wood furniture will make you feel at home. €€

B&B Ghibellino
This centrally located place has a colourful, welcoming and bright atmosphere, with private parking available nearby. €€

VASARI IN FLORENCE

Giorgio Vasari is primarily known for his Florentine works – the **Corridoio Vasariano** (p411) stretching above Ponte Vecchio, the loggia of the **Uffizi** (p411) and the frescoes adorning Palazzo Vecchio's **Salone dei Cinquecento** (p413).

Renaissance artists, still an influential source for the understanding of Tuscany's golden age.

In Arezzo the roots of Vasari's legacy are found on Via XX Settembre inside the **Museo di Casa Vasari**. The artist's family home was inherited by Vasari in 1541 and he decorated its rooms with marvellous frescoes between trips to Florence and Rome. The museum is also home to the Archivio Vasari, which preserves letters sent to Michelangelo, Cosimo I de' Medici and Pope Pius V, among other important figures of the Renaissance.

Many of Vasari's early paintings are scattered around the city. By walking down Via XX Settembre you'll soon reach the **Museo Nazionale d'Arte Medievale e Moderna**, housed inside the elegant Palazzo Bruni Ciocchi. Vasari's *Convito per le nozze di Ester e Assuero* – one of the largest panel paintings of the 16th century, measuring over 7m in length – is exhibited here next to works by Buonamico Buffalmacco, Andrea della Robbia and Pietro Lorenzetti. Nearby, the **Chiesa della Santissima Annunziata** showcases the *Deposizione dalla Croce* painting.

Further south, in Piazza della Badia, is the 13th-century **Badia delle Sante Flora e Lucilla**, whose bare, imposing facade hides the colossal altar designed by Vasari for his family chapel, under Andrea Pozzo's baroque illusion, the fake dome dominating the ceiling. This artistic journey ends with an architectural masterpiece by returning to the sloping **Piazza Grande**, where the Logge del Vasari, commissioned in 1572 by Cosimo I de' Medici, line the northern side of the square.

GETTING AROUND

Arezzo's train station is served by frequent daily trains from Florence, continuing onwards all the way to Rome. Faster Intercity trains take just 40 minutes from Florence, while slower (but more frequent) regional trains take approximately an hour and a half. The central train station is located one kilometre from the city centre, close to the archeological museum and the Roman amphitheatre. Another train line managed by the TFT (Trasporto Ferroviario Toscano) runs from Arezzo to Stia through the small towns of Casentino, offering great day trip opportunities if you choose to spend a longer time in Arezzo.

Stia   Camaldoli

Arezzo

Cortona

Beyond Arezzo

Find a place to disconnect in Casentino's forests or seek fresh inspiration in Cortona – it's your call.

TOP TIP

Be aware that Cortona's train station is in Camucia, 3km away from the city centre. Bus 4 runs throughout the day to the old town.

Surrounded by the Casentino, the Valdichiana and the Valdarno valleys, the province of Arezzo has long been admired by international film-makers for its combination of scenic countryside, ancient settlements and tranquil atmosphere embraced by the untamed nature of the Apennines. Besides a typically Tuscan character, however, this corner of the region hides a dynamic artistic drive, which blends international, contemporary influences with the traces left by legendary Renaissance masters such as Michelangelo and Piero della Francesca, born in the region. Get your fill of art and architecture in the small towns that dot the area before taking some time to reflect on your discoveries in the forest trails that link remote sanctuaries and hermitages.

Parco Nazionale delle Foreste Casentinesi (p491)

TRAVELVOLO/SHUTTERSTOCK ©

Piazza della Repubblica, Cortona

PHOTO FEST

One of Tuscany's most prominent contemporary photography festivals takes place in Cortona between July and October. **Cortona on the Move** gathers conceptual works of Italian and international photographers at the Fortezza del Girifalco and other city locations, wonderfully complementing Cortona's Renaissance art. Find out more at cortonaonthemove. com.

Picture-Perfect Hilltop Town

VISUAL JOURNEYS IN CORTONA

Perched on top of a 500m-tall hill, historic **Cortona** has attracted an increasing flow of international visitors after director Audrey Wells chose the town as the backdrop for her 2003 film *Under the Tuscan Sun*. Wells' choice was well justified – when it comes to picturesque scenery, Cortona is hard to beat.

The city, whose origins date back to Etruscan times despite the clearly medieval urban development, stretches out from the central **Piazza della Repubblica**, where the 12th-century Romanesque town hall stands imposingly at the end of a wide staircase, above the cafes and restaurants with tables spilling onto the stone pavement. Steps away is **Piazza Signorelli**, where you can find the neoclassical **Teatro Signorelli**, the heart of Cortona's cultural scene, built in the 19th century and accessible through its seven-arched loggia. You'll also find the town's most important museum, the **Museo dell'Accademia Etrusca di Cortona (MAEC)**, housed inside the 13th-century Palazzo Casali.

The first two floors of the MAEC showcase the findings of the academy (founded in 1727 by a group of scholars and historians),

WHERE TO EAT IN CORTONA

La Bucaccia
Brick arches, stone walls and dark-wood decor complement the Tuscan cuisine at this rustic restaurant. Try the *pici* pasta. €€

Osteria del Teatro
A flower-lined staircase leads to the elegant hall of this Renaissance palace where traditional fare is the star. €€

Birrificio Cortonese
This pub serves locally crafted beers and hearty classics like wild-boar *pappardelle*. There's even beer gelato. €€

gathered over the course of the past three centuries, including a precious bronze chandelier dating back to the 4th century BCE, found in 1840. The MAEC also functions as the information point for exploring the Etruscan remnants that surround Cortona, such as the **Tomba Etrusca di Mezzavia**, **Tumulo di Camucia** and the **Tanella di Pitagora**.

Around the town's core many great viewpoints await. Walk to the Romanesque **Cattedrale di Santa Maria**, home of fine paintings by Pietro da Cortona and Luca Signorelli, to admire the Valdichiana from above. Or head to the **Fortezza del Girifalco**, built by the Medici in the 16th century on the foundations of a former defensive structure, for a bird's-eye view over the city and its hilly surroundings.

Exploring a Lush Borderland

ANCIENT FORESTS AND QUIET RETREATS

Stretching across the border of Tuscany and Emilia-Romagna are the abundant forests covering the Apennines that form the **Parco Nazionale delle Foreste Casentinesi**, a mountainous nature reserve dotted by monasteries and hermitages praised for its scenery since Dante's time. The majority of the national park expands into the Emilia-Romagna side, where you can find the **Riserva Naturale Sasso Fratino** – the primeval beech forests given World Heritage status in 2017 – but hiking and bicycling trails are easily accessed from Tuscany as well.

From Florence or Arezzo you can drive up to **Stia**, the hamlet perched under Monte Falterona where the Arno river originates. Here you can visit the **Museo dell'Arte della Lana**, tracing the history of the textile industry in the area, and little **Museo del Bosco e della Montagna** (open Sundays), housing a collection of over 500 stuffed birds once belonging to Stia's former mayor Carlo Beni. Then continue to the **Camaldoli**, where a three-to-five-hour round hike leads to the **Eremo di Camaldoli** and back through the pristine forests of the Casentino. Camaldoli's hermitage – founded by Benedictine monks in the 11th century – is a tiny, peaceful monastery nestled in the greenery at an altitude of 1100m.

Those looking for more challenging hikes can tackle long-distance trails such as the seven-day **Sentiero delle Foreste Sacre**, crossing the border back and forth between Tuscany and Emilia-Romagna from Lago di Ponte to the La Verna sanctuary (GPS track available atparcoforestecasentinesi.it), or the 27-day **Alta Via dei Parchi** (*altaviadeiparchi.eu*), running across Emilia-Romagna, Tuscany and Le Marche through eight nature reserves, including the Parco Nazionale delle Foreste Casentinesi.

ST FRANCIS OF ASSISI'S TRAIL

One of Italy's most prominent religious figures, Giovanni di Pietro di Bernardone – better known as St Francis of Assisi – spent much of his life roaming eastern Tuscany attempting to spread the gospel and searching for spiritually favourable remote retreats. His wanderings led to the hermitage of La Verna in 1224, where Francis is said to have received the stigmata. Since then, the **Santuario della Verna**, located in a remote corner of the Parco Nazionale delle Foreste Casentinesi above a towering rock formation among beech trees, has become a pilgrimage destination, which can be reached on foot from Florence over six days (or in a few hours by car). The historic complex includes the beautifully frescoed Corridoio delle Stimmate and the Cappella delle Stimmate, built in 1263 and adorned with Andrea della Robbia's glorious *Crucifixion* (1481).

GETTING AROUND

Arezzo is conveniently located on the A1/E35 highway, which allows you to easily explore the Chianti region and the Valdichiana valley by car. The city is also well connected by train to major cities like Florence and Rome, with an additional railway line running to Stia in the Casentino region. Several buses run daily to the towns and hamlets of southern and eastern Tuscany as well.

GROSSETO

Grosseto

✦ Rome

Despite the city of Grosseto being the heart of Maremma and the main transport hub of southern Tuscany, it hardly makes it on tourist maps. Beginning its expansion as a result of the collapse of the Etruscan then Roman city of Roselle, Grosseto fell under the rule of both the Sienese and the Florentines. They viewed the city as important for acquiring the minerals found in the nearby Colline Metallifere, and for agricultural products from the Ombrone valley, but neglected its value as a social and cultural centre, obstructing the city's development. And then there was malaria, a disease that heavily affected coastal Maremma, forcing the inhabitants of Grosseto who could afford it to relocate to higher grounds during summer months to avoid infection. The malaria problem wouldn't be fully solved until after WWII, during which Grosseto was heavily bombed, making its current appearance a result of work done from the 1950s onwards

TOP TIP

Direct trains run from Pisa and Siena to Grosseto in approximately 1½ hours, but visiting the sights around Grosseto can be difficult without your own vehicle.

**BEST
RESTAURANTS
IN GROSSETO**

Trattoria Il Giogo €
Family-run and as homely as it gets, this trattoria is rooted in Maremma's traditions, as their *acquacotta* vegetable soup demonstrates.

Osteria Canapino €€
This sophisticated *enoteca* (wine bar) will find the perfect vino for any food you choose – they have over 400 labels in their cellar.

Gabbiano 3.0 €€€
This Michelin-starred restaurant in Marina di Grosseto's port serves a fish-based menu with a Balinese touch.

Maremma's Capital

YOUR BASE TO EXPLORE THE REGION

At first glance, Grosseto may seem to have little to offer compared to other Tuscan cities, but as soon as you look at a map you realise that not visiting means missing out on more than you accounted for. It's the largest Tuscan province by size, and Grosseto's surroundings make up in wilderness for what they lack in art and architecture. Driving through empty, two-lane roads towards Maremma's countryside means you'll encounter forgotten ruins, little-known wineries and spectacular scenery, all a short distance from each other.

Crowd-free and surrounded by natural and cultural gems, Grosseto is the optimal base from which to explore Etruscan ruins, pristine reserves and remote rural communities, connecting to both the Alta Maremma to the north and the Bassa Maremma in the south. The historic centre is locked within the 16th-century Medicean walls – a defensive structure that has remained intact to this day despite the city's convoluted history.

Grosseto's most important sights are found in the adjacent Piazza del Duomo and Piazza Dante, location of the pink-hued **Cattedrale di San Lorenzo**, dating to 1302, and the much more recent **Palazzo Aldobrandeschi**, which, contrary to what its Gothic influences may suggest, was built in the early 20th century.

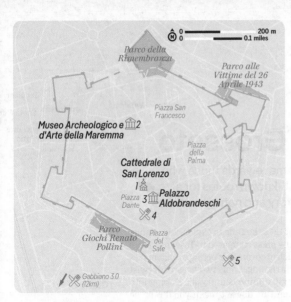

HIGHLIGHTS
1 Cattedrale
di San Lorenzo
2 Museo Archeologico e
d'Arte della Maremma
3 Palazzo
Aldobrandeschi

EATING
4 Osteria Canapino
5 Trattoria Il Giogo

Besides strolling through a mix of its architectural styles, it's worth stopping at Grosseto's **Museo Archeologico e d'Arte della Maremma (MAAM)** to get a better understanding of the region's early history before heading out to explore Maremma's archaeological sites. The MAAM houses a large collection of artefacts retrieved during the excavation of former Etruscan cities, some of which date back to the 6th century BCE.

 GETTING AROUND

Grosseto's historic centre, locked within the city walls, is closed to car traffic but can be easily explored on foot. If you are travelling with your own vehicle you can get to Grosseto via the E80 motorway from Rome or the SS223 road from Siena. Park your car outside the city walls (parking approximately €0.70/hour). The main railway crossing Grosseto is the Rome–Genoa line. From Florence, you will likely have to change trains in Pisa or Livorno. The train station is a 15-minute walk north of the inner city.

Beyond Grosseto

Massa Marittima

Seggiano

Vetulonia   Arcidosso   Santa Fiora

Grosseto   Rocchette
di Fazio

Alberese   Scansano

Vast, diverse Maremma rewards those who leave behind the well-known routes for a blend of ancient history and natural wonders.

Few are the travellers that take the time to explore Maremma, an area that hardly gets any press compared to Tuscany's more iconic destinations. The lack of coverage is perhaps what makes this part of the region so intriguing. Long, two-way roads twist and turn through seemingly infinite countryside sloping into the Mediterranean, though this doesn't mean you'll only be drifting through photogenic landscapes – you'll find there are plenty of reasons to break your journey, from discovering millennia-old Etruscan relics, to immersing yourself in the inebriating local wine culture and swimming in the numerous coves carved into the coastline. Plan for the unexpected.

TOP TIP

Buses run from Grosseto to the larger seaside towns, but a car is essential to explore beyond city centres, especially if your time is limited.

Pitigliano

CEZARY WOJTKOWSKI/SHUTTERSTOCK ©

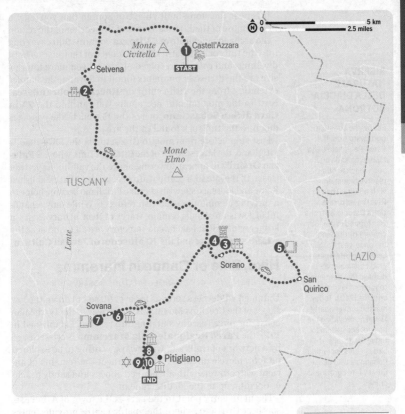

Città del Tufo Road Trip

ETRUSCAN CAVES & JEWISH CULTURE

A triangle of land in Tuscany's deep south forms the area known as Città del Tufo, a network of settlements that emerged during the Etruscan era. The three main (and most impressive) towns of the Città del Tufo are **Pitigliano**, **Sovana** and **Sorano**, around which the 60-hectare **Parco Archeologico Città del Tufo** extends. A round trip from Grosseto first heads to 1 **Castell'Azzara** along a twisting country road and then south to Sorano, after a brief stop at the abandoned 9th-century castle of 2 **Rocca Silvana**. The 12th-century 3 **Castello Orsini** dominates Sorano's skyline, best appreciated by climbing the fortress 4 **Masso Leopoldino**.

SATURNIA'S HOT SPRINGS

As you leave Città del Tufo to return to Grosseto, stop by the public baths of **Cascate del Mulino** in Saturnia, where sulphurous waters pour into pools (free to access) at a constant 37°C.

 WHERE TO EAT NEAR THE PARCO REGIONALE DELLA MAREMMA

Ristorante da Remo
In the centre of Rispescia, close to Alberese, is this locally loved seafood restaurant that makes freshness its trademark. €€

L'Ambientino del Pescatore
By Marina di Grosseto's port, L'Ambientino is known for its old-school hospitality and hearty seafood dishes. €€

Altro?
In Alberese, Altro? is almost stereotypically Tuscan, serving generous portions of Maremma classics. €

It is near the stone-built village of Sorano that you'll get a first glimpse of the Etruscan roots of this corner of the region – the archaeological site of **5 Vitozza** contains 200 caves dug into the tuff rock that still show evidence of their use as both dwellings and *colombari* (pigeon farms). Even more impressive are the Etruscan remnants found in Sovana, the hamlet extending from the 11th-century **6 Rocca Aldobrandesca**. Next to the monumental necropolis you can find the **7 Via Cava di San Sebastiano**, one of the 15 trench-like passages dug into the tuff rock found in the area.

Last stop before returning to Grosseto via the SR74 road is Pitigliano, the largest town of the Città del Tufo, whose **8 Palazzo Orsini** will appear towering above the tuff hill as you get closer. In the late 16th century, after racial laws that established Rome and Florence's Jewish ghettos, Pitigliano became home to a thriving community of Jewish refugees. While only a handful of Jewish residents remain, traces of their history exist – a kosher wine cellar, bakery and cemetery are all found near the **9 1598 synagogue** and the **10 Museum of Jewish Culture**.

RISERVA NATURALE DELLA DIACCIA BOTRONA

Follow the coastline northward from the Parco Regionale della Maremma and you'll soon reach another reserve brimming with wildlife. The **Riserva Naturale della Diaccia Botrona** was formed in the 18th century by draining the once-vast Preglio Lake in an attempt to eradicate malaria – a disease that continued to torment Maremma until the 1940s. Today, marshes cover nearly 13 sq km, providing the perfect ecosystem to thrive for dozens of bird species, including flamingos, wild geese, great white egrets and cranes.

Flamingos, Riserva Naturale della Diaccia Botrona

Hike, Bike or Canoe in Maremma

SOUTHERN TUSCANY'S LARGEST NATURE RESERVE

Untamed wilderness spreads for over 90 sq km down the low slopes of the Uccellina Mountains all the way to the Tyrrhenian coast, forming Tuscany's first nature reserve. Established in 1975, the **Parco Regionale della Maremma** is crisscrossed by a network of trails and waterways, waiting to be explored on foot, bicycle or canoe, which connect the remains of ancient watchtowers with abandoned abbeys and sandy beaches opening up to the Mediterranean.

The main entry point to the park is the town of **Alberese**, south of Grosseto, where the visitor centre provides entry tickets, maps and information. Eight cycling routes and 12 hiking paths offer the chance to experience Maremma's nature and wildlife, with trails such as the relatively flat 10km A3 'Caves' itinerary, to the circular C1 route leading to the **Salto del Cervo** beach, with over 600m of ascents.

The heart of the park is marked by the mysterious ruins of the **Abbazia di San Rabano**, a monumental Benedictine abbey built between the 11th and 12th centuries and abandoned in the 16th century. The 16km A1 circular path leading to San Rabano through the thick woods takes approximately seven hours to complete, passing through the 14th-century Uccellina watchtower before returning to the starting point, by the Casetta dei Pinottolai. As you

---

 WHERE TO EAT IN PITIGLIANO

Forno del Ghetto
Come here to try *lo sfratto*, a cylindrical pastry shell filled with honey, chopped walnuts, nutmeg and aniseed. €

Trattoria Il Grillo
A chequered-tablecloth-style trattoria serving handmade *pici* pasta, wild boar, local cheeses and many seasonal dishes. €€

Il Tufo Allegro
Chef Pichini Domenico brings history to the table here with exceptional flavours paying tribute to local traditions. €€€

walk through the park, keep your telephoto lens ready – over 270 species of birds, including ospreys and peregrine falcons, populate the forested grounds, together with deer, wild boars and foxes. If birdwatching is your thing, consider joining a canoe tour on the Ombrone river at sunrise (book via parco-maremma.it).

Not all the park is left to the fauna. Human settlements in the area have been traced back to the Palaeolithic era, and more recent agricultural heritage remains a prominent presence within the reserve's borders. The **Tenuta di Alberese**, one of Europe's largest organic farms, covers over 40 sq km of land – here you might spot some of the last remaining *butteri* – the horse-riding cowboys herding the long-horned Maremmana cows that roam the protected lands of the park. Tours led by the *butteri* can be booked via alberese.com.

Note that during the summer period of 15 June to 15 September, hiking is only allowed with certified guides due to the risk of wildfires.

ROWING REGATTA

On 15 August each year, Monte Argentario hosts its own version of the Palio. The **Palio Marinaro dell'Argentario** sees four teams in traditional costumes, representing the four historic districts, competing in a 4km rowing regatta off Porto Santo Stefano.

Mediterranean Escapes in Monte Argentario

VIEWS, COVES AND THE MYSTERY OF CARAVAGGIO

Connected to the rest of Tuscany via three narrow strips of land forming two lagoons, Monte Argentario can't be called an island, though its atmosphere suggests otherwise. Sleepy during winter and lively in summer, Monte Argentario has a unique geography and attracts holidaymakers who arrive by land and sea to enjoy its 20-plus coves and beaches. **Via Panoramica** links the two main cities, Porto Santo Stefano and Porto Ercole, by the coast, offering breathtaking views in between. Many of its more appealing beaches, however, can't be reached by car.

Cala del Gesso, for instance, is found at the end of a steep 700m walking path on the western coast – a great place to snorkel under the shadow of the 15th-century cliff-hanging watchtower. Similarly, the cobble beaches of **Cala Grande** and **Cala Piccola** require some nature walking – unless you have a yacht. Between dips in the sea, visit **Porto Santo Stefano** and step into **Chiesa della Santissima Trinità** to check out the modern mosaics (produced in the early 2000s) – uniquely surprising pieces of decorative work, incomparable to traditional religious wall art.

Porto Ercole, the main Monte Argentario city where part of Anthony Minghella's *The Talented Mr Ripley* (1999), starring Matt Damon, was filmed, houses the tomb of Renaissance

 WHERE TO EAT IN MONTE ARGENTARIO

Ristorante La Sirena
This busy establishment in Porto Ercole serves freshly caught seafood dishes in a classic trattoria atmosphere. €€

Cala Piatti
This seaside restaurant on the west coast is far from easy to reach, but the views hardly get any better. €€€

Il Pellicano
Splurge on creative flavour blends by Michelin-starred chef Michelino Gioia while listening to the sound of the waves. €€€

artist Michelangelo Merisi, better known as **Caravaggio**. Caravaggio died here in 1610, shortly after he arrived to retrieve a series of paintings mistakenly shipped to Monte Argentario. The artist's remains have long been contested by historians, but a 2010 DNA test found there was an 85% chance of them being authentic, leading to a funerary monument being placed in the centre of town. In 2019 the tomb was moved to the local cemetery.

Between Nature & History

NATURAL SURROUNDINGS AND SPANISH LEGACY

The enduring symbol of **Orbetello** is found by the tip of the peninsula – the small, cylindrical grain-grinding **Mulino Spagnolo**. Dating back to the Sienese era and restored by the Spanish, it rises from the lagoon on the west side of the dam. It's not the only piece of architecture reminiscent of the Spanish State of the Presidi – the 1692 Polveriera Guzman that once housed tonnes of explosive material has now been converted into Orbetello's **Archaeological Museum**, and the **Palazzo del Podestà**, once the residence of Spanish viceroys, rises from Piazza Eroe dei Due Mondi with its iconic clock tower.

Orbetello's urban landscape retreats as you leave the city centre, opening onto long sandy beaches and the WWF-protected oasis. The two beaches most people come here for during summer months stretch out on the outer edge of the two sandy tombolos that connect Monte Argentario with mainland Tuscany – **Giannella** and **Feniglia**. The 6km-long, tree-lined Giannella beach is a great spot to admire the sun setting on the Mediterranean, while Feniglia is a protected park known as **Riserva Naturale Duna Feniglia**, where deer, wild boars, foxes and other animals live between the lagoon and the open sea.

BEST RESTAURANTS IN ORBETELLO

L'Asino d'Oro €€
Lucio Sforza's little eatery is great for trying the diverse cuisine of lower Maremma, with a rich menu of seasonally changing dishes. Book ahead.

La Mi Casa €€
No fuss and no frills, La Mi Casa means fresh ingredients cooked according to tradition in the homely atmosphere the name suggests.

Trattoria Rugantino €€
Many Roman classics, including *cacio e pepe* and carbonara, are available for those looking for a break from Tuscan cuisine.

GETTING AROUND

A large network of trails extends within the limits of the Parco Regionale della Maremma, accessible via the town of Alberese located close to the E80 motorway. A regional train line connects Grosseto with Ortebello. Buses do run to Monte Argentario from Ortebello's railway station, although a car will make reaching panoramic viewpoints and hidden beaches much easier.

LIVORNO

Livorno

⭐ Rome

Though it's not at the top of everyone's agenda, the shabby port city of Livorno is full of unlikely charms. It's a worthwhile stopover on your way to the seaside, and a good spot to linger away from the crowds of more picturesque Tuscan cities. When Pisa's harbour silted up, the Medici dynasty founded Livorno as a 'free port' in 1606. The result was a multicultural merchant population – in particular Jews, Armenians, Dutch, English, Spanish and Greeks. Venetian workers were recruited to build houses, churches and canals in their own style, and the city flourished as a safe haven for persecuted minorities and pardoned criminals. It lost its status as a free port when Italy was unified more than 150 years ago, and was heavily bombed during WWII. Still, the centuries of cosmopolitan legacy live on – in the vibrant markets, diverse architecture and the Livornese people themselves. Oh, and you can expect some of the best seafood on the entire Tyrrhenian coast.

TOP TIP

Livorno is easy to navigate on foot, but cycle-hire app Bicincitta (bicincitta. com) provides a fun way of getting around. The station is a 30-minute walk from the town centre, all the way down Viale Giosuè Carducci.

Historic Old Town

LIVORNO'S BEATING HEART

With a couple of hours to spare, walking around Livorno's historic **Venetia Nuova** – the Venetian-style canal quarter – is the perfect way to soak up the Renaissance city. Start in grand **1 Piazza della Repubblica**, with Medici statues at each end. From here, follow the historic moat round to **2 Fortezza Nuova**, a vast pentagonal fortress, which retains the charm and layout given to it by Bernardo Buontalenti in the 16th and 17th centuries. Continuing on your walk, vast octagonal **3 Chiesa di Santa Caterina** is the next landmark. Venture inside to admire Giorgio Vasari's luminous altarpiece detailing the coronation of the Virgin Mary. The back of the church is a little grittier, as the site of the convent-turned-prison in which socialist politician Sandro Pertini was imprisoned during the Fascist era. A few metres further on, **4 Museo della Città di Livorno** breathes new life into a magnificent 18th-century olive-oil warehouse and baroque church. If you look down Viale Caprera from the museum, you'll get a glimpse of **5 Fortezza Vecchia**, a medieval fort and tower dating to the 11th century, now all but surrounded by ferry terminals. Instead of going there, weave through graffiti-lined streets and over canal bridges to the **6 Duomo**, also variously known as the Cathedral of St Francis of Assisi, the Virgin Mary, and Julia of Corsica (a patron saint of Livorno). Subjected to bombing during WWII, the

WHERE TO HAVE A DRINK IN LIVORNO

Fortezza Elettrica
Inside the walls of historic Fortezza Nuova, this edgy bar specialises in tequila cocktails and light evening snacks.

Cantina Nardi
Stop for a glass of wine from the large collection of bottles in this historic *enoteca*, served with a platter of *stuzzichini* (snacks).

Alphonse
This trendy canal-side *aperitivo* spot turns into a late-night drinking den, with live music and experimental cocktails.

BEST PLACES TO EAT SEAFOOD IN LIVORNO

La Barrocciaia €
A perennial favourite, this lively evening-only restaurant serves delectable fish from nearby Mercato delle Vettovaglie.

Melafumo €
The huge seafood platters at this rowdy trattoria are popular with both Livornese regulars and tourists.

L'Antica Venezia €€
Tucked away by the canals, this family-run spot hasn't changed for decades. The clientele is local, and the *baccalà alla Livornese* (cod) unmissable.

Azzighe €€
Try top-notch, Barcelona-inspired seafood tapas with a contemporary Livornese soul.

Il Sottomarino €€
Sample traditional daily specials, with what purists say is the best *cacciucco* (mixed seafood stew) in town.

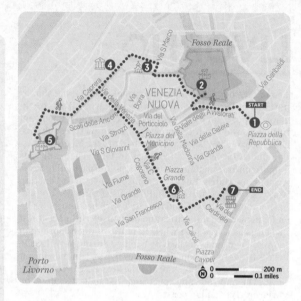

cathedral was restored and reconsecrated in 1952. Inside, look out for Fra Angelico's early-Renaissance fresco *Christ Crowned with Thorns* in the Eucharist chapel. The Duomo backs onto Via Grande, an impressive main shopping street with porticoes on both sides. Stroll under the arches back to where you started, or veer right for a snack in the **7 Mercato delle Vettovaglie**, before heading to the spectacular **Terrazza Mascagni** for an evening *passeggiata* – the very Italian tradition of a leisurely, people-watching stroll. Complete with 34,000 black-and-white tiles, the 1920s promenade is the world's largest checkerboard floor, with views over the faraway islands of Gorgona and Capraia on a clear day.

GETTING AROUND

As one of Tuscany's most significant ports, Livorno is for many a jumping-off point for ferries to Sardinia, Corsica, Sicily and the Tuscan Archipelago. Public buses from the train station (a 30-minute walk from the city centre) and Livorno itself are unreliable at best, so consider taking a taxi to navigate the maze of motorway exits and ferry terminals, and

allow plenty of time. Getting along the Etruscan Coast from Livorno is a breeze, on the other hand, with regular regional trains stopping at Castiglioncello, Cecina, Bolgheri, San Vincenzo and Piombino, among other destinations. The Via Aurelia, a Roman road that traces along the coast all the way down to Rome, is equally enjoyable.

Beyond Livorno

Travelling down the coast from Livorno, scruffy seaside towns morph into Slow Food eating spots, Super Tuscan vineyards and white sandy beaches.

Livorno

Castiglioncello • Cecina

Bolgheri

Elba

The Etruscan Coast takes its name from the pre-Roman civilisation that dwelt here in the 9th century BCE. Taking the train south of Livorno, you can be on the beaches of Castiglioncello or Cecina within 30 minutes, snacking on *fritti di mare* (fried seafood) with your toes in the sand as the sun goes down. Inland, a car gives you the freedom to weave through vineyards and olive groves, and explore on a whim medieval hilltop villages such as Bolgheri. And then there's Elba, the third-largest Italian island after Sicily and Sardinia. Elba's beaches and roads become jam-packed in August, but for the rest of summer, it's paradisical, with around 147km of glorious coastline to roam. The rugged hills and chestnut forests are just as enchanting as the beaches and are popular with hikers, cyclists and Slow Food enthusiasts.

TOP TIP

Take a train from Florence or Pisa to Piombino Marittima ferry port. Ferry services from Piombino to Portoferraio (Elba's biggest harbour) are run by Toremar, Moby Lines, Blu Navy and Corsica Ferries. All are similar in quality and cost, but Corsica Ferries are slightly faster.

Bolgheri village (p503)

SIMONA BOTTONE/SHUTTERSTOCK ©

Sorgente beach, Elba

UNFORGETTABLE DINING SPOTS

Marina Cacciapuoti, founder of Italy Segreta, spent childhood summers sailing around the island. (@italysegreta)

Agriturismo Montefabbrello
Head inland to this wine estate with extensive vegetable gardens and a secluded courtyard. Order the *antipasto dell'orto* followed by a traditional *fiorentina* steak, washed down with local organic wine.

Calanova
Swim and lunch at this peaceful, pebbly oasis between the beaches of Malpasso and Istia. In the shade of ancient cork trees, savour Simona and Cristophe's seafood menu before unwinding under umbrellas.

Capo Nord
An unmissable dinner spot in quaint Marciana Marina. Start with sunset cocktails at Bleep, next to the Bagni Capo Nord rainbow-coloured cabins, before enjoying this restaurant right on the water.

Elba Beach Vibes

SWIMMING, SNORKELLING AND SUNBATHING IN THE ARCHIPELAGO'S LARGEST ISLAND

Long sandy bays, lunar landscapes, windswept headlands, secluded coves and pebbly peninsulas... But with 126 beaches to visit, how do you choose? Luckily, there's an app for that: **Elba Spiagge** ('Beaches in Elba') gives up-to-the-minute information on weather conditions throughout the island, right down to which way the wind is blowing on any given beach.

Closest to Portoferraio, **Spiaggia di Capo Bianco** has striking white rocks and cliffs – a good (but sometimes crowded) option if you can only squeeze in a couple of hours before leaving. **Capo d'Enfola** is not far beyond, where the clear sea and strong breeze are popular for water sports. Beach town **Procchio** and adjoining resort **Biodola** are 10km west of Portoferraio, with lovely sandy beaches and clear water. West from Procchio, the road hugs cliffs above **Spartaia** and **Paolina**, beautiful little beaches requiring a steep clamber down.

Further afield, other top picks include the three sandy coves of **Morcone**, **Pareti** and **Cala dell'Innamorata**, framed by sweet-smelling pine trees. On Elba's northern extremity, **Cavo**

 HOTELS & CAMPSITES ON ELBA

Villa Ottone
A palatial 19th-century villa overlooking a private beach, where five-star facilities meet vintage interiors. €€€

Hotel Ilio
It's all about the sleepy beachside location for this simple yet welcoming boutique hotel in Sant'Andrea. €€

Tenuta delle Ripalte
A wine resort in the northern extremity of Capoliveri, with glamping, villas, farm stays and a grand old hotel. €€

is worth considering if you want to take a ferry straight there and stay put. A walk away, **Spiaggia di Frugoso** is a dreamy spot looking onto tiny Isola dei Topi. Active types may like to be based around **Porto Azzurro** and **Narengo** for the best windsurfing, canoeing and dinghy sailing off the beach. Pretty **Marina del Campo** also has a sailing school, Club del Mare, with small boats for all levels. Finally, the white shingle beaches of **Sansone** and **Sorgente** stand out for their crystal-clear, turquoise waters.

Wine Road

THE RISE OF THE SUPER TUSCANS

Until the 1980s, Chianti Classico was the only Tuscan wine to have a name on the international market. Cue the 'Super Tuscans', a handful of plucky and experimental winemakers from the **Bolgheri** region who decided to grow French grapes on the clay-rich soil. Planting merlot, syrah and cabernets sauvignon and franc on the fertile land, they created a new era for Tuscan winemaking. Today, an acre of land in Bolgheri DOC has the highest value in Italy, with its wine often selling for 20 times the price of Chianti.

To explore the cypress-lined roads and hilltop towns of the Bolgheri wine region, begin outside the village of **Castagneto Carducci** with a visit to **Michele Satta**, a founding Bolgheri winery. Next, weave through country roads to **I Greppi**, one of the most innovative winemakers in the region, where solar-powered roofs and ground-source heat pumps mean a carbon-neutral operation. At their brand-new 'cellar door' tasting space on the road into Bolgheri, the hanging log fire and glass-walled tasting room feel more like California than rural Italy. Book ahead for a private tasting, winemaker's tour, vineyard stroll and more, or drop in for a wine flight and some snacks for around €20. Just over the road, Chianti powerhouse **Antinori** also have their fingers in the Bolgheri pie, with Tenuta Guado al Tasso a magnificent spot for a sunset *aperitivo*.

Bolgheri itself is a minuscule but picturesque hilltop hamlet, with one road in and one road out. You can wander around the whole place in a few minutes – especially since the main historical attraction, the castle, isn't open to the public – but the real magic, of course, is in tasting the wines while looking out over the lands where they grow.

WHERE TO STAY AROUND BOLGHERI

Villa Caprareccia €
Homely cooking lessons, vineyards and orchards make this traditional *agriturismo* and campsite a haven for foodies on a budget.

Il Chiassetto €€
This quaint B&B offers a rare chance to sleep within the medieval hamlet of Bolgheri itself.

Relais Sant'Elena €€€
A fairy-tale hotel on the Tenuta Gardini country estate, where you'll find exquisite farm-to-table gastronomy and sumptuous cottagey decor.

GETTING AROUND

The Etruscan Coast is known for its driving routes, and in particular the ancient Roman Via Aurelia, a gloriously straight, tree-lined road that goes all the way to Rome. There's also touristic Strada del Vino *(lastradadelvino.com)*, which weaves through 150km of vineyards and olive-oil farms between Livorno and Piombino. Note that Bolgheri train station is misleadingly not in the city itself, but on the outskirts of Marina di Bibbona, where you can take a taxi to the hilltop town (buses are few and far between).

UMBRIA & LE MARCHE

ITALY'S GREEN HEART & SOUL

The oft-overlooked centre of the country has something to offer everyone, whether you're looking to immerse yourself in culture, nature or chocolate.

When the poet Giosuè Carducci called Umbria the 'green heart' of Italy, he could hardly have thought of a better metaphor. The heart is, after all, that vital organ that animates the body. Stroll through the alleys of Perugia or stand at the base of Assisi and you'll immediately feel a familiar pulse, constant and consistent.

Of course, every heart has secret chambers that it reveals only to the most dedicated lovers. Admirers of Umbria are rewarded when Le Marche unfolds in a procession of formidable mountain ranges that encircle cities like Ascoli Piceno and Urbino. Even bustling port cities are not always what they seem when they are so intimately traced back to the heart. Ancona may be a gritty threshold between land and sea but it is also the point where the vulnerable heart opens to the world beyond.

But every heart is bound to break. The great spine between Umbria and Le Marche has suffered from earthquakes that have ruptured towns through terrible tremors. However, broken hearts mend; those cracks become the most resilient points, where the greatest loves are inscribed. The green heart of Italy grows ever more resilient, ever more alive. So ignore the crowds going elsewhere and don't worry if you wind up falling in love along the way. The heart is, after all, built precisely for these things.

PAOLOGAETANO/GETTY IMAGES ©

THE MAIN AREAS

PERUGIA
The capital built on a kiss. p510

URBINO
Perfectly preserved Renaissance mystique. p521

ANCONA
The Adriatic at your fingertips. p526

ASCOLI PICENO
The shining white city. p534

ORVIETO
Northern beauty, southern charm. p539

N

0 ____ 50 km
0 ____ 25 miles

EMILIA-
ROMAGNA

SAN MARINO

SAN MARINO

Rimini

Riccione

Cattolica

Adriatic Sea

San Leo

Pesaro

Fano

Urbino, p521
This walled city looks like a fairy tale and has legends to match, along with some of the country's most dramatic panoramas and tastiest dishes.

Urbino

Urbania

Fermignano

Calcinelli

Metauro

Fossombrone

San Michele

Alpe della Luna

Sansepolcro

San Giustino

Cagli

Montevarchi

Arno

TUSCANY

Arezzo

Città di Castello

Sasso Ferrato

Scheggia

Monte Cucco

Parco Regionale del Monte Cucco

Perugia, p510
From medieval art to modern jazz to timeless chocolate, you'll find it in the regional capital, a stone's throw from classic hill towns.

Castiglion Fiorentino

Cortona

Umbertide

Gubbio

Sigillo

Fabriano

Appennines

Camucia

Terontola

Tuoro

Passignano

UMBRIA

Tevere

Gualdo Tadino

Nocera Umbra

Castiglione del Lago

Lago Trasimeno

Magione

San Feliciano

Corciano

Perugia

Parco Regionale del Monte Subasio

Assisi

Monte Subasio

Chiusi

Lago di Chiusi

Panicale

Torgiano

Santa Maria degli Angeli

Spello

Deruta

Bevagna

Foligno

Città della Pieve

Marsciano

Montefalco

Trevi

Arcidosso

Abbadia San Salvatore

Bastardo

TUSCANY

San Giacomo

Spoleto

Lente

Todi

Parco Regionale del Tevere

Orvieto

Parco Regionale di Coscerno Aspra

Pitigliano

Manciano

Bolsena

Lago di Bolsena

Baschi

Bagnoregio

Lago di Corbara

Montecchio

Lago di Alviano

San Gemini

Acquasparta

Ferentillo

Monteleone di Spoleto

Terni

Amelia

Narni

Rieti

Orvieto, p539
From underground Etruscan tunnels to the spires of Gothic cathedrals, this ancient city will take your breath away.

Orte

Tevere

LAZIO

Find Your Way

As its central position implies, Umbria and Le Marche form a bridge between northern and southern Italy. Of course, sometimes getting across it is easier said than done, especially if you're relying on public transport.

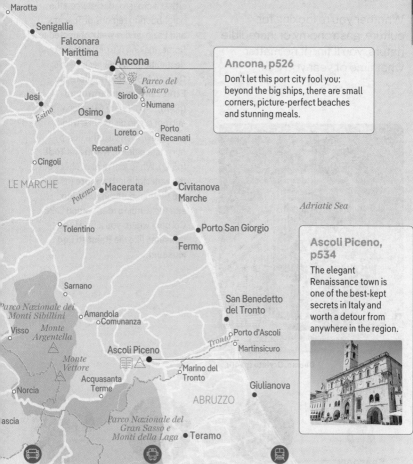

Ancona, p526

Don't let this port city fool you: beyond the big ships, there are small corners, picture-perfect beaches and stunning meals.

Ascoli Piceno, p534

The elegant Renaissance town is one of the best-kept secrets in Italy and worth a detour from anywhere in the region.

CAR

The best way to tour the area is by car. Roads are well maintained and signposted, and while you may run into the occasional 'strada bianca', you'll avoid the heavy traffic typical of other regions.

BUS

Umbria and Le Marche have bus links with major hubs but service is spotty and often doubles travelling time (or more). Buses are tricky if you don't speak Italian (or even if you do).

TRAIN

Perugia is roughly a two-hour train journey from both Rome and Florence but is not served by high-speed lines, so settle in and enjoy the scenery.

Plan Your Time

Whether you're looking for culture, gastronomy or incredible nature, you'll find it no matter what time of year you visit.

Duomo, Orvieto (p540)

An Umbrian Weekend

● The southern corner of Umbria sits at a crossroads between the neighbouring regions of Tuscany and Lazio, and is well connected to Rome, making it a perfect weekend destination. Marvel at Orvieto's **Duomo** (p540) and explore the **Etruscan city underground** (p540). Sip Orvieto Classico wine and eat rustic dishes like wild boar stew, then visit the nearby fairy-tale cities of **Narni** and **Todi** (p542). While you're at it, check out the waterfalls in **Marmore** (p541), the thermal baths in **Amerino**, and the winding roads along Lake Corbara where you'll find little treasures like the **Painted Egg Museum**.

Seasonal highlights

Umbria and Le Marche are two regions for all seasons, with festivals year-round and plenty of spots to soak up the summer sun.

JUNE
Watch summer bloom at the **Infiorate** flower festival in Spello.

JULY
Umbria Jazz in Perugia is the biggest party of the year, when the city comes alive.

AUGUST
Pick up your joust and head to Ascoli for the **Quintana** festival.

Three Days in Le Marche

● If you've got an insatiable appetite for the finer things, a holiday in Le Marche will satisfy every craving. Soak up the Renaissance splendour of **Urbino** (p521) and taste the prosciutto and truffles that have made it a gourmet paradise, then travel south to **Ascoli Piceno** (p534) to sample the famous olives in one of the most elegant cities in the country.

● The Marche coast and **Riviera del Conero** (p528) are made for sun-worshippers. If you're looking for an adrenaline rush, head inland to stand on the clouds at **Monte Vettore** (p537), one of the highest points in Italy.

A Week in Perugia

● Basing yourself in the regional capital is the best way to explore all of its nooks and crannies (above and below ground), and taste some of the incredible food for which Umbria is known. Oh, and don't miss a visit to the **Perugina factory** (p515) to get your fill on delectable chocolate.

● When you're done, walk the pilgrim's path in **Assisi** (p510), sample **Sagrantino di Montefalco** (p519) in its namesake town, and learn about cashmere and harmony in **Solomeo** (p518). Soak it all up in the **San Francesco thermal baths** (p539) or on the banks of **Lake Trasimeno** (p517).

SEPTEMBER

Head to **Jesi** for the wine harvest and a taste of the world's best.

OCTOBER

Live out your Willy Wonka fantasies at **Eurochocolate** in Perugia.

NOVEMBER

The **White Truffle Festival** in Acqualagna will spoil you rotten with copious amounts of this gastronomic delicacy.

DECEMBER

Ring in the New Year at **Umbria Jazz** in Orvieto.

PERUGIA

Not every city can claim the title of artist haven, jazz epicentre and chocolate kingdom. But Perugia isn't just any city. The Umbrian capital, nestled between Rome and Florence, has been breaking the mould since the Etruscans dominated here, becoming one of the most important cities of what was then a vast region known as Tuscia. One of the city's best-known sons, the artist Pietro Vanucci would become the master Perugino in the 15th century and bring the city to global prominence. Nearly five centuries later, in 1973, that same allure would bring a spontaneous festival called Umbria Jazz.

But in Perugia, not all heroes wear painter's caps or play the oboe. Some of them, like Luisa Spagnoli, are simply brilliant women who realise that chopped hazelnuts and chocolate should never go to waste. And so, in 1922, the Baci Perugina was born.

TOP TIP

This is a hill town par excellence, which makes driving and parking an absurd pursuit. Park your car in one of the many car parks at the foot of the city and make your way up through convenient lifts around town. Pack light.

INTERNATIONAL JOURNALISM FESTIVAL

Festivals in Perugia aren't just about chocolate and jazz. Since 2007 the International Journalism Festival has gathered journalists from around the world to share their work and their stories in a multi-day event that is free and open to the public. Where else will you get to mingle with Al Gore, Seymour Hersh and Edward Snowden while eating homemade *torta al testo* bread and washing it all down with a bold local red? The festival takes place every spring and sessions are in both Italian and English. Visit www.journalismfestival.com for more information on how to attend or how to support the project.

Outdoor Living in the Historic Centre

SOAK IN MEDIEVAL CHARM

Despite its moody climate, Perugia is a city that feels destined to be lived outdoors. It's difficult to say whether the sizeable student population makes it feel that way, or if the students have come as a result of it, but the result is an almost constant buzz in the air that tends to reach a fever pitch during the summer, on weekends and at the city's many festivals. Perugia seems both intimate and expansive, and accessible yet ever so slightly mysterious. It's a gritty type of place that runs from the highest points in the old centre to the tunnels underground.

If people-watching was a sport, Perugia would be its champion and there's no better place to do it than the steps of the **Cattedrale di San Lorenzo** in Piazza IV Novembre. All roads will lead you in and out of the piazza at some point, and the striking **Fontana Maggiore** will be your meeting point and reference for when the wine, chocolate or history goes to your head. The piazza sits at one end of **Corso Venucci**, the main artery of the *centro storico* (historic centre) that is bookended by **Giardini Carducci**, a green perch high above the town where perfect views are par for the course. On balmy summer nights you'll find families sitting on benches and young lovers trying to steal their first kiss. Then again, you'll probably find the very same thing on chilly winter evenings, too.

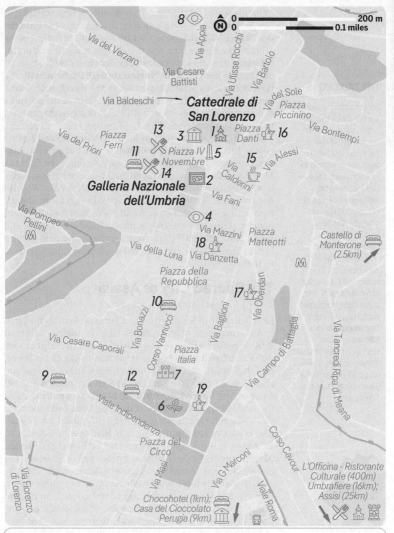

HIGHLIGHTS
1 Cattedrale
di San Lorenzo
2 Galleria Nazionale
dell'Umbria

SIGHTS
3 Capitularies
Museum of Saint
Lorenzo

4 Corso Vannucci
5 Fontana Maggiore
6 Giardini Carducci
(see 2) Palazzo dei Priori
7 Rocca Paolina
8 Via dell'Acquedotto

SLEEPING
9 Bio B&B Della
Mandoria

10 Hotel Locanda
della Posta
11 Priori Secret Garden
12 Sina Brufani

EATING
13 Il Cantinone
14 Osteria ai Priori

DRINKING
& NIGHTLIFE
15 Caffe Dal Perugino
16 Dempsey's Perugia
17 Kundera Bistrot
18 Mercato Vianov
19 Punto di Vista

On this stretch of road, you'll see one of the best examples of how architecture is always allegory, in the form of the **Palazzo dei Priori**. This colossal structure was built over the course of more than a century and the changing aesthetics, political landscape and society are all evident in its many styles. It also houses the **Galleria Nazionale dell'Umbria**, with the largest Umbrian school collection in the world, with works ranging from the 13th to 19th centuries. Many of the artworks depict morbidly obese men with facial expressions that beg to be made into memes. That is, of course, just a suggestion.

Perhaps one of the most unique stretches of road in this city is the **Via dell'Acquedotto**, which began as an ancient engineering project that brought water to the Fontana Maggiore but as times changed (and bricks were removed), it was decided that the road was best left scenic. And indeed, what it lacks in hydraulics it makes up for in charm, connecting the *centro storico* and Porta Sant'Angelo neighbourhood through a narrow pathway lined with houses and secret gardens. You'll likely have to manoeuvre past couples lost in each other's embrace but don't worry, they're used to that sort of thing.

The Sacred City of Assisi

WHERE TOURISTS BECOME PILGRIMS

Less than half an hour's drive from Perugia, Assisi is the birth and resting place of St Francis, one of the patron saints of Italy. Whether it was the town that created the saint or vice versa is difficult and perhaps irrelevant to say, but it is certain that Assisi will leave you speechless whichever angle you approach it from. The **Basilica di San Francesco** and accompanying **Sacro Convento** are utterly monumental, and the scale of the structure is stupefying both from the road and upon entering. It is enough to qualify Assisi for its well-deserved Unesco status, but it is just one in a series of stunning points in the town. The 14th-century **Rocca Maggiore** offers its own dramatic panorama of Assisi and the entire landscape around it, and is worth the considerable climb.

Assisi attracts more tourists than almost anywhere else in Umbria, and there is no shortage of restaurants, hotels and shops. But it remains a site of profound importance to the Catholic Church and is filled with pilgrims and followers of the Franciscan order. Don't be surprised to find yourself side by side with monks in ascetic brown robes from com-

---

THE TAU CROSS

Shop windows in Assisi are filled with the Tau Cross, the distinctive symbol of St Francis. *Tau* is the last letter of the Hebrew alphabet and was used in the Old Testament as well as by St Anthony of Egypt. St Francis adopted it as his personal seal and, later, his followers used it as a sign of their devotion. It symbolises protection and redemption, and is available in souvenir shops around Assisi. **Tomassetti Arte Sacra** has a vast selection of handmade items made from olive wood, all produced by local artisan Marcello Tomassetti.

 WHERE TO STAY IN PERUGIA

Sina Brufani
Five-star digs with all the bells and whistles, including a spa and panoramic views. €€€

Bio B&B Della Mandorla
Cosy, budget-friendly rooms with organic products in the heart of the city. €

Castello di Monterone
Just 3km from the city centre, this castle feels like another world. €€€

ARTMEDIAFACTORY/SHUTTERSTOCK ©

BEST DRINKS IN PERUGIA

Punto di Vista
The cocktails are the perfect compliment to the panoramic views.

Kundera Bistro
Though not technically a cocktail bar, the wine and beer list more than make up for it.

Mercato Vianova
The kitchen is chic, the decor is sleek, and the experience is both.

Dempsey's
Sure, it's a student dive but with better drinks than they need to have.

Dal Perugino
Nothing fancy, but it's open at 6am when only the street cleaners and you are up.

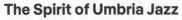

Via dell'Acquedotto

munities around the world, and if you're in the town during a holy day you'll find it overflowing with religious symbols and celebrations.

The Spirit of Umbria Jazz

THE BIGGEST PARTY IN TOWN

It is said that St Francis of Assisi prayed that God would perform miracles through him, and it only took 750 years for God to deliver and bring Miles Davis to Perugia.

Jazz music has a few spiritual homelands, and for nearly half a century Umbria has been one of them. What started in 1973 with a series of free outdoor concerts in cities around the region has become an institution. **Umbria Jazz** has, by its very existence and the opportunities it has given to performers over the years, come to embody the very spirit of the music itself. The proof is in the line-up of prolific artists, from Charles Mingus to Lady Gaga to Dee Dee Bridgewater,

Priori Secret Garden
Eco-chic suites in the heart of the centre, with a fantastic terrace for cocktails. €€

Hotel Locanda della Posta
Classic with modern finishes – an oasis in the middle of the action. €€€

Chocohotel
A bit out of town and a bit out of the world, it's a sweet bed for a sweet tooth. €€

PERUGIA UNDERGROUND

As alluring as the city centre is, there is an entire world underground that may just rival anything above. The **Rocca Paolina** fortress was built to contain the rebellions against the Papacy during the Salt War of 1540, and was destroyed sometime after. Its remnants, and those of the 36m Etruscan well, still lurk underneath Perugia and offer an incredible glimpse into medieval life.

Tours of underground Perugia begin at the **Museo del Capitolo di San Lorenzo**, next to the cathedral, and must be booked in advance. Visit www.cattedrale.perugia.it/museo-e-percorso-archeologico for information and opening hours or better yet, swing by the Cattedrale di San Lorenzo in Piazza IV Novembre for the most current information.

DREVS/SHUTTERSTOCK ©

Street musicians, Umbria Jazz (p513)

who performed at the outset in 1973 and returned in 2022.

Umbria Jazz takes place throughout the year but its most frenetic chapter unfolds in Perugia in July every year. Expect boisterous international crowds getting lost among the alleyways and partaking enthusiastically in the local grape variety, while rooms and reservations will be at a premium. But you'll also find a city possessed by the spirit of jazz itself, New Orleans on the hill or Montreux on the mountain. Whatever it is, enjoy it. After all, it took a miracle to make it happen.

For information on tickets, lineups, and travel, check out the Umbria Jazz website *(umbriajazz.it)* or Instagram *(@umbriajazzofficial)*. Parking in town is nearly impossible during the festival, but there are plenty of buses running to the centre as well as the trusted lift system.

 WHERE TO EAT IN PERUGIA

Osteria ai Priori
Local specialities in a quaint dining room with a shop to take home products. €

L'Officina – Ristorante Culturale
Innovative tasting menus featuring local ingredients and an extensive wine list. €€

Il Cantinone
You won't get more traditional, or more delicious, than this local mainstay. €€

A Kiss to Build a Dream On

EXPLORE THE CHOCOLATE OF PERUGIA

Perugia is a city built on stories and the very best of them involve love and chocolate. The intrepid entrepreneur Luisa Spagnoli came from a poor family and married young. She could have settled down instead chose to build her life on the *bacio*, a joyful mixture of chocolate and hazelnut upon which Perugia became a global brand and Perugia the host of its confections. Though her life was brief, Spagnoli became an enormous success in both food and fashion. Her dedication to Perugina was due in no small part to her partner in business and in life, Giovanni Buitoni. Their respect, admiration and love for one another put their city on the global map and is one of the stories upon which Perugia proudly stands.

You can visit the Perugina factory **Casa del Cioccolato Perugina** *(perugina.com/it/casa-del-cioccolato/la-cas)* throughout the year and there are countless chocolate shops all over the city. But if you're a true lover, make plans to attend **Eurochocolate** *(eurochocolate.com)*, a 10-day Perugia-wide festival that features chocolate art displays, chocolate-inspired street performances and chocolate sculpting. Perugia is proudly displayed along with other brands from Italy and abroad, all of which offer tastings in locations around the historic centre. The main event takes place at the **UmbriaFiere**, a 14,000-sq-metre space that features pavilions with immersive experiences.

OH, CHRISTMAS TREES!

Every year, just outside the city of **Gubbio**, the slopes of Mount Ingino are illuminated by the world's largest Christmas tree, according to the Guinness Book of Records. Standing 650m high and 350m wide, the Gubbio tree can be seen from 50km away, making it one of the oddest yet most popular holiday attractions in Umbria.

If you're looking for something a little more delicate you'll love the **Deruta** Christmas tree, made entirely from the ceramics for which the town is world-famous.

Both trees are on display from early December until after New Year's, giving you plenty of time to get into the Christmas spirit whichever you choose to visit.

 GETTING AROUND

Perugia is a big city on a big hill, so get ready to go vertical.

If you're arriving by car, find one of the car parks just outside of the city centre and reserve online *(sabait.it/en/parking-perugia)*, then grab one of the lifts into the city centre. Many hotels also have private parking facilities that usually cost €20 per day, so enquire in advance.

Perugia is well connected to other Italian cities via train but does not have high-speed links. It's roughly 2½ hours from Roma Termini and two hours from Florence. The train station is at the bottom of the hill, so use the Mini Metro to reach the centre.

Lake Trasimeno   Perugia

Solomeo   Spello

Montefalco Trevi

Beyond Perugia

You don't have to go far from the capital to get a taste of the best that Umbria has to offer.

If you haven't gotten your fill of decadent food, copious wine and seductive scenery, then the area just outside of Perugia will undoubtedly satiate you. Venture east towards the border with Le Marche and you'll hit some of the most picturesque towns in the region. While it may not be on the ocean, Umbria has plenty of watering holes that won't disappoint. Trasimeno Lake, a short drive west, is one of the most pristine and well-kept secrets in Italy; on your way over, don't forget to stop at Solomeo for what might be the holiest shopping experience you'll ever have. Finally, have a look at the Fonte di Clitunno and the Insta-famous hamlet of Rasiglia.

TOP TIP

Hill towns can be steep, so make sure you've got the right shoes for walking!

Passignano sul Trasimeno on Lago di Trasimeno

GIMAS/SHUTTERSTOCK ©

Panicale

WHY ARE DERUTA CERAMICS SO SPECIAL?

Since the Middle Ages, this tiny town just outside of Perugia has been famous for its majolica ceramics. The technique involves covering earthenware with an opaque tin glaze and decorating it before firing, which allows for intricate patterns and family crests to maintain their colours over the centuries. Deruta ceramic tiles were so sought after that they were used to decorate the Church of San Francesco in Deruta, Santa Maria Maggiore in Spello and San Pietro in Perugia. But the town has become most famous for its tableware, and you'll find iconic Deruta platters, pitchers and mugs in towns all over Umbria.

Floating on Lago di Trasimeno

UMBRIA'S SECRET SHORE ESCAPE

Though it's the fourth-largest lake in Italy, Trasimeno feels like your own personal watering hole wherever you happen to find yourself taking a dip. This is perhaps due to the stunningly well-preserved towns that line the lake and make it seem as though time forgot to tell anyone around here that it was ticking. For every paddleboarder or windsurfer, there are 10 birdwatchers or fishermen waiting silently for their catch to appear. Life moves slowly on the lake, and if you're looking to unwind you'd have a hard time finding a better place anywhere in the world.

Above the lake, the picturesque towns of **Panicale** and **Paciano** are full of character, with local shops and bars all benefitting from the panoramic views that never get tiring. The towns of **Castiglione del Lago** and **Passignano sul Trasimeno** offer majestic views from their medieval turrets, and

 WHERE TO STAY BEYOND PERUGIA

Antico Sipario
Theatrically themed rooms in Paciano that look onto their courtyard above Lake Trasimeno. €€

Rastrello
A boutique hotel with sumptuous rooms and even more lustrous olive oil, high in the hills of Panicale. €€-€€€

Hotel Castello di Reschio
Live like actual royalty on the Umbria–Tuscany border. €€€€

VALERIOMEI/SHUTTERSTOCK ©

Rasiglia

STRADA DEL VINO COLLE DI TRASIMENO

Though the tradition dates to the Etruscan era, the wines around Trasimeno are some of the least known outside of Italy (and even inside, to be fair). Which is a shame, because the microclimate of the lake and its surroundings produces a number of excellent whites, reds and rosés, all of which resemble and often surpass those of their more famous neighbours over the border in Montepulciano. Visit some of the wineries that have been operating for generations with the Strada del Vino Colle di Trasimeno, a collective of local producers who design itineraries, offer wine pairings and host guests in their *agriturismi* (farm-stay accommodation). For information visit trasimenodoc.it or stradadelvino trasimeno.it.

in the summertime the passing traffic hums without ever reaching fever pitch.

If you need even more quiet, take the ferry from Passignano to **Isola Maggiore**, one of three islands in the lake and the only one that is still inhabited, with a robust population of 35. If that's still too bustling for you, the other two islands, **Minore** and **Polvese**, are uninhabited.

A Designer's Dream Come True

A HAMLET OF CASHMERE & HARMONY

Just outside of Perugia on the road to Trasimeno, the hamlet of **Solomeo** is what would happen if you took Plato's Academy and made it about fashion. Designer Brunello Cucinelli, who was born and raised in Solomeo, has transformed the town into a living monument to philosophy and the art of living well, which mirrors the philosophy of his cashmere empire. If you've got the funds, you can book a private tour of

---

 WHERE TO STAY BEYOND PERUGIA

Torre di Moravola
Sleep like royalty in a medieval tower near Gubbio. €€€

Vicolo Fabbri
Luxe apartments in the medieval walls of Montefalco. €€

NUN Relais & Spa
Pamper yourself in the converted ancient Roman ruins in Assisi. €€€€

the town, its flagship store, the factory and the nearby park, which features the 22m Monument to Human Dignity. But Solomeo isn't a shopping mall and reservations aren't required. Instead it is a beautifully kept, slightly surreal and strangely captivating open-air museum that lives up to its name as 'the Hamlet of Cashmere and Harmony'.

Visitsolomeo.it for more information on the history of the town and how to book an appointment for a tour.

Montefalco, Trevi & Spello

THE MOST PERFECT TRIANGLE

We've all dreamt of those classic Italian hilltop villages that, based on some alchemy of altitude and ambiance, make us feel as though we've only ever made good decisions in life. All too often, however, we are disappointed to find out that everyone got there before us, and that all the magic has been lost to overcrowded piazzas and overburdened waiters. But then you find Umbria.

Pythagoras himself could not have plotted a more perfect triangle than that which links the towns of Montefalco, Trevi and Spello. The drive is scenic and straightforward, with only an hour of driving time between all three spots. Of course, you'll want to take your time in each, because there is plenty to enjoy.

Named in honour of Frederick II's penchant for falcon hunting during his stint on the hill, Montefalco has all of the drama and dominance that its imposing name implies. The approach to the walled city is lined with old-school vegetable stands selling local Cannara onions and old women sitting on the pavement outside their homes. Once you enter the gates, you're immediately greeted by beautifully preserved cobblestone streets dotted with cosy restaurants and inviting shops, most of which will serve or sell the town's prized commodity, **Montefalco di Sagrantino DOC**, a voluptuous red wine for which the town is world-renowned. You can drink it just about anywhere but head to the lively Piazza del Comune and grab an outdoor table at **Enoteca L'Alchemista**, one of the best restaurants in Umbria.

Across the valley, you'll spot a town that seems to have latched itself onto the face of an opposing hill. This is Trevi, unrelated to the Roman fountain in all ways apart from serving as a reservoir for precious liquid: in the capital it is water, in the town it is olive oil. If you're lucky enough to visit at the end of October you'll celebrate the new oil harvest

FONTE DI CLITUNNO & RASIGLIA

The hamlet of Rasigilia gained sudden fame when its canal-filled streets started to flood social media, having been dubbed the 'Venice of Umbria'. It does indeed look that way as crowds converge on this postage stamp–sized attraction every weekend. It is a lovely place but the sheer volume of tourists, souvenir shops and restaurants that have popped up make it difficult to get that perfect shot in front of the waterfall. Opt instead for a visit to the Fonte di Clitunno, the park and natural springs that inspired poets to christen this region 'Italy's green heart'. The park charges a symbolic fee to enter, which goes towards sustaining the Unesco temple on the grounds.

 WHERE TO EAT BEYOND PERUGIA

Enoteca L'Alchemista
Inventive dishes with local ingredients and a stunning wine list, all in the cosy medieval town of Montefalco. €€

Osteria Piazzetta dell'Erba
Who would have predicted Japanese-Italian fusion in the heart of sacred Assisi? But it works, really. €€

Taverna del Sette
This elegant, understated locale is one of the highlights of the scenic olive oil route that runs through Trevi. €€€

with the entire town. If not, you can always walk the **olive trail** through the groves outside of the town walls and finish at the **Olive Oil Museum**. Of course, one couldn't leave without thoroughly sampling the oil, along with the famous black celery for which Trevi is known. Try both at **La Taverna del Sette**.

If you should find yourself in the area around the ninth Sunday after Easter, head to Spello for the **Infiorate**, a celebration of the Corpus Domini that covers the winding medieval streets of this already gorgeous hill town with floral sculptures created by hand. If you can't get there for the Infiorate, the tiny **Museo delle Infiorate** in town has a lovely series of photos and drawings from years past. But if you want to take the memory of those sweet flowers with you, visit **Acqua ai Fiori di Spello**, an artisanal fragrance shop that designs bespoke fragrances using flowers from around the region. They also ship internationally and have a fantastic online presence so if your bags are already bursting, it'll be waiting for you on your return home.

BEST UMBRIAN WINES

Montefalco di Sagrantino
A tannic-heavy red that will pair with the hearty dishes of the area.

Trebbiano di Spoletino
An intense, fruity white that only grows in the region.

Cannara Rosso Passito
A sweet red that ends any meal on a high note.

Rosati di Trasimeno
A rosé that might be the best kept secret outside of Provence.

Grechetto
A bright, balanced white that is as close to Umbria in a glass as you can get.

GETTING AROUND

Though some of the larger hill towns are connected by train stations, service can be sporadic and transfers between the lower-lying stations and the town centres can be unreliable (or non-existent). The best option for travelling is to have your own car: parking is usually well indicated outside of the city centre and reasonably priced. Rental cars are available at the airport in Perugia, which hosts all major companies.

URBINO

The city of Urbino is so vertiginous that as you approach it, you may experience a moment of dizziness. You're not alone: many of the streets in the medieval centre are so steep that steel handrails are fixed to the stone walls, and they have helped people scale the town for centuries. Powerful duke Federico da Montefeltro loved Urbino and was so instrumental to the Renaissance that he was called 'the Light of Italy'. The city he built remains slightly frozen in time, perhaps in his honour. Today, Urbino cannot help but maintain its majesty, if only for its soaring altitude. Luckily, there is more than enough there to keep it the best city you've never heard of in Italy and the only one you must absolutely get to know.

TOP TIP

Whatever time you plan to spend in and around Urbino, budget at least one more day, especially if your trip coincides with any of the not-to-be-missed festivals in the area.

Exploring the Palazzo Ducale

DISCOVER THE DUKE'S TREASURES

The dimensions of the Palazzo Ducale are so imposing that they seem barely real; it's as if the entire formation has been ripped from the pages of a comic book and brought to life in brick and mortar. To call it a fortress does it no justice, nor does a castle seem to be quite the right term. It is so massive that the hills upon which it stands might be in danger of toppling over, unable to sustain the gigantic proportions of its towers and turrets. And yet it survives almost perfectly intact, like Urbino itself, an architectural marvel that has almost no equal anywhere else in what remains of Renaissance Italy.

Much like Federico da Montefeltro, the stern exterior of the Palazzo Ducale hides a bounty of treasures in its interior. The duke's patronage is displayed on par with his military prowess, in frescoes and sculptures throughout the complex. One of the most stunning features of the palace is the **Studiolo**, a small room that was built for contemplation and faced away from the city. The Studiolo is entirely decorated with inlaid wood that mimics shelves, benches, and scientific and musical instruments along with weapons and armour. It is as if Federico wanted to be surrounded by the things he loved most in the world, encased in the glossy finish of polished wood. More than the mammoth scale of the palace, this room tells the story of Urbino, with its attention to the smallest detail and the playfulness hiding just beneath the surface. After

FESTA DEL DUCA & FESTA DELL'AQUILONE

Over the final weeks of summer, while the rest of Italy is fighting over one last beach day, Urbino comes alive with two entirely unique celebrations. The **Festa del Duca** fills the city with an entire week of music, theatre and reenactments celebrating the greatest action hero of them all, Federico da Montefeltro. Then, on the first Sunday in September, the **Festa dell'Aquilone** fills the sky above Urbino with thousands of kites in a competition that has taken place since 1955. The two events couldn't be more different but together, they perfectly encapsulate the spirit of this very nearly ideal city.

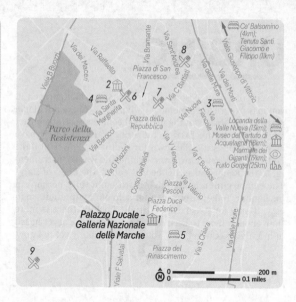

HIGHLIGHTS
1 Palazzo Ducale –
Galleria Nazionale
delle Marche

SIGHTS
2 Casa Natale
di Raffaello

SLEEPING
3 Hotel Boncorte
4 Hotel Raffaello
5 Hotel San Domenico

EATING
6 Antica Osteria
da la Stella
7 Piadineria L'Aquilone
8 Portanova
Ristorante in Urbino
9 Tartufi Antiche Bonta

UNESCO STATUS

The Palazzo Ducale was designated
a Unesco World Heritage Site in
1998, two years before **Assisi**
(p510).

all, in a city that has welcomed artists, poets and philosophers, a sense of humour is better than a suit of armour. Art has always been a serious business in Urbino, however, and the placement of the **Galleria Nazionale delle Marche** in the Palazzo Ducale highlights how important it was and remains to the identity of the city. The gallery houses one of the most important collections of Renaissance art in the world, and because it is less trafficked than its contemporaries in Florence, Rome or London, you can spend hours soaking up works from Titian, Piero della Francesca or Paolo Uccello. You'll also happen upon a painting of unknown provenance called *The Ideal City*, one of three that exist in the world. Though it bears little resemblance, you won't be hard-pressed to figure out why it hangs in Urbino.

Tasting Urbino

BIG FLAVOURS & BOLD DISHES

While every region of Italy has its own culinary canon, the cuisine of Le Marche may be one of the richest in the country. In Urbino, products are revered and dishes remain faithful to

 WHERE TO SLEEP IN URBINO

Hotel San Domenico
A modern, well-curated hotel directly opposite the Palazzo Ducale. €€

Hotel Raffaello
The art on the walls honours the hotel's namesake but the views over the city are even better. €€

Hotel Bonconte
A restored villa with charm and a sense of humour. €€€

Palazzo Ducale (p521)

NOSE TO TAIL AT LA TAVOLA MARCHE

New Yorkers Ashley and Jason Bartner moved to Italy in 2007 and founded La Tavola Marche cooking school on their farm just outside of Urbino. But this is no ordinary cooking school: classically trained chef Jason shows students how to make sausage and butcher a whole hog while Ashley wrangles chickens, teaches people how to relocate to Italy, and keeps it all looking effortless. Courses run year-roun and you can enquire about renting the farmhouse for events or coming to stay a while. Visit www. latavolamarche.com for more information on everything they offer.

their Renaissance origins. When you come to the city make sure to bring a scorecard and an extra suitcase.

Anywhere in the world, you'll likely find a butcher selling prosciutto from Parma or San Daniele. But you'll need to come to Urbino to taste *prosciutto di Carpagna*, a prized and protected label that you'll be hard-pressed to find elsewhere. The combination of Urbino's microclimate, painstaking preparation and secret spice blend make this one of the most well-known, and jealously guarded, foods in the region. If there is a rival in the form of cheese, it's *Casciotta di Urbino*, a blend of sheep and cow's milk that was said to be the favourite of Michelangelo. It too is a protected brand but can often be found at global festivals, where it has been named among the best in the world. Try them both at **Tartufi Antiche Bontà**, located near **Casa Raffaello** (the birthplace of Raphael).

Even the most studied pasta scholars might not know about *passatelli*. A speciality of Urbino and Pesaro, *passatelli* consists of breadcrumbs, eggs, salt and *parmigiano reggiano* (Parmesan) cheese. The mixture is passed through a ricer and cooked like a dumpling, then traditionally served in a broth with even more cheese. If that's still a bit too light for your taste, get your hands on *crescia*. This flat bread, a distant cousin of the

 WHERE TO SLEEP OUTSIDE URBINO

Tenuta Santi Giacomo e Filippo
Just outside of Urbino, this sprawling estate is an oasis.
€€€

Locanda della Valle Nuova
A sustainable, family-run farm-stay in Fermignano that's as comfortable as it is well run. €€

Ca' Balsomino
A luxury country house divided into chic apartments with an artistic flair, a stone's throw from central Urbino. €€

KNOW YOUR TRUFFLES!

In Acqualagna, there are four types of truffles that are harvested at different points in the year. If you stumble across anyone selling truffles outside of these periods, chances are they're not the real thing. Best to wait until the next festival.

**Marzuolo
(off-white truffle)**
Found from mid-January to late April.

**Perigord
(black truffle)**
Emerges from December to March.

**Scorsone
(summer truffle)**
Appears from June to August and then again from October until the end of December.

**Magnatum Pico
(white truffle)**
Only found from the last Sunday in September to the end of December.

DOUBLE YOUR PLEASURE

For true gourmands, pair the White Truffle festival in Acqualagna with **Eurochocolate** in **Perugia** (p515). Don't worry, you'll work it all off climbing the streets of Urbino.

Truffles, Museo del Tartufo di Acqualagna

better-known *piadina*, gets extra crispy thanks to a slathering of lard just before wood frying. *Crescia* is then filled with all manner of meats, cheeses and, on occasion, vegetables. Get your *passatelli* fix at **Antica Osteria della Stella** and load up on *crescia* at **Piadineria L'Aquilone**.

The Acqualagna Truffle Festival

A TRULY GOURMET ADVENTURE

We can only wonder who it was that first dug a rather questionable tuber from the ground and proclaimed it a food of the gods, but ever since then, the truffle has been the very definition of culinary luxury. There are those who don't see what all the fuss is about, and couldn't tell the difference between Perigord and Philadelphia. Others are so passionate that they follow the fluctuations in price in real time, on the running exchange that dates from 1890. That exchange, incidentally, has it origins in a tiny town in the hinterlands of Le Marche, which has become its own pilgrimage site for those who count themselves members of the Church of the Foodie. Welcome to Acqualagna.

WHERE TO EAT IN URBINO

**Portanova
Ristorante in Urbino**
The lofty ceilings and inventive dishes are a perfect tribute to the city's legendary cuisine. €€

Tartufi Antiche Bontà
To skip this hidden gem and its magical tubers would be an offence to Federico di Montefeltro himself. €€€

Antica Osteria da la Stella
Your new favorite spot in your new favourite city. €€€

This town of 4000 just outside of Urbino may seem at first glance like many others. But upon closer look, you'll notice that everything is covered in the scent and suggestion of the mighty truffle. The town is known globally as a centre for truffles and is one of only two locations in Italy where the prized white truffle is a protected foodstuff. Throughout the year, Acqualagna hosts truffle festivals that coincide with the various harvests. The most important of these is at the end of October when the white truffle is celebrated for three weekends like the icon it's become. Visit acqualagna.com/en/fiere-tartufo for information on all of the fairs and to map out the different ways you're planning to eat truffles over the weekend.

Outside of the festivals, however, you can still visit the town and sample the delicacies in shops and restaurants. If you want to dig even deeper, visit the **Museo del Tartufo di Acqualagna**, which has exhibits, interactive experiences and tasting courses for those looking to hone their gourmet palate.

Furlo Gorge & Marmite dei Giganti

CANOE THROUGH ANCIENT CANYONS

Once you've had your fill of truffles, head down the ancient Roman road Via Flaminia through the **Furlo Gorge**, the deep ravine from which the surrounding nature reserve takes its name and why this area is known as 'The Grand Canyon of Italy'. After that, don't miss the **Marmitte dei Giganti**, a series of cylindrical cavities that resemble cauldrons carved into the massive rock formations. Legend has it that giants used the cauldrons to cook soup – and with the culinary heritage of the area, you'd be inclined to believe it. But put away your potholders and get your swim gear on, because the best way to see this area is a canoe trip through the gorge. **Happy River** (*marmittedeigigantiincanoa.it*) runs 90-minute, budget-friendly canoe tours that will leave you breathless and work up a healthy appetite for some well-earned stuffed *crescia*.

THE UGLIEST TOWN IN THE WORLD

Since 1879, the tiny, picturesque town of **Piobbico** has been the home of the Club dei Brutti, or the Ugly Club. Founded on the belief that beauty really is in the eye of the beholder, the club's slogan is, 'Ugliness is a virtue, beauty is slavery'. The society, though founded in jest, now counts thousands of members from all over the world. Many converge on the first Sunday in September for the **Festa dei Brutti** in Piobbico, where a president is elected and new members are sworn in. All this is of course accompanied by food, drink and music, making it a true celebration.

GETTING AROUND

Although it doesn't have an airport or train station, Urbino isn't hard to reach via public transport. Look for trains to Pesaro and from there you can catch a bus to the city, which is usually about an hour's drive. Buses normally run once every half-hour throughout the day but on Sundays that could be reduced and during peak season it might increase. Tobacco shops and bars in the train station have updated timetables and ticket windows. The centre of Urbino is a ZTL (*zona a trafica limitata* or limited traffic zone) so most cars are prohibited from entering. The city has a handy map of available car parks with times and prices (*urbinoservizi.it/gestione-parcheggi*).

ANCONA

Ancona

Rome

Some ports have all the luck. They become destinations unto themselves, eclipsing their main function as points of passage or transit to adopt a carnival-like atmosphere. Ancona is not that kind of port. Its prowess as a commercial hub for the Italian economy has come at the expense of its reputation for tourism, consigning it to the back pages of most travellers' agendas, if it winds up there at all. But every port city has a story and Ancona has more to say than you might think. There are curves here, just as there are anywhere that land meets the sea, lurking in passages overshadowed by the refineries that dot the coastline. If you give it a chance, Ancona will surprise you. And if you venture just a bit further, you'll find some of Italy's best-kept secrets, hiding in plain sight.

TOP TIP

Along with many of the most precious beaches in Italy, the famed Spiaggia delle Due Sorelle has limited the number of people who can access the beach during the high season. Book a spot through the spiaggia.it app or risk a fine into the hundreds of euros!

THE BEST WHITE IN THE WORLD

The title of world's best white wine went to the 2019 **Verdicchio dei Castelli di Jesi Classico Superiore** from Villa Bucci, a family-run farm in Ostra Vetere. The winery is run by the enigmatic Ampelio Bucci, known in wine circles as 'the Professor'. The wine is incredibly difficult to find, and the winery is currently not open to the public for tastings or visits. For now, avid fans will have to be content reading excerpts from the Professor's book, *Infinite Infancy*.

Sunrise in Ancona

A WALK TO REMEMBER

The best time to really understand a port city is at first light, when the only sound you can hear is wayward seagulls calling out to each other. Though it benefits from a long and level coastline, Ancona is a gently sloping city that undulates like a lapping wave. It may seem flat in contrast to the dramatic slopes of the interior, which, coupled with the intense industrial development of the port, tend to dwarf the regional capital. Indeed, it is a city whose contrasts tend to form its character: even its weather is a relatively rare combination of Mediterranean and Continental, known as the 'Adriatic effect'. Snow is not uncommon in winter, winds can lash throughout the year, and an eerie fog may descend upon the city at the most inconvenient moments. But at sunrise, when the seagulls glide over the bobbing masts at **Marina Dorica** and their plaintive cries ring out across the gulf, you cannot help but be beckoned to explore.

As they have since Greek settlers first arrived in the 6th century BCE, most of Ancona's 100,000 inhabitants live in the crook between nearby Monte Conero, Monte Astagno and Monte Guasco, the 'elbow' from which the city takes its name. Having gone through countless iterations over the ensuing millennia, Ancona's ancient history mixes in with its modern industry, perhaps nowhere more than at the massive port. The **Arco di Traiano** dates to 115 CE and stands as a tribute to the Emperor Trajan

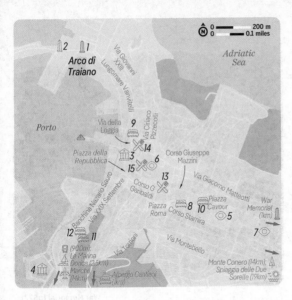

HIGHLIGHTS
1 Arco di Traiano

SIGHTS
2 Arco Clementino
3 Loggia dei Mercanti
4 Mole Vanvitelliana
5 Piazza Camillo Benso di Cavour
6 Piazza del Plebiscito
7 Viale della Vittoria

SLEEPING
8 B&B Arts And Music
9 Grand Hotel Palace
10 Metropolitan Suites
11 NH Ancona
12 SeePort Hotel

EATING
13 Bontà delle Marche
14 La Degosteria
15 Trattoria La Moretta

who first built the city. More than a millennia later, the **Arco Clementino** and pentagonal **Mole Vanvitelliana** were commissioned by Pope Clement to symbolise the importance of Ancona as a gateway to the Adriatic. These monuments may now look out of place on the busy harbour, but finding them in the tangle of steel is almost like picking out a familiar face in a long-forgotten family photo.

The centre of Ancona is refreshingly genteel, with winding streets and plenty of shops, bars and restaurants that rival any classic Italian cityscape. It unfolds from the ornate **Loggia dei Mercanti** and proceeds towards the **Piazza del Plebiscito**, whose angular design is unlike any other in Italy. Past the requisite **Piazza Cavour**, the leafy **Viale della Vittoria** connects the old and new parts of town through its wide promenade, which finishes at the **War Memorial**, one of Ancona's iconic sights. If you've timed it just right you'll end up in **Passetto**, an enclave that feels like another world with an idyllic beach surrounded by 'caves' that were dug into the cliffs as fishermen's shacks and have since become a colourful collection of intrepid dwellings. The sun

BOMBETTI IN PORCHETTA

Ancona's original street food has nothing to do with the slow-cooked suckling pig that you normally think of when you hear 'porchetta', and it is absolutely unrelated to the Tuscan doughnut known as 'bombolone'. Instead, 'bombetti in porchetta' is a native sea snail found off the coast of the city, which is prepared 'in porchetta', using the same flavour profile as the pork dish. The dish is so well known in Ancona that there is a festival dedicated to it every June, where it is naturally served with Le Marche's most famous white wine, Verdicchio dei Castelli di Jesi.

 WHERE TO SLEEP IN ANCONA

Grand Hotel Palace
After a massive refit, this hotel combines classic opulence with necessary mod cons. €€

SeePort Hotel
Living up to its name, the SeePort has great rooms and a better bar, all with killer views. €€€

Arts & Music B&B
Central, intimate, full of character, and deserves every award it's received. €€

UNDERGROUND CITIES: OSIMO & CAMERANO

The ancient town of Osimo is a short distance from the capital, and like much of the area, remnants of Greek and Roman settlements are visible everywhere. However, Osimo's real treasure lies underground. There you'll find a series of tunnels that run for hundreds of metres beneath the city and are adorned with countless symbols and designs that have been left over hundreds of years. Make a slight detour on the return to visit Camerano, another town with an extensive tunnel complex. They were once thought to have been built as cellars but actually date from the Romans and were used as a refuge from Moorish invasions during the Middle Ages.

War Memorial (p527)

will have made its way high into the sky by that point, the working day will have begun, and you'll have a full day of exploring ahead of you.

Riviera del Conero

PARADISE ON THE ADRIATIC

Picture it: you arrive in Italy in the middle of summer and witness the throngs of tourists heading to fight for umbrella space on one of the iconic postage stamp–sized beaches along the Amalfi Coast and Portofino. Or, you spy the infinite traffic jams snaking south towards Puglia as holidaymakers desperately try to find a bit of sand to call their own. And you are utterly unbothered because you know that you're headed to Conero.

Make no mistake that in the high season you'll find plenty of sun-worshippers in this **nature reserve** located just south of Ancona. But the 20km of sandy beaches always seem to have

 WHERE TO SLEEP IN ANCONA

Albergo Cantiani
Freshly renovated, centrally located and, most importantly, pet-friendly. €€

NH Ancona
Within walking distance of all the major sites and offers every mod con imaginable. €€

Metropolitan Suites
A high-tech, high-style refuge with a sense of humour in the middle of the city. €€€

room for everyone, and the 16 municipalities that make up the area have an eye towards sustainability in every sense of the word. They are well aware of what's at stake in opening the park to tourism, and the Riviera del Conero e Colli dell'Infinito Association has been protecting this area for almost 50 years. The result is some of the most unspoiled coastlines in Italy, a wide range of activities, and an enormous variety of protected wildlife species that you can both observe and taste.

As the closest town to Ancona proper, and thanks to a bus connection that takes but a few minutes, **Portonovo** sees the biggest influx of tourists in the high season. Of course, they're not coming merely for convenience: this uninhabited promontory is riddled with gorgeous swimming holes that will blow you away. While Portonovo Bay has many beach clubs and services, the more rugged 'wild' beaches are accessible only via a hearty walk through the **Monte Conero** park. There are few services and visitors are expected to leave the sand and take their rubbish: fines are issued regularly and locals are fiercely protective of the area. Once you've been there, however, you'll understand why.

Just a bit further down the coast sits **Sirolo**, the village known as 'the pearl of the Adriatic', with good reason. This utterly charming medieval town refers to the sea without being dependent on it: come in the shoulder season and you'll find it just as beautiful. The tiny, manicured streets are filled with quaint restaurants, shops and accommodation, and theatres throughout the town overflow with music and live performances. That said, Sirolo is home to some of the most stunning beaches on the coast, which have retained the coveted Blue Flag status since 1994. **Spiaggia delle Due Sorelle**, named for the rock formations that resemble two nuns, is considered one of the most beautiful beaches in Italy. It is only accessible by sea, making it that much more romantic.

Leave the car and take your trainers because a short walk from Sirolo brings you to **Numana** on the southern end of the Riviera del Conero and one of the largest towns on the coast. Not only does Numana boast a beautiful coastline and a medieval town that will charm the flip-flops off you, but it is also the home of a protected turtle species that the town works hard to care for throughout the year. They're very happy to get visitors involved as well. During the summer months the town, along with the Riccione Turtle Association, organises

CASTELFIDARDO, HOME OF THE ACCORDION

If you're a fan of the dulcet tones of an accordion, you cannot miss a trip to the small town of Castelfidardo, just south of Ancona. And once there, you must visit the Accordion Museum, **Museo della Fisarmonica**. If you don't happen to be a fan of accordions, you will nonetheless marvel at the intricate craftsmanship of the instruments on display. Should you be in the area at the end of September, the **International Accordion Festival** redefines the esoteric and will have you humming for weeks afterwards. For information on the festival visit pifcastelfidardo.it and for the museum opening times and tickets visit museo dellafisarmonica.it/en.

WHERE TO EAT IN ANCONA

La Degosteria
Brilliant chefs offering a fresh take on the city's traditional dishes and ingredients. €€

Trattoria La Moretta
Try the classics in the dining room that's been serving for more than a century. €€

Bontà delle Marche
Stellar products served at the table and available to take home from the deli counter. €€

BEST OF CONERO BEACHES

Spiaggia delle Due Sorelle
One of the best-known beaches on the Riviera del Conero, but there are plenty more to choose from.

Mezzavalle
Only accessible by foot, but it is worth the hike.

Il Trave
Must be seen to be believed.

Spiaggia San Michele
It's not heaven, it's in Sirolo.

Spiaggia dei Frati
Get your snorkelling fix in Numana.

a series of release dates called **Tartaday**, during which you can learn about the loggerhead turtle on a boat to Due Sorelle beach where the turtles are released into the sea. For tickets and information, visit traghettatoridelconero.it/en/tartaday.

Verdicchio Tasting in Castelli di Jesi

GOLD IN A GLASS

There are over 500 unique grape varieties in Italy, many of them so dependent on the microclimate of their place of origin that you may never find them outside of that area. Luckily, you're on holiday in Ancona, which means you're a Fiat 500 away from the Castelli di Jesi, home of the world's best white wine.

If you've never heard of Verdicchio di Jesi before, don't feel too bad. Even amongst Italians, the varietal is less well-known than a great many others from around the country. Verdicchio has been cultivated in the towns around Jesi for thousands of years, and owing to its particular mix of sea and mountain terroir, the result is a white wine that reflects every mystery and discovery you've had in Le Marche. The more time you spend here, the more you'll need another glass of the crisp white wine that tastes like every good thing you've ever had in equal measure.

You'll have ample opportunities to sample Verdicchio di Jesi wherever you are in Le Marche, but it will be especially appropriate as you tuck into one of the classic dishes of the region like *stoccafisso*, a fish stew, or the lasagne-like *vincisgrassi*. But if you're feeling particularly studious and want to get as much research in before you head home to humblebrag, book a few nights at **Filodivino**. This wine resort and spa in the Castelli di Jesi is the closest you'll get to immersive education; it's a tough job but someone's got to do it.

 GETTING AROUND

Ancona International Airport is about 19km from the city centre and is served by bus, train and rental car companies. From Rome it takes about three hours to reach Ancona whether by car or train. From Milan, the 400km trip takes about four to five hours.

The city itself is best explored by foot, as it's relatively compact and easy to navigate.

However, the bus service is easy, accessible and covers the greater Ancona region ,so it is worth getting to know. You can find Conerobus information throughout the city or through apps like Moovit, which give you real-time information on routes and departures in multiple languages.

Ancona

Grotte di
Frasassi

Macerata

Archaeological Park
of Urbs Salvia

Beyond Ancona

You don't have to go far from the shore to find
some of the greatest treasures in Le Marche.

The more time you spend in Le Marche, the more you
realise that it is simply overflowing with natural beauty, historical significance and cultural appeal. Often, the three
collide in magnificent fashion. So while the coastline is full
of idyllic beaches and wonderful towns, venturing into the
interior from Ancona is an opportunity to explore the glorious national parks that are the jewel of central Italy. Sloping
across the upper Apennine Mountains along the spine of Italy, the centre of Le Marche is a nature-lover's dream come
true, with plenty left over for amateur archaeologists and
seasoned explorers alike.

TOP TIP

Whenever you're
travelling be sure to
have warm clothes when
you go cave-diving in
Frasassi, which stays
at a constant, cool
temperature year-round.

Sferisterio di Macerata (p532)

PROFIMEDIA.CZ A.S./ALAMY STOCK PHOTO ©

Opera & Archaeology in Macerata & Urbs Salvia

IMMERSE YOURSELF IN HISTORY

Though it is up for some debate, the name of the classically provincial town of Macerata derives from the various occasions of its sacking and rebuilding throughout the Roman era, which thankfully settled down by the 12th century. Since then, Macerata has stayed firmly in one place, which has allowed it to host one of the oldest still-functioning universities in Europe. But visitors will be particularly struck by the massive **Sferisterio di Macerata**, an enormous open-air stadium that anchors the historic centre. Originally built as a centre for handball (which must have been pretty popular in the mid-19th century), this grand structure has become the seat of the **Macerata Opera Festival**, one of the most famous celebrations of opera in the world. Now a century old, the month-long summer festival has an incredible history all its own.

If you've come to explore ancient Roman history, your curiosity will be more than satisfied by the **Archaeological Park of Urbs Salvia**, located just a short distance from Macerata in Urbisaglia. Spread out over more than 40 hectares, the park is one of the best-preserved sites in Italy, with the visible remains of a reservoir that connected to the lower settlement and supplied it with water, ornately decorated tombs and temples, and an extraordinary system of tunnels that run throughout. The town of Urbisaglia also houses an **archaeological museum** that displays artefacts from the site.

PIT STOP IN TREIA

If all of this history has whetted your appetite, head to picture-perfect Treia for a *calcione*, a tasty, ravioliesque snack for which the town is well-known. It's somewhere between savoury and sweet, but it's undoubtedly delicious. Pick up a few, along with some other freshly baked goodies, from **Le Delizie del Forno** on Corso Italia.

The Frasassi Caves

GET DEEP INTO LE MARCHE

There are places in the world that must have been absolutely wild to stumble upon and the **Grotte di Frasassi** is a perfect example. This karst complex is one of the largest public cave systems in the world and it's a jaw-dropping experience. Open to the public since 1974, Frasassi is available to visit through guided tours only, where you have the option to take an easy route along well-trodden paths, or a more challenging trek into some of the nooks and crannies. Within the complex, some of the chambers include: **Grotta delle Nottole**, named for the resident bats hanging around (they won't

 WHERE TO STAY BEYOND ANCONA

Il Gallo Senone
A lush resort outside of Senigallia with family-run warmth and five-star services.
€€€

Terme di Frasassi Active Hotel
A stone's throw from the Genga caves, this thermal spa and retreat is a true refuge. €€

Coroncina Country Relais
A Vegan Eco Retreat with sumptuous spas and rolling hills just outside of Macerata.
€€

Tempio del Valadier

bother you); 13km **Grotta Grande del Vento**, or 'Great Cave of the Wind'; **Abisso Ancona**, which stands at nearly 200m tall; and **Sala delle Candeline**, named for the many stalagmites that resemble candles.

The temperature is a constant 14°C, so it's a perfect place to visit any time of the year. Plus, small and medium-sized dogs are welcome to join you on the tour (they must be carried), and there are unsupervised pens where larger dogs can be safely moored while you explore.

GENGA & THE TEMPLE OF VALADIER

The hamlet of **Genga** overlooks the Grotte di Frasassi. Houses are carved out of limestone and fairy-tale bridges span the clear waters that issue from underground. The 11th-century **Abbazia di San Vittore delle Chiuse** dominates the skyline above Genga and leads to the town's most famous landmark, the **Tempio del Valadier**. Built in 1828, the temple's perfectly symmetrical neoclassical design could not be more different from the context in which it's been placed, but its striking juxtaposition has made it a haven for sinners seeking absolution. It's also a theatrical backdrop for one of the best-known living nativity performances, which takes place over the Christmas holidays.

GETTING AROUND

Though a car is the most direct way to travel around the region, greater Ancona is served well by buses, particularly along the coast. From the city centre you'll find frequent services to many of the Riviera del Conero beaches, and within those smaller towns, free shuttles operate throughout the day.

If you do opt for a rental car, keep in mind that many towns and cities will not allow you to drive in the historic centre. Look for parking just outside the centre to avoid hefty fines that can and will follow you home.

ASCOLI PICENO

● Ascoli Piceno

Rome ✪

Some cities vibrate or hum. A few may sparkle, or shine. But rarely does a city glow. Then again, Ascoli Piceno is rare, indeed.

There are said to be several sources for the glow. Firstly, Ascoli's centre is mostly formed out of travertine, the same luminous stone that captured the echoes of gladiators in the Colosseum and formed the pools of the Trevi Fountain. The second might be linked to Caffè Meletti, whose selection of liquors has drawn the likes of Hemingway and Sartre into its incandescent embrace. After all, everything glows once you've had enough *anisette*. Another possibility may lie in nearby Monte Sibillini National Park – the phosphorescence of its lakes and caves is said to emanate from the underworld itself.

Ascoli Piceno predates the Romans and outlasted them; it has weathered the great tremors of the land around it, bowed but never unbroken. Truth be told, the city is radiant because it is lit from within, illuminated by its own resilience.

TOP TIP

Consider doing a night-time hike up Monte Vettore with an experienced guide in the area. Just watch out for any necromancers.

THE STONE THAT BUILT ITALY

Though it may look like marble, and these days can cost as much, travertine is a type of limestone that's been Italy's principal building material for millennia. This was partly a matter of convenience: travertine forms around mineral springs and in central Italy, where thermal waters flow almost as much as wine, the stone is abundant. Travertine is also pliable and durable, making it ideal to build houses that last and sculptures that amaze. Ascoli Piceno is illuminated by the lustre of its travertine. And when you see how it's held up the walls of the Colosseum and the contours of the Trevi Fountain, you'll have a new appreciation for this ancient stone.

A Tale of Two Squares

THE LIVING ROOM OF ITALY

Your first introduction to Ascoli Piceno will almost inevitably be the vast, monumental **Piazza Arringo**. The oldest square in the city, it's dominated by the **Cattedrale di Sant'Emidio** and the **Palazzo Vescovile**, which houses the still-under-restoration Diocesan Museum. The Palazzo Comunale, or Palazzo dell'Arengo, takes up that mantle with the **Pinacoteca**, a stunningly beautiful civic museum. Just opposite, the **Museo Archeologico** finds its home in Palazzo Panichi and contains some of the pre-Roman artefacts that show just how long the region has been the source, or perhaps the product, of alchemy.

Piazza del Popolo is commonly referred to as the *salotto*, or living room, of Ascoli, a sign of the affection that the *ascolani* have for the most remarkable feature of their remarkable city. It's an apt title: the square is the hearth around which the rest of Ascoli gathers, the hub for its many spokes. Piazza del Popolo is a reference point and the natural beginning of the classic *passeggiata*, an afternoon or evening walk that is known locally as *fare le vasche* or doing laps, as every stroll through this mercifully flat centre will always bring you back around for another pass.

But Ascoli's soft-hued Piazza del Popolo is never taken for granted by those who live here. Like everything else in the city, there is an air of mystery that borders on the magical,

HIGHLIGHTS
1 Caffè Meletti
2 Palazzo dei
Capitani del Popolo
3 Piazza del Popolo
4 Pinacoteca

SIGHTS
5 Cattedrale
di Sant'Emidio
6 Museo Archeologico
7 Palazzo Vescoville
8 Piazza Arringo

SLEEPING
9 Migliore Olive
Ascolane B&B
10 Palazzo dei Mercanti
11 Residenza
dei Capitani

EATING
12 La Nicchia
13 Siamo Fritti

and the movement of people in and out of its centre is fluid and constant. Couples glide arm in arm across the geometric pavement with movements so deft that they seem to float, while teenagers idle under arcades in their own time-honoured rituals. They are keeping up a tradition that spans millennia, after all.

Back up above, the geometrical slabs of the piazza, which were laid after a restoration in the 1960s, reflect a spectrum of soft colour from the buildings that line it. There are other places to explore in Ascoli, but none are quite like the Piazza del Popolo, the living room where we will all inevitably find each other once again, lapping up the amber rays of a setting sun.

One of the most unmistakable points on the piazza is the **Palazzo dei Capitani**, first constructed in the 13th century and subsequently added to over the next 300 years. It is now an archaeological treasure trove in the very heart of the city, and the seat of the Municipal Department of Culture. The archaeological area is open to the public during working hours, but check with visitascoli.it/en for the most up-to-date information.

 WHERE TO EAT OLIVE ASCOLANE IN ASCOLI

Migliori Olive
This tiny outpost has been living up to its name (which means 'best') for generations. €

Siamo Fritti
This place is more than olives, but they honour the great green fruit like no other. €€

Eccellenze Ascolane
Takes their product very seriously, and the world is a better place for it. €

BIBIANA CASTAGNA/SHUTTERSTOCK ©

View of Piazza del Popolo from Caffè Meletti

OLIVE ASCOLANE & CREMINI

The cuisine of Le Marche is full of delicious dishes, but none have become so well-known and loved as *olive ascolane*, named for the city of Ascoli Piceno. Beginning with particularly supple green olives that have been grown in the area since antiquity, *olive ascolane* are stuffed with a mixture of pork, beef, vegetables and *parmigiano*, breaded, and finally deep-fried.

Olive ascolane are often served as part of a *fritto misto all'ascolana*, which includes a fried pastry cream known as *cremini fritti all'ascolani*. How best to justify tucking into fried sage leaves, lamb chops, artichokes and the obligatory courgette? By having an after-dinner *anisetta* and doing a few laps around Piazza del Popolo, of course.

If you're in the mood to stay a while (you will be), **Palazzo dei Mercanti** is steps from the Piazza del Popolo and is one of the most stunning historical residences in Italy. Now a luxury hotel, it is more than worth the splurge to soak in every bit of that unmistakable glow.

Historic Caffè Meletti

TOAST WITH THE GHOSTS

One of the iconic features of the already iconic Piazza del Popolo didn't actually begin life that way. The candy-coloured building was originally the Customs Office, then the Post Office, before finally being purchased at auction by Silvio Meletti in 1905. After an extensive, art deco–influenced renovation, **Caffè Meletti** opened its doors in May 1907. Save for a few emergencies and a restoration project that took the better part of the 1990s, the cafe has stayed open. Its status was cemented in 1981 when the Italian Ministry of Culture listed Caffè Meletti as one of 11 Italian cafes of historical and artistic interest.

 WHERE TO SLEEP IN ASCOLI PICENO

Palazzo dei Mercanti
The luxe rooms in this historic residence may be a splurge, but one you definitely won't regret. €€€

Residenza dei Capitani
You won't find a more comfortable (or affordable) hotel that lets you admire Piazza del Popolo from your bed. €€

Migliore Olive Ascolane B&B
Eat the best olives in town and head upstairs to the comfiest bed in Piazza Arringo. One-stop shopping at its finest. €€

What is it that makes this cafe so special? The ambiance is so alive that it seems to exist wholly outside of the machinations of its patrons. It lives in the porticoes and frescoes, the marble tables inside, and the pink travertine facade outside, in the light that glints off of Murano chandeliers and dances onto the art deco mirrors behind the bar. Of course, the cafe's signature *anisetta meletti* may well be what truly sets the place apart. The bracing, verdant liquor is served with a roasted coffee bean that is famous enough to warrant its very own nickname (*la mosca*, or 'the fly') and has become an obligatory element of any meal in Ascoli. One cannot finish dinner until one has had an *anisetta meletti*, whether here or anywhere else in the city.

It is these things, to be sure. But what makes Caffè Meletti exceptional is the same thing that makes the city in which it lives so unique. Sitting at one of its tables doesn't feel like stepping back in time; it feels like stepping into another dimension entirely, where the ghosts of poets, writers and philosophers challenge each other to finish the last bottle of *anisette* with the noise of glasses clinking in the background. Carlo Alberto Salustri, the writer better known as Trilussa, once wrote: 'So many stories and sonnets of mine were inspired by *anisetta meletti*', and it isn't hard to see why. For there are a thousand cafes in Paris, and a million poets have tried desperately to leave their mark. But here in Ascoli, on these walls, the ghosts of Hemingway, de Beauvoir, Sartre, Guttuso and others flicker and dance off the light. You can still hear them laughing, still imagine them searching for the perfect word. And then you can see their faces as they find it, floating in front of them, like a perfectly roasted coffee bean resting on the surface of an anise-flavoured sea.

Grande Anello dei Sibillini

THE MAGIC MOUNTAIN RANGE

Few places in Italy are as blatantly mythical as Monte Sibillini, which is saying quite a lot for a country that believes in wolf kings and Epiphany witches. Once a favourite spot for necromancers, this mountain range is part of the Apennine system and has been a protected national park since 1993. Make it to **Monte Vettore**, the highest point in the park at 2476m for sweeping views of Le Marche, Umbria and Abruzzo on a clear day. If you're looking for a particularly rewarding challenge, the well-travelled Grande Anello dei Sibillini (Great

THE LAND OF DEMONS & FAIRIES

During the Middle Ages, the Sibillini mountains were known as a realm of demons, necromancers and fairies. Let that keep you company as you seek out the **Grotta della Sibillia**, which, legend has it, is the access point to the underground kingdom of Queen Sibil, a powerful sorceress. If you're not creeped out yet, visit the **Lago di Pilato**, where it is said that the dead body of the Roman procurator who famously condemned Christ to death was dragged by a herd of angry buffalo into the red waters of the 'devilish' lake near Monte Vettore. Because of seismic activity in the area, unaccompanied hikes are not advised – see the park's official website for a list of qualified guides.

MEDIEVAL MARCHE

Just like **Urbino** (p521), Ascoli celebrates its medieval spirit with the raucous Quintana every August. Make it a double bill and get your jousting fix for the year!

 FARM-STAYS IN MONTE SIBILLINI

B&B Il Rifugio di Marsi
This one-of-a-kind country retreat in Roccafluvione has retrofitted huge wine barrels into sleeping cabins. €€€

La Cascina di Opaco
Sparkling rooms, stunning views and hearty breakfasts in Norcia. What more do you need? €€

Terra di Magie
A magical atmosphere, tasty vegetarian food and otherworldly swimming pool in Amandola. €€

WHY I LOVE ASCOLI PICENO

Virginia DiGaetano,
writer

There are a few places in the world that feel as though they have been put here specifically for writers, and Ascoli Piceno is one of them. Whether it's the luminosity of the city itself, the love it's historically shown for creative expression, or the preponderance of finger foods, Ascoli inspires me. Walking into **Caffè Meletti** and looking out onto the same square that held the gaze of Simone de Beauvoir, strolling through the mystical arch of **Ponte Cecco**, or just listening to my own feet tap on the travertine pavement is an elixir that I could write about forever.

Ring) is a nine-stage, 120km walking route that covers the entire mountain chain. It is truly one of Italy's most spectacular outdoor experiences.

The trail is fully signposted, meaning that you get to concentrate on the stunning diversity of the landscape and the incredible wildlife, particularly if you're a birdwatcher. But some of the most unique features of the ring are the renovated mountain refuges for walkers, many of which have stood since the Middle Ages and where you can sleep during a multi-day itinerary. Not all of the stops have working facilities, but the park's official website *(sibillini.net/en)* has up-to-date information (in English) on the status of the structures and contact information to book with them.

If you're not feeling quite so intrepid, there are plenty of guided walks to take for all levels, as well as those adapted for children and animals. The park's official site also has a list of certified guides, the languages they speak, and the tours they offer. Several night-time hikes are also available, offering an extraordinary experience of the park and its surroundings.

GETTING AROUND

Getting to Ascoli from other parts of Italy requires a little creativity if you're travelling by public transport. Buses run from major cities and most will require a change in either Ancona or San Benedetta del Tronto. The train is a bit more scenic and takes quite a bit longer from nearly every point in the country but if you're looking to embrace slow travel, this is it. If you're arriving with your own car, parking lots are available outside of the city and can be booked through Saba *(sabait.it/en)*. Driving is the most direct means to reach the city and environs, following a mix of state highways and smaller provincial roads that will take you through some of the most stunning landscapes in Italy.

ORVIETO

Proudly fixed on a dramatic, almost vertical cliff, Orvieto has been an important destination since the Etruscan era. Even being annexed by Rome hardly fazed its citizens, who simply took to the underground networks that had been built centuries before. The impossibly grand Duomo in the centre of the city has withstood comparisons to other cathedrals in more heavily trafficked towns for almost a thousand years and if it's bothered anyone, it's impossible to tell.

Perhaps Orvieto is too distracted by the abundant thermal baths that spring up all over the territory, within easy reach of the city. It may also be the equally charming hill towns that rival and often beat anywhere else in central Italy. But it's most likely the knowledge that anywhere you go in town, you're guaranteed to find a chilled glass of Orvieto Classico white wine waiting for you, best served with a generous helping of Umbria Jazz.

TOP TIP

If you drive to the city, park your car at one of the underground facilities indicated on the approach. On your way into the centre, you'll get a free glimpse of the underground tunnels and caves for which Orvieto is famous.

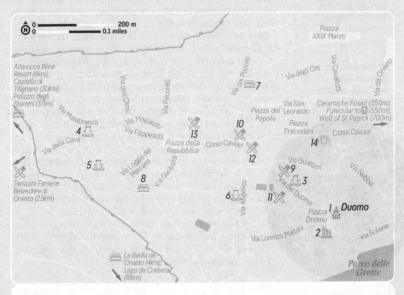

Orvieto, Over & Underground

ETRUSCAN TUNNELS & GOTHIC SKYSCRAPERS

BEST BARS FOR ORVIETO CLASSICO

Al Mercato
A shabby-chic refuge on the Via del Duomo with the perfect terrace for people-watching.

L'Oste del Re
A traditional setting and generous pours of the local grape.

Oleoteca Bartolomei
A great selection of Orvieto Classico, paired with their family olive oil and local snacks.

Trattoria dell'Orso
A hidden gem for a bottle or three with homemade pasta.

Terrazza Farnese Belvedere
The view onto Orvieto pairs perfectly with their generous selection.

DUELLING DUOMOS

Though the Duomo of Orvieto often draws comparisons with that of Florence, it's more closely related to the **Duomo of Siena** (p457) – visit them both to see for yourself.

Officially known as the Cattedrale di Santa Maria Assunta in Cielo, the **Duomo** of Orvieto is the nucleus of the ancient city centre. Once you've seen it, you'll have no problem understanding why. Depending on your approach, you may first get an inkling of its presence by the striped walls of white travertine and blue-grey basalt stone that peek out from alleyways. As you turn into the piazza and that golden Gothic facade reveals itself, you'll realise that you've been using the word 'masterpiece' way too lightly all these years. The golden frontage, a result of nearly three centuries of craftsmanship, captures the same sunlight today as the day it was first laid 700 years ago.

As you step inside, the frescoes soar overhead, mingling with a trussed timber roof created in 1320 and later fortified in the late 1800s. This blend of sturdy beams with delicate figures is enough to spark delirium and probably would do so if the rest of the interior were not left so uncluttered. The two main chapels, **Cappella del Corporale** and **Cappella di San Brizio**, anchor the structure and overflow with frescoes from the 13th and 14th centuries.

But Orvieto's treasures are more than gold. Indeed, the wealthiest families in antiquity measured their status not by what they displayed in their homes but rather by what was hidden underneath them. This is the story of **Orvieto Underground**, a vast system of over 1200 tunnels and caves that were dug over 2500 years and protected its inhabitants from the swings and roundabouts of history. A guided tour of the underground city explores some of the tunnels, galleries, stairs, quarries, cellars and pigeon roosts that were built to resist invasion. The fortifications were so effective that Pope Clement VII took refuge in Orvieto during the sacking of Rome in 1527 by the Holy Roman Emperor Charles V, and decided he should complement the design with a well to ensure a steady water supply. **Il Pozzo di San Patrizio**, or St Patrick's Well, was completed in 1537. The double-helix staircases allowed mules to carry empty and full water vessels separately in opposite directions without obstruction to and from the 53.15m depth.

A pass to visit the Duomo, Orvieto Underground, St Patrick's Well and more can be purchased on the Carta Unica website *(cartaunica.it/en)*, which also offers discounts on trains, hotels and restaurants.

 WHERE TO STAY IN ORVIETO

La Badia di Orvieto
A carefully restored Cistercian abbey in the valley, with fabulous rooms and even better views. €€€

Grand Hotel Italia Orvieto
You can't get more central, or more historic. €€

Palazzo Piccolomini
Centrally located with all the perks of a country villa for the best of both worlds. €€€

FRANCESCO BONINO/SHUTTERSTOCK ©

Cascata delle Marmore

UMBRIA JAZZ ORVIETO

Although the Umbria Jazz Festival is headquartered in Perugia, **Umbria Jazz Winter** takes place in Orvieto and is one of the best times to visit the city. Held over the holiday period between Christmas and New Year, the city is lit up by festive decorations. Concerts take place in locations around the historic centre, including Palazzo del Popolo, Palazzo dei Sette, Palazzo Soliano and the elegant **Teatro Mancinelli**. Add to this the many spontaneous performances that take place in squares and on street corners around town, and you've got the perfect recipe for a unique holiday season.

The Dancing Waterfall at Marmore

WATER, WATER (ALMOST) EVERYWHERE

The ancient Romans really did think of everything. Sometime around 271 BCE, the city of Rieti was suffering from a mysterious illness thought to be caused by a wetland in the neighbouring valley. The Roman consul at the time ordered a canal to be built that would drain the stagnant waters off the cliff at nearby Marmore. The ancient Roman engineers probably didn't realise that they were dealing with a likely malaria outbreak or that the solution they came up with would become the largest artificial waterfall in the world.

But indeed, the **Cascata delle Marmore**, or Marmore Falls, have stood just outside of the provincial capital of Terni for more than 2000 years. Over the centuries they have been tweaked and fixed to avoid flooding neighbouring towns, and they now stand as a particularly impressive engineering feat and a testament to the durability of ancient structures.

THE CENTRE WARS

Narni, the town closest to Marmore, claims to be the exact geographical centre of Italy but has been challenged by Rieti in **Lazio** (p130), which is also known as the 'navel' of the country.

 WHERE TO EAT IN ORVIETO

Trattoria dell'Orso
This cosy nook just off the Corso does traditional, local recipes just right. €€

Al Mercato
Practise people-watching on the Via del Duomo with a glass of Orvieto Classico and delectable nibbles. €€

La Pergola Orvieto
Tucked in the alleyways near the Duomo, this tiny bistro boasts creative dishes and a secret garden. €€

WHERE TO BUY CERAMICS IN ORVIETO

Rosarja
Traditional with a twist and offers classes to boot.

La Bottega del Pozzo
Sells traditional Orvieto patterns as well as having a great wine bar attached.

La Corte de Miracoli
This place is as artisanal as it gets, in the heart of Orvieto.

Ceramiche Fusari
The keepers of tradition in Orvieto, offering the city's signature patterns for more than 50 years.

Fravolini Ceramiche
They've kept it all in the family for more than 20 years, and have now added a great selection of locally made leather goods and jewellery.

Todi

Today, some of the water that flows down the 165m chute is used for hydroelectric power generation, which would be impressive enough on its own. But what makes Marmore worth visiting are the specific times throughout the day when the flow of water is increased, allowing visitors to watch the waterfall come to life and dance across the canyon. There are also guided tours that will take you through the forest around the falls. Or even better, take a tour at night when the falls are lit from underneath.

A Drive along the Lake

GET YOUR CONVERTIBLE TOP DOWN

Italy is a driver's dream, where the drive becomes an experience in itself. Those who venture around Orvieto will be rewarded with an almost perfect drive to nearby **Todi**, an idyllic hill town almost 40km to the west.

There are a few fine country roads and rolling landscapes to choose from, but take your time and enjoy the winding curves and fabulous scenery along the **Lago di Corbara**. The lake

WHERE TO STAY AROUND ORVIETO

Castello di Titignano
This truly special property outside Orvieto is well worth the short trip along Lago di Corbara. €€€

Altarocca Wine Resort
For an adults-only holiday break, look no further than this chic spot in Terni. €€€

Palazzo degli Stemmi
Just up the road in Todi, this is the ultimate immersion in fairy-tale luxury. €€€

was artificially formed in the 1960s after the River Tiber was dammed close to the town for which it is named, and it subsequently filled out the valley below the ancient Forello gorges. The lake is now part of the **Tiber River Park** and has become a well-known area for birdwatching and carp-fishing.

For the rest of us who want to roll down our windows and take a drive to remember, the road around the lake has become one of the best-kept secrets in the area. Indeed, you'll often find sports cars from far-flung counties and countries stopping at some of the small bars along the road or pulling into the tiny lanes of Todi. You could do worse than to follow their lead, particularly when it comes to visiting the lovely town in the very bosom of Umbria. And since you're in the neighbourhood, **Osteria Basico** has some of the freshest cuts of unctuous Italian beef that you'll find anywhere in central Italy. All of it is wood-fired in front of you and served piping hot. It's almost as if they knew you'd be stopping by.

THE SILENT HIKE OF UMBRIA

If you're more inclined towards walking than driving, the **Cammino dei Borghi Silenti** is a five-day excursion through some of the historic towns around the Amerini Mountains in southern Umbria. The trek is structured to encourage reflection rather than consumption, and much of the walk is spent in silence. The 90km trail is mostly on dirt roads, forest paths and limited asphalt, so a certain degree of preparedness is necessary, but the organisation has partnered with B&Bs and restaurants in the area to make sure that no matter how hard you walk, the landing is always a soft one. If you are looking for a true holiday, this may well be it.

WALKS TO REMEMBER

If you're planning to walk the **Via Francigena** (p463) through Italy, the Cammino dei Borghi Silenti would be excellent practice!

GETTING AROUND

Orvieto is very well connected to many other cities in central Italy, making it a great stopping point whether you're travelling by train, bus or car. Its position on the main A1 highway means it takes just over an hour to get here from Rome and a little under two hours from Florence. Parking is available in car parks under the city

and lifts into the historic centre pass through some of the Etruscan ruins for which Orvieto is so well-known.

Trains also run frequently to Orvieto Scalo, a more commercial area at the foot of the city. From the station, you can take the five-minute funicular railway ride up to the top.

NAPLES & CAMPANIA

BUCKET LIST ITALY

From the birthplace of pizza to the birthplace of Hades, this region is as comforting as a *nonna*, and as explosive as a volcano.

Welcome to Naples and Campania, an area with beauty so irresistible it's been the setting for Homeric myths and has attracted invaders from all over Europe. There's barely a rock or street corner that isn't smudged with the fingerprints of those who came before, from the ancient Greeks to the Camorra. Yet the region is known primarily for its contemporary virtues: its mozzarella-smothered dishes, its active volcanoes, its bougainvillea-draped coastal Italian dreamscapes.

To truly understand this (literally) explosive region, start 3000 years ago in Greece and head through ancient Rome, making stops along the way in Normandy, Spain and the Bourbon dynasty. Then look to its farthest reaches. Salerno, at its southernmost edge, is home to the first medical school in the Western world and the birthplace of the Mediterranean diet; Campi Flegrei, at its northern limit, is the site of one of the world's most dangerous supervolcanoes (not Vesuvius).

Before the Amalfi Coast was considered the height of all Italian glamour, it was a string of humble fishing villages, their scenery and culture catapulted to celebrity status by the writers and poets who stumbled through. The three islands dotting the Gulf of Naples charm with whitewashed city centres and thrilling natural escapes that swing from rugged hikes to phosphorescent caves. And then there's Naples itself, where you'll find lasagne-like layers of ancient architecture and the best pizza in the world. Grab a fork.

ARCADY/SHUTTERSTOCK ©

THE MAIN AREAS

Procida (p566)

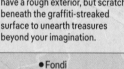

Naples, Pompeii & Around, p550

Naples and its outskirts may have a rough exterior, but scratch beneath the graffiti-streaked surface to unearth treasures beyond your imagination.

MOLISE

Campobass

Isernia

Bojano

Cassino

Fondi

LAZIO

Lago del Matese

Terracina

Formia

Minturno

Sessa
Aurunca

Teano

Gaeta

Volturno

Caiazzo

*Gulf of Gaeta
(Golfo di Gaeta)*

Mondragone

Grazzanise

Capua

Santa Maria
Capua Vetere

Montesárchio

Castèl
Volturno

Villa
Literno

Caserta

Maddaloni

*Mor
Vergi*

Villaggio
Coppola

Aversa

Arienzo

Avella

Qualiano

Acerra

Avella

Nola

CAR

Due to intense traffic and a tragic parking situation, unless you're in a crowd, driving through the Amalfi Coast, Capri, Salerno and Naples is discouraged, although a car will be useful for navigating Campi Flegrei, the Cilento and the various villages of the Sorrento Peninsula.

Cuma

Baia

Naples

Somma
Vesuviana

Pozzuoli

Portici

Sarr

Torregaveta

Bagnoli

Mt
Vesuvius

Casamicciola

Procida

Bacoli

Ercolano

Forio

Procida

Torre del Greco

Pompeii

Ischia

Torre Annunziata

Nocera

Ischia

Castellammare di Stabia

Ca

Vico Equense

Ravell

PUBLIC TRANSPORT

Ferries run regularly between Naples, Positano, Amalfi, Sorrento, Salerno and the smaller cities on the eastern Amalfi Coast, with services declining sharply in low season. Naples' public transport is excellent, and there is an extensive network of buses on the Amalfi Coast and the islands.

*Bay of Naples
(Golfo di Napoli)*

Sorrento

Positano

Ama

Anacapri

Sant'Agata sui
Due Golfi

Capri

Capri
Town

The Islands, p566

There's nothing deserted about these islands. Procida was Italy's 2022 Capital of Culture, while Capri offers jet-set glamour and Ischia's waters (may) have healing powers.

*Gulf of Salerno
(Golfo di Salerno)*

The Amalfi Coast, p577

This 50km stretch of dramatic cliffs and rugged coastline, punctuated by fishing villages and lemon groves, is everyone's favourite version of Italy.

WALKING

Walking will be a delight in Naples' neighbourhoods and in Sorrento, Salerno and the small towns of the Amalfi Coast. But unless you're hiking, opt for wheels in widely dispersed areas like the islands, Campi Flegrei and between Amalfi Coast cities.

*Tyrrhenian
Sea*

Find Your Way

No doubt about it: Naples is massive and its surrounding areas are widely dispersed. We'll show you how to make sense of this sprawling yet wildly diverse terrain to get the most out of your trip, from Greek ruins to secluded beach escapes.

Lago di Occhito

San Bartolomeo in Galdo

Cerignola

PUGLIA

Ariano Irpino

Benevento

Melfi

CAMPANIA

Monticchio   Venosa   Spinazzola

Avellino

Montella

Bagnoli

Monte Cervialto

Acerno

Salerno

Montecorvino

Salerno & Cilento, p587

Salerno is home to immaculately preserved Greek ruins, while Cilento's citizens have a life expectancy that's on average 10 years longer than in the rest of Italy.

Eboli

Battipaglia

Postiglione

Monte Alburno

ContrORONE   Polla

Capaccio Scalo

Capaccio   Roccadaspide

Paestum   Roscigno Vecchia   Teggiano   Sala Consilina

BASILICATA

Corleto Perticara

Agropoli   Sassano   Padula   Viggiano

Santa Maria di Castellabate   Castellabate

Parco Nazionale del Cilento, Valle di Diano e Alburni   Monte Cervati

Marina di Casal Velino   Vallo della Lucania   Sanza

Acciaroli

Ascea

Pisciotta

Palinuro   Sapri   Lagonegro

Golfo di Policastro

Marina di Camerota   Porto di Maratea

CALABRIA

0   40 km
N
0   20 miles

Plan Your Time

These sweet sojourns let you experience the best of Naples, the islands, the Amalfi Coast and Salerno in tiny, medium-sized and big bites.

Castello Aragonese, Ischia (p569)

Five Days on the Coast

● Spend your first two days on the lush volcanic island of **Ischia** (p568). Discover a medieval castle and underwater Roman ruins and spa break at Ischia's famous thermal parks. Explore its hamlets for hiking and spectacular beaches. On day three, ferry into glamorous **Capri** (p569) and tour the historic villas, labyrinthine historic centre and celebrity-magnet *piazzetta*.

● On the fourth day, wander **Sorrento's** (p582) historic centre and visit a lemon orchard to sip flights of 100% organic *limoncello*. Enjoy fresh seafood at the port. On your fifth day, ferry to romantic **Positano** (p578) to climb endless flights of steps and shop for artisanal beach wear. Enjoy the magical views.

Seasonal highlights

This deeply Catholic region of Italy is awash in religious feast days and *sagre* (food festivals) celebrating the harvest. Chilly and rainy in the off-season, blisteringly hot and crowded in late summer.

FEBRUARY

Wet and rainy, but it's **Carnevale** and the **feast day of Sant'Antonio**; sweets and celebrations abound.

MARCH

Settimana Santa (Holy Week) kicks off a series of celebrations. The weather is notoriously temperamental; an umbrella is a must.

MAY

The sun is shining; the first **beach clubs** are open and prices haven't yet skyrocketed. The sweet spot.

If You Have a Week

● Kick things off with two days in **Naples** (p550), exploring its cultural treasures, lively side streets and seaside promenades. Enjoy pizza in its birthplace.

● Dedicate day three to **Pompeii** (p560). Linger over magnificent mosaics and frescoes; climb the volcano that destroyed it all. Then unwind with a drink in **Capri's** (p569) famous *piazzetta* before overspending at superb boutiques on day four.

● Next, climb romantic **Positano's** (p578) endless steps for magical coastline views. Spend day six learning about seaside **Amalfi's** (p577) paper-making traditions and how its famous lemons are cultivated. Waltz through **Ravello's** (p580) spectacular 800-year-old villas on your last day.

The 10-Day Grand Tour

● Spend two days wandering **Naples** (p550), then another exploring history's most tragic ruins at **Pompeii** (p560). On days four and five, hike in volcanic **Ischia** (p568) and cure what ails you at its famous thermal spas.

● Get lost in **Capri's** (p569) beautiful boutiques and whitewashed streets on your sixth day, before arriving in magical **Positano** (p578) to see the Italian coastal panorama of your dreams on day seven.

● On day eight, ramble **Ravello's** (p580) 800-year-old villas with lush gardens and dazzling views of the coast. Devote your last two days to exploring cliff-side **Salerno** (p587) and the mountains of the **Parco Nazionale del Cilento, Vallo di Diano e Alburni** (p593).

JULY
Summertime is in full swing, with notable music festivals in **Naples, Sorrento** and **Ravello**.

AUGUST
Late summer is the hottest, most crowded time of year throughout the coastal region. Many places of worship and attractions are closed.

SEPTEMBER
The beginning of **grape harvest season**; a wonderful time to visit vineyards. In Naples, it's the feast day of **San Gennaro**.

DECEMBER
The **Christmas season** starts; see beautiful light displays in Salerno and the magical atmosphere of Via San Gregorio Armeno in Naples.

NAPLES

Italians sometimes joke that there's Italy and then there's Naples – so singular is its character, so potent its historical legacy. And yet so few visitors are prepared for its uniqueness and capacity to surprise.

The story of Naples begins with the Greek colony of Neapolis, founded in 474 BCE. Norman, Spanish and Bourbon rulers made Naples wealthy, leaving behind architectural splendours like the imposing Castel Sant'Elmo and the Palazzo Reale. Naples' reputation began its slow decline after the 1861 unification of Italy, a fate eventually sealed by the rise of the Camorra. Indeed, passing through some graffiti-streaked neighbourhoods in Naples today can be a sombre experience. But every few paces reveals another eye-popping monument. Funky street murals and modern art installations in the metro remind the world of the city's artistic excellence.

Take it all in; Naples is exactly what you expect while being not what you expect at all.

TOP TIP

Travel past the *centro storico* to the far edge of Naples and beyond; Posillipo, Mergellina's beaches and the Campi Flegrei are chronically overlooked by visitors. Wherever you roam, no proper Neapolitan experience begins without an espresso.

THE LEGACY OF SAN GENNARO

In 305, Gennaro, the bishop of Benevento, was beheaded for his faith. Then something strange happened: his blood, collected in two ampoules, began to liquefy at odd times. Gennaro was buried in the catacombs in Capodimonte, but his skull and blood were brought to Naples' Duomo centuries later. In gratitude for his protection during the 1631 eruption of Vesuvius, Neapolitans put up a spire to him in the *centro storico*.

San Gennaro's blood is said to liquefy three times a year: on his feast day (19 September), and again in December and May. Thousands flock to the Duomo to see it. If the blood doesn't liquefy, it's considered a bad omen for the city.

Centro Storico Treasures

PRICELESS ECCLESIASTICAL ART

The **Duomo** of Naples, an opulent 13th-century cathedral, houses more than 30 pieces of stunning ecclesiastical art. Walk through the sumptuous nave towards the altar by Francesco Solimena; to the left are the **Basilica di Santa Restituta** and the **Battistero di San Giovanni in Fonte**, with 4th-century mosaics.

You'll also find the **Cappella di San Gennaro**, dedicated to Naples' most beloved patron saint. There you'll find (more) frescoes by Luca Giordano and the 14th-century silver bust of San Gennaro, containing his skull and two vials of his blood, which are said to liquefy three times a year – a deeply important event for Neapolitans. You can see precious jewels and ceremonial objects in the Museo del Tesoro di San Gennaro next door.

Cappella Sansevero – a chapel on Via Francesco de Sanctis with foundations in the 17th century – is home to numerous examples of baroque art, such as the vivid *Gloria del Paradiso* ceiling fresco by Francesco Maria Russo. But the most famous artwork in the chapel is undoubtedly Giuseppe Sanmartino's 1753 reality-defying marble sculpture the *Cristo velato*, depicting a freshly slain and 'veiled' Christ. The incredible realism of what appears to be a whis-

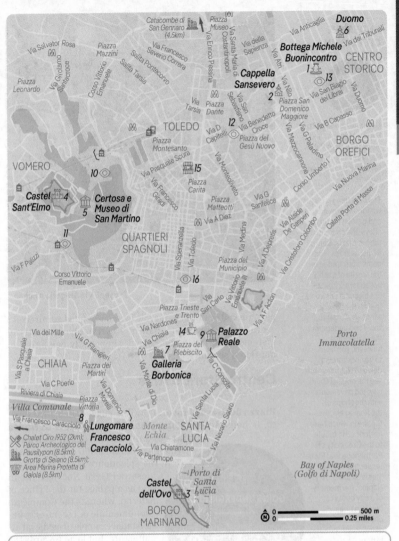

HIGHLIGHTS

1 Bottega Michele Buonincontro
2 Cappella Sansevero
3 Castel dell'Ovo
4 Castel Sant'Elmo
5 Certosa e Museo di San Martino

6 Duomo
7 Galleria Borbonica
8 Lungomare Francesco Caracciolo
9 Palazzo Reale

SIGHTS

(see 4) Museo del Novocento

10 Pedamentina di San Martino
11 Petraio Stairs
12 Piazza del Gesù Nuovo
13 Via San Gregorio Armeno

DRINKING

14 Caffè Gambrinus

SHOPPING

15 Via Pignasecca
16 Via Toledo

UNDER THE CITY'S SKIN

Gianmarco Pagotto, Export Manager and Host of Le Petit Palais Naples, tells us his favourite *centro storico* experience.

The best thing is just wandering around and getting lost in the alleys, the churches or the historic buildings, to discover the hidden gems, surrounded by the smells of freshly baked *taralli* (pretzel-like biscuits) or sweets that fill the bakery windows. To get to know and understand the real Naples, however, you need to go underground, down to Neapolis and see the original Greek city; the pavements with the shops of the Roman era, the theatre in which Nero performed in tribute to the Greek city of Parthenope that Rome respected so much. This is 'Underground Naples', the memory of a city built in layers, a treasure chest, a testimony of millenary history.

Presepi, Via Gregoria Armeno

per-thin veil sculpted in marble has confounded admirers for centuries. There's also a pair of preserved human arterial systems underneath the chapel, supposedly belonging to murdered servants.

Centro Storico Arts

CENTURIES OF ARTISANAL EXCELLENCE

Piazza del Gesù Nuovo, at the very edge of the *centro stori-co*, is home to the **Complesso Monumentale di Santa Chiara** and the **Chiesa del Gesù Nuovo**.

You'll have to turn 360 degrees to take in the splendours of the mammoth Chiesa del Gesù Nuovo, built in 1470 as a palace for the Prince of Salerno, whereas the Complesso Monumentale is a seemingly understated example of medieval architecture. But head towards the

GOING UNDERGROUND

Learn more about San Gennaro's cult at the Catacombs in Naples' **Rione Sanità** (p558).

WHERE TO EAT IN THE CENTRO STORICO

La Campagnola
Cosy yet classy space off Piazzetta Nilo serving huge portions of Neapolitan favourites. €€

Tandem
Serving pasta with *ragú* or *genovese* meat sauces, as well as the famous *ragú*-stuffed cuzzetiello *sandwich.* €

Da Michele
Eat at this much-loved historic pizza joint and pray the line isn't too long (but it will be). €

LAZYLLAMA/SHUTTERSTOCK

back of the complex to find the monastery, commissioned by Robert of Anjou, with its Angevin portico and stunning cloisters decorated with 17th-century frescoes and bright 18th-century majolica-tile columns. A small museum features the remains of a 1st-century spa. Anchoring the piazza is the **Guglia dell'Immacolata**, one of Naples' three baroque marble spires.

Exquisitely detailed and lovingly crafted, *presepi* (nativity scenes) are treasured throughout Campania, and especially in Naples. With origins in the 13th century, *presepi* are traditionally displayed at Christmastime and depict elements of once-typical southern Italian life, from fishmongers to shepherds to trees bulging with lemons. Stroll the cobblestones of **Via Gregorio Armeno** to see nativity craftsmen toiling on *presepi* all year long. You'll sometimes see mass-produced nativity sets, though you can still find artisans like **Bottega Michele Buonincontro**, who carries on his family's traditional *presepe*-making techniques. It's a pleasant stroll any time of year, but the atmosphere becomes downright magical during the Christmas season.

Two Hundred Years of Spanish Rule

NAPLES' SPANISH PHASE

Running north from the magnificent Piazza del Plebiscito, **Via Toledo** is Naples' historical Spanish neighbourhood's main artery. Look left to see the gritty Quartieri Spagnoli – originally built to house Spanish troops. Look right for popular chain shops, boutiques and art museums. The **Palazzo Reale** (Royal Palace), built in the 16th century, was home to the Spanish royal family. Today the massive complex houses the **Romantic Gardens** and **MeMus** art museum, as well as the **National Library of Naples** with its hidden gem, the 19th-century **Biblioteca Lucchesi Palli**. Book a tour of the palace's **Historic Apartment** and prepare to be awed by the opulent marble *scalone d'onore* staircase, the gilt and marble **Royal Chapel**, and the **Teatrino di Corte** – the private theatre commissioned by Ferdinando Fuga in 1768. Or visit the impossibly opulent **Teatro San Carlo**, the oldest continuously operating opera house in Europe. Originally built in 1737, the current building is an exact replica of the original, which burned to the ground in 1816. Don't miss the lavish **Caffè Gambrinus**, built in 1860. This belle-époque

WHERE TO SEE METRO ART IN NAPLES

Stazione
Commuters silk-screened onto a mirror (Garibaldi Station).

Dante e Beatrice
Colourful images of the Renaissance-era lovers, painted on two staircases (Università Station).

Spulcinellando, Sguazzando, Scugnizzando
Intricate mosaic depicting Neapolitan street children frolicking in the sea with Pulcinella and mythical monsters (Materdei Station).

Universo Senza Bombe, Regno dei Fiori, 7 Angeli Rossi
A vibrant blue background splattered with colourful geometric shapes (Dante Station).

Crater de Luz/Olas/Relative Light
A voyage under the sea amid mosaics, waves and light (Toledo Station).

 WHERE TO DRINK IN THE CENTRO STORICO

Intra Moenia
A sprawling historic literary cafe on Piazza Bellini serving cocktails, wine and *aperitivi* (pre-dinner drinks).

Shanti Art Musik Bar
Artsy tiki bar off Piazzetta Nilo; cocktails, small bites and comfy couches.

Libreria Berisio
Browse the stacks as you sip your wine at this vintage bookshop/wine bar near Port'Alba.

cafe with its lavish frescoes and tapestries is known for the *caffè sospeso* – a tradition where you buy a coffee for the next espresso hound to come along. Just a few coins to brighten someone's day.

Naples' Tastiest Quick Bites

STREET-FOOD MARKET

Heading north on Via Toledo, you'll come to a fork in the road leading towards **Via Pignasecca**, the oldest street market in Naples. With origins in the 1500s, **La Pignasecca** runs from Piazza Carità to the Montesanto funicular station. It's a hive of whole-food vendors, from fruit to bread to organ meats dangling from hooks behind glass, but La Pignasecca's biggest draw is undoubtedly its multitude of street-food joints.

Arrive early in the morning to get the freshest ingredients and catch the best buzz. Choose from fried snacks such as *frittatine di pasta* (pasta-and-béchamel croquettes) or a *montanara* (fried dough topped with tomato sauce, basil and cheese). Time your visit right and snag a fish-market *cuopp'* – an oil-spotted paper cone stuffed with fried calamari, octopus, shrimp and sardines. You'll need two hands to hold a *cuzzetiello* – a baguette sandwich stuffed with *ragù*. You may like calzones...but have you tried them deep-fried and stuffed with ricotta, black pepper and pork cracklings? If not, get thee a *pizza fritta*, pronto. Or try *pizza al portafoglio* (wallet style): mini pizzas you can fold up and eat on the go. And for something on the lighter side, consider *taralli n'zogna e pepe* – crunchy, ring-shaped biscuits flavoured with pepper and almonds. Whoops – and lard. Don't resist! Everything fried and porky is good.

Imposing Structures

A NORMAN CASTLE & A LABYRINTHINE BOMB SHELTER

Castel dell'Ovo, the oldest of Naples' seven castles, has been used as a monastery, a fortress, a prison and a royal residence. The imposing 12th-century Norman structure gets its name (Castle of the Egg) from the antics of the Roman poet Virgil who, according to legend, buried an egg where the castle stands today. Virgil claimed that when the egg broke, the castle would fall. So far, so good: the castle is still

BEST STREET FOOD IN TOLEDO & QUARTIERI SPAGNOLI

Passione di Sofi €
A modern take on street food, offering fried snacks like *pizza fritta* or fanciful *frittatine di pasta* made with gnocchi.

Pescheria Azzurra €
Brave the market crowd for a *cuopp'* heaped with sardines and calamari, or a plate of *spaghetti alle vongole* (spaghetti with clams).

Antica Pizzeria e Trattoria al 22 €
Classic neighbourhood pizzeria serving excellent *pizza al portafoglio*.

Friggitoria Fiorenzano €
There's nothing fancy about this stand, 'cept for its tasty fried calorie bombs. Another *montanara*, please!

WHERE TO EAT IN TOLEDO & QUARTIERI SPAGNOLI

Trattoria da Nennella
As famous for its wild waiters as it is for its down-home Neapolitan dishes. Prepare to queue. €

Ristorante Pizzeria Al Cucciolo Bohemien dal 1963
Classic Italian fare with homemade *primi piatti* (pasta) and *fritti* (fried appetisers). €€

Osteria della Mattonella
Old-school Neapolitan favourites served in an intimate space decorated with 18th-century majolica tiles. €€

TOMASZ WOZNIAK/SHUTTERSTOCK ©

Castel dell'Ovo

standing, and you can visit its elegant halls and climb up to its terrace for 360-degree views of the Gulf of Naples and the Santa Lucia and Mergellina promenades.

The historical layers of Naples are unending, but for an underground dive into the more recent past, visit the **Galleria Borbonica**, a repurposed Bourbon tunnel running beneath Monte Echia commissioned by Ferdinand II in 1853 to link the Palazzo Reale with the barracks. The tunnel was dug into the 17th-century Bolla Aqueduct system, and was more recently occupied by an estimated 5000 to 10,000 Neapolitans escaping the horrors of WWII bombing. A guided tour takes you through the tunnels that formed the refugee colony, past the ghostly playgrounds, the cramped latrines and the infirmary where residents were sprayed with DDT in a bid to combat sickness. The Galleria Borbonica also hosts theatrical events and concerts.

BY THE SEA

For more beautiful fishing villages and idyllic seaside strolls, hit the **Amalfi Coast** (p577).

 WHERE TO STAY IN TOLEDO & QUARTIERI SPAGNOLI

Hotel il Convento
Gorgeous, beautifully renovated boutique hotel in what was a 16th-century convent. €€

Real Toledo
Chic yet cosy rooms in this boutique B&B, featuring balconies and flatscreen TVs. €€

Art Resort Galleria Umberto
Lavishly decorated hotel located in Galleria Umberto I. Marble bathrooms, modern art on the walls. €€

MARCOBRIVIO PHOTO/SHUTTERSTOCK ©

Certosa e Museo di San Martino

FUNICULÌ FUNICULÀ

You've almost certainly heard the beloved Neapolitan song 'Funiculì Funiculà' – if not, YouTube it; great, huh? – but did you know what the title means? While considered 'Italian music' abroad, this song is 100% Neapolitan. Written in 1880 by the journalist Giuseppe Turco and set to music by Luigi Denza, it celebrated the inauguration of the funicular line connecting Herculaneum and Naples. The titular lyrics *'funiculi funiculà'* refer to the funicular (*funicolare* in Italian), while the lyrics to the instantly recognisable, internationally beloved chorus, *'jamm' jamm''*, mean 'let's go, let's go', in Neapolitan dialect. And now you know!

The Heights of Vomero

THE HIGH LIFE

Situated 250m above sea level on San Martino Hill, the 14th-century **Castel Sant'Elmo** is one of the city's most famous and imposing landmarks. The massive star-shaped structure is the largest of Naples' seven castles, most famous today for its amazing 360-degree views of Naples and its gulf. Originally a church dedicated to St Erasmus, it is also linked to the nearby **Museo del Novecento**, a museum housing exhibits of 20th-century Neapolitan art. The funicular and metro will get you close, but prepare for a leisurely stroll: the castle and museum are only accessible on foot.

Originally a Carthusian monastery built between 1325 and 1368, the nearby **Certosa e Museo di San Martino** is now home to priceless frescoes and paintings by Neapolitan baroque masters such as Jusepe di Ribera and Cosimo Fanzago. Lose yourself strolling through the sumptuous sacristy and and grand cloisters, then wander outside to the hanging gardens and viewpoint, overlooking the *centro storico* of Naples and the gulf. The *certosa* (charterhouse) is only

 WHERE TO EAT IN SANTA LUCIA & CHIAIA

Muu Muuzzarella Lounge
Everything's about fresh Campanian *mozzarella di bufala* at this contemporary restaurant. €

L'Ebbrezza di Noè
'The Drunkenness of Noah' wine shop turns into a trendy restaurant at night. €€

Antica Trattoria da Ettore
Well-loved cosy trattoria with an Italian celebrity following that serves classic Neapolitan comfort food. €€

accessible on foot. As you leave, stop at the historic family-run cameo boutiques; they've been selling their beautiful shell, mother-of-pearl and agate wares for over a century. Consider heading back via the Pedamentina stairs, tucked behind the stone wall directly facing the shops, and leading down to the Quartieri Spagnoli.

Secret Vomero Views

ONE-OF-A-KIND PANORAMAS

The funicular may be the speediest way to reach the San Martino Hill, but it's nowhere near the most beautiful. Vomero is also connected to terra ferma by two not-so-secret ancient stone staircases: the **Pedamentina di San Martino**, leading up from Corso Via Emanuele and ending at the Certosa e Museo di San Martino, and the **Petraio pathway**, starting in Chiaia and ending at the Morghen funicular station. The staircases may be steep – clocking in, respectively, at 414 and 530 steps – but the views and tranquil respite are sensational. Pass by typical local homes and under leafy overhangs, while looking down at the bustling city, worlds away.

Hugging the Gulf of Naples, the **Lungomare Francesco Caracciolo** is a 2.5km stretch of rocky coastline as distracting as it is delightful. Stroll past chalets – small bars pocking the waterfront – selling assorted snacks and granitas. Linger at a kiosks selling shells and crafts, and watch the boats bobbing in the water. Don't fight it; you're about to have the quintessential Naples experience: buying hot *taralli* from a chalet and munching it as you walk. Or if you're feeling sweet rather than savoury, stop at Chalet Ciro 1952; its sweets are fried to order, so plush and soft they melt in your mouth.

Off-the-Beaten Track Wonders

DON'T MISS THESE GEMS

Head up to Posillipo Hill to find the **Parco Archeologico del Pausilypon**, the remains of a luxurious Roman seaside villa. The villa belonged to Publius Vedius Pollo, a man so important he had his own amphitheatre, and so nasty he bred his own eels.

The villa is accessed through the imposing **Grotta di Seiano**, a Roman-era tunnel more than 770m long connecting the Bagnoli plain with the peaceful Gaiola Valley. The park also offers activities for children, including hands-on archaeology workshops. In keeping with its roots, the villa's

BEST RESTAURANTS IN VOMERO

Osteria
Donna Teresa €
Boisterous and family-run, this tiny *osteria* (tavern) serves high-quality old-school dishes, such as *pasta e patate*.

Gorizia 1916 €€
Trendy gourmet pizzeria. Try the delicious *fritti*, too – especially the *mozzarella in carrozza*.

Godot
Restaurant €€€
Carefully prepared Italian *crudo* (raw fish) and seafood dishes with a modern edge served in a small, hip space.

Trattoria Vanvitelli €€
Get the light yet tasty pizza at this uber-popular vintage-style pizzeria-restaurant. There's wholegrain crust, too.

 WHERE TO STAY IN VOMERO

Le Petit Palais Naples
B&B in a renovated 16th-century space on the Pedamentina staircase. Beautiful rooftop; amazing views. €€€

Vanvitelli Domus
Minimalist yet colourful interiors in this comfortable B&B with private bathrooms and flatscreen TVs. €

La Chambre
Comfortable, well-appointed B&B with breezy blue-and-white interiors. King rooms have balconies. €€

BEST PLACES TO EAT IN RIONE SANITÀ

Concettina ai Tre Santi €€€
Pricey but delicious and wildly inventive 'new Neapolitan' pizzas. Good list of cocktails.

Pasticceria Poppella €
Try a *fiocco di neve*, a sweet brioche bun filled with ricotta and cream, from this famous 100-year-old pastry shop.

La Campagnola €€
Rustic Neapolitan food, done perfectly. The fritti are excellent and so is the *pasta e patate*.

amphitheatre hosts summertime sunset events called Pausilypon: Suggestioni all'Imbrunire. The ruins are in association with the nearby **Area Marina Protetta di Gaiola** marine park, where you can enjoy snorkelling and glass-bottomed boat tours.

In Rione Sanità, the **Catacombe di San Gennaro** is one of the largest networks of catacombs in southern Italy and home to some of its oldest paleo-Christian frescoes. Admire its impressive vaults and the first grave of San Gennaro before his bones were transferred to the Duomo. The frescoes show an artistic shift from ancient Roman mythology to paleo-Christian symbolism. The catacombs are linked to the Basilica di San Gennaro *fuori le mura* (outside the walls) which, though almost entirely rebuilt after WWII, holds enormous significance for Neapolitans, who consider it a conduit between past, present and future.

GETTING AROUND

Get around using Naples' excellent public-transport network, including buses, funicular lines, and a metro system with spectacular modern art installations. Get a *biglietto giornaliero* (day pass) to all of Naples' public transit options for € 5.10. Despite its overall size, Naples' many *quartieri* (neighbourhoods) are small, making it a richly walkable city. Use a little more caution in crowded places and at night. Unless you're in a large group, driving in Naples is discouraged due to insane traffic and scarcity of parking.

Beyond Naples

Come for the Greco-Roman ruins, baroque palace and active volcano; stay to dive underwater ruins and sip ancient wines.

Caserta

Cuma · Naples
Parco · Herculaneum
Sommerso · Pompeii
di Baia

Few natural disasters in history capture the imagination like the eruption of Mt Vesuvius on 24 August 79 CE. The event signalled its arrival with a pine-tree-shaped plume of smoke; over the following 24 hours, lethal pyroclastic currents destroyed grand Pompeii and mudslides smothered the nearby seaside holiday village of Herculaneum. Excavations in the 18th century revealed magnificent homes, palaces, baths, temples and businesses decorated with breathtaking frescoes and mosaics.

Further inland, you'll find the lavish Reggia di Caserta palace, built by the legendary Neapolitan baroque architect Luigi Vanvitelli. And west of Naples lie the Campi Flegrei (Phlegraean Fields), home to the first Greek settlement on the Italian mainland and one of the world's most dangerous supervolcanoes.

TOP TIP

Campi Flegrei's €15 Circuito Flegreo multi-ticket includes admission to Parco Archeologico di Baia, Castello di Baia, Parco Archeologico di Cuma and Anfiteatro Flaviano.

Pompeii (p560)

ENRICO DELLA PIETRA/SHUTTERSTOCK ©

Casa di Nettuno e Anfrite, Herculaneum

TOP TIPS

- Explore the far side of Pompeii. It's less crowded.
- It's easy to get overwhelmed, so use The MyPompeii app or join an official tour.
- Yellowsudmarine Food Art & Tours offers guided and shared tours of Pompeii.
- Budget half a day for Pompeii (two to three hours for Herculaneum) to see things properly and avoid rushing through.
- Not all structures and exhibits are open every day; check the website.
- Wear sturdy shoes: sandals and high-heeled wedges are no match for rocky volcano paths and cobblestone streets.
- The free Pompeii ARTE shuttle can take you from Pompeii to the park's other archaeological sites, including Oplontis and Stabiae.

The Splendour of Pompeii

THE ERUPTION HEARD ROUND THE WORLD

A tragic thing happened on the way to the **Foro** (Forum), but we can still visit. Here you'll find the **Tempio di Giove**, a temple dedicated to Jupiter, Minerva and Juno; it was thoughtfully designed to line up with Mt Vesuvius. You'll also find the **Tempio di Apollo**, the *macellum* (produce market) and the *granai* (ex-granary), now housing more than 9000 recovered household items.

You can't miss the **Anfiteatro** (Amphitheatre), a hulking beast with 20,000-seat capacity; it's one of the oldest known Roman theatres. Frescoes of gladiatorial battles are visible on the parapet and the inscriptions of magistrates' names can be found on the upper level.

During the excavations, Italian archaeologist Giuseppe Fiorelli engineered the technique of pouring plaster into the voids the victims' bodies had left in the earth in order to get a perfect cast of the victims at the moment of their death. The **Orto dei Fuggiaschi** has Pompeii's largest collection of casts. Here you'll find 13 prone figures locked in various positions of defence or distress as they sought refuge.

WHERE TO EAT IN THE CAMPI FLEGREI

Angelina
Celebrity chef Marianna Vitale helms this 'modern *tavola calda* (cafeteria)' in Pozzuoli, serving high-quality street-food faves. €

Caracol
Small, Michelin-starred seafood restaurant in Bacoli serving fusion 'revisited' Italian fare on a sea-facing terrace. €€€

Coevo
Tiny Bacoli restaurant in a beautiful location overlooking the gulf, with creative Italian seafood dishes. €€€

The 2nd-century-BCE **Terme Stabiane** (Stabian Baths) had *tepidariums* (tepid baths), *frigidariums* (cold baths) and *caldariums* (hot baths), as well as a massive courtyard, a lavish marble colonnade and a large pool. A beautiful vault in the men's changing room has an ornate stuccoed ceiling depicting *putti* (winged babies) and saucy nymphs.

Wood Preserved in Volcanic Mud

HERCULANEUM'S GHOSTLY LEGACY

The volcanic mudslide that buried **Herculaneum** basically mummified organic matter such as cloth, metal and wood. The **Casa del Tramezzo di Legno** (House of the Wooden Partition) yields the spectacular, if slightly charred, treasures of a large, folding wooden 'privacy' screen and the remains of a wooden bedframe. The partition featured profiled panels and supports for hanging oil lamps, and separated one of the atriums from the common room, where the owner most likely dealt with clients. Also preserved are the marble covering of the impluvium tub, the wall paintings and a geometric mosaic near the entrance.

The vaulted rooms that open onto Herculaneum's beach, **L'Antica Spiaggia**, were most likely used as port warehouses and storage. During the eruption they became a refuge for those attempting to escape the blast. In 1980 approximately 300 human skeletons were found there, along with necklaces and coins. Two years later, archaeologists made an incredible discovery: there, beneath layers of volcanic mud, was the keel of a wooden boat, very likely used by the victims in a futile attempt to flee. The boat is over 9m long and is reminiscent of a modern-day *gozzo* (dinghy). You can see this ancient marvel of naval engineering in the pavilion adjacent to the ruins, as well as other artefacts recovered from the area.

Glorious Mt Vesuvius

STILL-ACTIVE VOLCANO

Bad news: in 79 CE, a volcano called Vesuvius erupted. More bad news: Vesuvius is still active and experts say it will strike again.

The twin-peaked mountain has been erupting for thousands of years. In 79 CE the local villages were still recovering from a terrible earthquake just 17 years before. Pliny the Younger wrote that residents largely ignored the warning tremors 'because they are frequent in Campania'. He

UNMISSABLE FRESCOES & MOSAICS IN POMPEII & HERCULANEUM

Casa del Fauno (Pompeii)
Tiled entrance reading *'have'* ('welcome' in Oscan dialect); mosaics of wildlife and battles.

Casa della Venere in Conchiglia (Pompeii)
Venus on a half-shell; fresco power.

Casa del Frutteto (Pompeii)
Fresco of an orchard with Egyptian motifs against a dramatic dark-green background.

Casa dello Scheletro (Herculaneum)
Spectacular *lararium* (shrine) inlaid with tiny mosaic tiles.

Casa di Nettuno e Anfrite (Herculaneum)
Intricate and strikingly vivid mosaic depicting Neptune and Aphrodite.

Colegio degli Augustali (Herculaneum)
Frescoes of Hercules fighting everyone.

Villa dei Misteri (Pompeii)
Massive Dionysiac frieze depicting Dionysus and Ariadne welcoming a young girl into his cult via ritual flagellation.

 WHERE TO EAT IN POMPEII & HERCULANEUM

Melius (Pompeii)
Gourmet deli/restaurant offering dishes made with local ingredients like Gragnano pasta or anchovies from Cetara. €€

Zi'Caterina (Pompeii)
Spacious old-school restaurant that looks touristy but serves delicious traditional southern Italian food. €€

La Bettola del Gusto (Pompeii)
Innovative Italian food like seared octopus couscous, made with artisanal ingredients. €€

witnessed the eruption from across the Gulf of Naples, comparing the volcano's initial puff of smoke to a pine tree. That 'pine tree' eventually claimed thousands of lives.

Then life went on: feast, famine, wars. Vesuvius erupted again in 1944, but almost three million people currently live within a 32km radius of it. Many locals refuse to live in fear. They challenge it, taking selfies with it, scaling it, sometimes even ignoring it entirely.

Vesuvius National Park, covering 85 sq km, was established in 1995. Each year millions hike to the gaping crater, thrilling at its 450m diameter.

Ignore touts who will try to mislead you into buying overpriced tour services. Hike – or ride horseback! – up that rough terrain with its black streaks of lava. (Or take the Vesuvius Active shuttle direct from Herculaneum train station in 40 minutes.) Spend three to four hours rambling across the site, relish the life-changing views of the Gulf of Naples, and at the end of it all celebrate with a beer at the park's crater-top cafe.

But if you ever see smoke rising from the crater, run.

Beyond the Ruins

THE AREA'S INSIDER EXPERIENCES

Oplontis, buried underneath modern-day **Torre Annunziata**, was an idyllic suburb of Pompeii. Currently, only one of its structures, **Villa Poppaea**, receives visitors. Villa Poppaea features splendid frescoes and elegantly decorated gardens, as well as private thermal baths.

Just 11km south are the ruins of **Stabiae**. Situated on the panoramic Varano Hill overlooking today's Castellammare di Stabia, it was home to many luxurious residential villas. Two are currently open to visitors: the 11,000-sq-metre Villa San Marco, and Villa Arianna, named for its fresco of Ariadne abandoned by Theseus at Naxos. You can easily reach these two sites from Naples, but getting from one to the other is tricky without wheels.

You could just head back to Naples after ruin-hopping, but then you'd miss out on the area's lovely non-archaeological experiences. **Cantina del Vesuvio**, a long-running vineyard on the slopes of Mt Vesuvius, is just a short drive from Pompeii and Herculaneum. The popular vineyard is especially known for its Lacryma Christi (tears of Christ), an ancient wine only grown in the vicinity of the volcano and said to be very similar to the wine of the ancient Romans. The vineyard offers cooking classes as well as tastings.

NEIGHBOURHOOD BEATS

Pompeii and Herculaneum are ancient, but it's astonishingly simple to imagine what life must have been like 2000 years ago. Their ample streets are instantly recognisable as neighbourhoods; you'll find wine shops with prices scribbled out the front, and bakeries equipped with kilns and grist mills. There were handsomely decorated *palestrum* (gyms), and Pompeii's famous *lupanare* (brothel) is notorious for its blushingly graphic frescoes.

As it was customary to go out for lunch, *thermopoliums* (snack bars where drinks and hot food were served) have been found in both cities, including the one in Pompeii's Regio V, its counter featuring a painting of a Nereid on horseback. The Large Thermopolium in Herculaneum even has cynical graffiti in the back room. Ancient Romans – they were just like us.

 WHERE TO EAT IN POMPEII & HERCULANEUM

Ro.Vi Pizzeria (Herculaneum)
Serving classic and innovative pizza made with curated local ingredients. Modern interiors; epic *pizza fritta*. €€

Pappamonte (Herculaneum)
Traditional Neapolitan dishes with innovative twists in a chic yet inviting setting. Veg-friendly; outdoor seating. €€–€€€

Ristorante President (Pompeii)
Elegant Michelin-starred restaurant with creative, beautiful dishes. €€€€

PI03/SHUTTERSTOCK ©

Reggia di Caserta

MODERN HERCULANEUM & POMPEII

As odd as it might be to think of Pompeii and Herculaneum in a modern light, give it a shot. **Via Sacra**, modern Pompeii's idyllic main thoroughfare, is lined with cafes, restaurants and shops, and the main piazza is home to a beautiful 19th-century basilica. Before heading to the ruins of Herculaneum, make a quick pit stop at the morning **Mercato di Resina** vintage street market. And just 300m from the Herculaneum ruins, the **Museo Archeologico Virtuale** (MAV) museum offers more than 70 multimedia exhibits depicting recreations of the various structures in the cities and a film about the fateful day of the eruption.

You can also visit **Castellammare di Stabia** for lunch at one of its seaside chalets, then take the cable car up to **Mt Faito** for incredible views.

A Baroque Masterpiece

LAYERS OF ARCHITECTURAL GENIUS

By 1752 the Spanish had weighed anchor out of Naples and the Bourbon dynasty was in full command. It was as good a time as any for Charles II to commission a royal residence so massive, so opulent, so unabashedly baroque that it would blow the minds of anyone who gazed upon it.

Nearly 300 years later and minds are still being blown. Charles II's fantasy became **Reggia di Caserta**, an enormous 6100-sq-metre palace with four courtyards, 1200 rooms, 34 staircases, its own theatre and library, and what is still one of the most impressively landscaped gardens in Europe. The master architect was, naturally, Luigi Vanvitelli, whose opulent creations defined the Italian baroque. The chosen site was Caserta, a small town roughly 25km outside Naples – close to the city yet far enough away to be safe from pirates. With its marble interiors and acres of gardens, the ornate structure

 WHERE TO DRINK IN POMPEII & HERCULANEUM

Sofi' (Pompeii)
This chic space serving cocktails, *aperitivi* and pizza turns into a bar at night, with DJ sets.

La Vineria – Ambulatorio Alcolico (Herculaneum)
A great people-watching spot. Enjoy a tasty *aperitivo* with *salumi* (cured meats).

The Roof/Habita79 (Pompeii)
A thumping hotel rooftop bar may be the last thing you associate with Pompeii, but here we are.

Roman statue, Parco Sommerso di Baia

VANVITELLI'S GREATEST HITS

Reggia di Caserta is just a taste of Luigi Vanvitelli's architectural genius. Apart from collaborating on Naples' Palazzo Reale, Vanvitelli also designed the Lazzaretto di Ancona – a mammoth pentagonal military quarantine station – the lavish Palazzo Colonna in Rome, and Naples' Villa Comunale. One of his most interesting works in Campania is the Casina Vanvitelliana in Bacoli, a quirky peach-coloured bi-level house that seems to float in the Gulf of Naples, connected to the mainland by a wooden arched bridge. It served, naturally, as a Bourbon hunting lodge.

is often compared to the palace at Versailles. But Reggia di Caserta was also an administrative centre for the entire kingdom, and it ended up even larger. The entrance is crowned by a massive staircase with 117 steps leading up to the royal apartments, which, like the rest of the palace, are decorated with priceless art and frescoes, the furnishings showpieces of lacquered wood, gilt and crystal.

Visitors can tour the humongous palace, as well as its gardens and their bevy of statues, fountains, waterfalls and pools. Take your time.

Active Volcanoes & Greek Myth

EXPLORE THE MYSTERIOUS CAMPI FLEGREI

After settling the colony of Pithecusae (today's Ischia), the Cumaean Greeks arrived on the Italian mainland in 750 BCE. They called their new colony **Cuma**, and it became one of the most important strongholds in Magna Graecia. You can see its ruins today at the **Parco Archeologico di Cuma**. Still visible are the acropolis, and two temples: the Tempio di Giove (Temple of Jupiter) and the Tempio di

BEFORE CUMA, ISCHIA

Cuma was the first Greek settlement on the Italian mainland, but the island of **Ischia** (p568) was settled first.

WHERE TO HAVE AN APERITIVO IN THE CAMPI FLEGREI

Beach Brothers (Miseno)
Beachfront resto-bar with a great *aperitivo* and live music from local Neapolitan artists.

Il Gozzetto (Pozzuoli)
Chic and relaxed cocktail bar at Pozzuoli's docks for a relaxing *aperitivo* in front of the sea.

Royal Capo Miseno (Bacoli)
Stylish beach club with DJ sets and a large menu of cocktails, wines and beers.

Apollo (Temple of Apollo). But Cuma was more than just history; it was myth, too, the setting for many Greek legends. Apollo was believed to speak to the people through one of its caves, and the Temple of Apollo is the legendary site of Daedalus' ill-fated voyage to the sun.

In 1538 a volcanic bradyseismic disaster sunk the shores of Baia, Pozzuoli and Lucrino, swallowing their Roman ruins whole. Thus was created a magical underwater world of Roman mosaics and columns 10m below sea level, which are visible at the **Parco Sommerso di Baia** (Underwater Park of Baia). Head to the park's diving centre at Lucrino for boat tours plus diving and snorkelling excursions to see the ancient sunken columns, statues and spectacular mosaics, bathed in a watery turquoise glow and teeming with fish, rocks and reefs.

WHAT IS BRADYSEISM?

Apart from its unnatural beauty and Greco-Roman past, the Campi Flegrei are notable for their high levels of bradyseismic activity.

Bradyseism is a phenomenon where the filling or emptying of underground magma chambers causes the Earth's surface to lift or sink. The Campi Flegrei are continuously plagued by these shifts, as evidenced by their perpetually changing coastline and sea levels. The three remaining marble columns at Pozzuoli's Macellum bear mollusk boreholes 7m up the shaft, showing how the land sank below the sea, only to eventually reemerge. The disappearing-reappearing Rione Terra ancient quarter of Pozzuoli is another victim of bradyseism. Who knows? Perhaps the majestic Roman ruins currently 10m below sea level at the Parco Sommerso di Baia will come back to Earth one day as well.

GETTING AROUND

You can easily reach Pompeii and Herculaneum from Napoli Centrale with the Circumvesuviana or L1 metro. Trains and buses run regularly to Caserta. The Cumana train links Naples to the individual towns of the Campi Flegrei, but a car is ideal when travelling throughout the area.

THE ISLANDS

Rome

The Islands ●

Just a century ago, the Gulf of Naples islands were barely a blip on the tourism radar. But thanks to the filmmakers and artists who have fallen in love with their wild beauty, the former fishing isles of Capri, Ischia and now tiny Procida – named Italy's 2022 Capital of Culture – have become classic Italian island escapes.

Seaside and sun merely scratch the surface. The ancient Greeks and Romans settled here, leaving legends and villas in their wake. There are wisteria-draped *palazzi* to discover, rainbow-hued fishing villages to swoon over and extreme cliffs to hike. Ischia and Procida are located on the Phlegraean caldera, owing their dramatic topography to the constant activity beneath their seas. The Greeks marvelled over the healing powers of Ischia's volcanic waters, and so has every visitor since.

Each island has a distinct personality – rough yet arty Procida, laid-back yet adventurous Ischia, glamorous yet athletic Capri. Get to know them all.

TOP TIP

Ischia and Procida are manageable year-round, but consider visiting Capri in the off-season, as the crowds (and prices) explode in the high season. Many restaurants and hotels close on the islands in the off-season, but you'll find B&Bs year-round.

WHERE THE FISHERFOLK LIVE

One of Procida's most memorable views is the candy-coloured **Marina Corricella**, the historical fishing port and village. The port gets crowded during the day – and unbearably hot in summer due to its lack of cover – but sunset is the perfect time to take a stroll down the sloping stone street from **Piazza dei Martiri** until you reach the shore, flanked by bobbing boats and restaurants serving up fresh fish. Alternatively, come in by boat on a private tour or your own rented rig and admire the scene from afar. Local legend has it that the homes were painted in pastel hues so that the fishers could easily identify them while away at sea. True or not, they give Procida its unmistakable coastline.

From Paradise to the Abyss

PROCIDA'S HISTORIC ARCHITECTURE

Procida lacks the Greco-Roman ruins of its neighbours Ischia and Capri, but you can explore its fascinating medieval quarter, **Terra Murata** (walled city), once a refuge from Saracen raids. Come through the Terra Murata's vaulted *porta* (gate) and find the **Abbazia di San Michele Arcangelo**, a splendid 11th-century abbey devoted to San Michele (St Michael), Procida's patron saint. The abbey is richly decorated in silver and gold and hosts ecclesiastical art, but its more fascinating treasures lie in its basements; namely an 18th-century wood and terracotta *presepe* and an ossuary-necropolis.

Just outside Terra Murata is the **Palazzo d'Avalos**, an intriguing structure that began life as a 17th-century villa, home to the noble Avalos family. It was converted into a prison in the 19th century, and remained a functioning jail until the 1980s. The prison was remarkable for its history of rehabilitating prisoners by teaching them to weave linen, a traditional Procida art form. Today, the Palazzo d'Avalos allows guided tours, complete with visits to the preserved prison cells, and hosts cultural events and modern art exhibits, like 2022's surreal *Sprigionarti* art installation. Walk down from the Palazzo d'Avalos towards Piazza dei Martiri to reach **Casale Vascello**, Procida's oldest neighbourhood, with multi-hued bilevel homes and trippy 'donkeyback' staircases.

HIGHLIGHTS
1 Aenaria
2 Capri Town
3 Castello Aragonese
4 Ischia Ponte
5 Terra Murata

SIGHTS
6 Abbazia di San Michele Arcangelo
7 Spiaggia dei Pescatori
8 Torre di Guevara
9 Villa Jovis
10 Villa Lysis

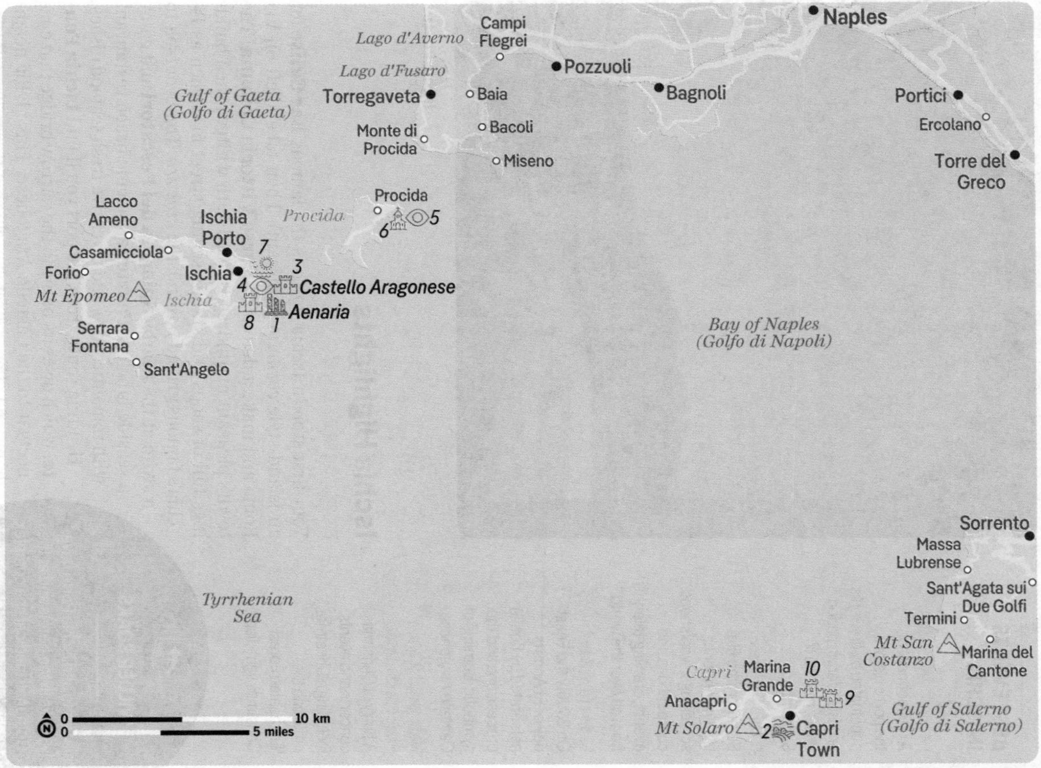

Naples

Portici
Ercolano
Torre del Greco

Bagnoli

Pozzuoli

Campi Flegrei

Baia
Bacoli
Miseno

Lago d'Averno
Lago d'Fusaro

Torregaveta
Monte di Procida

Procida

Procida

6 △ ⊙ 5

Castello Aragonese

Aenaria

Lacco Ameno
Casamicciola
Forio
Mt Epomeo △

Ischia Porto
Ischia
Ischia

Serrara
Fontana

Sant'Angelo

Gulf of Gaeta
(Golfo di Gaeta)

7
4 ⊙ 3
8 1

Bay of Naples
(Golfo di Napoli)

Sorrento

Massa Lubrense
Sant'Agata sui Due Golfi
Termini
Marina del Cantone

Mt San Costanzo △

Gulf of Salerno
(Golfo di Salerno)

Capri

Marina Grande △
10
9
2 Capri Town

Anacapri
Mt Solaro △

Tyrrhenian Sea

0 ——— 10 km
0 ——— 5 miles

N ▲

Capri (p569)

ROMAN PLESKY/SHUTTERSTOCK ©

BEST EVENTS IN ISCHIA

La Festa del Porto
A reenactment of the port's history, punctuated by fireworks and islanders in period dress; held on 17 September.

Ischia Film Festival
Summertime film festival featuring screenings, workshops, competitions and events, drawing talent from all over the world.

La Festa di Sant'Anna
On 26 July the Feast day of St Anne is celebrated by flotilla processions and the symbolic 'burning' of Castello Aragonese.

Natale ad Ischia: Il Bosco Incantato
A flurry of Christmas concerts and events, including a Christmas raffle and the 'Enchanted Forest' Christmas light display.

WILDER SOAKS

Ischia Ponte and Ischia Porto have lovely soaks in the hotels and at the Terme Comunali medical spa complex, but Ischia's best thermal spring experiences are undoubtedly found in Ischia's other hamlets, such as **Forio** (p573).

Ischia Ponte

Ischia Highlights

FIRST PORTS OF CALL

Your first stop in Ischia Porto is the famous **Bar Calise** for an island-style *cornetto* (croissant). Then take a left on Via Roma and make a detour to **Corso Vittoria Colonna**. The town's pleasant main drag is lined with whitewashed buildings full of shops and stands selling street food such as Ischia's famous grilled *panino*, the *zingara*. Treat yourself to a swim at the nearby **Spiaggia dei Pescatori** and enjoy a seaside lunch at **Pazziella** – a chic beach restaurant with romantic views and inventive fresh seafood dishes.

Heading south from the port you'll find **Ischia Ponte**, which owes its name to the narrow bridge that connects it to the Castello Aragonese. This idyllic neighbourhood offers a stretch of chic boutiques, art galleries and seafood restaurants leading down to the pier, with its sweeping views of the castle and the beautiful **Baia di Cartaromana**. High up in the cliffs above the beach

 WHERE TO STAY IN ISCHIA

Albergo Il Monastero
Castello Aragonese's adjacent guesthouse. Spartan but lovely monastic decor married with blue Mediterranean tiles. €€€

Hotel Mare Blu Terme
Sprawling hotel with breezy coastal decor. Pool, spa and views of Castello Aragonese. €€€

B&B Marcantonio
Renovated country home with outdoor terrace. Spacious sunny rooms; views of rolling hills. €€

is **Torre di Guevara**, the 14th-century home of the noble Guevara family.

End your visit to Ischia Ponte with a sunset *aperitivo* and dinner overlooking the sea at one of the pier's chic seafood restaurants. The energy at Ischia Ponte becomes lively as soon as the sun goes down and the area becomes a pedestrian zone.

The Treasures of Baia di Cartaromana

ISCHIA'S BEAUTIFUL BAY

At the end of Ischia Ponte looms **Castello Aragonese**. The imposing fort-city, built on an islet and attached to Ischia by a bridge, began its life as a Syracusan settlement in the 5th century BCE, serving as a refuge from Saracen raids. The structure was completely overhauled in the 1400s by King Alfonso of Aragon, and it has seen additions in every century since.

With the 18th-century as a starting point, you can literally see the castle's history as you stroll the grounds: the medieval gardens, the 11th-century crypt plastered with 14th-century frescoes inspired by Giotto, the 16th-century cemetery for Clarisse nuns. From the Terrace of the Immaculate Conception there are stunning views of Ischia Ponte, Spiaggia dei Pescatori beach and Monte Epomeo.

Just underneath the **Spiaggia di Cartaromana** lie the underwater ruins of the ancient Roman city of **Aenaria**. Aenaria existed on Cartaromana's shores from the 4th century BCE onward, replacing the Greek colony of Pithecusae as Ischia's main settlement, until it was swallowed up sometime between 130 and 150 BCE. Archaeology nuts can see the ruins for themselves on kid-friendly glass-bottomed boat tours led by archaeologists. Those who want to get even closer to ancient history can snorkel or dive as part of an expedition with authorised guides. At just 9m below sea level, ancient Rome is tantalisingly close.

Be Chic in Capri Town

JET-SETTERS, WELCOME

Like the other Gulf of Naples islands, **Capri** has only become a tourist destination within the last 100 years – particularly its eastern half, the village of Capri Town. Capri Town's beauty is so iconic that it has come to represent the island as a whole. And it's no wonder. Its whitewashed labyrinthine streets – with their tiled courtyards and

WHERE TO SWIM IN ISCHIA

There's no shortage of amazing places to swim on Ischia. Lucia La Monica, sommelier at Pignattello, gives her insider favourites.

Spiaggia dei Maronti
It's the longest beach on the island, and has so many great restaurants and live music, too.

Spiaggia di San Montano
This insider beach is in one of Ischia's most beautiful bays.

Baia di Sorgeto
A really special beach where you'll find hot natural springs.

Spiaggia di Cartaromana
It's just gorgeous, and has great views of Castello Aragonese.

VOLCANIC UNDERWATER RUINS

Aenaria isn't the only underwater ruin in Campania; the **Parco Sommerso di Baia** (p565) in Campi Flegrei is home to the ruins of Roman villas and stunning mosaics, sunk by a volcanic event in 1538.

WHERE TO HAVE AN APERITIVO IN ISCHIA

Ischia Salumi
Historic artisan laboratory turned gourmet sandwich shop. Seaside *aperitivi* with charcuterie boards.

Garden Fruit Ischia
Greengrocer by day, *aperitivo* spot in the evening. In a side street near Castello Aragonese.

Caffetteria del Monastero
Super exclusive *aperitivo* in the Albergo il Monastero's cafeteria; delicious cocktails.

hand-painted ceramic street signs, shaded by purple blooms – form the ultimate Italian island dreamscape.

Your first port of call is, naturally, **Piazza Umberto I**, called *la piazzetta* by locals; perfect for people- and celebrity-watching. Then wander into the centre's side streets, such as Via Le Botteghe, to be rewarded with fashionable boutiques, restaurants and, now and then, the odd fruit and veg vendor. Take a detour to the **Giardini di Augusto** and the charterhouse **Certosa di San Giacomo**; the walk over is a pleasant stroll, and you'll pass the **Carthusia** shop, one of Italy's oldest perfumers. Or enjoy one of Capri's lovely rambles, like the **Passeggiata del Pizzolungo**, which takes you to **Arco Naturale**, passing by lookouts and grottoes, or the walk to **Punta Tragara,** passing early-20th-century villas and stunning palatial hotels to reach a lookout terrace with a romantic view of Capri's Faraglioni rock formation. Turning back will take you through Via Camerelle, Capri's haute-couture street. Hopefully, you have some coins left; it's always *aperitivo*-o-clock at the *piazzetta*.

Villas to Dream About

ISLAND PALACES

Capri Town's most famous structures are undoubtedly its two historic villas high up in the hills: Villa Jovis and Villa Lysis. Two villas, two radically different stories.

Villa Jovis is an enormous Roman villa, commissioned by Emperor Tiberius in the 1st century BC. The sprawling ruins – now populated by roaming goats – include imperial quarters, bathing gardens and the **Salto di Tiberio** (Tiberius' Leap), where, according to local legend, insubordinate servants and undesirable guests were thrown into the sea at the emperor's whim.

Villa Lysis, by contrast, is an early-20th-century clifftop villa with art nouveau influences. French poet Count Jacques d'Adelsward-Fersen exiled himself here in 1904 following gay sex scandals, barricading himself with three floors of grand salons and even an opium den in the basement. Don't miss a stroll in the gardens where you'll see the knockout panorama of Capri's coastline.

The villas are only accessible by foot, and though the road is paved, make no mistake: it's a 40-minute uphill urban trek. You can easily make a morning out of seeing the two manors,

---

SEA MONSTERS & MERMAIDS

Capri's most iconic natural sight is undoubtedly the **Faraglioni** rock formation. The Faraglioni is formed by three stacked crags just off the island's coast: the 109m high Saetta; Stella with its 60m long central cavity; and Scopolo, home of the blue lizard, native only to Capri. You'll see countless Insta-photogs snapping new profile pics. Swimmers revel. Lovers kiss for luck as they sail through Stella's cavity. They must not know the legends.

The Faraglioni, like many of Campania's natural phenomena, are linked to Greek myth. Homer believed they were boulders hurled at Ulysses by the Cyclops Polyphemus. Virgil thought they were the legendary home of murderous mermaids, waiting to lure sailors to death. Squint; don't they look like a sea monster? Instagram at your own risk.

WHERE TO STAY IN CAPRI

Hotel Gatto Bianco
The island's most historic hotel, notable for its stunning tile floors. Associated with a nearby spa facility. €€€

Villa Marina Capri Hotel & Spa
Ultra-luxurious hotel with sprawling gardens, thermal baths and a seafront pool. €€€

La Minerva
Classic Capri glamour: whitewashed walls, blooming vines and pool-coloured tile floors. €€€

Piazza Umberto I

BEST RESTAURANTS IN CAPRI TOWN

Pescheria Le Botteghe €€€
Fish market by day, fantastic seafood bar by night. Pricey for a fish market bar, dead cheap for Capri.

Gelateria Buonocuore €
Historic gelateria known for its freshly made ice-cream cones, hot-pressed before your eyes.

Donna Rachele €€€
Popular trattoria with decorative tiles and walls lined with bottles. Vegetarian options.

for a true time travel experience that will be worth it at the end. Just before you reach Villa Jovis is **Astarita Park**. At first glance it appears neglected and unremarkable, but venture further in and find dramatic views of the gulf.

GETTING AROUND

You can get from Marina Grande to Capri Town via bus, scooter or the iconic funicular. Score tickets around the corner from the port; lines will be insufferably long in high season, and the funicular shuts down from January to March.

Ditch the car; Capri's roads are tortuously narrow and there's little parking. Taxis are, of course, expensive. Capri Town is a pedestrian zone.

Beyond the Islands

Forio Lacco Ameno
Serrara Fontana
Sant'Angelo

Anacapri
Monte Solaro

There's no shortage of experiences to be had in Ischia and Capri's outer reaches, from perilous walking trails to hot spring soaks that will bring you back to life. Almost.

You've had a taste of the Gulf of Naples islands; now get ready for dessert. Ischia's most adventurous and defining experiences are found in its five outlying *frazioni* (hamlets), where you'll find the island's most popular thermal spas and rugged wildlife ranging from blinding white tuff peaks to mountains. You'll also find fabulous beaches, including the Spiaggia dei Maronti, featured in Elena Ferrante's *My Brilliant Friend*.

While the name Capri immediately conjures up glamorous villas, that's (literally) only half of the story. This craggy island is split into two towns: the princess Capri Town, and Anacapri, her sporty sister. Here, you'll find the blue phosphorescent waters of the Grotta Azzurra, fantastic hikes and, yes, villas. Quiet ones.

TOP TIP

Certain spa parks in Ischia like Negombo are reservation-only and all have regulations. For better accommodation deals in Capri, try Anacapri, which is far less touristy and slightly less expensive, teeming with idyllic countryside B&Bs.

Giardini Poseidon, Ischia

AWP76/SHUTTERSTOCK ©

Giardini la Mortella (p574)

Lush Island Nature

GO BEYOND THE BEACH

Geologists have attempted to explain the phenomenon of **Ischia's** healing thermal waters, but spa-goers are less interested in science than the relief. The country club–like **Giardini Poseidon** in Ischia's *frazione* of Forio is unquestionably Ischia's most popular thermal park, offering outdoor pools, lavish spa treatments and access to the Spiaggia di Citara beach. For a more holistic experience, visit **Parco Negombo** in Lacco Ameno, surrounded by florals and therapeutic herbs. Destress amid 13 thermal pools, or enjoy the hammam, Japanese labyrinth pool, spa services and private beach.

For a 100% natural thermal adventure, head to **Baia di Sorgeto**. The waters coming out of its wellspring are boiling hot – literally; you'll find potatoes and ears of corn cooking away – but the waters further off are manageably toasty.

Ischia offers supreme hiking opportunities. The **Pizzi Bianchi** hiking trail in Serrara Fontana takes you hundreds of metres up into a bewildering landscape of white tuff menhir peaks with jaw-dropping views of Sant'Angelo and the Spiaggia dei Maronti. Hiking to **Monte Epomeo** in

TAKE A COLD SHOWER

The glossy spas of Negombo and Poseidon are an excellent way to practise self-care, but consider a thermal water park that's less about the pools and more about the water. The thermal water source of **Fonte delle Ninfe di Nitrodi** in Barano has been used since Greek times, its waters so renowned that people fill water jugs to take home. There are no pools here; just a network of refreshing showers, as well as an exquisitely manicured mountaintop setting, where you can take in stunning views of the valley hundreds of metres below. A basic entrance fee gets you a drink ticket to use at the health cafe plus a ticket for a face mask using products from Nitrodi's thermal water–infused line of products. A true insider experience.

WHERE TO EAT BEYOND ISCHIA

Sarace'
Forio restaurant with excellent inventive seafood dishes in a sophisticated yet friendly space. €€€

Pignatello
Michelin-star seafood restaurant in Lacco Ameno that specialises in fresh fish *crudo*. €€€

Bella Napoli
Delicious pizza and gourmet specialities in Forio with traditional, cosy decor. €€€

ADAM EASTLAND ART • ARCHITECTURE/ALAMY STOCK PHOTO ©

Cup of Nestor, Museo Archeologico di Pithescuae

Barano is another classic Ischia escape. The 789m hike up is relatively mild but the trails, caves, 15th-century chapel and views are nonetheless extremely rewarding.

For a less athletic green experience, visit the **Giardini la Mortella** in Forio. This bi-level paradise features a Mediterranean Hill, Greek theatre, aviary and Thai pavilion. Nearby is the **Giardini Ravino**, a 6000-sq-metre garden of succulents curated by local botanist Giuseppe D'Ambra.

Mushrooms & Chicken

SURPRISES IN ISCHIA'S OUTER REACHES

Lacco Ameno's pedigree goes further than its splashy town square, idyllic seafront and high-money boutiques; it was also most likely the site of Pithecusae, the first Greek colony in the Italian peninsula. You can further explore Lacco Ameno's Greek roots at the **Museo Archeologico di Pithecusae**, located in the hillside **Villa Arbusto**. The 18th-century villa was bought by the Council of Lacco Ameno expressly for the purpose of housing the numerous Greek artefacts uncovered during decades of exploration, namely red figure pottery and the Cup of Nestor. It was later repurchased by film director

 WHERE TO STAY BEYOND ISCHIA

Umberto a Mare
Stunning beachside property in Forio with coastal Mediterranean-inspired decor. On Chiaia Beach. €€

Terme Manzi
Historic property in Casamicciola with stunning Turkish-inspired interiors, an excellent spa and a pool. €€€

Hotel Terme Principe
Historic property just off Lacco Ameno beach with well-priced spa, lovely swimming pool and thermal bath access. €€

Angelo Rizzoli, who transformed the grounds into one of the island's most scenic parks.

Lacco Ameno is home to the **Parco Negombo** thermal spa, as well as the paleo-Christian **Basilica di Santa Restituta**. The pristine, lively sprawl of Lacco Ameno's beach owes its particular panorama to **Il Fungo** – 'the mushroom' – a squat, fungi-like rock formation rising up out of the sea.

Walk from the ancient village of **Sant'Angelo** or take a water taxi to **Le Fumarole dei Maronti** beach, so-called for its steaming-hot sands formed by volcanic gases escaping from the earth. Fun fact: savvy islanders use the sands to cook chicken (the birds are buried underneath). As you approach Le Fumarole, a sensational panorama unfolds before you of caramel-coloured sand, turquoise sea and steam rising from the ground.

Island Hiking Trail

FOLLOW THE LITTLE FORTS

'Bring water', is the first thing people say when you tell them you're doing the **Sentiero dei Fortini**. 'There's nothing out there.'

And desolate it is: just you, forests, steep rock steps, cliffs and the wine-dark sea, hundreds of metres below. This is **Anacapri**'s Trail of Little Forts, an invigorating 6km hike that takes you through the string of early-19th-century British military outposts that once formed the island's defence network. The *sentiero* (trail) runs on the west side of Anacapri between **Grotta Azzurra** at the north end and the lighthouse-topped **Faro di Punta Carena** at its southernmost tip. Hand-painted ceramic signs along the route describe local flora and fauna, including sea lions and rock-climbing octopuses.

The trail is of medium difficulty due to the steep, craggy terrain between **Forte Pepino** and **Forte Mesola**. The water problem is real; there's one water fountain near Fort Mesola, but otherwise there are no shops, and few hikers. Come as early as possible; there is little shade on this route. You can do the trail from the Faro di Punta Carena to Grotta Azzurra, but most do it the other way around so they can cool off with a dive at **Spiaggia di Faro** cliff beach – particularly rewarding at sunset. Do note, however, that the most difficult terrain is towards the lighthouse. Wear trail shoes, not your new Capri sandals.

QUIET VILLAGE LIFE & CULTURAL TREASURES

Just a short bus ride out of Capri Town, the centre of **Anacapri** is worlds away from the chichi elegance of Piazza Umberto I. Here you'll find a tangle of quiet streets lined with restaurants, boutiques, cultural treasures and quirky architectural sites, such as **La Casa Rossa** (The Red House), intriguing for its blend of architectural styles and bright brick-red colour. Also worth a visit is the **Villa di San Michele** – the former home of Swedish physician and author Axel Munthe – with its grand sitting rooms and neoclassical gardens, built on Roman ruins. But the real neighbourhood stunner is the opulent **Chiesa di San Michele**, a petite baroque jewel with a show-stopping hand-painted tile floor depicting a Garden of Eden scene.

 WHERE TO SWIM BEYOND ISCHIA

Spiaggia dei Maronti	**Spiaggia di San Montano**	**Spiaggia di San Francesco**
Ischia's most popular beach; sprawling and golden, full of great beach restaurants and shops.	Small insider beach between the green islets of Monte Vico and Zaro.	Long stretch of festive beach in Forio with lots of restaurants, shops and vintage hotels.

Looking Down on Creation

MOUNTAINS & NATURAL PHENOMENA

Just off Anacapri's city centre, at Piazza Vittoria, is the entrance to the chairlift up to **Monte Solaro**, Capri's highest peak. The 13-minute, 589m ride up will provide unforgettable views of terraced vineyards, white houses and lemon groves, with the gulf and the Amalfi Coast winking in the distance.

Vertigo? You can get to the top on foot by following Via Axel Munthe to Via Salita per il Solaro. Go right, then look for the iron crucifix marking La Crocetta pass. A left turn will take you to the hermitage of **Santa Maria a Cetrella** overlooking Marina Piccola; turning right will get you to the summit.

The hike takes about an hour each way. Ride up and walk down, or walk both ways if you're fit. Keep an eye out for mountain goats.

The world-famous **Grotta Azzurra** is an incredibly beautiful natural phenomenon, although the sheer tourist crush may harsh your buzz. The grotto technically opens at 9am, but try to get there are early as possible to (slightly) shorten your wait. A ticket to the grotto is €14 for a five-minute tour; duck as the gondolier ushers the boat inside, lest you crack your head open on the rock. Inside, the waters glow electric blue and the gondoliers serenade you with Neapolitan classics. Oh; so this is why you came to Capri.

BEST ACCOMMODATION IN ANACAPRI

Capri Palace €€€
Shameless luxury that you'll find only in Capri.

Giardino dell'Arte €€
Delightful B&B just outside Anacapri Centro with lovely blue and white rooms and a sprawling garden overlooking the island.

Boutique B&B Bettola Del Re €€
Charming B&B with tasteful coastal decor, a large outdoor terrace, and excellent food and *aperitivi*.

GETTING AROUND

You can easily reach individual spots on Ischia from Ischia Ponte and Ischia Porto with the circular CD and CS bus lines, but a personal set of wheels is more convenient for travelling between *frazioni*. Anacapri's greatest hits are connected by its bus service, but keep in mind that Anacapri and Capri buses are run by different companies.

THE AMALFI COAST

Ink-blue sea lapping at endless stretches of beach and pastel-coloured houses clinging to stacked cliffs. Sprigs of wild rosemary brush your arms; the perfume of lemons wafts through the air. Every time you look up, there's another colourful tiled cupola rising from the skyline; every time you look down, more stone steps. You pinch yourself. It's real; you're on the Amalfi Coast.

Lucky you! People wait lifetimes to experience this magical expanse of coastline. Amalfi, the medieval trading city and the region's namesake, was Italy's first Maritime Republic, and is still the area's principal hub. Richard Wagner famously took refuge in hilltop Ravello, today the site of the internationally acclaimed Ravello Festival. Few moments are as thrilling as watching Positano's cone-shaped panorama swim into focus from the ferry. But don't stop there. Be surprised by the coast's smaller villages, Roman ruins and rugged natural beauty – home of Ulysses' legendary mermaids. You're finally here. Make it yours.

Rome

The Amalfi Coast

TOP TIP

Amalfi, halfway between Sorrento and Salerno and the area's main ferry and bus hub, is the best base if you are planning on exploring the region. If the rates are too rich for your blood, consider staying in Salerno or the coast's other sleepy fishing villages instead.

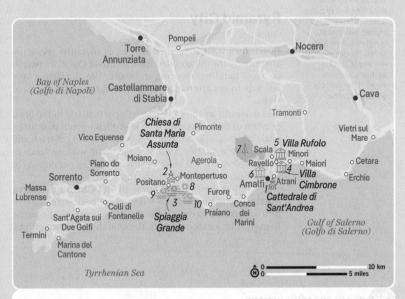

HIGHLIGHTS
1 Cattedrale di Sant'Andrea
2 Chiesa di Santa Maria Assunta
3 Spiaggia Grande
4 Villa Cimbrone
5 Villa Rufolo

SIGHTS
6 Museo della Carta
(see 1) Museo Diocesano di Amalfi
7 Riserva Statale Valle delle Ferriere
8 Spiaggia Arienzo
9 Spiaggia del Fornillo
10 Spiaggia Laurito

Positano

MONTEPERTUSO

Sometimes, Positano is a little *too* Positano. When that happens, take the shuttle bus from Piazza dei Mulini to Montepertuso up in the Lattari mountains for a radically different yet classic 'beyond Positano' experience. There are a number of restaurants and historical taverns up here, which make for a perfect lunchtime interlude. Try **Il Ritrovo**, a quiet bistro that serves inventive country cuisine made with local products – think fried *fiori di zucca* (zucchini flowers) stuffed with Provola di Agerola, Agerola's prized cheese. Il Ritrovo has ample outside seating and offers views of the gulf and woodland below.

Pyramid City

THE ROMANCE OF POSITANO

Positano's volcano-shaped skyline is instantly recognisable among the villages dotting the Amalfi Coast, its pastel-coloured buildings clinging on for dear life. But there's only one way to get around, and that's to climb its hundreds of steps.

As dastardly as the steps can be – particularly in the heat, or when dragging a suitcase to your B&B – you'll pass artisanal linen *pezze* (beachwear) boutiques and art galleries, and glide under a gnarled wood pergola, hung with garlands of purple blooms. You'll be rewarded by soaring panoramas of sea and sky when you reach the top.

The yellow Vietri-tiled dome of the **Chiesa di Santa Maria Assunta** is Positano's second-most iconic sight. But venture underneath to explore the recently-opened-to-the-public Roman villa, located beneath the church's medieval crypts.

 WHERE TO EAT IN POSITANO

Covo dei Saraceni
A middle ground between pizzas and higher-end fare – both delicious. Chic space just steps from the port. €€€

La Zagara
Historic bar and restaurant with iconic blue and orange Vietri-tiled floor, outdoor pergola and traditional pastries. €€€

Casa e Bottega
Delightful organic food bistro/boutique selling work by local artisans. Shop ceramics, textiles and objets d'art. €€€

The exquisitely frescoed grand villa is believed to have been another victim of the catastrophic eruption of Mt Vesuvius in 79 CE.

Positano is best known for it spectacular coastline, but it has great beaches, too. **Spiaggia Grande** at the port teems with beautiful people and flanks Positano's stretch of *locali* (bars) and restaurants, whereas **Spiaggia del Fornillo** is a secluded yet lively pebbly inlet beach. If even that's too much action, try **Spiaggia Arienzo**, 1km east of Positano, or **Spiaggia Laurito**, 3km away. These tiny pebble beaches are wrapped in striated cliffs, worlds away from Positano's swells.

Medieval Centre & Paper

AMALFI'S GREAT ARTISANS

It's just a few steps from **Amalfi**'s port to reach **Piazza Duomo**, dotted with historic coffee bars and the fountain of Sant'Andrea Apostolo. The Arabic-Norman **Cattedrale di Sant'Andrea** dominates the piazza with its massive 62-step staircase. Visit the cathedral to admire the frescoes in the idyllic Cloister of Paradise and the Basilica of the Crucifix, first constructed in the 6th century. The adjacent **Museo Diocesano di Amalfi** is home to ecclesiastical art and, in its crypt, the relics of Sant'Andrea (St Andrew), the city's patron saint. Strolling down **Via Lorenzo D'Amalfi** – the town's main drag – you'll find romantic alleys and restaurants, plus boutiques selling artsy clothing and artisanal ceramics.

Amalfi isn't merely a former maritime superpower; since the 13th century, it has also been a producer of artisanal paper. The area stretching from the Valle dei Mulini at the far end of town through the forested **Valle delle Ferriere** was once a hive of paper mills, powered by the forest's lapping waterfalls. Learn more at the **Museo della Carta** (Paper Museum), housed in one of the town's original 13th-century paper presses – the oldest in Europe.

The museum offers hands-on tours in Italian, Spanish and English. Visitors are able to view the historic instruments, and even try their hand at making their own artisanal paper. The gift shop sells beautiful notebooks and other paper gifts.

AMALFI'S MAIN CURRENCY

Lemons are prime currency in Campania. But there's just one place to get Amalfi lemons, and that's Amalfi. To learn more about the city's quintessential citrus fruit, head to the **Amalfi Lemon Experience**, an organic lemon orchard run by the Aceto family since 1825. You'll learn how lemon trees are sustainably grafted to make them more disease-resistant. Head to the orchard's spacious cafe area with peaceful valley views, where you'll sample homemade lemon sweets and 100% organic *limoncello* made onsite. *Limoncello* isn't considered proper *limoncello* unless it's over 30 proof – taste the difference for yourself.

EVEN MORE LEMONS!

The **Giardini di Cataldo** (p583) lemon orchard in Sorrento runs a bar, speciality shop and gelateria alongside its orchard. Everything is made with authentic organic *limone di sorrento*, of course.

 WHERE TO SHOP IN AMALFI

Dalla Carta alla Cartolina
Magical paper shop with art exhibit; drop postcards in a mailbox and see its beautiful story come to life.

Angela Romano
Artisanal boutique selling luxury coastal apparel for men and women.

L'Altra Costiera
Shop with a wide selection of traditional and modern coastal artisanal ceramic ware.

Eight-Hundred-Year-Old Villas

LET RAVELLO ENCHANT YOU

Ravello's sprawling **Villa Rufolo**, just off Piazza Duomo, is named after the noble family who founded it in the 13th century. In its 800 years, it's also been the residence of King Robert of Anjou, as well as several popes. You can literally see its history: the 14th-century entrance tower, the Gothic gateway, the curlicued Moorish courtyard and the 19th-century cascading gardens and lavish sitting rooms with sweeping views of the gulf. Here, Wagner got the inspiration for the second act of his opera *Parsifal*.

Villa Cimbrone is just 10 minutes away. Like Villa Rufolo, it's a medieval structure peppered with influences from subsequent eras, but Villa Cimbrone's major draw is its gorgeous garden. Allow yourself to be transported when you pass through its rose bushes or underneath its leafy shaded pergola, lush with purple blooms. Linger on the **Terrace of Infinity**, 280m above sea level, with its garden of marble busts and gasp-worthy views.

Both villas also function as hotels, with frescoed ceilings and Vietri-tile floors. Even if you can't afford a night there, you can enjoy a drink at Villa Cimbrone's **Grotto di Eva** hilltop garden bar.

BEST PLACES TO STAY IN RAVELLO

Hotel Parsifal – Antico Convento del 1288 €€€
Staying at this stunning luxury hotel situated in a 13th-century convent is a religious experience. Original antique tile floors, opulent upstairs salons.

Le Perle d'Italia €€
Extremely well appointed B&B on the edge of town. Mediterranean coastal decor; breakfast you can enjoy on the mountain-view terrace.

Palazzo Avino €€€
Ornate old-world decor that manages to be breezy in a stately 12th-century palace with fanciful Moorish touches.

GETTING AROUND

The infamous SITA bus running along the perilous SS163 highway is the principal mode of public transportation between the Amalfi Coast's cities. As nerve wracking as it can be, taking the SITA is vastly preferable to driving in this heavily trafficked region. Ferries run regularly between the major cities and the smaller cities on the eastern end of the coast. Note that the last ferry out of Positano leaves early in high season; in low season, service diminishes drastically, so if you're not staying over, plan to leave by SITA bus.

Beyond the Amalfi Coast

Tramonti
Vietri sul Mare
Agerola Scala
Sorrento Cetara
Nocelle Furore Amalfi

Mermaids, secret bays, Roman ruins, and a hike that lets you commune with the gods. Positano who?

From secluded beaches to charming villages, the areas surrounding Positano, Amalfi and Ravello are worth their own itinerary. Tackle epic hikes like the iconic Sentiero degli Dei and the Sentiero di Ieranto, the trails perfumed with lemons and wild rosemary. The ragged coast's mysterious cliffs and grottoes are deeply alluring for water sports and sailing adventures.

Allow yourself to be surprised by Amalfi Coast wines when you visit Furore or the hilltop winemaking area known as Tramonti. Along the way, you'll meet the oldest city on the Amalfi Coast, dine in a fishing village that produces a condiment so delicious gourmands hoard their supply, and see the rainbow burst in Vietri sul Mare, the birthplace of Vietri tiles.

TOP TIP

If a scooter isn't your speed, consider ferrying it along the coast. Though pricier than the bus, even in high season they're far less crowded and often quicker (Amalfi to Salerno in 35 minutes, Cetara to Vietri sul Mare in five).

Sentiero degli Dei (p583)

FRANCESCA SCIARRA/SHUTTERSTOCK ©

BEST NIGHTLIFE IN SORRENTO

Giuseppe Morvillo, journalist, travel planner and owner of sorrentovibes.com, tells you where to enjoy the best Sorrento nightlife.

Peter's Beach is great – you can drink until midnight and they have twice-weekly musical events and theme parties. They also organise cultural events like indie, classic and sometimes contemporary music. **Grand Hotel Excelsior Vittoria** is a historic property; they have a magnificent terrace where you can have an *aperitivo* or cocktail. **Hotel Mediterraneo** in Sant'Agnello is really famous for its rooftop bar; the views are incredible. Then there's **Bar Ercolano** in Piazza Tasso where they have live music. And **Vrasa** – it's got a garden. Amazing style and unique location. I'm sure it will boom!

Chiostro di San Francesco

A Town to Return To

DISCOVER SORRENTO'S MANY RICHES

The seaside city of **Sorrento** often gets lumped in with the Amalfi Coast, but it's 100% Sorrento Peninsula, baby. Scratch beneath the touristy plasticised menus and cookie-cutter souvenirs in its historic centre to find masterpieces of medieval, Renaissance and baroque architecture. The exquisite religious centres include the 11th-century **Basilica di Sant'Antonino** and the **Chiostro di San Francesco**, with its leafy courtyard and modern art exhibits. Dig even deeper for Roman ruins; Sorrento was a holiday destination for emperors, and before that, a Greek colony. Sorrento also boasts a healthy calendar of cultural events at great spaces like the beautiful **Parco di Villa Fiorentino**, which hosts tastefully curated revolving modern art and photography exhibits in a serene park setting. You'll find grand villas, some of which are now palatial hotels, like the Grand Hotel Excelsior Vittoria on Piazza Torquato Tasso. Don't miss the **Museo della Tarsia Lignea** – a museum dedicated to the intricate craft of inlaid wood, which originated in Sorrento in the 15th century.

 WHERE TO EAT BEYOND RAVELLO

La Cianciola
Somewhere between homey and chic, offering classic seafood dishes with a twist in Cetara's Piazza Cantone. €€

Pizzerie Da Giufè
This all-round star in Vietri sul Mare serves fantastic *fritti* and a surprisingly light Neapolitan-style pizza. €€

Pasticceria Sandra
Old-school pastry shop on Vietri sul Mare's Corso Umberto I with artisanal creations you won't find anywhere else. €

Enjoy *caffè* in **Piazza Tasso**, then head to the ancient quarter to browse boutiques and see Sorrento's artisanal woodworkers toiling in their shops. Then stroll **Villa Comunale**'s gardens, where you might crash a wedding. Decide: dinner at **Marina Piccola** with its excellent seafood restaurants, or in the historic centre for old-school eats under lemon groves? Whatever you decide, stop by **Giardini di Cataldo** to sample 100% artisanal *limoncello*.

Between Heaven & Earth

A WALK WITH THE DEITIES

Any traveller you meet here will ask, 'Have you done the Path of the Gods yet?', so famous is this mountain trail, so-called for the godly experience of being suspended somewhere between heaven and earth.

The **Sentiero degli Dei** is about 6km long each way – starting in **Agerola** (Bomerano) and ending in the hamlet of **Nocelle**. From its dizzying heights, you can spy terraces, olive groves and the blue-and-white dome of **Praiano** as you scale the side of the mountain, accompanied by the Greek gods and the ghosts of the writers and artists who hiked this trail before you. Inspired by the Greek legends surrounding the Sorrento Peninsula, Italo Calvino described it as 'the road suspended over the magical gulf of the Sirens'.

Instead of starting from Agerola and ending in Nocelle, you can take the trail to the halfway point, turning back to Agerola when you come to the fork between the trail's 'upper' and 'lower' paths. The route is clearly marked and you'll encounter many pilgrims along the way.

If you choose to end your hike in Nocelle, you'll be greeted by a lemon slushy stand; for a refreshing treat, try one mixed with a splash of orange juice. There are also bathrooms so you can freshen up before tackling the 1700-step hike down to Positano.

Wine & Fjords

A TIPPLE; A SECLUDED BEACH

Head east and you'll hit **Furore**, aka, *la citta' che non c'e'* – the city that doesn't really exist. There's no centre – just smatterings of nondescript buildings decorated with funky murals, creating a sort of open art museum.

CLIFF HIKES

Prefer hiking on the cliffs? Try the **Sentiero dei Fortini** (p575) in Capri.

ADVENTURE BEACHES

If you're gutsy (and in top shape), then try the Sorrento Peninsula's life-changing adventure beaches. The **Bagni di Regina Giovanna** – the ruins of the seaside Roman villa of Pollio Felix – today serves as a natural swimming hole, despite the danger signs blocking the cobblestone path. It's a long hike down (and back up) but the panorama, punctuated by Roman arches and bathers diving off the ruins into the sea, is mesmerising.

Alternatively, there's the **Baia di Ieranto**, the legendary home of the mermaids who attempted to seduce Ulysses. The 45-minute medium-difficulty trail starts from the hamlet of Nerano and leads to a secluded yet lively cliff beach facing the Faraglioni (rock towers) of Capri. The pebbly shore is tranquil, perfect for a lovely swim and people- (or mermaid-) watching.

 WHERE TO EAT AROUND AMALFI

Euroconca	**Le Arcate**	**Sal de Riso**
It may look like a roadside stand, but this is an elegant Conca dei Marini restaurant with fantastic *spaghetti alle vongole*. €€€	Just out of the tunnel between Amalfi and Atrani with lovely sea views; good pizza and seafood. €€€	Famous *pasticceria* and gelateria in Minori. Vintage wood and glass interiors; pastry case full of perfect sweets. €

QUIET BEACH HIDEAWAYS

Tiny **Atrani**'s postcard panorama attracted Dutch artist MC Escher in 1923, when he took inspiration for some of his labyrinthine works from its snaking alleyways. Further east are **Minori** and **Maiori**, with their idyllic waterfronts. For casual hikers, there's a 3km walking path between the two towns called the **Sentiero dei Limoni**, a beautiful lemon grove ramble. Minori is also known for its pasta, its biggest hits including *scialatielli* - thick ribbon pasta - and *'ndunderi*, ricotta and potato gnocchi. Maiori and Minori also make an excellent base for exploring the coast; they're both connected by ferry to its principal cities – just a 10- to 20-minute ride to Amalfi – and you can often get good (well, decent) accommodation deals.

PHOSPHORESCENT PILGRIMAGES

The phenomenon of phosphorescence cannot be missed if you're in the area. The **Grotta Azzurra** (p576) in Anacapri is the most dramatic; its waters are practically neon.

You'll need wheels to see it properly. Otherwise, stop by **Cantine Marisa Cuomo** – a woman-run winery that's the birthplace of the multi-award-winning Fiorduva wine. You can tour the hilltop vineyard with views of the sea and the cliffs, or opt for the tasting experience. Don't get too tipsy – you'll need your wits for the **Fiordo di Furore**, a secluded pebble and cliff beach crowned by a scenic arched bridge. There's only one way to get there. You guessed it: down hundreds of stone steps.

The 5070 SITA bus from Amalfi will drop you off at the overpass, where you'll start your downward hike. Hang in there; the crystal-clear waters and joyous atmosphere are worth it. Furore is a free beach and, according to Luigi, the sea wolf who's been renting out deck chairs here for the past 15 years, it's completely secluded except Sundays and the week of Ferragosto in August.

Just past Furore in Conca dei Marini, you'll find **La Grotta dello Smeraldo**, a phosphorescent cave with a beautiful underwater Vietri-made ceramic *presepe* at the bottom, 4m deep. Did we mention that the waters glow bright green? Guided tour only.

Up in the Mountains
CHASE WATERFALLS

Should you feel like trading medieval romance for mountain grit, there are two great hikes starting just outside of Ravello. To hike to the 12th-century ruins of the **Basilica di Sant'Eustachio**, you'll pass through ancient **Scala** – the oldest town in the Amalfi Coast – and the villages **Minuta** and **Pontone**, overlooking the Valle di Dragone, until you reach the Basilica with its stunning triple-apse facade studded with mosaic inlays. You can segue right into the **Sentiero delle Ferriere** trail, which runs between Amalfi and Scala, through the valley where Amalfi's ancient paper mills were located, amid lush forest and whispering waterfalls.

Tuscan reds are wonderful, but have you ever tried wines made from grapes that breathe salt water and mountain mist? Meet **Tramonti** – a dispersed mountaintop community of villages linked only by their historic clifftop vineyards. Campania vineyards produce bold red grape varietals like Tintore and Piedirosso, as well as crisp whites like the slightly sulphuric Biancolella, grown in volcanic soil. Enjoy a classic vineyard tasting tour plus a gourmet farm-to-table

WHERE TO STAY AROUND AMALFI

Amalfi Coast Agriturismo Serafina
A farmhouse B&B in Furore, with hotel-level amenities and charm, and sea views. €€€

Casa Amorino
Seaside B&B in Minori with breezy coastal decor and a lovely garden for guests; romantic for couples. €€

Casa Clotilde
Well-appointed B&B in Maiori with a charmingly rustic decor. Beautiful views of the coastline, and homemade sweets. €€

Vietri sul Mare

AMALFI COAST SEA ADVENTURES

Giovanni Fasano, owner of Vietri Rent multiservice agency, gives us his recommendations for the best sea adventures to be had on the Amalfi Coast.

Visit the promontory of **Capo d'Orso** and enjoy the sight of the *maquis* (herbal shrubland). Stop for a swim in the clear waters of **Pandora's cave** (Grotta di Pandora). The **Marmorata waterfalls** are also beautiful; you can only get there by boat. You can also have lunch at one of the area's small beaches like **Santa Croce**, or the bay of **Conca dei Marini**. Swim in the clear waters of **Fiordo di Furore** beach and watch adventure seekers try things like zip lining or cliff jumping.

experience at the sprawling **Tenuta San Francesco**, where you can take a cooking class or enjoy a home-cooked farm-to-table multi-course meal to pair with your artisanal wine. For something far more intimate, visit the family-run **Monte di Grazia Azienda Agricola Biologica**, where you'll sample a flight of bold wines in the owner's own mountaintop garden.

Jewels of the Coast

CERAMICS & ANCHOVIES

Vietri sul Mare is the birthplace of the exquisitely colour-ful hand-painted Vietri ceramics you've seen decorating the Amalfi Coast's villas and the majestic cupolas that domi-nate its cityscapes. Its city centre is an open-air museum, with ceramics lining stairways, storefronts and alleyways in a technicolour blaze. Even a simple water fountain can be a priceless work of art, like the turquoise blue '*ciuccia-rello*' donkey statue in **Piazza Matteotti**. Get lost in the ceramics workshops lining the streets, where you'll see the artisans hard at work on vases, decorations and tableware. Then visit the **Villa Comunale**, an urban garden noted for its series of rainbow-hued tiled steps leading down to the sea.

WHERE TO EAT BEYOND POSITANO

Ristorante Eughenes
Aggressively old school, economical eatery in Massa Lubrense, at the juncture for the Punta Campanella hike. €€

O'Parrucchiano
Serving high-end traditional Italian food in Sorrento since before Italy was a country. Has a lemon grove. €€€

La Cantinaccia del Popolo
Boisterous trattoria in Sorrento with gut-busting portions of traditional Campanian favourites. €€

Cetara

RAITO

The lovely mountaintop village of Raito is just a quick ride away on the 01 bus from Vietri's main piazza. Raito is home to the **Museo della ceramica a Raito** – Raito Ceramics Museum – where you can learn more about the tradition of ceramics-making and see some of the earliest examples of the art form, dating back to the 17th century. Further up the hill, you'll find **Le Vigne di Raito**, a woman-run *cantina* (winery). It not only has tasting menus but also relaxed picnics where – after touring the tranquil grounds and savouring the views – visitors can sample the winery's prize-winning and surprisingly robust rosé in a casual hilltop setting. Who said wine has to be stuffy?

Next, meet **Cetara**; a small fishing village that's big on charm. After docking, head up to the imposing **Torre di Cetara**, a 14th-century Angevin watchtower, to take in the panorama, then head down the steps to its left and arrive at the **Spiaggia di Lannio**. This tiny black-sand beach is sheltered by cliffs; a perfect secret beach experience. After a dip, it's time to experience Cetara's signature culinary speciality – *colatura di alici*, an umami-rich oil made from salt-cured anchovies. Enjoy a heaping plate of *spaghetti con colatura di alici* at La Cianciola on Piazza Cantone, a great location for catching the town's summertime seaside concerts.

GETTING AROUND

While Sorrento and Positano are wellconnected to the surrounding villages, the connections between the villages themselves are meagr eand unreliable. In general, a scooter is your best bet for reaching the area's dispersed attractions, but only if you're experienced; this is not the place to learn.

SALERNO & CILENTO

Rome ✪

Salerno & ● Cilento

Extending from the coast to a 900m-high mountain, Salerno is the second biggest city in Campania after Naples, counting 127,000 inhabitants to Naples' one million. It is often called 'little Napoli'.

Salerno has been inhabited since at least the 6th century BCE by Osco-Etruscans. In the 2nd century BCE, the Romans made Salerno a major maritime colony and built a proper port. Salerno became its own principality in the Middle Ages, and a prosperous melting pot of cultures, finding itself between the Byzantine and the Islamic worlds. This melting pot is part of the origin of the Schola Medica Salernitana. In the 1800s, many factories were built – Salerno was even dubbed the 'Manchester of the two Sicilies' – and by the time Italy was unified in 1861, the province of Salerno was the third-richest in Italy.

TOP TIP

Between the kindness of its people and the layout of its streets, Salerno is somewhere between a town and a city. If you intend to go shopping, check the stores' opening hours – in summer, they tend to take a rather long break after lunch.

Essential Salerno

BREATHTAKING VIEWS AND CENTURIES-OLD TRADITIONS

The **Castello di Arechi** dominates Salerno from 300m above the city, only a 10-minute drive from the centre. The castle was built by Prince Arechi II in the 8th century on the remains of a Roman fort. Fun fact: it has never been conquered. Visitors can walk along the castle battlements and towers for a unique view over Salerno and the entire gulf, then explore the adjacent **Museo Medievale**. The castle often organises cultural and social events such as **Rock alla Rocca** concerts.

If you're looking for a magical place to spend a few hours, head to Salerno's **Giardino della Minerva** (Garden of Minerva), the oldest modern botanical garden in the world. In the early 1300s, Matteo Silvatico – a noble physician at the **Schola Medica Salernitana** – created the garden to cultivate natural remedies and teach his students. Today, you can walk through the terraced orchard to admire over 300 species of plants and a spectacular view of the city and sea below.

The lower terrace is still dedicated to medicinal herbs and is divided according to the ancient plant classification system following the theory of the four humours (blood, yellow bile, black bile and phlegm). There is also an apothecary-style cafe offering all-natural infusions, a library and a multimedia lab.

SCHOLA MEDICA SALERNITANA

The legend of the foundation of Europe's oldest medical school, the Schola Medica Salernitana, goes like this: on a stormy night in the 9th century, a Latin man, a Greek man, a Jewish man and an Arab man sought refuge under an archway of Salerno's aqueduct. The four began discussing the Latin man's wounds and discovered that they were all physicians. They decided to open a school that would be based on traditions from all cultures. The Salerno Medical School took pride in allowing women to study, practise and teach medicine. These women went down in history as Mulieres Salernitanae (women of Salerno).

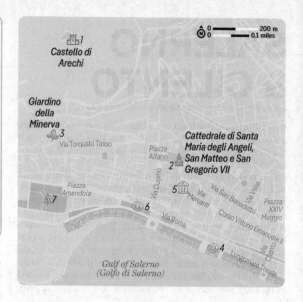

The Duomo & the Seafront

TREASURES OF THE CITY

Salerno's *duomo* (cathedral), the **Cattedrale di Santa Maria degli Angeli, San Matteo e San Gregorio VII**, was built by the Normans in the 11th century. As you walk inside, you'll see the influences through the centuries, with Renaissance frescoes, Byzantine columns, inlaid work, colourful marble, and three colourful mosaics behind the apse, made in the 1950s. The bronze door is framed by two lions that are said to have saved the city from a Saracen attack.

The cathedral's baroque crypt houses the remains of San Matteo (St Matthew), the city's beloved patron saint. The vault is covered in late-mannerist frescoes representing scenes from the saint's life by the Italian-Greek artist Belisario Coerenzio.

Salerno's seafront promenade, **Lungomare Trieste**, is considered one of Italy's most beautiful. In summertime, the beach hums with music, sports and games.

Walk through **Villa Comunale** and cross **Via Roma**, the main street studded with restaurants and bars, then delve

 WHERE TO EAT IN SALERNO'S HISTORIC CENTRE

Al Civico 90
This simple, tasteful restaurant wows with its signature cheese-filled dumpling dish, *noccioraviolo*. €€

La Botte Pazza
A homey Italian restaurant that uses local produce. Refill your wine glass at the self-service taps. €€

Da Michele
Renowned pizzeria perfect for eating on a budget. Go for the classic margherita or a *pizza fritta*. €

Crypt of San Matteo

BEST CHURCHES IN SALERNO

Other than Salerno's *duomo*, these two churches also deserve a visit.

San Pietro a Corte
This church shows the many steps in Salerno's history: a Roman thermal bath (1st century), an early Christian tomb (5th century), a prince's palace (8th century; the only surviving example of Longobard palatial architecture in Italy) and finally the church we see today.

Chiesa di San Giorgio
The myriad colourful frescoes in this church easily make San Giorgio the most visually pleasing and most baroque church in Salerno.

into the maze of alleys that constitute Salerno's historic centre. It's populated with stores of all kinds, including old workshops producing ancient crafts, from colourful ceramics to inlay works.

From November to January, Salerno attracts countless tourists thanks to **Luci d'Artista**: light installations strewn across Salerno. Every year the city chooses a theme, from fairy tales and myths to monuments and food. You can take pictures with the light sculptures and giant Christmas tree, and ride a Ferris wheel overlooking the gulf.

GETTING AROUND

Everything there is to see in Salerno, except for Castello di Arechi, is reachable on foot. If you get to Salerno by car, you can leave it in the massive, newly built parking lot under Piazza della Libertà, a stone's throw away from Villa Comunale. Salerno is on the ferry route from Naples, Sorrento and (in summer) the Amalfi Coast resorts and islands. It is also on the main train line between Naples and Reggio Calabria.

Beyond Salerno

A dramatically different side of Cilento than what we've seen so far.

Salerno

Parco Archaeologico di Paestum

Sala Consilina

Padula

Parco Nazionale del Cilento, Vallo di Diano e Alburni

A prosperous plateau on the eastern side of Cilento, Vallo di Diano sees little tourism, despite the entire area being a Unesco World Heritage Site. Its picturesque villages cling to ancient traditions and provide a rare type of slow life. Not far off, the caves of Pertosa contain the remains of a pile-dwelling village from the 2nd millennium BCE.

Past the Vallo di Diano, the Cilento Coast is a 100km-long coastal strip of hamlets facing emerald waters between the Gulf of Salerno and the Gulf of Policastro. The gem is undoubtedly Paestum with its well-preserved ancient Greek temples. Other beauties are enchanting beach towns such as Marina di Camerota, Ascea and Palinuro.

TOP TIP

Locals have a life expectancy that is on average 10 years longer than in the rest of Italy. Their secret to longevity? People in these remote villages take things slow. Don't rush them.

Certosa di San Lorenzo di Padula

FONT85/GETTY IMAGES ©

Battistero di San Giovanni in Fonte

Explore Padula

FROM MONASTERIES TO BAPTISTRIES

Go to the town of Padula and visit the **Certosa di San Lorenzo di Padula**, the largest Carthusian charterhouse in the world (51.5 sq metres). Built in 1306, its ornaments were embellished repeatedly until the 1700s – ranging from frugal monk cells to the Chiostro Grande, the massive cloister (104m by 149m), which took nearly two centuries to complete.

The iconic *scalone*, the elliptical staircase that became a symbol of the *certosa*, can sadly no longer be visited. The monastery also houses a rich museum hosting archaeological findings from Vallo di Diano, dated to the 10th to 6th century BCE.

Between Padula and the neighbouring town of **Sala Consilina**, you'll see brown street signs pointing to the impossibly picturesque 4th century **Battistero di San Giovanni in Fonte** – one of the oldest baptistries in the Western world and the only one built on water.

Time and the elements have not preserved the frescoes well, but you can see faces of the apostles on the walls, and still recognise the distinct Byzantine style. Sit on the ground, put your feet in the stream and let the water lull you. This is the

THE PRODUCTS OF CHEESE-MAKING

Milk is sometimes called *oro bianco* (white gold) here. Cheese-making is embedded in the history of this region, and cheese makers retain ancient traditions while keeping up with technology. The towns of Capaccio Paestum, Battipaglia and Eboli are home to some of the best *caseifici* (cheese-making factories). The queen of cheeses is undoubtedly the pure white round *mozzarella di bufala* (buffalo mozzarella), but there are many other products, like its mini-self (*bocconcini*), a smoked and darker version (*provola*), a flattened and braided version (*treccia*) or the delicate, soft ricotta. That's not even mentioning the hard, stretched-curd *caciocavallo*.

🧀 BEST CASEIFICI TO VISIT

La Perla del Mediterraneo
This *caseificio* specialises in *mozzarella di bufala*, all dairy-related products and lactose-free mozzarella.

Da Vannulo
Take a tour in the Museum of Rural Life of this *caseificio* that treats its 600 buffaloes with homeopathic care.

Caseificio Barlotti
This *caseificio* organises tastings of its many specialities: dairy, meat, vegetables, yoghurt, cakes and pastries.

STARS UNDERGROUND

The Grotte di Pertosa-Auletta hold one more secret: writings on the wall. There are six-pointed stars, names, the digits 1944 and 1945. The Stars of David attest that the authors of the graffiti must have been Jewish and the numbers provide enough context for an explanation. In those years, locals hid Neapolitan Jews in the caves so they wouldn't be deported to concentration camps. It's unknown whether the graffiti was penned by the Jews in hiding, or by the Jewish soldiers who landed in this area as part of the Allied troops. The darkness of the cave also hides one more inscription, in Hebrew; it reads 'this valley is beautiful, but the one waiting for us even more so'.

Parco Archeologico di Paestum

perfect place for a picnic in the shade of the tall trees that act as the perfect frame to this picturesque scene.

Temples & Caves

ECHOES OF AN ANCIENT TIME

Parco Archeologico di Paestum is home to the only Magna Graecian colony that has survived in its entirety, with ruins that are among the best preserved in the world. The heroes here are the three temples dedicated to Hera, built across the 5th century BCE. Then there are the ruins of a Roman amphitheatre, shops, houses, thermal baths and every component befitting a city popular among rich merchants and nobles. Don't miss the **museum**, where you can admire world-famous images like the Tomb of the Diver. Download the Paestum app for a solo guided tour.

The **Grotte di Pertosa-Auletta** have been around for 35 million years, with signs of being inhabited since the Bronze Age. Guided tours take you inside the caves, past thousands of stalactites and stalagmites, like the iconic 'Kiss' where a stalactite and a stalagmite resemble two faces kissing. But the real star of the visit is navigating the **Fiume Negro** on

 WHERE TO EAT IN PADULA

Locanda dei Trecento
Generous portions, friendly staff and authentic recipes and ingredients: one of the best restaurants. €

Agriturismo L'Aia Antica
Typical Cilento food using home-grown produce. At dinner, pizza is queen. €

Porticum Herculis
In an ancient villa with frescoes. The local food is delicious and comes at a very low price. €

a raft –this is the only site in Italy where you can sail on an underground river. The experience is magical because of the artificial lighting that makes the grotto look like the set of a horror movie. Every few years, the caves become the stage for special performances of Dante's *Inferno*, a thrilling sight to behold.

Trek, Hike, or Ride in Nature

CILENTO'S WILD SIDE

The **Parco Nazionale del Cilento, Vallo di Diano e Alburni** is Italy's second-largest national park, with over 360 sq km of uncontaminated nature, extending from the sea to the Apennines. It is, in its entirety, a Unesco World Heritage Site. The park is home to 1800 species of indigenous plants, 10% of which are rare. There are also hundreds of bird, mammal, reptile and fish species. Trek past streams and waterfalls, wander through meadows and forests. The many beautiful hiking trails will take you to lonely places of worship or even archaeological sites.

The Cilento Coast's treasures range from beaches to villages to archaeological sites. Hit the coast between the towns of **Agropoli** and **Marina di Ascea** for an idyllic stretch of sandy beach; there's also a fun, gay-friendly beach in **Eboli**. Driving south from Agropoli, you'll find **Castellabate**, a medieval hilltop village considered one of the most beautiful in Italy. Its sea hamlet, **Punta Licosa**, with its crystalline waters, was believed to be inhabited by sirens. Further down is **Acciaroli**, the enchanting village where Ernest Hemingway was inspired to write *The Old Man and the Sea*. Don't miss **Velia**, home to the Greek city of Elea, whose citizens keep ancient traditions alive by organising a theatre festival in a millennium-old amphitheatre. Heading south from Palinuro to **Marina di Camerota**, you can explore gorges and caves, where researchers have found prehistoric hominid remains.

 GETTING AROUND

There aren't many transport options in Vallo di Diano and the inland parts of Cilento. There are currently no trains – the stations exist but have been closed for years – but the national railway service (Rete Ferroviaria Italiana) runs a handful of buses every day to and from Napoli, Battipaglia (the closest operating train station) and other towns. The public bus company SITA Sud runs three daily services between Salerno and Pertosa (Monday to Saturday). That said, bus services can be unreliable. Driving is the best way to reach these areas, so you are fully autonomous and not dependent on bus departure/arrival times. The roads are good and the signals visible and in good shape.

Vieste (p615)

PUGLIA
TARALLI & VINO

Where olive-green seas intertwine with seas of green olive groves, and seafood is a feast for the eyes and stomach.

Puglia's obsession with good food and good wine makes it one of Italy's main destinations for foodies. So it seems appropriate that the Italian expression '*finire a taralli e vino*', literally meaning 'ending up with *taralli* and wine', was born here. Metaphorically, it is used to indicate a heated quarrel that ultimately ends in a friendly and calm atmosphere, just like the wine and *taralli* – a type of dried snack similar to breadsticks in texture – that were offered, once upon a time, to guests in Puglia.

This sun-kissed region has long been stereotyped as a warm and welcoming but poor land, that would attract tourists for a few dives in its clear waters, followed by tasty seafood and white wine, but push its own children to emigrate elsewhere.

After the pandemic, however, Puglia is finally being appreciated for its true richness. Many of its citizens lost to wealthier places in Europe have come back in a counter-exodus and have decided to stay, giving Puglia another chance. Amid its Greek-like villages and medieval towns, along with bigger cities like Bari, the Italian seafood capital, and baroque Lecce, you'll see an up-and-coming youth trying to boost Puglia's territory, beyond just summer.

SVITLANA BELINSKA/SHUTTERSTOCK ©

THE MAIN AREAS

ALBEROBELLO
Countryside relaxation. p600

LECCE
Folk dancing and nightlife.
p607

VIESTE
Hiking trails with sea views.
p615

Isole
Tremiti

● Termoli

Rodi
Garganico   ● Peschici

● Vieste

Lago di
Lesina   Lago di
Varano   Parco Nazionale
del Gargano

○ Ururi

● Lesina

Cagnano ○
Varano

San Giovanni
Rotondo   Promontorio
del Gargano   ○ Mattinata

MOLISE

● San Severo   ● Monte
Sant'Angelo

● Manfredonia

Lago di
Occhito   Golfo di
Manfredonia

Vieste, p615
The 'green lung' of
Puglia, the Gargano
is all about nature
and hiking trails
overlooking the
crystal-clear waters
of the Adriatic Sea.

● Lucera

● Foggia

○ Troia   ● Barletta
                                              Trani
                               Canosa di   ●
                               Puglia   ● Bisceglie
● Cerignola   ● Andria   ● Molfe

Ariano ●   Corato ●   Ruvo di
Irpino   Puglia

                               Minervino
                               Murge

● Melfi

● Venosa   Gravina di
                            Puglia   ● Altamur

CAMPANIA   ● Matera

○ Montella   Grassano ○   Lago di San
                                            Giuliano
                            ● Potenza

● Eboli   BASILICATA   Ferrandina ○

● Battipaglia

Golfo di   Corleto
Salerno   Roccadaspide ○   ○ Perticara
                              Sala ○
● Agropoli   Consilina   Viggiano ○

PLANE
The best way to reach
Puglia is to fly. There are
four main airports – the
biggest is Karol Wojtyla
International Airport in Bari,
which each year welcomes
over three million
passengers.

TRAIN
If you're already in Italy, then
hopping on a five-hour train
journey from Rome to Bari
could be a valid option if
you're up for a slow-paced
journey. You'll be rewarded
with romantic countryside
views of Italy's rural areas.

CAR
Hitting the road by car will
allow you to travel at your
own pace and stop for lunch
breaks at wineries and farms
for a genuine Pugliese food
experience.

Find Your Way

Puglia is the heel of Italy's boot and the country's longest region. Its coastlines, filled with environmental diversity and nightlife fun, stretch for almost 900km. We've picked Puglia's most iconic areas to help you unravel its many treasures.

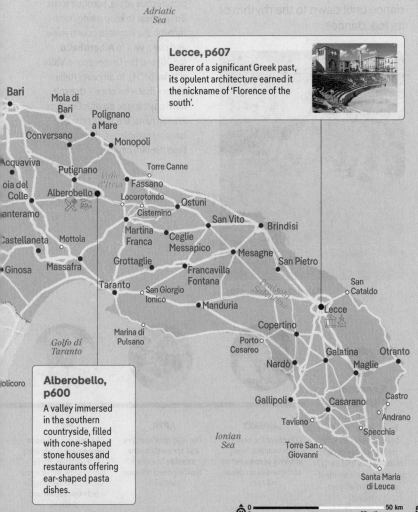

Adriatic Sea

Lecce, p607
Bearer of a significant Greek past, its opulent architecture earned it the nickname of 'Florence of the south'.

Bari

Mola di Bari

Polignano a Mare

Conversano

Monopoli

Acquaviva

Putignano

Torre Canne

Valle d'Itria

Fassano

oia del Colle

Alberobello

Locorotondo

Ostuni

anteramo

Cisternino

San Vito

Brindisi

Castellaneta

Mottola

Martina Franca

Ceglie Messapico

Mesagne

San Pietro

Ginosa

Massafra

Grottaglie

Francavilla Fontana

Penisola Salentina

San Cataldo

Taranto

San Giorgio Ionico

Manduria

Lecce

Golfo di Taranto

Marina di Pulsano

Copertino

Porto Cesareo

Galatina

Otranto

Nardò

Maglie

olicoro

Alberobello, p600
A valley immersed in the southern countryside, filled with cone-shaped stone houses and restaurants offering ear-shaped pasta dishes.

Gallipoli

Casarano

Castro

Taviano

Andrano

Specchia

Ionian Sea

Torre San Giovanni

Santa Maria di Leuca

0   50 km
0   25 miles

Plan Your Time

As the locals say, Puglia is 'a state of mind'. Bike or hike its nature trails, grab a grilled octopus sandwich by the coast, then dance until dawn to the rhythm of its folk dances.

Baia delle Zagare (p620)

A Couple of Days

● If you're a history buff, you will want to start off with a road trip to some of the 12 Greek villages of **Salento** (p607) to explore a piece of Greece in southern Italy. If you're pressed for time, end your tour in **Lecce** (p607), a picturesque white, baroque town. But it's best to keep going north through the Pugliese countryside and pay a visit to **Alberobello** (p600) and the Disneyesque **Valle d'Itria** (p604), to discover Italian history that – for once – doesn't have anything to do with Greek or Roman ruins: the *trulli*, primitive housing complexes, dating no later than the 14th century.

Seasonal highlights

Summer in Puglia can be quite hot, but its breezy beaches will help you stay cool. Mild winters and early springs make it an ideal destination all year-round.

JANUARY
Discover the beauty of reenacted 'living' **nativity scenes** set up across small medieval villages.

APRIL
The mild temperatures call for a walk by the **seaside** to enjoy a typical grilled octopus sandwich.

MAY
A three-day **religious procession** celebrating St Nicholas, Bari's patron saint, will lure you into an unknown Puglia between sacred and profane.

If You Have Just a Few Days

● Puglia should be on any food-lover's wish list. Even a short pit stop will tantalise your tastebuds, especially if you start on Puglia's eastern coasts, where you'll find the best seafood, fresh off fishers' small boats and served directly to the table. A quick stop by the seafront in **Bari** (p604) to try the town's iconic grilled octopus sandwich is a must. For the region's nationwide famous pasta dish – *orecchiette con le cime di rapa* ('little ears' pasta with turnip greens) – wait until you get to **Alberobello** (p600), just a few kilometres away from Bari, and have a traditional meal inside a cone-shaped restaurant.

If You Have a Week or More

● A week-long stay calls for a detour through Puglia's lesser-known nature and hiking spots. **Parco Nazionale del Gargano** (p619) is the ideal starting point: with its biodiversity, the park is a refreshing escape from the urban chaos you can find in even small villages in Italy. The Gargano promontory and its wonderful sea views are less than a 45-minute drive away from the park. Stop for a dive in the turquoise waters of **Baia delle Zagare** (p620), and if you feel like challenging yourself, hop on a two-hour bike trip from there to **Vieste** (p615).

JULY	AUGUST	SEPTEMBER	DECEMBER
Enjoy traditional Pugliese street food at **Festa te la Uliata**, which every year attracts thousands of foodies.	Be sure to wear comfortable shoes for the **Notte della Taranta**, a folk music festival that celebrates traditional dances of the Salento area.	**Grape-harvesting season** means open-gate weekends at local vineyards for visitors willing to have a look – and a try! – at grape-treading.	Challenge yourself with a *tarallo* **culinary class**, taught by local grandmas preparing them to celebrate the holiday season.

ALBEROBELLO

Rome

Alberobello

In a landscape of rolling green fields and vineyards, conical, white-tipped stone buildings sprout from the soil like something frm a fairytale, giving life to the village of Alberobello, in the province of Bari. Alberobello's long, yet melodic, Italian name comes from the Latin *'arboris belli'* (beautiful trees), as the area was once surrounded by a primitive oak forest. Today Alberobello is Puglia's most iconic landmark, a Unesco site which attracts thousands of tourists every year. It is home to about 2000 trulli, the typical cone-shaped, dry-stone buildings made from local limestone that earned the village its fame. Many have been turned from private houses to luxury hotels, affordable restaurants and pasta workshops. The view over Alberobello is dominated by the Church of Santi Medici Cosma e Damiano, an example of neoclassical architecture and a Catholic pilgrimage site.

TOP TIP

Rather than by foot, hit Alberobello's dusty alleys by bike, whether you're a skilled cyclist or a newbie. That's the best way to enjoy the unique views across the winding country lanes, and to grab a bite at local farms off the main roads.

TRULLI UNIQUE

Alberobello is the 'capital' of the surrounding *trulli* villages, and a historical landmark in which Italy takes great pride. It's like walking through an urban sprawl for gnomes, a theme park for history and culture geeks, where you can enjoy the unique view of buildings you will never see anywhere else in the world. People – especially older generations – are extremely welcoming and proud of the uniqueness of this place, despite it being a rural area sometimes overlooked by locals. Alberobello is special because it shows the beauty of country living, and how such small places can thrive despite globalisation.

Crafting Ear-Shaped Pasta

LEARNING PUGLIA'S RICH RECIPES

Dedicating two hours of your time in Alberobello to learning traditional Apulian recipes – the result of cultural mixes and centuries-old culinary experiences – will allow you to take home more than just a material souvenir, but knowledge for life. Knowledge you can acquire through a relaxing morning with Nonna Maria, the pillar of **Trulli del Bosco**, a trulli complex where you can sleep, eat or sign up for cooking workshops. You will attend your class surrounded by hills planted with centuries-old olive trees and fruit trees, and have the chance to hand-pick the ingredients you'll need to prepare Puglia's most famous dish: *orecchiette con le cime di rapa*.

Watching Maria's wrinkled hands kneading flour, you'll learn the exact finger movements needed to craft this challenging ear-shaped pasta (*orecchiette* means 'small ears' in Italian), traditionally cooked in boiling water together with *cime di rapa* (turnip greens) to better mix and absorb the aromas. Tradition says the pasta should be handmade, and your expert teacher, between a laugh and self-explanatory hand gestures, will not forget to highlight how important it is to keep this craft alive, despite new generations' fading interest and the use of industrial tools. Sharing her tips with you, she will make you a part of a centuries-old secret and make you feel like her own child.

HIGHLIGHTS
1 Trullo Sovrano

SIGHTS
2 Basilica di Santi Medici Cosma e Damiano

SLEEPING
3 Le Alcove Luxury Hotel
4 Tipico Resort
5 Trulli Holiday
6 Trullidea

EATING
7 Ristorante EVO
8 Ristorante Trullo d'Oro
9 Trattoria Terra Madre

Orecchiette will be your launching pad into Puglia's flavours of *cucina povera* (simple, poor man's cuisine). The traditional local cuisine is known across Italy for being humble, but also very nutritious and rich in flavours, revealing the varied mix of civilisations that have passed through this land, leaving indelible traces in its culinary legacy. National cookbooks have listed five food items not to be missed while in Alberobello: the Apulian focaccia, the Apulian mozzarella (commonly known as burrata), the wine, local seafood and, of course, *orecchiette con le cime di rapa.*

A Walk Through Time

A HOUSE MUSEUM, BEYOND THE FAIRY TALE

The **Trullo Sovrano** is located in the northern part of Alberobello, behind the **Basilica di Santi Medici Cosma e Damiano**. It's the only *trullo* to have an elevated floor, reachable from the inside via a masonry staircase, among the first to be built with mortar. It is considered the town's 'head' *trullo*, and today it acts as the main local museum, providing

MORE OF A SEASIDE PERSON?

Beaches with **love legend backstories** (p617) will uplift your spirit and satisfy your need to shake off life's responsibilities for an afternoon of relaxation.

 WHERE TO SLEEP IN ALBEROBELLO

Trullidea
Several restored and cosy *trulli* scattered across Alberobello's historic centre. €€

Casa Albergo Sant'Antonio
Spartan rooms for the unfussy in this former monastery located next to a church. €€

Trulli del Bosco
A small 'village' of four *trulli* (plus a swimming pool) deep in the woods. €€€

ALBEROBELLO'S BEST-KEPT SECRETS

Guido Convertino, map illustrator with a passion for local history

Abbazia di Santa Maria di Barsento
A few kilometres from Alberobello, this mysterious place is linked to many local legends, where recent archaeological excavations have revealed interesting discoveries.

Cycling Route of the Apulian Aqueduct
A panoramic route that closely overlooks the Canale delle Pile. In spring the route is filled with wild orchids – one year I counted 15 different types out of about 60 species that grow in Puglia.

Fornello Pronto
More than a place, it is a local tradition of the area. On specific days you can go to the butcher, choose the meat you want and the butcher cooks it on the grill for you.

TAKASHI IMAGES/SHUTTERSTOCK ©

Trullo Sovrano (p601)

insight into what life was like inside a *trullo* in the 17th century. It's a must stop for anyone travelling to Alberobello.

The 14m-high conical dome stands imposingly in the centre of a group of 12 cones. This *trullo* represents a transitional building that heralds the general change in the construction technique of the *trulli*. In fact the master mason, who remains unknown, adopted unique construction methods that make this building the most advanced and admired interpretation of *trullo* architecture.

The current left wing constitutes the building's original central point, which can be traced back to the early 1600s, while the remaining part was built in the first half of the 1700s on behalf of a wealthy family. Over time, the building has had various uses: courtyard, chapel, apothecary, monastery, country oratory, home. In the early 1800s the relics of Sts Cosma and Damiano – patron saints of Alberobello – lived here and from 1826 it was the seat of the Confraternity of the Holy Sacrament. At the end of the 19th century it was passed to the Sumerano family, who made the *trullo* their home and who are the owners to this day. The furnishings

 WHERE TO SLEEP IN ALBEROBELLO

Trulli Holiday
A multi-building hotel whose mission is to mix tradition and modernity and let guests enjoy the quiet. €€

Tipico Resort
The apartments and rooms feature elegant furnishings, a private bathroom, and stone walls and floors. €€€

Le Alcove Luxury Hotel
An unusual mix of modern comforts and ancient stone dwellings. €€€

and exhibits on display are all authentic memorabilia. On 19 September 1923, it was declared a National Monument.

The Birth of Burrata

PUGLIA'S CHEESE STAR

There are almost 500 officially recognised types of cheese in Italy, but burrata – Puglia's most famous dairy delicacy – easily makes the Top 5. Obtained from whole (raw or pasteurised) cow's milk, burrata is made up of an outer shell of solid mozzarella paste filled with fresh cream or butter, with a softer consistency than that of mozzarella itself.

Legend says burrata was born in the first half of the 20th century in the countryside surrounding Alberobello, during a heavy snowfall that isolated a farm. In order to save the milk from going bad, a local farmer recovered the cream that naturally emerged and, as in the butter preservation procedure, he created a wrap with mozzarella paste to protect the fresh product inside.

BEST RESTAURANTS

Trattoria Terra Madre €€
One of the few vegetarian-ish options in town. Vegetables come from the owners' organic garden outside.

Trullo d'Oro €€
The menu follows the seasonal cycle of local produce so it constantly changes throughout the year.

Ristorante Evo €€€
Enjoy centuries-old recipes with a modern twist inside a typical *trullo*.

GETTING AROUND

Alberobello is easily accessible by train or bus. Trains run hourly and last around an hour for the cost of two cappuccinos. Once you get off at the station, a journey of around 500m through Via Mazzini will bring you to Piazza del Popolo, the heart of town with a privileged view over the sea of *trulli*: once there, you'll have the whole place to yourself (and a few hundred more tourists). The village is small enough to walk or bike through, so there's no need to stress about navigating the public transportation system in Italian. Alberobello's narrow streets are sometimes dusty, especially in summer, and it's best to wear comfortable running shoes to tame its slippery cobbles.

Beyond Alberobello

Andria

Alberobello • Cisternino
Locorotondo • • Ostuni
Martina
Franca

Alberobello is set in a wider valley stretching as far as the eye can see. Venture into it.

Where the Ionian and Adriatic coasts intertwine, the 400m-high mountain plateau of the Murgia rises over central Puglia, giving life to the idyllic valley of Valle d'Itria. The area stretches from Bari, the region's major city, and the provinces of Brindisi and Taranto.

The *trullo* became the symbol of this enchanted valley, with Alberobello being proclaimed its unofficial, incommensurate capital. But there's much more beyond Alberobello, namely a sea of other smaller villages with just as beautiful limestone structures and white dry-stone walls, including the bright village of Ostuni and the baroque city of Martina Franca. Often overlooked by mainstream tourist trails, they deserve a visit of their own.

TOP TIP

If you're up for it, Valle d'Itria villages are best discovered through green, solo means of transport such as bikes.

Locorotondo

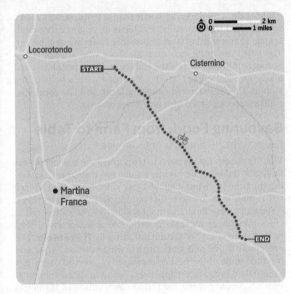

Biking the Valley

DRYSTONE, VINEYARDS & OLIVE GROVES

Locals know that the best way to experience the urban and rural views of their valley is on two wheels. That's why many of them have been raised as skilled cyclists, and some have decided to share their expertise with visitors. Like Damiano, who after years spent sitting at a desk behind a laptop decided to create a tourism venture that would economically help his region and give him a more active life. You can contact him via email, but it's best (and faster!) to reach out to him via WhatsApp at +393203526423, then meet him at his headquarters in the village of **Martina Franca**. Through his meticulously designed four-hour e-bike tours, he will share his valuable insider's knowledge of the places where he grew up.

The scenic biking adventure sets off near **Locorotondo** and continues by **Cisternino**, often included among the most beautiful villages in Italy. It then stops by a Roman aqueduct for a quick photo session accompanied by historical fun facts. After the tour wraps up, return to Martina Franca, a charming baroque village at the heart of the valley.

 WHERE TO STAY IN VALLE D'ITRIA

Truddhi
A tranquil place in Locorotondo surrounded by vineyards where you can take cooking courses, too. €€€

Masseria San Paolo Grande
Immersed in a nest of white stones, this Ostuni *masseria* comes with a restaurant, swimming pool and gym. €€€

Lama di Luna
A 'bio-*masseria*' in Andria offering organic products for a healthy, sustainable stay. €€€

Biking through the valley is safe thanks to its country roads, with limited traffic, that let you focus on appreciating landscapes that are otherwise impossible to fully enjoy by car. The paths are quite easy even for those who are not exactly sports buffs, as there's the chance of using pedal-assisted bikes. Physical efforts will be rewarded with a belly-filling stop at a local *masseria* (working farm) to taste local specialities accompanied by a nice glass of wine.

Savouring Food, from Farm to Table

FLAVOURS OF THE PUGLIESE COUNTRYSIDE

Visiting *masserias* is a must to truly grasp the way people eat in Puglia. It doesn't simply mean going to a restaurant, but taking the time to savour a long-ish car journey to reach a place in the middle of nowhere, that paradoxically has everything.

You can't leave Puglia without trying the iconic olive oil; to enjoy a high-quality example produced at a *masseria*, head to the white village of Ostuni and drop by **Il Frantolo**. The owners still live and work at this whitewashed farm, and produce some of the best cold-pressed oil, served over fresh oven-baked bread as an appetiser. For an updated version of Puglia's *cucina povera*, the little-known village of Manduria can be a worthy detour. This place is run by a Pugliese family who used to live in the north and came back to the valley; during dinner, as you make your way through their delicious dishes, they'll argue about why it was worth it.

Borgo Egnazia

GETTING AROUND

There are buses and trains linking Valle d'Itria villages that take about an hour from Bari, and a few minutes from Alberobello. The view is scenic, but can also be enjoyed if you're travelling by car. The historic centres of the main urban areas, Cisternino and Locorotondo, are pedestrian-only areas, while that of Martina Franca is a Limited Traffic Zone, labelled with the acronym ZTL. Most parking spaces in the valley are free of charge.

LECCE

Puglia's southernmost region of Salento is best known for its Greek allure, a legacy from the time when Puglia was a Greek colony in the 8th century BCE. In a dozen villages, locals still speak a variant of modern Greek. But it's more recent artistry that makes Lecce a gem not to be missed. With more than 40 churches and baroque buildings dating back to the 17th and 18th centuries, the city is the pearl of southern Puglia. Lecce's urban architecture earned it its own label, *barocco Leccese* (Lecce baroque), characterised by the detailed decorations that adorn the facades of its *palazzi* (mansions). The city's Piazza Duomo is its focal point, a feast for the eyes of architecture lovers, who will find in its white-blond stones – best appreciated at golden hour – a reason to call this place the 'Florence of the south'.

TOP TIP

Stick around an extra day in Lecce and get ready for a road trip across Salento to the 12 Greek villages for an off-the-beaten track experience.

On the Leccese Dance Floor

A CENTURIES-OLD FOLK DANCE

The *pizzica*, Salento's traditional folk dance, has ancient origins that seem to date back to the time when the area was under Greek rule. It was born with the intent to heal '*tarantate*' (meaning stung by a tarantula spider) women who behaved in an obscene, reckless or hysterical way. With the dance and specific chords of some instruments, it was believed that such women could free themselves from this poisonous spell. Today the *pizzica* is one of the most famous Italian folk dances, part of the wider family of *taranta* dances found in the Italian south, especially Naples. Every year in August an international festival celebrates its rhythms.

Lecce – as the area's main city – is the ideal place to immerse yourself in a practical demonstration of the dance's complex moves, which tell a wider cultural history of Salento. Inside the two-storey **ICOS building** in downtown Lecce, Serena D'Amato, an experienced Salento folk dance teacher, will put you at ease in her cosy dance studio. Her hour-long *pizzica* lessons begin with a few easy steps from the popular tradition that slowly evolve into the new forms of expression she has been studying for decades, to give a fresh flavour to this centuries-old dance. Her unique style combines ancient movements with a personal interpretation, emphasising the beauty, elegance and liberating force of this ancient dance. It is usually a dance for couples, but solo travellers can also

WHY I LOVE LECCE

Stefania D'Ignoti, writer

Everyone heads over to Bari because it's the capital of the region, but this smaller, charming town shows that not all *capoluoghi* (regional capitals) are a region's most representative place. Lecce is the beating heart of Salento, and possibly of the whole of Puglia. With monuments ranging from the Roman period to the 17th century, best seen when lit by the rays of sunset gleaming on the buildings' white-blond stones, it's a supremely romantic and scenic destination.

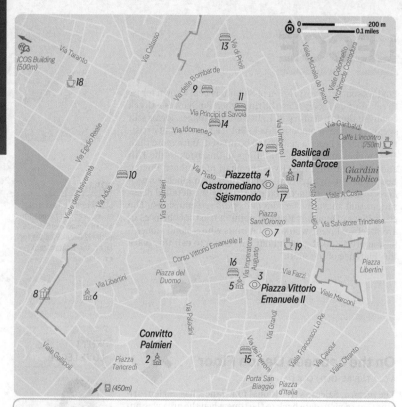

have a go at learning the basic movements. Serena will argue that her class counts as a therapy session for your soul – and not just the body! – and will introduce you to *pizzica* with a few twists, such as the concept of *pizzica* fencing, a dance

 WHERE TO SLEEP IN LECCE

Pollicastro Boutique Hotel
A historical manor dating back to the 16th century, with a huge terrace overlooking the city.
€€€

La Dimora dei Celestini
Right in the heart of Lecce, you won't need any public transport to get around, just your feet. €€€

Mantatelurè
The warm welcome here wraps you up like its name, which in local dialect means 'the king's cloak'. €€€

Pizzica dancer, Salento

SALENTO'S SALT OF THE EARTH

Salento has attracted wide international attention in recent years thanks to its rediscovery of popular music and local traditions. Many scholars have been intrigued by this area and have tried to analyse its peculiar phenomenon of perpetual parties and festivals. But only locals are aware of a new trend that has earned the area the nickname of 'Jamaica of Italy'. Reggae culture in Salento was born in the late 1990s in the Lecce area, from where it soon spread throughout Italy, thanks also to the growing fame of the Sud Sound System group. The best place to enjoy the rhythms of *reggae Pugliese* is Melendugno, about 30km from Lecce, which for the past 20 years has been a venue of reference for lovers of this genre.

between duelling opponents much like the concept of hip-hop. If you want to go the extra mile, you can dress in traditional Salentini clothing, although to blend in it'll be enough to wear a dark-coloured vest and a white, long-sleeved shirt for men, and a long, wide skirt for women to allow for ample leg and feet movements. For the ladies, Serena will add a final touch: a red foulard, to be swirled around the body to the rhythm of the music, a typical courtship object that women used to wear when the tradition was first born.

Classes take place year-round, and over summer this talented *pizzica* teacher will invite you for open-air sessions in her own garden, turning the experience into a more intimate workshop. The classes can be booked online and in-person as a one-off session for visitors willing to have a full-on cultural experience to grasp the vibrant Leccese way of life.

A Creamy Pastry Tour

TOURING LECCE'S BEST CAFES

The *pasticciotto* (also known as *bocconotto*) is the symbol of Salento pastry. It's typically made of a crunchy shortcrust pastry shell and a filling of custard, and the most common

Vico dei Bolognesi per Palazzo Personè
Owner Francesco moved to Lecce from Bologna to open a bistro, shop, then B&B. €€€

Amatè Suite & Rooms
A four-room B&B in Lecce's historic centre; an old Salentine house with a modern reinterpretation. €€€

Palazzo Guido
A historic residence from the 16th century that has always belonged to the Geltrude family. €€€

BEST-LOVED HAUNTS

Alessandra Ripa, manager of a Milan-based company, decided to come back to her native Lecce. She shares three gems of her hometown that she missed the most while living in the north.

The Giravolte District
One of the least gentrified neighbourhoods in the historic centre. This labyrinth of narrow streets and squares that ends with a giant fig tree in the cloister of the **Chiesa di Sant'Anna** is a masterpiece of nature.

The Covered Market of Porta Rudiae
Discover local products and chat with the sellers and people of the neighbourhood.

Chiesa di San Niccolò dei Greci
The only church where Mass is still celebrated with the Byzantine Orthodox rite in the city. A legacy of a not-too-distant past.

SABINO PARENTE/SHUTTERSTOCK ©

Pasticciotto leccese

variety also has a filling enriched with delicious black cherries. The best place to try them is **Caffè L'Incontro**, a small bistro away from the historical city centre, but worth a trip for its cheap, but tasty, *pasticciotto*. Order their equally tasty cappuccino to accompany it, but never outside breakfast time as that's considered a sin here. At **Caffè Alvino**, not far from Lecce's opulent **Basilica di Santa Croce**, owner Mr Peluso churns out the best *pasticciotti* filled with sweet ricotta cheese. If you're feeling extra indulgent, order them with freshly made gelato and dip pieces of your *pasticciotto* into the cup. Despite the post-COVID rise in prices, breakfast and *merenda* (afternoon snack) here are still affordable (5 euros on average for two people) as most of the ingredients are produced organically or bought from local producers.

Last but not least, your *pasticciotto leccese* tour should lead you to **Pasticceria La Fornarina**, a family-run cafe and bakery in business since 1979. A point of reference in Lecce, this place reminds locals of Sunday lunches with family featuring their iconic pastries, or quick breakfasts at their counter

 WHERE TO SLEEP IN LECCE

Arryvo
Less than 1km away from Piazza Sant'Oronzo, in the heart of the historical city centre. €€

Suite Hotel Santa Chiara
Housed in an 18th-century baronial palace, overlooking the splendid Piazza Vittorio Emanuele II. €€€

B&B Palazzo Paladini
A wonderful historic home in Lecce stone, but completely renovated. €€

before the school bell rang. The cafe's furniture and ambiance dating back to the 1970s will trick you into believing you've actually returned to the past.

Lecce Beyond Culture

NIGHTLIFE IN THE CITY

If you want to have fun in Lecce, you can find the heart of the *movida* (evening fun) in **Piazza Vittorio Emanuele II**. Among locals this is known as Piazzetta Santa Chiara, named after the **Chiesa di Santa Chiara** that is on one side of the square. There are a lot of pubs here where you can have a typical *aperitivo*.

On the other side of **Piazza Sant'Oronzo**, you'll find **Piazzetta Castromediano Sigismondo**. This is a simple small square where, through windows on the floor, you can see historical evidence of the Roman Empire as well as a Renaissance oil store. At night, it becomes a perfect place to hang out with friends, close to one of Lecce's most significant baroque treasures: **Basilica di Santa Croce**.

Moving towards one of the city gates, **Porta Rudiae**, you'll find **Convitto Palmieri** – a place chosen by the director Ferzan Özpetek as a location for one of his most famous movies, *Loose Cannons (Mine vaganti)*. The building has been restored several times over the years, but it was built as a convent in 1273. Nowadays, it is possible to have a drink in one of the nearby bars and to sit on the steps of the convent, just like the characters in the movie.

A DIALECT FROM THE PAST

Salento's Griko is one of the two varieties of neo-Greek spoken in Italy (the other is the Grecanic spoken in Calabria). Passed down almost exclusively through oral traditions, Griko is still officially spoken today in the 12 municipalities of Greek Salento. And after centuries, it's finally been put into writing. Take advantage of your time around Lecce to discover unusual sounds and dive into this unique linguistic history and culture.

NIGHTLIFE FUN

More of a night owl than a culture geek? **Gallipoli** (p612) less than 40 km from Lecce, will give you the crazy holiday vibes you've been craving so you can let out your party animal.

GETTING AROUND

Since Lecce's centre is quite small, it's easy to tackle it on foot – the best way to appreciate its wonderful baroque buildings. You can use public transport to reach more distant areas in the suburbs, but the best way to get around Puglia's smaller cities is by bike. Thanks to the 'Lecce safer by bike and on foot' project, the city has a new bike-sharing service. To hit the ground running, you can download the municipality's BicinCittà app, which lets you purchase, add or renew seasonal subscriptions or daily services, and unhook the bicycles without the card.

Lecce

San Mauro
Gallipoli

Beyond Lecce

Salento is not just history and culture. It's also vibrant nightlife and beaches.

A not-to-be-missed historical destination, Salento is also the 'pearl of the Ionian' and, thanks to its magnificent beaches, it's known for its decadent nightlife, best represented by the medieval seaside village of Gallipoli. The alleys of its historic centre are packed with people all summer long, its bars serving freshly fried seafood and refreshing Negronis. The typical local routine involves taking an afternoon nap to recharge for the night and then heading downtown to the seafront for an *aperitivo* at a table overlooking the Sant'Andrea island, 2km off the coast. A trendy destination with sparkling offerings typical of a seaside tourism resort, Gallipoli is the soul of the party for anyone with a youthful soul.

TOP TIP

At sunset you can have an *aperitivo* at the fish market – a way cheaper option than *aperitivi* at bars off the main street.

Gallipoli

PIOT/SHUTTERSTOCK ©

Fish market, Gallipoli

A Night Dive into Movida Salentina

UNWIND BY THE BEACH

Young Italians refer to evening fun – from *aperitivi* to clubbing – as *movida*. Gallipoli is famous for attracting thousands of young people, both locals and international, to its beaches that turn into discos after sunset. To live the Gallipoli experience like a local, after a lazy day chilling by the nearest beach and a well-deserved nap (the sea can be tiring!), head over to **Riobo**, one of Italy's most famous clubs, in this business for over two decades. Nestled in the hills of San Mauro, on a provincial road 8km from Gallipoli's downtown, it is the perfect setting for a decadent night on the tiles. The evening begins with a seafood main course and glass of white wine, as Riobo also serves as a decent – albeit overpriced – restaurant and cocktail bar. Slowly around 11pm, the sound of internationally renowned DJs begins to fill the venue, inviting guests onto the dance floor, which is covered with fluorescent lights. Customary practices suggest heading towards the nearby **Lido delle Conchiglie**, for a few impromptu *pizzica* dance moves by the beach, feet stomping fiercely on the

THE SERENE MARINE LIFE OF GALLIPOLI

Here you feel the deep and intense flavour of the sea. Gallipoli is a place that lies by the sea and lives on the sea, impregnated with its perfume and positive influence. From the fish market, dominated by the mix of bright colours of the fresh fish displayed on the fishmongers' stalls, to the fishing boats docked at the harbour and the seashells decorating shop windows – everything echoes the marine world.

WILDER TRAILS

Nightlife not your thing? If you prefer quieter areas but still love the beach and seafood, then opt for the northern villages of **Vieste** (p615) and **Peschici** (p619) in Gargano.

WHERE TO EAT IN GALLIPOLI

La Puritate
Anything fishy and fried or grilled is good, and the windows afford splendid views. €€

Baguetteria de Pace
For when you're ready to try the art of Italian fish sandwiches. €

Osteria Enoteca 15 Gradi
A relaxing atmosphere and decent prices in the new part of town, but still close to the city centre. €€

**BEST
COCKTAIL BARS**

Buena Vista
The perfect bar to
enjoy a sunset sea
view with a frozen beer
in one hand and fried
seafood in the other.

Sciarock Brewery
Taking its name from
the local word for
scirocco, you'll be
served their iconic beer
brewed in-house.

Blue Café
Good cocktails
accompanied by
plenty of finger food at
one of the few bars by
the seafront.

white sand until sunrise. Finally, **Parco Gondar** organises
an annual program of concerts and artists in its wide green
space. Open every evening, it's the place to go if you want to
grab a quick bite or sip a cocktail while enjoying a selection
of music by DJs or local bands. In summer, it's impossible to
get bored in Gallipoli.

Gallipoli's Hidden History

ITALY'S OLDEST FOUNTAIN

Not just sea and wind, Gallipoli also has historical and architectural features that are unfortunately too often overlooked.
By the bridge that connects the new to the old part of town
lies Gallipoli's Greek fountain. It's the oldest in Italy and is
said to have been built around the 3rd century BCE, though
other sources claim it dates back to the Renaissance. Scholars have recently agreed that the fascinating work is the result of several interventions that have changed its primitive
appearance, after an 18th-century counterfacade was added
to the oldest one facing south. On one facade, three scenes
from Greek mythology are depicted, as well as the coat of
arms of the King of Spain, Philip II, with the symbol of the
city on the right and left. On the other facade, dating to 1765,
are engraved the coat of arms of Gallipoli, an epigraph in
Latin and the insignia of Charles III of Bourbon, who used
to rule the area. Today this is Gallipoli's most iconic monument, a stop not to be missed even if you're in town for less
'cultural' purposes.

GETTING AROUND

Walking is the best way to explore the historic
centre of Gallipoli. But if you can't live without
the thrill of an engine, you can rent a Vespa,
and feel like a local. Keep in mind that the
city centre has the usual limited traffic areas
common to small villages, so vehicle access is
limited to certain users and hours.

Probably the most fun option to get around
and enjoy a full Italian-style experience is to
take an Ape rickshaw, a motorised gig-style
van that you can find parked at the entrance
of the old town. These vehicles are perfect for
navigating city traffic and also for reaching
the most distant beaches, such as Punta della
Suina, just a few kilometres away.

VIESTE

Rome

Vieste

Nestled between two sandy beaches atop steep white cliffs, Vieste clings to the Promontorio del Gargano, one of the most scenic places in northeastern Puglia. With its narrow alleys, draped with lines of drying clothes and its bird's eye view over the Mediterranean, the old town is an essential stop away from the bustling nightlife, and a chance to enjoy the Pugliese seaside at a slower pace. Vieste and its surroundings are for sports and nature lovers: the town's gritty harbour offers water sports for all skill levels and the surrounding Parco Nazionale del Gargano, with its scenic trails overlooking the area's white cliffs and olive-green waters, is a must for a day of cycling and hiking. Here you'll find all the ingredients you need for a big city escape and a journey through nature's tranquillity.

TOP TIP

Watch the sunset while surfing with a small group of strangers at Vieste's famed Pizzomunno beach.

Local Legends, Sea Lovers

A FISHING DEMONSTRATION

If you want to experience the real, traditional Vieste, look no further than the town's harbour. Learn secret marine legends and historical fun facts from Vieste's fishers. Like the brothers Gianni and Michele, who through their few broken English words, but lots of hand gestures, will share with you the legend of **Pizzomunno** – Vieste's iconic symbol, an imposing, 25m-high limestone monolith by the beach – handed down through oral history by locals for generations. All this as they show you how to fish with their centuries-old fishing machine, the *trabucco*.

Locals say that *trabucchi* do not only concern the work of fishers, but are a symbol of unity and nostalgia among the wider Gargano community. Every Tuesday and Thursday between May and October, a local association responsible for the historical preservation and maintenance of *trabucchi* – which are slowly disappearing with the advancement of technological tools and fishing techniques – schedules these encounters between visitors and local fishermen through the payment of a small contribution to sustain their work. And beyond fishing itself, you'll also get an engineering lesson because, once upon a time, the fishers turned into self-taught carpenters and engineers in order to build their own fishing machines. Their technical skills have been handed down orally and practically, so much so that today's construction

THE LEGEND OF PIZZOMUNNO

Vieste manages to disrupt any traveller's cynical side and awaken their love for romance. The legend of Pizzomunno, Vieste's iconic white beach, even made it into a romantic song at San Remo Festival, the Italian National Song contest. Listening to locals sharing the story of this legend – the details of which change with every person telling it – could not be any more southern Italian. This place helps you connect with the sea and its magic.

HIGHLIGHTS
1 Baia dei Porci
2 Pizzomunno
3 Pugnochiuso

SIGHTS
4 Torre del Porticello

SLEEPING
5 Albergo La Botte
6 B&B Rocca sul Mare
7 Hotel La Caravella
8 Le Ginestre
Family & Wellness
9 Relais Parallelo 41
10 Sciali

EATING
11 Masseria Sgarrazza

MORE INTO BUSTLING HOLIDAYS?

The sea is relaxing, but if for you the seaside also means partying hard then you might want to venture through Gallipoli and an evening of *aperitivi* in **Salento** (p607).

---

professionals have to refer to their teachings to learn about *trabucchi*. This is an easily accessible, yet unique activity that will help you to get under the skin of Vieste, as you listen to locals tell their stories about how people here live beneath the surface of mass tourism. And if you're lucky, you'll get to share a meal of fish fresh from the sea with them.

A Vieste Beach Tour

DIVE INTO GARGANO'S CRYSTAL WATERS

With its 800km of coastline bathed by the Ionian and Adriatic seas, Puglia is a top destination for sea lovers. In 2022 the region's beaches were awarded the

---

 WHERE TO SLEEP IN VIESTE

Albergo La Botte
The owners don't speak much English, but are incredibly friendly and will help you get around the area. €€

B&B Rocca sul Mare
In a former convent in the old quarter, it has a rooftop terrace with panoramic views. €€

Relais Parallelo 41
A small, renovated B&B with rooms decorated with hand-painted ceilings, in the heart of the old town. €€€

Pizzomunno

VIESTE ESCAPES

Matteo Silvestri, a civil engineer who comes from a family of fishermen, shares his favourite little-known gems.

Torre del Porticello
Admire one of the most beautiful sunrises in the Gargano area. The sun rises from above the sea and colours a well-kept Saracen Tower, as well as the nearby *trabucco* of Porticello, with all shades of red. Perfect for a romantic escape.

Masseria La Sgarrazza
A garrison of food and wine culture that will make your lunch, your dinner or even your overnight stay special. At night, looking at the stars from the garden will make you feel like being wrapped inside a blue blanket with glittering dots.

highest number of blue flags (a sort of Michelin star ranking for beaches). Travellers looking for less mainstream destinations than the overcrowded – albeit still stunning – Polignano a Mare in the Bari metropolitan area may find Vieste's quieter beaches a worthy detour. The area is better known by Italian tourists, and something of a hidden gem for foreign visitors, who tend to stick around Salento's seaside.

Vieste's beach tour should start with its most famous stretch of sand, the **Pizzomunno**, a romantic beach close to Vieste's old town, cradle of a poignant love legend. It is best enjoyed at golden hour, when the high temperatures fade to make room for a refreshing breeze and a majestic sunset. Just a 40-minute trip from Vieste, one of the symbolic beaches of the Gargano will unveil its landscape as you arrive by car from above. With high white cliffs dominating the view, it gives visitors a glimpse into the Gargano's wild beauty and nature. Bring a sandwich, as there aren't many food spots around.

If you're looking for a beach with better access to services, especially restaurants and snack bars, **Pugnochiuso** might be your best bet. A mixed sand and pebble beach, with

Le Ginestre Family & Wellness
Within the Parco Nazionale del Gargano, 8km from Vieste, it offers swimming pools and a wellness centre. €€

Scialì
At 300m from the sea, guests have free beach access and the use of an umbrella and sun loungers. €€

Hotel La Caravella
A modern building situated 50m from the iconic Pizzomunno beach. €€€

IL TRABUCCO

Coming down from the Adriatic, the visitor's gaze is captivated by strange wooden structures, with antennas thrown towards the sea and suspending gigantic fishing nets. This giant of the sea, the *trabucco*, was born in ancient times from the need to face the sea while keeping your feet firmly planted on the ground, as it allowed people to fish without sailing. Today, it has become a historical and cultural symbol of the simple lifestyle of locals before the tourism boom. These unique and rudimentary fishing tools, built with complex techniques by simple fishers, today seem to want to sing the ancient poetry of lost times for curious visitors.

Trabucco (fishing tower), Vieste

parking space for motorboats, it is only accessible through the entrance of a nearby resort (by paying a fee) or by sea if you rent a boat. Locals also love to suggest **Baia dei Porci**, more commonly known as 'narrow beach'. To get there, you will have to go down and up a sand dune of about 30m before you reach a small hidden corner of paradise where you can relax and take a swim in peace with yourself and nature.

GETTING AROUND

Be prepared to get around mainly on foot or by bike, because there's a consistent lack of free parking in the city centre. During the summer, due to the large influx of tourists, it is not easy to find parking spots in Vieste, which are usually not free; when you see blue lines on the ground next to a pavement, remember you'll have to pay for an hourly parking ticket, or you'll get a fine. Pedestrian islands and Restricted Traffic

Zones for residents are enforced between 8pm to 8am in the whole of downtown. So be careful if you park in the centre when these come into effect, or your vehicle may be removed. The best option is to park just outside the centre. If you stay in the historic centre, you'll have everything within easy reach. The main street is closed to vehicles at 8pm, so there'll be no need for public transport or a car to get around.

Beyond Vieste

Experience nature beyond a swim.

Although you'll find the most picturesque villages by the sea, the paths and hiking trails leading towards Parco Nazionale del Gargano are definitely worth a visit. The creeping urbanisation of this area was thankfully halted in 1991 through the foundation of this park. At 1181 sq km, it's one of Italy's largest protected areas, and represents a paradise of biodiversity, culminating in the Umbra Forest, a Unesco site rightly referred to as the 'green lung' of Puglia. With its 800m altitude, you'll find ideal temperatures for trekking even in summer. Make the most of it.

TOP TIP

On your way to the national park, make a quick detour for a snack or lunch break in Peschici; it will add around 40 minutes to reach your final destination, but the view will be worth it.

Baia delle Zagare (p620)

ANGELO CHIARIELLO/SHUTTERSTOCK ©

BEST RESTAURANTS

Al Trabucco da Mimì €€
Sitting beneath a Peschici *trabucco*, you'll eat the freshest seafood, prepared with expertise and zero fuss.

Porta di Basso €€€
Choose from one of three tasting menus at this clifftop Peschici restaurant, and prepare to be delighted.

Casa li Jalantuúmene €€
A renowned restaurant with seasonal menus and good vegetarian options.

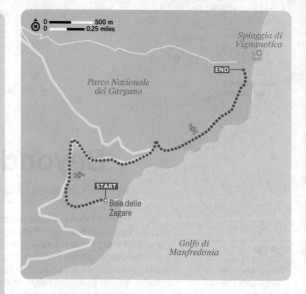

Hiking Trails with Sea Views

EXPLORING BIODIVERSITY

The **Path of Love** is one of the most scenic treks in the Gargano area, and perhaps in all of Puglia. Each step is a new surprise. Breathtaking views appear between the lush vegetation, the white cliffs plunging steeply and the intense blue sea on the horizon mingling with the sky. This 3km trek runs between two of the most famous beaches of the Gargano, and was given its nickname because of its romantic views it gained the nickname Path of Love. It can be covered in about an hour and is about 140m above sea level.

The route can be hiked in both directions: either from near **Baia delle Zagare** towards **Spiaggia di Vignanotica**, or vice versa. The trail does not start directly from Baia delle Zagare but from an access point along the SP53 road, which is located about 2km after the bay towards Vignanotica. At the access point there is a small, free parking area, with only a few spots and no services. The first steps of the trek are almost flat, then a slight climb begins.

 WHERE TO SLEEP BEYOND VIESTE

Rifugio Sfilzi
Eight rooms with three- and four-bed configurations, making them ideal for groups or families. In Vico del Gargano. €€

Locanda al Castello
Staying here is like entering a large, welcoming family home. By the cliffs in Peschici, with fantastic views. €€

Cantoniera d'Umbra
A working farm in Monte Sant'Angelo where you can rest and eat homemade food before hitting the hiking trails. €€

Shortly after, on the right, the most photographed spot in the Gargano appears in all its glory: Baia delle Zagare. This is often included among the most beautiful beaches in Italy and from the Path of Love, the view is enchanting.

You will have a picture-perfect postcard in front of you: white cliffs that plunge into the blue sea, small bays set in the rock, stacks that emerge from thewater and the vegetation that dominates and frames the entire view. Continuing on, you enter a pine forest with shaded areas and tables where you can relax. The tree you'll see here is the Aleppo pine, a species that thrives in the arid climate and lives up to 200 years.

The path finally descends and among the vegetation the high cliffs begin to appear, announcing your arrival at Spiaggia di Vignanotica, a gem in the green of the forest and the white of the cliffs. The Path of Love overlooks the sea throughout the trek but, except for the point of arrival (or departure) at Baia di Vignanotica, it never actually descends onto the beach.

The path retraces an old mule track and a wooden fence accompanies the whole journey. The route is not demanding, but the ground can sometimes be bumpy and is not suitable for buggies. It is a dirt path, with stretches of stones and pebbles, so it's better to wear suitable shoes and not flip-flops.

The pine forest that covers this promontory was damaged by a large fire in the 1990s. In the following years, maintenance and safety works were carried out on the route by the Municipality of Mattinata and the Puglia Region, so it is now a very safe trekking trail.

GARGANO'S ANIMAL MASCOT

The Gargano roe deer is an endangered native species that can only be found in the **Umbria Forest**. It is considered one of the symbolic species of the park, and is unfortunately at risk of extinction due to environmental changes. However, a few more specimens have been spotted lately, raising the hopes of local researchers. The roe deer of the Gargano promontory is a native breed isolated from the rest of Italy and therefore not genetically 'polluted' over time; for this reason, it is believed to represent the original Italic deer breed.

GETTING AROUND

From the coastal road SP53, turn towards the road that leads to Vignanotica beach. Turn left if you're coming from Vieste, or right if you're coming from Mattinata. Follow the sign for Camping Vignanotica and pass it. On the left there are various areas where you can park your car for a fee. At this point do not follow the steps to the beach (and do not take the shuttle that goes down to the sea) but head towards the path that enters the woods, near the Baia delle Zagare.

CALABRIA & BASILICATA

HISTORY AMID SOARING MOUNTAINS

Another Italy altogether, Calabria and Basilicata offer a candid travel experience full of ancient history, sparkling seas, unusual food and intriguing small-town culture.

Deeply rural Calabria and Basilicata are two of Italy's least visited regions . They're the right place to be if you want to immerse yourself in authentic local realities – not the folkloric version of Italy, but the real deal made up of many contradictions.

Calabria is Italy's slender toe, while Basilicata is the wedge between Campania and Puglia. The area is a natural marvel, ringed by 800km of blue sea backed by the thickly forested slopes of the southern Apennines. The regions contain some of Italy's most intact ecosystems in three vast parks (the Pollino, Sila and Aspromonte), quilted with villages harpooned on rocky ridges. Some shelter cultural pockets of Griko and Arbëreshë people, others medieval castles and rare relics of Byzantium and Magna Graecia.

The area's inaccessible and sometimes inhospitable nature is a blessing and a curse. It has preserved innate characteristics but also stymied development. The regions are still among Italy's poorest and there's a long history of brigandage in these hills. The 'ndrangheta, Calabria's home-grown Mafia, is considered the richest crime syndicate in the world.

Long-held stereotypes paint a picture of a backward and unchanging southern scene. But in an era of climate change and over-tourism, the slow pace of life, a strong sense of community, locavore cuisine and largely unspoiled environment make this an increasingly attractive destination.

KLIOLI/SHUTTERSTOCK ©

THE MAIN AREAS

MATERA	MARATEA	LA SILA	COSTA DEGLI DEI	REGGIO DI CALABRIA
One of Europe's oldest cities. **p628**	Low-key coastal glamour. **p635**	Immense forests, lakes and canyons. **p640**	Stunning views, beaches and boating. **p645**	Gritty art nouveau capital. **p650**

Matera (p628)

Find Your Way

Italy's toe touches two seas and features the country's most spectacular coastline, yet it's a region defined by towering mountain ranges and village culture. We've picked the best of both to get you started.

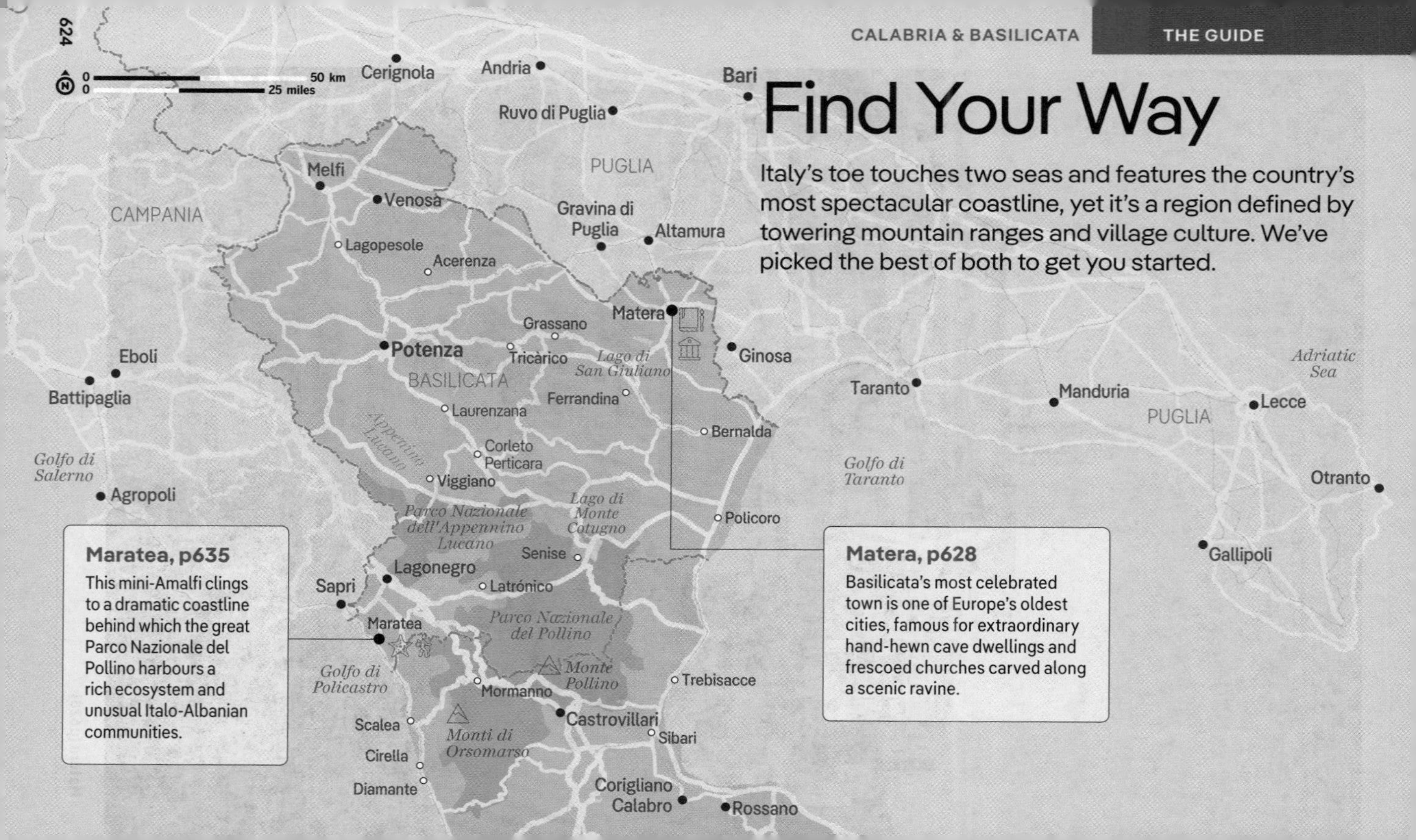

Matera, p628

Basilicata's most celebrated town is one of Europe's oldest cities, famous for extraordinary hand-hewn cave dwellings and frescoed churches carved along a scenic ravine.

Maratea, p635

This mini-Amalfi clings to a dramatic coastline behind which the great Parco Nazionale del Pollino harbours a rich ecosystem and unusual Italo-Albanian communities.

La Sila, p640

Some 736 sq km of forest interspersed by huge mirror-like lakes make up Europe's largest high plateau, where you can go boating in summer and skiing in winter.

TRAIN

Regional trains run right alongside the gorgeous Tyrrhenian coast to Scilla, Tropea and Maratea, and also to Catanzaro on the Ionian coast. A minor rail route runs through Basilicata, connecting Potenza with Metaponto and Salerno.

BUS

For mountain towns, buses are your best bet, but they are slow going. SAM Autolinee operates around Pollino's Basilicatan villages, ATAM runs a service from Reggio Calabria to Gambarie in the Aspromonte, and Ferrovie della Calabria services La Sila from Cosenza and Crotone.

CAR

The best way to explore the secluded bays and mountain villages of these regions is by car. Be prepared to navigate hairpin bends or drive long distances around large mountains; thankfully, traffic is light. In the southern Aspromonte some roads are poorly maintained.

Tyrrhenian Sea

Stromboli

Aeolian Islands *Panarea*

Salina *Lipari*

Ionian Sea

Crotone
Capo Marina
Le Castella
Cutro
San Giovanni in Fiore
Cotronei
Sersale
Taverna
Lago Arvo
Lago Ampollino
CALABRIA
Parco Nazionale della Sila
Monte nero
Cosenza
Paola
Amantea
Soveria Mannelli
Sant'Eufemia Lamezia
Golfo di Sant'Eufemia
Pizzo
Vibo Valentia
Tropea
Nicotera
Capo Vaticano
Golfo di Gioia
Gioia Tauro
Rosarno
Polistena
Palmi
Bagnara Calabra
Taurianova
Scilla
Villa San Giovanni
Messina
SICILY
Taormina
Strait of Messina
Reggio di Calabria
Melito di Porto Salvo
Bova Marina
Parco Nazionale dell'Aspromonte
△Montalto
Bianco
Locri
Siderno
Roccella Ionica
Stilo
Soverato
Catanzaro Lido
Golfo di Squillace
Catanzaro

Costa degli Dei, p645

Calabria's most stunning stretch of coastline, lapped by azure seas and dotted with cliff-backed beaches, most famously at Tropea.

Reggio di Calabria, p650

Calabria's capital is a balcony gazing towards Sicily. It's also a lively and characterful city, furnished with beaches and backed by Italy's last true wilderness.

Plan Your Time

These mountainous regions are logistically challenging. Allow plenty of time to get around, and combine coastal honeypots with forest hikes to mountaintop eyries for the full experience.

Matera (p628)

A Long Weekend

● **Matera** (p628) is unmissable. Book accommodation in the sassi (cave dwellings) area to immerse yourself in the extraordinary setting. Spend a day walking the jigsaw of alleys, making sure to visit the **Palombaro Lungo** (p630), **Madonna dell'Idris** (p630), **Casa Noha** (p630) and **MUSMA** (p631). Then trek the gravina (gorge) and book an afternoon visit to the **Cripta del Peccato Originale** (p631) for a spectacular sunset.

● With another day or two, strike out to **Montescaglioso, Bernalda** (p633) or the villages of **Tursi** (p633) or **Aliano** (p633). You can tackle one of them in the morning and then head to the beach at **Marina di Pisticci** (p634).

Seasonal highlights

Cool and constant sea breezes make summer here idyllic. But for hiking, wine tasting, foraging and mountain exploration, late spring and autumn are best.

FEBRUARY

Aliano celebrates **Carnevale** in ancient Lucanian style with masked figures and plenty of feasting.

MARCH/APRIL

Easter marks the start of the 'season' with impressive processions and re-enactments. The best are in Catanzaro, Badolato and Laino Borgo.

MAY

Hike among wildflowers in the parks and celebrate folkloric festivals like the **Madonna della Stella** in San Costantino Albanese.

GIUMA/SHUTTERSTOCK ©, FRANCESCA SCIARRA/SHUTTERSTOCK ©, REDA &CO SRL/ALAMY STOCK PHOTO ©

LAURAVL/SHUTTERSTOCK ©

A Weeklong Stay

● Pick two bases on the Tyrrhenian coast, such as Maratea and Tropea, and spend two to three days in each. In **Maratea** (p635), you can hike the incredible coastal paths or walk up a million stairs to see the Redeemer. Lounge on the cute beaches of **Fiumicello** (p636) and **Acquafredda** (p636), then head inland to the Parco Nazionale del Pollino for a day of hiking around **Rotonda** (p638 or **Raganello** (p639).

● In **Tropea** (p646), you won't be able to take your eyes off *those* views of the Aeolian Islands, which you can day-trip to. Spend your days beachside and your evenings dining and drinking in quaint clifftop towns.

If You Have More Time

● Start in **Reggio di Calabria** (p650). Visit the archaeological museum, walk Italy's finest seaside promenade and dine at some of Calabria's best restaurants. Then head into the wild **Aspromonte** national park to explore the ghost towns of **Pentedàttilo** (p655), **Roghudi** (p655) and **Bova Superiore** (p655).

● Move on to **Badolato** (p649), a stunning mountain village just 6km from the sea. From here you can visit the Greco-Byzantine villages of **Gerace** (p655) and **Stilo** (p655), and the ruins at **Locri** (p655), and still go swimming in the afternoon. Finally, head north to **Cirò** (p644), visiting the Aragonese castle at **Le Castella** (p644) en route before finishing with a world-class dinner at **Dattilo** (p644).

JULY	AUGUST	SEPTEMBER	DECEMBER
Beaches start to fill up and **festival season** breaks out, the best of which is the week-long celebration commemorating Matera's patron saint.	A party atmosphere is in full swing at the **beach**, while **hikers** head for the hills and river canyons of Pollino and La Sila.	Balmy weather at the beach; the **grape harvest** commences; festivals celebrate Diamante's *peperoncino* and Camigliatello Silano's wild mushrooms.	**Skiing** is possible in La Sila, while **Christmas** heralds living nativity scenes (*presepe vivente*) throughout the region, most atmospherically in Matera.

MATERA

Rome

Matera

Matera, *la città sotterranea* (the underground city), is an extraordinary place. It's said to be Europe's oldest city, ancient like Aleppo and Jericho. Natural caves hollowed out of a steep gorge provided shelter for Palaeolithic people, first to shepherds and farmers and later, in the 8th century, to Orthodox Basilian monks who painted their caverns with affecting frescoes recognised as unique by Unesco in 1993.

Periods of prosperity during the Middle Ages and Renaissance saw the city expand with a grand cathedral and the addition of Renaissance facades. All that was eclipsed by punishing latter-day poverty after Italian unification. In his impactful 1945 book *Christ Stopped at Eboli*, exiled writer Carlo Levi wrote, 'Christ never came this far...nor hope'.

Now, the wheel has turned full circle. Following mass public works and much EU investment, the 'Shame of Italy' (as Matera was once dubbed) is now a worthy 2019 European Capital of Culture and the location of choice for the latest Bond film.

TOP TIP

The two gorge-side *sassi* (cave dwellings) districts are accessible via an entrance off Piazza San Francisco, or take Via delle Beccherie to Piazza del Duomo and follow the tourist itinerary signs to enter either Barisano or Caveoso. Caveoso is also accessible from Via Ridola.

WHY I LOVE MATERA

Paula Hardy, writer

While anyone who comes to Matera will be blown away by its extraordinary character, seeing the city evolve over the decades has been a privilege. When I first came in the 1990s, the *sassi* still carried the weight of a hard history. Now it's a Capital of Culture with a Bond film under its belt, and its golden tufa stone literally glows in the sunlight. Better still is talking to confident young Materans about how lessons from their city's humble and self-sufficient past hold the key to many modern global problems.

Creative Conservation

A GENTLER KIND OF TOURISM

Sextantio Le Grotte della Civita is one of Italy's most unusual hotels. Distributed across a cluster of cave dwellings (including a scenic 13th-century church), it sits at the edge of Matera's spectacular ravine in the oldest part of the *sassi*, Civita. It's the brainchild of Italian entrepreneur Daniele Kihlgren, who for the last 15 years has been on a mission to save some of Italy's most beautiful *borghi fantasma* (abandoned villages), which he finds too often dismissed as 'minor' patrimony in a country of weighty historical sites.

Part philosopher, part anthropologist, Kihlgren has a vision to stay as true as possible to the character of his rural locations, offering guests a unique immersive experience. There are no frills such as television, air-conditioning or even lights. Instead, the 18 cave rooms are furnished with rough-hewn furniture and bed linens woven on traditional looms, while the chiselled walls and smooth flagstones are unadorned, leaving you to appreciate the golden glow of the tufa stone in the candlelight.

Evening aperitifs on the terrace overlooking the ravine are magical, and knowledgeable staff can arrange superb cultural tours, trekking, yoga and in-room massages. Best of all is the multicourse dinner prepared by Nunzia and Mirella, which showcases the best home cooking of the region with sophisticated simplicity.

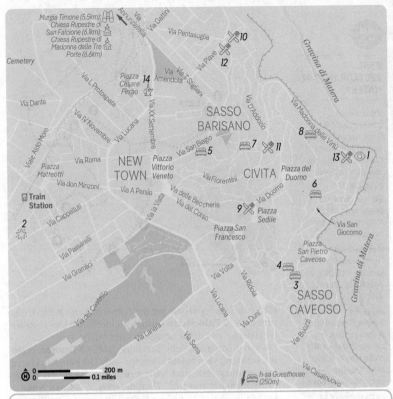

HIGHLIGHTS
1 Monasterio di Santa
Lucia e Agata alla Civita

**ACTIVITIES,
COURSES & TOURS**
2 Ferula Viaggi

SLEEPING
3 Corte San Pietro
4 Il Vicinato
5 La Casa di Ele
6 Le Dodici Lune
7 L'Hotel in Pietra

8 Sextantio L
e Grotte della Civita

EATING
9 La Gattabuia
10 MateraMi
11 Oi Marì

12 Stano
13 Vitoantonio
Lombardo

DRINKING
14 Bar Sottozero

Epic Views, Caves & Palace Museums

A WALK THROUGH DEEP TIME

Orient yourself in Piazza Vittoria Veneto, where you'll get your
first view of the Sasso Barisano from the **1 Belvedere Guer-
ricchio**. This was the richer of the two *sassi* districts, with

 WHERE TO STAY IN MATERA

Corte San Pietro
One of Matera's most
comfortable, design-led
boutique hotels in Sasso
Caveoso. €€€

Il Vicinato
A lovely B&B in a building
dating to around 1600, with
views of the Murgia Plateau. €

L'Hotel in Pietra
Nine zen-like, rock-cut rooms
furnished in understated style.
Bathrooms have stylish sunken
tubs. €€

Vitoantonio Lombardo €€€
Complex and daring cooking showcasing the best of Basilicata in a stunning cave.

Oi Marì €
Perfect pizza; the house special is topped with *pezzente* sausage.

materaMì €€
Honest country cooking including an unusual spread of antipasti.

Stano €€
Simple, flavourful dishes such as *cavatelli* pasta with *crusco* pepper, fried breadcrumbs and *caciocavallo* cheese.

La Gattabuia €€€
Contemporary fine dining in a one-time prison with an impressive Lucanian wine list.

Bar Sottozero €
Panzerotti (fried crescents of dough) stuffed with delicious local produce.

elaborate facades disguising the cave structures behind. Also here is the **2 Palombaro Lungo**, an incredible 15m-deep water cistern – one of the largest in the world.

Wander down Via delle Beccherie to the **3 Duomo**, enjoying stunning viewpoints along the way. The honey-coloured, 13th-century cathedral has recently had its frescoed interior gorgeously restored. Then descend to **4 Casa Noha**, a faithfully reconstructed cave dwelling with a multimedia exhibit that tells the story of Matera's painful recent past in unvarnished detail.

Climb back up to Piazza Sedile and turn left down Via Ridola, where you'll find **5 Museo Ridola** and **6 Palazzo Lanfranchi**. The former houses an interesting ethnographic exhibit about the region, plus some remarkable Greek pottery, while the latter holds Carlo Levi's paintings, including the panoramic mural *Lucania '61*.

Behind Palazzo Lanfranchi is the Sasso Caveoso, the site of the frescoed cave churches of **7 Santa Lucia alle Malve** and **8 Santa Maria di Idris**, the latter hewn out of a towering craggy rock. Finally, walk along Via Madonna delle Virtù

 WHERE TO STAY IN MATERA

h-sa Guesthouse
A contemporary guesthouse with a garden outside the *sassi* with free off-street parking. **€**

La Casa di Ele
A 17th-century palace whose atmospheric rooms with balconies overlook the *sassi*. **€€€**

Le Dodici Lune
A characterful cave hotel offering guests a 10% discount at the Palazzo Gattini spa. **€€**

enjoying panoramic views over the gorge to reach the atmospheric contemporary sculpture museum **9 MUSMA** and the richly frescoed **10 Chiesa San Pietro Barisano**, Matera's largest cave church.

Parco della Murgia Materana

DOWN INTO THE CANYON

In the picturesque landscape of the Murgia Plateau, the Matera Gravina cuts a rough gouge in the earth, a 200m-deep canyon pockmarked with abandoned caves and villages, and roughly 150 mysterious *chiese rupestri* (cave churches). The 80-sq-km protected park was formed in 1990 and, since 2007, included in Matera's Unesco World Heritage Site. You can hike from the *sassi* into the gorge; steps lead down from the parking place near the **Monasterio di Santa Lucia**. At the bottom of the gorge you have to ford a river and then climb up to the **belvedere** (viewpoint; the location of the crucifixion in Mel Gibson's *The Passion of the Christ*) on the other side; this takes roughly two hours and is particularly scenic at sunset.

Cave churches accessible from the *belvedere* include **San Falcione** and **Madonna delle Tre Porte**. The *belvedere* is connected by road to the **Jazzo Gattini** visitors centre, housed in an old sheepfold. Guided hikes can be organised here, as can walks to the nearby Neolithic village of **Murgia Timone**. For longer forays into the park, including a long day trek to the town of Montescaglioso, consider a guided hike with **Ferula Viaggi**. They also rent out mountain bikes and detail self-guided itineraries on bikebasilicata.it.

MATERA'S SISTINE CHAPEL

For years the myth of an immense cave church larger than any in the city circulated among the Murgia's shepherds, but it was only in 1963 that the **Cripta del Peccato Originale** (Crypt of Original Sin) was discovered. This stunning Benedictine monastery dating to the Lombard period houses 41 sq metres of impressively preserved frescoes from the 8th and 9th centuries. The apostles, Virgin Mary and scenes from Genesis are vividly depicted in a unique Byzantine style. The artist was dubbed 'the Flower Painter' due to the recurring motif of red flowers typical of the Murgia Plateau. The cave is 7km south of Matera; visits must be booked through the website, then joined at the ticket office (at Azienda Agricola Dragone).

 GETTING AROUND

Cars are prohibited in the *sassi*, so park at Piazza della Visitazione or Piazza Matteotti, or ask your hotel to advise on a private garage. Miccolis runs city services, which will get you to Murgia Timone, while Linea Sassi does a loop around the *sassi*. Small Ape rickshaws offer a taxi service in the historic centre.

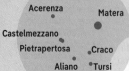

Acerenza Matera

Castelmezzano

Pietrapertosa Craco

Aliano Tursi

Beyond Matera

Matera's hinterland packs a punch with wild soaring mountains, surreal sculpted plateaus and cheerful sandy beaches strewn with ancient ruins.

TOP TIP

A car is essential in the mountains. Fuel stops are infrequent, so fill up before you leave and carry some cash.

Basilicata is one of Italy's smallest and strangest regions. There are no gently rolling hills or honey-coloured villas here. Instead, the soaring Lucanian Apennines rise to the north of Matera like an iron curtain, before plunging southwards to sunny Ionian beaches where ancient Greeks built civilised cities such as Metaponto where Pythagoras taught his theorem. The mountains are old and secretive, harbouring ruined cities like Roman Grumentum and monasteries such as Venosa's vast Abbazia della Santissima Trinità. Escher-like stone villages made of a million stairs cling to the rock face, and ghost towns like Craco hold the memory of other lives long gone.

Aliano

MASSIMILIANO MARINO/GETTY IMAGES ©

Calanchi, Aliano

The Badlands & Beaches

TRAVEL INTO THE UNKNOWN

Parts of Basilicata are like the blank spaces on old seafaring maps: a modern-day terra incognita. The area just south-west of Matera (about an hour's drive) has that feeling. Here, the bone-white terrain starts to erode into bizarre geological gullies, ridges and pinnacles as the clay plateau collapses towards the coastline. This strangely sculpted landscape is known as the *calanchi* (badlands).

The most evocative towns of the *calanchi* are eerie **Craco** (fully abandoned and the star of numerous Passion films), **Tursi** with its frescoed Arabo-Romanesque sanctuary of **Santa Maria di Anglona**, and **Aliano** where exiled Carlo Levi wrote *Christ Stopped at Eboli*. There's a small museum dedicated to Levi there, and in February the town holds Basilicata's most atmospheric masked carnival, the Maschere La Cornute (the Horned Mask Festival).

By car, you can visit the villages on a day trip, but travelling more slowly allows you to drop down from the plateau via stunning, whitewashed **Pisticci** (where Amaro Lucano was invented) to **Metaponto**, a one-time Greek colony. There you

HOLLYWOOD'S DARLING

Basilicata may fly under the tourist radar, but this otherworldly region hasn't escaped the attention of Hollywood. Films are regularly shot here and famous moviemaker Francis Ford Coppola hails from the area. His grandfather Agostino emigrated from **Bernalda** to the US in 1904, and since he sought out his ancestral home in the 1960s, Francis has been a regular visitor. He bought the 19th-century **Palazzo Margherita** on Corso Umberto and had Jacques Grange convert it into a hotel draped in frescoes and Carrara marble. It's fantastically expensive, but the **Cinecittà Bar** is open to all and worth a visit for its killer Negroni. Bernalda is a great base for exploring the area's beaches, vineyards and hill towns.

 WHERE TO STAY IN THE BADLANDS

San Teodoro Nuovo
Originally a hunting reserve, now an upscale farm-stay amid citrus groves and vineyards. €€€

Borgo San Gaetano
A beautifully renovated olive mill set around a pretty garden in lively Bernalda. €€

Taverna La Contadina Sisina
A sensational traditional restaurant with five simple rooms in Aliano. €

**Al Becco della
Civetta €€€**
Seasonal cooking
showcasing
typical dishes of
Castelmezzano; try
the forest-inspired
antipasti. There are
rooms upstairs.

**La Locanda
di Pietra €€**
A palace restaurant in
Pietrapertosa serving
top-notch Lucanian
fare, particularly cold
cuts, mountain lamb
and pork from black
pigs.

**La Dimora dei
Cavalieri €€**
A farm-stay serving
traditionally made
cheeses, pastas and
pizzas, home-grown
grains and hyper-
local wines. In Vaglio
Basilicata, near
Potenza.

Al Becco della Civetta

can visit the temple ruins of **Tavole Palatine**, where Crusaders convened, and the **Museo Archeologico Nazionale**, which houses finds from the Greco-Roman site. The best beach is at **Marina di Pisticci**, where 8km of pine-backed sand gently slope into a limpid blue sea.

Lucanian Apennines

THE MINI DOLOMITES

Weathered by wind and rain for 15 million years, the Lucanian Apennines are a dramatic mountain range that rises sharply 80km west of Matera (about 1½ hours' drive). Their weathered peaks are identified with evocative names such as Owl's Beak, Anvil and Golden Eagle. Hard as it is to believe, people have lived here since the 6th century BCE, building extraordinary villages and hulking churches above the cloud line. The most incredible are **Castelmezzano**, **Pietrapertosa** and **Acerenza**; the latter is one of Basilicata's most ancient towns, an impregnable fortress with a frescoed basilica said to hide the Holy Grail.

Atmospheric Pietrapertosa and Castelmezzano are hidden in the thick Gallipoli Cognato forest. The name Pietrapertosa (1088m) means 'pierced rock', as the village is wedged in a crack in a cliff. It is Basilicata's highest village and offers spectacular views of the Basento valley. From here you can walk the 7km trail of the **Sette Pietra** (Seven Stones) down into the valley and up to the neighbouring eyrie of Castelmezzano, which is strung out along a heart-stopping mountain ledge. Or, simply fly across between May and October on Italy's longest zip line, **Il Volo dell'Angelo**.

Those with a head for heights can also tackle the tremendous *vie ferrate* – the **Via Ferrata Salemm** or the **Via Ferrata Marcirosa** – or climb the 54 rock-cut stairs to the top of Castelmezzano's castle for a view you won't forget.

GETTING AROUND

You'll need a car and sturdy walking boots to get around these parts.

MARATEA

A sparkling, sun-drenched contrast to Basilicata's rugged interior, Maratea is a pure delight. It's the centrepiece of Basilicata's tiny strip of Tyrrhenian coast and is, in fact, a loose collection of coastal villages tumbling steeply through pine forests. The setting is idyllic and the twisting coastal road from Sapri, which hugs the cliff face above the sea, is reminiscent of the Amalfi Coast minus the throngs of tourists.

Those in the know come here seeking a refined beach holiday, although there's a surprising amount to do in the area. Of course, days can be spent lolling around in picturesque beach lidos or zipping out on boat excursions, but you can also take to the pine-clad hills for some stunning coastal hikes or make short forays inland to visit rural villages or revered mountain sanctuaries in the epic Parco Nazionale del Pollino.

Rome ✪

Maratea

TOP TIP

Maratea is a collection of small settlements with a train station located in their midst. The port is a 10-minute walk below while the historic centre, Maratea Borgo, is perched in the hills above. A bus leaves every 30 minutes from the station.

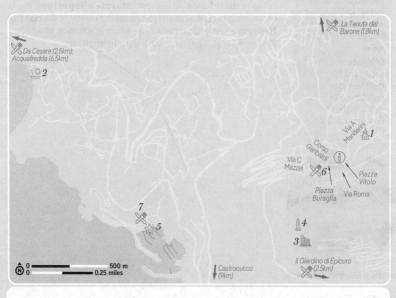

SIGHTS		ACTIVITIES,	EATING
1 Convento di Sant'Antonio	3 Maratea Superiore	COURSES & TOURS	6 Il Sacello
2 Fiumicello	4 Statue of Christ the Redeemer	5 Nautilus Escursioni	7 Ristorante 1999

BEST PLACES TO EAT IN MARATEA

Il Giardino di Epicuro €€
A Slow Food restaurant serving silky handmade pasta and fabulous antipasti.

Ristorante 1999 €€€
Simple, sophisticated seafood dishes in the port. Try the tuna with sweet onion jam.

Il Sacello €€
Elegantly executed local dishes and views over the Maratea Borgo rooftops.

Da Cesare €€
Heavenly fish dishes include ravioli stuffed with grouper, served on a terrace with gulf views.

La Tenuta del Barone €€
Meat from farm-reared Podolica cattle is the highlight. The *fiorentina* steak is immense.

Ravioli, Il Giardino di Epicuro

Coastal Views, Lidos & Cafe Lifestyle

A RETRO AMALFI

The best thing to do in Maratea is kick back and marvel at the natural beauty surrounding you. Pretty **Fiumicello** has a chic lido on an idyllic pebbled beach, while the coastline at **Acquafredda** is dotted with deep grottoes and tiny coves. Families head south to **Castrocucco**, where a large sandy beach is backed by restaurants. Boat trips with Nautilus will ferry you to secret swimming spots, or hook up a diving excursion with Centro Sub Maratea (in Porto di Maratea).

Maratea itself doesn't have a beach, but rather a chichi little port filled with yachts and ringed with restaurants. Up above, **Maratea Borgo** (the historic centre) has dozens of pastel-coloured churches. You can while away hours here wandering the alleys snapping photos or eating gelato in Piazza Buraglia. Further up the hillside is ridiculously quaint **Rivello** with its beautifully frescoed **Convento di Sant'Antonio**.

The best experience, however, is hiking the coastal paths around the headland, which offer views of the Gulf of Policastro. The tourist office in Piazza Vitolo has a booklet detailing the trails, and Maratea Outdoor Experience leads treks and horse hacks. From Via Cappuccini, you can also climb the steep hill above Maratea to poke around the picturesque ruins of the original settlement, **Maratea Superiore**. It sits on an escarpment beneath the towering statue of **Christ the Redeemer**, which overlooks the whole coast atop Monte San Biagio (644m). The drive up is equally thrilling.

GETTING AROUND

Maratea is on the railway line between Naples and Reggio di Calabria, and the station is located midway between Maratea Borgo and Porto di Maratea. Local buses pick up here. There are also local buses that connect Maratea with Fiumicello and the big sandy beach at Castrocucco. However, a car is best for beach-hopping and reaching coastal restaurants.

Beyond Maratea

Maratea ● Viggianello ● ● Terranova di Pollino
Rotonda ● ● Gole del Raganello

Rising steeply behind sleepy Maratea is the Parco Nazionale del Pollino, the largest national park in Italy, full of rare flora and fauna.

The 'Mountains of Apollo' (Pollino) are a vast 1960-sq-km range encompassing varied landscapes that are a repository of rare plants and animals. The snowcapped peaks include Monte Pollino (2248m), Serra Dolcedorne (2267m) and Serra di Crispo (2053m), also known as the 'Garden of the Gods' due to its forest of Bosnian pine, a relict species from the last ice age.

Rich in oaks, maple, beech, pine and fir, the Pollino is often snowbound, but in spring and autumn the meadows burst with flowers, fruit and edible fungi, while tiny towns celebrate esoteric arboreal festivals. Some, like San Costantino and San Paolo, are home to Arbëreshë communities, descendants of Albanians who sought refuge here from the Ottomans in the 15th century.

TOP TIP

In Rotonda, the national park information office can recommend guides, itineraries, accommodation and where to buy maps.

Parco Nazionale del Pollino (p638)

NELLA/SHUTTERSTOCK ©

FEDERICO RANO/ALAMY STOCK PHOTO ©

Ponte del Diavolo, Gole del Raganello

ART & ARCHITECTURE IN THE POLLINO

Driving through the Pollino, you'll be amazed by what you see. But if you pass a children's carousel on a summit near San Severino Lucano, you may think you're hallucinating. Don't worry, you're simply staring at Carsten Höller's contribution to **Arte Pollino**. This international art project encourages people to ponder the landscape from alternative perspectives. Swinging in the breeze on this dinky, slow-moving carousel above vast forests is a unique and meditative experience.

Further south, in Campotenese, you'll also pass a towering wedge of logs. This is **Catasta Pollino**, a cultural hub and one of the best restaurants in the park. The structure sits on the award-winning **Ciclovia dei Parchi** cycling route.

Parco Nazionale del Pollino

PRISTINE NATURE, RURAL LIFE

Given its vast scale and sparsely populated ranges, the Pollino offers a chance to experience a way of life little affected by development. Amid the flower-strewn alpine meadows and thickly forested hillsides, traditional communities go about small-scale farming and celebrate important rural festivals, such as the Marriage of the Trees, honouring the environment they live in.

Viggianello, Terranova di Pollino and Rotonda are all good bases for excursions and can be reached in one to two hours from Maratea. Rotonda is the park's official HQ where you'll find the main information office and the L'Ecomuseo del Pollino, which gives you an overview of the park's cultural and natural heritage.

Expert English-speaking guide **Giuseppe Cosenza** *(viaggiare nelpollino.it)* leads varied excursions, including summiting Monte Pollino and treks to see the 'warrior trees', as the epic Bosnian pines are known. Birdwatching, river trekking, mountain biking and mushroom foraging are also possible. **Discover Pollino** can sort foraging permits, guides and arrange mushroom-themed dinners.

 WHERE TO STAY IN THE POLLINO

Villa Crawford
A stunning, cliffside villa in the village of San Nicola Arcella at the foot of the Parco Nazionale del Pollino. €€

Agriturismo Colloreto
Set amid rolling hills outside Morano Calabro, this farm-stay has country-style rooms and a hearty restaurant. €

Albergo Villa San Domenico
An 18th-century palace with antique-filled rooms next to Santa Magdalena church in Morano Calabro. €€

If conquering summits isn't your thing, there are historic routes that connect some of the park's ancient villages, such as San Paolo Albanese and San Costantino Albanese. These isolated communities fiercely maintain their unique Italo-Albanian culture, and the Greek liturgy is retained in the main churches. Visiting during Easter and the second week of May, during the **Festa della Madonna della Stella** and the **Festa dei Nusazit**, is especially interesting. The latter involves dramatically exploding giant folkloric papier-mâché puppets (the Nusazits).

The Raganello Canyon

RIVER RUNNING, LOCAL CONNECTIONS

Plunging through frothing Class I and II white-water rapids, beneath an overarching canopy of green leaves in the gorges of the **Gole del Raganello**, is a first-rate adrenaline rush. As the Pollino drops southwards into Calabria, once-small mountain streams pick up speed and power, carving steep gashes and dark caves in the karst landscape as they power towards the sea. It is a stunning location, a Unesco Geosite and one of the 10 deepest canyons in Europe.

An hour's drive inland from Maratea, in Laino Borgo, **River Tribe** offers thrilling multi-day rafting, raftpacking, kayaking and river-walking excursions into the canyon. It was set up by professional sportsman Antonio Trani, who rafted many of the world's major rivers before returning home to reclaim a waste dump and transform it into his rafting basecamp with scenic camping and glamping sites.

It is a model of sustainable tourism – their trips are full of information about the dramatic environment you're experiencing while also working hard to connect you with local culture. Examples of this include the river trek to dramatically sited Civita, which you ascend to from beneath the Ponte del Diavolo (Devil's Bridge); mountain biking (or e-biking) to Mormanno and Morano Calabro; and the 29km rafting excursion to Grotta del Romito to see a perfectly preserved Upper Palaeolithic rock engraving of an auroch.

DEEP DIVE INTO SAN NICOLA ARCELLA

Andrea Fama, owner of Villa Crawford in the pretty seaside village of San Nicola Arcella, shares his tips on the town. *(@villacrawford sannicolaarcella)*

San Nicola Arcella
The pastel-coloured village is lovely in the evening. Explore its narrow lanes and have a drink or dinner at cool Qcècè.

Spiaggia dell'Arcomagno
This secluded cove is famous for its gigantic natural rock arch, translucent water and dazzling sunsets.

Belvedere
From this viewing terrace you get an amazing view of the Crawford Tower, Dino Island and Gulf of Policastro.

Note del Borgo
A magical festival in August when poets, painters and musicians perform all night in the most beautiful spots in the village.

 GETTING AROUND

Public transport isn't well developed in Pollino and you'll find logistics hard without a car. Your best bet is to book organised walks and arrange transfers through a walking guide or your hotel.

If you're relying on buses, SAM Autolinee serves Castelluccio, San Severino Lucano, Viggianello and Rotonda, and connects with the long-distance services of SLA to Naples from Rotonda.

LA SILA

Rome

La Sila

At the heart of Calabria are the immense forests of La Sila, now a protected national park that spans 130 sq km. Some believe it is Dante's *selva oscura* (dark forest), the place of mid-life meanderings where life's sureties are lost in a labyrinth of obscure trails. Certainly, the 12th-century theologian, Joachim of Fiore – who lent his name to the park's main town, San Giovanni in Fiore, and is buried in its medieval abbey – is given a favoured spot in *Paradise* (Canto XII).

Rather than a single unified forest, La Sila is a layer cake of different plateaus, zones and distinct woodland. The highest peaks (over 2000m) are in the Sila Grande, which is covered in beech trees, white firs and the park's signature Calabrian pine trees (from which Roman and Greek ships were built). The Sila Greca, to the north, retains strong Albanian influences, while the Sila Piccola, near Catanzaro, is swathed in a thick cloak of holm oaks.

TOP TIP

For information in English, try the visitors centre at Lorica and Taverna, or the tourist office in Camigliatello Silano. The owners of Scigliano's B&B Calabria are very helpful. Cammina Sila runs scheduled hikes and canoeing excursions.

THE GLOOMY VALLEY

From **Sersale**, in Sila Piccola, trek into the so-called **Valli Cupe** (Gloomy Valleys) – a series of deep gashes in the soft tufa bedrock. The valleys have a distinct biotope: the pinkish granite walls are hung with dangling ferns, refreshed by waterfalls and rock pools. Guides at the local cooperative (*riservanaturale vallicupe.it*) lead treks, donkey rides and 4WD excursions into the canyon, interspersing trips with visits to remote monasteries and churches.

The Dark Forest

HIKING AND LAKESIDE LOUNGING

The forests of La Sila are an arboreal wonderland: lush, cool and deeply verdant. They feel more Scandinavian than Mediterranean, and even in summer the climate is coolly alpine. Spring brings forth fields of endemic wildflowers, and in autumn the trees glow red and gold while mushrooms and truffles send locals out foraging in droves.

There are 66 park trails (600km in total) and, given their remote nature, a guide (listed on the park website) is recommended. Certainly, check in at the visitors centres in Cupone, Villagio Mancuso or Cotronei before heading out.

The best routes include the hike to **Montenero** (1881m), a bare summit offering sweeping views across the park's valleys and lakes, and to **Monte Gariglione** (1772m) on Sentiero CAI 312, which wends through ancient larch pine and silver fir forests. From **Longobucco** there's an easy hike up **Monte Sordillo** (1551m). From **Camigliatello Silano** (1272m),

 WHERE TO STAY IN LA SILA

San Lorenzo si Alberga
An acclaimed restaurant in Camigliatello with simple but chic rooms serving a stunning homemade breakfast. €€€

LorichiAmo
A contemporary chalet with balconied rooms overlooking Lake Arvo. The sauna is a bonus for trekkers. €€

B&B Calabria
A comfortable B&B in Scigliano with a terrace overlooking the forest, and a knowledgeable host. €

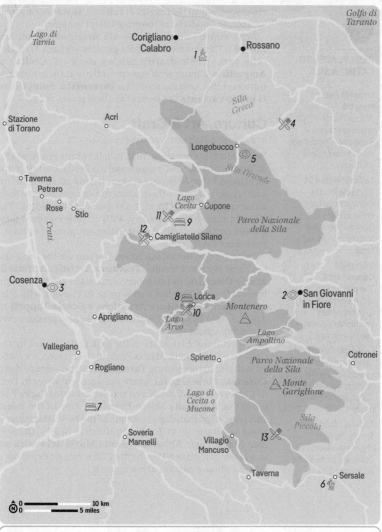

BEST PLACES TO EAT IN LA SILA

Locanda Pecora Nera €€
A Slow Food-approved tavern in Buturo serving dishes made from organic produce.

La Tavernetta €€€
First-rate food in Camigliatello based on local ingredients, from wild aniseed to mountain-raised lamb.

Silafunghi Campanaro €
The place to go in Camigliatello to satisfy every mushroom craving you've ever had.

Le Vie del Gusto €
Salami and dried vegetables are the highlights at this Camigliatello *osteria* (tavern).

Fattoria Franco €€
Simply the best cheese products in Calabria can be found in Longobucco.

make your way to the Giganti di Fallistro (Giants of Fallistro), an ancient woodland of towering Calabrian pines.

Come winter, skiing is possible at Camigliatello Silano and **Lorica** (1370m), which overlooks picturesque Lago Arvo. One of the park's four huge artificial lakes, along with **Cecita** and **Ampollino**, it hums with summer activity at the resorts and trattorias that ring the shore. **La Tavernetta**, **Spineto** and **Il Brillo Parlante** are some of the best places to eat.

Culture, Art & Craft

BYZANTINE INFLUENCES, BEAUTIFUL BLANKETS

Despite La Sila's remote setting, its folk culture reaches as far as Turkmenistan, the Caucasus and old Persia. Certainly, the local hand-loomed blankets share a striking affinity with Oriental rugs in terms of their geometric designs and the technique used to create them, known as weft brocading. The effect is much like embroidery, with brightly coloured flowers and patterns in silk floss standing out proudly against a plain wool background.

There are two workshops where you can see the craft and buy these beautiful textiles. **Tessitura Artistica a Mano di Mario Celestino** in Longobucco has made pieces for royal households and also has a showroom in Camigliatello Silano. At **Caruso Tessiture Artistiche e Scuola Tappeti** in San Giovanni in Fiore, Domenico Caruso also presides over a weaving school.

Other cultural highlights in the park include work by the Calabrian Caravaggio, Mattia Preti, in the Museo Civico and cathedral of his hometown, **Taverna**; an art promenade down **Cosenza**'s Corso Mazzini, where you'll see sculptures by Dalí, de Chirico and Modigliani; and the Unesco-listed Codex Purpureus in **Rossano**'s Museo Diocesano. One of the oldest surviving illuminated manuscripts of the New Testament, it glows as gorgeously as Rossano's cathedral. Nearby, the Norman-Romanesque **Abbazia di Santa Maria del Pàtire** set in a lovely glade has a 12th-century floor mosaic depicting a lion, a griffon, a centaur and a unicorn.

GETTING AROUND

You can reach Camigliatello Silano and San Giovanni in Fiore via regular Ferrovie della Calabria buses from Cosenza or Crotone. But you really need your own car to explore the park properly.

Beyond La Sila

Dattilo
La Sila

Shielded by La Sila's forests, the Ionian coast is a sheltered nook with sandy beaches and rolling hills covered in Italy's oldest vines.

Covering three regions, La Sila's foothills harbour Calabria's largest cities: Cosenza, Crotone and Catanzaro. Despite their outsized histories – all three were important Greek settlements in the 8th century BCE – they now have a raw, workaday feel to them.

More picturesque are the coastal vineyards that cloak the eastern seaboard. Planted by the Greeks, the local Gaglioppo grape is one of the oldest in the world, and the centre of production focuses on Cirò, Cirò Marina, Crucoli and Melissa. Indulge in a little adventure around these parts to find surprising Michelin-starred cooking, fine wineries and excellent beachside restaurants amid rolling hillsides grazed by sheep and Podolica cows.

TOP TIP

Cirò holds an epic wine festival in early August in the old Saracen markets. Cellars open to the public and restaurants put on themed dinners.

Podolica cow, La Sila

MARCO FINE/SHUTTERSTOCK ©

643

CIRÒ VINTNERS

This group of artisanal vintners are dedicated to micro-vinification using the best grapes of the local terroir. Most production focuses on the distinctive black grape Gaglioppo, which shares many characteristics with Piedmont's Nebbiolo grape.

Sergio Arcuri
A fourth-generation winemaker producing from old vines. His Più Vite has an intense deep red cherry and blood orange flavour.

'A Vita
Francesco de Franco creates surprising tastes like the masterful Leukò Bianco with hints of grapefruit, almonds and apricots.

Ippolito 1845
The oldest winery in Calabria, producing complex wines such as Ripe del Falco.

Tenuta del Conte
Mariangela Parilla produces beautiful whites from Greco Bianco that pair wonderfully with seafood.

Dattilo: A Gastronomic Detour

BEACHSIDE WINING & DINING

Krimisa, once made in Cirò Marina, was the official wine of the Greek Olympics. That's easy to believe when you find your way to Dattilo, Caterina Ceraudo's Michelin-starred *agriturismo* (farm-stay accommodation) housed in a 400-year-old mill (an hour's drive east of San Giovanni in Fiore). In 1973 her father Roberto bought some land in Strongoli on the chalky hills overlooking the Ionian Sea. A pioneer in biodynamic farming, he revived the autochthonous Pecorello grape, and now Caterina's restaurant is doing the same for Calabrian food.

Staying here is an experience. Guests can tour the vineyards with Roberto, whose love of the land is evident in his highly personal guided tastings. On other days, they'll pack a gourmet picnic for you and send you off on smart boat trips or explorations of other vineyards.

The highlight is the 12-course dinner menu, which showcases Caterina's elegant cooking. It focuses on essential ingredients, elevating flavour to an intense pitch. Local seafood, farm-grown beef and all manner of vegetables are showcased. A single, achingly sweet carrot, a bowl of intense mushroom *tortelloni*, and snapper with bergamot and sweet pink pepper are some of the highlights.

From the farm you can easily reach the beaches and seafood restaurants of Cirò Marina, other nearby vineyards and the **Marine Reserve of Capo Rizzuto**, where an Aragonese castle stands on the mythic island of Calypso.

GETTING AROUND

There are buses between Cosenza, Catanzaro and Crotone. But to explore the countryside, you'll need a car.

COSTA DEGLI DEI

Calabria's 800km Tyrrhenian coast is a combination of the beautiful and the beastly. The Autostrada del Mediterraneo (A2), one of Italy's great coastal drives, twists and turns along its length through tunnels blasted through mountains, past huge swaths of dark-green forest and endless views of cerulean-blue sea.

From the border of Basilicata, beaches link resort towns from tired Praia a Mare to quaint Diamante, famous for its chillies and bright murals. Inland, villages like Aieta and Tortora sit at the end of tortuous, ribbon-like roads. Meanwhile, the faithful flock to Paola's great sanctuary, where St Francis (the patron saint of Calabria) was born in 1416.

But the jewel in the Tyrrhenian crown is undoubtedly the Costa degli Dei (Coast of the Gods), a bulbous peninsula dressed in Mediterranean *macchia* (shrubbery) and pine trees that plunges dramatically into crystalline waters. At its centre is Tropea, a stage-set tourist town buzzing with visitors in high summer.

TOP TIP

During July and August, Tropea gets very busy. Pizzo, Parghelia, Capo Vaticano and Vibo Valentia are great alternative bases within easy reach of the town. Villa Zufrò and Porto Pirgos are two of the nicest hotels in the area.

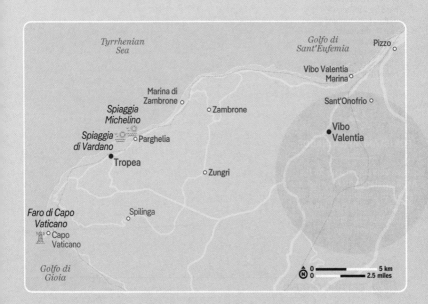

Abigail Johnson, founder of Explore Calabria with iitaly (@explorecalabria)

Don't leave the Costa degli Dei without getting out on the turquoise water! There are plenty of excursions departing from Tropea, but I prefer to explore at my own pace and rent a small motorboat from the port for the day. Fill the cooler with ice, wrap up some 'nduja arancini, and discover all the tiny beaches that are only accessible by sea. Be sure to snorkel at Capo Vaticano, then head back to Tropea by sunset for the best seats in the house – the view from the water as the sun dips behind Stromboli volcano is one of Italy's finest.

The Coast of the Gods

A SLICE OF PARADISE

This scenic, 56km spur of coastline between Pizzo and Nicotera is Calabria's most lovely, characterised by white sandy beaches, vertiginous granite cliffs and water so translucent you can watch the fish swimming in the shallows. **Tropea**, perched on a sheer cliff at its centre, is a tangle of tiny lanes and piazzas. Its crescent beaches are bath-warm and you can swim around the picturesque island atop which sits the lovely monastic church of Santa Maria dell'Isola.

At the height of summer, Tropea throngs with visitors, so it's best to spread out along the coastline. There are fabulous sandy beaches and hotels at **Zambrone** and **Parghelia**, such as **Spiaggia Michelino** and **Spiaggia di Vardano**. **Pizzo** is another pretty cliff-side town, famous for its intense *tartufo* ice-cream ball (a death-by-chocolate hazelnut truffle bomb) and charming cave-church, the Chiesetta di Piedigrotta (p648).

The best swimming, though, is at **Capo Vaticano**, the tip of the rocky headland, which sheers away into the sea and offers perfect views of the Aeolian Islands (you can visit on day trips from Tropea). Hire a pedalo from Grotticelle beach and spend the day snorkelling and paddling about. Then head up to the lighthouse, **Faro di Capo Vaticano**, for one of the most beautiful sunset views in all of Italy.

FOR ISLAND AFICIONADOS

Boat trips depart daily for the **Aeolian Islands** (p674), which are closer to Calabria than they are to Sicily. See what the different islands are like and decide where to go.

GETTING AROUND

If you're based at a resort like Tropea or Pizzo, you can manage without a car. The train line along the coast is slow but incredibly scenic and something of a highlight in itself. But if you'd like the freedom to explore all the beaches along the coast, you'll need a car.

Costa degli Dei

• Badolato

Beyond Costa degli Dei

The 43km-wide hinterland between the Tyrrhenian and Ionian coasts is packed with quaint villages, ancient monasteries and good eating.

TOP TIP

Calabria's famous *'nduja* (a spicy spreadable sausage) is made in Spilinga, which holds a festival dedicated to it on 8 August. Stock up at Salumificio Latteria Monteporo.

From Pizzo in the west to Soverato in the east is a mere 43km – the narrowest point on the Calabrian peninsula. Therefore, it has always been an important pathway, as the enormous castle in Vibo Valentia and the monastery at Serra San Bruno attest. It's walkable in three days thanks to a new georeferenced trail.

Once you hit the Ionian coast, you'll feel a change of pace. Gone are the dramatic cliffs – instead, the gentle, citrus-lined Bay of Squillace spreads before you with acres of white sandy beach. Soverato is the smart town at its centre with a fabulous beach, a botanical garden and some great summer music festivals.

Chiesetta di Piedigrotta (p648)

TOMMASO LIZZUL/SHUTTERSTOCK ©

647

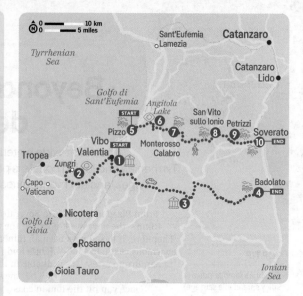

Coast to Coast

CAVES, CULTURE & THE KALABRIAN TRAIL

Behind the coastline rises the Serre massif. **1 Vibo Valentia**,
40 minutes' drive from Tropea, is the regional capital and is
set on the hillside with lovely views of the Golfo di Sant'Eufemia and a well-preserved medieval centre paved with lava
stones. Head up to the Norman-Hohenstaufen castle to potter around the Museo Archeologico 'Vito Capialbi'. It has a fine
collection of artefacts, including a large collection of unusual terracotta votive statues from the necropolis of Hippon-
ion, the Greek city on which Vibo is built. The best time
to come to Vibo is during Easter for the Affruntata, one
of Calabria's biggest festivals.

Other places to explore inland by car are **2 Le Grotte
degli Sbariati di Zungri**, an ancient cave settlement
carved into the tufa stone by Basilian monks during
the 11th century. There are about 100 caves connected
with stone stairways and a system of water channels and
cisterns. More impressive is the enormous charterhouse,
3 Certosa di Serra San Bruno, founded by the namesake
monk who turned down a bishopric to retire here. Stop for

 WHERE TO EAT IN SERRE MASSIF

Trattoria Vecchi Tempi A grill bar in Vibo Valentia where you can choose your cured meat and cuts from the counter. €€	**Il Normanno** A deeply traditional trattoria in Miletto serving *fileja* pasta and excellent salami. €€	**Lo Speziale** A restaurant in a palace in Petrizzi where you can try pasta with Calabrian liquorice. €€

lunch at Zenzero before continuing down a winding mountain road to the village of **4 Badolato**

Alternatively, you can hike across the peninsula a little further north. Georeferenced during the COVID-19 lockdown, the Kalabria Coast-to-Coast Trail *(kalabriatrekking.it)* starts at **5 Pizzo** and traverses olive groves and mountain pastures via **6 Lake Angitola**, **7 Monterosso Calabro**, **8 San Vito sullo Ionico** and **9 Petrizzi** on the Tyrrhenian coast before reaching **10 Soverato** on the Ionian coast. It takes three days and is marked with waypoints, simple B&Bs and rural restaurants.

Calabria's Kindest Village

MODERN MOUNTAIN LIFE

A two-hour drive east from Tropea, **Badolato** is an 11th-century mountain town set between two plunging valleys. It nearly joined other Calabrian *borghi fantasma* but found a route to resurrection by welcoming a ship of desperate Kurdish refugees in 1997. The *Ararat* was carrying 836 people. In contrast, Badolato's handsome old town – founded by the first Duke of Calabria, Robert Guiscard – had just 350 residents left, down from a peak of 8000.

So, instead of turning the desperate families away, the then mayor Gerardo Mannello offered to house them in the old town. The Kurds were immensely grateful and set about renovating some old homes and helping farm the surrounding fields. The effort was a huge success and attracted worldwide attention. More and more curious people arrived, including celebrities Oliver Stone and Wim Wenders. New businesses appeared, like the fantastic Torinese ice-cream parlour **Fabbrica del Gelato** and **Cicchinella** wine bar, and *badolatesi* returned from the diaspora.

Now it's a vivacious place – an unusual phenomena in a region emptied by emigration. Take a walk with **Badolato Slow Village** to hear more incredible stories and read the 'Talking Stones' carved in the walls around town. Attend the friendly Easter festivities and visit the village's 15 churches. Hike to the tranquil **Convento Santa Maria degli Angeli**, and stay for the August **Festival Insegui L'Arte**. Then return for the olive and grape harvest in autumn.

EXPLORE BADOLATO

Guerino Nisticò, a member of Badolato Slow Village *(@badolatoslow village)*

Badolato Marina
Badolato is just 15 minutes from a beautiful beach. Head to Lido Solesi for great seafood and Calabrian wine.

Easter
This is a magical time in Badolato, full of folk events, authentic encounters and an ancient religious procession called the Cumprunta.

Badolato Slow Village
Take a walk around the village with one of our guides to understand its unique history and meet some locals.

Catojo dello Spinetto
Dine in this old wine cellar overlooking the valley. Chef Ciro Piedimonte's cooking is incredible.

Nido di Seta
This silk farm is reviving the ancient art of silk production.

GETTING AROUND

A train runs along the coast between Badolato Marina, Soverato and Catanzaro Lido, but to reach the old village of Badolato and explore inland, you'll need a car. Traffic is restricted in Badolato, so check ahead with your hotel about parking.

REGGIO DI CALABRIA

Rome

Reggio di
Calabria

Port, transport nexus and the main arrival and departure point for Sicily, Reggio seems more functional than fascinating. That is up until the point you set foot inside its fabulous national museum, custodian of some of the most precious artefacts of Magna Graecia.

The city's architectural eclecticism and attractive art nouveau centre is a result of its tectonic liveliness: in 1908 the last big earthquake triggered a tsunami that killed over 100,000 people. By Italian standards, little of historical merit remains, although the *lungomare* (seafront promenade) with its views across the strait to Mt Etna is, arguably, the finest in Italy for an evening *passeggiata* (stroll).

Fortunately, there's no need to doubt the food. Reggio hides some of Calabria's best restaurants. You can work up an appetite by hiking in the nearby Parco Nazionale dell'Aspromonte or exploring the coastline, especially the charming fishing village of Scilla.

TOP TIP

The elongated grid of streets behind the *lungomare* is sprinkled with bars and pubs. They generally begin opening up around 6pm or 7pm. For a more refined drink and a bite to eat, head to Lievito or Vesper.

BEST PLACES TO EAT IN REGGIO

Lisca Bianca €€
Superbly cooked fish, like red shrimp tartare, fragrant spaghetti with clams and swordfish skewers.

La Cantina del Macellaio €€
Famous for its mixed grill, pasta with pork sauce and veal rolls. Excellent Calabrian wines, too.

La Vie del Gusto €€
A friendly place known for its sprawling antipasti plates and meaty dishes.

Cèsare €
The most popular gelateria in town, in a kiosk by the *lungomare*. Try the bergamot flavour.

Southern Warriors

ANCIENT & REAL-LIFE HEROES

Set in Marcello Piacentini's monumental marble and lava stone **Museo Nazionale di Reggio Calabria** is southern Italy's finest collection of artefacts from the colonies of Magna Graecia, which dotted the Calabrian peninsula in the 8th century BCE. Spend half a day here, and you can work your way through time from Calabria's earliest Neolithic communities to glorious Hellenistic, Byzantine and Roman periods.

The museum's crown jewels are the *Bronzi di Riace*, two godlike bronze statues of Greek warriors discovered on the seabed near Riace in 1972. They are probably the world's finest examples of ancient Greek sculpture. The finer of the two has ivory eyes and silver teeth parted in a faint Mona Lisa–like smile. Their provenance is a mystery, although they are known to date from around 450 BCE.

On a par with the museum is **L'A Gourmet L'Accademia**, Reggio's finest restaurant. It's run by Filippo Cogliandro, a world-class chef and anti-Mafia activist, whose creative dishes showcase Calabria's surprising produce, like liquorice from Rossano, swordfish from Scilla, Tropea's sweet red onions and bergamot from Reggio that once perfumed Versailles.

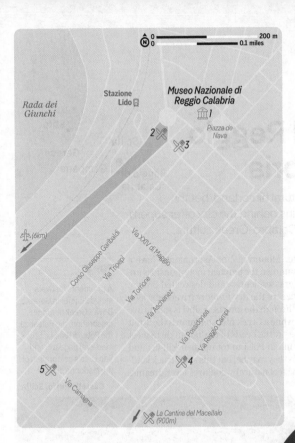

HIGHLIGHTS
1 Museo Nazionale di
Reggio Calabria

EATING
2 Cèsare
3 L'A Gourmet
L'Accademia
4 La Vie del Gusto
5 Lisca Bianca

**MORE SPLENDID
GREEK RUINS**

If you're heading over the Strait of
Messina to Sicily, you can continue
exploring the legacy of Magna
Graecia at **Syracuse**, **Selinunte**
and Agrigento's **Valle dei
Templi** (p696).

GETTING AROUND

Reggio is the gateway to Sicily. There are two
main departure ports: the Stazione Marittima in
Reggio Calabria, and the ferry port in Villa San
Giovanni, 14km north and accessible by train.
Passenger ferries depart from both. Car ferries
depart from Villa San Giovanni. This is also the
port used by Trenitalia's train-ferry.

Reggio's main train station, the Stazione
Centrale, is at the town's southern edge. Of more
use to ferry foot passengers is the Stazione Lido,
near the harbour. Trains depart to Milan, Rome and
Naples. Regional services run along the coast to
Scilla, Tropea and Catanzaro.

Reggio's airport at Ravagnese, about 5km south,
has flights to Rome, Turin and Milan.

Beyond Reggio di Calabria

Sicily is Reggio's natural hinterland, but the mysterious mountains behind the city offer superb hikes and a unique Calabro-Greek culture.

Stilo

Scilla

Gerace

Reggio di Calabria

Gambarie

Calabria's so-called 'Bitter Mountains', or Aspromonte, have a fearsome reputation. In summer, the parched mountainsides are covered in brittle blond grasses, lentisk and desiccated broom. The exposed white boulders of the dry *fiumare* (riverbeds) look like bony gashes slashed through the forests. A sibyl is said to live near Montalto's summit, while a Greek monster guards the Strait of Messina at Scilla. Some say the heads of the 'ndrangheta meet at the feast of the Madonna di Polsi to tot up their kill-list and elect a new *capo*. Tall tales they may be, but this sun-struck landscape with its lost-in-time feel naturally conjures fever dreams.

TOP TIP

Aspromonte festivals include Easter in Gerace; Bova's Greek heritage celebration, the Paleariza; the Palio di Ribusa, Stilo's medieval pageant; and San Luca's celebration of the Madonna di Polsi.

Castello Ruffo, Scilla

ANDREW MAYOVSKYY/SHUTTERSTOCK ©

MARCO RUBINO/SHUTTERSTOCK ©

Chianalea

Mythical Scilla

SNORKELLING AND SEASIDE CHARM

Scilla's painted houses cling on for dear life to the jagged promontory, ascending in jumbled ranks to the hill's summit, which is crowned by **Castello Ruffo** and, just below, the dazzling white **Chiesa Maria Santissima Immacolata**. There's not much to see in town (a half-hour train ride from Reggio), but it's worth hiking up to **Piazza San Rocco** both for the view and the epic statue of monstrous namesake Scylla. This beautiful Greek nymph angered the jealous witch Circe and was thus transformed into a monstrous half-fish, half-woman with six ferocious dog heads that thereafter terrorised sailors in the strait.

Scilla's hillside town is separated from the fishing district **Chianalea** by a tiny port. The latter sits almost directly in the water, its terraces propped up on pontoons. It is only accessible on foot or by little Ape taxis that ferry people up and down. Swimming off the town's sandy beach is glorious, as is boating and diving in the rich volcanic waters. **Scilla in Barca** runs excursions along the coast, while **Scilla Diving Centre** can get you kitted up for dives.

VIEWS OF THE VIOLET COAST

For heavenly views of the Strait of Messina, head out along the **Sentiero dei Tracciolino**, a dramatic panoramic footpath that starts above Palmi and hugs the coast all the way to Bagnara Calabra. It's 7km long and takes 2½ hours to hike with glorious views of the Aeolian Islands all the way. More demanding is the circular, 18km-long **Sentiero dell'Aquila**, or Path of the Eagle (aspromonteoutdoor. it), which takes eight to nine hours.

Otherwise, drive up to **Monte Sant'Elia**, above Palmi, for a breathtaking view from the belvedere. Come at sunset to see the sky blur from gold to pink to that deep shade of violet that gives this coastline its name.

✖ WHERE TO EAT IN SCILLA

Caluna
A contemporary osteria with a limited menu of seafood and regional wines. The pasta is the highlight. €€

Osteria del Centro
Behind the church of San Rocco, this place serves great meat dishes and the ubiquitous swordfish. €€

Glauco
Enjoy delicious grilled fish and ravioli stuffed with aubergine and shrimp on a romantic deck over the water. €€

POLONIO VIDEO/SHUTTERSTOCK ©

Gerace

APHRODITE'S APPLE

Citrus bergamia (Calabrian bergamot) grows in the final foothills of the Aspromonte between Villa San Giovanni and Gioiosa Ionica. Its essential oil is a key ingredient in perfumes, as it is used to fix aromatic bouquets and heighten fragrance. It also has antiseptic and antibacterial qualities prized by big pharma and can be used in teas, confectionery and cakes. This makes it the most sought-after citrus in the world.

Azienda Agrituristica 'Il Bergamotto' is a bergamot plantation and a fine *agriturismo* run by Ugo Sergei. Here you can stay amid the citrus and olive groves and dine on tasty country cooking. Ugo can help arrange excursions into the Aspromonte on foot or on donkeys.

Otherwise, head for **Lido Paradiso**, from where you can squint up at the castle while sunbathing with your fellow Calabrian holidaymakers. Then follow their lead and head to **Dali City Pub**. This Beatles tribute beach bar serves cold beer and *pesce spada* (swordfish) sandwiches with a view of Stromboli.

Aspromonte Grecanica

INTO THE WILD

Carved up by seasonal torrents, Aspromonte's mountains are awesomely beautiful. Underwater rivers keep the peaks covered in coniferous forests and ablaze with flowers in spring. It's wonderful walking country, crisscrossed by trails. **Gambarie**, an hour's drive from Reggio, is the main town and the easiest approach to the park. The roads are good and the park office can advise on activities and guides.

More challenging to reach are the last Grecanico communities in the jagged peaks at the tip of the peninsula. They cluster around Bova and preserve the last vestiges of a Greek community descended directly from the western Byzantine Empire of the 6th century CE, harking back to Magna Graecia. Access is from the SS106 south of Reggio. From here

WHERE TO STAY & EAT IN THE ASPROMONTE

Borgo Pentedattilo
An unforgettable experience – a renovated rural house in a spectacular ghost town; see borgopentedattilo.it. €

Al Borgo di Mafrica Marcello
Fresh ricotta, stewed goat and *lestopitta* are served at this Greek-influenced trattoria in Bova Superiore. €

Qafiz
Fine dining from Nino Rossi; the tasting menu is enhanced by foraged wild herbs and mountain produce. €€€

you can climb inland up hairpin roads to the superbly sited Byzantine castle of **San Niceto**, the abandoned village of **Pentedàttilo** on the slopes of Monte Calvario, and ghostly **Roghudi Vecchio**, which nearly fell from its rocky ridge during the 1971 floods, prompting the villagers to evacuate.

From Roghudi it's possible to hike to **Gallicianò**, **Condofuri**, **Amendolea** and **Bova Superiore**, where you'll have a sweeping view of the mountains and Mt Etna. Calabria's last Greek-speaking people inhabit this handful of towns, preserving their ancient traditions and dialect. Co-operative San Leo in Bova and Naturaliter in Condofuri can help you find guides and accommodation.

Ancient Villages, Monasteries & Ruins

ARCHITECTURAL TREASURES

At the northern fringes of the Aspromonte are the charming Byzantine villages of **Gerace** and **Stilo**. They sit in the hills behind ruined **Locri Epizephyrii**. Once a powerful Greek city, Locri was reputedly settled by Greek slaves who eloped with the wives of their masters. You can wander the ruins and visit their treasures in the **Museo e Parco Archeologico Nazionale**, 3km south of Locri.

Due to constant Saracen harassment, Locri was abandoned in the 10th century and the residents moved uphill to **Gerace**, a spectacular and unspoilt medieval hill town, a 20 minutes' drive inland. It is full of striking architecture like the Byzantine **Chiesa di Santa Maria del Mastro**, the Gothic **Chiesa di San Francesco** and the epic **Castello Normanno**. The soaring Byzantine-Romanesque **Basilica Concattedrale di Gerace** is the largest church in Calabria and contains tapestries by Jan Leyniers. Give yourself time to wander Gerace's quaint streets. In July, there's a street art festival called Borgo di Incanto.

An hour's drive further north is **Stilo**, a Byzantine beauty with a dramatic mountain backdrop. It, too, is scattered with charming churches. From the clay-brick **Cattolica**, a Greek-Byzantine temple, the view over the Ionian coast is stunning. It gets better if you climb up **Monte Consolino**, where you'll find the grottoes of Basilian hermits. A community of six Orthodox Romanian monks still tends to the atmospheric **Monastero di San Giovanni Theristis**, which sits 8km outside of town.

Aspromonte villages host fantastic festivals, including the Easter celebrations in Gerace; Bova's Greek heritage celebration, the Paleariza; Pentedattilo Film Festival; the Palio di Ribusa, Stilo's medieval pageant; and, San Luca's celebration of the Madonna di Polsi, the most revered pilgrimage site in these mountains.

BEST PLACES TO EAT ON THE IONIAN COAST

A Squella €
Traditional Calabrian cooking in Gerace with valley views. Try the homemade pasta.

Gambero Rosso €€€
Stunningly elegant, Michelin-starred fish dishes in Gioiosa Ionica. Its *crudo* (raw seafood) is famous.

La Buca del Re €€
Ancient oil cellar in Stilo serving top-notch charcuterie and handsome plates of homemade pasta.

'A Lanterna €€
A fabulous *agriturismo* with organic country cooking near the Greek ruins of Caulonia.

GETTING AROUND

It is possible to reach Gambarie from Reggio Calabria by bus on the ATAM city bus 319. For any further exploration, you'll need your own car and a head for hairpin bends. Note that the roads to the mountain villages in the south are not well maintained.

ROLF E. STAERK/SHUTTERSTOCK ©

Cefalù (p670)

THE MAIN AREAS

PALERMO
Architectural masterpieces
and extraordinary food. p662

LIPARI
Island-hopping paradise
promising slow escapes. p672

CATANIA
Urban springboard for
Mt Etna forays. p680

SICILY

ETERNAL CROSSROADS OF THE MEDITERRANEAN

Byzantine to baroque, Arabic to anti-Mafia: nowhere else in Italy does the ancient and modern collide with such attitude and cultural sass.

In the Sicilian capital, footsteps from the sea, Palazzo Butera slumbers in the shadow of an ornate elevated walkway, designed in the 19th century for mourning widows to promenade in peace. The experimental gallery inside offers no descriptive panels or labels with displayed artworks – it's all about using your intuition to appreciate the ensemble.

The same goes for the entire intoxicatingly storied island – a mash-up of old, new, chaos and calm, which, with its offshore archipelagos, forms an autonomous region in Italy. For centuries, Sicily enticed Greeks, Carthaginians and Romans into its bewitching, devilishly handsome lair. Later rule by Byzantines, Saracens, Normans, Germans, Angevins and Spanish blessed Sicily with an embarrassment of artistic and architectural riches that remain a star attraction. Stirring your soul with shimmering-gold Byzantine mosaics, baroque stucco or toe-tapping jazz in a medieval monastery is a drop in the ocean when it comes to encountering Sicilian dolce vita – even dolce far niente (p770).

The Sicilian kitchen, crafted from multiple cuisines, only intensifies the sensory feast. Island produce – sun-spun capers, olives, almonds and pistachios, wild saffron, ricotta, shellfish, tuna and swordfish – has been the magic ingredient ever since Bacchus planted vines near Taormina and the Greek god of blacksmiths fired up his forge inside Mt Etna. In the face of earthquakes, volcanoes and modern Mafia menace, it is farmers and artists who keep the Sicilian cart turning.

VINCENZO SCARANTINO/SHUTTERSTOCK ©

SYRACUSE	AGRIGENTO	TRAPANI
Theatrical Greek ruins and superstar baroque towns. p687	Sicily's most magnificent archaeological site. p695	Small port town with nature-rich seascapes. p699

Find Your Way

Lounging in sun-spangled turquoise waters between the toe of Italy and Tunisia, 160km southwest, Sicily promises seafaring and land adventures in spades. This is the Mediterranean's largest island, but the major sights still remain eminently navigable in a couple of weeks.

THE GUIDE

SICILY

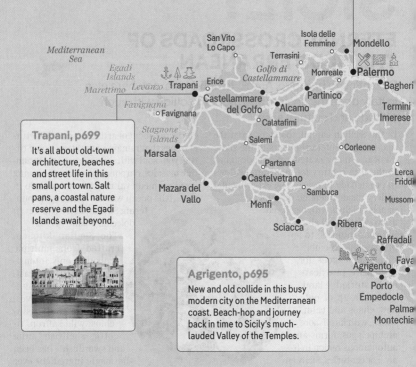

Tyrrhenian Sea

Ustica

Mediterranean Sea

Egadi Islands

Marettimo *Levanzo* **Trapani**

Favignana ○ Favignana

Stagnone Islands

Marsala

Mazara del Vallo

Menfi

San Vito Lo Capo

Erice

Castellammare del Golfo

Calatafimi

Salemi

Partanna

● Castelvetrano

Sambuca

Sciacca

Terrasini

Golfo di Castellammare

Alcamo

Isola delle Femmine

Monreale

Partinico

Corleone

Ribera

Mondello

Palermo

Bagheri

Termini Imerese

Lerca Friddi

Mussom

Raffadali

Fava

Agrigento

Porto Empedocle

Palma Montechia

Trapani, p699

It's all about old-town architecture, beaches and street life in this small port town. Salt pans, a coastal nature reserve and the Egadi Islands await beyond.

Agrigento, p695

New and old collide in this busy modern city on the Mediterranean coast. Beach-hop and journey back in time to Sicily's much-lauded Valley of the Temples.

Pantelleria
○ Pantelleria

CAR

Driving in traffic-busy Palermo and Catania is a headache, but motoring along the coast and inland is generally pleasurable and stupendously scenic. Rural mountain roads can be single-lane and pot-holed. The A18 and A20 *autostrade* (motorways) are toll roads. Away from towns, electric vehicle charging stations are scarce.

BUS & TRAIN

With the exception of Trenitalia trains trundling scenically along the Tyrrhenian coast between Catania and Trapani, buses are generally faster and more frequent. Private operator Ferrovia Circumetnea *(www. circumetnea.it)* runs trains around Mt Etna. Across the board, Sunday services are limited.

BOAT

Regular car-passenger ferries cross the Strait of Messina from the Italian mainland to Sicily, and once on the island a flurry of high-speed hydrofoils and slower *traghetti* (ferries) sail to Sicily's off-shore Aeolian and Egadi islands. Boats run year-round, with reduced schedules in winter.

Palermo, p662

Sicily's capital is an intoxicatingly chaotic city, seductively spiced with Byzantine mosaics, Arabic domes, frescoed cupolas and sensational food.

Lipari, p672

An ideal island-hopping base, the Aeolians' largest and liveliest island delivers pebble beaches, tasty dining, artsy shopping and a rugged hinterland to hike.

San Vincenzo (Stromboli Town)

Stromboli

Aeolian Islands

Panarea

Salina

Santa Marina Salina

Alicudi   *Filicudi*

Lipari   Lipari Town

Vulcano Porto

Vulcano

Palmi

Golfo di Milazzo

Milazzo

Golfo di Patti

Villa San Giovanni

Messina

Capo d'Orlando

Patti

Barcellona

Reggio di Calabria

Golfo di Termini Imerese

Cefalù

Santo Stefano di Camastra

Sant'Agata di Militello

Straits of Messina

Castelbuono

Tusa

Parco Regionale dei Nebrodi   Mt Soro

Mistretta

Francavilla di Sicilia

Mélito di Porto Salvo

Caltavuturo

Pizzo Carbonara

Randazzo

Taormina

Petralia Sottana

Cesarò

Linguaglossa

Giardini-Naxos

Parco Naturale Regionale delle Madonie

Nicosia

Troina

Parco dell'Etna   Mt Etna

Bronte

Giarre

Leonforte

Agira

Regalbuto

Adrano

Zafferana Etnea

Enna

Catenanuova

Nicolosi

Acireale

San Cataldo

Caltanissetta

Paternò

Catania

Pietraperzia

Misterbianco

Canicattì

Barrafranca

Piazza Armerina

Golfo di Catania

Riesi

Scordia

Lentini

Ravanusa

Mazzarino

Caltagirone

Augusta

Grammichele

Golfo di Augusta

Niscemi

Vizzini

Sortino

Licata

Gela

Chiaramonte Gulfi

Canicattini Bagni

Floridia

Syracuse

Golfo di Gela

Vittoria

Comiso

Palazzolo Acreide

Fontane Bianche

Ionian Sea

Scoglitti

Ragusa

Noto

Avola

Modica

Marina di Ragusa

Scicli

Rosolini

Ispica

Pozzallo

Pachino

Catania, p680

Bargain with fish vendors at dawn, scale an active volcano by day, and dance until dawn in a Unesco-listed old town in Sicily's second-largest city.

Syracuse, p687

Ancient Graeco-Roman splendour meets antique island elegance and a string of towns stitched from late-baroque architecture on Sicily's southeastern coast.

Mediterranean Sea

N   0   50 km
    0   25 miles

659

LEONORI/SHUTTERSTOCK ©

Plan Your Time

Avoid cramming your itinerary with too many glittering *palazzi* (mansions), gem-packed galleries and time-wizened ruins. Pepper sightseeing with sea dips, scenic walks and memorable feasts.

Cattedrale di Palermo (p665)

If You Only Do One Thing

● Throw yourself into the labyrinthine historic centre of **Palermo** (p662), where dizzyingly beautiful churches, artisan workshops, street markets and edible temptations enthral. Begin with crown jewel **Cappella Palatina** (p664) in **Palazzo dei Normanni** (p663) and the **cathedral** (p665). Skyline views from its roof terrace are unmatched. Grab street food for lunch at **Mercato del Capo** (p662).

● Hop on a bus to **Cattedrale di Monreale** (p669). Back in Palermo, watch the setting sun turn **Fontana Pretoria** (p662) pink over drinks at rooftop **Le Terrazze del Sole** (p663). Dine at **Gagini** (p666) and enjoy late-night cocktails at **Farmacia Alcolica** (p664).

Seasonal Highlights

Summer is sizzling hot. Spring, with its bouquet of wildflowers, and summer's tail end are ideal for hiking, swimming and diving. Autumnal harvests are a foodie delight.

APRIL
Religious processions, barefoot parades and marzipan lambs mark **Easter week**. On the Aeolian Islands the first capers ripen.

MAY
Roses bloom and the first sun-spun fruits are picked. Salt is harvested (until August) from shimmering **salt pans** in western Sicily.

JUNE
The first beach lovers descend on the coast. Rooftop bars, beach restaurants and sun-lounger rentals usher in the **summer season**.

EMILY MARIE WILSON/SHUTTERSTOCK ©, IPICS/SHUTTERSTOCK ©, ALEX SEGRE/SHUTTERSTOCK ©

Three Days to Travel Around

● Begin in **Catania** (p680), rebuilt in lava after an earthquake in the 17th century. Explore its markets, shopping and buzzy nightlife. Day two, climb the lofty heights of **Mt Etna** (p684) to appreciate the Herculean proportions of this active volcano and the rich biodiversity – vineyards included – it fuels.

● Take a train to **Syracuse** (p687) to explore one of the ancient world's most powerful cities, rival to Athens. Amble from the papyrus-fringed spring of **Fonte Aretusa** (p688) on Ortygia island to altars and grottos in the **Parco Archeologico** (p688). After dark, watch a summertime play beneath stars in the ruined **Greek theatre** (p689).

If You Have More Time

● Trace the footsteps of 18th-century romantics on a Grand Tour. Begin in **Palermo** (p662), regal home of Norman kings. Day-trip to beach-bum fave **Cefalù** (p670). Head southwest to port city **Trapani** (p699) and beyond to awe-inspiring temple ruins at **Segesta** (p704), **Selinunte** (p705) and the Valley of the Temples at **Agrigento** (p695). Linger to explore wild beaches and the photogenic **Scala dei Turchi** (p695) along Agrigento's coastline. From **Syracuse** (p687), serenade baroque beauties in the Unesco-listed **Val di Noto** (p691) and catch Greek drama in **Taormina** (p686). End on a natural high with fireworks on **Mt Etna** (p684) or an island adventure in the **Aeolian archipelago** (p675).

JULY	AUGUST	SEPTEMBER	OCTOBER
Prices and temperatures soar. Open-air concerts entertain. Blockbuster sights like the **Valley of the Temples** stay open late.	Beaches sizzle (temperature and crowds). Islanders feast on figs and fresh carob pods. Segesta's **theatre festival** opens.	Wine towns celebrate the **grape harvest**. Beach clubs and restaurants shut by the month's end. The first pomegranates ripen.	Autumn brings wild mushrooms, colourful foliage and **harvest festivals** in mountain villages. The olive harvest is in full swing.

PALERMO

With a history stretching back nearly 3000 years, Siciliy's complex metropolitan capital is the result of centuries of dizzying highs and crushing lows. Palermo was conquered by the Arabs in 831 CE and when the Normans invaded in 1072, Roger I (1031–1101) made the old Greek port the seat of his enlightened 'kingdom of the sun', encouraging resident Arabs, Byzantines, Greeks and Italians to remain.

Contemporary Palermo is stitched from rebellion, bravery, squalor and solidarity. It's a place where Piero wraps a huge block of ice in cloth each morning for another day at the market; where reformed juveniles bake biscuits to sell in artisan kitchens. Talented street artists take up arms against the Mafia, and locals chat in Albanian and Arabic in this heavily spiced melting pot of history and cultures. Be inquisitive. Peek into that citrus-filled cloister, bewitching cherub-spun chapel or trash-strewn back alley, and you will be astonished by what you find.

★ Rome

Palermo ●

TOP TIP

Lap up Palermo's chaotic vibe on foot. New town main streets Via Maqueda and Via Vittorio Emanuele meet at Quattro Canti (Four Corners) to slice the historic centre into four vibrant quarters: Alberghería, Il Capo, La Kalsa and Vucciria.

LUNCH STOP

Palermo's premier fruit-and-veg market, **Mercato del Capo** feels as souk-esque as it did when Arab traders, pirates and slave merchants peddled goods in its streets in the 9th century. Watch your pockets as you mill with the crowd through **Porta Carini**, an original city gate rebuilt in 1782. Stalls piled high with fist-sized lemons, beakers of fresh coconut and wild strawberries pack **Via Porta Carini**. Sample the morsels on sticks offered by boisterous street-food vendors push. **Sit & Mancia** (No 63) is one of several spots to sip local Birra dei Vespri craft beer and lunch on *pastelle* (deep-fried slices of seasonal veg), pistachio-stuffed sardines or marinated swordfish.

Quattro Canti

BACKSTAGE AT THE SUN THEATRE

Not only does Quattro Canti – as the elegant intersection of Via Vittorio Emanuele and Via Maqueda is commonly known – mark the epicentre of Palermo's sizeable old city. The iconic square (officially Piazza Vigliena) is also nicknamed **Il Teatro del Sole** (Theatre of the Sun) because of the light show that unfolds each day on its perfect circle of curvilinear facades.

Return to these bustling crossroads at different times of the day to catch the sun lighting up a different building – unlit facades disappear up to the china-blue vault of the sky in a clever display of perspective. Religious believers preaching 'speakers-corner style', waiting taxis blaring music on portable loudspeakers and horse-drawn carriages only add to the show.

Fontana Pretoria

SUNSET DRINKS AT THE FOUNTAIN OF SHAME

So scandalised were Sicilian churchgoers by the flagrant nudity of the cheek-baring nymphs, tritons and frolicking river gods sculpted in marble on **Piazza Pretoria**'s monumental fountain that they dubbed it Fontana della Vergogna (Fountain of Shame). Designed by Florentine sculptor Francesco Camilliani between 1554 and 1555 for the Tuscan villa of Don Pedro de Toledo, it was bought by Palermo in 1573

HIGHLIGHTS
1 Cattedrale di Palermo
2 Chiesa e Monastero
di Santa Caterina
d'Alessandria
3 Fontana Pretoria
4 Museo Archeologico
Regionale Antonio
Salinas
5 Palazzo dei Normanni
6 Quattro Canti

EATING
7 Gagini
8 Grattatella all'antica
no Zu' Vicè
(see 6) Grattatella da
Tonino
9 I Segreti del Chiostro

**DRINKING
& NIGHTLIFE**
10 Le Terrazze del Sole

in an effort to outshine the newly crafted Fontana di Orione in Messina.

The play of light on the nudes posing in Fontana Pretoria's tiered basins is theatrical any time of day – and never the same twice. Return several times to admire the whimsical scene in different lights. Come sunset, enjoy it from above over alfresco drinks at **Le Terrazze del Sole**, the rooftop bar of Palermo's historic Grand Albergo Sole (now Hotel B&B Palermo Quattro Canti) on Via Vittorio Emanuele.

Palazzo dei Normanni

GLITTERING MOSAICS IN A ROYAL PALACE

Norman Sicily's compelling cultural complexity is beautifully evoked at Palermo's star attraction: Cappella Palatina, squirrelled away like a rare jewel inside the **Norman Palace** (also called Palazzo Reale). The landmark monument, built by conquering Arabs on the highest point of the city in the 9th century, morphed from defensive fortress to pleasure palace with the arrival of the Normans in Palermo in

 WHERE TO SAVOUR STREET FOOD IN THE HISTORIC CENTRE

Mercato di Ballarò
Vintage pushcarts hawking *sfincione* (Sicilian-style pizza) and stalls grilling *stigghiola* (goat intestines) alfresco. €

Biga
Pizza slices with seasonal toppings, many Slow Food-endorsed, on dough naturally leavened for 48 hours. €

Friggitoria Chiluzzo
A kerbside kiosk with Palermo's best *pane e panelle* (sesame bread with chickpea fritters) and *cazzilli* (potato croquettes). €

BEST MAFIA INSIGHTS

No Mafia Memorial
Learn Mafia history and tune into the anti-Mafia movement at Via Vittorio Emanuele 353.

Teatro Massimo
Stand on the steps where the iconic Mafia shooting scene from Francis Ford Coppola's *Godfather III* was shot.

Muro della Legalità (Wall of Legality; 2022)
This mural on Piazza degli Aragonesi honours 26 unsung heroes who've died in Sicily's ongoing anti-Mafia fight.

Falcone & Borsellino Mural (2017)
Street artist Rosk e Loste's portraits of slain anti-Mafia magistrates Giovanni Falcone and Paolo Borsellino dominate La Cala port.

ECSTK22/SHUTTERSTOCK ©

Fontana Pretoria (p662)

ARAB-NORMAN TREASURES

From 1130 to 1194 the Normans collaborated with Byzantine and Arab architects to transform Greek temples into basilicas. Palermo's Capella Palatina, **Cattedrale di Monreale** (p669) and Cefalù's **Duomo** (p670) are the stars of this period.

the 11th century. Since 1947 it has been the seat of the Sicilian Regional Assembly.

The lavish **royal apartments** can be visited Friday to Monday: admire the Sala d'Ercole (Hall of Hercules) where the Regional Assembly convenes on the other days of the week; the king's bedroom; and the Sala dei Venti (Hall of Winds) with Byzantine mosaics and 18th-century wooden ceiling.

But it is the shimmering-gold **Cappella Palatina**, designed by Roger II in 1130 in the palace loggia, that takes your breath away. The Norman king brought in the finest Byzantine Greek craftsmen to inlay the chapel's interior with gemstones and marble. The detail, expression and movement captured by the figurative mosaics are extraordinary. Revel in the life of Christ, the Saints, Prophets and Evangelists in the presbytery; *Cristo Pantocratore* (*Christ All Powerful*) and angels in the apse and dome; and the Old Testament in the central nave.

WHERE TO GO FOR LATE-NIGHT COCKTAILS

Mak Mixology
Cocktails are paired with modern cuisine at this chic bar in a 1930s shopping gallery off Via Maqueda.

Terzo Tempo Cocktail Lab
Superb signature cocktails (try Sicilian Shepherds!) or customise with your favourite boutique gin, rum or whisky.

Farmacia Alcolica
Chink cocktails with urban hipsters in a funky interior crafted from flea-market finds.

Cattedrale di Palermo

ROYAL TOMBS, TREASURES & ROOFTOP WALK

A sensual feast of geometric patterns, ziggurat crenellations, majolica cupolas and blind arches, Palermo's **cathedral** is a larger-than-life example of Sicily's unique Arab-Norman architectural style. Above its magnificent triple-arched entrance, admire the beautiful painted intarsia decoration depicting the tree of life in a complex Islamic-style geometric composition of 12 roundels featuring fruit, humans and all kinds of animals. It's thought to date back to 1296.

The cathedral's interior, while impressive in scale, is essentially a marble shell whose most interesting features are the **royal Norman tombs** (to the left as you enter, containing the remains of two of Sicily's greatest rulers, Roger II and Frederick II of Hohenstaufen) and the **treasury** (see Constance of Aragon's gem-encrusted 13th-century crown, made by local craftspeople in fine gold filigree, and silver reliquaries safeguarding a tooth and ashes of Santa Rosalia). Save the best for last: the cinematic spiral up 110 steep stone steps to the cathedral's **roof terraces**, with panoramic city views.

On the cathedral's southern porch, look for a column inscribed with a passage from the Koran. This detail is all that remains of the 9th-century mosque on which construction of the cathedral began in 1184. Over time the building has been much altered, sometimes with great success (as in Antonio Gambara's 15th-century three-arched portico that took 200 years to complete and became a masterpiece of Catalan Gothic architecture), and sometimes with less fortunate results (Ferdinando Fuga's clumsy dome, added between 1781 and 1801).

Museo Archeologico Regionale Antonio Salinas

ANCIENT TREASURES IN A CLOISTER GARDEN RETREAT

Bookworms rejoice: the **cloister garden** at this Renaissance monastery-turned-Sicily's oldest public **museum** is heaven on earth. Plant yourself on an old stone bench beneath banana trees and contemplate the courtyard collection of Phoenician sarcophagi from the 5th century BCE (or simply read your book in meditative silence).

All three courtyards at Palermo's archaeological museum are stunning: water turtles frolic in a

FATIMID ART

In the **Cappella Palatina's** trio of naves, don't forget to look up. A lively menagerie of camels, lions, griffins, scribes, musicians, wrestlers, nude belly dancers and various other profane court entertainers of the day practically pop off the vaulted ceilings. Carved in wood and painted by Muslim artists, the ceiling is a rare example of 12th-century Fatimid art in the Mediterranean basin and unique for a Christian church. Inscriptions in Kufic script surround the blaze of Islamic star-shaped polygons, while between the ceiling and walls, ornately wood-carved *muqarnas* drip down like honeycomb.

FOR ARCHAEOLOGY EXPLORERS

The ancient powerful city of **Selinunte** (p705) ranks among Sicily's most captivating archaeological sites. Pair it with Greek ruins at **Segesta** (p704) to make a thrilling road trip. Visit in March and April when surrounding fields blaze yellow with wild fennel.

 WHERE TO DINE EXCEEDINGLY WELL

Le Cattive	**Osteria Ballarò**	**Ciccio ... in pentola**
Sophisticated dining by Sicily's Tasca d'Almerita winery, with sea-facing tables on the Mura delle Cattive. €€€	It's strictly Sicilian produce all the way at this stylish, Slow Food–approved *osteria* (tavern) in former *palazzo* stables. €–€€	Creative fish and seafood dishes paired with excellent service make this elegant *ristorante* a local foodie favourite. €€

fountain in the first; and ancient and modern worlds collide in the centrepiece glass-ceilinged courtyard displaying a life-size reconstruction of a pediment from Temple C at Selinunte (p705). Allow ample time for the original decorative friezes from Selinunte – the detail, such as Actaeon being torn apart by dogs as punishment for seeing Artemis naked, is utterly thrilling.

Chiesa e Monastero di Santa Caterina d'Alessandria

BAROQUE ART & BIRD'S EYE VIEWS

A 360-degree old-city panorama jostles for the limelight with baroque masterpieces at this early-14th-century **hospice-turned-convent**. Its rooftop terraces alone demand unlimited swooning.

Allow two hours to explore the elaborate, richly decorated interiors. The single-nave church, built between 1580 and 1596, tips its hat to the Italian Renaissance with its frescoed dome depicting the *Triumph of the Holy Dominicans* (1751) by Vito D'Anna and intricate filigree ornamentation in gold leaf and marble inlays. On the sumptuous main altar, a tabernacle encrusted in amethyst and lapis lazuli gemstones dazzles. Prolific baroque artist Filippo Randazzo executed the vault fresco depicting the *Triumph of St Catherine* (1744), and notable 17th-century paintings by Vincenzo Marchese and Giacomo Lo Verdo – students of baroque master Pietro Novelli – adorn the side chapels.

End your visit with a sinfully good *minni di vergine* ('virgin's breasts', a white cake with a candied cherry on top) from Santa Catarina's 1st-floor *pasticceria* **I Segreti del Chiostro** ('The Cloister's Secrets'). Devour it in peace in the monastery's majolica cloister, ringed with perfumed orange trees and balconied cells overlooking an 18th-century fountain by late-baroque Palermo sculptor Ignazio Marabitti (1719–97).

Gagini

FINE DINING IN A RENAISSANCE ART STUDIO

Palermo sumac, Nubia garlic, Mediterranean crab and lobster, yellow Monreale plums, Ispica sesame and pungent *cucina* (caper flowers) from the Aeolian island of Salina: experience gourmet heaven with local foodies at the contemporary kitchen of Italian-Brazilian chef **Mauricio Zillo** – Palermo's only Michelin-starred address. Reserve well in advance to bag a

---

 WHERE TO STAY IN PALERMO

B&B Dimora Sinibaldi	**Stanze al Genio**	**B&B Hotels – Hotel Palermo Quattro Canti**
Enjoy lavish, homemade breakfasts and 360-degree city views from rooftop terraces at this *palazzo* B&B in La Kalsa. €€	Overnight among majolica tiles in the extraordinary, 16th-century *palazzo* house-museum of art collector Pio Mellina. €€	Unmatched central location and rooftop restaurant-bar render this hotel excellent value. €–€€

table in the 16th-century mansion – the Renaissance workshop of Palermitan sculptor Antonello Gagini (1478–1536), it's a contemporary gallery for local artists whose canvases hang on exposed gold-stone walls. Skip lunch to max out on the eight-course tasting menu.

Grattatella Carts

THE OLD-FASHIONED ART OF KEEPING COOL

Track down a roving pushcart selling *grattatella* – ice scratchings, hand-scraped from a hefty block of ice wrapped in a cloth and served in a plastic beaker with fresh fruit syrup. Lemon is classic, but **Grattatella da Tonino** serves mint, tropical rose, orgeat, cola and a rainbow of other modern flavours from the brightly painted cart often parked around the intersection of Via Maqueda and Via Vittorio Emanuele on Quattro Canti.

Piero Caccamo works the cart of his late father-in-law Vincenzo Tirenna, a Palermo legend nicknamed '*il re della grattatella*' ('the king of *grattatella*'), who crafted the city's iconic summertime thirst-quencher for 40-odd years from his **Grattatella all'antica no Zu' Vicè** cart in front of Teatro Massimo. Look for Piero juicing fresh pomegranates and scratching ice to order opposite Via Porta Carini 20 in Il Capo.

MORE STREET FEASTS

Follow your nose (literally) to Vucciria's market-busy Piazza Caracciolo where weather-beaten *mèusari* Rocky Basile doles out some of Palermo's best *pani câ mèusa* (spleen-and-lung buns) from his mobile pushcart. In Catania, **La Pescheria** (p682) is another unforgettable spot for foodies to street feast.

THE GUIDE

SICILY

BEST HIDDEN GARDENS

Giardino Bistro Al Fresco
Drinks and zero-kilometre cuisine by reformed juveniles, in a plumeria flower garden.

Chiesa di San Giovanni degli Eremiti
Escape to a stone bench beneath a pomegranate tree at this soulful, ruined, 12th-century church.

Giardino Garibaldi
Grab *panelle* to go from celebrated sandwich shop Francu U Vastiddaru and scoff under the aerial roots of Palermo's oldest fig tree.

Orto Botanico
Solace for weary urban souls, these prestigious botanical gardens tell the story of Palermo's diverse landscape.

GETTING AROUND

Getting to town from Palermo's Aeroporto Falcone Borsellino, 35km northwest of downtown, is swift and efficient. Whether you opt for the train or the bus, count on about 50 minutes to Palermo Centrale train station and adjoining Via Tommaso Fazello bus station.

Hands down, the best way to explore central Palermo is on foot. Wear sturdy, comfortable shoes or sandals – flimsy flip-flops don't fly – to combat uneven pavements, dusty streets and slippery stone paving.

Or use apps to find free-floating wheels: try Ridemovi for regular and electric bikes; Tier, BiT, Link, Helbiz or Bird for e-scooters. There's almost always a line-up of scooters and bikes – alongside three-wheel Piaggio Ape city taxis – on Piazza Giuseppe Verdi, Piazza del Parlamento and other major squares.

Mondello
Palermo Cefalù
Monreale

Beyond Palermo

Palermo's location assures restful green landscapes, sandy beaches and serene islands – all only a short bus trip, electric scoot or boat ride away.

From patron saints who sought peace and solitude on Monte Pellegrino to Sicilian kings and nobles who landscaped hunting grounds rich with partridges and pheasants, the need to flee the noise, dirt and crowds of old Palermo is an intrinsic element of the city fabric. Urban Palermo's natural charisma is indisputable, but when the need for respite kicks in, the city delivers with soul-soothing side trips.

A Sicilian proverb says that whoever visits Palermo without visiting Monreale arrives a donkey and leaves an ass. The reason: this hillside village claims one of Europe's greatest examples of Norman architecture, World Heritage–listed Cattedrale di Monreale. Shimmering gold mosaics coupled with commanding views over Palermo and the Tyrrhenian Sea make a half-day here non-negotiable.

TOP TIP

Tours whisk day-trippers off to Mondello and Monreale (hotels have details), but it's cheaper and easy to DIY with public transport or hop-on hop-off City Sightseeing (city-sightseeing.it/en/palermo).

Cattedrale di Monreale

ROMAN BABAKIN/SHUTTERSTOCK ©

Statue of William II, Cattedrale di Monreale

Cattedrale di Monreale

SICILY'S TEMPLE OF GOLD

Travel back in time to the architectural pomp of the Italian Middle Ages in a hilltop village. Walking up from the bus stop at the foot of **Monreale** (take AMAT line 389 from Palermo's Piazza Indipendenza), it's hard to believe that such a humble spot could have ensnared Sicily's finest example of Norman architecture, built by William II to upstage his grandfather Roger II's efforts in Cefalù and Palermo.

In the cathedral's golden mosaic interior, scout out Noah's ark perched atop the waves, Rebecca watering camels, Christ healing a leper infected with leopard-sized spots, the murder of Abel, and Adam and Eve. Medieval mosaicists hailed from Sicily and Venice, but the stylised influence of the Byzantines pervades their work, completed in 1184. To know what you're searching for, buy the €1 brochure mapping out all 42 biblical scenes in the cathedral bookshop. In the romantic **cloister**, look for William II offering the cathedral to the Madonna. End with the cathedral **terrace** with celestial aerial views of the cloister garden, the cathedral's majolica rooftops and the city of Palermo lounging on the horizon by the sea.

REDISCOVERING BAGHERIA

Suzanne Edwards, co-author of *Sicily: A Literary Guide for Travellers*.

Long in decline, Bagheria has undergone something of a rebirth. The town was a summer retreat for Palermitan aristocracy and several of their *palazzi* can be visited. The most fascinating is **Villa Palagonia** (1715). The circular building is beautiful in itself, but the garden wall displays the most surprising aspect: fantastical statuary, from periwigged aristocrats to horse-headed gargoyles and hunch-backed gnomes. Rumours circulated about the owner's motivation, the most colourful of which suggested that the statues were satirising his wife's many lovers. Locals refused to look at them – especially pregnant women – believing they were cursed.

WHERE TO GET GREAT GELATO

Gelateria della Piazzetta
Crunchy almond, liquorice and cinnamon are standout flavours at this Monreale hang-out, with tables on a teeny piazza.

Caffè Traina
Hike up the steps from Ustica's port to the village to uncover the islander favourite for gelato since 1931.

Latte Pa
Does it get any better than brioche oozing mulberry, pistachio or watermelon gelato on Mondello's beachfront?

JOIN THE PARTY

Only the sons of local fishers can take part in **Ntinna a mari**, the grand finale of Cefalù's annual festival on 6 August celebrating its patron saint. The ancestral tradition sees 17 men in swim shorts attempt to walk across a 16m-long pole balanced above the water at il Molo to retrieve a flag of San Salvatore. The narrow pole is greased with fat, assuring hilarity all round.

Traditionally, this four-day fest – ending with midnight fireworks on the beach – is the time to devour Cefalù's signature dish, *pasta 'a taianu*. Derived from the Arabic *taoio*, the word for a terracotta dish, it layers two types of shredded meat (beef, lamb or pork meat) with aubergine, tomato sauce and *pecorino* cheese in a terracotta dish.

Ntinna a mari, Cefalù

Mondello Beach Life

PALERMO'S SUMMER PLAYGROUND

On summer weekends, don your shades and hop aboard AMAT bus 806 on Palermo's Piazza Sturzo or charter a motorboat from La Cala to decamp to the city's favourite beach resort. A one-time muddy, malaria-ridden port, golden-sand Mondello has been fashionable since the 19th century when aristocrats built opulent summer villas here. Gorge on old-school glamour on the Liberty-style pier and bathing establishment from 1913, now top-notch restaurant **Alle Terrazze** with on-trend *crudo* (raw seafood) bar and unmatched sunset sea views.

Sacred Allure in Cefalù

CATHEDRAL MOSAICS, GELATO & APERITIVO

You only have to follow the crowd streaming along Cefalù's pedestrian, shop-lined **Corso Ruggero** to Piazza Duomo to feel its sacred allure. Go with the flow – and be prepared to stop dead in your tracks at first sight of Cefalù's soaring golden-hued fortress of an Arab-Norman **Duomo**.

Entering on Via Passafiume, climb the spiral staircase at the back of the nave to scale one of the cathedral's twin towers. Bird's-eye views of Cefalù's enchanting old town tease as you climb, and the rooftop panorama of town, mountains and Tyrrhenian Sea is quite dizzying.

Back down by the altar, show your ticket to access the privileged viewing point of the cathedral's celebrated mosaics in the central apse. A towering figure of Cristo Pantocratore (Christ All Powerful) is the shimmering focal point of these elaborate Byzantine mosaics – Sicily's oldest and best preserved, predating those of Monreale by 20 or 30 years. Take your time to absorb the scene of a compassionate-looking Christ, holding an open Bible bearing a Latin and Greek inscription. Spot the Virgin with Four Archangels dressed as Byzantine officials. Continue to the sacristy, with an altar in front of a window opening onto the sea; the treasury bursting with 12th- to 19th-century treasures; and a romantic cloister garden with ancient columns supporting graceful Arab-Norman arches.

Back amid the crowds on cafe-clad Piazza Duomo, relax over a morning coffee or *aperitivo* (pre-dinner drink) spritz at **Duomo Gelatieri dal 1952**, with terrace tables spilling across the square. Or grab a signature cannolo-flavoured gelato or *affogato al caffè* (espresso with vanilla gelato) to go.

 WHERE TO SCOFF CEFALÙ'S 'PASTA IN A PAN'

Tinchité
This taverna, with a foliage-shaded terrace, celebrates local produce. Kudos for the backstories on its menu. €€

La Botte
For over three decades, this family-run restaurant in the old town has served flavoursome local and Sicilian classics. €€

La Trinacria
Sea views and top-notch *pasta 'a taianu* justify the 10-minute walk to this clifftop eatery in an old pasta factory. €€

Climb La Rocca

SUNRISE HIKE, RUINS & VIEWS

Looming large over Cefalù, this imposing rocky crag was once the site of an Arab citadel, superseded in 1061 by the **Norman castle** whose ruins still crown the summit. Climbing its heady heights along **Salita Saraceni**, an enormous staircase that winds dramatically through Aleppo pines and three tiers of city walls before emerging onto rock-strewn upland slopes, rewards with spectacular coastal views.

Below the windy summit, drone-esque views of the cathedral and old-town red rooftops from the castle's old crenellated ramparts are equally dramatic. Lower down again, picnic tables beneath trees by the ruined 4th-century-BCE **Tempio di Diana** (signposted 'Edificio Megalitico') provide a peaceful lunch spot. To access La Rocca, follow Vicolo Saraceni uphill from Corso Ruggero, and expect the hike to take around 45 minutes.

Escape to Capo Cefalù

LOCAL BEACH LIFE & SNORKELLING

Downtown Cefalù's sweep of action-packed golden sand needs no introduction – crescent-shaped **Spiaggia di Cefalù** is one of Sicily's best sand beaches. To flee the crowd, follow locals to Capo Cefalù, a cape with a vintage **lighthouse** (1900) and clear, turquoise and emerald waters for snorkelling.

From the Duomo, walk downhill along Corso Ruggero then right along Via Porpora until you reach dry limestone walls built by the Greeks in the 4th and 5th centuries BCE. Duck through the *postierla* – a passage cut in the megalithic walls so dwellers could access a fresh spring flowing out of the cliff – to arrive by the sea. Follow the paved path, steps and bridges along rocks to dip in beautiful shallow pools and snorkel in the sparkling big blue.

SNORKELLING IN PARADISE

Rising out of cobalt-blue waters off Sicily's northeastern coast, the volcanic **Aeolian Islands** (p675) pepper 1600 sq km in the Tyrrhenian Sea and were clearly created with snorkelling enthusiasts in mind. Nowhere else are gin-clear waters quite so rich in aquatic flora and fauna.

ITALY'S TASTIEST LENTILS

Sampling the famous brown lentils cultivated on tiny volcanic **Ustica** is well worth the 90-minute hydrofoil ride from Palermo's ferry port. Try them as *polpettine di lenticchie* (lentil meatballs) in Ustica village at **Trattoria Da Umberto**. Or head 1.8km west to **Agriturismo Hibiscus**, an organic lentil farm with self-catering accommodation and a small museum exploring the island's agricultural and seafaring traditions. Learn how lentil plants are sown with horse-drawn ploughs in December, harvested and dried in June, then crushed and 'sieved' by hand to sort the lentil from the 'straw' during the traditional *Pistata delle lenticchie*.

GETTING AROUND

Buy return bus tickets (€2.80) for Monreale before boarding the bus from the ticket kiosk next to the bus stop, on the eastern (Royal Palace) side of Palermo's Piazza Indipendenza. Watch for pickpockets – ditto for jam-packed buses to/from Mondello. Liberty Lines hydrofoils to Ustica fill last in high season – book return tickets online a day or so in advance *(https://booking.libertylines.it)*.

LIPARI

Rome
Lipari

Home to some 12,000 islanders year-round – double in summer – lively Lipari is the Aeolians' largest and most accessible Island. For first-time visitors, stepping off the boat from the Sicilian 'mainland' in bijou port Marina Lunga is a relaxing introduction to laid-back island life. If you're returning from the outer Aeolians, the intrusive din of screeching *motorini* and shouting street touts pushing boat trips is tantamount to landing in a big city.

Lipari town was settled by the Greeks and destroyed by an earthquake in 365 CE. Its pastel-coloured waterfront and car-free main street today bely its standing as the archipelago's transport hub. A dozen volcanoes sculpted the island's windswept highlands, precipitous cliffs and rugged Mediterranean *macchia* (scrubland); and many islanders still mete out a living selling pumice stones and jewellery embedded with glassy deep-black obsidian extracted from ancient volcanic deposits on the island's northeastern coast.

TOP TIP

A grand tour of Lipari takes about an hour by car or scooter. With more time, hike or use buses and private minivans: check bus schedules, including for pebble beaches on the northeast coast (Spiaggia di Canneto is the closest to Lipari town), at the port.

THE LIPARI PAINTER

In the ancient Greek empire, prized pottery came from Lipari. Vases containing jewellery, cosmetics and other goods to be placed in sarcophagi with the deceased were formed in terracotta and painted with intricate patterns. By the 4th century BCE ceramists were illustrating sophisticated stories of the deceased (always female) preparing for the marriage of their soul to a divinity. One such master was the Lipari Painter who, between 300 and 260 BCE, painted elaborate compositions on ceramics in rich earthy colours. His signature was an egg-shaped motif, from which laurel branches burst forth.

Historic Castello di Lipari

FIVE MILLENNIA OF HISTORY

After 'red beard' pirate Barbarossa rampaged through Lipari in 1544, murdering most of the town's menfolk and enslaving its women, the island's Spanish overlords sensibly fortified the settlement. It is in their impressive clifftop **citadel** (1556) that island history comes alive.

Approach it on **Via del Concordato**, a steep photogenic stairway that climbs up from central Via Garibaldi (opposite No 104) to **Cattedrale di San Bartolomeo**. A beautiful example of 17th-century baroque architecture, the Aeolians' 'mother church' replaced the 11th-century Norman cathedral also destroyed by the ruthless Barbarossa. Head next door to 18th-century Palazzo Vescovile (Bishop's Palace), home to the prehistory section of the top-drawer **Museo Archeologico Regionale Eoliano**. Unravel Lipari's intriguing backstory, from early Neolithic settlers to Roman Lipára, through trichrome painted pottery, copper and bronze artefacts, lava-stone votive offerings, marble carvings and finely sculpted tools handcrafted from obsidian.

The archaeological museum romps through six further citadel buildings. Shipwrecked amphorae, the world's largest collection of miniature Greek theatrical masks and exquisite painted ceramics from the Greek necropolis of Lipari steal the show in the **Sezione Classica**. A riveting portrait of the Aeolians' oldest industries – the extraction of sulphur

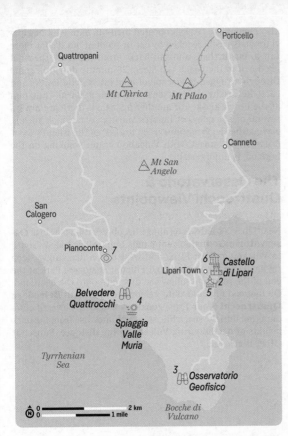

HIGHLIGHTS
1 Belvedere Quattrocchi
2 Castello di Lipari
3 Osservatorio
Geofisico
4 Spiaggia Valle Muria

SIGHTS
5 Cattedrale di
San Bartolomeo
6 Museo
Archeologico Eoliano
7 Pianoconte

on Vulcano and of alum, pumice and obsidian on Lipari – and its volcanoes unfolds in the **Sezione Vulcanologica**. Break between sections in the tree-shaded **archaeology garden**, littered with remounted sarcophagi from the 4th and 5th centuries BCE. Catching a summer performance with sea views at the open-air amphitheatre here is a treat.

Swim at Spiaggia Valle Muria

A DAY AT THE BEACH

Cradled by cliffs and sun-spangled emerald waters, this **pebbly beach** on Lipari's southwestern shore is a dramatically beautiful swimming and sunbathing spot. The journey is

 WHERE TO EAT IN LIPARI TOWN

Kasbah
Trendy candle lit garden with wood-fired pizzas, creative pasta and local swordfish (fresh from May to September). €€

Osteria Liparota
Tuck into burrata with island figs and anchovies or seared tuna at this jovial *osteria* with tables in one long line on the street. €€

Gilberto e Vera
Well-stuffed *panini* named after customers embrace every taste and mood at this decades-old, family-run icon. €

WANDER AEOLIAN PATHWAYS

Centuries-old mule tracks and steep footpaths stray across the island's rugged interior. Where only farmers once trod to reach isolated vineyards, terraced olive groves and caper fields, hikers now explore. Signage can be erratic; it's best to walk with a naturalist guide or conservation biologist from **Nesos** (nesos.org). The local environmental organisation sells the excellent hiking guide *15 Best Walks in the Aeolian Islands* (€7) at its Lipari office at Corso Vittorio Emanuele 24 and arranges guided birdwatching and botanical walks, archaeology treks and mountain-bike tours (minimum five people, €20 per person, reserve in advance).

also memorable. The signposted turn-off, 3km west of Lipari town, is easily reached by car or scooter, but it's far more fun to bus it there and sail back. From the road, the final leg down to the beach is a steep, 25-minute downhill romp through a rugged landscape of long grass, wildflowers and cacti. Return by sea with local boat captain Barni – find him at the beach kiosk – or another boat taxi; there are always several on the quays at Lipari's Marina Corta (book ahead). Navigating the *faraglione* (rock towers) of the island's western shore at sunset, with Vulcano's crater smoking on the horizon, is unforgettable.

The Osservatorio & Quattrocchi Viewpoints

ISLAND PANORAMAS AT SUNSET

Near Lipari's southwesternmost tip, observation platform **Osservatorio Geofisico** commands unparalleled views south to Vulcano and Mt Etna, and west into a dizzyingly steep ravine backed by Alicudi and Filicudi at sunset. Park at the end of the road and follow the dirt path onto the headland. On the road to Pianoconte, celebrated viewpoint **Belvedere Quattrocchi** (Four Eyes) cooks up giddying views of cliffs plunging into the sea, while smoke plumes rise from the dark heights of neighbouring Vulcano in the distance. Sunset at either is celestial.

Hiking, Lipari

GETTING AROUND

Many hotels outside of Lipari town include transfer from the port in their rates; if they don't, they can arrange a minivan pick-up. Beach restaurants and bars can give you the name and mobile telephone number of taxi boats they work with; otherwise find taxi boats at Marina Corta and Molo di Canneto. Book ahead by phone.

March to October, kiosks at Marina Lunga and numerous agencies in town sell tickets for organised day trips to other Aeolian islands. It's also easy to DIY: buy tickets at least a couple of days ahead in high season, either online or at the Liberty Lines ticket office at Marina Lunga.

Download the smartphone app to buy tickets for local Urso buses (ursobus.it).

Beyond Lipari

Island-hopping around the Aeolians is a treat for seafaring adventurers sailing off into the Tyrrhenian Sea.

Filicudi   Salina

Alicudi   Lipari
               Town

    Vulcano

Book scooters, rental cars and taxis before arrival. Few outlets stock bikes; the few roads are steep and perilously narrow. On Stromboli, book guided volcano treks to 400m (any higher is off-limits) well before arrival.

While the island of Lipari has a generous share of crystalline waters and beautifully remote beaches, most visitors can't resist a boat trip to another Aeolian island. Salina (20 minutes north by hydrofoil) and Vulcano (10 minutes south) are each close enough to fit into separate half-day jaunts from Lipari – although both warrant far longer. To really appreciate the raw beauty, languid pace and harsh reality of island life on bijou Alicudi and volcanic Stromboli – roughly two hours west and northeast respectively – stay a couple of days; Alicudi and Salina make a practical pairing.

Wherever you choose to sail to, set your compass for spectacular vistas and whitewashed villages, dazzling black-sand beaches, naturally sustainable marine cuisine (don't miss *spaghetti alla stromboliana* with wild fennel, mint, anchovies, cherry tomatoes and breadcrumbs on Stromboli) and a privileged sprinkling of off-beat adventure.

Harbour, Santa Marina Salina (p677)

ALFIYA SAFUANOVA/SHUTTERSTOCK ©

AEOLIAN ECO-PADDLES

Explore Aeolian coastlines, caves and beaches from a different perspective – afloat a sea kayak or stand-up paddleboard, during the day, at sunset or by night. From his home base on Vulcano, passionate kayaker, guide and eco-warrior Eugenio Viviani at **Sicily in Kayak** leads half-day, day and multi-day expeditions around the different islands. Sea adventurers eager to dip, duck and dive can combine paddling with swimming, snorkelling and coasteering (rock scrambling, climbing and diving) on a sit-on-top kayak trip. If you're an eco-paddler, sign up for one of Eugenio's beach cleanups by kayak – he organises four full weekends a year dedicated to cleaning up beaches in Vulcano and Lipari.

PASCAL BOEGLI/ALAMY STOCK PHOTO ©

Boat tour, Grotta del Cavallo

Scoot Around Vulcano

TWO-WHEEL ROAD TRIP

Stepping off the hydrofoil at the port, the overpowering bad-egg reek instantly makes you question the wisdom of a day trip to the volcanically active island of Vulcano. Rest assured, away from the hydrofoil dock the vile pong of sulphurous fumes emanating from the island's dramatically smoking crater dissipates.

Head south along the waterfront, past kiosks selling boat tours to iridescent sea cave **Grotta del Cavallo** and natural swimming pool **Piscina di Venere**. Turn right along Via Provinciale to rent wheels at **Luigi Rent** (*nolosprintdaluigi.com*). The island is only 20.9 sq km but surprisingly hilly, so you're probably best with a classic Italian, Hepburn-style scooter or e-bike (Luigi's open-sided Mini Mokes are hot too). If you've forgotten your snorkel, hiking boots or want to dump your rucksack for the day, this is the place.

Hit the main road south, cruising sinuously uphill for 7km to **Capo Grillo**. The island panorama from this breathtaking viewpoint – of Lipari and Salina, with Panarea, Stromboli and Filicudi floating in the distance – is unmatched. Continue south to the minuscule fishing port of **Gelso**. Lunch on the morning's

 WHERE TO STAY & EAT ON VULCANO

Hotel Faraglione
Location alone renders this two-star, port-side hotel exceptional value. €

Malvasia
Try the finest *pane cunzato* – plate-sized bread soaked in olive oil and piled with toppings – in the Aeolian archipelago. €

Trattoria da Pina
Two local men do the fishing and their families do the cooking at this seaside trattoria in Gelso. €€

catch at family-run **Trattoria da Pina**, and enjoy a siesta and afternoon swim on black-sand **Spiaggia Cannitello**. Returning north to Porto di Ponente, taste island wine with passionate winemaker and artist Giuseppe Livio at **Soffio sulle Isole**. A sunset *aperitivo* at this beautiful vineyard estate, glass of volcanic red or sweet Malvasia in hand, is out of this world.

Taste Produce in Salina

SALINA CAPERS & HONEY-SWEET WINE

Salina's good fortune is its freshwater springs. It is the only Aeolian island with significant natural sources and residents on this green, twin-peaked island have put them to good use: they produce their own style of wine, Malvasia, and – as proud *salinari* will tell you – the archipelago's finest capers (caper rivalry between islands is fierce).

From port town **Santa Marina Salina**, bus it to the seaside hamlet of **Lingua**, 3km south. Handwritten signs outside islanders' homes advertise home-grown capers, *caperoni* (caper berries), curcuma and oregano for sale. Next to the bus stop, look for the trailhead to the Aeolians' highest point **Monte Fossa delle Felci** (962m; 2½ hrs). On lower slopes the trail passes the pea-green vineyards of **Azienda Agricola Carlo Hauner**. Call ahead to arrange a winery tour and guided tasting of its classic reds, whites and signature Malvasia delle Lipari Passito DOC with Carlo, Andrea or another family member. Grandfather and painter Carlo Hauner nurtured the first vines in the late 1960s and also painted the original wine-bottle labels – miniature works of art evoking traditional island architecture, the startling greens of Salina's verdant vegetation, sea blues, sunsets. Estate-grown capers and other delicious nibbles accompany tastings – forget dinner afterwards (catch sunset in **Pollara** instead).

Granita Legends

STAY COOL ISLAND-STYLE

If you're on Salina with kids, it's not only the shallow pools formed by the concrete breakwaters on Lingua's Spiaggia Biscotti that will ensure you love this family-friendly island. Across the street from its pebble beach is the lavender-blue terrace of **Da Alfredo**, famed across Sicily for its *granite*. Flavours handcrafted from fruits of the land include pistachio, watermelon, lemon, fig and mulberry. Go local with glass beakers of blackberry *granite* and a basket of brioche – rip off chunks of the sweet bread and dunk in the crushed ice.

NECTAR OF THE GODS

It is thought that the Greeks brought **Malvasia** grapes – a name derived from the Greek city Monemvasia – to Salina in 588 BCE, and the wine is still produced using traditional techniques. Malvasia and Corinto Nero (black Corinthian) grapes are harvested in mid-September and dried in the sun on *cannizzi* (woven reed mats) for 15 to 20 days. This drying process is crucial: the grapes must dry out enough to concentrate the sweet flavour but not too much, which would caramelise them. The result is a sweet, dark-golden or light-amber wine that tastes, some say, of honey – 'nectar of the gods' for the Greeks. The sweet dessert wine is usually drunk in very small glasses and pairs well with cheese, sweet biscuits and almond pastries.

📖 WHERE TO STAY & EAT ON SALINA

Hotel Signum
Michelin-starred eco-dining and sensational thermal spa make this Malfa retreat the island's top boutique address. €€€

Agriturismo Al Cappero
Simple rooms on a caper farm in Pollara, with terrace serving Sicilian homecooking and sensational sunset views. €

Nni Lausta
Grape must and Malvasia wines feature on the veggie-rich menu at Santa Maria Salina's most creative contemporary table. €€

The sublime ricotta *granita* with candied capers and toasted capers at **Pa.Pe.Ro** is reason enough to visit bijou fishing hamlet **Rinella**, on Salina's southern coast.

Alicudi

ISLAND OF STEPS

Magical and mesmerising, the Aeolians' second-smallest island feels like a mischievous afterthought on the map. As isolated a place as you'll find in the entire Mediterranean basin, the 5.2 sq km island has no roads – just a relentless succession of time-wizened, volcanic-stone steps staggering mercilessly up to **Monte Montagnola** (675m). This is the kind of place where you have to ask around for rooms or a boat taxi, where you whittle away hours watching fishers unload and clean fish. Old-timer donkeys and mules, boats and wheelbarrows are the only means of transport and lugging stuff around.

Stepping off the hydrofoil at the sleepy port, simply head uphill. Count two hours along the **Filo dell'Arpa** trail of steps to reach Alicudi's central peak; **Chiesa di San Bartolo** marks the hike's midpoint. At the T-intersection up top where the trail dead-ends at a stone wall, turn left to circle the crater of the extinct volcano or right to continue to dramatic cliffs at Alicudi's western edge. Near the summit, look for Timpone delle Femmine, huge fissures where women are said to have taken refuge during pirate raids. The sea views are beyond heavenly. Back down at the port, cool off in the crystal-clear sea – either from the pebble beach right by the hydrofoil dock or from rocks immediately south.

Stromboli

SUNSET HIKES & CRATER FIREWORKS

On the strangely hypnotic and intoxicating island of Stromboli, the force of nature doesn't get mightier or feel closer than from the night-time slopes of its beloved **volcano**. Sit on a rock or stand at one of two viewpoints on the lower slopes of the imposing 924m-high volcano to watch spectacular fireworks explode from the hidden crater. The show is more dramatic some nights than others – during active periods, explosions occur every 20 minutes or so and are preceded by a ferocious belly-roar as gases force hot magma into the air. The occasional cascade of red-hot rock crashing down the lava-blackened mountainside into the sea below is breathtakingly spectacular. Linger past nightfall when the volcano's vivid, fire-orange glow burns brighter.

 WHERE TO STAY & EAT ON STROMBOLI

Hotel Villagio Stromboli
A 1950s icon. Rooms with ceiling fans open onto a sea-facing flower courtyard. Private beach and rooftop terrace. €€

L'Osservatorio
Feast on pizza by candlelight against a backdrop of volcanic fireworks at Stromboli's favourite garden restaurant. €€

L'Angolo del Pesce
Sushi burgers, poke bowls, tomato and caper doughnuts in a fairy light-lit garden; party vibe after dark. €

Stromboli eruption

Two viewpoints facing the **Sciara del Fuoco** – the blackened laval scar running down Stromboli's northern flank – are accessible on foot from Stromboli village. You can hike up to the 290m platform alone, but to access the 400m viewpoint, you need a guide. Informative, small-group treks (8km, five hours) led by a volcanologist guide depart from **Magmatrek**, on Via Vittorio Emanuele near the church, two or three hours before sunset and return around 10pm. Bring a picnic to enjoy at the viewpoint and a torch (flashlight or head torch) for the return hike. Rent walking boots (you'll need them), head torch, rucksack and other equipment from **Totem Trekking**.

If you plan to DIY to 290m, check the current trail route with local guides. **Stromboli Adventures** at Via Roma 17 also provides a visitor information service, with a family-friendly exhibition on one of the world's most active volcanoes. Volcanic activity is monitored by Florence University's Laboratory of Experimental Geophysics (LGS) in Stromboli; download its View Stromboli app for daily reports and real time images.

GETTING AROUND

Of the seven Aeolian Islands, Vulcano is closest to mainland Sicily, meaning that Liberty Lines' hydrofoils are especially frequent: all Lipari-bound boats from Milazzo and Messina stop here first. If sailing to Salina, check which ferry port you want – the island has two. Boats to Stromboli typically stop at Santa Marina Salina (eastern shore); boats from Lipari to Alicudi stop at Rinella (southern shore).

Private boat taxis operated by individual boat captains operate on every island, and are eminently useful for accessing more remote beaches and caves. Call their mobile numbers to reserve. On Stromboli, don't be alarmed by taxi drivers driving around in their electric golf carts and three-wheeled Apes barefoot – no shoes is the hardcore islander norm.

CATANIA

Given its proximity to Mt Etna, Sicily's second-biggest city has dealt with devastating volcanic activity on numerous occasions. It was engulfed by boiling lava in 1669, and in 1693 an earthquake hit the region. On Catania's Porta Ferdinandea city gate, an inscription reads '*Melior de cinere surgo*' ('I rise stronger from the ashes'), summing up Catanians' pride in their rebuilt, Unesco-listed city.

Over the centuries Greeks, Romans, Byzantines, Arabs, Normans, French, Aragonese and Spaniards have passed through here and the city's impressive black-and-white *palazzi* and dizzying domes, towering over grandiose baroque piazzas and vivacious street life, continue to attract a huge mix of admirers today.

Rome
Catania

BEST CITY VIEWPOINTS

Chiesa Badia di Sant'Agata
Swoon over a 360-degree panorama of the city's rooftops, domes and a brooding Mt Etna to the north from the church's terrace.

Ostello degli Elefanti
Enjoy an *aperitivo* at sunset in the rooftop bar of this popular hostel, in a 17th-century *palazzo* a stone's throw from the cathedral.

Chiesa di San Nicolò l'Arena
Spiral up 141 steps to the roof of the church, with striking unfinished facade, in the Benedictine monastery complex on Piazza Dante – the panorama is top-drawer.

Tour the Resurrected City

SOAK UP BAROQUE ARCHITECTURE

Walk looking up so you don't miss any of Catania's magnificent, Unesco-listed baroque buildings crafted in black lava and white limestone. Begin on **Piazza del Duomo** with the city symbol: **Fontana dell'Elefante** (1736), known as U Liotru in the local dialect, a lava-stone elephant surmounted by an obelisk. The splash-happy waters of 19th-century **Fontana dell'Amenano** pour into the underground River Amenano, which once ran above ground. The star of the piazza is **Cattedrale di Sant'Agata**, dedicated to the city's patron saint, who is celebrated on 5 February during one of Sicily's largest festivals. World-famous Catanian composer Vincenzo Bellini rests here. Next door, the concave-convex facade of **Chiesa Badia di Sant'Agata** is an architectural masterpiece by Giovanni Battista Vaccarini.

Walk along Via Etnea to reach Piazza Università, framed by **Palazzo Sangiuliano** and **Palazzo Università**, with a beautiful cobblestone courtyard designed by Vaccarini. Turn left to follow Via Alessi up to **Via Crociferi**, a triumph of baroque: visit **Chiesa di St Giuliano** and **Arco di St Benedetto**, and walk to the opposite end of the street to admire Vaccarini's **Villa Cerami** (today the university's law faculty). Return to Via Etnea via Via Penninello, and at the **Quattro Canti** intersection, walk east along Via Sangiuliano to neo-baroque **Teatro Bellini**. The theatre was

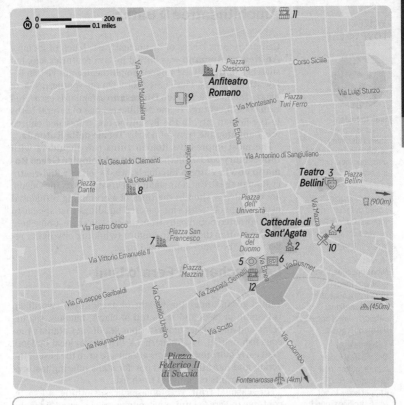

HIGHLIGHTS
1 Anfiteatro Romano
2 Cattedrale di Sant'Agata
3 Teatro Bellini

SIGHTS
4 Church of San Placido
5 Fontana dell'Amenane
6 Museo Diocesano
7 Parco Archeologico Greco Romano
8 Terme della Rotonda
9 Villa Cerami

EATING
10 I Dolci di Nonna Vincenza

SHOPPING
11 Fera 'o Luni
12 La Pescheria

inaugurated in 1890 with the opera *Norma*, inspiration for *pasta alla norma* (pasta with basil, eggplant, ricotta and tomato). End with a mooch around nearby **Chiesa di St Placido** and memorable *cannoli* at neighbouring **I Dolci di Nonna Vincenza**.

 WHERE TO STAY & EAT IN CATANIA

Habitat
A 19th-century factory-turned-boutique hotel near Teatro Massimo. €€

Mè Cumpari Turiddu
Small producers and Slow Food sensibilities underline sophisticated dishes at this quirky, vintage-styled bistro. €€

Fud Off
One of the coolest spots for casual bites with cocktails. €€

Amphitheatres & Baths

ROMAN CATANIA

Catania retains traces of its ancient past. Much of its huge **Anfiteatro Romano** was buried by lava centuries ago, but snatches of the ruined Roman amphitheatre are visible below street level on Piazza Stesicoro. On the southern side of Piazza Duomo, the **Museo Diocesano** safeguards excavated ruins of 5th-century Terme Achilleane, one of several baths in the Roman city. In the Byzantine era, a frescoed church was built atop the ruins of nearby **Terme della Rotonda**.

The most impressive Roman ruins rub shoulders with 18th-century *palazzi* in the **Parco Archeologico Greco Romano** on Via Vittorio Emanuele: what's left of a 2nd-century Roman theatre and its small rehearsal theatre, the Odeon, are evocatively sited in the thick of a crumbling residential neighbourhood, with vine-covered buildings that appear to have sprouted organically from the sunken stage. Come here at night, after the rain, to admire twinkling city lights reflected in the water-submerged stage.

La Pescheria & Fera 'o Luni

VISIT THE MARKETS

Tables groan under the weight of decapitated swordfish, ruby-pink prawns and trays full of clams, mussels, sea urchins and all manner of mysterious sea life at Catania's raucous fish market, La Pescheria (A' Piscaria in local dialect). Visit early morning – it opens at 7am – to grab the best of the action and morning catch. Look for stalls offering tastings and restaurants cooking up fresh fish.

For seasonal fruit, vegetables, spices, clothing, all sorts, continue to Fera 'o Luni, a morning market around since the Middle Ages and filling Piazza Carlo Alberto with the din of hawking vendors since 1832.

GETTING AROUND

Catania Airport is 7km southwest of town, with frequent train and bus (Alibus) connections to the central train station. From the latter, it's a 20-minute walk or short metro ride (alight at the Piazza Stesicoro stop) to the historic centre – compact, walkable and hilly in places. To zip around swiftly, use the local e-scooter sharing system; download Helbiz, Dott or Lime apps to locate wheels. Think twice before renting a bicycle – road traffic is chaotic and lava-stone pavements can be a bone-rattling challenge.

A hop-on hop-off panoramic bus departing from Piazza del Duomo loops around the main sights in the centre. Take Catania's one-line metro from the Giovanni XXIII stop (across the street the central train station) to the Cantania Borgo stop, from where you can pick up the Ferrovia Circumetnea train encircling Mt Etna.

Beyond Catania

Bronte Mt Etna

La Timpa Nature Reserve

Riviera dei Ciclopi Acireale

Catania

A mythical coastline much-loved by Homer and the hissing craters of brooding Mt Etna usher in outdoor adventure in spades.

Beyond Catania spills the Ionian Coast, a stretch of cobalt-blue seaside stitched from ancient myths, pretty fishing villages and enough Sicilian icons to fill a souvenir tea towel. Halfway up a rocky mountainside, sophisticated Taormina is the hot spot to lounge with holidaying celebs, VIPs and day-tripping tourists.

No single experience trumps hiking Mt Etna. Brooding menacingly on Catania's doorstep, Europe's tallest active volcano promises walkers surreal moonscapes, unparalleled views of mainland Italy and a deep, rare silence hard to find elsewhere. Its storied lower slopes are a dream for outdoor enthusiasts who mountain bike here in summer, ski and snowshoe in winter, and play out the shoulder seasons in a bewitching underworld of lava-carved caves and clandestine ice-blue glaciers.

Greek theatre, Taormina (p686)

TOP TIP

Walking on Mt Etna is best in April, May, September and October. Even if it's hot at lower altitudes, it's windy (and sometimes freezing) up top. Bring walking shoes, wind jacket, warm headgear, gloves and sunglasses. Rifugio Sapienza rents kit.

K. ROY ZERLOCH/SHUTTERSTOCK ©

PARCO DELL'ETNA

Dominating eastern Sicily, **Mt Etna** (3326m) is Italy's highest mountain south of the Alps and Europe's largest active volcano. It's in a constant state of activity and eruptions occur frequently, most spectacularly from the four summit craters, but more often from the fissures and old craters on the mountain's flanks. This activity, closely monitored by 120 seismic activity stations and satellites, means Mt Etna is occasionally closed to visitors.

Since 1987 the volcano has been protected by the national park, Parco dell'Etna (*parcoetna. ct.it*). Embracing 581 sq km and 21-odd villages and towns, its natural landscapes range from snowcapped mountaintop to lunar deserts of barren black lava, beech woods and lush vineyards.

TRABANTOS/GETTY IMAGES ©

Crateri Silvestri, Mt Etna

Hiking Mt Etna's Lower Slopes

WILD LAVA TRAILS ON AN ACTIVE VOLCANO

Explore Etna's lower slopes on foot. While many dramatic hiking trails can be tackled independently, it is forbidden to trek above 2450m without a professional guide; recommended trekking companies include Guide Vulcanologiche Etna Nord and Etna Exclusive Guide. From the **Rifugio Sapienza** car park on the southern slope – the closest to Catania, an hour by car or two by bus – it's a five-minute walk to the lower crater of inactive **Crateri Silvestri**, dating to an eruption in 1892, and 20 minutes to the upper crater along an easy, signposted footpath.

With more time and energy on your hands, pick up the two-hour **Schiena dell'Asino** trail (5.5km) not far from the car park. Easy but uphill, it edges along the Valle del Bove where lava flows collect. Birds of prey circling in the sky above and great views of Catania and the Ionian Sea keep you company along the way.

On Etna's eastern slope in the fertile Val Calanna, the **704 path** (two hours, 4km) tangoes between woods and lava (dating from eruptions between 1991 and 1993 that completely

 WHERE TO STAY & EAT ON ETNA

Rifugio Sapienza
Right next to the lower cable-car station. Stay overnight, eat, rent a bike, book a tour. €

Rifugio Ragabo
Family-run mountain eatery in a beautiful pine forest near Piano Provenzana; the handmade *maccheroni* is sublime. €

Osteria del Siciliano
Excellent Sicilian cuisine in Nicolosi. Abundant portions. Try the pistachio ravioli. €€

swamped the valley) to the top of Mt Calanna. Find the trail-head in Piano dell'Acqua in **Zafferana Etnea**. This town is the place to taste local honey and Sicilian pizza, aka fried cal-zone filled with *tuma* (cheese) and anchovies.

Summiting Mt Etna

CLIMB TO 3000M WITH A GUIDE

Park in **Piano Provenzana** (1800m), a small ski station and gateway to Etna's quieter northern slopes. From here, join a 90-minute 4WD guided tour with **Etna Freedom** (*etna freedom.it*) up to the **Observatorio Volcanologico** (Volcanic Observatory) looking out across the Valle del Leone at 2900m. Volcanologist guides point out lava flows and extinct craters en route up the mountain and take you on a short half-hour walk around the observatory to unravel the extraordinary view before driving back down.

Summit seekers can book an add-on guided hike from the observatory up to 3300m; count four to five hours walking. Buy tickets for both tours in advance online or at Etna Freedom's ticket office in the Piano Provenzana car park.

To summit Etna from the south, ride the **Funivia dell'Etna** cable car from Rifugio Sapienza up to **Montagnola** (2500m). Clamber aboard a 4WD jeep operated by Star (buy tickets in situ) and continue to **Torre del Filosofo** (2920m). From here, you can continue on foot with a guide hired at a small wood-en hut by Torre del Filosofo.

For an unforgettable experience, catch the last cable car up to 2500m, revel in the glorious sunset, and walk back down by moonlight. You can't get lost: cable-car pylons guide you.

Subterranean Etna

EXPLORING LAVA TUNNELS & CAVES

Delve into Etna's hidden underworld, a labyrinth of tunnels and caves sculpted by lava flows and used as burial places, shelters and storage spaces for snow and ice in ancient times. **Grotta del Lamponi** (Raspberry Cave) extends for 700m and **Grotta del Gelo** (Ice Cave), carved by a 17th-century erup-tion, is considered Europe's most southern glacier. Uncover both on a challenging day hike (20km, eight hours) through pine forest and lava flows from Piano Provenzana. Trekking company **Gruppo Guide Alpine Etna Nord** arranges guid-ed hikes to both.

VOLCANIC WINE TASTING

Mt Etna's rich volcanic soils produce some of Italy's finest wines – **Etna DOC** is among 23 Sicilian wines with the Denominazione di Origine Controllata denomination. With a car and a little planning, the mountain sets a stunning scene for hunting out the perfect vintage. Dozens of wineries offer *degustazione* (wine tasting), but most require booking.

Some, such as **Donnafugata Randazzo**, offer vineyards, walks with Mt Etna views and cellar tours. Others, such as **Cantine Palmento Costanzo**, are testimony to the Herculean determination of Etna winemakers who cultivate vines on steep dry-stone terraces staggering up a 19th-century lava flow. At **Tenuta di Fessina**, an abandoned village-turned-winery, you can stay the night.

✂ WHERE TO EAT IN TAORMINA

Osteria RossoDiVino
On a romantic and intimate staircase, serving excellent fish cuisine with a good wine list. €€

Bam Bar
Best *granita* in town – no wonder it is constantly busy. Try a fruit-based seasonal flavour. €

Pasticceria D'Amore
Do not leave without tasting the freshly filled *cannoli*. €

A Date with Fashionable Taormina

THE PEARL OF THE IONIAN SEA

Since the Grand Tour era when 18th-century aristocrats lapped up a dashing dose of Sicilian dolce vita here on their extended journey around Europe, celebrity-loved Taormina has been one of Sicily's hottest tourist destinations. From **Porta Messina**, join shoppers on boutique-lined **Corso Umberto I**. Admire 10th-century **Palazzo Corvaja** and stroll southwest for a spectacular view of the bay from **Piazza IX Aprile**. Facing the square is early-18th-century **Chiesa di San Giuseppe**. Walk west through 12th-century clock tower Torre dell'Orologio onto **Piazza del Duomo**, with its baroque fountain and 13th-century cathedral. From here, lose yourself in the rabbit warren of side streets hiding time-worn *palazzi*, tiny churches and ceramic-decorated alleys.

When a green oasis of calm beckons, make your way to the stunningly sited public gardens of **Villa Comunale**. Created by Englishwoman Florence Trevelyan in the late 19th century, this is a wonderful place to escape the crowds, with tropical plants, delicate flowers punctuated by whimsical follies and breathtaking views of the coast and Mt Etna.

Showtime at Teatro Greco

TWO SHOWS IN ONE

Sensational Etna views loom from Taormina's remarkable clifftop **Greek theatre**. Built in the 3rd century BCE and still in use, this perfect horseshoe-shaped theatre suspended between sea and sky is the world's most dramatically situated Greek theatre and Sicily's second largest (after Syracuse). Bag a gold-dust ticket for a summer concert and enjoy the thrilling double act: the performance on the stage and the fire-red flow of erupting Etna beyond.

 GETTING AROUND

Hourly buses (interbus.it) link Catania and Taormina in 1¼ to two hours. The two main approaches to Etna are from the north and south. The southern route, signposted as Etna Sud, is via Nicolosi and Rifugio Sapienza, 18km further up the mountain. The northern approach, Etna Nord, is through Piano Provenzana, 16km southwest of Linguaglossa.

Etna is hard to reach by public transport. Daily AST buses only depart from Catania (opposite the train station) to Rifugio Sapienza (two hours) on the southern slope. To reach the other sides of Etna, take a car or organised tour *(excursionsetna.it)*. To enjoy the hissing craters from afar by train, jump on the 114km-long Ferrovia Circumetnea line from Catania Borgo metro station.

SYRACUSE

Rome

Syracuse

More than any other city, Syracuse encapsulates Sicily's timeless beauty. Ancient Greek ruins rise out of lush citrus orchards, cafe tables spill onto dazzling baroque piazzas, and honey-hued medieval side streets lead down to the sparkling blue sea. It's difficult to imagine now, but in its heyday this was the largest city in the ancient world, bigger even than Athens and Corinth.

Its 'once upon a time' begins in 734 BCE, when Corinthian colonists landed on the island of Ortygia (Ortigia) and founded the settlement, setting up the mainland city four years later. Almost three millennia later, the ruins of that then-new city called Neapolis form one of Sicily's greatest archaeological sites. Across the water from the mainland, deeply atmospheric Ortygia remains Syracuse's most beautiful corner, rammed in summer with Instagram romantics seeking beautiful streetscapes and attractive dining, drinking and shopping.

TOP TIP

To escape the tourist crowds, explore the mesmerising maze of La Giudecca, Ortygia's old Jewish quarter around Via della Maestranza and the Via della Giudecca Jewish ghetto. Accessed by Ponte Umbertino or Ponte Santa Lucia, the area is best explored on foot.

Antico Mercato di Ortygia

FOODIE FINDS AT THE MARKET

Ortygia's open-air market sets up shop by the Tempio di Apollo every morning except Sunday. Weave your way through the kaleidoscope of stalls selling seafood, fruit, veggies, herbs and cheeses, to **Fratelli Burgio**. Take a pew on the terrace, order a charcuterie board and glass of wine, and enjoy the dress-circle spectacle of vendors shouting and gesticulating to catch shoppers' attention. Freshly shucked oysters and giant *panini* prepared in front of you with locally sourced products are the star attraction of legendary **Caseificio Borderi**. If fish rocks your boat, hit **La Lisca** for red tuna tartare spiked with *friggitelli* (sweet chilli pepper).

The Ortygia Loop

WALK THE ISLAND'S PERIMETER

Count less than an hour to walk a complete loop of Ortygia, along its handsome perimeter. Start at **Forte San Giovannello**, part of the island's 16th-century fortification system, and drink in perfect views of modern Syracuse on the mainland. Continue along Lungomare di Levante to **Forte Vigliena** – snap photos of waves crashing against the crenellated fort walls. Visit 13th-century **Castello Maniace** on the island's southern tip, host to July's electronic-music festival **Ortigia Sound System**. Don't miss the castle's vaulted central hall. Continue your walk along the western shore

BEST SWIM SPOTS

Forte Vigliena
Right next to the fort, metal stairs lead to rocks below. Space is limited but the water is deep enough for diving. In summer there is an additional wooden platform.

Cala Rossa
For those who prefer a proper beach. This sandy crescent is very small and can get crowded in summer.

Zefiro Solarium
Just below the Fonte Aretusa, this wooden platform sports sun loungers, parasols, music and drinks. Come dusk, it morphs into a sunset lounge bar.

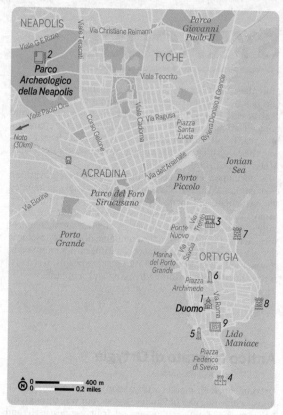

HIGHLIGHTS
1 Duomo
2 Parco Archeologico della Neapolis

SIGHTS
3 Antico Mercato di Ortygia
4 Castello Maniace
5 Fontana Aretusa
6 Fontana di Diana
7 Forte San Giovannello
8 Forte Vigliena
9 Galleria Regionale di Palazzo Bellomo

to **Fonte Aretusa**, the legendary spot where goddess Artemis transformed Aretusa into a bubbling spring, now a pretty pond of papyrus plants. End on the pedestrian jetty – a magical place to enjoy sunset.

Parco Archeologico della Neapolis

ANCIENT GREEK DRAMA ON & OFF STAGE

It's pretty wild to think you can sit in the very theatre – potentially even the same seat – where ancient Greek playwright Aeschylus watched his tragedies unfold on stage for the first time. Syracuse's 16,000-capacity **Teatro Greco**, dating to the 5th century BCE and rebuilt two centuries later, remains one

 WHERE TO STAY & EAT IN ORTYGIA

Alla Giudecca
In a restored 15th-century building, above an ancient Jewish ritual bath. Gorgeous courtyard. €€

Hotel Gutkowski
Simple yet chic mix of vintage details and industrial vibes. Book in advance for a sea-view room. €

A Putia delle Cose Buone
Lovely atmosphere, great home-style food, generous portions. A nice lunch stop; reservation recommended for dinner. €€

of Sicily's most prestigious theatres and watching a summertime play here is unforgettable. Mid-May to early July, during the **Festival del Teatro Greco**, Syracuse's Istituto Nazionale del Dramma Antico (INDA) – the only school of classical Greek drama outside Athens – stages classical Greek plays (in Italian). Bag tickets in advance online or from the ticket booth outside the theatre.

Pre-performance, time-travel to ancient Greek Syracuse with an evocative amble around the **archaeological park**. Beside the theatre, the mysterious **Latomia del Paradiso** is a precipitous limestone quarry from which stone for the ancient city was extracted. Riddled with catacombs and perfumed with citrus and magnolia trees, this is where 7000 survivors of the war between Syracuse and Athens in 413 BCE were imprisoned. The tyrant Dionysius eavesdropped on his prisoners from the entrance of **Orecchio di Dionisio**, a grotto with perfect acoustics, 23m high and extending 65m back into the cliffside.

Up to 450 oxen could be killed at one time on the 3rd-century BCE **Ara di Gerone II**, a monolithic sacrificial altar to Hieron II, and gladiatorial combats and horse races provided entertainment at the 2nd-century **Anfiteatro Romano**. End at the **Museo Archeologico Paolo Orsi**, a one-stop shop covering Syracuse's backstory from prehistory to Roman times.

An Ortygia Walking Tour

TEMPLES, CHURCHES, FOUNTAINS & ALLEYS

Cross Ponte Umbertino and admire the ruins of Sicily's oldest Doric temple, **1 Tempio di Apollo**. Walk south along Corso Matteotti to Giulio Moschetti's **2 Fontana di Diana** (1906–07) on Piazza Archimede. The fountain's leading lady is Artemis, goddess of hunting, who transformed her handmaiden Aretusa into a spring to protect her from the bothersome advances of pesky river god Alpheus.

Continue south along Via Roma and turn right onto Piazza Minerva. Observe the Doric columns of the 5th-century BCE temple to Athena on which Syracuse's 7th-century cathedral was built. Before entering the **3 Duomo**, contemplate Syracuse's showpiece square and its sweep of baroque, pale golden-stone *palazzi* that appear to be built from light. Spot the signature stone lizard of Spanish architect Juan Vermexio on the left corner of the cornice at **4 Palazzo Municipale** (1629). Opposite, 17th-century **5 Palazzo Arcivescovile** hosts the **Biblioteca Alagoniana** with rare 13th-century manuscripts. In **6 Chiesa di Santa Lucia alla Badia**, uncover a nuns' parlour with beautiful blue majolica floor. Before leaving Piazza

BEST LATE-NIGHT DRINKS

BOATS
Despite the nautical decor, 'Boats' stands for 'Based on a True Story'. A good drinks list, guest bar staff and great vinyl.

Muciula
Good vibes and a great place for *aperitivo* with a huge platter of street-food nibbles while listening to live music on the Piazzetta San Rocco.

Cortile Verga
Enjoy drinks and chilled music in an 18th-century courtyard at one of Ortygia's top cocktail bars.

 WHERE TO EAT GELATO IN ORTYGIA

Voglia Matta
Best ice cream in town. Try the brioche with gelato inside instead of a classic ice-cream cone.

Crema & Cioccolato
Welcoming staff and outdoor tables. Highly recommended flavours: *nocciola* (hazelnuts) and pistachio.

Il Cucchiaino
The pistachio is absolutely divine. Try it together with ricotta flavour: a heavenly ice cream.

BEST PLACES FOR A SWEET TREAT

I Cannoli del Re
The *cannoli* here are not served in the traditional shell but in a cone so you can eat it as you walk around. You also choose the filling.

Bar Condorelli
Right on Piazza Duomo. Sit and watch the world go by: children play and musicians busk while you savour a *granita* (flavoured crushed ice drink).

Pasticceria Artale
It's not fancy but the delicious pastries are to die for. Fill your eyes at the counter, then fill your belly.

del Duomo, sit and watch the world go by – children playing, musicians busking – over pistachio *granita* from **Bar Condorelli** at No 16 on the square.

Or walk five minutes south to 13th-century Catalan-Gothic *palazzo* **7 Galleria Regionale di Palazzo Bellomo**, stopping at Cannoli Del Re en route for typical Sicilian *cannoli* in a cone instead of the traditional shell. Among the gallery's collection of early-Byzantine to 19th-century art, *Annunciation* (1474) by Sicily's greatest 15th-century artist, Antonello da Messina, is a highlight.

GETTING AROUND

Most of Ortygia is restricted to resident motorists only. Find two paying car parks (Marina and Talete) at the entrance of the island.

Arriving by train is only really convenient from Catania – from elsewhere, take the bus. Count 20 minutes on foot from Syracuse train station to Ortygia, or 10 minutes by electric minibus 1. To reach the Parco Archeologico della Neapolis, take minibus 2 from Molo Sant'Antonio (just west of the bridge to Ortygia). Buy bus tickets on board. Siracuse Tour Bike (siracusatourbike.it) rents bicycles and organises city bike tours.

Beyond Syracuse

History and nature are deeply intertwined around Syracuse. Lose yourself in the hypnotic web of scenic and storied landscapes they weave.

Gole della Stretta
Sortino
Pista Ciclabile Rossana Maiorca
Buccheri
Buscemi
Palazzolo Acreide
Syracuse
Area Marina Protetta del Plemmirio

TOP TIP

Don't miss a glass of fragrant Moscato di Noto or sweet flowery Passito, produced from the grapes grown around Noto. Join a wine-tasting tour or visit wineries independently along the Strado del Val di Noto (*stradadelvaldi noto.it*).

The area around Syracuse is the cinematic Sicilia of TV series *Inspector Montalbano* – a swirl of luminous hill towns, sweeping topaz beaches and olive-laden hillsides luring everyone from French artists to Milanese moguls in search of new beginnings. The emerald sea panders to outdoor explorers with dramatic sea caves dotting golden cliffs and rich marine life begging to be viewed through a snorkelling mask (*ortigiadiving. com*). May to September, boat trips yo-yo along the coast from Syracuse's port and guided bike tours (*siracusatourbike.it*) dive into the rocky peninsula inland. For history buffs, a prehistoric necropolis carved into a rocky gorge and exquisite baroque towns promise endless discovery.

Corso Vittorio Emanuele, Noto (p693)

STEPNIAK/SHUTTERSTOCK ©

MARCO OSSINO/SHUTTERSTOCK ©

Necropoli di Pantalica

PIZZOLO IN SORTINO

Typical Syracusa *pizzolo* (local pizza) originates in Sortino. Scraps of leftover bread dough were traditionally used in family kitchens to make focaccia rounds spiced with thyme, salt and oil. Today *pizzolo* is topped with an additional layer of dough to resemble a pizza sandwich stuffed with cheese, oregano, pepper and whatever else the *pizzarolo* chef chooses to add. La Castellina and Le Monache in Sortino both cook up some wild combos. Sweet variations ooze ricotta and honey – sample for dessert at **La Pizzoleria**.

Into the Valle dell'Anapo

BAROQUE VILLAGES AND BRONZE AGE TOMBS

There are three great reasons to visit **Sortino**, 40-minutes northwest of Syracuse: it's a delightful baroque village; you can taste authentic native *pizzolo* (pizza); and the town's *fascitrari* (beekeepers) produce excellent honey, hence its 'city of honey' nickname. Don't miss the **Chiesa di Santa Sofia**, dedicated to the town's patron saint, and the dazzling baroque gem of **Chiesa di Monevergine**. Traditional Sicilian puppetry tradition comes alive in the small Museo dell'Opera dei Pupi and beekeeping paraphernalia fills house-museum Casa ro Fascitraru.

Sortino is also the springboard for explorations in the wild, unspoilt Valle dell'Anapo (Anapo Valley). The deep limestone gorge was forged by the Anapo and Calcinara rivers, and is laced with scenic walking trails (paths marked 'B' are slightly more challenging). Peering down on it from a huge plateau is the Unesco World Heritage–listed **Necropoli di Pantalica**. This was Sicily's most important Iron and Bronze Age necropolis, and more than 5000 tombs of various shapes and sizes honeycomb its limestone cliffs. The site is terribly ancient, dating between the 13th and 8th century BCE, but its origins are largely mys-

WHERE TO DINE IN NOTO

Manna
In a former prince's wine cellar, this is Noto's best restaurant. Expect Sicilian cuisine with contemporary flair. €€€

Dammuso
Cosy seafood restaurant. Try the tuna in pistachio crust. €€

Trattoria Giufà
Rabbit cooked in red wine and squid meatballs with sultanas and toasted almonds are superb at this beloved trattoria. €€

terious. Little survives of the town itself other than the Anak-tron or prince's palace. Hike in the archaeological park independently or with a guide *(scopripantalica.it)*.

Baroque at its Peak

NOTO, HONEY-GOLD GARDEN OF STONE

An earthquake in 1693 razed **Noto** to the ground, but a grander legacy arose from the tragedy. Unesco-listed Noto is an elegant baroque beauty, dubbed 'garden of stone' for its flamboyant *palazzi*, churches, bell towers and balconies strung with sculpted masks and cherubs. At sunset the city really works its magic: limestone buildings glow honey-gold.

Plunge through Porta Reale into Noto's beautiful historic centre. Walk west along Corso Vittorio Emanuele to 18th-century **Chiesa di San Francesco d'Assisi all'Immacolata** and **Basilica del Santissimo Salvatore**, adjoining a Benedictine convent. Spot the ornate original portal of **Chiesa di Santa Chiara**, made redundant after the street was lowered in the 19th century. The church's elliptical interior is awash with whimsical stuccowork and stars one of Noto's finest baroque altars, but it's the rooftop terrace with soul-soaring view that steals the show.

The peachy dome dominating the skyline is that of **Basilica Cattedrale di San Nicolò**, a renovated baroque beauty. In front of the cathedral, **Palazzo Ducezio** is now the town hall, with a Versailles-style Hall of Mirrors. **Palazzo Landolina** and **Palazzo Nicolaci di Villadorata**, wrought-iron balconies propped up by grotesque figures, are other fantastical facades flanking architectural jewel box Piazza Municipio. Continue west along Corso Vittorio Emanuele to **Chiesa di San Domenico**, one of Noto's finest baroque buildings, designed to a Greek-cross plan by baroque starchitect Rosario Gagliardi who is reputedly buried here. Duck a block north to uncover a bounty of noble, 18th-century *palazzi* on **Via Cavour**.

Baroque Towns

A TWO-DAY ROAD TRIP

A land of remote rocky gorges, sweeping views and silent valleys, Sicily's southeastern corner is home to the 'baroque triangle', an area of Unesco-listed hilltop towns famous for their lavish baroque architecture.

Just over 35km south of Syracuse, **1 Noto** has arguably Sicily's most beautiful street – Corso Vittorio Emanuele. Head south along SP19, pausing at **2 Villa Romana del Tellaro** to admire its Roman mosaics. Continue to **3 Ispica**, a hilltop

NOTO ANTICA

The Noto you see today dates from the 18th century, but a town called Netum existed here for centuries before. The ruined medieval city, Noto Antica, is a short drive from the city centre. Find it languishing on a plateau overlooking the green river valley of Asinaro awash with almond, olive and citrus groves.

 WHERE TO HAVE A DRINK IN NOTO

Anche Gli Angeli
Have an *aperitivo* while you browse books or a late-night drink while listening to live music in this old church. €€

Il Brillo Parlante
A family-owned wine bar serving local cheeses and wines. Let Giuseppe, the sommelier, guide you. €€

Il Libertyno
The perfect spot to have a good beer or a cocktail accompanied by Sicilian tapas. €€

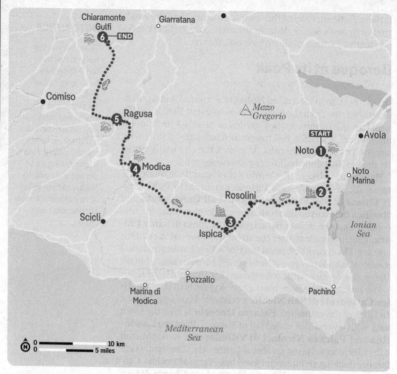

town overlooking a huge canyon, Cava d'Ispica, riddled with prehistoric tombs. Follow the SS115 a further 18km to the bustling town of **4 Modica**, set in a rocky gorge. With superb accommodation and restaurants, it's an ideal overnight stop. The best baroque sights are in Modica Alta, the upper town; preserve energy for a *passeggiata* (late-afternoon stroll) along Corso Umberto I and dinner at Michelin-starred Accursio or the family-run Osteria dei Sapori Perduti.

Next morning, wind up and down rock-littered hilltops to **5 Ragusa**. The town is divided in two: Ragusa Ibla is a claustrophobic warren of grey stone houses and elegant *palazzi* opening onto Piazza Duomo, a superb example of 18th-century town planning. Lunch on food like Mamma makes at La Bettola or Sicilian cuisine with a contemporary twist at Camùri. Or push onto **6 Chiaramonte Gulfi**, a tranquil hilltop town some 20km to the north along the SP10. Dubbed the 'Balcone della Sicilia' (Sicily's Balcony) for its breathtaking panorama, it's famous for its coveted olive oil and blue-ribbon pork. Savour it at Ristorante Majore.

GETTING AROUND

Your own wheels are essential for exploring this area around Syracuse. Train and buses connect Noto with Catania airport in 1½ to two hours.

AGRIGENTO

Rome

Agrigento ●

Ancient Greek myth claims Agrigento was founded by Cretan inventor and architect Daedalus and his son Icarus. Historical records date the ancient city-state of Akragas to 580 BCE. The presence of a ready water supply ensured its rapid growth and by the 5th century BCE it had become one of the Mediterranean's great cities, with a population of 200,000 and a reputation as a party hot spot. Greek poet Pindar described Akragas as the most beautiful city ever built by mortals, while Agrigentine philosopher Empedocles famously said that its inhabitants 'feast as if they will die tomorrow and build as if they will live for ever'.

Situated about 3km below the modern city of Agrigento, the Unesco-listed Valley of the Temples is one of the most mesmerising sites in the Mediterranean, boasting the best-preserved Doric temples outside Greece. Today they are Sicily's single biggest tourist site, with more than 600,000 visitors a year – to dodge crowds and summer heat, visit in the early morning or at sunset (open until midnight in summer).

TOP TIP

Download the official Valley of Temples app, with audio guide and itineraries, and – to better grasp how the valley originally appeared – visit the Museo Archeologico housing artefacts from the site (like the telamon, an 8m-high statue once supporting the now-ruined Temple of Zeus).

Agrigento Old Town

NOBLE PALAZZI AND HISTORIC CHURCHES

Sitting at the medieval core of Agrigento is pedestrianised main street **Via Atenea**, lined with shops, restaurants and bars. Narrow alleys and stairways wind upwards and downwards off the main street, past noble palaces and historic churches. Start inside 11th-century **Cattedrale di San Gerlando**, altered over the centuries, with a facade reached by a wide stairway flanked by an unfinished 15th-century bell tower. Among the treasures it safeguards is a Normand painted wooden ceiling and an outstanding Roman sarcophagus. No one has ever been able to decipher the enigmatic 'letter of the devil', a 17th-century manuscript addressed to a nun in undecipherable characters.

From Via Duomo, walk five minutes southeast along Via de Castro and Via Garufo to **Chiesa di Santa Maria dei Greci**. Inside the enchanting bijou church, look up to admire the Norman ceiling, Byzantine frescoes and traces of the original Doric columns of the 5th-century temple on which the church was built. Another 10-minute wiggle east along old-town streets brings you to **Monastero di Santo Spirito**, a Cistercian convent founded in 1290 with magnificent stuccowork by late baroque and rococo genius Giacomo Serpotta (1656–1732). Nuns in residence here bake delicious sweets, including *cuscusu* (sweet couscous made with local pistachios) – press the doorbell to enter and buy.

BEST BEACHES AROUND AGRIGENTO

Scala dei Turchi
Gorge on bold views of this spectacular white cliff from the neighbouring sandy beach – climbing on the cliff itself is forbidden.

Riserva Naturale Torre Salsa
This WWF nature reserve protects a sandy coastline with beaches, turquoise blue waters, dunes, chalk cliffs and wetlands.

Spiaggia di Punta Bianca
This wild beach is a divers' paradise; no facilities so come prepared.

Spiaggia di Nicolizia
Another wild, unequipped beach surrounded by Mediterranean shrubs.

HIGHLIGHTS
1 Cattedrale di
San Gerlando
2 Giardino
della Kolymbetra
3 Valley of the Temples

SIGHTS
4 Chiesa di Santa Maria
dei Greci
5 Monastero di
Santo Spirito
6 Via Atenea

Favara (9km)

*Cattedrale di
San Gerlando*

Piazza
Don
Minzoni

Piazza
Lena

Via Atenea

Via Gioeni

Piazza
Rosselli

*Piazzale
Aldo Moro*

Via Manzoni (Circonvallazione)

Viadotto Akragas

Viale della Vittoria

Via Demetra

Via Petrarca

*Porto Empedocle
(5km)*

Via Crispi

*Giardino della
Kolymbetra*

Via Panoramica dei templi

*Valley of
the Temples*

0 — 500 m
0 — 0.25 miles

Valley of the Temples Walking Tour

UNESCO-PROTECTED DORIC TREASURES

Begin your exploration in the eastern zone, home to Agrigento's best-preserved temples. From its **1 ticket office**, a short walk leads to the 5th-century BCE **2 Tempio di Hera Lacinia** (also called Tempio di Giunone), perched on the ridgetop. The colonnade and sacrificial altar remain largely intact. Red traces are the result of fire damage likely dating to the Carthaginian invasion of 406 BCE.

Descend past a 500-year-old olive tree and Byzantine tombs to **3 Tempio della Concordia**. This remarkable edifice, the

WHERE TO STAY IN AGRIGENTO

Cortile Baronello
A stylish place to stay in a
renovated old house right in
the city centre. Very friendly
hosts. €

Camere a Sud
A B&B located in the heart of
the historical centre. Modern
design and traditional Sicilian
touches throughout. €

Terrazze di Montelusa
In an atmospheric old *palazzo*
with original furniture along
with lovely plant-filled
panoramic terraces. €

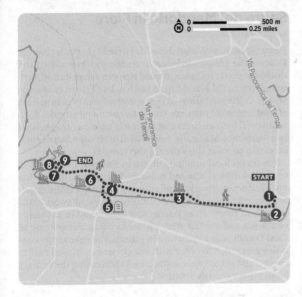

BEST NIGHTLIFE IN AGRIGENTO

Erika Cancialosi, content creator and @ig_agrigento admin, shares her best places to enjoy nightlife in Agrigento.

Cantina Granet Enobistrot €€
In the *dammuso* (vaulted stone room) of a historic building on Via Atenea, it is the perfect spot to taste very good wines accompanied by great food. In summer you can also sit outdoors.

Café Girasole €
A trendy hangout with DJ set and outdoor seating. Stop by to have an *aperitivo* or a cocktail.

'Nzolia €€
A wide selection of wines in a very nice atmosphere. You can also eat amazing finger food.

Caffè San Pietro €
Adjacent to the 18th-century church of San Pietro, now used as a cultural venue, this hip cafe serves wines and *aperitivi*.

model for Unesco's logo, has survived almost entirely intact since its construction in 430 BCE, partly due to its conversion into a Christian basilica in the 6th century, and partly thanks to the shock-absorbing, earthquake-dampening qualities of the soft clay underlying its hard rock foundation. Further downhill, 4 **Tempio di Ercole** is Agrigento's oldest, dating from the end of the 6th century BCE. Down from the main temples, miniature 5 **Tomba di Terone** dates to 75 BCE.

Cross the pedestrian bridge into the western zone, stopping at 6 **Tempio di Giove**. This would have been the world's largest Doric temple had its construction not been interrupted by the Carthaginian sacking of Akragas. Take a brief look at the ruined 5th-century BCE 7 **Tempio dei Dioscuri** and the 6th-century BCE complex of altars and small buildings known as the 8 **Santuario delle Divine Chtoniche**, before ending your visit in the 9 **Giardino della Kolymbetra**, a lush garden in a natural cleft near the sanctuary, with more than 300 (labelled) species of plants and welcome picnic tables. On summer evenings, sip an aperitif and enjoy live music in the citrus grove.

WHERE TO EAT IN AGRIGENTO

Aguglia Persa
Find well-presented seafood at this mansion-*ristorante* with a leafy courtyard. €€

Kalòs
Balcony dining, great *pasta all'agrigentina* (tomatoes, basil and almonds) and homemade *cannoli* to die for. €€

A' Putia Bottega Siciliana
This is the place for a more informal dinner, with platters of local cheese, focaccia, grilled veggies and craft beers. €

BEST FOOD SPOTS

La Scala €€€
Vincenzo Santalucia
makes the perfect
host at this fabulous
restaurant on Via
Atenea. Parties of
two can dine on a tiny
balcony overlooking the
main street.

Il Re di Girgenti €€€
Fine-dining experience,
with innovative menu
and views of the Valley
of the Temples in the
distance. Book ahead to
sit outside.

Sagra del Mandorlo in Fiore

ALMOND BLOSSOM FEST

There is possibly no more beautiful time of year to savour the
Valley of the Temples in its natural serenity – crowd-free and
cloaked in pretty soft-pink almond blossom – than during Agrigento's Sagra del Mandorlo in Fiore in late February or early
March. Celebrated since 1934, the festival ushers in nine days
of food and wine tastings, concerts, costumed parades with
traditional Sicilian carts and other folkloric events spanning
two weekends. Magically, the festival opens and closes amid
evocative ruins at the Valley of the Temples.

Gen up on local almond culture in **Favara**, 15km west of
town. Exhibits at almond museum **Marzipan** unravel the
nut's history, cultivation and culinary uses. Don't miss *agnello pasquale di Favara*, a beautifully decorated sweet crafted around Easter from *pasta reale* (marzipan) in the shape
of a lamb and stuffed with pistachio paste. Sample one at
Cosi Dunci near Favara's main square. The cake shop's *cannoli* shells, filled to order with velvety lemon-infused ricotta
cheese, and other sweet distractions showcasing the region's
almonds are equally sublime.

Porto Empedocle

SEAFARING GATEWAY TO ANCIENT AGRIGENTO

In ancient Akragas sulphur and rock salt were shipped from
Porto Empedocle, 10km southwest of the Valley of the Temples on the coast. Originally called Marina di Girgenti, the
port changed its name in 1863 to commemorate the Greek
philosopher Empedocle who was born here. The town's best-
known modern son is Sicilian novelist Andrea Camilleri (1925–
2019), whose wildly popular detective novels starring Inspector Montalbano are set in the fictional city of Vigàta – Porto
Empedocle in disguise. Find a street mural dedicated to the
writer on Via Salita Chiesa.

GETTING AROUND

The historic centre is best explored on foot. To
get to the Valley of the Temples, hop on city
bus 1, which runs half-hourly from Agrigento's
bus station on Piazzale Rosselli to the Porta
V entrance (20 minutes) on Via Caduti di
Marzabotto.

Buses 2 and 2/ – the quicker route, just 10
minutes – use the 'Tempio di Giunone' stop
on Via Panoramica dei Templi by the temples'

eastern entrance. See schedules online
(trasportiurbaniagrigento.it) and at bus stops;
buy tickets at tobacconists or onboard.

Alternatively, Agrigento's Temple Tour Bus
(templetourbusagrigento.com) includes the
Valley of the Temples on its hop-on hop-off
tourist circuit. Motorists can use official car
parks at both entrances.

TRAPANI

A melting pot of old and new, this small port town seduces with ancient churches, gold-stone *palazzi* and traditional dining spun from local produce and fair trade. In the historic centre, pedestrian Via Garibaldi is a mellow place to stroll, both for locals enjoying a *passeggiata* and travellers awaiting their next boat.

Food is of utmost importance to this town where trattorias cook up couscous, *busiate alla trapanese* (hand-twirled pasta with pesto made from tomatoes, basil, garlic and almonds) and dishes peppered with capers from Pantelleria island. On Spiaggia di San Giuliano, a 30-minute walk from Piazza Vittoria Emanuele, sun-worshippers chink cocktails in beach clubs and queue for fresh corn on the cob – chargrilled to order, salted and wrapped in a leaf from a pushcart on the golden sand. At the town cemetery, the Murale di Licuado wall mural by Uruguayan street artists Camilo Nuñez and Florencia Durán is an artistic shout-out to Trapani's rich multicultural heritage.

Rome

Trapani

TOP TIP

Watch for summertime events: organ concerts at the cathedral; free guided tours of Palazzo Riccio di Morana; the street-food festival Stragusto *(stragusto.it)* in July, three days of absurdly delicious tastings and live cooking shows.

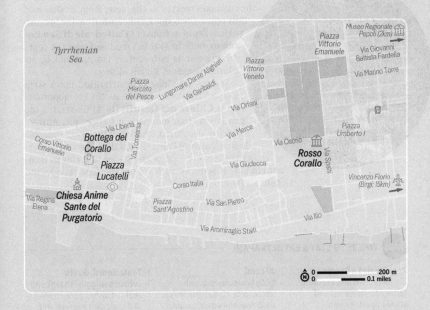

BEST DRINKING SPOTS

BrigBar
Serious coffee and food made using local produce. Coffee and beer are transported sustainably to Trapani by sailing ship.

Moai
DJs spin lounge tunes and hipsters bag dress-circle stools by the wall to enjoy sunset cocktails; unmatched sea/sunset views.

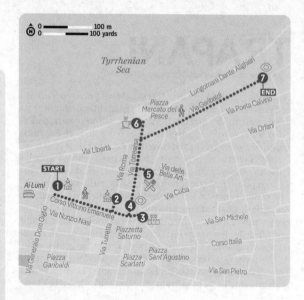

MORE BAROQUE

Baroque masterpieces lure architecture aficionados all over Sicily. To plot your own tour, consider visiting the I Tesori della Loggia collection of churches showcasing Giacomo Serpotta's dazzling stuccowork in **Palermo** (p662); cathedrals in **Noto**, **Modica** and **Ragusa** (p694); and Agrigento's **Monastero di Santo Spirito** (p695).

Waltz through 17th- & 18th-Century Baroque

CHURCHES, PALAZZI AND HANDSOME ARCHITECTURE

While Trapani's golden-hued historic centre is Moorish, the city takes most of its character from its 17th- and 18th-century baroque architecture from the Spanish period. Begin in front of **1 Cattedrale di San Lorenzo**, built in 1421 but modified over the years to arrive at its 18th-century baroque look by architect Giovanni Biagio Amico.

Waltz east along pedestrianised main strip Corso Vittorio Emanuele. At No 12, monumental **2 Chiesa dei Gesuiti** (1614) illustrates the transition from mannerism to baroque. Admire its richly decorated interior, with ornate marble inlays evocative of Palermo's dazzling baroque churches. At the eastern end of the street, **3 Palazzo Senatorio** (1672) seduces with its peach-stone facade and elegant statues in niches.

 WHERE TO STAY & EAT IN TRAPANI

Residenzia La Gancia
Elegant rooms and a rooftop terrace for breakfast and sunset cocktails with Favignana craft gin. €€

Ai Lumi
Little beats this B&B with kitchenette-clad apartments in an 18th-century *palazzo*; enter via a verdant courtyard. €

Tentazioni di Gusto
Lobsters wriggle in a tank and seafood dishes ooze creativity at this elegant address, with tables filling a tiny lane. €€

Walk north along **4 Via Torrearsa** and turn right onto Via Carosio for old-school coffee, *biscotti di fichi* (fig biscuits) and Trapani's best *cannoli* at **5 Antica Pasticceria Colicchia** (1885), in 18th-century Palazzo dei Signori Carosio. Continue north for an iced latte or cold brew at **6 BrigBar**, with a terrace overlooking Trapani's historic open-air fish market on **Piazza Mercato del Pesce**. The 19th-century ensemble of arched porticoes by Venetian architect Giambattista Talotti, cradling a fountain of Venus emerging from the sea, is pure romance. End with a handsome stroll east along **Via Garibaldi**, bejewelled with baroque *palazzi*. To sleep and dream baroque, check into **7 Ai Lumi** (p700) inside 18th-century Palazzo Berardo Ferro (No 71–73).

Trapani Coral

MEET ARTISANS & MODERN MASTERS

Delve into Trapani's rich coral tradition at **Rosso Corallo**, the family workshop of Platimiro Fiorenza (b. 1944). Son of a coral-goldsmith and Unesco Living Human Treasure, Trapani's most distinguished coral master famously sculpted a *Madonna di Trapani* in coral, gold and precious stones for the Pope (displayed in Rome's Vatican Museums) and created a red-leather handbag covered in coral and silver for Italian fashion house Fendi to celebrate its iconic 'baguette' bag. Workshop visits at Via Osorio 36 tango through local coral-working history and demonstrate Platimiro's *retroincastro* (reverse-embedding) technique, introduced by Trapani craftsmen in the 17th century.

For more affordable coral necklaces, earrings or a simple droplet of red coral straight from a coral fisher's net, browse **Bottega del Corallo**, the workshop-boutique of coral jeweller Marzia Cipriano Novata at Corso Vittorio Emanuele 47.

Coral carving dates to 1416 when local fishermen uncovered coral reefs offshore from Trapani and later San Vito Lo Capo. Dazzling chalices, relic boxes and *presepi* (nativity scenes) at the **Museo Regionale Pepoli** illustrate the prized craftsmanship of Trapani *corallari* between the 16th and 18th centuries. The decorative-arts museum, hidden like a precious gem in the cloister of a 14th-century monastery, showcases the collection of local count Agostino Pepoli (1848–1910). He devoted his life to salvaging Trapani's local arts and crafts, notably coral carvings, all the rage in Europe until the 18th century when Trapani's coral banks were decimated.

 WHERE TO HAVE A DRINK IN TRAPANI

Bar Il Salotto
Pomegranate juice squeezed to order; street terrace with sofa seating cocoons.

Tenuta Adragna
Rustic *vineria* (wine bar) with pavement cushions and excellent wine from its out-of-town vineyards.

Bardia Nuova
June to September ushers in this chic rooftop lounge-bar – a near-perfect spot for an *aperitivo* or after-dark drinks.

La Processione dei Misteri

MEET THE CITY'S CELEBRATED STATUES

It goes without saying. If you're in town at Easter, witnessing Trapani's traditional four-day celebration of the Passion of Christ is non-negotiable. Even if you're not religious, feeling the delirious fervour of the crowd – matched only by that of the Semana Santa parades in Seville, Spain – as the town's celebrated *misteri* (life-sized wooden statues of Mary, Jesus and other biblical figures), accompanied by a Trapanese band, process through town is unforgettable.

If you're not in town over Easter, devote a morning to studying the *misteri* in **Chiesa Anime Sante del Purgatorio** (*processione misteritp.it*). Carved in cypress or cork wood, painted by hand and clothed, the statuary groupings represent 20 scenes from the Passion and Death of Christ. Most are originals from the 17th century; some were heavily repaired or replaced after WWII.

On the Tuesday before Easter Sunday, Trapani inhabitants – represented by 20 traditional *maestranze* (guilds) – parade the life-sized Virgin Mary through town. Nightly processions of the other *misteri*, accompanied by musicians playing dirges to the slow steady beat of a drum, make their way to a chapel on **Piazza Lucatelli** before returning to Chiesa Anime Sante del Purgatorio. Celebrations peak around 2pm on Good Friday when the 20 guilds emerge from the church. Bearers carry the statues at shoulder height on flower-adorned floats and walk with a forward-side step to heighten the drama. The all-night procession weaves through the old town, returning to the church on Saturday afternoon.

COUSCOUS ALLA TRAPANESE

Trapani's unique position on the sea route to Tunisia has made couscous a local speciality. Table reservations are essential at side-street **La Bettolaccia**, with a sharp white interior, and family-run **Caupona Taverna di Sicilia**, with summer terrace eyeballing the sculpted facade of Chiesa Anime Sante dei Purgatorio. Both are unwaveringly authentic, Slow Food favourites for traditional *couscous alla trapanese* – couscous accompanied by a broth of seafood, garlic, chilli, tomatoes, saffron, parsley and wine, which you ladle over according to taste. Share as a *primi* or order as a meal in itself.

COUSCOUS FOR DOLCI

For a sweet version of couscous studded with local pistachio nuts, make a beeline for the cake shop run by Cistercian nuns at **Monastero di Santo Spirito** (p695) in Agrigento.

GETTING AROUND

AST buses link Trapani–Birgi Vincenzo Florio Airport with Trapani port; taxis to either Trapani or Marsala charge a fixed €30 rate. Once in town, ATM city buses are useful to the beaches and the lower funicular station for Erice.

Beyond Trapani

Whether you're atop a medieval hilltop village, amid Greek theatre ruins or striding along salt pans, views here are out of this world.

San Vito
Lo Capo

Riserva Naturale
dello Zingaro

Trapani   Bonagia   Scopello
            Erice

Via del Sal   Segesta

Mozia

Trapani's busy port buzzes primarily with ferries sailing overnight to the mysterious volcanic rock island of Pantelleria, not far from Tunisia, and zippy hydrofoils whisking holidaymakers to pebble beaches in the Egadi archipelago. Protected by the Egadi Marine Protected Area – Europe's largest marine reserve – Favignana and its smaller sister islands promise slow food, pristine nature and evocative history in spades.

Along the coast, between Trapani and the wine town of Marsala, are beguiling salt pans where the prized salt used to conserve artisanal Tre Torri tuna in tins is harvested. Inland, the remarkable preservation of ancient ruins and the majesty of their sublime rural setting at both Segesta and Selinunte further south combine to form two of Sicily's enduring highlights. So large is the archaeological site of Selinunte that excavations have never really stopped since 1823 when the first metopes were unearthed.

TOP TIP

Plan your trip to Trapani's salt pans; the most interesting activities at Saline Ettore e Infersa must be booked. Cool down after exploring Selinunte's ruins with a sea dip from Lido di Zabbar, a beach hidden below the archaeological site.

Greak theatre, Segesta (p704)

ATLANTIDE PHOTOTRAVEL/GETTY IMAGES ©

ANCIENT CIVILISATIONS

Long before the arrival of the Greeks, Segesta was the principal city of the Elymians, an ancient civilisation claiming descent from the Trojans that settled in Sicily in the Bronze Age. The Elymians were in constant conflict with Greek Selinunte, whose destruction (in 409 BCE) they pursued with bloodthirsty determination. More than 100 years later the Greek tyrant Agathocles slaughtered over 10,000 Elymians and repopulated Segesta with Greeks.

TRABANTOS/SHUTTERSTOCK ©

Castello di Venere, Erice

Segesta

MAGIC AMID ANCIENT RUINS

GREEK THEATRE

Watching a performance in Segesta's Greek theatre during August's **Segesta Teatro Festival** is goose bump stuff. Elsewhere in Sicily, Taormina's Teatro Greco stages theatre and classic concerts with a Mt Etna backdrop during July's **Taormina Arte festival** and Greek tragedies unfold in Syracuse at the summer-long **Festival del Teatro Greco** (p689).

It's not hard to create your own magic in Segesta, 32km west of Trapani. Simply staring in wonder at its centrepiece **Doric temple** in fields of wildflowers and grasses, or watching drama unfold on a hot summer night beneath the stars in a 3rd-century BCE **Greek theatre**, is nothing short of celestial. Set on the edge of a deep canyon amid desolate mountains, these 5th-century BCE ruins are among the world's most evocative ancient sites.

The remarkably well preserved temple, a five-minute walk uphill from the ticket office, has retained all of its 36 columns – on windy days they become an organ, producing mysterious notes. The theatre, a 1.25km walk or shuttle-bus ride from the office, crowns the summit of Monte Bàrbaro and affords sweeping views north to the stunning Golfo di Castellammare. Allow at least a half-day to fully take in the ruins' remarkable state of preservation and the majesty of their bucolic, rural setting.

WHERE TO LUNCH IN ERICE

Gusto Il Panino Gourmet
Gourmet *panino*, salads and Bruno Ribadi craft beer brewed an hour along the coast.

Ristorante Monte San Giuliano
A stone archway leads into a vine-shaded patio garden.

Liparoti
Skip *dolci* for outstanding *granita*: try almond, pistachio and lemon peel or salted caramel and peanut.

Medieval Erice

RUINS, VIEWS & SENSATIONAL CAKES

It's difficult to pinpoint one highlight of a day trip to Erice, a medieval hilltop village watching over Trapani from its mountain perch atop the legendary peak of Eryx. The funicular ride up is a treat in itself – be sure to choose a sunny day for it – as a spectacular panorama extending from San Vito Lo Capo to Trapani's salt pans unfolds.

Inside the walled 12th-century village, get lost in a mesmerising tangle of polished, slippery, stone-paved lanes – wear shoes with decent grip. Spend an hour exploring the grassy, evocative ruins of 12th- to 13th-century **Castello di Venere**, built by the Normans over the Temple of Venus, and break over coffee and cakes in the secret garden of legendary **Pasticceria di Maria Grammatico**.

Selinunte Ruins Explorer

UNCOVER EUROPE'S LARGEST ARCHAEOLOGICAL PARK

Don your safari hat and lose yourself Indiana Jones–style in the temples and acropolis of ancient Greece's most westerly colony. Dating to the 7th century BCE, Selinos (Selinunte) was a prosperous metropolis of 100,000 people – one of the world's richest and mightiest cities – until the Carthaginians destroyed it in 409 BCE.

As you walk from the ticket office, the almost-complete **Temple E** looms large in the Eastern Temples zone. Built in the 5th century BCE and reconstructed in 1958, this is the park's showpiece. The other temples here, including 6th-century **Temple G**, which was one of the largest temples in the Greek world despite never being completed, are rubble.

Explore the **Acropolis** next, about 2km from the entrance, with five temples on a slanted plateau. The sea views are stunning. **Temple C** is the oldest temple and, because 14 of its 17 original columns are still intact, the most photographed. Smaller **Temple B**, from the Hellenistic period, was possibly dedicated to the Agrigentan physiologist and philosopher Empedocles, whose water-drainage scheme saved the city from the scourge of malaria.

Walk about 20 minutes west next, across the now-dry river Modione and up a dirt path, to the **Sanctuary of Malophoros**. Among the ravaged ruins of this temple dedicated to Demeter, the goddess of fertility, look for two altars, one of which was used for sacrifices. End in the **Ancient City**, north of the acropolis on Manuzza hill, where most of Selinunte's inhabitants lived.

SYRACUSE V CARTHAGE

Originally allied with Carthage, Selinunte switched allegiance after the Carthaginian defeat by Gelon of Syracuse in 480 BCE. Under Syracusan protection it grew in power and prestige, resulting in territorial disputes with its northern neighbour, Segesta. The final showdown came in 409 BCE when the latter called for Carthaginian help. Selinunte's former ally happily obliged and arrived to take revenge. Troops commanded by Hannibal destroyed the city after a nine-day siege, leaving only those who had taken shelter in the temples as survivors.

Around 250 BCE, with the Romans about to conquer the city, its citizens were relocated to Lilybaeum (Marsala), the Carthaginian capital in Sicily, but not before they destroyed as much as they could. What they left standing, mainly temples, was finished off by an earthquake in the Middle Ages.

 WHERE TO STAY & EAT BEYOND TRAPANI

Agriturismo Vultaggio
Safari tents, B&B rooms and a zero-kilometre farm restaurant make this countryside retreat hard to resist. €

Baglio La Luna
Escape to this hillside farmhouse B&B with hypnotic sea views, 2km north of the Zingaro reserve. €€

La Tonnara di Scopello
Scopello's historic *tonnara* (tuna fishery) has self-catering apartments and hotel rooms on the water's edge. €€

DECORATIVE TREASURES

Enrich your understanding of Selinunte with a half-day at Palermo's fascinating **Museo Archeologico Regionale Antonio Salinas** (p665). The stunning metopes found in 1823 are displayed in this world-class museum, alongside decorative friezes and the Gorgon's mask adorning Temple C.

The Salt Road

HELP HARVEST ITALY'S FINEST SALT

Along the coast between Trapani and the wine town of **Marsala** lies an evocative landscape of *saline* (shallow salt pools) and decommissioned *mulini* (windmills). As you drive along the Via del Sal or Salt Road in summer from Trapani – SP21 on maps – spot salt workers harvesting Italy's finest salt from rosy-pink salt pans glinting in the sun. Only a cottage industry remains today, providing discerning tables with prized *fior di sal* (rock salt), *cristalli di sal* (salt crystals) and *sale marino di Trapani* IGP (table salt).

Learn about salt production and take part in a guided salt-pan walk or salt tasting at **Saline Ettore e Infersa** *(seisaline. it)*, a salt museum in a 16th-century windmill, 25km south of Trapani. May to August, try being a salt worker for a half-day, harvesting salt (boots provided); or sail 20 minutes in a traditional lagoon boat across **Stagnone di Marsala** to the uninhabited islet of Isola Lunga. Back at the mill, tuck into an alfresco lunch, sunset drinks or dinner overlooking salt pans at **Mamma Caura**.

Favignana

ONE-DAY ISLAND ADVENTURE

Take a slow boat (or speedy hydrofoil) from Trapani or Marsala to this island idyll and spend the morning exploring the 19th-century tuna cannery, **Ex-Stabilimento Florio delle Tonnare di Favignana e Formica** – a vast, elegant complex built from local tufa stone overlooking the port. Inside, you can still see the sheds with vintage boats ready to roll out to sea; the terrace where tuna were hung; *la batteria de cottura*, with a trio of huge red-brick chimneys, where tuna were cooked; and the cavernous hall with the original assembly tables where the cans were filled. Short films document different aspects of the cannery's history and tuna fishing traditions, including the island's famous *Mattanza*. The *tonnara*, built in 1859 and operational until 1977, was one of many in Sicily to be owned by Favignana's famous Flavio family.

In the afternoon, rent two wheels – old-school push bike, e-bike or 50cc scooter – at the port and take the scenic 3km route to the **Giardino dell'Impossibile**, an incredible Mediterranean garden flourishing in sunken tufa-stone courtyards (some 25m deep), tunnels, caves, grottos and galleries quarried in the 1950s and 1960s. Privately owned, the gardens are the love child of owner and visionary

 WHERE TO STAY & EAT ON FAVIGNANA

La Casa del Limoneta
An enchanting sunken garden full of lemon trees frames this cosy whitewashed B&B. €€

Villa Margherita
Peace and tranquillity reign at this enchanting villa hotel in Favignana's botanical gardens. €€

Osteria del Sotto Sale
The *busiate alla norma* (pasta with aubergine, tomato and ricotta) at this casual-chic *osteria* is spot on. €€

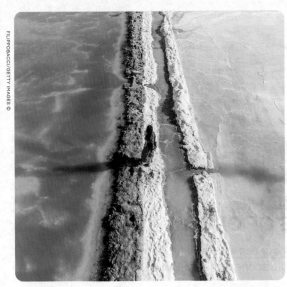

Salt pools, Trapani

WHY I LOVE FAVIGNANA

Nicola Williams, writer

It's the unpretentious grassroots cuisine and nonchalance with which quarried blocks of tufa are scattered around like a child's Lego bricks that I love. The global desire for island escapes might have rocketed over the years, but islanders make no attempt to manicure their island. Favignana is, first and foremost, their home where the day's catch ends up in brown-paper cones of deep-fried *frittura mista* (mixed seafood) at **Tunafish City**; where the old-fashioned grocery store on Piazza Madrice chalks *'ricotta fresca'* (fresh ricotta) on a blackboard outside; where Roman camomile, rosemary, wormwood and other indigenous botanicals watered with naturally salty water from an artisan well end up in Isola di Favignana craft gin.

Maria Gabriella Campo, now in her 80s, who personally planted and nurtured most of the 300-odd different flora species – indigenous and exotic – that defiantly thrive in the dusty, tufa-stone landscape. Visits are by guided tour. You can also stay overnight in its upmarket **Villa Margherita** hotel or a self-catering cottage on the estate.

Riserva Naturale dello Zingaro

A HIKER'S SEASIDE PARADISE

Stride along a 7km walking trail bejewelled with blockbuster sea views in this wild coastal **nature reserve**. Wild carob and yellow euphorbia dust the hillsides, and narrow paths dive down to rocky coves with pebble beaches and emerald waters to swim in. The hot spot for snorkelling is **Cala Marinella**, midway along the path. Buy admission tickets and pick up a trail map at the park's southern entrance, 2km north of Scopello, or the northern entrance in San Vito Lo Capo.

 GETTING AROUND

In Trapani, to get the funicular up to Erice, take bus 21 or 23 from the western end of Via GB Fardella (by Piazza Vittorio Emanuele) to the end. Tarantola *(tarantolabus.com)* buses between Trapani bus station and Segesta (40 to 50 minutes) are limited. In Segesta, motorists must park in a purpose-built car park and walk 1.5km or take a shuttle bus to the ruins.

Getting around Segesta and Selinunte on foot requires stamina, especially in summer when water, sun protection and sunhat (even an umbrella to use as a parasol) are survival essentials. At Selinunte, electric golf carts at the main entrance cut out some of the legwork.

Pre-book tickets for Liberty Lines hydrofoils to Favignana. Bring your passport, ID card or driving licence to rent a bike at Favignana port.

SARDINIA

WALK IN THE FOOTSTEPS OF GIANTS

Just beyond the glamour lies an island full of myth, tradition and incredible scenery that will leave you breathless.

Legend has it that when Karim Aga Khan first visited the land he had purchased in Sardinia, he arrived by donkey to find sleepy fishing villages with no electricity, running water or paved roads. He was, unsurprisingly, concerned about the folly of his investment. Returning by yacht, however, he envisioned what would become the Costa Smeralda. This tiny stretch of curated beach would eventually become one of the most prized bits of real estate on the planet and make Sardinia synonymous with wealth, celebrity and excess.

But a world awaits beyond the erstwhile glamour of Porto Cervo, from the forbidding cliffs of the Supramonte to the *tombe dei giganti* (giants'

tombs) to the sultry winds of Cagliari. It feels more than different: it is mythic, immortal. Though reverence for tradition is palpable in every corner of Sardinia, there is an almost fearless embrace of the future. Iconic locations are taking radical steps to preserve their resources, and regions once considered off-limits have opened their courtyards to the world.

Those who venture even slightly off the beaten track are well rewarded. Hospitality is expansive here, so don't be surprised to find yourself in someone's workshop or living room getting a dizzying history lesson served with homemade treats you'll never be able to replicate. No matter. You'll be back, whether by donkey, yacht or anything in between.

SCHWARZE NINA/SHUTTERSTOCK ©

THE MAIN AREAS

CAGLIARI	BARBAGIA & THE SUPRAMONTE	ALGHERO & THE WEST COAST	LA MADDALENA & GALLURA	COSTA SMERALDA
The cosmopolitan capital. p714	The heart of Sardinian culture. p723	Haute cuisine and wild nature. p631	From wine tasting to snorkelling. p739	An undeniable bucket-list destination. p743

Capriccioli Beach, Costa Smeralda (p743)

Find Your Way

The second-largest island in the Mediterranean has been called a 'micro-continent' thanks to its incredible natural and cultural diversity. But don't worry about seeing it all – wherever you go will be a breathtaking discovery.

La Maddalena & Gallura, p739

The beauty of the archipelago, the incredible history and miles of golden vineyards make this a must-visit corner of the island.

Costa Smeralda, p743

Forget all you think you know about the billionaire's playground and focus on the stunning, surreal coastline that seems to go on forever.

Alghero & the West Coast, p731

Marvel at how diverse the island can be within a short distance, and celebrate it at the most beautiful beach in the world.

Mediterranean Sea

Tyrrhenian Sea

Parco Nazionale dell'Asinara

Golfo dell'Asinara

Parco Nazionale dell'Arcipelago di La Maddalena

Iles Lavezzi

CORSICA (FRANCE)

Propriano

Porto-Vecchio

Bonifacio

Santa Teresa di Gallura

La Maddalena

Palau

Porto Cervo

Arzachena

Porto Rotondo

Golfo Aranci

Golfo di Olbia

Olbia

San Teodoro

Siniscola

Golfo di Orosei

Orosei

Cala Gonone

Dorgali

Oliena

Orani

Nuoro

Bitti

Monti

Budduso

Oschiri

Ozieri

Tempio Pausania

Monte Limbara

Coghinas

Isola Rossa

Castelsardo

Sorso

Perfugas

Ploaghe

Thiesi

Pozzomaggiore

Macomer

Ottana

Tirso

Cuglieri

Bosa

Bosa Marina

Montelcone

Villanova

Ittiri

Sassari

Porto Torres

Fertilia

Alghero

Stintino

Argentiera

Barbagia & the Supramonte, p723

With some of the most distinct cultural traditions anywhere on the island, this region is truly the heart of Sardinia.

Cagliari, p714

From bustling markets to sandy beaches, the capital has everything you could ask for in a holiday hub – within walking distance.

50 km
25 miles

CAR

The well-maintained network of roads and highways (all toll-free) make Sardinia a fantastic road-trip destination – or, to channel your inner *Easy Rider*, go by motorcycle. Seasoned travellers bring their cars on the ferry but renting a car is just as simple.

BUS

There are a number of companies operating local, provincial and longer-distance bus services that can bring you to just about anywhere on the island. But be aware that trips can be long, delayed, and confusing if you don't speak Italian or Sardinian.

TRAIN

Trains are clean, budget-friendly and efficient, but they only link larger cities or transport hubs along the western spine of the island. The scenic Trenino Verde is a great way to see the countryside, as long as you're not in a rush.

711

Plan Your Time

Sardinia is a year-round destination with an endless amount of possibilities. Whether you're looking to stimulate your mind, body or appetite, something on the island will stir your soul.

Carloforte (p721)

If You Only Do One Thing

● The heady mix of ancient fortifications, breezy cafe terraces and lively streets give **Cagliari** (p714) a vitality that seems to roll in from the sea itself. Explore the **Marina** (p717) district for a mix of traditional restaurants and ambitious upstarts, all of which adhere to an ethos of local, sustainable food. Nearby beaches and nature reserves mean you're never too far from a walk through unspoilt natural beauty. Take the time to explore the western shores of **Sant'Antioco** (p720) and **Carloforte** (p721), where time does more than stand still – it simply stops existing altogether.

Seasonal highlights

Though widely considered a quintessential summer destination, Sardinia is worth visiting almost all year-round. Festivals featuring traditional food, crafts and dance are not to be missed.

JANUARY/ FEBRUARY

Get spooked by the *mamuthones* masks in Barbagia's village of Mamoiada to banish evil during **Carnevale**.

MAY

Come for the **Festa di Sant'Efisio** (honouring Cagliari's patron saint), stay for the **Cavalcata Sarda** (Sassari's cavalcade).

JUNE

Fall in love with **Cagliari**'s winding alleys, rich museums and stellar nightlife, all a stone's throw from lovely Poetto beach.

CHIARA PAOLINI/SHUTTERSTOCK ©, PAOLO CERTO/SHUTTERSTOCK ©, ALF/GETTY IMAGES ©

A Week-Long Stay

● Once considered a no man's land due to a complicated history of banditry and resistance, **Barbagia** (p723) is today the custodian of Sardinia's cultural heritage. The towns of **Oliena** (p736) and **Dorgali** (p726) keep artisanal crafts alive, while **Orgosolo** (p723) displays its history through stunning murals that decorate the town. Hike through the **Supramonte** (p723), the **Valle di Lanaittu** (p726) and **Tiscali** (p726) for a glimpse of the earliest human settlements in Europe. Grab your snorkel and hop into a *gommone* (rubber boat) on the **Golfo di Orosei** (p729) to bathe in pristine seas, then celebrate with *pecorino* cheese and ruby Cannonau wine.

If You Have More Time

● It would be unforgivable not to visit the most famous corner of Sardinia, but there's much more to do than lament rising costs in **Porto Cervo** (p743) and stalk celebrity yachts in the marina. The northern province of **Gallura** (p739) is home to **La Maddalena** (p739) archipelago, a cluster of 60 islands that have the audacity to be increasingly more beautiful as you explore. But a visit to the interior is just as rewarding, with hikes through towns like **Luogosanto** (p740) offering a window into the history of Sardinia, along with generous tastings of the rightfully famous Vermentino white wine.

JULY

Brave the crowds (if you must) to people-watch in Porto Cervo, with plenty of **swim breaks** around La Maddalena.

SEPTEMBER

Breathe in the aromas of cured *bottarga* (mullet roe) in Cabras and get to know the **giants' tombs** around Tharros and Barumini.

OCTOBER

Make the pilgrimage to **Barbagia** to sample its traditional cuisine, including suckling pig and *pecorino* cheese.

NOVEMBER

Explore the **Cortes Apertas** (Open Courtyards) of Barbagia to experience the food, culture and traditions at the heart of the island.

CAGLIARI

Of the many types of port cities, there is no category so evocative as those that seem to have grown out of the sea to form on great hills in the embrace of a bay. These cities live not only next to but in tandem with the sea; if the waves are not visible from every tenement window, they are palpable all the same. They are places which possess and are possessed by an energy so unique that it is almost intoxicating. Every distant whistle that drifts back to shore is a reminder of the world beyond, and every warm embrace under the amber lights of an ancient alleyway is a siren's song to return ashore. Cagliari is one of these cities, one of the very best. From the Castello district above to the Marina below, its rhythm is unmistakable. Cagliari is the soul of Sardinia.

Rome

Cagliari

TOP TIP

Driving in central Cagliari is restricted for nonresidents, particularly in the Castello, Marina, Stampace and Villanova neighbourhoods. Find a free parking spot (within the white lines), avail yourself of the expansive bus network, or better yet, walk.

MORNINGS AT THE MARKET

At one of the largest covered markets in Europe, **Mercato di San Benedetto**, over 200 stalls overflow with fresh produce and local specialities like *porcheddu* (suckling pig) and a host of cuts you're unlikely to find elsewhere. Cheeses like *pecorino*, Fiore Sardo and *ricotta salata* all fight to perfume your palate first. At the lower level, fishers arrive with their catch around dawn – while you may get the best deals nearer to closing time, there's nothing like the early-morning scent of saltwater. Afterwards treat yourself to a cappuccino and brioche from **Pasticceria Piemontese**.

Cagliari's Nature Escapes

WHITE BEACHES, PINK FLAMINGOS

Perhaps one of the best reasons to visit Cagliari is the opportunity to mix the culture of the city with the unrivaled natural beauty just outside its centre. No place is better for a quick jaunt than **Poetto Beach**.

If you're feeling sporty, the nearly 7km walk from the centre of Cagliari to Poetto is mostly flat. There are also easy bus connections – the 'P' on any bus is a sign it stops there (during the warmer months, look for locals with umbrellas at the bus stop). Once you arrive, you'll find a wide sandy beach that evokes nostalgia for anyone who grew up near the sea: the boardwalk is a haven for cyclists and runners, and filled with kiosks selling all manner of snacks and drinks. Poetto stretches along the Golfo degli Angeli (Angel's Gulf) towards the **Sella del Diavolo** (Devil's Saddle), establishing a clear theme for sightseeing. But there's no debate – you're much closer to heaven here.

Before heading back to the centre, stop at the **Parco Naturale Regionale Molentargius**, an ancient salt basin and the nesting ground of pink flamingos. Once the main salt extraction point on the island, today it extends across 16 sq km with architectural remnants from the 19th and early 20th centuries dotting the peaceful, verdant landscape. It's truly an oasis, lined with walking trails and observation points set against the backdrop of the beckoning Cagliari skyline.

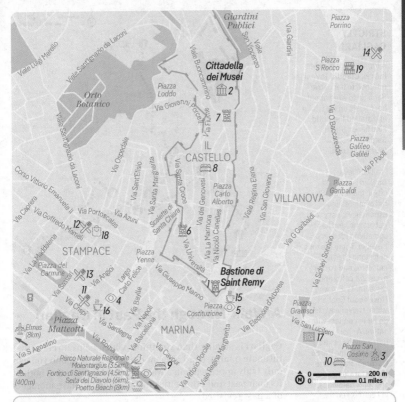

HIGHLIGHTS
1 Bastione di Saint Remy
2 Cittadella dei Musei

SIGHTS
3 Basilica di San
Saturnino
4 Largo Carlo Felice

5 Piazza Costituzione
6 Torre dell'Elefante
7 Torre di San Pancrazio

SLEEPING
8 Birkin Hotel – Castello
9 Palazzo Dessy
10 Palazzo Doglio

EATING
11 Ditrizio Pasticceria
12 Framento
13 Josto
14 Pasticceria
Piemontese

DRINKING
15 Antico Caffè

16 Caffè Svizzero

ENTERTAINMENT
17 Exmà

SHOPPING
18 Etto Macelleria
19 Mercato di
San Benedetto

 WHERE TO SLEEP IN CAGLIARI

Birkin Hotel Collection
Beautifully curated rooms,
luscious breakfasts and stellar
service; locations in Castello,
Marina and the port. €€€

Palazzo Dessy
Elegant guesthouse tucked
away in Marina – no matter
how lively it gets outside, you'll
sleep like a baby. €€

Palazzo Doglio
Looking to treat yourself?
There's no better place than
this historic hotel that has
thought of every detail. €€€

715

I truly believe Cagliari is the best city in the world. It's full of interesting experiences, easy to get around, and has something for every traveller. There are tons of historic sites and museums and so many excellent cafes and restaurants. But what I love about Cagliari is that I never have to go far to connect with nature. A short bus ride from the centre takes me to the **Parco Naturale Regionale Molentargius** to spot pink flamingos, or I can hike up the **Sella del Diavolo** promontory for a great workout and views of Poetto beach. When I need inspiration, I head to the **Fortino di Sant'Ignazio** for magnificent sunsets.

A Walk Through the Past in Cagliari

A STROLL FOR ANY SEASON

Cagliari is smaller than you think, which helps it retain that intimate quality of all ancient cities by the sea, one you can only truly apprehend on a walk. The city is evocative both of its own past and other cities like it – you will have moments of a past revisited.

Even in the warmest months of July and August the balmy *maestrale* carries northward to the Castello district, bordered by medieval fortifications nearly 100m above sea level. The story of Cagliari begins here: its Sardinian name, Casteddu, means 'castle', and the neighbourhood houses the stunning **1 Cittadella dei Musei** on Piazza Arsenale. While you could easily spend days here, if you only see one part of the citadel let it be the Museo Archeologico Nazionale, with the impossible yet real Giganti di Monte Prama on display along with a stellar collection of mysterious *bronzetti* (bronze figurines) presumably dating back to the nuraghic period.

WHERE TO GO FOR COFFEE IN CAGLIARI

Antico Caffè
A historic spot where DH Lawrence once scrawled. Great coffee, and staff who tolerate your genius for hours.

Ditrizio Pasticceria
This Marina gem will inspire you with an endless selection of sublime pastries, perfect coffee and sumptuous decor.

Caffè Svizzero
Stunning for more than a century, centrally located, and serving the smoothest coffee you'll taste all day.

The mildly serpentine streets of Castello rarely feel claustrophobic, though you'll catch the scents of *sugo* (meat sauce) bubbling in a ground-floor kitchen or spot a family gathered around the television through open doors. Wander between the two towers that overlook the city – **2 Torre di San Pancrazio** was completed in 1305, and **3 Torre dell'Elefante** in 1307; each was designed to ward off invaders and the latter is named for its marble elephant statue. While both are impressive, they perhaps pale in comparison to the **4 Bastione di Saint Remy**. The magnificent structure connects Castello with the rest of the city via striking marble stairs added at the very end of the 1800s along with the panoramic Umberto I terrace.

Head left at the foot of Saint Remy towards the boho shopfronts of Villanova or make a right to the lively sidewalks and piazzas of Marina. But don't rush off – **5 Piazza Costituzione**, connecting some of Cagliari's main arteries, is a lovely place to linger and appreciate the very human scale of the city. If you're in the mood for shopping (window or otherwise), **6 Via Garibaldi** takes you through the heart of Villanova by way of impossibly quaint boutiques. A straight shot down Via San Lucifero leads to **7 Exmà**, a former slaughterhouse turned contemporary arts centre, with the ancient **8 Basilica di San Saturnino** ruins just steps further in Piazza San Cosimo. You'll find no shortage of parks, squares or cafes to stop by.

All great port cities begin and end their stories where land meets sea, and Cagliari is no exception. Though now a genteel progression of overflowing terraces and lively banter, Marina retains a hint of those rough edges where sailors and merchants would have lit up the night. Take Via Manno towards **9 Piazza Yenne** to enter Marina from its liveliest point. The piazza is filled with bars serving *aperitivi* (pre-dinner drinks) late into the night to a steady stream of revellers. Head towards the sea on **10 Largo Carlo Felice**, peering down the labyrinthine alleys that smell of grilling fish and vibrate with the sound of plates. You'll inevitably find yourself under the porticoes of **11 Via Roma**, in the shadow of cruise ships, sailboats, and perhaps traditional Sardinian fishing boats. Drink in hand, you'll swear you've been here before, or someplace just like it.

CAGLIARI'S DINING SCENE

Cagliari has a well-established culinary scene, but ambitious young chefs are reinvigorating traditional cuisine with local ingredients, sustainable practices and a healthy dose of humour. Chef **Pierluigi Fais** is at the forefront of this new scene, with a number of restaurants that are sure to satisfy any appetite. **Etto Macelleria** serves a tiny menu of fresh local dishes sliced to order, day and night from their stylish outpost on Corso Vittorio Emanuele II. If you're craving pizza, he's way ahead of you: **Framento** has the best sourdough crust in the city and a fine range of craft beers to pair it with. For those looking for fine dining, look no further than **Josto**, a showcase for traditional dishes reinvented with Fais' signature flair.

 GETTING AROUND

Cagliari is well served by both air and sea, with Elmas Airport a short drive from the centre and the main port just steps from the porticoes of Via Roma. If you're planning to stay in the city, you'll find it entirely walkable and where not, well served by an efficient bus network. However, if you want to venture out towards any of the natural parks, beaches or parts unknown, you'll need a car. Rental agencies abound, both at the airport and in town.

Barumini

Montevecchio

Isola di San Pietro • Iglesias • Cagliari

Sant'Antioco • Carbonia

Beyond Cagliari

Southern Sardinia has a complex and fascinating history that goes far beyond its crystalline shores, and is well worth exploring.

The story of Sardinia could be told in a thousand different ways, and each one would illustrate how distinct the island is from the rest of Italy. As you travel further from the well-established resort towns, you'll notice fewer holiday caravans and more of the sprawling, mountainous countryside that characterises much of the island's interior. This is perhaps because the southwestern corner of Sardinia – while no less beautiful than the other parts – was for centuries a hub for industry rather than holidays. However, instead of making it less accessible, this complicated history makes it one of the most rewarding places to explore.

TOP TIP

Plan for an overnight stay to soak up all the strange beauty of Sant'Antioco and the stellar setting of Carloforte.

Su Nuraxi di Barumini (p722)

VALERY ROKHIN/SHUTTERSTOCK ©

Porto Flavia, Masua (p720)

Exploring the Ghost Mines of Iglesias

DIG DEEP INTO SARDINIAN HISTORY

Since the Bronze Age, Sardinia has been called 'The Island of Silver Veins' due to its vast mineral resources. Empires from the Phoenician to the Byzantine took their turn exploiting them, and when the Maritime Republics of Genoa and Pisa arrived on the island in the 9th century, it had a well-developed infrastructure for extracting and processing raw materials. Until well into the 20th century, Sardinia – especially the southern town of Iglesias – was a hub for coal, zinc, lead and silver mining. This industrial development came at a cost to both the land and its inhabitants: mining was a notoriously dangerous job, with safety protocols often sacrificed in favour of speedy delivery. Countless lives were lost over generations.

Whether by necessity or intention, Sardinia has preserved many of these mining villages and opened them to the public as some of the best examples of industrial archaeology in the world. One of the oldest mines, the stunning ghost village and geomineral park at **Montevecchio** is about an hour's drive northwest of Cagliari. It's in a decrepit state,

SARDINIAN SHIPBUILDING

The craft of small shipbuilding is integral to the history of Sardinia's Sulcis archipelago, where both Sant'Antioco (p720) and Carloforte (p721) are located. The small but incredibly bright and cheerful **Museo del Mare e dei Maestri d'Ascia** takes you through the history of small ships in Sant'Antioco with displays of equipment, vessels and video testimony from some of the islands' best-known shipbuilding families. Don't miss the gift shop, which is full of quirky items from local designers like Cagliari's Silvia Congiu.

WHERE TO STAY IN SANT'ANTIOCO AND CARLOFORTE

MuMA Hostel
Part of Sant'Antioco's shipbuilding museum, MuMA has clean, cheerful rooms with a fabulous local breakfast. €

Lu'Hotel Riviera
Panoramic sea views in Carloforte, breezy rooms and a beachy vibe that will instantly relax you. €€

Poecylia Resort
This digital detox in Carloforte is so welcoming that you'll forget all about the rest of the world. €€€

Carloforte

SANT'ANTIOCO GEMS

Paola from **Gioielleria Malia** (with boutiques in Sant'Antioco and Carloforte) not only has a stunning collection of traditional Sardinian filigree jewellery, but she'll tell you the best place to eat and make you a reservation. Speaking of which, **S'unda Manna** is a seaside restaurant in Sant'Antioco that serves impossibly fresh fish straight off the grill located just behind your table. You'll be busy watching the sunset, but the nose knows. Get the tuna, of course.

almost frozen in time like a sunken ship, which makes it even more moving. Further south, the Museo del Carbone in **Carbonia** blends the impossible scale of these engineering projects with the human dimension of the workers who made them possible. But to truly comprehend the Herculean nature of these endeavours, head to **Masua** where two 600m-long tunnels were dug into cliffs to reach the Pan di Zucchero sea stack, where they loom 50m over the water's edge. This marvel of modern engineering was christened Porto Flavia after the daughter of the engineer who designed it. However, the true miracle of this site is that, despite ignoring all safety protocols, it didn't cost any lives when it was built in the early 1920s.

The Art of Sea Silk in Sant'Antioco

GET BEWITCHED BY THE MASTER

There are legends in Sardinia – if you are lucky, you'll occasionally find them hiding in plain sight. The 'Maestro di Bisso', **Chiara Vigo**, is one such legend. Her home is on the main street of Sant'Antioco (an hour and a half by car from Cagliari), and there's no signage. The front door is barely

BEST BEACHES IN SANT'ANTIOCO AND CARLOFORTE

Il Giunco
The longest beach in Carloforte offers disabled access and it's dog-friendly. Bring your own drinks and snacks!

Maladroxia
About 10km outside Sant'Antioco, this is an ideal place for families to spend the day.

Conca
Head to this Carloforte beach to cliff-dive or cave-dive, depending on your mood.

open, offering the most tepid invitation inside. Keep going, because the **Museo del Bisso** is not the cluttered, ground-floor room you've just entered, overflowing with strange wall hangings and frames. The museum is the woman whose piercing glare will make you want to run back down the street. You'll be convinced that you've made a mistake. No matter; keep going.

The giant *Pinna nobilis* mollusc, which can grow up to 1.5m, uses byssuses (*bisso* in Italian) to attach itself to rocks, forming a filament known as sea silk. This delicate, rare material has been harvested and used for millennia to decorate clothing or wall hangings. A Sant'Antioco native, Vigo is – in her own words – the 30th generation of *bisso* divers from the island. Her studio, filled with sea-silk hangings that she refuses to sell, is open to the public in the morning and afternoon, with a generous break for lunch. Whether her legend is apocryphal hardly matters: sit back and watch her incantations as she slowly coaxes the tiny threads from their algae, and allow yourself to be enchanted as she sings strange songs from her youth. She doesn't speak English, often looks like a disapproving schoolteacher, and seems to come from another universe altogether. Stick around for a while anyway – you'll be glad you did.

Discovering Carloforte's Genoese Heritage

A LITTLE BIT OF LIGURIA

Just when you think you're starting to get the slightest grasp on some of the Sardinian language, U Pàize throws you a curveball. This Ligurian enclave, interchangeably referred to as **Isola di San Pietro** (St Peter's Island), is the loveliest bit of delirium you're likely to come across on any holiday. However, the story doesn't end there: the original founders were from just outside Genoa but they shared the permission to settle the island with fishing families from Tabarka in Tunisia. Confused? Don't fret, the island is so beautiful that you won't need to know where you've landed.

The 6000 residents of Carloforte, San Pietro's main town, still maintain strong links to Genoa, which is evident in the language of the island (known as *tabarkino*) as well as its architecture. Indeed, the narrow streets and gentle slopes will evoke the pastel colours of the Boccadasse neighbourhood, where the sea peeks in through every angle. There is no shortage of perfect beaches,

CARLOFORTE'S FESTIVALS

Carloforte was built on the tuna fishing industry, and every June it honours this heritage with **Girotonno**, a multiday festival that culminates with a tuna cooking competition featuring international chefs and local stars. Girotonno also hosts a tuna village in Carloforte and live cooking throughout the city.

Lest we forget, the island shares a dual heritage with the Arab world, and every autumn this is celebrated with **Cascà**, the international festival of couscous. Chefs from around the Mediterranean gather to share recipes, stories and endless variations of this all-important staple in both the cuisine and history of Carloforte.

IF YOU'RE HEADING NORTH

Leave early enough to have a day at **Barumini** (p722), the largest nuraghic site in Sardinia and an easy stop on the SS131.

WHERE TO EAT TUNA IN CARLOFORTE

Al Tonno di Corsa	**Osteria della Tonnara**	**Ristorante da Andrea**
Michelin-rated, with an intimate dining room and inventive menu based almost entirely on the catch of the day. €€	The gold standard for tuna in Carloforte – the relaxed atmosphere means you can take your time tasting everything. €€	Come here to feast on *cascà* (couscous) and the freshest tuna you can imagine. €€€

either, and each of them has its own subtle charm. Swim at family-friendly **La Caletta** beach, then treat yourself to some local tuna and white wine at **Ristorante da Nicolo**, where you can watch the world go by on Corso Cavour. It will feel like nowhere you've been before, and everywhere you've ever wanted to go.

The Prehistoric Marvels of Barumini

FINDS FROM ANOTHER WORLD

As you travel through Sardinia, you'll begin to notice a strange reoccurring structure in the fields or on the hilltops. It will appear to be a cross between a Stonehenge tribute and a Pugliese *trullo* (circular stone-built house) without being either; some will be in almost perfect condition while others will look like they've seen better days (or centuries). Eventually, you'll be compelled to ask what these curious shapes are, and the answer will do nothing to satisfy you. They are *nuraghi*, the principal structures and most tangible evidence of a prehistoric culture that vanished leaving no written records. And though you'll find the *nuraghi* in nearly every corner of Sardinia, perhaps nowhere are they better experienced than at the Unesco World Heritage Site of **Su Nuraxi di Barumini** (a two-hour bus ride from Cagliari).

The nuraghic civilisation is thought to have existed between the 18th century BCE and somewhere between the 6th and 11th centuries CE, depending on who you ask. But chronology is the least of your concerns – when you stand at the foot of the site, you'll have no words for what is in front of you. The rounded structures are built with rock formations so symmetrical that they bring to mind the rhyming couplets of poets who wouldn't be born for millennia. The sheer scale of these monuments is baffling. No one knows what purpose these settlements served, but if the present is any indication, they were imposing and inspiring places to gather.

MORE ON THE NURAGHI

Beyond the Su Nuraxi site itself, visit the **Centre Giovanni Lilliu**, named after the renowned archaeologist and political figure who first discovered the *nuraghe* (stone tower) in the 1950s. The centre is filled with a photographic chronicle of the excavations as well as exhibits of artisanal crafts from around Sardinia. The **Casa Zapata** museum in Barumini also houses an impressive array of nuraghic artefacts from the Su Nuraxi 'e Cresia, another site that is still being explored.

GETTING AROUND

Trains run from Cagliari as far as Carbonia in the southwest; if you're looking to explore the peninsula it's best to hire a car. Sant'Antioco is connected by a land bridge to the rest of Sardinia, making it an easy one-hour drive from Cagliari. Getting to Carloforte, however, requires a ferry from Calasetta. The trip takes about 30 minutes and ferries run frequently between the two ports, so if you're in the mood for a tuna lunch, there's nothing stopping you.

BARBAGIA & THE SUPRAMONTE

Rome
✪

● Barbagia & the
Supramonte

If Cagliari is the soul of Sardinia, the central Barbagia region is its heart. Though largely contiguous with Nuoro province, Barbagia remains an important cultural, historical and geographical distinction. Cicero used the term to describe the 'barbarians' that Rome's armies never came close to conquering.

Indeed, a ferocious sense of independence permeates Barbagia – nowhere more so than in the Supramonte mountain range, running along the northeastern spine of the Gennargentu massif. This spirit has helped preserve Sardinia's distinct language and customs. But the forbidding landscape also made it a haven for banditry in the 19th and 20th centuries.

Hospitality in Barbagia is so genuine it will change the way you think about Sardinia. It is said that giants once roamed this land – whether hiking through nuraghic ruins, watching *pane carasau* (flat bread) fired in a homemade oven or diving into pristine waters that even Venus couldn't resist, you'll believe it.

TOP TIP

September is the perfect time to enjoy everything that makes the island so special. You'll avoid the summer crowds, the sea is still warm enough for snorkelling, and you're just in time for Autumn in Barbagia, a three-month-long celebration of Sardinian culture.

The Town of 700 Murals

A BRILLIANT HISTORY OF RESISTANCE

There are places in the world that, owing to some particular alchemy, remind us how very small we are. It may occur in large cities when we are overwhelmed by the flow of human traffic, or it may come over us in the midst of an unexpected bout of solitude. In some rare cases, it materialises when we find awe-inspiring beauty that blends the natural with the handcrafted, humbling us in the best possible way. Anywhere you go in Barbagia has this potential, but nowhere more so than the formidable mountain town of **Orgosolo**, where the complicated and compelling history of the region is written on nearly every wall.

The notion of *banditismo Sardo*, a specifically Sardinian type of banditry, has existed since the ancient Roman era. Over the centuries it developed as a response to violence and oppression inflicted on the poverty-stricken agro-pastoral population by large landowners; in the absence of any laws or protection, the kinship and family networks that kept towns in Barbagia alive came to depend on these small crimes. Of course, that was fertile ground for anti-heroes and *banditi* soon became folklore, Robin Hood–type figures in thick woollen coats nobly vanishing into the mountains. Though banditry existed throughout the island, by the 20th century the areas around Nuoro were considered particularly difficult to govern, which only increased the force applied. Banditry

BARBAGIA'S OPEN COURTYARDS

In 1996 the town of Oliena organised an event known as **Cortes Apertas**, where historic homes would open their doors and allow visitors to observe the cultural traditions that had been maintained for generations. The project was such a success that other towns in Barbagia soon followed suit and by 2001, **Autumn in Barbagia** was born. Every year from September to December, 31 towns in the region welcome visitors into their homes to experience a bit of Sardinia. Each town has a distinct heritage, and all are worth exploring during this seasonal festival. For the annual schedule, visit *cuoredellasardegna. it* or the Sardinian tourism board's website *(sardegnaturismo.it)*.

in turn grew more violent: by the 1960s, kidnappings were rampant in the mountainous region and more than 150 were reported until the practice largely ended in 1997. The stain it left on the region, and on Sardinia as a whole, has taken a generation to wipe clean.

But it has not been erased in Orgosolo, and by design. In 1969, a collective of anarchists known as **Dioniso** painted the first mural in the town to honour the nonviolent resistance of the people of Orgosolo, known as the Pratobello revolt. Soon, schoolteachers began to encourage their students to paint murals, and artists from around the world began

 WHERE TO STAY IN BARBAGIA

Agriturismo S'Ozzastru
This *agriturismo* (farm-stay accommodation) in Dorgali blends tradition and modern comfort; the pool is superb. €€

Rifugio Gorropu
Also in Dorgali, Gorropu offers warm, family- and pet-friendly hospitality with stunning views and local cuisine. €

Su Lithu
Not your average *agriturismo* (it bills itself as a 'boutique hotel'), serving traditional food and hospitality in Bitti. €€€

ANDREA ETZI/SHUTTERSTOCK ©

Su Gorropu (p726)

WHY I LOVE BARBAGIA

Virginia Di Gaetano, writer

There is a common thread that runs through those places in the world that tend to get called 'difficult'. Too often they are undervalued and overlooked, deemed not worth the trouble it takes to get there. But 'difficult' places share a brilliant, unrelenting sense of humanity because if you do go there with the willingness to give and receive kindness, you will be rewarded with the most incredible experiences imaginable. Barbagia is that kind of place, and it will leave an imprint on your heart if you let it, just as it has done on mine.

flocking to this small town whose story was unfolding in the open air. Today, there are over 700 murals in Orgosolo: many depict the struggles of Sardinians, many more depict their triumphs. Still others evoke international themes and sing out against far-away wars and universal injustice. While Orgosolo still grapples with its complex history, thousands of people come to witness one of the most unlikely yet incredible examples of street art in the world.

Hidden Sardinia in the Supramonte

BE CHALLENGED, BE HUMBLED

Some things reach such a level of infamy that the mere mention of their name elicits a reaction somewhere between awe and intimidation. The untamed Supramonte mountain range will garner just that response from those in the know. Its peaks are staggeringly vertiginous, its valleys misty repositories of an almost primitive air. If giants did indeed roam this land and left any magic behind, surely they left it in the Supramonte.

Lollovers
This place in tiny Lollove is just about as close as you can get to going back in time while keeping your creature comforts. €€

Agriturismo Guthiddai
Taking a bite out of Su Gologone's overflow in Oliena, Guthiddai is full of experiences, services and charm. €€

Agriturismo Testone
If you want to feel like a shepherd for a day, Nuoro's Testone is a fine, cosy place to spend a holiday. €

GIUMA/SHUTTERSTOCK ©

Tiscali

OLIENA'S EXPERIENCE HOTEL

Oliena locals may somewhat derisively call it a *mosca bianca* (rare bird), but they will also tell you about the incredible meals they've enjoyed at **Su Gologone** for decades. Beginning as a restaurant in 1967, when the area was known more for its criminals than its cuisine, over time it bravely expanded into accommodation and evolved into a luxury retreat. The rates for rooms can veer into the eye-watering, but if you're going to splash out, there's no better place than this oasis at the foot of the Supramonte, cocooned in extraordinary local arts and crafts. Oh, and the restaurant is as good as ever.

The mountains have long since been liberated from both behemoths and bandits, but it's still best not to wander off too far alone. Though well patrolled, the Supramonte is a wild, largely uninhabited place with almost no phone signal throughout. Besides, a trek through the range without someone to tell you about the millennia of history would be a shame: there are treasures to discover around every corner if you know where to look, or who to ask.

Luckily, Fabrizio Caggiari organises treks, hikes and cultural visits through his company, **Sardegna Nascosta**, based out of his hometown of **Oliena**, one of the most vibrant towns in Barbagia. Few people have the same kind of passion – more than a guide, Caggiari is the amiable ambassador of a land that is surprisingly responsive to his tenderness. Tours include visits to the natural spring of Su Gologone at the foot of the Supramonte, the linked caves of **Sa Ohe** and **Su Bentu**, the nuraghic village of **Tiscali**, the majestic canyons of **Su Gorropu** and the **Valle di Lanaittu**, cultural visits to Oliena and Orgosolo, and traditional mountain meals prepared by shepherds.

 BEST OF BARBAGIA'S ARTISANS

Dorgali
Dorgali is known for its incredible filigree jewellery, and you'll find a wealth of shops in town dedicated to the art.

Sarule
This small village stands out among many for its brightly coloured, hand-woven traditional rugs and tapestries.

Desulo
Visit Desulo to watch the famously vibrant ceremonial costumes being hand-stitched before your eyes.

Museum-Hopping in Barbagia

ANCIENT CULTURE MEETS CONTEMPORARY ART

If you're based in or around the provincial capital of **Nuoro**, you're a stone's throw from some of the most fascinating and varied museums on the island. And while it is fair to say that many parts of Sardinia are an open-air museum, the care that has been shown to collect and preserve this cultural heritage demonstrates how highly valued (and valuable) it truly is.

The **Museo Deleddiano** occupies the childhood home of Grazia Deledda (1871–1936) in the centre of Nuoro and takes visitors on a multimedia tour of a house that not only retraces Deledda's development as a writer but shows how truly groundbreaking her work was and is. The first Italian woman to win the Nobel Prize for Literature in 1926, Grazia Deledda remains one of the most important figures in modern Sardinia, and her home is a tribute to this.

Also in Nuoro, the **Museo Etnografico Sardo**, or Museo del Costume, is the most comprehensive collection of the history, customs and traditions unique to Sardinia. It's housed in a purpose-built complex based upon a traditional village and contains over 8000 items including clothes, jewellery, tools, weapons and masks from around the island. Don't miss the Traditional Bread room, displaying more than 600 types of ceremonial loaves that different towns use to celebrate weddings, births and holy days.

One of the most iconic images of Sardinia is the fearsome sheepskin figure with a wooden mask that stomps evil spirits away during the festival of *mamuthones* in **Mamoiada**. These and other masks are on display at the **Museo delle Maschere Mediterranee** where the origin and significance of these distinct festivals is explored through written and recorded material. The town of Mamoiada itself is one of the most fascinating in Barbagia, and is worth exploring after the museum. If you close your eyes, you can hear the *mamuthones* marching.

The newly inaugurated **Museo Diffuso di Arte Contemporanea (MAC)** in the tiny, ancient town of **Lula** shows how Barbagia honours its past while continuing to look towards the future. The museum, set within the former mining zones and the towns that grew up around them, features contemporary artists from around Sardinia as well as international names. Like Orgosolo, Lula is decorated with murals and the museum engages with them both inside and out. If you were starting to think you had Barbagia all figured out, the MAC will keep you on your toes.

BARBAGIA'S TRADITIONAL CUISINE

Every corner of Italy has its own cuisine, and in Barbagia, tradition reigns supreme.

The ubiquitous *pane carasau* is a large, impossibly thin toasted bread. It's sometimes known in Italian as 'music paper' (but no one actually calls it that).

During any kind of celebration you may see the town centre filled with iconic *su porcheddu* (spit-roasted suckling pig). It's meticulously prepared and delicious.

The story of Sardinia could be told through the art of *pecorino* cheesemaking: the Cyclops of Homer's *Odyssey* was a purveyor of sheep's milk cheese, the very same produced here.

Nothing is eaten without being washed down by a generous gulp of Cannonau, the red wine made throughout Sardinia and prevalent in Barbagia. It's tangy, spicy and often homegrown.

GETTING AROUND

The closest airport is Olbia Costa Smeralda, which is about 80km north of Nuoro and 100km north of Dorgali and Orgosolo. Olbia also has a ferry service to/from mainland Italy, making it the most convenient departure point. Once in the area, you'll need a car to get around as there are scant public transport links, particularly into the Supramonte. If you plan on doing any solo driving into the mountains, you'll need a 4WD or SUV, but the best advice is to leave the mountain driving to the professionals.

Beyond Barbagia & the Supramonte

Just when you thought you couldn't be surprised by the beauty of Barbagia any more, turn your head towards the sea.

Barbagia   • Cala Gonone

Though not technically beyond Barbagia, the craggy coves and breezy towns along the Golfo di Orosei will feel like a world away from the rugged interior. The town of Cala Gonone offers the most services and is the best departure point to explore the area. While it sees its fair share of tourism, the Golfo di Orosei is largely undisturbed and outside the high-season months of July and August, you'll find that life moves at a charmingly relaxed pace. Pick your *cala* (cove), gaze at the turquoise sea in front of you, and let yourself enjoy the extra effort you put in to get here. It was well worth it.

TOP TIP

This is a protected area, so make sure you know the rules before sailing solo. Better yet, give an experienced skipper the wheel.

Golfo di Orosei

PICS721/SHUTTERSTOCK ©

VALERIOMEI/SHUTTERSTOCK ©

Cala Goloritzè

CALA GOLORITZÈ

Tucked on the tail end of the Golfo di Orosei, Cala Goloritzè truly lives up to every expectation, due in large part to the conservation efforts that have been enacted around it. Created by a landslide in 1962, it was declared a national monument in 1995 and as such is afforded a protected status that prohibits boats from approaching the shore.

You can get to the beach overland by taking a 90-minute, intermediate-level trek. However, the more comfortable route may be from the back of a Zodiac boat – you can dive in at a safe distance with your snorkelling gear. It's just as stunning under the water as it is over the waves.

Cruising the Golfo di Orosei

PREPARE TO BE BLOWN AWAY

Part of the same nature reserve that protects the Gennargentu massif, the Gulf of Orosei is delineated by the curvature that goes from Marina di Orosei in the north to Capo di Monte Santu in the south. Between those two poles, land and sea meet in a dramatic confrontation. Reminded of how small you are, you'll wonder how the cliffs could be so sheer, the sand so alabaster and the water so impossibly blue.

Most of the *cale* along the Gulf are either inaccessible by land or can only be reached on a trek through the Gennargentu. To see as much as possible and do minimal damage to the fragile ecosystem of the area, hop aboard one of the ubiquitous *gommoni* (rubber dinghies) at **Cala Gonone**, the largest town in the Gulf. Better yet, **Blue and Green Best** *(blubest. it)* run by locals Paolo Insolera and Maria Lucia Cossu offers guided tours that allow you to see the beauty of the area and appreciate the efforts being made to protect it. Their skippers are unambiguous: the Gulf is a gift and must be respected.

You'll quickly understand why locals are so fiercely protective of the Gulf. Whether it's the surreal beauty of the Piscine

CHOOSE YOUR OWN CALA

Cala Luna
You'll want to spend an afternoon at the Gulf's longest beach, with the Su Neulagi restaurant tucked in the valley.

Cala Mariolu
One of the most picture-perfect spots in the Gulf has been limiting the number of visitors to keep it that way.

Cala dei Gabbiani
This otherworldly cove will give you chills, but its warm waters will make you forget the rest of the world exists.

DECODING THE SARDINIAN LANGUAGE

Italy has a seemingly endless number of dialects, but Sardinian is a distinct language that has been recognised by the state. Sardinian was denigrated for decades and considered a language of the poor, uneducated population. However, it has been reclaimed and is a source of pride for new generations – so wherever you are on the island, don't be afraid to ask a native speaker to explain. There are variations clustered around the north, south and centre of the island and no one will expect you to know your way around them as a visitor. But it's a sign of respect to acknowledge the singularity of Sardinian – greet your Sardinian friend with a hearty *'Ajò!'* and laugh along with them as they answer.

A. EMSON/SHUTTERSTOCK ©

Cala Luna (p729)

di Venere or the striking Grotta del Bue Marino, you'd be hard pressed to think of another area with so many riches in such concentration. And then there are the *cale*. Take your pick from nearly 10 of them, all slightly different – some that can only be reached by sea and others whose sandy beaches beckon you to stay a while. Luckily, you hardly have to choose: Paolo and Maria Lucia offer a five-night/five-*cala* cruise, visiting the Gulf's most famous nooks.

 GETTING AROUND

You'd wait quite a long time if you were reliant on public transport in this part of the country, as buses along the coast are few and far between. Some ferries do run between Orosei and Baunei/Arbatax, but the best way to get around is by car. Be warned, however: much of the coast is not for those with a fear of heights, or anyone whose stomach quakes at the idea of curves. Pack your motion-sickness pills!

ALGHERO & THE WEST COAST

Alghero &
the West
Coast

⭐Rome

Sardinia is arguably the most distinct region of Italy, yet it is also the one that most closely mirrors the country itself: venture out in any direction and you're in a different culture with its own dialect, traditions and cuisine. You think you know cosmopolitan Cagliari, or that you've won the heart of Barbagia, but then you head west and everything changes as you work your way north from ancient Oristano to charming Alghero, where you'll swear that you blinked and woke up in Barcelona.

This, too, is Sardinia, just as authentic as any other corner and just as beloved by its inhabitants. The variation is striking but never dizzying, perhaps because you can always fix your eyes on the horizon of the stunning Riviera del Corallo (Coral Riviera). Or perhaps it is the knowledge that when the northerly road ends, the most beautiful beach in the world is waiting to welcome you.

TOP TIP

Conservation efforts are taken seriously, especially when it comes to the many beaches on the coast. You can be heavily fined for taking sand as a souvenir. Best to enjoy it while you're there and leave the beach for the next traveller.

Carnevale, Quartz & Caviar, Oh My!

HISTORIC CARNIVAL AND QUARTZ BEACHES

Despite its small stature, the provincial capital of **Oristano** has built up an impressive CV over the centuries. You'll have to avoid tripping over ancient monuments, and its position on a gulf meant that it was an important trading post throughout the Middle Ages. The evidence of this is ubiquitous around the genteel city centre – a statue on the main piazza honours Eleonora d'Arborea who enacted the Carta de Logu (the legal code in Sardinia from 1395 until 1827).

Like many Sardinian cities, Oristano has a long tradition of celebrating Carnevale – but unlike many others, **Sa Sartiglia** feels like you've actually travelled 500 years back in time to its origins. An enthralling blend of jousting, racing and theatrics, Sa Sartiglia takes place on the last Sunday and Tuesday of Carnevale and has just celebrated its 557th year. While summers are glorious along the western coast, February is the month where Oristano's star shines brightest.

But it wouldn't be Sardinia without summer, the endless quartz beaches of the Sinis Peninsula and the salty breeze floating into **Cabras** from its eponymous lagoon. The town itself brings to mind the sun-bleached roofs of Almería in miniature, but it's a meeting point for the natural, archaeological and gastronomic treasures of the entire peninsula – from the immortal *bottarga* (mullet roe) to the artefacts from the ancient city of **Tharros**. Likely founded by the Phoenicians in the

THE MAGIC OF BOTTARGA

It's called Sardinian caviar, but that's selling it short. For centuries, fisherfolk have carefully extracted the pale-blond egg sacs of the native mullet before deftly tying and hanging them dry, creating the *bottarga*. Legend has it that the *maestrale* was the only wind capable of performing the magic trick that deepened the colour into its trademark amber, and that in the old days people used to whisper out to the sea to beckon the wind to shore. Nowadays such incantations are simulated in family-run cooperatives around Cabras, all year-round. You can still hear the whispers along the lagoon as the *bottarga* cures in the wind, and it's magic all the same.

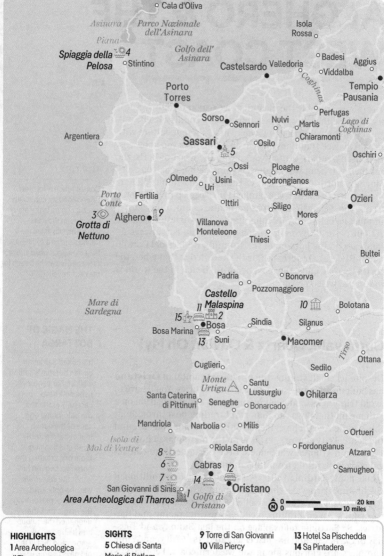

o Cala d'Oliva

Asinara
Piana

Parco Nazionale
dell'Asinara

Isola
Rossa o

Spiaggia della ≋4
Pelosa o Stintino

Golfo dell'
Asinara

Castelsardo • Valledoria

o Badesi   Aggius
o
• Viddalba

Tempio
Pausania

Porto
Torres

Sorso •
• o Sennori

Nulvi
o

o Perfugas

Martis
o

Lago di
Coghinas

Argentiera o

Sassari ⛪5

o Osilo

o Chiaramonti

Oschiri o

o Ossi

Ploaghe
o

o Olmedo
Uri o

Usini
o

o Codrongianos

Ardara
o

Ozieri
•

Porto
Conte

Fertilia
o

o Ittiri

Siligo
o

Mores
o

3 ◎ Alghero ▮9
Grotta di
Nettuno

Villanova
Monteleone
o

Thiesi
o

Bultei
o

Mare di
Sardegna

Padria
o

o Bonorva

• Pozzomaggiore

Castello
11 *Malaspina*
15 ⌂▦2
Bosa Marina • **Bosa**
13 Suni

10 ⛪   Bolotana
o

Sindia
o

Silanus
o

• Macomer

Tirso

Ottana
o

Cuglieri o

Sedilo
o

Monte
Urtigu △
Santa Caterina
di Pittinuri o

Santu
Lussurgiu
o
Seneghe o   • Bonarcado

• Ghilarza

Mandriola
o

Narbolia o   o Milis

o Ortueri

Isola di
Mal di Ventre

8
6
7

o Riola Sardo

Cabras
14 ●12

o Fordongianus   Atzara
o

o Samugheo

San Giovanni di Sinis o
Area Archeologica di Tharros 🏛 1

Golfo di
Oristano

Oristano

Ⓝ 0   20 km
  0   10 miles

HIGHLIGHTS
1 Area Archeologica
di Tharros
2 Castello Malaspina
3 Grotta di Nettuno
4 Spiaggia della Pelosa

SIGHTS
5 Chiesa di Santa
Maria di Betlem
6 Is Aruttas
7 Maimoni
8 Mari Ermi

9 Torre di San Giovanni
10 Villa Piercy

SLEEPING
11 Aghinas
12 Hotel Regina d'Arborea

13 Hotel Sa Pischedda
14 Sa Pintadera

DRINKING
15 Enoteca Su Camasinu

7th century BCE, Tharros had already hosted nuraghic settlements. Spend the day between the ruins and the archaeological museum in Cabras, where you'll wander through artefacts from Tharros as well as those from the nearby Monte Prama.

Indeed, Cabras may be tiny but in the many chapters that tell the story of Sardinia, it's mighty.

The Painted Tuscan Town
BOSA'S UNLIKELY BEAUTY

If your mood boards are filled with images of the colourful villages of Burano, Vernazza or Portofino, you'll be stunned when you happen upon **Bosa**, nestled in between Oristano and Alghero on the western coast of Sardinia. This town of 9000 people descends from the heights of the spectacular **Castello Malaspina**, built in the 12th century by Tuscan nobles who knew a good thing when they stumbled upon it. Unlike other seaside towns in Sardinia, Bosa benefits from its position on the banks of the Temo river, the only navigable body of water on the island and thus an important trade route. It was also an ideal spot for tanneries – you can see the remains of many of these if you take one of the absurdly romantic boat tours along the Temo.

No one knows precisely why or when Bosa's old town, known in the local dialect as Sa Costa, first acquired its festive, rainbow facade. Depending on who you ask, it may have as much to do with the nobles who once roamed the castle as it does with the spirits that come calling during **Carrasegare**, the local Carnevale celebration featuring townspeople in black masks and a doll they collectively weep over. Or maybe, it all started with the first bottles of Malvasia, a locally produced sweet wine. Spend an afternoon trying to find out, but don't be surprised if you wind up staying a night or two. Towns like this have a habit of growing on you, and of colouring much more than your camera roll.

Treasure Hunting in Alghero
RUN WITH THE GREAT EXPLORERS

A rather elegant delirium greets you on arrival in Alghero, particularly after having visited other parts of Sardinia. First, you'll find an entirely different language: the Catalan dialect of Algherese is an officially recognised minority language and many of the city's 43,000 inhabitants still use it regularly. You'll also

THE GUIDE

SARDINIA

MEDITATING ON MALVASIA

If you've never had the fortune to encounter a 'meditation wine' in Italy, a generous gulp of **Malvasia di Bosa** will give you a level of enlightenment that the Buddha himself would envy. This sweet wine truly evokes nectar and has been one of Bosa's most important products since the Middle Ages. Today it enjoys DOP status under Italian law and can only be produced in seven areas around Bosa. Book a tasting at **Enoteca Su Camasinu** in the old town, the retail outpost of famed Cantina Giovanni Battista Columbu. Afterwards, they're happy to carry you to their *albergo diffuso*, **Aghinas** ('grape' in local dialect) to sleep it off.

A FOOD LOVER'S AUTUMN

The Sagra della Bottarga in Cabras often takes place around the same time as the **Cascà festival** (p721) in Carloforte, making it a foodie's dream itinerary.

 WHERE TO STAY ON THE WEST COAST

Hotel Regina d'Arborea
Palatial elegance and prime location are the twin attractions at this quirky and historical hotel on Oristano's main square. €€€

Sa Pintadera
Traditional yet mod-con apartments in Cabras with a shared garden and local specialities for breakfast. €€

Hotel Sa Pischedda
Near the Ponte Vecchio in Bosa, this grand hotel has an excellent restaurant and a few rooms with riverside terraces. €€

DESCEND INTO NEPTUNE'S GROTTO

There are two very different ways into the legendary **Grotta di Nettuno**. You can arrive by car or bus to the entrance at Capo Caccia and join one of the obligatory guided tours that depart on the half-hour. And let's be clear: the Escala del Cabirol is 400m long, precipitous and hugs the mountain for 654 steps. If you've ever wanted to channel your inner mountain goat (or roe deer, for which the staircase is named), this is the time. If you're not a fan of dizzying heights, boats from Alghero reach the cave in just over half an hour, which is also a great chance to see the stunning Riviera del Corallo. Either way, you won't want to miss it.

VIVIANO TEDDE FOTOGRAFIA/SHUTTERSTOCK ©

Cavalcata Sarda, Sassari

notice a decidedly different type of architecture, perfectly captured in the distinctive walls that encircle the old city. The maritime wars of the 11th century made defensive structures a necessary battle strategy, and while Genoa and Pisa fought over Alghero, the former erected walls to keep invaders out. By the time Catalan invaders finally made their way in, the city was fortified.

The fortifications were built to last. Alghero's bastions are among the best preserved in all of Italy and are now one of the nicest promenades this side of the Mediterranean. Each of the ramparts is dedicated to great explorers: Columbus, Pigafetta, Magellan and Marco Polo all look out onto the far horizon. These wide elevated lanes are punctuated by bulbous watchtowers, which you'll begin to notice as you move around the city. Succumb to their charms and allow yourself to get lost for a while.

Or, get found. You can't miss the 16th-century **Torre di San Giovanni**, now host to projects like #playalghero, the interactive treasure hunt that's part of an EU-funded initiative and created in partnership between Fondazione Alghero and

 BEST QUARTZ BEACHES OF THE SINIS PENINSULA

Is Aruttas
Once a well-kept secret but those days are gone. Outside August, though, finding a spot on the sand is no problem.

Maimoni
It changes from pink to white quartz along its 2km-long stretch. And the water? Blue as far as the eye can see.

Mari Ermi
This beach is known for its placid undertow and flat expanse, and it does not disappoint.

organisations in Lebanon, Spain and Jordan. From historical maps to murder mysteries, #playalghero showcases the city as it always should be: delirious, whimsical and proud.

The Festivities of Sassari
FROM CAVALCADA TO CANDELIERI

It seems wrong to squeeze the second-largest city in Sardinia into a whirlwind trip along the west coast, but Sassari doesn't mind. In fact, it's the most serious city on the island, or at least the most studious. The University of Sassari was founded by Jesuit priests in 1562 and it remains one of the top institutions in Italy. You'll find students all over the city, which makes it feel welcoming yet transitory; you'll hear the Sassarese dialect spoken, but it will often be in a chorus of Italian, French or Spanish. The cuisine reflects this utilitarian melange, typified by dishes like *fainé*, a chickpea-flour fritter that can be bulked up with any number of meats or vegetables.

Sassari does let its hair down a couple of times a year, in spectacular fashion. The **Cavalcata Sarda** is almost the 'best of' Sardinian culture, as the unique identities from every part of the island converge on the city on the second-last Sunday in May, just like they have done since 1711. The parade winds through the city along with floats pulled by oxen and the impossibly beautiful costumes, dresses and crafts from around Sardinia.

Every 14 August, the **Faradda di li Candareri**, or Candlesticks Festival, pays tribute to the Madonna of the Assumption for having protected the island from a plague. Thirteen massive wooden candles are carried on the participants' shoulders across the city streets to finish at the **Chiesa di Santa Maria di Betlem** – the same route they have followed for more than five centuries.

AN ENGLISH VILLA IN SARDINIA

Benjamin Piercy developed railway lines in France, India and his native Wales throughout much of the 19th century, but it was his work in Sardinia that changed the course of his life. As a civil engineer with the Royal Sardinian Railroad Company, Piercy built the first train lines to ever cross the island, along the way becoming a friend of Garibaldi. He later purchased lands outside Macomer for what would become an English manor and working farm. Today, **Villa Piercy** is open to the public after a 2010 renovation. Take an afternoon to wander the lush gardens and ponder the man who built a town around a dream.

GETTING AROUND

Alghero's historic centre is a limited-traffic zone (ZTL in Italian), meaning that if you aren't a resident you might be facing heavy fines for parking in unauthorised zones. There are cameras posted around the city so instead of testing your luck, head for one of the parking lots in Piazza dei Mercati, Piazzale della Pace or Via XX Settembre and expect to pay around €15 per day. Public transport in Alghero is reliable and quick, and tickets can be purchased at tobacco shops all over the city. It's a good place to try out your Italian (or Sardinian) without getting too lost, as the city is compact and people are very willing to help.

Isola dell'Asinara
Stintino
Porto
Torres
Alghero

Beyond Alghero & the West Coast

Leave the eclectic cityscapes behind you and dive into the wild nature of the northernmost tip of Sardinia.

By the time you reach the hamlet of Stintino in Sardinia's remote northwest, you'll likely have passed through dramatic landscapes, explored stimulating cities and enjoyed ever so slightly hedonistic meals. None of that will stop you from gasping when you see the fabled Spiaggia della Pelosa. But while the lion's share of people come to strike a pose and take a swim at what may well be the most beautiful beach in the world, don't miss the chance to play among the wild scrub of Isola dell'Asinara, which was once known as Italy's Alcatraz.

TOP TIP

Booking at La Pelosa during the high season is necessary, and simple to do via its bilingual website.

La Pelosa beach

DENIS BELITSKY/SHUTTERSTOCK ©

Credit: GIUMA/SHUTTERSTOCK ©

Torre del Falcone

Sardinia's Celebrity Beach

MORE THAN BEAUTIFUL SANDS

The word 'paradise' is overused these days, which is a shame because when you actually stumble upon one there is often nothing to say that will convey how idyllic it is. The **Spiaggia della Pelosa**, or simply La Pelosa, is one of the finest stretches of beach anywhere in the world and the throngs of people who descend upon it are living proof. But don't mind them, because the water is so shallow and placid that you'll be able to walk over to your own little corner, listen to the waves calmly pass over alabaster sand, and fix your eyes on the iconic **Torre del Falcone**, an Aragonese watchtower. La Pelosa is also popular with wind- and kitesurfers, thanks to the *maestrale* wind.

You can walk to La Pelosa from Stintino, or catch one of the frequent buses that come from as far away as Alghero and Sassari. Driving and parking, especially in the high season, are tasks best left out of your itinerary. There are also strict rules for visiting the beach, including a ban on smoking, trash, animals between certain hours, and taking any sand with you, and local authorities will issue fines for disrespecting them.

BOOKING THE BEACH

Since 2018 the number of daily visitors to **La Pelosa** has been capped at 1500 between the months of June and September, in an effort to control erosion and damage to the beach. In order for you to spend the day, you'll need to reserve a spot for a nominal fee through its website, lapelosastintino.com. You'll also have to bring or buy a straw mat to avoid tracking sand with your towel, so be prepared. However, if you want to walk on the beach or have a swim without setting your umbrella or beach chair up for the day, you can do so anytime. It is still a public beach, but one that people are working hard to protect.

🍴 WHERE TO HAVE A SEASIDE LUNCH IN CASTELSARDO

Il Cormorano
On the main square of one of Sardinia's best-preserved medieval villages, inventive dishes pay tribute to tradition. **€€€**

Ristorante Baga Baga
Dramatic views over Castelsardo and the sea, plus a menu of fresh seafood and traditional Sardinian recipes. **€€**

Rocca'ja
A no-frills Sardinian restaurant with copious portions, beautiful views and tables that fill up throughout the year. **€€**

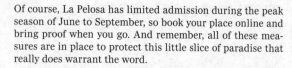

TUNA-FISHING NOSTALGIA

An ideal refuge for notable kooks, **Stintino** has just the right balance of seaside nostalgia and modern comfort. It's worth stopping here and tucking into some of the great restaurants on the main drag, which appropriately get much of their supply from the local catch. The town's **Museo della Tonnara** is an unexpectedly fascinating look at the bygone era of tuna fishing – don't be surprised if it brings a tear to your eye. After that, drown your sorrows in some fine Vermentino at **Albergo Ristorante Silverstrino** in the town centre, and while you're at it, stay the night in one of their classic rooms.

Harbour, Stintino

Of course, La Pelosa has limited admission during the peak season of June to September, so book your place online and bring proof when you go. And remember, all of these measures are in place to protect this little slice of paradise that really does warrant the word.

Escape to the Former Prison Island

ALCATRAZ, BUT MAKE IT WILD

Like much of Sardinia, the **Isola dell'Asinara** is humble but not modest. Named after the albino donkeys (*asini bianchi*) that roam here, the island's 51 sq km of rocky coasts, hidden coves and craggy trails is the closest you can get to leaving civilisation behind. Indeed, that may be why Asinara used to host one of Italy's harshest maximum-security prisons, and why the heroic Palermo prosecutors Borsellino and Falcone exiled themselves there to prepare for their anti-Mafia trials. They don't call it 'the Italian Alcatraz' for nothing.

These days, Asinara is a national park and a haven for wildlife; while it is still remote, it's less of a punishment and more of a pleasure to visit. It still has only one small town, **Cala d'Oliva**, but the newly built **Locanda del Parco** has welcoming rooms that are open all year-round. There are hiking trails, remote sandy beaches, nuraghic remains and the old barracks of the *carcere* (prison) to explore. But most of all there is silence, and the feeling of being a million miles away from anywhere else.

The only way to reach Asinara is with a licensed boat operator from Stintino or Porto Torres; agencies in Stintino also offer a range of guided tours.

 GETTING AROUND

If you really want to explore the winding roads of the west, the best way to do so is by car or motorcycle. A word of advice: if you're embarking on a camper-van holiday, you might find yourself facing considerable crowds during the high season, as ferries from nearby Porto Torres tend to mean lots of trailers disembarking on the same beaches. Public transport is refreshingly present but characteristically sparse: the trip from Alghero to Stintino takes about two hours by bus, and there are five to seven trips per day.

LA MADDALENA & GALLURA

La Maddalena & Gallura ☀ Rome

There's a word in Italian that, like many others, gets butchered by translation: *suggestivo*. It means to evoke, resonate and gently guide towards a deep expression of feeling. A place that captures this spirit must be more than beautiful, perhaps even more than inspiring – it must stir something within you. Follow the paths of statesmen and troubadours to the northeastern corner of Sardinia and you may get close, because this meeting of land and sea is the very essence of *suggestivo*. After all, it's where Italy was made.

Parco Nazionale dell'Arcipelago di La Maddalena sits across the Strait of Bonifacio from the region of Gallura, which stretches across the northeastern digit of Sardinia. Its supernatural landscape draws throngs in the summer months, but there's a lot more history here than meets the eye. Cross back onto land and into the interior, where giants roamed, rock stars were captured, and Vermentino wine keeps flowing.

TOP TIP

Avoid driving on La Maddalena. Ferries from the mainland bring crowds, cars and congestion to this fragile ecosystem. Boats are reasonably priced and take you everywhere.

A Pilgrimage to Garibaldi's Island

THE REFUGE OF THE REVOLUTIONARY

He was called 'the Hero of Two Worlds', but upon further examination they may have left one out. No one knows exactly why Giuseppe Garibaldi bought half of **Isola Caprera** in 1855, but legend has it that he was en route to a Tunisian prison in 1849 when the captain of the ship – an ardent admirer originally from La Maddalena – absconded with Garibaldi and brought him to the archipelago. He stayed there for a month, and there he would return until the end of his days.

Indeed, the clock in Garibaldi's home on the island, called the **Casa Bianca**, is frozen at the time of his death in June 1882. During his lifetime, the house was an exile and a refuge, a political centre and a subsistence farm. It was where he created Italy and where he came to get away from it when his hopes were (all too frequently) dashed. It was – and is – a sanctuary that honours the hero who, of all the worlds he could have chosen, came and stayed here.

No matter how long you plan to spend in the archipelago, make a trip to the **Compendio Garibaldino** on Caprera, which comprises both the Casa Bianca and the memorial to him. Consult the website for opening hours as they do change with the season, and keep in mind that this is considered a sacred space so if you're coming from the sea make sure you have appropriate clothing. Of course, red shirts and ponchos are always welcome.

SUSTAINABLE SAILING

Of course, it wouldn't be La Maddalena without excursions around the seven main islands and plenty of swimming during the season. Private boats are fairly priced and a good option for groups: the best skipper in town is Daniele from **Emerald Cruises**. If you're looking for a day cruise with all the amenities on board, look no further than **Luxury Virginia**. There are bells, whistles, a DJ and a one-of-a-kind look, but that's not what really makes it stand out. Instead, the company made the decision to retrofit the vessel so that it wouldn't have to dock on any of the islands to let passengers out, thus cutting down on sand depletion and proving that sustainability can be sexy.

The Granite Hills of Gallura

ARTISTS' RETREAT, SACRED VILLAGE

Sardinia is one of those places that get underneath people's skin. Many are so changed that they only feel complete upon returning. Garibaldi was one; legendary musician Fabrizio de Andrè was another. The Genoa native may not have known how deeply his city was linked to Sardinia when he bought a *stazzi* (stone home typical for Gallura), but he chose it as his home nonetheless. **L'Agnata**, located near Tempio in the granite hills of Gallura, became a haven for poets, artists and musicians from around the world during the years in which De Andrè lived there with his wife. It was also the site from where the couple were kidnapped and held for ransom in the turbulent 1970s, which inspired his famous song, 'Hotel Supramonte'. Today, L'Agnata is a one-of-a-kind hotel, restaurant and cultural monument to one of modern Italy's most influential artists. It's also a tribute to Gallura and its singular beauty.

Tucked in the foothills of Monti Ghjuanni, the tiny village of **Luogosanto** is an undeniably sacred place, as its name attests. Though it counts fewer than 1000 inhabitants, it has

WHERE TO TASTE WINE IN GALLURA

Petra Bianca
Organic winery and hotel overlooking the iconic Isola dei Gabbiani – plenty of reasons to make it an overnight trip. €€

Tenute Filigheddu
Visit the vineyard and chat with the family over lush platters of local meats and cheeses; tastings by appointment only. €

Capichera
One of the region's most iconic names; visit the winery and you'll see it's well deserved (by appointment only). €€

La Maddalena

ISLAND-HOPPING AROUND LA MADDALENA

Isola Budelli
Famous for the Spiaggia Rosa (Pink Beach) – while access to the beach is forbidden, don't miss getting a glimpse of it from the sea.

Isola Santa Maria
It hosted the Benedictine monks who first inhabited the archipelago, and still has some of the most stellar beaches in the area.

Isola Razzoli
The island's dramatic cliffs and spooky ghost stories only add to the otherworldly beauty of the beach at Cala Lunga.

been an important pilgrimage site since the Middle Ages and has a uniquely generous sense of hospitality. With over 20 religious structures around town, Luogosanto is still visited by worshippers, but the more adventurous pass through on treks or come for one of the many festivals that take place throughout the year. Perhaps none is as important as the **Festa Manna**, which celebrates all of the Gallura region's religious traditions during the first two weeks of September.

PROTECTING THE BEACH

Much like **La Pelosa** (p737), La Maddalena is committed to preserving the park, and many beaches are off limits. If you're planning to rent a Zodiac alone, make sure you know where you can't go.

The Timeless Charm of La Maddalena

CHIC BOUTIQUES AND CRYSTAL SEAS

Although it's often a quick stop on boat tours from Palau or a meeting point for excursions around the islands, the town of La Maddalena is well worth taking the time to visit. The only inhabited town in the archipelago, La Maddalena has an enchanting history of pirates, monks and, of course, Napoleon; the young general fought (and lost) his

 WHERE TO STAY IN GALLURA

Gallicantu
A stunning mix of historical preservation, sustainable construction and chic style in Luogosanto. €€€

Lu Ciaccaru
A family-run, restored property that makes guests feel perfectly at home while also spoiling them rotten. €€€

Agriturismo Saltara
A working farm with charming rooms, suites and *stazzi* that offer comfort and charm for a modest budget. €€

THE WHITE GOLD OF GALLURA

It would be sacrilege to leave Gallura without venerating its most important resource, the famed **Vermentino white wine**. Luckily, one of its most devoted disciples is a stone's throw from Luogosanto and hosts tastings at the winery throughout the year (by appointment only). **Piero Mancini** grew up visiting his grandparents' land in Gallura but, like with many others, the land got under his skin. In the 1960s he came back, and fortunately for anyone who's ever tasted his Vermentino, he stayed. Visit the winery website for information on bookings and directions.

first battle here and the victory against him is commemorated throughout the town. Nonetheless, there is something distinctly Provençal about La Maddalena, whether it's the charming port that hints at Marseille or the chic yet unobtrusive shops in the old town that you could swear you visited in Nice. And you won't mind one bit, because it is still perfectly, authentically Sardinia.

The ferries from Palau, directly opposite La Maddalena on the mainland, run frequently and efficiently. **B&B Clelia**'s is a gem in the old town whose charm is only complemented by the hi-tech, sustainable features that owner Luca Marogna has cleverly implemented. **Bottega Sfusa**, just around the corner on Corso Vittorio Emanuele, has a terrific selection of locally made organic soaps, shampoos and accessories to replace anything you left on land. Once you've got all of that out of the way, **Osteria Cocò** near the port makes the best *fregola ai frutti di mare* (Sardinian seafood pasta) in town, best washed down with a glass of Vermentino.

GETTING AROUND

Getting onto the archipelago is a quick ferry ride from Palau, with boats running throughout the day and night and the trip taking less than 30 minutes. You can also bring your car on the ferry but be aware that Maddalena and Caprera are the only islands on which you can drive, as they're connected by the 600m Passo della Moneta or Caprera Bridge. If you want to get to the less visited islands, you'll need to hit the water. Boat rentals are ubiquitous around Maddalena town and if you're in a group, they can be quite reasonable.

COSTA SMERALDA

Rome

Costa
Smeralda

It helps to mentally prepare yourself for the gobsmacking amount of money you'll likely spend if you're planning to visit the Costa Smeralda, just as it's best to prepare for swarms of people eagerly scanning the verdant piazzas for celebrity sightings. You might also do well to ignore those pesky declarations of the enclave being 'soulless' or 'superficial' by those who claim to have found better, because there's simply nothing like it anywhere in the world. Legend has it that this is exactly what millionaire Karim Aga Khan intended.

After all, it's not called the Emerald Coast for nothing. The viridian beaches (almost) make up for the eye-watering price point, and gliding through the suspended reality of those well-manicured villages will make anyone feel like a mogul. So what if it's all artifice? For a moment, you'll feel like you're on top of the world. For a moment, you are.

TOP TIP

Accommodation is sparse and does not come cheap on the Costa Smeralda. Look inland to Arzachena for cheerful B&Bs, and don't miss the market in nearby San Pantaleo on Thursdays for local products from all over the island.

Coastal Glamour

BATTLE OF THE BILLIONAIRES

You'll try and fail to play it cool as you wander around **Porto Cervo** – but don't worry, even the billionaires have imposter syndrome if they think about it too much. The most famous of the Costa villages, Porto Cervo remains the crown jewel in Aga Khan's vision; the 420 permanent residents now live on one of the most expensive pieces of real estate in the world. The original old town looks like what Gaudí would have done with Bedrock, and it's lined with all the high-end boutiques you'd expect. Both the old port and new Marina overflow with yachts in the summer; it's great fun to take a walk down the promenade and see them being seen.

The other towns of the original plan have far fewer attractions to offer nonresidents, but further down the coast you'll find **Porto Rotondo**, the wild stepchild of Porto Cervo. This glittering cove has a yacht club of its own, slightly bigger than that of its competitor and slightly more audacious. Only slightly, however, because the real chutzpah lives closer to the source at **Billionaire**. Teetering between famous and infamous, the club and restaurant has become synonymous with the excess of the Costa Smeralda. Yet it remains one of the hottest tickets in town, year after year. If you want to experience it, be prepared to pay dearly for the privilege – and as with all things, it helps to know someone.

**BEST BEACHES
ON THE COSTA
SMERALDA**

Principe
This magnificent crescent of white sand is one of the top beaches in the world.

Cala di Volpe
It shares the name and real estate with a luxe hotel just above; a once-in-a-lifetime experience.

Capriccioli
The calm, shallow water makes this a popular spot for families.

**Grande &
Piccolo Pevero**
Play spot-a-celebrity while you pedal in the azure waters.

Liscia Ruia
The longest of the Costa beaches is also one of the more challenging to get to, but it's worth it.

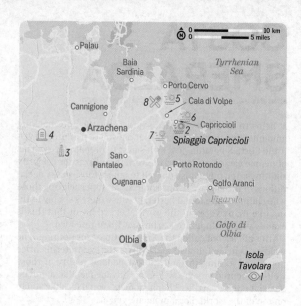

Explore the Emerald Coast

HIDDEN GEMS

The glitzy villages of the Costa Smeralda are heavy on luxury but lighter on local culture – still, you don't have to venture far to get an authentic taste of Sardinia. **Arzachena** is about 20km inland and is actually the coast's main town, with a rich cultural heritage and fabulous cuisine. It's also known for the *Rainbow Staircase* mural by Manuel Maratto that descends from the Church of Santa Lucia. The town is a fascinating mix of old and new: traditional *stazzi* homes are converted into chic B&Bs, while festivals take place at the foot of nuraghic ruins.

One of the most striking examples of the Bronze Age monuments that dot the island, **Coddu Ecchju** is located just a few kilometres outside Arzachena and absolutely merits a detour. The megalith is stunning to behold – the bas-relief of the large entranceway stones will leave you speechless. A short drive leads to the sculpture garden at **Li Muri**, a necropolis thought to date from the 4th millennium BCE.

In nearby **San Pantaleo**, the party begins on Thursday with an open-air market that has become one of the best-

BEST OF SARDINIAN BEAUTY BRANDS

Soha Sardinia
A line of natural hair, facial and body products started by two friends from Nuoro.

Acqua di Sardegna
Originally from Alghero, the brand is known around the world for its fragrances.

FarmAsinara
Cosmetics produced on Isola dell'Asinara using locally sourced ingredients.

Open-air market, San Pantaleo

THE KINGDOM OF TAVOLARA

Long ago, rumours circulated that there was a James Bond–style villain's lair on **Isola Tavolara**, inspired perhaps by the fact that parts of *The Spy Who Loved Me* were filmed in Porto Cervo. It may also have been due to the top-secret NATO base on the island's eastern half. But this enormous limestone massif that rises precipitously out of the sea is the sort of place that would inspire tall tales. Indeed, it even became 'the smallest kingdom in the world' that was bestowed by King Carlo Alberto to the Bertoleoni family of local shepherds. As you swim in its gargantuan shadow, you'll certainly believe that giants once stood there.

known attractions in the area. From local cheeses to crafts to cashmere, this tiny mountain town is a slice of authentic Sardinia that also knows the way to a traveller's heart. Expect warm smiles, broken but earnest English or French, and lots of free samples. Let the rest of them fight over a seat at the yacht club – you're fine just where you are.

SAILING AROUND THE COAST

Boat trips to **La Maddalena archipelago** (p739) are also frequent and simple from the Costa Smeralda and make a fabulous day trip.

GETTING AROUND

Olbia Costa Smeralda Airport is one of the best connected to the northern and eastern regions of Sardinia, and continues to expand its capacity. The ferry terminal at Olbia operates crossings to/from Italy throughout the year. The overnight journey is particularly popular, and a cabin is definitely recommended.

TOOLKIT

The chapters in this section cover the most important topics you'll need to know about in Italy. They're full of nuts-and-bolts information and valuable insights to help you understand and navigate Italy and get the most out of your trip.

Arriving
p748

Getting Around
p749

Money
p750

Accommodation
p751

Family Travel
p752

Health & Safe Travel
p753

Food, Drink & Nightlife
p754

Responsible Travel
p756

LGBTiQ+ Travellers
p758

Accessible Travel
p759

Nuts & Bolts
p760

Language
p762

Rickshaw drivers, Battistero di San Giovanni, Florence (p408)

✈ Arriving

Italy's main intercontinental airports are Rome's Fiumicino Airport (Leonardo da Vinci) and Milan's Aeroporto Malpensa. Venice's Marco Polo Airport and Naples International (Capodichino) Airport are also served by a few intercontinental flights. There are also plenty of options for entering Italy by train, bus or ferry. Depending on distances, rail can be highly competitive with air travel.

Border crossings
As part of the unified Schengen area, there are no border formalities between Italy and its European neighbours. At most, you may occasionally be asked to show ID or a passport.

Visas
EU nationals don't need a visa. Travellers from the UK, Canada, New Zealand, the US and Australia can stay for up to 90 days with no visa. See www.schengenvisainfo.com.

SIM cards
The cheapest way to use your mobile phone is to buy a prepaid (*prepagato*) Italian SIM card. SIM card kiosks are located at the airport, or you can pick them up in town. You'll need ID or passport.

Wi-fi
Free wi-fi is usually available at the airport, and is widely available in hotels, hostels and cafes, though signal quality can vary in older or rural properties.

Public transport from airport to city centre

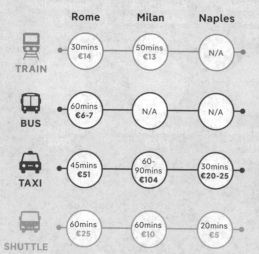

	Rome	Milan	Naples
TRAIN	30mins €14	50mins €13	N/A
BUS	60mins €6-7	N/A	N/A
TAXI	45mins €51	60-90mins €104	30mins €20-25
SHUTTLE	60mins €25	60mins €10	20mins €5

ETIAS

In late 2023, the European Commission's new electronic vetting system – European Travel Information and Authorisation System (ETIAS) – will begin operating. Similar to the US's Esta Visa Waiver, ETIAS aims to pre-screen travellers from non-EU, visa-exempt countries. Under the terms, all non-EU travellers will have to fill in an online form and pay a €7 fee before travelling into the Schengen area. Once registered, travellers will be able to visit all Schengen countries for up to 90 days, for tourism or business. For updates, see etiasvisa.com.

Getting Around

Italy's long profile lends itself to high-speed train travel, which is well priced and efficient. Major cities also have good public transport networks. Still, you'll need a car to really explore the countryside.

TRAVEL COSTS

Rental
From €30/day

Petrol
Approx €1.80/ litre

Bike hire
From €10/day

Train ticket from Milan to Rome
From €58

Urban transport

Italian cities have extensive bus, tram and metro networks (or, in Venice, *vaporetti* – passenger ferries). Most cities offer good-value travel cards. Bike and scooter-sharing schemes are increasingly popular in large cities.

Hiring a car

Car hire is only really useful for the countryside. Booking hire cars online is cheaper, and opting for a smaller model makes parking a lot easier. Renters must be 21 or over. Automobile Club d'Italia (www.aci.it) is an excellent resource.

TIP

Download the Citymapper app for multi-modal transport information (including cycling and scootering), based on real-time data, for major Italian cities.

VALIDATING TICKETS

On state-run buses, trams, trains and Venice's *vaporetti*, you will need to validate (date/time stamp) your ticket. On regional trains, this is done at the green machines found at the head of the platform; on buses and trams, it is the yellow machine found on board. An unvalidated ticket may incur a fine between €50 and €110.

Validating tickets isn't required on high-speed trains such as Frecciarossa, Frecciargento, Frecciabianca, Italo, InterCity and EuroCity, as these are valid for a specific service and seat.

DRIVING ESSENTIALS

Drive on the right.

Tolls & ZTLs

Italy has an extensive motorway (*autostrada*) network, some of which have tolls. Pick up a ticket at the entry barrier and pay (by cash or card) as you exit. Many historic centres are Limited Traffic Zones (ZTL), and can only be entered with a permit. Check with your hotel before arrival.

Taxis

Taxi ranks are widespread in cities. Alternatively, phone for a radio taxi. Note, radio taxi meters start running from their departure point rather than when you're picked up. Most city-centre journeys cost €10-15. Uber is generally banned in Italy – only Uber Black is available in Rome and Milan. An alternative is MyTaxi.

Train & bus

Train is the most popular mode of transport in Italy, which has a well-connected, high-speed network as well as extensive regional services. They work in conjunction with an efficient regionalised bus network. Train travel is best between major cities and along the coast. Buses are better in rural areas.

50

Speed limit is 50km/h in urban areas, 90-110km/h on secondary roads, 130km/h on motorways.

.05

Blood-alcohol limit is 0.05%; zero for under-21s and those who've held a licence for less than three years.

€ Money

CURRENCY: **EURO (€)**

Credit cards

Major credit cards are widely accepted (Amex less so). Businesses are obliged by law to accept digital payments, though exceptions persist, particularly in the south, in small establishments. Don't rely on cards at small museums.

ATMs

ATMs (*bancomat*) are widely available, accepting cards tied to Visa/MasterCard/Cirrus/Maestro systems. Avoid Euronet ATMs, which charge inflated fees. There's a daily limit of €250 on withdrawals.

Taxes & refunds

A 22% value-added tax known as IVA (Imposta sul Valore Aggiunta) is included in the price of most goods and services. Non-EU residents who spend more than €154.94 in one shop (displaying a 'Tax Free' sign) at a single time can claim a refund when leaving the EU. See www.taxrefund.it.

Tipping

Restaurants The *coperto* (cover) is included in the bill and includes service.

Hotels Tourists may tip at high-end hotels.

Taxis No.

Bars No, although some people leave small change (€0.10–€0.20).

HOW MUCH FOR A…

Pizza slice
€2.50

Negroni with *aperitivo*
€8-10

Mid-range meal
€25-35

Museum ticket
€10-20

HOW TO… Save some euros

City tourist cards Discounts on local museums, tours and sometimes transport.
Bus/train Purchase multi-ticket transport passes rather than individual tickets.
Bars/cafes Take your coffee/breakfast at the bar to avoid table service charges.
ID or student cards Italy's state museums and sites are free to EU citizens under 18. Discounts also apply to people aged 18 to 25.
First Sunday of the month Many sites are free of charge.

PAYING THE BILL

In a restaurant, you must ask for the bill ('*il conto, per favore?*'), though it's not uncommon to simply walk up to the register and ask to pay. For your own protection, as well as discouraging tax avoidance, do not let a restaurant drop a piece of paper with nothing but a scribbled total – ask for an itemised bill ('*il conto dettagliato*'). Overcharging in very touristy areas unfortunately happens – sometimes even making international headlines – so pay attention while dining out.

LOCAL TIP

Public toilets charge a fee of €1 to €1.50. You can use the facilities at a bar or cafe, but it's considered rude to do so without buying something.

Accommodation

Rural idylls

Live out your bucolic fantasies at one of Italy's characterful *agriturismi* and *masserie* (farm stays). A long-booming industry in Tuscany and Umbria, farm stays now spread across the country, from the alpine meadows of Trentino Alto-Adige to the vineyards of Sicily. They are perfect for families, relaxation and cultural immersion experiences such as truffle hunting, olive harvesting and cookery classes.

Heavenly hotels

Convents and monasteries offer some of Italy's most memorable lodgings. Many religious houses let out cells or rooms as a modest revenue-making exercise and happily take in tourists, while others only take in pilgrims or people who are on a spiritual retreat (popular in Assisi, for example). Elsewhere, ancient religious retreats, such as Umbria's Eremito, have been converted into luxury lodgings. Some operate an evening curfew.

Mountain refuges

Italy's user-friendly network of *rifugi* (mountain huts) in the Alps, Apennines and other mountains are usually only open from June to late September. Offerings range from rudimentary shelters (known as *bivacchi*) to hostel-like alpine lodges with heating, electricity and often hot meals. Club Alpino Italiano (cai.it) keeps an updated *rifugi* directory.

HOW MUCH FOR A NIGHT IN...

an *agriturismo*
€40-80

a hostel dorm
€20-60

a designer hotel
€200-250

Budget sleeps

Youth hostels (*ostelli per la gioventù*) are run by the Associazione Italiana Alberghi per la Gioventù, affiliated with Hostelling International (www.hihostels.com). Following the trend in other major European cities, Milan, Venice, Rome, Turin, Florence, Bologna, Naples and Palermo all have fabulous designer hostels with shared and private rooms and great facilities.

B&Bs & pensione

There's a fine distinction between a B&B (a room in someone's house) and family-run *pensione* (effectively a small hotel) in Italy. These two types of accommodation are the backbone of Italy's tourist industry and they range from restored farmhouses, to small townhouses and even city *palazzi* (palaces). Prices vary hugely, too – anywhere from €60 to €140.

AIRBNB

Before the COVID-19 pandemic, concerns were raised that Italy's great art cities – Rome, Venice and Florence – were being damaged by a surge of Airbnb rentals. Locals complained of being pushed out by rising rents. With lockdown, the extent of the problem became clear as once-thriving cities became ghost towns. In 2021 Florence and Venice submitted a Decalogo (literally, Ten Commandments) to the Italian government, outlining 10 actions needed to manage tourism. One of them is to better regulate Airbnb by classifying rentals under 30 days as for tourism purposes, limiting to two the number of rentals per person, and imposing a 90-day annual limit on rentals.

Family Travel

Italy is an endlessly entertaining destination for families. Cities are crammed with cultural riches that can be explored with audio guides, smartphone apps and high-quality tours. The countryside offers similar diversity: snorkelling and swimming in beach-rich Puglia, Calabria, Sicily and Sardinia; mountain hikes and lake swims in the Alps and Apennines; and a host of cycling, horse riding and walking in between.

Sightseeing

Italy's museums and monuments beat schoolbooks hands down. Few organise specific tours and workshops for children, but many cater to young minds with multimedia displays, touchscreen gadgets and audio guides; some even have augmented-reality headsets. To get your kids in the mood for sightseeing, share tales of Italy's legendary past like volcanic destruction at Pompeii and brave gladiators at the Colosseum.

Best regions for kids

Rome & Lazio Ancient ruins, eerie catacombs and sensational pizza.

Tuscany Fabulous villas, country walking, cycling and horse riding.

Naples & Campania Ruins in Naples, Pompeii and Vesuvius.

Sicily & Sardinia Volcanoes, dazzling beaches, interesting island-hopping and water sports.

The Dolomites Italy's best family-friendly ski resorts; hiking and biking in summer.

KID-FRIENDLY PICKS

Colosseum (p66) Conjure up the drama of ancient Rome at this global icon.

Aeolian Islands (p673) Seven tiny volcanic islands with everything from spewing lava to black-sand beaches.

Venice (p268) Learn to row standing up like a gondolier in a watery wonderland.

Puglia (p294) Italy's best sandy beaches, charming seaside towns and kid-friendly cuisine.

Discounts

Discounted admission for children is available at most attractions. At state-run sites, admission is free for under-18s, and EU citizens aged between 18 and 25 pay €2 for tickets. Many other places offer reduced admission for those aged six to 18.

Facilities

- Very few restaurants (or other public facilities) have nappy-changing facilities.
- Most hotels (but rarely budget places) have cots; reserve one in advance.
- Car seats are compulsory for kids up to 150cm tall and 12 years of age. Book seats in advance.

EATING OUT

Eating out is one of the joys of Italian travel, with kid-friendly gelato, pizza and pasta regular staples.

Kids are welcome pretty much everywhere, especially in casual trattorias, which are usually pretty informal with menus of simple pasta dishes and grilled meats.

Italian families eat late and few restaurants open much before 7.30pm. Some serve a *menu bambino* (child's menu), but if not it's perfectly acceptable to order a *mezzo porzione* (half-portion) or a simple plate of pasta with olive oil and Parmesan. High chairs (*seggioloni*) are occasionally available, but if your toddler needs to be strapped in, bring your own portable cloth seat.

Health & Safe Travel

TRAVEL SCAMS & THEFT

Pickpockets are active in touristy areas and on crowded public transport. Ticket touts can also be a problem at major sites like the Colosseum. Watch out for people asking for signature/donations in the street if they don't have appropriate ID. Report any theft to police within 24 hours and ask for a statement.

Quakes & volcanoes

Due to its position at the juncture of the African and Eurasian tectonic plates, Italy has high seismic risk, especially around the central Apennines, Rome, Florence and Bologna. Active volcanoes are part of this tectonic liveliness. Naples' Mt Vesuvius and Sicily's Mt Etna and Stromboli have the potential for eruptions. Italy's Protezione Civile (www.protezionecivile.gov.it) monitors threat levels.

Forest fires & floods

Increasingly hot European summers are resulting in more Italian wildfires. Nearly 30% of the country is forested and the south is particularly affected, especially Puglia, Calabria and Sicily. Extreme thunderstorms typically follow heatwaves, often with devastating effect, such as mudslides on Stromboli in summer 2022. If you're caught up in a fire or flood, follow evacuation orders immediately.

TAP WATER

Tap water in Italy is safe to drink, unless a tap is marked *'acqua non potabile'* (water not suitable for drinking).

SWIM SAFELY

Green flag
Safe to swim

Yellow flag
Caution; you can swim near the shore

Red flag
Danger; swimming not advised

Double red flag
Swimming forbidden

Purple flag
Marine pest, such as jellyfish, present

Drugs

If you're caught with enough drugs to deal, you risk a prison sentence of up to 22 years. Cannabis possession for personal use is decriminalised, but possession of other drugs is punishable by administrative sanctions, although first-time offenders may get away with a warning.

HEALTH CARE

Health care is readily accessible throughout Italy. Pharmacists can advise on medical matters and sell medications for minor illnesses. They can also advise on more specialised help. Outside of normal trading hours, pharmacies are required to open on a rotational basis and post a list of open places in the vicinity. Call 118 for an ambulance.

Food, Drink & Nightlif

Eating etiquette

A full-blown Italian meal in a restaurant usually consists of an *antipasto* (starter), a *primo piatto* (first course), a *secondo piatto* (second course) with an *insalata* (salad) or *contorno* (vegetable side dish), *dolci* (sweet), fruit, coffee and *digestivo* (liqueur). Few Italians eat meals this large, though. When eating out, do as most Italians do: mix and match.

Where to eat

Popular and fine-dining restaurants need to be booked in advance, particularly in peak season.

Trattoria: Informal, family-run restaurant cooking up traditional regional dishes.

Ristorante: Formal dining, often with comprehensive wine lists and more sophisticated local or national fare.

Osteria: Similar to a trattoria, with a focus on traditional cooking.

Enoteca: Wine bars invariably double as casual places to graze or dine.

Agriturismo: A working farm with rooms and a farm-to-table restaurant.

MENU DECODER

Piatto del giorno: Dish of the day.

Antipasto: A hot or cold appetiser. For a tasting plate of different appetisers, request an *antipasto misto* (mixed antipasto).

Primo: First course, usually a substantial bowl of pasta, risotto or *zuppa* (soup).

Secondo: Second course, often *pesce* (fish) or *carne* (meat).

Contorno: Side dish, usually *verdura* (vegetable).

Carte dei vini: Wine list.

Dolce: Dessert, including *torta* (cake).

Frutta: Fruit; usually the epilogue to a meal.

Nostra produzione: Made in-house; used to describe anything from bread and pasta to *liquori* (liqueurs).

Surgelato: Frozen; usually used to denote fish or seafood that has not been caught fresh.

Menù fisso: An affordable fixed-price menu; quite rare in Italy and usually only found at lunchtime in popular trattorias frequented by working people.

HOW TO... Order a coffee

Think of your first Italian coffee order as an unofficial initiation ceremony. Rule number one: don't ask for a large double-shot, skinny, vanilla latte. Most coffee orders can be made by uttering a single word: *caffè* (the term 'espresso' is rarely used in Italian coffee bars).

A macchiato is an espresso with a dash of steamed milk. An americano is an espresso with added hot water. The king of all white coffees is the cappuccino, an espresso topped with frothy milk with an optional sprinkling of chocolate.

All coffee in Italy is served at the perfect temperature for flavour – that's *tiepido* (tepid). This means that the *crema* – that caramel-coloured foam on top – preserves the aroma. It also means the milk is heated with steam to create a rich, dense foam (*schiuma*) that captures the essence of the *crema*. If you want your coffee hotter, ask for it 'molto caldo'.

HOW MUCH FOR A...

Cornetto
(croissant)/
brioche
€1.10-2

Aperitivo
€8-10

Espresso
€1.10

Small
ice-cream cone
€2-3

Lunch at a trattoria
€15-20

Dinner at a
Michelin-star
restaurant
€200-250

Beer
€4-6

Glass of wine
€5-8

HOW TO... Navigate vegetarianism

To many Italians, being vegetarian means not eating red meat. Few are strictly vegetarian – many eat meat in limited quantities, particularly in the south.

In big cities, there's an increasing number of vegetarian, vegan and raw-food restaurants and cafes. High-end restaurants typically offer vegetarian menus and bar-cafes increasingly serve *cornetti vegani* (vegan croissants) and *latte di soia* (soya milk).

On regular menus, be mindful of hidden ingredients in vegetarian-sounding dishes – steer clear of anything that's been stuffed (like zucchini flowers, often spiced up with anchovies) or pastas with tomato sauce that might be enriched with *guanciale* (pork jowl). To be sure, check that your dish is *senza carne o pesce* (without meat or fish).

Vegans are in for a tougher time. This is particularly true in the north where all things dairy (milk, cheese, yoghurt, butter) play a central role in the diet. Cheese is used universally, so specify that you want something *senza formaggio* (without cheese).

Plant-based popularity

Although vegetarianism has grown exponentially in Italy over the last decade, vegetarians and vegans still only represent 8.9% of the population. Carlotta Perego, founder of Cucina Botanica (https://cucinabotanica.com), is a pioneer of the movement.

Useful phrases

Io sono vegano/vegana: I'm vegan (male/female)
Non mangio prodotti di origine animale: I don't eat animal products
Non mangio i latticini: I don't eat dairy products
Contiene uova? Does it contain eggs?
Avete latte di soia? Do you have soya milk?

APERITIVO

Aperitivi are often described as a 'before-meal drink and light snacks'. Don't be fooled. Italian happy hour can easily turn into a budget-friendly dinner disguised as a casual drink (otherwise known as *apericena*). This is particularly true of *aperitivi* accompanied by a buffet of antipasti, pasta salads, cold cuts and some hot dishes. As a result, *aperitivo* bars are popular places for first dates and singles looking to meet new people. You can methodically pillage buffets in cities, including Milan, Turin, Rome, Naples and Palermo, from about 5pm or 6pm to 8pm or 9pm for the price of a single drink – which crafty diners nurse for the duration – while Venetians enjoy *ombre* (half-glasses of wine) and bargain seafood *cicheti* (Venetian tapas).

Despite its national popularity, Italy's *aperitivo* roots lie in Turin. It was in Piedmont's capital that, in 1786, Antonio Benedetto Carpano infused Moscato white wine with herbs and spices to create vermouth. The drink quickly gained a reputation for piquing the appetite, turning the bar in which Carpano worked into Turin's pre-dinner hot spot. These days, favourite *aperitivo* libations include the spritz – a mix of prosecco, soda water and either Aperol, Campari or the more herbacious Cynar. Not surprisingly, *aperitivi* are wildly popular among the many young Italians who can't afford to eat dinner out, but still want a place to enjoy food while schmoozing with friends – leave it to Italy to find a way to put the glam into budget.

Responsible Travel

Climate change & travel

It's impossible to ignore the impact we have when travelling, and the importance of making changes where we can. Lonely Planet urges all travellers to engage with their travel carbon footprint. There are many carbon calculators online that allow travellers to estimate the carbon emissions generated by their journey; try resurgence.org/resources/carbon-calculator.html. Many airlines and booking sites offer travellers the option of offsetting the impact of greenhouse gas emissions by contributing to climate-friendly initiatives around the world. We continue to offset the carbon footprint of all Lonely Planet staff travel, while recognising this is a mitigation more than a solution.

Ethical accommodation

Italy's network of farm stays (agriturismo.it) offer affordable, authentic experiences, often with farm-to-table meals. Other organisations support a cleaner economy – these include Fairbnb.coop, which aims to better connect travellers with local hosts, and Addiopizzotravel.it, which promotes ethical, anti-mafia travel.

Slow Food

The Slow Food organisation (www.slowfood.it) promotes projects that protect genuine culinary traditions and local ecosystems. Seek out restaurants recognised by Slow Food's guide, Osterie d'Italia (published annually), to support regional biodiversity and the people who care about it.

Cruise ships

Forgo cruise ships – although the largest cruise ships are now banned from Venice's lagoon, cruise-ship pollution is still a serious issue in port towns.

Cultural considerations

Don't picnic on or at historic steps, fountains, museum entrances, ruins or monuments as the constant wear and spilled food causes damage. Instead, look for the nearest bench and dispose of rubbish in a bin or take it with you.

According to Legambiente, Italy's most prominent environmental association, there are over 2500 'dying villages' in less-trodden regions like Umbria, Calabria, Basilicata and Molise. Support them by travelling off-the-beaten path. Sextantio.it is a model project.

Support social enterprises such as Rome's Binario95 (binario95.it), which has been providing shelter to the homeless for the past 20 years. Check out legacoopsociali.it for other ideas.

Cycle paths and bike-sharing schemes are prevalent in major cities and towns, as well as the Amalfi Coast. There's also an increasing number of regional and national cycle routes, the longest of which is the Via Francigena. Check out eurovelo.com/italy.

Shop local

Seek out souvenirs from local businesses, especially in small towns where tourist cash goes a long way. Italy has some amazing artisanal products, such as Murano glass from Venice, Amalfi and Sicilian ceramics, Roman leatherwork and Florentine textiles.

Water, water everywhere

Le fontanelle (little fountains) and *nasoni* (big noses, or large fountains) are found all over Italy, with extensive networks in Rome, Venice, Turin and Florence – ditch the bottled water and bring your own reusable bottle.

Sp.accio *(https://spaccio. sanpatrignano. org)* pizzeria in the therapeutic rehabilitation community of San Patrignano near Rimini is run by community members.

Get out in Italy's national parks *(parks. it)* and support organisations conserving wildlife and biodiversity.

15

The Global Sustainability Index ranks Italy in 15th place worldwide. Italy has invested heavily in renewable energy in order to reach a 30% share by 2030. It's also the first country to incorporate climate change sustainable development into its national curriculum.

Scooter, bike & trolley etiquette

Take care with e-scooters, bikes and trolley suitcases in historic centres. It is illegal to drag them up/down historic staircases. In 2022 a tourist caused €25,000 worth of damage to the Spanish Steps with an e-scooter.

RESOURCES

wwoof.it
Volunteer opportunities on organic farms

aitr.org
Has a map of responsible tourism initiatives.

legambiente turismo.it
Italy's most important environmental association

Stay longer and travel slower. The longer you stay, the lower your carbon-per-day bill. Seek out less famous destinations: instead of Venice, try Padua or Trieste; instead of Florence, visit Lecce or Matera; instead of Tuscany, venture to Piedmont o Puglia.

LGBTIQ+ Travellers

Homosexuality, cross-dressing and sex reassignment are legal (over the age of 16) and even widely accepted in Italy. In 2016 a civil union law was passed providing same-sex couples with many of the rights of marriage, although marriage itself remains banned. That said, Italy remains a fairly conservative society and outside larger cities discretion is still wise.

Gay districts

In Rome, the Colosseum end of Via di San Giovanni is a gay-friendly haunt, while in Milan, Via Lecco, Via Tadino and NoLo are popular LGBTIQ+ areas. In Turin, Bananamia is a huge club night hosted weekly at the Centralino nightclub. In Genoa, the place to be is the Virgo Club. Queer and Crisco Club are Florence's two big gay clubs, and the southern region of Puglia is something of a queer mecca, given its former president, Nichi Vendola, was one of Italy's first openly gay politicians.

COMPLEX MINDSETS

Italian attitudes to the LGBTIQ+ community are complex. Polls repeatedly show that the majority of Italians support equality and legal recognition of same-sex relationships, yet traditional Catholic values concerning sexuality and gender roles prevail. As a result, overt displays of affection can attract a negative response, especially in smaller towns.

PINK CITY

Bologna is home to Italy's national Arcigay organisation. It was also the birthplace of two iconic LGBTIQ+ personalities: filmmaker Pier Paolo Pasolini and singer Lucio Dalla. Bologna's Villa Cassarini has one of only three European monuments commemorating the WWII persecution of LGBTIQ+ people. A ceremony is held here on 27 January and 25 April.

Partying with Pride

Rome, Milan, Turin, Padua, Bologna, Florence, Naples, Palermo and Catania are all recognised as gay-friendly cities, along with the coastal holiday resorts of Rimini, Capri, Torre del Lago (Tuscany), Taormina (Sicily) and Gallipoli (Puglia). They all host great Pride parades (as do 30 towns and cities across Italy) in June and July. Head to www.gay.it for LGBTIQ+ news, features and gossip.

SAFE NETWORKS

Arcigay *(arcigay.it)* Italy's national organisation for LGBTIQ+ rights was established in 1980.

Coordinamento Lesbiche Italiano *(clrbp.it)* The national organisation for lesbians holds regular cultural events in Rome.

Circolo Mario Mieli di Cultura Omosessuale *(mariomieli.org)* Rome-based cultural centre that organises debates, cultural events and social functions.

Pride *(prideonline.it)* Culture, politics, travel and health with an LGBTIQ+ focus.

Gay Village

Running every night from mid-June to mid-September, Gay Village *(facebook.com/GayVillage)* sees Parco del Ninfeo transformed into an outdoor cinema, exhibition space, open-air gym, dance, performance and party venue.

Accessible Travel

Italy is not an easy country for travellers with disabilities. Cobblestone streets make getting around difficult for wheelchair users, and many buildings have no lift. The situation is similar for hearing- and vision-impaired travellers. However, awareness of accessibility issues and a culture of inclusion are steadily growing.

Free museum access

If you have a visible disability and/or appropriate ID, many museums and galleries offer free admission for yourself and a companion.

Airport

Airlines will arrange assistance at airports if notified in advance. Trains and buses from Rome's Fiumicino and Ciampino and Milan's Malpensa airports to the city centre are wheelchair accessible. Otherwise, the nationwide 3750.it taxi service has wheelchair-adapted vehicles.

Accommodation

Newer and larger hotels tend to have some adapted rooms, though facilities may not be up to scratch; ask at the local tourist board. Many newer hostels have accessible facilities. Villageforall. net lists accessible accommodation.

PARKING PERMITS

If you are driving, EU disabled parking permits are recognised in Italy, giving you the same parking rights as local drivers with disabilities.

Street obstacles

With its cobbled historic centres and hilltop rural villages, Italy can be difficult for wheelchair users. Even in largely flat cities, such as Milan, many pavements are blocked by parked cars and scooters.

Public transport

If travelling by train, arrange assistance through SalaBlu (https://salabluonline. rfi.it). Many urban buses are wheelchair-accessible, though some of the stops may not be – ask before you board.

TAXIS

Some taxis are equipped to carry passengers in wheelchairs; ask for a taxi for a *sedia a rotelle* (wheelchair). Fausta Trasporti *(https://accessibletransportationrome. com)* and 3750.it have wheelchair-accessible vehicles.

RESOURCES

Accessible Italy (*accessibleitaly. com*) Runs guided tours and offers services including equipment rental, accommodation booking and adapted-vehicle hire, and can arrange personal assistants.

Rome & Italy (*romeanditaly.com/ accessible*) Offers tours, accessible accommodation, and equipment and vehicle hire. Its Wheely Trekky service uses a specially designed sedan/ rickshaw to access many otherwise inaccessible archaeological sites.

Village for All (*villageforall.net/ en*) Performs on-site audits of tourist facilities in Italy and San Marino.

ACCESSIBLE BEACHES

Fondazione Cesare Serono (fondazioneserono. org) provides a list of accessible beaches.

 # Nuts & Bolts

OPENING HOURS

We've provided high-season opening hours. Hours decrease in winter.

Banks 8.30am–1.30pm and 2.45–4.30pm Monday to Friday

Bars & cafes 7.30am–8pm, sometimes to 1am or 2am

Restaurants noon–3pm and 7.30–11pm (later in summer)

Shops 9am–1pm and 3.30–7.30pm (or 4–8pm) Monday to Saturday. In cities some shops stay open all day. Some shops close Monday.

Dress code

Cover shoulders, torso and thighs when visiting churches and dress smartly when eating out – Italians don't appreciate beach attire in restaurants.

Smoking
Smoking is banned in enclosed public spaces, which includes restaurants, bars, shops and public transport.

Drinking age
The legal age to be served alcohol in a restaurant or bar in Italy is 16.

GOOD TO KNOW

Time zone
UTC plus one hour

Country code
39

Emergency number
112

Population
59.3 million

Electricity 220–230V/50Hz

Type L
220V/50Hz

Type F
230V/50Hz

PUBLIC HOLIDAYS

Most Italians take their annual holiday in August. Many businesses and shops close for at least part of the month, particularly around Ferragosto (Feast of the Assumption) on 15 August.

Capodanno (New Year's Day) 1 January

Epifania (Epiphany) 6 January

Pasquetta (Easter Monday) March/April

Giorno della Liberazione (Liberation Day) 25 April

Festa del Lavoro (Labour Day) 1 May

Festa della Repubblica (Republic Day) 2 June

Ferragosto (Feast of the Assumption) 15 August

Festa di Ognisanti (All Saints' Day) 1 November

Festa dell'Immacolata Concezione (Feast of the Immaculate Conception) 8 December

Natale (Christmas Day) 25 December

Festa di Santo Stefano (Boxing Day) 26 December

Rome (p58)

Language

TOOLKIT

Italian comes from the Romance language family and is closely related to Spanish and French.

Basics

Hello. Buongiorno. *bwon·jor·no*
Goodbye. Arrivederci. *a·ree·ve·der·chee*
Yes. Sì. *see*
No. No. *no*
Please. Per favoire. *per fa vo·re*
Thank you. Grazie. *gra·tsye*
Excuse me. Mi scusi. (pol)/ Scusami. (inf). *mee skoo·zee/ skoo·za·mee*
Sorry. Mi dispiace. *mee dees·pya·che*
What's your name? Come si chiama. *ko·me see kya·ma*
My name is ... Mi chiamo... *mee kya·mo...*

Do you speak English? Parla/parli inglese? (pol/inf). *par·la/par·lee een·gle·ze*
I don't understand. Non capisco. *non ka·pee·sko*

Directions

Where's (the station)? Dov'è. *do·ve ...*
What's the address? Qual'è l'indirizzo. *kwa·le leen·dee·ree·tso*
Could you please write it down? Può scriverlo, per favore?. *pwo skree·ver·lo per fa·vo·re*
Can you show me (on the map)? Può mostrarmi (sulla pianta)? *pwo mos·trar·mee (soo·la pyan·ta)*

Signs

Aperto/a Open
Chiuso/a Closed
Informazione Information
Bagno WC/Toilets
Prohibito/a Prohibited
Uscita Exit

Time

What time is it? Che ora è?. *ke o·ra e*
It's 1 o'clock. È l'una. *e loo·na*
Half past (1). (L'una) e mezza. *(loo·na) e me·dza*
morning mattina. *ma·tee·na*
afternoon pomeriggio. *po·me·ree·jo*
evening sera. *se·ra*
yesterday ieri. *ye·ree*
today oggi. *o·jee*
tomorrow domani. *do·ma·nee*

Emergencies

Help! Aiuto! *a·yoo·to*
Leave me alone! Lasciami in pace!. *la·sha·mee een pa·che*
I'm ill. Mi sento male. *mee sen·to ma·le*
Call ...! Chiami. *kya·me*
a doctor un medico. *oon me·dee·ko*
the police la polizia. *la po·lee·tsee·a*

Eating & drinking

What would you recommend? Cosa mi consiglia? *ko·za mee kon·see·lya*
Cheers! Salute! *sa·loo·te*
That was delicious. Era squisito! *e·ra skwee·zee·to*
Vegetarian. vegetariano. *ve·-je·ta·rya·no*

NUMBERS

1
uno *oo-no*

2
due *doo-e*

3
tre *tre*

4
quattro *kwa-tro*

5
cinque *cheen-kwe*

6
sei *say*

7
sette *se-te*

8
otto *o-to*

9
nove *no-ve*

10
dieci *dye-chee*

DONATIONS TO ENGLISH

Numerous - you may recognise **ciao, bella, pasta, mafia, maestro**

10 Phrases to Sound Like a Local

What's up – Cosca c'é – *ko-za-che*
All OK? – Tutto a posto? – *too-ta pos-to*
It's OK – Va bene – *va be-ne*
Great! – Fantastico! – *fan=tas=tee-ko*
That's true – È vero –*e ve-ro*
Sure – Certo – *cher-to*
No way! – Per niente! – *per nyen-te*
You're kidding! – Scherzi! – *fsker-tsee*
If only! – Magari! – *ma-ga-ree*
Really? – Davvero? – *da-ve-ro*

DISTINCTIVE SOUNDS

The only sound that differs from English is the 'r', which is rolled and stringer than in English.

False Friends

Some Italian words look like English words but have a different meaning, eg *camera* (*ka*-mer-ra) is 'bedroom', not 'camera', which is *macchina fotografica* (*ma*-kee-na fo-togra-fee-ka).

Must-Know Grammar

Italian has a formal and informal word for 'you' (*Lei* and *tu* respectively). Verbs have different endings for each person, like the English 'I do' vs 'he/ she do**es**'.

Italian in Italy

Italians are very proud of their language's rich history and influence – rightly so, since it claims the closest relationship with the language spoken by the Romans. For example, Italy is one of the few countries in Europe where dubbling of foreign-language movies is preferred to subtitling.

WHO SPEAKS ITALIAN?

Thanks to the widespread migration and the enormous popularity of Italian culture and cuisine – from 'spaghetti Western' to opera – Italian is often a language of choice in schools all over the world, despite that fact that Italy never established itself as a colonial power.

65 million speak Italian as their first language

20 million speak Italian as their second language

Switzerland
Italy ,
San Marino,
Vatican City)
Istria (Croatia & Slovenia)

STORYBOOK

Our writers delve deep into different aspects of Italian life

Trulli village, Alberobello (p600)
WJAREK/SHUTTERSTOCK ©

Selunte (p705)

A HISTORY OF ITALY IN
15 PLACES

The history of Italy is characterised by two periods of unity – the Roman Empire and the current democratic republic that was born from the ashes of WWII. Between these two eras, there has been a millennium and a half of division and disruption, invasions and conflicts. By Stefania D'Ignoti

BETWEEN THE 6TH and the 3rd centuries BCE, the city of Rome conquered the Italian Peninsula; in the following centuries, it spread its influence over the majority of Mediterranean and Western Europe, evolving into an empire dominating much of the then-known world. Roman civilisation left a remarkable legacy to Western society, and still defines much of Europe's history.

But after the Empire 'fell' in the 5th century CE, the geographical area of modern Italy was the target of several barbaric invasions. The previously united entity broke into several smaller, independent nations, including the Papal States. The chaos that followed gave life to one of Western history's most flourishing periods for the arts, the Renaissance (circa 1400–1600). It wasn't until the mid-19th century that that disruption came to an end with Italy's short-lived unification as a nation state and kingdom, only to be briefly fragmented again between the two world wars, until in 1946 it became the modern republic we know today.

1. Su Nuraxi
BEFORE THE ERA OF GREAT EMPIRES

Between 1900 and 730 BCE, the *nuraghe* represented the main type of prehistoric megalithic structure in Italy. Seven thousand of these mysterious stone towers are scattered across Sardinia. Nuraghe Su Nuraxi – a Unesco World Heritage Site – in Barumini is Sardinia's biggest and most famous one. Today, the complex consists of a majestic *nuraghe* surrounded by an extensive nuraghic village. Historians haven't decided on the purpose of this settlement, but it may have been a symbol of wealth or power, or they may have signalled that that part of land already had an owner.

For more on Su Nuraxi, see page 772

2. Selinunte
GREEK TEMPLES AND VALLEYS

Southern Italy was under Greek rule between the 8th and 11th centuries BCE, and the impressive ruins of Selinunte tell the story of the colony's rise and decline. Today this vast complex, covering around 270 hectares, is the largest archaeological park in Europe. It includes seven ruined temples with over 2500 years of history. The city is located on top of a promontory, and the ruins of the ancient temples overlooking the Mediterranean Sea are a charming place to wander, not to be missed on a trip to Sicily.

For more on Selinunte, see page 705

3. Foro Boario

THE ORIGINS OF ROME

Piazza della Bocca della Verità is where, in ancient Rome, the area of the Foro Boario (Latin for cattle market) stood. Its presence dates back to earlier times, to the actual foundation of Rome, and because of this, it's considered to be a symbolic place of interest that witnessed Rome's escalating urban change. It was considerably enlarged in the 2nd century BCE, to meet the needs of a rapidly expanding Rome. Today, it is one of the Italian capital's most famous squares.

For more on Piazza della Bocca della Verità, see page 71

4. Arena di Verona

BEYOND GLADIATORS

Although smaller than the Colosseum in Rome, the Arena di Verona is one of the largest examples of Roman architecture, and also one of the best-preserved ancient amphitheatres, thanks to the frequent restorations carried out since the 16th century. During the summer months it hosts the Arena Opera Festival, whose concerts have taken place regularly since 1913; the rest of the year it becomes a popular destination for many international singers and musicians.

For more on Arena di Verona, see page 352.

5. Torre degli Asinelli

ITALY'S OTHER LEANING TOWER

In the 13th century, in a period of conflict between the popes and the Holy Roman Emperor, Italy was divided into two political factions – the *guelfi* and the *ghibellini* – as narrated in Dante Alighieri's *Divine Comedy*. It is still not possible to say with certainty when and by whom Bologna's Torre degli Asinelli was built, but it is assumed that the leaning tower owes its name to Gherardo Asinelli, a noble knight of the Ghibelline faction whose family may have owned the tower.

For more on Torre degli Asinelli, see page 368.

6. Palazzo dei Priori

MEDIEVAL TALES

Built in Gothic style between 1293 and 1443, Perugia's Palazzo dei Priori is one of the best examples of a public palace of this period, which was dominated by the rising phenomena of city-states. Accessed through a 13th-century portal decorated with statues of the griffin and the lion, it houses the magnificent Galleria Nazionale dell'Umbria, whose artistic heritage boasts the masterpieces of the famous Duccio di Buoninsegna, Piero della Francesca, Beato Angelico, Pinturicchio and Perugino, Raffaello's maestro.

For more on Palazzo dei Priori, see page 512

7. Basilica di San Lorenzo

RENAISSANCE BEAUTY

Less well known than the Cattedrale di Santa Maria del Fiore, the Basilica di San Lorenzo in Florence represents one of the best architectural examples of the Renaissance. It is known for being the mausoleum of the Medici, the family that ruled and, most of all, contributed to the greatness of Florence, and to the birth and development of the Renaissance. Important artists such as Brunelleschi and Michelangelo contributed to its construction.

For more on Basilica di San Lorenzo, see page 425

8. Ponte dei Sospiri

(UN)ROMANTIC LEGENDS

Many people who have been to Venice have passed beneath the Ponte dei Sospiri (Bridge of Sighs) aboard a gondola. But what for many is the Lovers' Bridge was originally an access ramp from the halls of the magistrates to the Palazzo delle Prigioni, where prisoners who had just been tried and sentenced were transported. Through the windows of the bridge the condemned would have seen the sky for the last time before being locked up in prison; the sighs sounded their longing for freedom. Over time, however, the bridge has taken on a more romantic meaning, linked to the sigh of lovers.

For more on Ponte dei Sospiri, see page 277

9. Teatro San Carlo

LYRIC PRESTIGE

Next to Piazza del Plebiscito, iconic symbol of Naples, stands the Italian lyric temple of San Carlo, predating the more famous Scala in Milan by 41 years. This ginormous theatre was built in 1737, by the will of King Charles III of Bourbon, a French-Spanish dynasty that for centuries dominated southern Italy. All the greatest artists sooner or later walked the stages of the rheatre, a symbol of Bourbon power that for decades challenged the birth of a united Italy.

For more on Teatro San Carlo, see page 553

10. Palazzo Carignano

TOWARDS UNITY

Every corner of Turin screams Risorgimento – a historical period characterised by political movements that led to the unification of Italy, for the first time since the Roman Empire. Turin was the first capital of the kingdom, and the symbol of this period is the Palazzo Carignano, seat of the first Italian parliament and birthplace of Vittorio Emanuele II, the first king of Italy. In 2011, for the 150th anniversary of the birth of Italy, it was a place of colourful national celebrations.

For more on Palazzo Carignano, see page 167

11. Vittoriano

CELEBRATING NEWBORN ITALY

At the end of the 19th century, the capital of Italy was moved from Turin to Rome; as a result, the city went through a profound process of urban renewal. It was at this time of renovation, during Italy's first steps as a united country, that the construction of the Vittoriano took place. Begun in 1885, this monument was designed to honour the memory of Vittorio Emanuele II, the king under whom unification of the country was achieved. It was inaugurated on 4 June 1911 for the 50th anniversary of the unification, and since 4 November 1921 it has hosted the body of the unknown soldier.

For more on Vittoriano, see page 67

12. Forte di Osoppo

ITALY AND THE GREAT WAR

Some of the main battles Italy was involved in during WWI took place in this area in Friuli Venezia Giulia. Declared a national monument in 1923, it was demilitarised in 1951 and it features a significant number of remains dating back to the period of the Great War. Today, despite being a scene of horrible war atrocities, its beautiful landscape over the Tagliamento river, overlooking wonderful nature and hiking trails, hosts several cultural events.

13. Monumento alla Vittoria

TROUBLED FASCIST LEGACY

In Trentino Alto Adige, urban planning and architecture were used as instruments of internal colonialism that fascism used to 'Italianise' the unredeemed northern border territories, torn from Austria after WWI. In Bolzano, this legacy is most visible in the fascist Monumento alla Vittoria (Monument to Victory). The building is at the same time a shrine dedicated to the fallen of WWI and a reminder of the fascist rhetoric used to Italianise South Tyrol. With the end of the dictatorship, the monuments and buildings linked to fascism have become the reason for clashes between the Germans and Italians who live in this autonomous province, and with the return of the far-right in Italy, there have been several protests to get rid of it.

14. Piazza Umberto I

THE ECONOMIC BOOM

With the end of WWII and following a slow economic recovery, Italy went through a boom symbolised by holidays on the island of Capri, off Naples' coast. People would wear their Sunday best and dance until sunrise in summer at Piazza Umberto I. In the 1960s, the Piazzetta became the beating heart of the island's social life; it was nicknamed the living room of the world and a symbol of Italy as a flourishing international tourist destination for the next several decades.

For more on Piazza Umberto I, see page 570

15. Porta d'Europa

ITALY'S REFUGEE CRISIS

A monument almost 5m high, the 'door to Europe' was inspired by the dramatic stories of the thousands of migrants who, facing incredible adversities, try to reach Europe by boat from Africa. Since 2015 Italy has been greatly affected by the refugee crisis, and more than half a million people have passed through Lampedusa, Italy's southernmost point and home to the country's biggest refugee camp. This monument pushes future generations not to forget the tragedies of migrants, and to invite them to understand how close they are geographically.

DOLCE FAR NIENTE:
MYTHS & TRUTHS

An attitude, a lifestyle, the soul of the Italian summer – caught between stereotypes and real life. By Benedetta Geddo

YOU MIGHT HAVE heard of the dolce vita. An idea that was immortalised by Federico Fellini's 1960 film of the same name, which inspired a thousand and one dreams across the world of people wishing to recreate Marcello Mastroianni's and Anita Ekberg's iconic scene in the Trevi Fountain in Rome.

The movie propelled the idea of the dolce vita into the mainstream, turning Italy – and certain locations in particular, from Portofino through to Rome and the Amalfi Coast – into a dreamland of endless glamour veiled by a bittersweet nostalgia for the happy days of the postwar economic boom.

But at its core the dolce vita is mostly that – a cinematic invention that built on some real aspects of everyday Italian life. It captured the zeitgeist of that particular moment in time – Cinecittà Studios in the 1960s, international stars milling around, the glitz and glamour of cinema. The idea of the dolce far niente, however, is another thing entirely.

Or, well, not entirely. The two ideas are not unrelated, if only by virtue of sharing the same sweetening adjective. The dolce far niente – the 'sweet doing nothing' – overlaps with the dolce vita somewhat, in its leisurely and unhurried sense. But its roots can be traced much further back than the second half of the 20th century.

In Italian, the word that best encapsulates the idea of dolce far niente is *ozio*. This acquired some negative connotations over the centuries, but has arrived into the modern language of Italy directly from the Romans – and they themselves noticed the same concept being used by the Greeks before them.

In his *Eclogues*, written in the 1st century BCE, Roman poet Virgil describes how the Greeks despised work and spent their time in nobler ways, devoting themselves to gymnastics, philosophy and poetry. In the first eclogue, he describes leisure as a divine gift.

Many of Virgil's fellow ancient Roman writers and philosophers shared this idea, that the true measure of people isn't just in what keeps them busy, but also in what they do when they're not busy. With a much-needed distinction – *ozio* and dolce far niente don't refer to being idle. They

are about being at leisure. It's a subtle difference but a vital one.

From the Romans onwards, the idea ebbed and flowed with the centuries. The subtle distinction was lost, and leisure became something to be criticised with the sweeping arrival of Catholic morals, and later something to praised once more. Today, leisure seems to be something that fewer and fewer people can afford, but which more and more people seek scraps of in order to feel grounded. All in all, the idea of the dolce far niente remains deeply rooted in Italian culture, and you see it popping its head up around you to this day.

This may be one of the reasons why the stereotype of Italians being generally lazy still prevails – because society hasn't been able to once again grasp the fundamental distinction that the Romans made centuries ago between being at leisure and being idle. That difference is key to the dolce far niente.

Here's an example... During a long, golden Italian summer, you'll find many shops closed in the hours immediately after lunch. And this is not because of a simple 'Italians are lazy' stereotype. You have to take into consideration the physical realities of Italy – a country with scorching hot summers, where the sun is at its most unforgiving between midday and four in the afternoon. So people stay inside to protect themselves, and shops remain closed. It's not laziness, and it's not even dolce far niente.

Let's bring it back to summer, the queen of all Italian seasons. In his book *Call Me By Your Name*, Egyptian–American writer André Aciman gives one of the best descriptions of the dolce far niente I have ever read. He writes, 'What did one do around here? Nothing. Wait for summer to end. What did one do in the winter, then? I smiled at the answer I was about to give. He got the gist and said, 'Don't tell me: wait for summer to come, right?'

That really is the point – it's what you do while waiting for summer to end. To Italians, the dolce far niente means getting time to do what you usually have to

cut out of your busy day. Whatever it is, really – reading, baking, collecting stamps, going out for a walk or a bike ride. And especially catching up with people. Italians are social creatures, and for us dolce far niente means gathering around a table with your friends, chatting until lunch turns into a mid-afternoon snack, which turns into *aperitivo* time.

And that scene is one that most Italians associate with the long days of summer, where everything seems to be magically suspended in a haze of golden hours, childhood memories and time that moves honey-slow. I'm not saying that you can't have some dolce far niente time in spring, winter or autumn, quite the contrary – each season has its own brand and flavour of it. However, the dolce far niente you have in summer is another creature altogether.

But no matter what season you're in, whether you're sipping wine as you watch the summer sun go down or you're bundled up inside on a winter afternoon, dolce far niente is, at its core, this – not laziness, not idleness, but doing what you love best on time that isn't borrowed or stolen from what you should be doing. Instead, it's exactly where you should be – here and now, sweetly doing nothing.

Finally, here come some clarifications. Of course, too much dolce far niente does turn into laziness eventually – this is as true in Italy as it is in any other corner of the world, and the Romans themselves were very much aware of this as they were enjoying their time of *ozio*, or *otium* as they knew it. And another thing that is true for everyone is that generalisations only work up to a certain point.

There are more than 60 million people living in Italy. And while dolce far niente is an undeniable part of Italian culture, that doesn't mean that every single Italian will interpret it in the same way or even dedicate time to it. The reality of everyday life needs to be afforded complexity and depth, one that goes beyond what you might have heard about Italians and their lifestyle. Take it from an Italian herself – I am just one of us, after all.

ITALIAN FOOD DOESN'T EXIST

The search for 'authentic' cuisine has turned too many holidays into hunts for holy grails, when the secret is hiding in plain sight. By Virginia DiGaetano

ONE OF MY first assignments as a travel concierge was for a group of self-proclaimed 'foodies' who wanted to arrange a tour of central and southern Italy. Despite my visceral aversion to the terms 'foodies' and 'tour', I built an itinerary around traditional ingredients, dishes and locations. Over two weeks they tried Roman *porchetta*, Umbrian truffles, and still-warm *mozzarella di bufala* just outside of Naples. The responses were tepid yet tactful: the fattiness of one or the sourness of another was always just a bit too much for their tastes.

At one of our busiest stops, we arrived in that temporal purgatory between lunch and dinner, meaning that only the most forlorn establishments would be open. An 'authentic' farm visit earlier that day had fallen flat, so the famished group roamed the desolate streets until someone spied a neon sign that said 'home cooking' in English. Before I could protest they entered a storefront whose only discernible sign of a kitchen was a prominently displayed microwave and the suggestion of their famous 'aubergine parmigiana'. If the dish they served had ever been aubergine or parmigiana at any point in its short life cycle, it certainly wasn't any more. Yet every single person tucked in with pure, unadulterated joy. 'Finally,' the most vocal of them said. 'Real Italian food.'

Not since Joseph of Arimathea decided to send the world on a wild chase for a cup has a quest been more misdirected, and just like the grail that spawned a thousand falsehoods, we've forgotten what it is that even makes Italian food special. We are so obsessed with 'authentic' experiences that we accuse our meals of adultery and perjury, never stopping to consider that we're the ones who are guilty of betrayal.

So, what does authenticity taste like, and why do we pathologically expect it in Italy? Each of the 20 regions in this unlikely federation could claim custody of 'the quintessential Italian recipe' and every city, town or hamlet has infinite variations therein. Stop someone on the street in Genoa and ask them how to prepare pesto: in less time than it's taken them to get their mother on the phone, a crowd will amass to debate whether garlic should be

Caponata and bruschetta

included. Wander through bustling Sicilian alleyways tasting *caponata* in Palermo or Catania, and then dare to declare whose version is the original.

The finest restaurants of Piedmont or Veneto all have their signature risotto, and each will claim the most faithful rendition. None will rival the unctuous *mantecato* that you'll have visiting a friend's family somewhere along the flat rice plains of the Po valley. Make your way to Bologna into one of the mythical trattorias where *ragù bolognese* bubbles on the stove for so long that it leaves deep amber streaks on the walls that date the dining room like rings on a redwood. There too, you'll hear endless, forensic discussions about the correct temperature and time frame that every batch requires. Everyone will have a different opinion and to your uninitiated ears, everyone will be right.

As all roads do, yours will inevitably lead to Rome and the search for the Platonic form of carbonara. Aggressive advice on everything from the correct cured meat (*guanciale*) to pasta shape (rigatoni) to the origin story (who really knows) would be imparted like sacred runes on a pilgrimage. But for every person who swears to be the Keeper of the Carbonara, there are five more to challenge them. Every dish will feel 'authentic' until it all merges into a delicious miasma. All you'll remember is that microwaved imitation at wherever was open at the one moment in the day when you simply couldn't be bothered to think about it anymore. You will have been vanquished by the sheer immensity of the Italian culinary canon. Don't worry, it happens to the best of us.

But there is a secret hiding so plainly in sight that you will wonder how you missed it. To eat in Italy is to bathe in its multitudes, to succumb and surrender to the inherent, enveloping sensuality of

every plate, every bite, every spoonful. It is laughter and communion and passion, all mingling together like the musky flavours of that perfect *ragù*. Our search for 'authenticity' has become a desperate plea that what we're eating, drinking and feeling is objectively and Instagrammably 'real'. What we really want is to connect, and the radical truth is that any time we seek out someone to share those moments with, it is real. 'Authentic' experiences give us that sense of belonging to something, sometime. In Italy, everything is tenuous, ephemeral and fragile but the food, no matter what it may be, is real. It's how we connect but it is not why. There is no national dish because every meal is proof that we exist; if only until the last traces of sauce are polished off. This is an old country, with old blood coursing through it, and nothing is a guarantee. But today, tonight, or on Sunday afternoon, we will break bread together and whether that bread has salt in it or not, it will be 'real Italian food' because it will nourish something deeper, something real.

Years after that tour I went for lunch with a dear, beautiful friend in one of the oft-overlooked neighbourhoods of Naples. It was the kind of scorching, dazzlingly humid day that required copious amounts of Fiano di Avellino, a white wine made to combat exactly these sorts of conditions. I could only order an *insalata caprese* with ripe tomato and plump mozzarella but he, native to the area, chose unflinchingly: aubergine parmigiana. It arrived bubbling like the lava that would have issued from nearby Mt Vesuvius but he was undeterred, typically courageous in front of a torturously hot tureen. I asked what possessed him to undergo such anguish. He gulped that golden Fiano and said simply, beautifully:

'I wanted real food.'

UNGOVERNABLE ITALY

Italian politics often seems disorganised, chaotic and bewildering. That's the point. By Virginia DiGaetano

IF YOU'VE EVER so much as had an extended layover in Italy, chances are you've been present for a government collapse. Of course, you probably didn't notice: at most you would have caught snippets of conversations between taxi drivers and tax advisors but it would hardly have seemed urgent. Because with 70 governments in just under 75 years, the Italian political system is like a phantom limb that forges a lucrative career as a hand model. It is, after all, an anachronism.

And though the country may seem to be constantly teetering on the brink of catastrophe, the system is designed to prevent the concentration of power in the hands of one individual. In Italy, success is measured by how often leaders are removed from power rather than whether they hold on to it. It's working perfectly.

To say that Italy was fractured in the aftermath of WWII does not do justice to the trauma: the Mussolini years had economically ravaged the economy, and the very fabric of society had unravelled. But the wound ran deeper: after more than two decades of fascism, there was a moral and almost psychic aversion to the ideals of 'order', 'discipline' and 'authority'. Thus, when a 1946 referendum asked Italian citizens to choose between restoring the shredded prewar monarchy and forming a republic, the latter won as much out of desperation as it did out of inclination.

When the time came to write a constitution for this nascent nation in 1948, there was little upon which its representatives would or even could agree except for the need to guard against another seizure of power. As such, the seat of prime minister was kept deliberately weak and dependent on both houses of Parliament. But like many things that happened in those strange, surreal postwar years, the Italian Republic was formed in a vacuum. No one was ready to think of the past, and no one really had a roadmap for the future. Anything was better than what had just been, even if it meant that 'leadership' would be a fictitious concept in 20th-century Italy. The constitution established a never-ending present in political life paved with good intentions, a road that famously leads in one general direction.

The new Italian constitution should have empowered citizens to chart a new course for the future. Instead, clauses were added to allow a very small section of the government to effectively topple the rest, which has led to the revolving door of prime ministers. No one, no matter how powerful, escapes a no-confidence vote in the Italian Parliament. Even Giulio Andreotti, who wielded so much power in postwar Italy that he was nicknamed Beelzebub, was forced to reorganise seven governments. In fact, he holds the dubious honour (one among many for him) of one of the shortest periods in office before a no-confidence vote was triggered: nine days. He lost the vote.

As time moved on the names changed but the song remained the same. As the era of former cruise ship singer Silvio Berlusconi took shape, Italian politics evolved (or devolved) from a complex issue into a cruel joke. The never-ending technocratic governments and grand coalitions made it impossible to follow who was elected and who was allied with whom. Increasingly byzantine electoral laws turned the political system into a labyrinth. But this wasn't chaos, and it wasn't unplanned. Instead, it was the perfection of a system that cultivates mediocrity rather than risk another brush with totalitarianism.

The result, that crisis becomes a default position in the daily performance of political life, should and indeed has spelled ruin for many another state. Yet remarkably, Italy has survived, and perhaps even flourished because of rather than despite this discord. Everything that you love about Italy, from the art to the architecture to the beauty of every hand-hewn pasta shape, stems from this inherent conundrum. Italy's divinity is its manifest impossibility, the very notion that it exists at all.

Democracy asks us to commit to imperfection yet simultaneously strive towards an ideal, another funny anachronism. All over the world, that pursuit is facing a stress test. In some places it bends, in others it has broken. In Italy, it curves gently through the alleyways and canals and boulevards and mountain paths that connect this impossible place. Those paths also contain the spectre of fascism, which continues to haunt the Italian consciousness. Sometimes it even seems poised to take over again, as all trauma tends to do. But the *poltrona*, or the throne of the modern Italian republic, is lined with nails and intentionally crafted to make sure that no one ever gets too comfortable. It is an imperfect solution, but it buys us time.

To truly love Italy means in part to reconcile the chaos with the transcendent. Those of us who live here do so under our own great compromise: our administrative lives will be subject to rules that go beyond any possible human comprehension, but in return, we will develop relationships that help us navigate the roughest seas. We will occasionally be cursed by the dark magic that is *burocrazia*, and the spell will be lifted through an equal and opposite reaction. We will wonder aloud why so many laws exist to govern so little and why it is that the entire system cannot somehow undergo a reboot and then be grateful that somehow the great treasures of this fine place are protected. We will look at undeveloped or abandoned parcels of land and see nothing but potential, for as far as the eye can gaze towards the horizon. If only, if only it all worked a bit better, we'll say, as the next government falls to make way for the one after.

And then we'll go back to the lives that are only possible through this impossible mix of fatalism and hope, glad for what may still yet come. And Italy, the best and worst of both worlds, will go on. It is, after all, eternal.

DOV'ERA, COM'ERA:
WHY ITALY LIVES ITS PAST

From buildings reconstructed perfectly when they're damaged, to artisans practising centuries-old trades – why Italy's love of the past created la dolce vita. By Julia Buckley

WHAT DO LEONARDO da Vinci's *Last Supper*, Bologna's Sala Anatomica and Venice's Teatro La Fenice have in common? None of them are quite what they seem. While *The Last Supper* is – thank goodness – original, the Milanese convent in which it sits was reconstructed after being bombed during WWII. The other two? Modern reconstructions of the originals. Not that you'd know, looking at any of them. And that's thanks to Italy's love of history and tradition, and the need to keep everything unchanged.

Dov'era, com'era ('Where it was, as it was') is the Italians' motto. If a bomb hits, as it did the Sala Anatomica, they clear the rubble and rebuild. If a fire destroys an entire building – as happened to La Fenice in 1996 – do they take advantage of the engineering innovations that have taken place in the 200 years since it was reconstructed after the last fire? Absolutely not: they rebuild it to 19th-century standards. Attend a performance in La Fenice today, and you'd have no idea that the stucco topless mermaids and gilded cupids were sculpted in 2003. Another

Venice icon is also surprisingly modern. The Campanile – that huge brick bell tower soaring above Piazza San Marco – was built in 1912. It's a perfect replica of the original medieval tower, which was begun in the 10th century, completed in 1514, and collapsed in 1902.

The Last Supper, in a way, is different. Art is sacred here, so instead of reproducing frescoes that were on the bombed-out walls, they left the newly reconstructed sides of Santa Maria delle Grazie's refectory blank. *Dov'era, com'era* – before Leonardo and chums got their paintbrushes out.

In many ways, Italy is a country stuck in the past. Speak to anyone about their town, and they'll wax lyrical about its Renaissance history, or get granular about the medieval church down the road. They'll feed you meals that have been cooked for centuries – the traditional food of Ferrara, for example, comes from the Renaissance court of the Este family – and show you the traces of an Early Christian church under a baroque cathedral, as they do in Bergamo.

They protect their languages – both the dialects and standard Italian. Go to

a city like Naples, Venice or Palermo and you'll hear the local dialect spoken in every bar and newsagent. In small towns, kids learn Italian at school, dialect at home. And while citizens fight to keep their pre-unification dialects alive, the country as a whole is standing up to the inexorable encroachment of English on Italian. The Accademia della Crusca (literally 'the Bran Academy'), founded in Florence in 1584, is responsible for separating the linguistic wheat from the chaff, coming up with Italian words to defy cheap anglicisations and keep language on a tight leash. In 2020 they pronounced that COVID was a masculine, not feminine noun, in a 3500-word essay.

Even in the shops, you'll find this love of history. Not just when it comes to the myriad pasta shapes found throughout the country (we defy you to like *croxetti*, a disc-like medieval pasta from Liguria that looks like communion wafers – and can taste just as stodgy), but also when it comes to souvenirs. Italian artisans practise centuries-old trades, from paper-marbling in Venice (a technique lifted from Turkey during the Silk Road days) to basket-weaving and hat-making in the Macerata province of Le Marche, and the *botteghe* of San Gregorio Armeno in Naples who've been making Nativity scenes in the same street since the medieval period.

The respect for history is perhaps most visible in the architecture. Although there was a wave of modern construction during the fascist regime (more on that later), in most towns and cities you'll find the *centro storico* devoid of contemporary buildings. Not that they don't exist – they're just kept away from the history. In cities from Padua to Lecce, the historic centre is looped by an ugly modern sprawl, while places known for their setting like Urbino and Matera hide their 1950s concrete blocks on the less spectacular side of the hill or canyon.

Does that make being an architect in modern Italy frustrating? Probably. Celebrated Venetian architect Carlo Scarpa developed a deliberately unassuming style – his (few) projects in his hometown slip under the radar, making no attempt to compete with the bombastic buildings around it. Meanwhile, contemporary architect Claudio Nardi, having taken inspiration from Sicilian baroque architecture while designing shops for the likes of Dolce & Gabbana, stripped things right back when building his own hotel in his native Florence. Riva Lofts is an old factory, which Nardi then converted into his own studio, before transforming it again into a simple but modern hotel. He calls it a 'collective memory' in which you can see the building's past. When you put it like that, who needs a skyscraper?

There *is* modern architecture in Italy – much of it world-leading – but you'll usually find it outside the city centre. For example, Milan's Bosco Verticale, or Vertical Forest – two apartment blocks planted with 17,000 trees – are in the modern Porta Nuova district north of the centre, beside Piazza Gae Aulenti, a 2012-inaugurated square that seems more at home in the States than in Italy. One rare place where modern design takes centre stage is Genoa, where the waterfront Porto Antico area was designed by Renzo Piano. But there's a reason – this, the city's first port, from which Christopher Columbus set sail to America, fell out of use when Genoa's 'new' port was built in the 19th century. Piano's 1992 redevelopment of the area gave it new life.

There's a darker side, too, to Italy's devotion to historic architecture. During the 1920s and 1930s, the fascist dictatorship used it to mould a country in its own image. Mussolini – who was highly involved in this architectural drive – went on a building spree, constructing entire new towns around the country, and inserting fascist architecture into Italy's iconic sites such as Milan's Piazza del Duomo. The regime took the classical structures of ancient Rome and added the streamlined shapes of art deco to create what it styled rationalist architecture. The result – think Milan's Centrale train station, or the EUR area in

Rome – is spectacular, but it's also pure propaganda. By linking himself to ancient Rome, Mussolini wanted to make it look like a second empire was Italy's divine right – a revival of the glory days of Augustus – as he invaded countries including Ethiopia, Albania and, later, Egypt. Through architecture linked to the past, he planned to make fascism an unshakeable part of the country.

Some past styles are more equal than others. You'll hardly find any late-19th- or early-20th-century industrial architecture in Italy – it was knocked down and rebuilt on as soon as fashions changed. Places like Brescia's Areadocks – a block of railway warehouses turned into the kind of hipster nightlife space you expect from Downtown Los Angeles – are few and far between. Out of all Italy's cities, only Turin has hung on to its industrial heritage in any real way, turning old factories into galleries and event spaces.

But as these kinds of venues get more popular, expect to see more industrial heritage spots rejuvenated and preserved. In Venice, the Arsenale (former shipyard) is now one of the most coveted spaces for the film festival, and is taken over by the Biennale. And while most of Sardinia's tourism industry is all about the beach, the area around Iglesias and Carbonia is valorising its old mining heritage, with the Serbariu mine turned into the Museo del Carbone (Coal Museum) and Porto Flavia (a cliff-cut mining tunnel) providing a very different experience of Sardinia's breathtaking coastline.

ATZORI RICCARDO/SHUTTERSTOCK ©

WOULD ITALY BE SUCH A HUGE TOURIST DESTINATION WITHOUT THE CONCEPT OF DOV'ERA, COM'ERA? ALMOST CERTAINLY NOT.

Even Carbonia itself is a modern heritage site – it's one of the towns that were built from scratch by Mussolini. Practically untouched today, it's a time capsule of the rationalist era.

Of course, that great love – almost worship – of the past has served Italy well since the days of the Grand Tour. We travel here for that history: for that unspoiled *centro storico*, for that Tintoretto painting still hanging in the church, for the Biennale in that old shipyard. A huge part of la dolce vita is that ability to step back in time. Would Italy be such a huge tourist destination without the concept of *dov'era, com'era*? Almost certainly not.

Today, ancient and modern are locked in a dance – delicate and ever-changing. During the COVID lockdown in January 2021, Venetians escaping to the Lido for their permitted daily walk noticed a huge deposit of bricks, washed up on the beach during a harsh winter storm. They were, it turned out, from the original Campanile – a mixture of Byzantine, medieval and even Roman bricks that had been swept up after the collapse, and dumped at the mouth of the lagoon.

Fittingly, they appeared just when they were needed to boost morale, as Venetians rushed to collect bricks for themselves: a precious link to the past at a time of uncertain future. *Dov'era, com'era* – the Campanile may have fallen, but it never died.

ALBERTO MASNOVO/SHUTTERSTOCK ©

Vittoriano, Rome (p67)

THE COUNTRY OF A
THOUSAND CULTURES

Italy's history – from rival city-states to the nation's unification in 1861 – means that it's a country of huge diversity. By Julia Buckley

ASK ANY ITALIAN about their favourite place in Italy, and they may well look at you as if it's a trick question. Rome, Florence, Venice? Of course not – there can only be one response, and that's always their hometown.

More than most Europeans, Italians feel deeply rooted to their place of birth. Not for nothing do country-dwellers talk about their *paese* – literally their 'country' – when referring to their village. Here, cities and hamlets alike are their own little worlds. They have their distinct food traditions, artisan heritage and even dialects.

The reason is rooted in Italy's history as one of Europe's younger countries. While

Portugal was established in 1143 and Denmark in 965, the Italian Peninsula only became a single state in 1861. Before that, it was a disparate group of rival regions, which formed alliances, battled and practised diplomacy amongst themselves for centuries as foreign powers constantly tried to invade. While the word 'Italia' dates back several thousand years, it wasn't always used to refer to the entire peninsula. Dante chose to describe what we now know as Italy as *il bel paese là dove 'l sì suona* – that beautiful country that resounds with the word *sì*, or yes. And – *sì* – that's where Italy's nickname of the *bel paese* originates.

783

That 1861 date – when Vittorio Emanuele II was pronounced king by the newly assembled parliament in Turin – doesn't even tell the whole story. *Il Risorgimento* (The Resurgence) was a decades-long political battle to unify the country, lasting from 1848 to 1871. By 1830 the peninsula was made up of no fewer than eight states, all with their own customs and laws. Today, several of the names you'll see given to streets in every town belong to those who fought for unification: Cavour, Mazzini and, of course, Garibaldi. By 1861 they had brought together all states except Rome and the Veneto (the former was under papal rule, the latter under Austrian occupation). The process was completed a decade later, and Italy grabbed more mountainous regions after WWI.

That rich history has always been Italy's forte, and is responsible for much of what we love about the country today. The Renaissance was spearheaded by rival courts commissioning art, literature and architecture to outdo each other. Even Dante wrote his *Divine Comedy* in exile in Ravenna from his native Florence, filling it with bile about his former city. If Italy had been one country, we might never have been given some of the world's greatest works of art. It's also the reason for the wealth of sublime architecture you'll find across the peninsula. Instead of one capital city, Italy had one for every state. No wonder that today there's so much to see.

Not only did those states create intense loyalty, but much of Italy spent centuries under foreign rule, which made for even tighter-knit societies. Venetians still speak scathingly of the French – to this day, many still demand reparations for Napoleon's destruction and looting – while Sardinians tell how the Spanish stripped the island to the bone.

It's not only foreigners they dislike. Venice's patriarch, or head priest, is from Genoa – locals shake their head, or say *poverino* (poor thing), Genoa being Venice's long-time maritime superpower rival. (All four former maritime republics – Venice, Genoa, Pisa and Amalfi – still have a fiercely contested annual regatta, to judge their dominance of the seas.) The Neapolitans, meanwhile, largely hate Garibaldi, who passed through in 1860 – many tell ugly tales about priceless treasures of the city that he supposedly made off with. The unification of Italy drained the country's south, formerly prosperous, of money. In bringing the country together, Garibaldi forged a chasm between north and south that still exists – and has driven the success of political parties like the Lega Nord, or Northern League.

What creates damaging politics makes for fascinating travel, however. Garibaldi's red-shirt troops were known as *I Mille* (The Thousand) and today this feels like a country of 1000 cultures. Different traditional dishes, food festivals and rituals are everywhere, from menus filled with obscure lake fish on Iseo and Como, to the autumn chestnut festivals in the Tuscan Apennines, celebrating the *albero del pane* (bread tree) whose flour fed the poor for centuries.

The more you travel you'll also be able to discern broader regional differences – for example, in the Po valley, the traditional food base is risotto, not pasta, while Liguria's street-food tradition is true to its medieval origins (there's not a tomato in sight). Tuscany is big on pulses, while in the Veneto they still eat lots of polenta. Generally, in the north butter is the traditional fat, whereas it's oil in the south. It's not just about food, either. That famous southern friendliness? It's real, and it's *not* the same higher up.

Italians may move cities, but their loyalties always lie with their place of origin – ask a Milan resident where they're from, and it's rare they'll say Milan, instead waxing lyrical about their birthplace. In Sicily's Cammarata, a famous one-euro home scheme is being run by millennials who moved away to find work, and returned during the pandemic to reboot their hometown.

The hyper-local fixation has its drawbacks – good luck finding a restaurant in Bologna that serves anything other than Bolognese food, for example (try Oltre for modern Bolognese, or Ristorante Ponterosso in Monteveglio for more outlandish takes on traditional cuisine). In Rome, you will be eating *cacio e pepe* and *gricia*, like it or not.

But overall, this diversity is what makes Italy one of the most fascinating countries to visit – there's a different culture on every hilltop, in every valley and cliffside cove. From the cuisine to the language and atmosphere, you'll find a different *paese* in every corner. Time to get exploring.

INDEX

Map Pages 000

Map Pages **000**

Map Pages **000**

Map Pages **000**

Map Pages **000**

Map Pages **000**

'San Giorgio Maggiore island (p307) is Venice in miniature, with a knockout Palladian basilica and a *campanile* (bell tower) to rival St Mark's.'

'Giorgio Vasari's and Federico Zuccari's *Last Judgement* (1572–79) can be admired as you climb the 463 steps leading to the rooftop of Florence's Cattedrale di Santa Maria del Fiore (p408).'

THIS BOOK

Design development
Marc Backwell

Content development
Mark Jones, Sandie Kestell, Anne Mason, Joana Taborda

Cartography development
Katerina Pavkova

Production development
Sandie Kestell, Fergal Condon

Series development leadership
Darren O'Connell, Piers Pickard, Chris Zeiher

Commissioning Editor
Daniel Bolger

Product Editor
Clare Healy

Book Designer
Fergal Condon

Cartographer
Anthony Phelan

Assisting Editors
Janet Austin, Andrew Bain, Andrea Dobbin, Alison Killilea, Amy

Lysen, Mani Ramaswamy, Brana Vladisavljevic

Cover Researcher
Hannah Blackie

Thanks Ronan Abayawickrema, Katie Connolly, Gwen Cotter, Esteban Fernandez, Karen Henderson, Kate James

MIX
Paper from responsible sources
FSC™ C021741
www.fsc.org

Paper in this book is certified against the Forest Stewardship Council™ standards. FSC™ promotes environmentally responsible, socially beneficial and economically viable management of the world's forests.

Published by Lonely Planet Global Limited
CRN 554153
16th edition – May 2023
ISBN 978 1 83869 810 2
© Lonely Planet 2023 Photographs © as indicated 2023
10 9 8 7 6 5 4 3 2 1
Printed in Singapore